Contents

OPPOSITE MONKS COLLECTING ALMS, KO LIPE **PREVIOUS PAGE** VIEW FROM KO WUA TALAB, ANG THONG MARINE PARK

Introduction to
Thailand's
Beaches & Islands

Despite myriad cultural attractions, sand and sea are what most Thailand holidays are about, and with over three thousand kilometres of tropical coastline there are plenty of stunning white-sand beaches to choose from. In addition, the peculiar shape of the country – which is often likened to an elephant's head, with Bangkok as the eye, the east coast as the chin, and the peninsular Andaman and Gulf coasts forming the trunk – means you can dive, swim and sunbathe all year round, for when the monsoon rains are battering one coast you merely have to cross to the other to escape them.

Geographical differences have given distinctive character to each of the coasts. The **Andaman coast** is the most dramatic, edged by sheer limestone cliffs carved by wind and water into strange silhouettes, and interleaved with thick bands of mangrove forest. The **Gulf coast** begins and ends quietly with relatively flat, featureless stretches to the south of Bangkok and down towards the Malaysian border, but peaks at its midpoint, where the peninsular mountains march into the sea to form the wildly varied landscapes of the Samui archipelago and the Ang Thong National Marine Park. A fair chunk of the **east coast** is dominated by the rigs of offshore oil and gas exploration, but the islands that lie further out have forested spines and gorgeous strands. In short, you'll find great beaches on all three coasts: idyllic confections of clear turquoise waters at invitingly balmy temperatures, sand so soft that it squeaks underfoot, and palm trees laden with coconuts.

The Thai royal family started the craze for seaside holidays by making regular trips to Hua Hin in the early 1900s, and the subsequent construction of the Southern Railway Line soon opened up the region to the rest of the population. Inspired by American GIs who'd discovered Thailand's attractions during their R&R breaks from Vietnam, it wasn't long before foreign holidaymakers followed suit, and these days

FACT FILE

- Divided into 77 provinces or *changwat*, Thailand was known as **Siam** until 1939 (and again from 1945 to 1949); some academics suggest changing the name back again, to better reflect the country's Thai and non-Thai diversity.

- The **population** of 63 million is made up of ethnic Thais (75 percent) and Chinese (14 percent), with the rest comprising mainly immigrants from neighbouring countries as well as hill-tribespeople.

- Buddhism is the national **religion**, Islam the largest minority religion, but nearly all Thais also practise some form of animism (spirit worship).

- Since 1932 the country has been a **constitutional monarchy**. King Bhumibol, also known as Rama IX (being the ninth ruler of the Chakri dynasty), is the world's longest-ruling head of state, having been on the throne since 1946; the current prime minister, Yingluck Shinawatra, entered politics only six weeks before winning the general election in 2011 with an absolute majority.

- Thailand fell to 153rd out of 178 countries on Reporters without Borders' index on **press freedom** in 2010, because of a surge in the use of the *lèse majesté* laws.

- The world record for **non-stop kissing** was set by two Thai men in Pattaya on Valentine's Day, 2012, at a gobsmacking 50 hours, 25 minutes and 1 second.

tourism is the main industry in nearly all Thailand's coastal areas. Many of the most beautiful spots have been well and truly discovered, and a number have developed into full-blown high-rise resorts that seem to have more in common with the Costa del Sol than the rest of Southeast Asia. But you need only venture a few kilometres from such anomalies to encounter a more traditional scene of fishing communities, rubber plantations and Buddhist temples. Some forty percent of Thais still earn their living from the land or the sea, and around 85 percent of the population are **Theravada Buddhists**, a faith that colours all aspects of daily life – from the tiered temple rooftops that dominate the skyline, to the omnipresent saffron-robed monks and the packed calendar of festivals.

Where to go

Airline schedules decree that many beach holidays begin in **Bangkok**, and despite initial impressions, Thailand's crazy, polluted capital is well worth at least a couple of days of your time. Within its historic core you'll find the country's most dazzling works of art and architecture, which are complemented by a seductive array of traditional markets and contemporary boutiques, hip bars and outstanding restaurants, in the fashionable downtown area.

Within easy striking distance of Bangkok, the east-coast resort of **Pattaya** is the country's most popular – and least interesting – destination, a concrete warren of hotels and strip joints that makes its money from package tourists who are unaware of what they're missing. Yet just a few kilometres beyond sits the diminutive island of **Ko Samet**, whose superb sands are lined with more conducive beach bungalows. East again, just inside the Cambodian border, **Ko Chang** has retained its upland forest despite the relentless march of resort-style facilities along its shores; but for old-style Thai beach charm, you'll need to press on, to tiny, charming **Ko Mak** and wild, unsullied **Ko Kood**.

OPPOSITE KO SIMILAN (KO MIANG)

After an interesting inland diversion at the atmospheric, temple-filled town of **Phetchaburi**, the peninsular Gulf coast kicks off with the historic resort of **Hua Hin**, now disfigured by excessive hotel development; better to keep going to **Pak Nam Pran**'s arty boutique hotels or unspoilt **Prachuap Khiri Kan**, with its handsome promenade and shady sands. The main draw on this side of the peninsula, though, is the Samui archipelago to the south: **Ko Samui** itself is the most developed of the three main islands here, but has largely kept its good looks and offers an appealing variety of beachside accommodation, restaurants and facilities; **Ko Pha Ngan**, with its small resorts and desolate coves, is still firmly backpacker territory, drawing party people – to **Hat Rin** – and solitude seekers in equal parts; and **Ko Tao** is the remotest outcrop of the three, but has established itself as one of the world's leading centres for scuba-diving courses. On the mainland to the south, **Nakhon Si Thammarat** is a great place to recharge your cultural – and culinary – batteries.

RAT OR RAJA?

There's no standard system of **transliterating** Thai script into Roman, so you're sure to find that the Thai words in this book don't always match the versions you'll see elsewhere. Maps and street signs are the biggest sources of confusion, so we've generally gone for the transliteration that's most common on the spot; where it's a toss-up between two equally popular versions, we've used the one that helps best with pronunciation. However, sometimes you'll need to do a bit of lateral thinking, bearing in mind that a classic variant for the town of Satun is Satul, while among street names, Thanon Rajavithi could come out as Thanon Ratwithi – and it's not unheard of to find one spelling posted at one end of a road, with another at the opposite end.

Across the peninsula, there's extraordinary drama and beauty all along the Andaman coast. Underwater highlights include the polychromatic reefs of the **Ko Similan** island chain, while above water there's the islet-studded bay of **Ao Phang Nga**, the curvy white-sand shores of party-island **Ko Phi Phi** and the primeval cliffs of **Krabi's Railay peninsula**. There's grandeur inland, too, in the lofty tropical rainforests of **Khao Sok National Park**. Sadly, the big resort island of **Phuket** is increasingly denuded of its natural beauty, but five million visitors a year are still drawn to its dozen different beaches, which offer everything from luxurious five-star seclusion to seedy nightlife. **Ko Lanta** is, for the moment at least, a calmer alternative for families, while independent travellers will much prefer the uncommercial islands of **Ko Jum, Ko Yao Noi, Ko Chang** and **Ko Phayam**.

Spectacular limestone backdrops continue down the Andaman coast into the provinces of the deep south, where the main attractions are teeming sea life and unfrequented sands. The quietest spot of all is the beautiful national park of **Ko Tarutao**, though **Ko Lipe** is a rather rowdy neighbour, with the fastest development on this stretch of littoral; half a dozen other varied islands down here offer an appealing balance of remoteness and facilities. There's now the intriguing possibility of **island-hopping** your way down through them – in fact, all the way from Phuket to Penang in Malaysia – without setting foot on the mainland.

When to go

The **climate** of most of Thailand is governed by three seasons (see p.55): **rainy** (roughly May–Oct), caused by the southwest monsoon dumping moisture gathered from the Andaman Sea and the Gulf of Thailand; **cool** (Nov–Feb); and **hot** (March–May). The rainy season is the least predictable of the three, varying in length and intensity from year to year, but it's never a case of the heavens opening in May and not closing again till October: there'll be rain most days, but often only for a few hours in the afternoon or at night. The rains usually gather force between June and August, coming to a peak in September and October, when unpaved roads are reduced to mud troughs and some islands become inaccessible.

Within this scheme, slight variations are found from region to region. In southern Thailand, temperatures are more consistent throughout the year, with less variation the closer you get to the equator. The rainy season hits the **Andaman coast** harder than anywhere else in the country: rainfall can start in April and usually persists until November. The **Gulf coast** of the southern peninsula lies outside this general pattern – with the sea immediately to the east, this coast and its offshore islands feel the effects of the northeast monsoon, which brings rain between October and January, especially in November, but suffers less than the Andaman coast from the southwest monsoon.

Overall, the cool season is generally the **best time** to come to Thailand, and the most popular: as well as having more manageable temperatures and less rain, it offers waterfalls in full spate and the best of the flowers in bloom.

Author Picks

Having finally settled down in Thailand after twenty years of toing and froing, our author, Paul, has plenty to write home about. Here are some of his personal favourites.

Messing about in boats It's hard to beat a short, richly diverse boat trip around Ko Tao and the causeway beaches of Ko Nang Yuan. p.267

Kneads must A good pummelling at the massage pavilions amid the historic, kaleidoscopic architecture of Wat Pho is one of Bangkok's unmissable experiences. p.85

Best view Among dozens of contenders along Thailand's vast coastline, in the end it has to be the implausible concentration of limestone turrets in Phang Nga bay. p.350

Unspectacular islands Ko Mak and Ko Phayam lack the spectacular scenery of some of their neighbours, and their beaches, though beautiful, are not quite as stunning, but they both have a lovely, laidback atmosphere for chilling out and just enough facilities to keep most beach bums happy. p.194 and p.297

Aaaaaah-roy "Deliciousness" is never far away in Thailand, be it fluffy deep-fried catfish with a tangy mango salad, toothsome beef green curry, or mango with sticky rice and coconut milk. p.39

Sundowners Anywhere along Ko Lanta's vast swathe of west-facing beaches is great for watching the sun set with an ice-cold beer – the restaurant at *Lanta Coral Beach*, on a small promontory at Hat Khlong Nam Jud, particularly sticks in the mind. p.388

> Our author recommendations don't end here. We've flagged up our favourite places – a perfectly sited hotel, an atmospheric bar, a special restaurant – throughout the guide, highlighted with the ★ symbol.

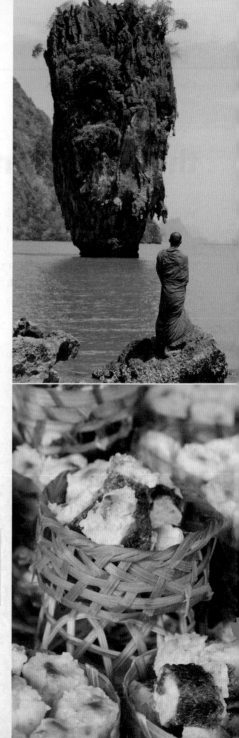

FROM TOP JAMES BOND ISLAND, PHANG NGA BAY; KHANOM JEAP (*DIM SUM*)

18

things not to miss

It's not possible to explore every inch of Thailand's coastline in one trip – and we don't suggest you try. What follows, in no particular order, is a selective taste of the highlights: beautiful beaches, outstanding national parks, exuberant festivals and thrilling activities. All highlights have a page reference to take you straight into the guide, where you can find out more.

1 DIVING AND SNORKELLING
Page 51

There's another world of teeming colours under the water, and Thailand's coastline offers hundreds of opportunities to explore it.

2 NIGHT MARKETS
Page 40

After-dark gatherings of dramatically lit pushcart kitchens, which are usually the best-value and most entertaining places to eat.

3 ANG THONG NATIONAL MARINE PARK
Page 253

Stunning vistas of this dense cluster of jungle-clad islands set in the deep-blue Gulf of Thailand, and some truly remote accommodation.

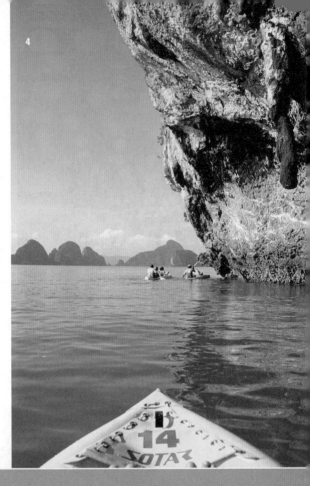

4 SEA-CANOEING
Low-impact paddling is the best way to explore the natural beauty of the Ko Chang, Ang Thong, Ao Phang Nga and Tarutao archipelagos.

5 PHETCHABURI
Many of the temples in this charming, historic town date back three hundred years and are still in use today.

6 SEAFOOD
Fresh fish, curried with vegetables, steamed whole with ginger and mushrooms or simply barbecued…the only problem is knowing when to stop.

7 FULL MOON PARTY AT HAT RIN, KO PHA NGAN
Apocalypse Now without the war…

8 KO TAO
Take a dive course, or just explore this remote island's contours by boat or on foot.

9 SONGKHRAN
Page 47
Thai New Year is the excuse for a national water fight – and tourists are definitely fair game.

10 ROCK-CLIMBING
Pages 348, 368 & 372
Even novice climbers can scale the cliffs at Ko Yao Noi, Phi Phi or the Railay peninsula for an unbeatable perspective on the Andaman seascape.

11 THE GRAND PALACE, BANGKOK
Page 78
No visitor should miss this huge complex, which encompasses the country's holiest and most beautiful temple, Wat Phra Kaeo, and its most important image, the Emerald Buddha.

12 KO KOOD
Page 198
An untamed beauty, fringed by very pretty beaches.

13 KO PHA NGAN
Page 254
The island is dotted with beautiful beaches, so head out to secluded Bottle Beach or Thong Nai Pan, or gear up for the fun at Hat Rin.

12

14

15

Itineraries

The following itineraries cover Thailand's coastline in all its diversity, from snorkelling the Similans to beach-bumming your way through the Andaman archipelagos. Whether you want to feel the buzz of adventure in the great outdoors, feast on the never-ending variety of Thai cuisine, or find the nearest thing to a desert island paradise, these will point the way.

FOR ADVENTURE SEEKERS

Thailand offers an astonishing range of good-value adventure sports, especially in, on and over the teeming tropical seas.

❶ Ko Tao dive courses The best place to hone your skills, whether you're a beginner, advanced or speciality diver. **See p.270**

❷ Khao Sok National Park Halfway between the southern peninsula's two coasts, Khao Sok offers guided and self-guided hikes, caving, tubing and kayaking. **See p.307**

❸ Diving and snorkelling off Ko Similan Camp out on this remote chain of national park islands or take a live-aboard trip to make the most of the spectacular turquoise waters and shallow reefs. **See p.316**

❹ Sea-canoeing in Ao Phang Nga Day, night or multi-day paddling trips are the best way to explore the secret caves and mangrove swamps of this extraordinary bay. **See p.352**

❺ Ko Yao Noi This relaxing island on the edge of Phang Nga bay is a low-key hub for active visitors, who kayak, snorkel, dive and climb rocks. **See p.345**

❻ Rock-climbing on the Railay peninsula Offering courses for beginners, as well as equipment rental and guides, this is Thailand's premier site for climbers, with over seven hundred bolted routes amid awesome scenery. **See p.372**

FOR FOOD LOVERS

The seafood's great all around Thailand's coastline, but the places mentioned below are at least one notch above your average bungalow kitchen: they're all locally famous restaurants serving a wide range of regional specialities, where you can eat extremely well.

❶ Bangkok Among fifty thousand places to eat in the capital, a couple of restaurants can be singled out for special mention: *Taling Pling*, with a long list of dishes from the four corners of the country praised by Thai food critics; and *Bolan*, for its meticulous commitment to traditional recipes and the "Slow Food" philosophy. **See p.135 & p.136**

❷ Hua Hin Long the favourite seaside retreat of Bangkok's food-loving middle classes, Hua Hin has built up a thriving culinary scene – *Baan Itsara*'s creative seafood dishes stand out. **See p.220**

❸ Phuket Among Phuket's swanky, big-name restaurants, *The Seacret* may seem an unlikely choice, but it delivers fantastic local dishes such as dried and smoked shrimp relish (*nam prik kung siap*) and stewed pork belly with cinnamon. **See p.340**

❹ Krabi You may have to queue for a table at *Ko Tung*, but it's worth the wait for the fresh, southern-style seafood such as delicious sweet mussels and baked crab. **See p.360**

❺ Nakhon Si Thammarat *Krua Thale* is almost reason in itself to go to Nakhon – don't miss the chunky mussels in herb soup. **See p.282**

❻ Ko Samui The island now has some great hotel restaurants, though our favourite spot is still *Ban Hua Thanon Seafood*, a wooden shophouse with waterfront tables and superb shredded prawns with mango salad. **See p.253**

FOR RESTLESS ISLAND-HOPPERS

Ferries now join up the karst islands of the southern Andaman coast, so it's possible to get from Phuket to Penang in Malaysia without setting foot on the mainland. You can avoid the crowds, and save yourself money and hassle, by bypassing the kiss-me-quick honeypots of Phuket, Ko Phi Phi and Ko Lipe in favour of these island beauties.

❶ Phuket Town Base yourself among the Sino-Portuguese architecture of the island capital, which has better-value and more interesting places to stay and eat than the big-name beaches, and much better transport links. **See p.323**

❷ Ko Jum Half a dozen wild and lonely beaches facing the sunset, with boat trips to enjoy, a small mountain to climb, and paraffin lamps in some of the resorts. **See p.380**

❸ Ko Lanta With around 20km of west-facing sands and a laidback, family-friendly atmosphere, Lanta offers a wide range of affordable accommodation. **See p.384**

❹ Ko Hai A variety of good resorts for all budgets and a gorgeous panorama of jagged limestone islands. **See p.406**

❺ Ko Mook The main draw here is the stunning Emerald Cave, with its inland beach of fine sand at

the base of a spectacular natural chimney. **See p.409**

❻ Ko Kradan A remote island that's uninhabited apart from its half-dozen resorts, with a long, powdery, east-facing strand, crystal-clear waters and a reef for snorkellers to explore. **See p.410**

❼ Ko Tarutao Huge national park island with mangroves and jungle tracks to explore, and the most unspoilt beaches in the area. **See p.414**

Underwater Thailand

Dip your head beneath the surface of the Andaman Sea or the Gulf of Thailand and a whole new world of outrageous shapes and colours opens up. The figures speak for themselves: together these two tracts play host to nearly a thousand species of fish and some 270 species of hard coral. On these pages we highlight just a few of the most fascinating examples, so you'll know more about what you're seeing while out diving or snorkelling (see p.51).

Coral

Coral reefs are living organisms composed of a huge variety of marine life forms, which provide a habitat for hundreds of species of fish, but the foundation of every reef is its stony coral constructions such as **boulder**, **leaf**, **table**, **mushroom**, **staghorn** and **brain coral**. Though seemingly inanimate, stony coral is actually composed of colonies of polyps – minuscule invertebrates which feed on plankton, generally depend on algae and direct sunlight for photosynthesis, and extract calcium carbonate (limestone) from sea water in order to reproduce. The polyps use this calcium carbonate to build new skeletons outside their bodies and this is how a reef is formed. It's an extraordinarily slow process, with colony growth averaging between 0.5cm and 2.8cm a year.

Fleshy, plant-like **soft coral**, such as **elephant's ear**, is also composed of polyps, but has flaccid internal skeletons built from protein rather than calcium. The lack of an external casing means the polyps' vivid colours are much more visible and, as they do not depend on direct sunlight, they flourish at greater depths, swaying with the currents and using tentacles to trap microorganisms.

Horny coral, or **gorgonians**, like **sea whips** and **sea fans**, are a cross between stony and soft coral, while **sea anemones** have the most obvious, and venomous, tentacles of any member of the coral family, using them to trap fish and other large prey.

Reef fish

The algae and plankton that accumulate around coral colonies attract a catalogue of fish known collectively as **reef fish**. Most are small in stature, with vibrant and exotically patterned skins for camouflage against the coral, and flattened bodies, broad tails and specially adapted fins for easy manoeuvring around the tiniest of reef crannies.

Butterfly fish are typically well designed: named for the butterfly-like movements of their thin, flat, yellow-white-and-black bodies, they can swim backwards, and some also have elongated snouts for nosing into crevices; a number even sport eye-like blotches near the tail to confuse predators.

Vibrantly coloured with flattened bodies that are well adapted for reef-dwelling, **angelfish** are distinguished from the similar butterfly fish by the strong spines on their gill flaps. **Emperor angelfish**, with their tangerine and blue stripes, make a clicking sound when disturbed and can grow up to 30cm in length.

There are approximately one hundred different species of **surgeonfish**, each with its own distinctive markings, but they all share the feature that gives them their name – a sharp blade on either side of their tail-base that becomes erect when antagonized and can inflict serious damage. More innocuous is the distinctive long pennant fin that trails from the dorsal fin of the **moorish idol**, which is also recognizable by its pronounced snout and dramatic bands of colour.

Among the most impressive reef fish that school are the huge shoals of silvery **fusilierfish**, which move as one, changing direction in an eye-catching flash of rippling

1 PARROTFISH; 2 BUTTERFLY FISH; 3 CORAL HIND AND CLEANER WRASSE; 4 MORAY EEL; 5 EMPEROR ANGELFISH >

silver. Growing up to 60cm in length, they have extensible upper jaws, adapted for picking plankton. Some reef fish, among them the ubiquitous **parrotfish**, eat coral. With the help of a bird-like beak, which is in fact several teeth fused together, the parrotfish scrapes away at the coral, leaving characteristic white scars, and then grinds the fragments down with another set of back teeth – a practice reputedly responsible for the erosion of a great deal of Thailand's reef.

Anemonefish are so called because, having covered themselves in the sea anemone's mucus, they are able to move among and gain protection from the anemone's venomous tentacles, which would paralyse other fish on contact. Since the film *Finding Nemo* came out, their most famous species, the **clown anemonefish**, is generally just referred to as "Nemo".

Equally as predictable as sightings of anemonefish is the presence of cleaner fish, or **cleaner wrasse**, on the edges of every shoal of reef fish. Streamlined, with a long snout and jaws that act like tweezers, a cleaner fish spends its days picking parasites off the skins of other fish, such as the normally voracious **grouper fish** – a symbiotic relationship essential to both parties. A close but more colourful relative of the grouper is the commonly sighted **coral hind**, which is often found among staghorn coral.

Larger, less frequently spotted visitors to Thailand's offshore reefs include the **moray eel**, whose elongated jaws of viciously pointed teeth make it a deadly predator; it hunts mainly at night and often holes up in coral caves during the day. The similarly be-fanged **barracuda** can grow to 2m and is one of the world's fastest-swimming fish, using its speed – up to 40kmh – to prey on other fish of any size.

Sharks and rays

One of the few shark species – along with the white-tip shark – that can breathe while stationary, the **leopard shark** is often found on sand bottoms, camouflaged by its grey-to-brown body with dark spots and blotches. Sometimes found up to 3m in length, they're completely harmless to humans and live off such things as fish, shellfish and worms.

Curious but very rarely aggressive unless provoked, small **white-tip reef sharks** are named for the white tips on their dorsal and tail fins. They hunt, mostly at night, for fish, crustaceans and octopus. With its white belly and greyish back with light spots and stripes, the **whale shark** is quite harmless, feeding on plankton and small fish that are filtered into its huge mouth as it cruises the seas. The largest fish in the world, at up to 18m long, the whale shark lives for around seventy years and migrates every spring to feed on the abundant plankton off the west coast of Australia.

You have to keep your distance if you encounter a stingray (see p.24), but it is sometimes possible to swim with a graceful **manta ray**, whose extraordinary flatness, strange wing-like fins, and massive size – up to 6m across and weighing some 1600kg – make it an astonishing presence.

Turtles

Occasionally seen paddling around reef waters, turtles come in four local species, all of them endangered: the green, the leatherback, the olive ridley and the hawksbill (considered critically endangered). The loggerhead turtle also once swam in Thai waters, until the constant plundering of its eggs rendered it locally extinct. Most of the Thai beaches favoured by turtles for egg-laying are now protected as marine parks and are off-limits to visitors.

Of the remaining four species, the **green turtle** is the commonest, a mottled brown creature named not for its appearance but for the colour of the soup made from its flesh. Adults weigh up to 180kg and are herbivorous, subsisting on sea grass, mangrove leaves and algae.

The **leatherback**, encased in a distinctive ridged shell, is the world's largest turtle, weighing between 250kg and 550kg; it eats nothing but jellyfish. Weighing up to 50kg and feeding mainly on shrimps and crabs, the small **olive ridley** is named partly after its olive-green, heart-shaped carapace (no one knows who or what "ridley" was).

Named for its peculiar beak-like mouth, the **hawksbill** is prized for its spectacular carapace (the sale of which was banned by CITES in 1992), with light and dark streaks on an amber background and a serrated appearance towards the tail; it weighs up to 75kg and lives off a type of sea sponge.

Invertebrates

Thailand's reefs support countless species of **invertebrates**, including spiral-feathered **Christmas-tree worms**, also sometimes evocatively known as bottle-brush worms, which embed their lower bodies in coral heads; all sorts of multi-celled, multi-hued **sponges**, both encrusting and free-standing; neon-bright squamose **giant clams**, which burrow into the reef, exposing only their soft, flamboyantly coloured mantle; and a thousand-plus species of hermaphroditic, shell-less mollusc known as **nudibranchs** or sea slugs, which come in an arresting array of patterns and shapes and live in shallow waters.

Of the reef's numerous spiny echinoderms, the commonest **sea urchins**, which also tend to live in shallow areas near shore, are those with evil-looking black spines up to 35cm in length, though some varieties are covered in short, blunt spines or even excruciatingly painful flower-like pincers.

The magnificent **crown-of-thorns starfish** is also protected by highly venomous spines, which sheath the twenty or so "arms" that extend from a body that can measure up to 50cm in diameter. Disastrously for many reefs, the crown-of-thorns starfish feeds on coral, laying waste to as much as fifty square centimetres of stony coral in a 24-hour period. The much more benign **feather stars** also have multiple feather-like arms arranged in star formations and come in many versions; they feed at night, crawling along reef surfaces with the help of tiny jointed limbs, or cirri, to sway in the current.

Though hideous, the **sea cucumber**, which looks like a large slug and lies half-buried on the sea bed, is quite harmless. Deceptively slothful in appearance, sea cucumbers are constantly ingesting and excreting so much sand and mud that the combined force of those in a three-square-kilometre area can together redistribute one million kilograms of sea-bed material a year.

OTHER BITERS AND STINGERS

Thailand is home to 25 species of **sea snake**, whose tails are flattened to act as an efficient paddle in water. Most sea snakes are venomous, though not aggressive. Of the venomous ones, the commonest and most easily recognized is the banded sea snake, which is silvery grey with thirty to fifty black bands and a slightly yellow underside at its front end. It grows to 1.5m and inhabits shallow coastal waters, coming onto land to lay its eggs.

Other harmful creatures to be avoided include the highly camouflaged sea-bed-dwelling **stonefish** and **scorpionfish**, both of which can be very hard to spot but have extremely venomous spines which are dangerous when trodden on. The magnificent **lionfish** should also be admired from afar as its impressive plumes are venomous if brushed against, as are the tentacles of the **jellyfish**.

The **blue-spotted ray** or **stingray** has two venomous spines on its long tail with which it lashes out when threatened; as it tends to bury itself with almost complete disguise in the mud or sand near reefs, it can be a particular hazard to unwary divers. Another thing to be wary of is so-called **fire coral** (not actually a true coral but a coral-like brownish encrustation), which is found in shallow waters on the edge of the reef and is covered in a mass of tiny, fuzz-like tentacles that can inflict a painful burn.

LONGTAIL BOAT

Basics

Getting there

The vast majority of travellers fly into Bangkok's Suvarnabhumi Airport. There are also four international airports in southern Thailand, at Hat Yai, Krabi, Phuket and Ko Samui.

Air fares to Thailand generally depend on the **season**, with the highest being approximately mid-November to mid-February, when the weather is best (with premium rates charged for flights between mid-Dec and New Year), and in July and August to coincide with school holidays. You will need to book several months in advance to get reasonably priced tickets during these peak periods.

The cheapest way of getting to most **regional Thai airports** is usually to buy a flight to Bangkok and then a separate domestic ticket (see p.33). However, there are dozens of potentially useful, mostly seasonal, international routes into **Phuket**, including direct flights with several airlines from Australia. For **Ko Samui**, there are flights from Singapore, Hong Kong (both Bangkok Airways) and Kuala Lumpur (Berjaya Airlines and Firefly); and for **Krabi** you can fly from KL with Air Asia, from Singapore with Tiger Airways or nonstop on seasonal, mostly charter, flights from Scandinavia.

Flights from the UK and Ireland

The fastest and most comfortable way of reaching Thailand **from the UK** is to fly nonstop from London to Bangkok with Qantas (@qantas.com.au), British Airways (@ba.com), Thai Airways (@thaiair.com) or Eva Airways (@evaair.com), a journey of about eleven and a half hours. These airlines sometimes have special promotions, but a typical fare in high season might come in at around £900. Fares on indirect scheduled flights to Bangkok are always cheaper than nonstop flights – about £600 in high season if booked well in advance with Qatar Airways (@qatarairways.com), for example – though these journeys can take anything from two to twelve hours longer.

There are no nonstop flights from any **regional airports** in Britain or from any **Irish airports**, and rather than routing via London, you may find it convenient to fly to another hub such as Frankfurt (with Lufthansa; @lufthansa.com), Zurich (with Swiss; @swiss.com), Abu Dhabi (with Etihad; @etihadairways.com) or Dubai (with Emirates; @emirates.com), and take a connecting flight from there. Return flights from Newcastle upon Tyne with Emirates, for example, currently start at around £675 in high season, from Dublin via Copenhagen with SAS (@flysas.com), at around €800.

Flights from the US and Canada

Thai Airways (@thaiair.com) offers convenient flights from LA to Bangkok, with a one-hour stop in Seoul, charging around US$1600 in high season. Plenty of other airlines run to Bangkok from East and West Coast cities with one stop en route; it's generally easier to find a reasonable fare on flights via Asia than via Europe, even if you're departing from the east coast. From New York, expect to pay upwards of US$1375 return in high season, including taxes, US$1250 from LA. Air Canada (@aircanada.com) has the most convenient service to Bangkok from the largest number of Canadian cities; from Vancouver, expect to pay from around Can$1450 in high season; from Toronto, Can$1675. Cheaper rates are often available if you're prepared to make two or three stops and take more time.

Minimum **flying times** are twenty hours from New York or Toronto (westbound or eastbound), including stopovers, seventeen hours (nonstop) or nineteen and a half hours (with one stop) from LA, and eighteen hours from Vancouver.

Flights from Australia and New Zealand

There's no shortage of **scheduled flights** to Bangkok **from Australia**, with direct services from major cities operated by Thai Airways (@thaiair.com), Qantas (@qantas.com.au) and half a dozen others (around nine hours from Sydney and Perth), and plenty of indirect flights via Asian hubs, which take at least eleven and a half hours. You can also fly nonstop to Phuket from Sydney (with Jetstar; @jetstar.com), Melbourne, Brisbane (both Air Australia; @airaustralia.com) and Perth (on Thai and Virgin Australia; @virginaustralia.com). There's often not much difference between the fares on nonstop and indirect flights with the major carriers, nor between the fares from the major eastern cities. From Sydney, if you book far in advance, you should be able to get a ticket to Bangkok in high season for around Aus$900, on a low-cost carrier such as Jetstar or through a special promotion with one of the major airlines; nonstop flights with the major airlines more typically cost around Aus$1200. Fares from Perth and Darwin are up to Aus$200 cheaper.

From **New Zealand**, Thai Airways runs nonstop twelve-hour flights between Auckland and Bangkok, costing from around NZ$1700 (including

A BETTER KIND OF TRAVEL

At Rough Guides we are passionately committed to travel. We believe it helps us understand the world we live in and the people we share it with – and of course tourism is vital to many developing economies. But the scale of modern tourism has also damaged some places irreparably, and climate change is accelerated by most forms of transport, especially flying. All Rough Guides' flights are carbon-offset, and every year we donate money to a variety of environmental charities.

taxes) in high season. British Airways/Qantas flights from Auckland make brief stops in Sydney, adding about three hours to the trip, and other major Asian airlines offer indirect flights via their hubs (from 13hr, but more typically 17hr): fares for indirect flights can start as low as NZ$1500 in high season.

Flights from South Africa

From South Africa, Thai Airways (W thaiair.com), code-sharing with South African Airways (W flysaa .com), currently operate three nonstop flights a week from Johannesburg to Bangkok, taking eleven and a half hours and costing from around ZAR9500 return for an advance booking in high season, including taxes. Otherwise, you'll be making a stop either in the Middle East or in Hong Kong or Southeast Asia, with fares starting at around ZAR8000 in high season.

AGENTS AND OPERATORS

Adventure Center US ☎ 1-800/228-8747, W adventurecenter .com. Hiking and "soft adventure" specialist agent, offering dozens of packages to Thailand with well-regarded tour operators from all over the world.

All Points East UK ☎ 023/9225 8859, Thailand ☎ 081 885 9490; W allpointseast.com. Southeast Asia specialist operating small-group adventure holidays with off-the-beaten-track itineraries.

Andaman Discoveries Thailand W andamandiscoveries.com. Village-based homestay community tourism programmes around Khuraburi on the north Andaman coast, lasting from one to five days, which allow visitors to experience daily activities such as soap making, cashew-nut farming and roof thatching. Other tours include four-day trips to Ko Surin National Park to learn about Moken life.

Asian Trails Thailand W asiantrails.net. Well-regarded company that offers self-drive tours, cycling adventures, homestay programmes, river and sea cruises, plus more typical package tours.

Creative Events Asia Thailand W creativeeventsasia.com. Wedding specialists for everything from paperwork to the ceremony and guest accommodation.

Crooked Trails US ☎ 206/383-9828, W crookedtrails.com. Not-for-profit community-based tourism organization offering homestays along the Andaman coast, featuring volunteer work as well as cultural tours.

ETC (Educational Travel Centre) Thailand W etc.co.th.

Unusual tour programmes including Thai cooking holidays and community-based programmes and homestays that might include trekking and teaching.

Flight Centre Australia ☎ 13 31 33, Canada ☎ 1-877/967 5302, New Zealand ☎ 0800/243 544, South Africa ☎ 0860 400 727, UK ☎ 0870/499 0040, US ☎ 1-877/992 4732; W flightcentre.com. Guarantees to offer the lowest international air fares.

Grasshopper Adventures Australia ☎ 03/9016 3172, Thailand ☎ 02 280 0832, UK ☎ 020/8123 8144, US ☎ 818/921-7101; W grasshopperadventures.com. Cycling day-tours around Bangkok and longer rides to Ko Samui.

Intrepid Travel Australia ☎ 1300/018 871, Canada ☎ 1-866/360-1151, Ireland ☎ 01/524 0071, New Zealand ☎ 0800/600 610, South Africa ☎ 087 985 2798, UK ☎ 0800 781 1660, US ☎ 1-800/970 7299; W intrepidtravel.com. Well-regarded, small-group, off-the-beaten-track tour operator that offers over sixty trips to Thailand.

North South Travel UK ☎ 01245/608 291, W northsouthtravel .co.uk. Friendly, competitive travel agency, offering discounted fares worldwide. Profits are used to support projects in the developing world, especially the promotion of sustainable tourism.

Responsible Travel UK ☎ 01273/600030, W responsibletravel .com. One-stop shop for scores of fair-trade, ethically inclined holidays in Thailand, including trips that focus on wildlife, meditation, family activities and village life.

Spice Roads Thailand W spiceroads.com. Escorted bike tours through Thailand.

STA Travel Australia ☎ 134 782, New Zealand ☎ 0800/474 400, South Africa ☎ 0861/781 781, Thailand ☎ 02 236 0262, UK ☎ 0871/230/0040, US ☎ 1-800/781-4040; W statravel.com. Worldwide specialists in independent travel. Good discounts for students and under-26s.

Symbiosis UK ☎ 0845/123 2844, W symbiosis-travel.com. Upmarket, off-the-beaten-track tours with an environmentally sensitive, fair-trade focus, including kayaking at Khao Sok and Ko Tarutao.

Telltale Travel UK ☎ 0800/011 2571, W telltaletravel.co.uk. Tailor-made, upscale company that offers off-the-beaten-track wildlife, cultural, family, cooking and well-being tours, as well as group trips for solo travellers.

Thailand Birdwatching Thailand W thailandbirdwatching.com. Specialist bird-watching tours in national parks and nature reserves.

Trailfinders UK ☎ 0845 058 5858, Ireland ☎ 01 677 7888; W trailfinders.com. One of the best-informed and most efficient agents for independent travellers, with 24 branches in Britain and Ireland.

Travel Cuts Canada ☎ 1-800/667 2887, US ☎ 1-800/592-2887;

W travelcuts.com. Popular, long-established specialists in budget travel, including student and youth discount offers.

USIT Australia **☎** 1800 092499, Ireland **☎** 01/602 1906; **W** usit.ie. Ireland's main outlet for discounted, youth and student fares, with a branch in Sydney.

Travel via neighbouring countries

Sharing land borders with Burma, Laos, Cambodia and Malaysia, Thailand works well as part of many overland itineraries, both across Asia and between Europe and Australia. Bangkok is also one of the major regional flight hubs for Southeast Asia.

The main restrictions on overland routes in and out of Thailand are determined by where the permitted land crossings lie and by **visas**. Details of visa requirements for travel to Thailand's immediate neighbours are outlined below, but should be double-checked before you travel. All **Asian embassies** are located in Bangkok (see p.145), where many Khao San tour agents offer to get your visa for you, but beware: some are reportedly **faking the stamps**, which could get you into pretty serious trouble, so it's safer to go to the embassy yourself.

The right paperwork is also crucial if you're planning to **drive your own car or motorbike** into Thailand; see the Golden Triangle Rider website (**W** gt-rider.com) for advice.

Burma

There is no overland access from **Burma (Myanmar)** into Thailand, and access in the opposite direction is restricted. Western tourists are only allowed to make limited-distance overland trips into Burma, usually just for the day, including at Kaw Thaung (Victoria Point) near Ranong (see p.292).

Cambodia

At the time of writing, six overland crossings on the **Thai–Cambodia border** are open to non-Thais. See the relevant town accounts for specific details on all the border crossings; for travellers' up-to-the-minute experiences, plus an account of the common **scam** on through-transport from Bangkok to Siem Reap, consult **W** talesofasia.com /cambodia-overland.htm.

Most travellers use either the crossing at Poipet, which has transport connections to Sisophon, Siem Reap and Phnom Penh and lies just across the border from the Thai town of Aranyaprathet (see p.153), with its transport to Bangkok and, with a change in Sa Kaew, to Chanthaburi; or they follow the route from Sihanoukville in Cambodia via Koh Kong and Hat Lek to Trat (see p.178), which is near Ko Chang on Thailand's east coast.

Thirty-day tourist **visas** for Cambodia are issued to travellers on arrival at Phnom Penh and Siem Reap airports, and at all the above-listed land borders; you need US$20 and one photo for this. If you want to buy an advance thirty-day visa, you can do so online at **W** mfaic.gov.kh/evisa which takes three working days and costs US$25; these "e-visas" can only be used at the international airports and at Poipet and Ko Kong land borders, but might help you to avoid the more excessive scams at the land borders.

Laos

There are five main points along the **Lao border** where tourists can cross into northern and north-eastern Thailand: Houayxai (for Chiang Khong); Vientiane (for Nong Khai); Khammouan (aka Thakhek, for Nakhon Phanom); Savannakhet (for Mukdahan); and Pakse (for Chong Mek). All these borders can also be used as exits into Laos.

Visas are required for all non-Thai visitors to Laos. A thirty-day **visa on arrival** can be bought for US$30–42 (depending on your nationality), plus one photo, at Vientiane, Luang Prabang and Pakse airports, and all the above-listed land borders. Or you can buy one in advance from either the Lao Embassy in Bangkok or the Lao Consulate in Khon Kaen for about the same fee.

Malaysia and Singapore

Travelling between Thailand and **Malaysia and Singapore** has in the past been a straightforward and very commonly used overland route, with plentiful connections by bus, minibus, share-taxi and train, most of them routed through the southern Thai city and transport hub of Hat Yai. However, because of the ongoing **violence in Thailand's deep south** (see p.401), most major Western governments are currently advising people not to travel to or through Songkhla, Pattani, Yala and Narathiwat provinces, unless essential (and consequently most insurance companies are not covering travel there). This encompasses Hat Yai and the following border crossings to and from Malaysia: at Padang Besar, on the main rail line connecting Butterworth in Malaysia (and, ultimately, Kuala Lumpur and Singapore) with Hat Yai and Bangkok; at Sungai Kolok, terminus of a railway line from Hat Yai and Bangkok, and at adjacent Ban Taba, both of which are connected by road to nearby Kota Bharu in Malaysia; and at the road crossings at Sadao, south of Hat Yai, and at Betong, south of Yala. (The routes towards Kota Bharu and Betong pass through particularly volatile territory, with martial law declared in Pattani, Yala and Narathiwat provinces; however, martial law is not in effect in Hat Yai itself.)

Nevertheless, the provinces of Trang and Satun on the west coast are not affected, and it's still perfectly possible to travel **overland via Satun**: by ferry between Satun's Thammalang pier and Kuala Perlis or the island of Langkawi, or overland between Ban Khuan and Kangar (see p.420); or by boat between Ko Lipe and Langkawi (see p.417). For up-to-the-minute advice, consult your government travel advisory (see p.57).

Most Western tourists can spend thirty days in Malaysia and fourteen days in Singapore without having bought a visa beforehand, and there are useful Thai embassies or consulates in Kuala Lumpur, Kota Bharu, Penang and Singapore (see p.60).

Getting around

Travel in Thailand is inexpensive and efficient, if not always speedy. Unless you travel by plane, long-distance journeys in Thailand can be arduous, especially if a shoestring budget restricts you to hard seats and no air conditioning.

Nonetheless, the wide range of transport options makes travelling around Thailand easier than elsewhere in Southeast Asia. **Buses** are fast, cheap and frequent, and can be quite luxurious; **trains** are slower but safer and offer more chance of sleeping during overnight trips; moreover, if travelling by day you're likely to follow a more scenic route by rail than by road. Inter-town **songthaews**, a/c **minibuses** and **share-taxis** are handy, and **ferries** provide easy access to all major islands. Local transport comes in all sorts of permutations, both public and chartered.

Inter-town buses

Buses, overall the most convenient way of getting around the country, come in four main categories. In ascending order of comfort, speed and cost, they are **ordinary** buses (*rot thammadaa*; not air-conditioned, usually orange-coloured) and three types of **a/c** bus (*rot air* or *rot thua*; usually blue): second-class, first-class and VIP. Ordinary and many a/c buses are run by Baw Khaw Saw (BKS), the government-controlled transport company, while privately owned, licensed a/c buses (*rot ruam*, usually translated as "join buses"), some of which operate from Baw Khaw Saw terminals, also ply the most popular long-distance routes. Be warned that long-distance overnight buses, on which some drivers are rumoured to take amphetamines to stay awake, seem to be involved in more than their fair share of accidents; because of this, some travellers prefer to do the overnight journeys by train and then make a shorter bus connection to their destination.

Ordinary and second-class

On most routes, including nearly all services out of Bangkok, **second-class** (*baw sawng*; look for the "2" on the side of the vehicle) a/c buses have now replaced **ordinary buses** as the main workhorses of the Thai bus system, though you'll still see plenty of the latter on shorter routes in more remote parts of the country. Whether a/c or not, these basic buses are incredibly inexpensive, generally run frequently during daylight hours, pack as many people in as possible and stop often, which slows them down considerably.

It's best to ask locally where to catch your bus. Failing that, designated **bus stops** are often marked by **sala**, small, open-sided wooden structures with bench seats, located at intervals along the main long-distance bus route through town or on the fringes of any decent-sized settlement, for example on the main highway that skirts the edge of town. Where there is only a bus shelter on the "wrong" side of the road, you can be sure that buses travelling in both directions will stop there for any waiting passengers; simply leave your bag on the right side of the road to alert the bus driver and wait in the shade. But if you're in the middle of nowhere with no *sala* in sight, any ordinary or second-class bus should stop for you if you flag it down.

First-class and VIP

Express services, with fewer stops, are mostly operated by **first-class** (*baw neung*; look for the "1" on the side of the vehicle) and **VIP** (usually written in English on the side) buses. These are your best option for long-distance journeys: you'll generally be allotted specific seats, there'll be a toilet, and on the longest journeys you may get blankets, snacks and nonstop DVDs. The first-class services have fewer seats than second-class and more leg room for reclining, VIP services fewer seats again. Other nomenclature for the top-of-the-range services is also used, especially by the **private "join" companies**: "999", "super VIP" (with even fewer seats), "Gold Class" and, confusingly, sometimes even "First Class" (in imitation of airlines, with just eighteen huge, well-equipped seats).

On a lot of long-distance routes private "join" buses are indistinguishable from government ones and operate out of the same Baw Khaw Saw bus terminals. The major private companies, such as Nakhon Chai Air (T02 936 0009) and Sombat Tour (T02 792 1444), have roughly similar fares, though naturally with more scope for price variation, and offer comparable facilities and standards of service. The opposite is unfortunately true of a number of the smaller, private, unlicensed companies, which have a poor reputation for service and comfort, but gear themselves towards foreign travellers with bargain fares and convenient timetables. The long-distance tour buses that run **from Thanon Khao San** in Banglamphu to Surat Thani are a case in point; though promised VIP buses, travellers on these routes frequently complain about shabby furnishings, ineffective a/c, unhelpful (even aggressive) drivers, lateness and a frightening lack of safety awareness – and there are frequent reports of theft from luggage on these routes, too, and even the spraying of "sleeping gas" so that hand luggage can be rifled without interruption. Generally it's best to travel with the government or licensed private bus companies from the main bus terminals (who have a reputation with their regular Thai customers to maintain) or to go by train instead – the extra comfort and peace of mind are well worth the extra baht.

Tickets and timetables

Tickets for all buses can be bought from the departure terminals, but for ordinary and second-class a/c buses it's normal to buy them on board. First-class and VIP buses may operate from a separate station or office, and tickets for the more popular routes should be booked a day in advance. As a rough indication of **fares**, a trip from Bangkok to Surat Thani, a distance of 640km, costs B760–880 for VIP, B490–570 for first-class air-con and B370 for second-class a/c.

Long-distance buses often depart in clusters around the same time (early morning or late at night for example), leaving a gap of five or more hours during the day with no services at all. Local TAT offices occasionally keep up-to-date bus **timetables**, but the best source of information, apart from the bus stations themselves, is W thaiticketmajor.com, which carries timetables in English for 360 routes as well as useful information on how to **buy tickets** in advance. Options include buying them online through the site; by phone on T02 262 3456 (making your payment within five hours at, for example, any branch of 7–Eleven); and buying them at 83 major post offices (as listed on the site), including the GPO in Bangkok, the Ratchadamnoen post office in Banglamphu and the Thanon Na Phra Lan post office opposite the entrance to the Grand Palace in Ratanakosin.

Songthaews, share-taxis and air-conditioned minibuses

In rural areas, the bus network is often supplemented by **songthaews** (literally "two rows"), which are open-ended vans (or occasionally cattle-trucks) onto which the drivers squash as many passengers as possible on two facing benches, leaving latecomers to swing off the running board at the back. As well as their essential role within towns (see p.33), songthaews ply set routes from larger towns out to their surrounding suburbs and villages, and, where there's no call for a regular bus service, between small towns: some have destinations written on in Thai, but few are numbered. In most towns you'll find the songthaew "terminal" near the market; to pick one up between destinations just flag it down. To indicate to the driver that you want to get out, the normal practice is to rap hard with a coin on the metal railings as you approach the spot (or press the bell if there is one).

In the deep south (see p.400) they do things with a little more style – **share-taxis** connect many of the major towns, though they are inexorably being replaced by more comfortable **air-conditioned minibuses** (rot tuu, meaning "cupboard cars"). Scores of similar private a/c minibus services are now cropping up all over the country, generally operating out of small offices or pavement desks in town centres – or from the roads around Bangkok's Victory Monument. Some of these services have a timetable, but many just aim to leave when they have a full complement of passengers; then again, some companies publish a timetable but depart when they're full – whether before or after the published time. They cover the distance faster than buses, but often at breakneck speed and they can be uncomfortably cramped when full – they're not ideal for travellers with huge rucksacks, who may be required to pay extra. These services are usually licensed and need to keep up their reputation with their regular Thai passengers but, as with full-sized buses (see p.31), you should be wary of unlicensed private companies that offer minibuses solely for farangs from Bangkok's Thanon Khao San.

In many cases, long-distance songthaews and a/c minibuses will drop you at an exact address (for example a particular guesthouse) if you warn them far enough in advance. As a rule, the **cost** of inter-town songthaews is comparable to that of a/c buses, that of a/c minibuses perhaps a shade more.

Trains

Managed by the State Railway of Thailand (SRT), the **rail** network consists of four main lines and a few branch lines. In the area covered by this book is the little-used **Eastern Line**, which has two branches, one of which runs from Bangkok to Aranyaprathet on the Cambodian border, the other of which connects Bangkok with Si Racha and Pattaya. The **Southern Line** extends via Hua Hin, Chumphon and Surat Thani, with spurs off to Trang and Nakhon Si Thammarat, to Hat Yai (see p.401), where it branches: one line continues down the west coast of Malaysia, via Butterworth, where you usually change trains for Kuala Lumpur and Singapore; the other heads down the eastern side of the peninsula to Sungai Kolok on the Thailand–Malaysia border (20km from Pasir Mas on Malaysia's interior railway).

Fares depend on the class of seat, whether or not you want air conditioning, and on the speed of the train; those quoted here exclude the "speed" supplements (see below). Hard, wooden or thinly padded third-class seats are much cheaper than buses (Bangkok–Surat Thani B107), and are fine for about three hours, after which numbness sets in. For longer journeys you'd be wise to opt for the

padded and often reclining seats in second class (Bangkok–Surat Thani B248), which are sometimes available in air-conditioned carriages. On long-distance trains, you also usually have the option of second-class berths (Bangkok–Surat Thani B348–398, or B548–618 with a/c), with day seats that convert into comfortable curtained-off bunks in the evening; lower bunks, which are more expensive than upper, have a few cubic centimetres more of space, a little more shade from the lights in the carriage, and a window. Female passengers can sometimes request a berth in an all-female section of a carriage. Travelling first class (Bangkok–Surat B989–1189 per person) generally means a two-person a/c sleeping compartment, complete with washbasin.

There are several different **types of train**: slowest of all is the third-class-only Ordinary service, which is generally (but not always) available only on short and medium-length journeys and has no speed supplement. Next comes the misleadingly named Rapid train (B20–110 supplement), a trip on which from Bangkok to Surat Thani, for example, takes twelve or thirteen hours; the Express (B150 supplement), which does the same route in around twelve hours; and the Special Express (B170–190 supplement) which covers the ground in between nine and eleven hours. Among the last-mentioned, fastest of all are the mostly daytime Special Express Diesel Railcars, which can usually be relied on to run roughly on time (most other trains pay only lip service to their timetables). Nearly all long-distance trains have **dining cars**, and rail staff will also bring meals to your seat.

Booking at least one day in advance is strongly recommended for second- and first-class seats on all lengthy journeys, and sleepers should be booked as far in advance as possible (reservations open sixty days before departure). You can make bookings for any journey in Thailand at the train station in any major town, and it's now also possible to book online, at least two days in advance, at SRT's Ⓦthairailticket.com. The website is allocated only a limited number of seats, but it allows you to

---

TRAIN INFORMATION & BOOKING

The State Railway of Thailand (SRT) offers 24hr **train information** on its free hotline ☎ 1690 and publishes free **timetables** in English, detailing types of trains available on each route (the best place to get hold of them is over the counter at Bangkok's Hualamphong Station). Its main website (Ⓦrailway.co.th) carries English-language timetables and a breakdown of prices, but to buy tickets you'll need to go to its **booking** website, Ⓦthairailticket.com. For more comprehensive information and advice, go to Ⓦseat61.com/thailand.htm.

pay by credit card and simply print off your ticket. Otherwise, you can arrange advance bookings over the internet with reputable Thai travel agencies such as Thai Focus (W thaifocus.com) or Thailand Train Ticket (W thailandtrainticket.com). Trains out of Bangkok can be booked **in person** at Hualamphong Station (see p.115).

Ferries

Regular **ferries** connect all major islands with the mainland, and for the vast majority of crossings you simply buy your ticket on board. Safety standards are generally just about adequate but there have been a small number of sinkings in recent years – avoid travelling on boats that are clearly overloaded or in poor condition. In tourist areas competition ensures that prices are kept low, and fares tend to vary with the speed of the crossing: thus Chumphon–Ko Tao costs between B200 (6hr) and B600 (1hr 45min).

On the east coast and the Andaman coast boats generally operate a reduced service during the monsoon season (May–Oct), when the more remote spots become inaccessible. Ferries in the Samui archipelago are fairly constant year-round. Details on island connections are given in the relevant chapters.

Flights

Thai Airways (W thaiair.com) and Bangkok Airways (W bangkokair.com) are the major full-service airlines on the internal **flight** network, which extends to all parts of the country, using some two-dozen airports. Air Asia (W airasia.com), Nok Air (W nokair.com), which is part-owned by Thai Airways, and Orient Thai (formerly One-Two-Go; W flyorientthai.com) provide the main, "low-cost" competition; Thai Airways are also about to set up a new low-cost arm, Thai Smile. In a recently deregulated but ever-expanding market, other smaller airlines come and go with surprising frequency – and while they are operating, schedules tend to be erratic and flights are sometimes cancelled.

Book your flights early if possible – you can reserve online with all companies – as fares fluctuate wildly. For a fully flexible economy ticket, Bangkok to Phuket costs B4775 with Thai Airways, but you'll find flights on the same route with the "low-cost" carriers for under B1000 (with restrictions on changes), if you book online far enough in advance.

If you're planning to make lots of domestic flights, you might want to consider the **airpasses** offered by Thai or Bangkok Airways – their complex conditions and prices are posted on their websites.

Local transport

Most sizeable towns have some kind of **local transport system**, comprising a network of buses, songthaews or even longtail boats, with set fares and routes but not rigid timetabling – in many cases vehicles wait until they're full before they leave.

Buses and songthaews

A few larger cities such as Bangkok have a **local bus** network that usually extends to the suburbs and operates from dawn till dusk (through the night in Bangkok). Most vehicles display route numbers in Western numerals – see the relevant accounts for further details.

Within medium-sized and large towns, the main transport role is often played by **songthaews**. The size and shape of vehicle used varies from town to town – and in some places they're known as "tuk-tuks" from the noise they make, not to be confused with the smaller tuk-tuks, described below, that operate as private taxis – but all have the tell-tale two facing benches in the back. In some towns, songthaews follow fixed routes; in others, they act as communal taxis, picking up a number of people who are going in roughly the same direction and taking each of them right to their destination. To hail a songthaew just flag it down, and to indicate that you want to get out, either rap hard with a coin on the metal railings, or ring the bell if there is one. Fares within towns are around B10–20, depending on distance.

Longtail boats

Wherever there's a decent public waterway, there'll be a **longtail boat** ready to ferry you along it. Another great Thai trademark, these elegant, streamlined boats are powered by deafening diesel engines – sometimes custom-built, more often adapted from cars or trucks – which drive a propeller mounted on a long shaft that is swivelled for steering. Longtails carry between eight and twenty passengers: generally you'll have to charter the whole boat, but on popular fixed routes, for example between small, inshore islands and the mainland, it's cheaper to wait until the boatman gets his quorum.

Taxi services

Taxis also come in many guises, and in bigger towns you can often choose between taking a tuk-tuk, a samlor and a motorbike taxi. The one thing common to all modes of chartered transport, bar metered taxis in Bangkok, is that you must establish the **fare** beforehand: although drivers nearly always pitch their first offers too high, they do calculate with traffic and time of day in mind, as well as according to distance – if successive drivers scoff at your price, you know you've got it wrong.

Tuk-tuks

Named after the noise of its excruciatingly unsilenced engine, the three-wheeled, open-sided **tuk-tuk** is the classic Thai vehicle. Painted in primary colours, tuk-tuks blast their way round towns and cities on two-stroke engines, zipping around faster than any car and taking corners on two wheels. They aren't as dangerous as they look though, and can be an exhilarating way to get around, as long as you're not too fussy about exhaust fumes. Fares come in at around B60 for a medium-length journey (over B100 in Bangkok) regardless of the number of passengers – three is the safe maximum, though six is not uncommon. It's worth paying attention to advice on how to avoid getting ripped off by Bangkok tuk-tuk drivers (see p.58).

Samlors

Tuk-tuks are also sometimes known as samlors (literally "three wheels"), but the original **samlors** are tricycle rickshaws propelled by pedal power alone. Slower and a great deal more stately than tuk-tuks, samlors still operate in one or two towns around the country.

A further permutation is the motorized samlors, where the driver relies on a motorbike rather than a bicycle to propel passengers to their destination. They look much the same as cycle samlors, but often sound as noisy as tuk-tuks.

Motorbike taxis

Even faster and more precarious than tuk-tuks, **motorbike taxis** feature both in towns and in out-of-the-way places. In towns – where the drivers are identified by coloured, numbered vests – they have the advantage of being able to dodge traffic jams, but are obviously only really suitable for the single traveller, and motorbike taxis aren't the easiest mode of transport if you're carrying luggage. In remote spots, on the other hand, they're often the only alternative to hitching or walking, and are especially useful for getting between bus stops on main roads, around car-free islands and to national parks or ancient ruins.

Within towns motorbike-taxi fares can start at B10 for very short journeys, but for trips to the outskirts the cost rises steeply – reckon on at least B200 for a 20km round trip.

Vehicle rental

Despite first impressions, a high accident rate and the obvious mayhem that characterizes Bangkok's roads, **driving** yourself around Thailand can be fairly straightforward. Many roads, particularly in the northeast and the south, are remarkably uncongested. Major routes are clearly signed in English, though this only applies to some minor roads; unfortunately there is no perfect English-language map to compensate (see p.66).

Outside the capital, the eastern seaboard and the major tourist resorts of Ko Samui and Phuket, local drivers are generally considerate and unaggressive; they very rarely use their horns, for example, and will often indicate and even swerve away when it's safe for you to overtake. The most inconsiderate and dangerous road-users in Thailand are bus drivers and lorry drivers, many of whom drive ludicrously fast, hog the road, race round bends on the wrong side of the road and use their horns remorselessly; worse still, many of them are tanked up on amphetamines, which makes them quite literally fearless.

Bus and lorry drivers are at their worst after dark (many of them only drive then), so it's best **not to drive at night** – a further hazard being the inevitable stream of unlit bicycles and mopeds in and around built-up areas, as well as poorly signed roadworks, which are often not made safe or blocked off from unsuspecting traffic. Orange signs, or sometimes just a couple of tree branches or a pile of stones on the road, warn of hazards ahead.

As for local **rules of the road**, Thais drive on the left, and the speed limit is 60km per hr within built-up areas and 90km per hr outside them. Beyond that, there are few rules that are generally followed – you'll need to keep your concentration up and expect the unexpected from fellow road-users. Watch out especially for vehicles pulling straight out of minor roads, when you might expect them to give way. An oncoming vehicle flashing its lights means it's coming through no matter what; a right indicator signal from the car in front usually means it's not safe for you to overtake, while a left indicator signal usually means that it is safe to do so.

Theoretically, foreigners need an international **driver's licence** to rent any kind of vehicle, but most car-rental companies accept national licences, and the smaller operations have been known not to ask for any kind of proof whatsoever; motorbike renters very rarely bother. A popular rip-off on islands such as Ko Pha Ngan is for small agents to charge renters exorbitant amounts for any minor damage to a jeep or motorbike, even paint chips, that they find on return – they'll claim that it's very expensive to get a new part shipped over from the mainland. Be sure to check out any vehicle carefully before renting.

Petrol (*nam man*, which can also mean oil) currently costs around B38 a litre, gasohol, which can be used in most rental cars (though it's worth checking), B36 a litre. The big fuel stations are the least costly places to fill up (*hai tem*), and many of these also have toilets, minimarts and restaurants, though some of the more decrepit-looking fuel stations on the main highways only sell diesel. Most small villages have easy-to-spot roadside huts where the fuel is pumped out of a large barrel.

Renting a car

If you decide to **rent a car**, go to a reputable dealer, such as Avis, Budget or National, or a rental company recommended by TAT, and make sure you get insurance from them. There are international car-rental places at many airports, including Bangkok's Suvarnabhumi, which is not a bad place to kick off, as you're on the edge of the city and within fairly easy, signposted reach of the major regional highways.

Car-rental places in provincial capitals and resorts are listed in the relevant accounts in this book. The price of a small car at a reputable company can start as low as B900 per day if booked online.

Jeeps or basic four-wheel drives are a lot more popular with farangs, especially on beach resorts and islands like Pattaya, Phuket and Ko Samui, but they're notoriously dangerous; a huge number of tourists manage to roll their jeeps on steep hillsides and sharp bends. Jeep rental usually works out somewhere around B1000–1200 per day.

International companies will accept your credit-card details as surety, but smaller agents will usually want to hold on to your passport.

CAR RENTAL AGENCIES

Avis Ⓦ avisthailand.com
Budget Ⓦ budget.co.th
Master Ⓦ mastercarrental.com
National Ⓦ nationalcarthailand.com
Thai Rentacar Ⓦ thairentacar.com

Renting a motorbike

One of the best ways of exploring the countryside is to **rent a motorbike**. You'll never be asked for a driving licence, but take it easy out there – Thailand's roads are not really the place to learn to ride a motorbike from scratch. Bikes of around 100cc, either fully automatic or with step-through gears, are best for inexperienced riders, but aren't really suited for long slogs. If you're going to hit the dirt roads you'll certainly need something more powerful, like a 125–250cc trail bike. These have the edge in gear choice and are the best bikes for steep slopes, though an inexperienced rider may find these machines a handful; the less widely available 125–250cc road bikes are easier to control and much cheaper on fuel.

Rental **prices** for the day usually work out at somewhere around B150–200 for a small bike and B500 for a good trail bike, though you can bargain for a discount on a long rental. Renters will often ask for a deposit and your passport or credit-card details; insurance is not often available, so it's a good idea to make sure your travel insurance covers you for possible mishaps.

Before signing anything, **check the bike** thoroughly – test the brakes, look for oil leaks, check the treads and the odometer, and make sure the chain isn't stretched too tight (a tight chain is more likely to break) – and preferably take it for a test run. As you will have to pay an inflated price for any damage when you get back, make a note on the contract of any defects such as broken mirrors, indicators and so on. Make sure you know what kind of fuel the bike takes as well.

As far as **equipment** goes, a helmet is essential – most rental places provide poorly made ones, but they're better than nothing. Helmets are obligatory on all motorbike journeys, and the law is often rigidly enforced with on-the-spot fines in major tourist resorts. You'll need sunglasses if your helmet doesn't have a visor. Long trousers, a long-sleeved top and decent shoes will provide a second skin if you go over, which most people do at some stage. Pillions should wear long trousers to avoid getting nasty burns from the exhaust. For the sake of stability, leave most of your luggage in baggage storage and pack as small a bag as possible, strapping it tightly to the bike with bungy cords – these can usually be provided. Once on the road, oil the chain at least every other day, keep the radiator topped up and fill up with oil every 300km or so.

For expert **advice** on motorbike travel in Thailand, check out David Unkovich's website (Ⓦ gt-rider.com).

Cycling

The options for **cycling** in Thailand are numerous, and most Thai roads are in good condition and clearly signposted. The secondary **roads** (distinguished by their three-digit numbers) are paved but carry far less traffic than the main arteries and are the preferred cycling option. Traffic is reasonably well behaved and personal safety is not a major concern as long as you "ride to survive"; dogs, however, can be a nuisance on minor roads so it's probably worth having rabies shots before your trip. There are bike shops in nearly every town, and basic equipment and repairs are cheap. Unless you head into the remotest regions around the Burmese border you are rarely more than 25km from food, water and accommodation. Overall, the best time to cycle is during the cool, dry season from November to February and the least good from April to July (see p.55).

The traffic into and out of Bangkok is dense so it's worth hopping on a bus or train for the first 50–100km to your starting point. Intercity buses, taxis and most Thai domestic planes will **carry your bike** free of charge. Intercity trains will only transport your bike (for a cargo fare – about the price of a person) if there is a luggage carriage attached, unless you dismantle it and carry it as luggage in the compartment with you. Songthaews will carry your bike on the roof for a fare (about the price of a person).

Local one-day cycle tours and **bike-rental outlets** (B30–100/day) are listed throughout this book. There are also a number of organized **cycle tours** (see p.28). A very useful English-language resource is Ⓦbicyclethailand.com, while Biking Asia with Mr Pumpy (Ⓦmrpumpy.net) gives detailed but dated accounts of some cycling routes in Thailand.

Cycling practicalities

Strong, light, quality **mountain bikes** are the most versatile choice. 26-inch wheels are standard throughout Thailand and are strongly recommended; dual-use (combined road and off-road) tyres are best for touring. As regards panniers and **equipment**, the most important thing is to travel light. Carry a few spare spokes, but don't overdo it with too many tools and spares; parts are cheap in Thailand and most problems can be fixed quickly at any bike shop.

Bringing your bike from home is the best option as you are riding a known quantity. **Importing** it by plane should be straightforward, but check with

the airlines for details. Most Asian airlines do not charge extra.

Buying in Thailand is also a possibility: the range is reasonable and prices tend to be cheaper than in the West or Australia. In Bangkok, the best outlet is Probike at 237/2 Thanon Rajdamri (actually off Soi Sarasin next to Lumphini Park; ☎02 253 3384, Ⓦprobike.co.th); Velo Thailand (see p.118) also sell international-brand aluminium-frame bikes, as well as **renting** mountain bikes for B300 per day. You can also rent good mountain bikes through the Bangkok cycle-tour operator Spice Roads (☎02 712 5305, Ⓦspiceroads.com) for B280–400 per day.

Hitching

Public transport being so inexpensive, you should only have to resort to **hitching** in the most remote areas, in which case you'll probably get a lift to the nearest bus or songthaew stop quite quickly. On routes served by buses and trains, hitching is not standard practice, but in other places locals do rely on regular passers-by (such as national park officials), and you can make use of this "service" too. As with hitching anywhere in the world, think twice about hitching solo or at night, especially if you're female. Like bus drivers, truck drivers are notorious users of amphetamines, so you may want to wait for a safer offer.

Accommodation

For the simplest double room, prices start at a bargain B150 in the outlying regions, B200 in Bangkok, and B400 in the pricier resorts. Tourist centres invariably offer a tempting range of more upmarket choices but in these areas rates fluctuate according to demand, plummeting during the off-season, peaking over the Christmas fortnight and, in some places, rising at weekends throughout the year.

Guesthouses, bungalows and hostels

Most of Thailand's **budget accommodation** is in **guesthouses** and **bungalows**. These are small, traveller-friendly hotels whose services nearly always include an inexpensive restaurant and safe storage for valuables and left luggage, and often also run to internet access (sometimes even in-room wi-fi) and

ACCOMMODATION PRICES

Throughout this guide, the prices given for guesthouses, bungalows and hotels represent the **minimum** you can expect to pay in each establishment in the **high season** (roughly July, Aug and Nov–Feb) for a typical **double room**, booked via the hotel website where available; there may however be an extra "peak" supplement for the Christmas–New Year period. If travelling on your own, expect to pay between sixty and one hundred percent of the rates quoted for a double room. Where a hostel or guesthouse also offers **dormitory beds**, the minimum price per bed is also given; where a place has rooms in distinct categories (eg fan/air-con, shared bathroom/en suite), we've given the minimum price for a double in each category. Top-end hotels will add **seven percent tax** and **ten percent service charge** to your bill; the prices given in the guide are net rates after taxes have been added.

a tour desk. The difference between guesthouses and bungalows is mostly in their design, with "bungalows" – which are generally found on the beach and in rural areas – mostly comprising detached or semi-detached rooms in huts, villas, chalets or indeed bungalows, and "guesthouses" being either a purpose-built mini-hotel or a converted home. En-suite showers and flush toilets are common in both, but at the cheapest places you might be showering with a bowl dipped into a large water jar, and using squat toilets.

Many guesthouses and bungalows offer a spread of options to cater for all budgets: their **cheapest rooms** will often be furnished with nothing more than a double bed, a blanket and a fan (window optional, private bathroom extra) and might cost anything from B150–300 for two people, depending on the location and the competition. A similar room with **en-suite** bathroom, and possibly more stylish furnishings generally comes in at B200–600, while for a room with **a/c**, and perhaps a TV and fridge as well, you're looking at B350–1500.

In the most popular tourist centres at the busiest times of year, the best-known guesthouses are often full night after night. Some will take **bookings** and advance payment via their websites, but for those that don't it's usually a question of turning up and waiting for a vacancy. At most guesthouses **checkout time** is either 11am or noon.

Generally you should be wary of taking accommodation advice from a **tout** or tuk-tuk driver, as they demand commission from guesthouse owners, which, if not passed directly on to you via a higher room price, can have a crippling effect on the smaller guesthouses. If a tout claims your intended accommodation is "full" or "no good" or has "burnt down", it's always worth phoning to check yourself. Touts can come into their own, however, on islands such as Ko Lanta where it can

be a long and expensive ride to your chosen beach, and frustrating if you then discover your bungalows are full; island touts usually sweet-talk you on the boat and then transport you for free to view their accommodation, ideally with no obligation to stay.

With only a dozen or so registered **youth hostels** in the country, bookable via ⓦtyha.org, it's not worth becoming a Hostelling International member just for your trip to Thailand, especially as card-holders get only a small discount and room rates work out the same as or more expensive than guest-house equivalents. In addition, there are a small, but growing number of smart, modern, non-affiliated **hostels**, especially in Bangkok. They usually work out more expensive than budget guesthouses but are good places to meet other travellers.

Budget hotels

Thai sales reps and other people travelling for business rather than pleasure rarely use guest-houses, opting instead for **budget hotels**, which offer rooms for around B150–600. Usually run by Chinese-Thais, these functional three- or four-storey places are found in every sizeable town, often near the bus station or central market. Beds are large enough for a couple, so it's quite accept-able for two people to ask and pay for a "single" room (*hawng thiang diaw*, literally a "one-bedded room"). Though the rooms are generally clean, en suite and furnished with either a fan or a/c, there's rarely an on-site restaurant and the atmosphere is generally less convivial than at guesthouses. A number of budget hotels also double as brothels, though as a farang you're unlikely to be offered this sideline, and you might not even notice the goings-on.

Advance reservations are accepted over the phone, but this is rarely necessary, as such hotels rarely fill up. The only time you may have difficulty finding a budget hotel room is during Chinese New

---

BATHROOM ETIQUETTE

Although modern, Western-style bathrooms are commonplace throughout Thailand, it's as well to be forewarned about local bathroom etiquette.

Sit-down **toilets** are the norm but public amenities, especially at bus and train stations, and in some homes and old-style guesthouses and hotels, tend to be squat toilets. Thais traditionally don't use **paper** but wash rather than wipe themselves after going to the toilet. Modern bathrooms are fitted with a special hose for this purpose, while more primitive bathrooms just provide a **bucket of water and a dipper**. Thais always use their left hand for washing – and their right hand for eating (see p.41). As Thai plumbing is notoriously sluggish, where toilet paper is provided, it's normal to throw it in the waste basket and not down the U-bend. If a toilet is not plumbed in, you flush it yourself with water from the bucket. In really basic hotel bathrooms with no **shower** facilities, you also use the bucket and dipper for scoop-and-slosh bathing.

Year (a moveable three-day period in late Jan or Feb), when many Chinese-run hotels close and others get booked up fast.

Tourist hotels

The rest of the accommodation picture is all about **tourist hotels** which, like anywhere in the world, come in all sizes and qualities and are often best booked via online discount accommodation booking services such as ⓦsawadee.com. One way or another, it's a good idea to **reserve ahead** in popular tourist areas during peak season.

Rates for **middle-ranking hotels** fall between B600 and B2000. For this you can expect many of the trimmings of a top-end hotel – a/c, TV and mini-bar in the room, plus an on-site pool, restaurant and perhaps nightclub – but with dated and possibly faded furnishings and little of the style of the famous big names; they're often the kind of places that once stood at the top of the range, but were outclassed when the multinational luxury hotels muscled in.

Many of Thailand's **expensive hotels** belong to the big international chains: Sheraton, Marriott and Sofitel all have a strong presence in the country and are closely followed by upmarket home-grown groups such as Amari, Dusit and Centara. Between them they maintain premium standards in Bangkok and major resorts at prices of B3000 (£60/US$100) and upward for a double – far less than you'd pay for equivalent accommodation in the West.

Thailand also boasts an increasing number of deliciously stylish **luxury hotels**, many of them designed as intimate, small-scale **boutique** hotels, with chic, minimalist decor, exceptional service and excellent facilities that often include private plunge pools and a spa. A night in one of these places will rarely cost you less than B6000 (£120/US$200), and

may set you back more than twice as much, though they're still often outstanding value for the honeymoon-style indulgence that they offer; see accommodation listings for Bangkok, Ko Samui, Khao Lak and Phuket for some suggestions. As in the West, however, the term "boutique" is overused, and a "boutique" guesthouse or hotel may in practice be little more than "small". Some luxury hotels quote rates in US dollars, though you can always pay in baht.

Homestays

As guesthouses have become increasingly hotel-like and commercial in their facilities and approach, many tourists looking for old-style local hospitality are choosing **homestay accommodation** instead. Homestay facilities are nearly always simple, and cheap at around B150 per person per night, with guests staying in a shared spare room and eating with the family. Homestays give an unparalleled insight into typical Thai (usually rural) life and can often be incorporated into a programme that includes experiencing village activities such as rice farming, squid fishing, rubber tapping or silk weaving. They are also a positive way of supporting small communities, as all your money will feed right back into the village. As well as listed homestays in Ban Khiriwong (see p.282), Khuraburi (see p.302) and Krabi (see p.356), there are many others bookable through tour operators (see p.28) or via, for example, ⓦhomestaybooking.com /homestay-thailand.

National parks and camping

Nearly all the **national parks** have accommodation facilities, usually comprising a series of simple concrete bungalows that cost at least B600 for two or more beds plus a basic bathroom. Because most of their custom comes from Thai families and student groups, park officials are sometimes loath to discount them for lone travellers, though a few parks do offer dorm-style accommodation at around B100 a bed. In most parks, advance booking is unnecessary except at weekends and national holidays.

If you do want to pre-book, you can do so up to sixty days ahead of your stay at ⓦdnp.go.th. As credit-card payment is not possible on this website, you need to pay in cash or via bank draft within two days of booking, most conveniently at any branch of Krung Thai bank, at designated international banks, or at the National Park headquarters in question; see the website given above for comprehensive details. Affiliated with the National Parks department, a new website, ⓦthaiforestbooking.com, in theory allows booking with a credit card (up to 65 days in advance), though it doesn't work very well. If you turn up without booking, check in at the park headquarters, which is usually adjacent to the visitor centre.

In a few parks, private operators have set up low-cost guesthouses on the outskirts, and these generally make more attractive and economical places to stay.

Camping

You can usually **camp** in a national park for a nominal fee of B60 per two-person tent, and some national parks also rent out fully equipped tents from B150 (bookable through a separate section on ⓦdnp.go.th). Unless you're planning an extensive tour of national parks, though, there's little point in lugging a tent around Thailand: accommodation everywhere else is very inexpensive, and there are no campsites inside town perimeters, though camping is allowed on nearly all islands and beaches, many of which are national parks in their own right.

Food and drink

Bangkok is the country's culinary hub, boasting the cream of gourmet Thai restaurants and the best international cuisines. The rest of the country is by no means a gastronomic wasteland, however, and you can eat well and cheaply in even the smallest provincial towns, many of which offer the additional attraction of regional specialities. In fact

you could eat more than adequately without ever entering a restaurant, as itinerant food vendors hawking hot and cold snacks materialize in even the most remote spots, as well as on trains and buses – and night markets often serve customers from dusk until dawn.

Hygiene is a consideration when eating anywhere in Thailand, but being too cautious means you'll end up spending a lot of money and missing out on some real local treats. Wean your stomach gently by avoiding excessive amounts of chillies and too much fresh fruit in the first few days.

You can be pretty sure that any noodle stall or curry shop that's permanently packed with customers is a safe bet. Furthermore, because most Thai dishes can be cooked in under five minutes, you'll rarely have to contend with stuff that's been left to smoulder and stew. Foods that are generally considered high risk include salads, ice cream, shellfish and raw or undercooked meat, fish or eggs. If you're really concerned about health standards you could stick to restaurants and food stalls displaying a "**Clean Food Good Taste**" sign, part of a food sanitation project set up by the Ministry of Public Health, TAT and the Ministry of the Interior.

Most restaurants in Thailand are open every day for lunch and dinner; we've given full opening hours throughout the Guide. In a few of the country's most expensive restaurants, mostly in Bangkok, a ten percent service charge and possibly even seven percent VAT may be added to your bill.

For those interested in **learning Thai cookery**, short courses designed for visitors are held in Bangkok (see p.130) and dozens of other tourist centres around the country.

Where to eat

A lot of tourists eschew the huge range of Thai **places to eat**, despite their obvious attractions, and opt instead for the much "safer" restaurants in guesthouses and hotels. Almost all tourist accommodation has a kitchen, and while some are excellent, the vast majority serve up bland imitations of Western fare alongside equally pale versions of common Thai dishes. Having said that, guesthouses do serve comfortingly familiar Western breakfasts.

Throughout the country, most **inexpensive Thai restaurants** and cafés specialize in one general food type or preparation method, charging around B40–50 a dish – a "noodle shop", for example, will do fried noodles and/or noodle soups, plus maybe a

FRUITS OF THAILAND

You'll find **fruit** (*phonlamai*) offered everywhere in Thailand – neatly sliced in glass boxes on hawker carts, blended into delicious shakes and served as a dessert in restaurants. The fruits described below can be found in all parts of Thailand, though some are seasonal. The country's more familiar fruits include forty varieties of **banana** (*kluay*), dozens of different **mangoes** (*mamuang*), three types of **pineapple** (*sapparot*), **coconuts** (*maprao*), **oranges** (*som*), **limes** (*manao*) and **watermelons** (*taeng moh*).

To avoid stomach trouble, **peel all fruit** before eating it, and use common sense if you're tempted to buy it pre-peeled on the street, avoiding anything that looks fly-blown or seems to have been sitting in the sun for hours.

Custard apple (soursop; *noina*; July–Sept). Inside the knobbly, muddy green skin is a creamy, almond-coloured blancmange-like flesh, with a strong flavour of strawberries and pears, and a hint of cinnamon, and many seeds.

Durian (*thurian*; April–June). Thailand's most prized, and expensive, fruit has a greeny-yellow, spiky exterior and grows to the size of a football. Inside, it divides into segments of thick, yellow-white flesh, which gives off a disgustingly strong stink that's been compared to a mixture of strong cheese and caramel. Not surprisingly, many hotels and airlines ban durians.

Guava (*farang*; year-round). The apple of the tropics has green textured skin and sweet, crisp pink or white flesh, studded with tiny edible seeds. Has five times the vitamin C content of an orange and is sometimes eaten cut into strips and sprinkled with sugar and chilli.

Jackfruit (*khanun*; year-round). This large, pear-shaped fruit can weigh up to 20kg and has a thick, bobbly, greeny-yellow shell protecting sweet yellow flesh. Green, unripe jackfruit is sometimes cooked as a vegetable in curries.

Longan (*lamyai*; July–Oct). A close relative of the lychee, with succulent white flesh covered in thin, brittle skin.

Lychee (*linjii*; April–May). Under rough, reddish-brown skin, the lychee has sweet, richly flavoured white flesh, rose scented and with plenty of vitamin C.

Mangosteen (*mangkut*; April–Sept). The size of a small apple, with smooth, purple skin and a fleshy inside that divides into succulent white segments that are sweet though slightly acidic.

Papaya (paw-paw; *malakaw*; year-round). Looks like an elongated watermelon, with smooth green skin and yellowy-orange flesh that's a rich source of vitamins A and C. It's a favourite in fruit salads and shakes, and sometimes appears in its green, unripe form in salads, notably *som tam*.

Pomelo (*som oh*; Oct–Dec). The largest of all the citrus fruits, it looks rather like a grapefruit, though it is slightly drier and has less flavour.

Rambutan (*ngaw*; May–Sept). The bright red rambutan's soft, spiny exterior has given it its name – *rambut* means "hair" in Malay. Usually about the size of a golf ball, it has a white, opaque flesh of delicate flavour, similar to a lychee.

Rose apple (*chomphuu*; year-round). Linked in myth with the golden fruit of immortality; small and egg-shaped, with white, rose-scented flesh.

Sapodilla (sapota; *lamut*; Sept–Dec). These small, brown, rough-skinned ovals look a bit like kiwi fruit and conceal a grainy, yellowish pulp that tastes almost honey-sweet.

Tamarind (*makhaam*; Dec–Jan). A Thai favourite and a pricey delicacy – carrying the seeds is said to make you safe from wounding by knives or bullets. Comes in rough, brown pods containing up to ten seeds, each surrounded by a sticky, dry pulp which has a sour, lemony taste.

---

basic fried rice, but they won't have curries or meat or fish dishes. Similarly, a restaurant displaying whole roast chickens and ducks in its window will offer these sliced, usually with chillies and sauces and served over rice, but their menu probably won't extend to noodles or fish, while in "curry shops" your options are limited to the vats of curries stewing away in the hot cabinet.

To get a wider array of low-cost food, it's sometimes best to head for the local **night market** (*talat yen*), a term for the gatherings of open-air night-time kitchens found in every town. Sometimes operating from 6pm to 6am, they are typically to be found on permanent patches close to the fruit and vegetable market or the bus station, and as often as not they're the best and most entertaining places to eat, not to mention the least expensive – after a lip-smacking feast of savoury dishes, a fruit drink and a dessert you'll come away no more than B150 poorer.

A typical night market has maybe thirty-odd "specialist" pushcart kitchens (*rot khen*) jumbled together, each fronted by several sets of tables and stools. Noodle and fried-rice vendors always feature prominently, as do sweets stalls, heaped high with sticky rice cakes wrapped in banana leaves or thick with bags of tiny sweetcorn pancakes hot from the griddle – and no night market is complete without its fruit-drink stall, offering banana shakes and freshly squeezed orange, lemon and tomato juices. In the best setups you'll find a lot more besides: curries, barbecued sweetcorn, satay sticks of pork and chicken, deep-fried insects, fresh pineapple, watermelon and mango and – if the town's by a river or near the sea – heaps of fresh fish. Having decided what you want, you order from the cook (or the cook's dogsbody) and sit down at the nearest table; there is no territorialism about night markets, so it's normal to eat several dishes from separate stalls and rely on the nearest cook to sort out the bill.

Some large markets, particularly in Bangkok, have separate **food court** areas where you buy coupons first and select food and drink to their value at the stalls of your choice. This is also usually the modus operandi in the food courts found in department stores and shopping centres across the country.

For a more relaxing ambience, Bangkok and the larger towns have a range of **upmarket restaurants**, some specializing in **"royal" Thai cuisine**, which is differentiated mainly by the quality of the ingredients, the complexity of preparation and the way the food is presented. Great care is taken over how individual dishes look: they are served in small portions and decorated with carved fruit and vegetables in a way that used to be the prerogative of royal cooks, but has now filtered down to the common folk. The cost of such delights is not prohibitive, either – a meal in one of these places is unlikely to cost more than B500 per person.

How to eat

Thai food is eaten with a **fork** (left hand) and a **spoon** (right hand); there is no need for a knife as food is served in bite-sized chunks, which are forked onto the spoon and fed into the mouth. Cutlery is often delivered to the table wrapped in a perplexingly tiny pink napkin: Thais use this, not for their lap, but to give their fork, spoon and plate an extra wipe-down before they eat. Steamed **rice** (*khao*) is served with most meals, and indeed the most commonly heard phrase for "to eat" is *kin khao* (literally, "eat rice"). **Chopsticks** are provided only for noodle dishes.

So that complementary taste combinations can be enjoyed, the dishes in a Thai meal are served all at once, even the soup, and shared communally. The

---

VEGETARIANS AND VEGANS

Very few Thais are **vegetarian** (*mangsawirat*) but, if you can make yourself understood, you can often get a non-meat or fish alternative to what's on the menu; simply ask the cook to exclude meat and fish: *mai sai neua, mai sai plaa*. You may end up eating a lot of unexciting vegetable fried rice and *phat thai* minus the shrimps, but in better restaurants you should be able to get veggie versions of most curries; the mushroom version of chicken and coconut soup is also a good standby: ask for *tom kha hed*. Browsing food stalls also expands your options, with barbecued sweetcorn, nuts, fruit and other non-meaty goodies all common. The two ingredients that you will have to consider compromising on are the fermented **fish sauce** and **shrimp paste** that are fundamental to most Thai dishes; only in the vegan Thai restaurants described below, and in tourist spots serving specially concocted Thai and Western veggie dishes, can you be sure of avoiding them.

If you're **vegan** (*jay*, sometimes spelt "*jeh*") you'll need to stress when you order that you don't want egg, as they get used a lot; cheese and other dairy produce, however, don't feature at all in Thai cuisine. Many towns will have one or more **vegan restaurants** (*raan ahaan jay*), which are usually run by members of a temple or Buddhist sect and operate from unadorned premises off the main streets; because strict Buddhists prefer not to eat late in the day, most of the restaurants open early, at around 6 or 7am, and close by 2pm. Most of these places have a yellow and red sign, though few display an English-language name. Nor is there ever a menu: customers simply choose from the trays of veggie stir-fries and curries, nearly all of them made with soya products, that are laid out canteen-style. Most places charge around B40 for a couple of helpings served over a plate of brown rice.

SOUTHERN THAI FOOD

Southern Thai cuisine displays a marked Malaysian and Muslim aspect as you near the border and, as you'd expect in a region bounded by sea, the salty flavours associated with seafood are prevalent. Liberal use of **turmeric** is another distinctive feature, which gives many southern dishes a yellow hue, notably *plaa khluk khamin*, grilled fish rubbed with turmeric, garlic and salt.

A huge variety of **curries** is dished up in the south, many of them substituting shrimp paste for the fish sauce used elsewhere in Thailand. Two of the peninsula's most famous curries are *kaeng leuang* ("yellow curry"), which features fish, turmeric, pineapple, squash, beans and green papaya; and *kaeng tai plaa*, a powerful combination of fish stomach with potatoes, beans, pickled bamboo shoots and turmeric. Another very popular local dish, especially on the Andaman coast, is *nam prik kung siap*, a delicious relish of smoked, dried shrimps served with raw vegetables.

Satays feature more down here, as does delicious *hor mok* (sometimes known as *khai plaa mok*), a kind of seafood soufflé made with coconut milk and red curry paste. In Muslim areas, you'll come across *khao mok kai*, the local version of a biryani: chicken and rice cooked with turmeric, cinnamon, cloves and other Indian spices and served with clear chicken soup. Also popular, especially in Phuket, Nakhon Si Thammarat and Trang, is *khanom jiin* (literally, "Chinese pastry"), rice noodles topped with hot, sweet or fishy sauce (the latter Malay-style *naam yaa*, made with ground fish) and served with crispy raw vegetables.

Markets in the south often serve *khao yam* for breakfast or lunch, a deliciously refreshing salad of dried cooked rice, dried shrimp, grated coconut and lemon grass served with a sweet sauce. You'll find many types of **roti** in the south, too – pancake-like bread sold hot from pushcart griddles and, in its plain form, rolled with sickly sweet condensed milk and sugar. Other versions include *roti kluay* (with banana), *roti khai* (with egg), savoury *mataba* (with minced chicken or beef) and, served with curry sauce for breakfast, *roti kaeng*.

more people, the more taste and texture sensations; if there are only two of you, it's normal to order three dishes, plus your own individual plates of steamed rice, while three diners would order four dishes, and so on. Only put a serving of one dish on your rice plate each time, and then only one or two spoonfuls.

Bland food is anathema to Thais, and restaurant tables everywhere come decked out with **condiment sets** featuring the four basic flavours (salty, sour, sweet and spicy): usually fish sauce with chopped chillies; vinegar with chopped chillies; sugar; and dried chillies – and often extra bowls of ground peanuts and a bottle of chilli ketchup as well. Similarly, many individual Thai dishes are served with their own specific, usually spicy, condiment dip (*nam jim*). If you do bite into a **chilli**, the way to combat the searing heat is to take a mouthful of plain rice and/or beer: swigging water just exacerbates the sensation.

What to eat

Five fundamental tastes are identified in Thai cuisine – spiciness, sourness, bitterness, saltiness and sweetness – and diners aim to share a variety of dishes that impart a balance of these flavours, along with complementary textures. Lemon grass, basil, coriander, galangal, chilli, garlic, lime juice, coconut milk and fermented fish sauce are just some of the distinctive components that bring these tastes to life. A detailed food and drink glossary can be found at the end of "Contexts" (see p.448).

Curries and soups

Thai **curries** (*kaeng*) have a variety of curry pastes as their foundation: elaborate blends of herbs, spices, garlic, shallots and chilli peppers ground together with pestle and mortar. The use of some of these spices, as well as coconut cream, was imported from India long ago; curries that don't use coconut cream are naturally less sweet and thinner, with the consistency of soups. While some curries, such as *kaeng karii* (mild and yellow) and *kaeng matsaman* ("Muslim curry", with potatoes, peanuts and usually beef), still show their roots, others have been adapted into quintessentially Thai dishes, notably *kaeng khiaw wan* (sweet and green), *kaeng phet* (red and hot) and *kaeng phanaeng* (thick and savoury, with peanuts). *Kaeng som* generally contains fish and usually takes its distinctive sourness from the addition of tamarind. Traditionally eaten during the cool season, *kaeng liang* uses up bland vegetables, but is made aromatic with hot peppercorns.

Eaten simultaneously with other dishes, not as a starter, Thai **soups** often have the tang of lemon grass, kaffir lime leaves and galangal, and are sometimes made extremely spicy with chillies. Two favourites are *tom kha kai*, a creamy coconut chicken soup; and *tom yam kung*, a hot and sour prawn soup without coconut milk. *Khao tom*, a starchy rice soup that's generally eaten for breakfast, meets the approval of few Westerners, except as a traditional hangover cure.

Salads

One of the lesser-known delights of Thai cuisine is the *yam* or **salad**, which imparts most of the fundamental flavours in an unusual and refreshing harmony. *Yam* come in many permutations – with noodles, meat, seafood or vegetables – but at the heart of every variety is a liberal squirt of lime juice and a fiery sprinkling of chillies. Salads to look out for include *yam som oh* (pomelo), *yam hua plee* (banana flowers) and *yam plaa duk foo* (fluffy deep-fried catfish).

Noodle and rice dishes

Sold on street stalls everywhere, **noodles** come in assorted varieties – including *kway tiaw* (made with rice flour) and *ba mii* (egg noodles) – and get boiled up as soups (*nam*), doused in gravy (*rat na*) or stir-fried (*haeng*, "dry", or *phat*, "fried"). Most famous of all is *phat thai* ("Thai fry-up"), a delicious combination of noodles (usually *kway tiaw*), egg, tofu and spring onions, sprinkled with ground peanuts and lime, and often spiked with tiny dried shrimps. Other faithful standbys include fried rice (*khao phat*) and cheap, one-dish meals served on a bed of steamed rice, notably *khao kaeng* (with curry).

Desserts

Desserts (*khanom*) don't really figure on most restaurant menus, but a few places offer bowls of *luk taan cheum*, a jellied concoction of lotus or palm seeds floating in a syrup scented with jasmine or other aromatic flowers. Coconut milk is a feature of most other desserts, notably delicious coconut ice cream, *khao niaw mamuang* (sticky rice with mango), and a royal Thai cuisine special of coconut custard (*sangkhayaa*) cooked inside a small pumpkin, whose flesh you can also eat.

Drinks

Thais don't drink water straight from the tap, and nor should you; plastic bottles of drinking **water** (*nam plao*) are sold countrywide, in even the smallest villages, for around B10 and should be used even when brushing your teeth. Cheap restaurants and hotels generally serve free jugs of

boiled water, which should be fine to drink, though they are not as foolproof as the bottles. In some large towns, you'll come across blue-and-white roadside machines that dispense purified water for B1 for 1–2 litres (bring your own bottle).

Night markets, guesthouses and restaurants do a good line in freshly squeezed **fruit juices** such as lime (*nam manao*) and orange (*nam som*), which often come with salt and sugar already added, particularly upcountry. The same places will usually do **fruit shakes** as well, blending bananas (*nam kluay*), papayas (*nam malakaw*), pineapples (*nam sapparot*) and others with liquid sugar or condensed milk (or yoghurt, to make lassi). Fresh **coconut water** (*nam maprao*) is another great thirst-quencher – you buy the whole fruit dehusked, decapitated and chilled – as is **pandanus-leaf juice** (*bai toey*); Thais are also very partial to freshly squeezed **sugar-cane juice** (*nam awy*), which is sickeningly sweet.

Bottled and canned brand-name **soft drinks** are sold all over the place, with a particularly wide range in the ubiquitous 7-Eleven chain stores. Glass soft-drink bottles are returnable, so some shops and drink stalls have a system of pouring the contents into a small plastic bag (fastened with an elastic band and with a straw inserted) rather than charging you the extra for taking away the bottle. The larger restaurants keep their soft drinks refrigerated, but smaller cafés and shops add **ice** (*nam khaeng*) to glasses and bags. Most ice is produced commercially under hygienic conditions, but it might become less pure in transit so be wary (ice cubes are generally a better bet than shaved ice) – and don't take ice if you have diarrhoea. For those travelling with children, or just partial themselves to **dairy products**, UHT-preserved milk and chilled yoghurt drinks are widely available (especially at 7-Eleven stores), as is a variety of soya drinks.

Weak Chinese **tea** (*nam chaa*) makes a refreshing alternative to water and often gets served in Chinese restaurants and roadside cafés, while posher restaurants keep stronger Chinese and Western-style teas. Instant Nescafé is usually the **coffee** (*kaafae*), offered to farangs, even if freshly ground Thai-grown coffee – notably several excellent kinds of coffee from the mountains of the north – is available. If you would like to try traditional Thai coffee, most commonly found at Chinese-style cafés in the south of the country or at outdoor markets, and prepared through filtering the grounds through a cloth, ask for *kaafae thung* (literally, "bag coffee"; sometimes known as *kaafae boran* – "traditional coffee" – or *kopii*), normally served very bitter with sugar as well as sweetened condensed milk alongside a glass of black or Chinese tea to wash it down with. Fresh Western-style coffee (*kaafae sot*) in the form of Italian espresso, cappuccino and other derivatives has recently become popular among Thais, so you'll now come across espresso machines in large towns all over the country (though some of these new coffee bars, frustratingly, don't open for breakfast, as locals tend to get their fix later in the day).

Alcoholic drinks

The two most famous local **beers** (*bia*) are Singha (ask for "*bia sing*") and Chang, though many travellers find Singha's weaker brew, Leo, more palatable than either. In shops you can expect to pay around B30 for a 330ml bottle of these beers, B50 for a 660ml bottle. All manner of slightly pricier foreign beers are now brewed in Thailand, including Heineken and Asahi, and in the most touristy areas you'll find expensive imported bottles from all over the world.

Wine is now found on plenty of upmarket and tourist-oriented restaurant menus, but expect to be disappointed by both quality and price, which is jacked up by heavy taxation.

At about B80 for a hip-flask-sized 375ml bottle, the local **whisky** is a lot better value, and Thais think nothing of consuming a bottle a night, heavily diluted with ice and soda or Coke. The most palatable and widely available of these is Mekong, which is very pleasant once you've stopped expecting it to taste like Scotch; distilled from rice, Mekong is 35 percent proof, deep gold in colour and tastes slightly sweet. If that's not to your taste, a pricier Thai **rum** is also available, Sang Som, made from sugar cane, and even stronger than the whisky at forty percent proof. Check the menu carefully when ordering a bottle of Mekong from a bar in a tourist area, as they often ask up to five times more than you'd pay in a guesthouse or shop. A hugely popular way to enjoy whisky or rum at beach resorts is to pick up a bucket, containing a quarter-bottle of spirit, a mixer, Red Bull, ice and several straws, for around B200: that way you get to share with your friends and build a sandcastle afterwards.

You can **buy** beer and whisky in food stores, guesthouses and most restaurants; **bars** aren't strictly an indigenous feature as Thais traditionally don't drink out without eating, but you'll find plenty of Western-style drinking holes in Bangkok and larger centres elsewhere in the country, ranging from ultra-hip haunts in the capital to basic, open-to-the-elements "**bar-beers**".

Culture and etiquette

Tourist literature has marketed Thailand as the "Land of Smiles" so successfully that a lot of farangs arrive in the country expecting to be forgiven any outrageous behaviour. This is just not the case: there are some things so universally sacred in Thailand that even a hint of disrespect will cause deep offence.

The monarchy

It is both socially unacceptable and a criminal offence to make critical or defamatory remarks about the **royal family**. Thailand's monarchy might be a constitutional one, but almost every household displays a picture of King Bhumibol and Queen Sirikit in a prominent position, and respectful crowds mass whenever either of them makes a public appearance. The second of their four children, Crown Prince Vajiralongkorn, is the heir to the throne; his younger sister, Princess Royal Maha Chakri Sirindhorn, is often on TV and in the English-language newspapers as she is involved in many charitable projects. When addressing or speaking about royalty, Thais use a special language full of deference, called *rajasap* (literally "royal language").

Thailand's **lèse majesté laws** are among the most strictly applied in the world, increasingly invoked as the Thai establishment becomes ever more uneasy over the erosion of traditional monarchist sentiments and the rise of critical voices, particularly on the internet (though these are generally quickly censored). Accusations of *lèse majesté* can be levelled by and against anyone, Thai national or farang, and must be investigated by the police. As a few high-profile cases involving foreigners have demonstrated, they can be raised for seemingly minor infractions, such as defacing a poster. Transgressions are met with jail sentences of up to 15 years.

Aside from keeping any anti-monarchy sentiments to yourself, you should be prepared to stand when the **king's anthem** is played at the beginning of every cinema programme, and to stop in your tracks if the town you're in plays the **national anthem** over its public address system – many small towns do this twice a day at 8am and again at 6pm, as do some train stations and airports. A less obvious point: as the king's head features on all Thai currency, you should never step on a coin or banknote, which is tantamount to kicking the king in the face.

Religion

Almost equally insensitive would be to disregard certain **religious** precepts. **Buddhism** plays a fundamental role in Thai culture, and Buddhist monuments should be treated with respect – which basically means wearing long trousers or knee-length skirts, covering your arms and removing your shoes whenever you visit one.

All **Buddha images** are sacred, however small, tacky or ruined, and should never be used as a backdrop for a portrait photo, clambered over, placed in a position of inferiority or treated in any manner that could be construed as disrespectful. In an attempt to prevent foreigners from committing any kind of transgression the government requires a special licence for all Buddha statues exported from the country (see p.59).

Monks come only just beneath the monarchy in the social hierarchy, and they too are addressed and discussed in a special language. If there's a monk around, he'll always get a seat on the bus, usually right at the back. Theoretically, monks are forbidden to have any close contact with women, which means, as a female, you mustn't sit or stand next to a monk, or even brush against his robes; if it's essential to pass him something, put the object down so that he can then pick it up – never hand it over directly. Nuns, however, get treated like ordinary women.

See "Contexts" for more on religious practices in Thailand (see p.431).

The body

The Western liberalism embraced by the Thai sex industry is very unrepresentative of the majority Thai attitude to the body. **Clothing** – or the lack of it – is what bothers Thais most about tourist behaviour. You need to dress modestly when entering temples (see above), but the same also applies to other important buildings and all public places. Stuffy and sweaty as it sounds, you should keep short shorts and vests for the real tourist resorts, and be especially diligent about covering up and, for women, wearing bras in rural areas. Baring your flesh on beaches is very much a Western practice: when Thais go swimming they often do so fully clothed, and they find topless and nude bathing offensive.

According to ancient Hindu belief, the **head** is the most sacred part of the body and the **feet** are the most unclean. This belief, imported into Thailand, means that it's very rude to touch another person's head or to point your feet either at a human being or at a sacred image – when sitting on a temple floor, for example, you should **tuck your legs beneath you** rather than stretch them out towards the Buddha. These hierarchies also forbid people from wearing **shoes** (which are even more unclean than feet) inside temples and most private homes, and – by extension – Thais take offence when they see someone sitting on the "head", or prow, of a boat. **Putting your feet up** on a table, a chair or a pillow is also considered very uncouth, and Thais will always take their shoes off if they need to stand on a train or bus seat to get to the luggage rack, for example. On a more practical note, the **left hand** is used for washing after going to the toilet (see p.38), so Thais never use it to put food in their mouth, pass things or shake hands – as a farang though, you'll be assumed to have different customs, so left-handers shouldn't worry unduly.

Social conventions

Thais rarely shake hands, instead using the **wai** to greet and say goodbye and to acknowledge respect, gratitude or apology. A prayer-like gesture made with raised hands, the *wai* changes according to the relative status of the two people involved: Thais can instantaneously assess which *wai* to use, but as a farang your safest bet is to raise your hands close to your chest, bow your head and place your fingertips just below your nose. If someone makes a *wai* at you, you should generally *wai* back, but it's safer not to initiate.

Public displays of **physical affection** in Thailand are more common between friends of the same sex than between lovers, whether hetero- or homosexual. Holding hands and hugging is as common among male friends as with females, so if you're caressed by a Thai acquaintance of the same sex, don't assume you're being propositioned.

Finally, there are three specifically Thai **concepts** you're bound to come across, which may help you comprehend a sometimes laissez-faire attitude to delayed buses and other inconveniences. The first, **jai yen**, translates literally as "cool heart" and is something everyone tries to maintain: most Thais hate raised voices, visible irritation and confrontations of any kind, so losing one's cool can have a much more inflammatory effect than in more combative cultures. Related to this is the oft-quoted response to a difficulty, **mai pen rai** – "never mind", "no problem" or "it can't be helped" – the verbal equivalent of an open-handed shoulder shrug, which has its basis in the Buddhist notion of karma (see p.432). And then there's **sanuk**, the wide-reaching philosophy of "fun", which, crass as it sounds, Thais do their best to inject into any situation, even work. Hence the crowds of inebriated Thais who congregate at waterfalls and other beauty spots on public holidays (travelling solo is definitely not *sanuk*), the reluctance to do almost anything without high-volume musical accompaniment, and the national waterfight which takes place during Songkhran every April on streets right across Thailand.

Thai names

Although all Thais have a first **name** and a family name, everyone is addressed by their first name – even when meeting strangers – prefixed by the title "Khun" (Mr/Ms); no one is ever addressed as Khun Surname, and even the phone book lists people by their given name. In Thailand you will often be addressed in an anglicized version of this convention, as "Mr Paul" or "Miss Lucy" for example. Bear in mind though, that when a man is introduced to you as Khun Pirom, his wife will definitely not be Khun Pirom as well (that would be like calling them, for instance, "Mr and Mrs Paul"). Among friends and relatives, **Phii** ("older brother/sister") is often used instead of Khun when addressing older familiars (though as a tourist you're on surer ground with Khun), and **Nong** ("younger brother/sister") is used for younger ones.

Many Thai **first names** come from ancient Sanskrit and have an auspicious meaning; for example, Boon means good deeds, Porn means blessings, Siri means glory and Thawee means to increase. However, Thais of all ages are commonly known by the **nickname** given them soon after birth rather than by their official first name. This tradition arises out of a deep-rooted superstition that once a child has been officially named the spirits will begin to take an unhealthy interest in them, so a nickname is used instead to confuse the spirits. Common nicknames – which often bear no resemblance to the adult's personality or physique – include Yai (Big), Oun (Fat) and Muu (Pig); Lek or Noi (Little), Nok (Bird), Noo (Mouse) and Kung (Shrimp); and English nicknames like Apple, Joy or even Pepsi.

Family names were only introduced in 1913 (by Rama VI, who invented many of the aristocracy's surnames himself), and are used only in very formal situations, always in conjunction with the first name. It's quite usual for good friends never to know each other's surname. Ethnic Thais generally have short surnames like Somboon or Srisai, while the long, convoluted family names – such as Sonthanasumpun – usually indicate Chinese origin, not because they are phonetically Chinese but because many Chinese immigrants have chosen to adopt new Thai surnames and Thai law states that every newly created surname must be unique. Thus anyone who wants to change their surname must submit a shortlist of five unique Thai names – each to a maximum length of ten Thai characters – to be checked against a database of existing names. As more and more names are taken, Chinese family names get increasingly unwieldy, and more easily distinguishable from the pithy old Thai names.

The media

To keep you abreast of world affairs, there are several English-language newspapers in Thailand, though relatively mild forms of censorship (and self-censorship) affect all newspapers and the predominantly state-controlled media.

Newspapers and magazines

Of the hundreds of **Thai-language newspapers and magazines** published every week, the sensationalist daily tabloid *Thai Rath* attracts the widest readership, with circulation of around a million, while the moderately progressive *Matichon* is the leading quality daily, with an estimated circulation of 600,000.

Alongside these, two daily **English-language papers** – the *Bangkok Post* (ⓦbangkokpost.com) and the *Nation* (ⓦnationmultimedia.com) – are capable of adopting a fairly critical attitude to political goings-on and cover major domestic and international stories as well as tourist-related issues. The *Nation*, however, has recently adopted a split personality (and a more overt anti-red shirt stance) and now covers mostly business news. The *Post*'s *Spectrum* supplement, which comes inside the Sunday edition, carries investigative journalism. Both the *Post* and *Nation* are sold at most newsstands in the capital as well as in major provincial towns and tourist resorts; the more isolated places receive their few copies one day late. Details of local English-language publications are given in the relevant Guide accounts.

You can also pick up **foreign** magazines such as *Newsweek* and *Time* in Bangkok and the major resorts. English-language bookshops such as Bookazine and some expensive hotels carry air-freighted, or sometimes locally printed and stapled, copies of foreign national newspapers for at least B50 a copy; the latter are also sold in tourist-oriented minimarkets in the big resorts.

Television

There are six government-controlled, terrestrial **TV channels** in Thailand: channels 3, 5 (owned and operated by the army), 7 and 9 transmit a blend of news, documentaries, soaps, sports, talk and quiz shows, while the more serious-minded PBS (formerly Thaksin Shinawatra's ITV) and NBT are public-service channels, owned and operated by the government's public relations department. **Cable** networks – available in many mid-range and most upmarket hotel rooms – carry channels from all around the world, including CNN from the US, BBC World from the UK and sometimes ABC from Australia, as well as English-language movie channels, MTV and various sports and documentary channels. Both the *Bangkok Post* and the *Nation* print the daily TV and cable **schedule**.

Radio

Thailand boasts over five hundred **radio stations**, mostly music-oriented, ranging from Virgin Radio's Eazy (105.5 FM), which serves up Western pop, to Fat Radio, which plays Thai indie sounds (104.5 FM). Chulalongkorn University Radio (101.5 FM) plays classical music from 9.30pm to midnight every night. Net 107 on 107 FM is one of several stations that include English-language news bulletins.

With a **shortwave radio** – or by going **online** – you can pick up the BBC World Service (W bbc .co.uk/worldservice), Radio Australia (W radio australia.net .au), Voice of America (W voanews .com), Radio Canada (W rcinet.ca) and other international stations right across Thailand. Times and wavelengths change regularly, so get hold of a recent schedule just before you travel or consult the websites for frequency and programme guides.

Festivals

Nearly all Thai festivals have a religious aspect. The most theatrical are generally Brahmin (Hindu) in origin, honouring elemental spirits and deities with ancient rites and ceremonial costumed parades. Buddhist celebrations usually revolve round the local temple, and while merit-making is a significant feature, a light-hearted atmosphere prevails, as the wat grounds are swamped with food and trinket vendors and makeshift stages are set up to show *likay* folk theatre, singing stars and beauty contests.

Many of the **secular festivals** are outdoor local culture shows, geared specifically towards Thai and farang tourists. Others are thinly veiled but lively trade fairs held in provincial capitals to show off the local speciality, be it exquisite silk weaving or especially tasty rambutans.

Few of the **dates** for religious festivals are fixed, so check with TAT for specifics (W tourismthailand.org). The names of the most touristy celebrations are given here in English; the more low-key festivals are more usually known by their Thai name (*ngan* means "festival"). Some of the festivals below are designated as national holidays (see p.67).

A festival calendar

JANUARY–JUNE

Chinese New Year Nationwide (particularly Bangkok and Phuket; three days between mid-Jan and late Feb). The new Chinese year is welcomed in with exuberant parades of dragons and lion dancers, Chinese opera performances and fireworks displays.

Makha Puja Nationwide (particularly Wat Benjamabophit in Bangkok and Wat Mahathat in Nakhon Si Thammarat; Feb full-moon day). A day of merit-making marks the occasion when 1250 disciples gathered spontaneously to hear the Buddha preach, and culminates in a candlelit procession round the local temple's bot.

Kite fights and flying contests Nationwide (particularly Sanam Luang, Bangkok; late Feb to mid-April).

Songkhran Nationwide (particularly Bangkok's Thanon Khao San; usually April 13–15). The most exuberant of the national festivals welcomes the Thai New Year with massive waterfights, sandcastle building in temple compounds and the inevitable parades and "Miss Songkhran" beauty contests.

Visakha Puja Nationwide (particularly Bangkok's Wat Benjamabophit and Nakhon Si Thammarat's Wat Mahathat; May full-moon day). The holiest day of the Buddhist year, commemorating the birth, enlightenment and death of the Buddha all in one go; the most public and photogenic part is the candlelit evening procession around the wat.

Raek Na Sanam Luang, Bangkok (early May). The royal ploughing ceremony to mark the beginning of the rice-planting season; ceremonially clad Brahmin leaders parade sacred oxen and the royal plough, and interpret omens to forecast the year's rice yield.

JULY–DECEMBER

Tamboon Deuan Sip Nakhon Si Thammarat (Sept or Oct). Merit-making ceremonies to honour dead relatives accompanied by a ten-day fair. See p.277.

Vegetarian Festival Phuket, Trang and Satun (Ngan Kin Jeh; Oct or Nov). Chinese devotees become vegetarian for a nine-day period and then parade through town performing acts of self-mortification such as pushing skewers through their cheeks. Celebrated in Bangkok's Chinatown by most food vendors and restaurants turning vegetarian for about a fortnight. See p.133, p.325, p.402 and p.419.

Tak Bat Devo and Awk Pansa Nationwide (Oct full-moon day). Offerings to monks and general merrymaking to celebrate the Buddha's descent to earth from Tavatimsa heaven and the end of the Khao Pansa retreat.

Chak Phra Surat Thani (mid-Oct). The town's chief Buddha images are paraded on floats down the streets and on barges along the river. See p.234.

Thawt Kathin Nationwide (the month between Awk Pansa and Loy Krathong, generally Oct–Nov). During the month following the end of the monks' rainy-season retreat, it's traditional for the laity to donate new robes to the monkhood and this is celebrated in most towns with parades and a festival, and occasionally, when it coincides with a kingly anniversary, with a spectacular Royal Barge Procession down the Chao Phraya River in Bangkok.

Loy Krathong Nationwide (full moon in Nov). Baskets (*krathong*) of flowers and lighted candles are floated on any available body of water (such as ponds, rivers, lakes, canals and seashores) to honour water spirits and celebrate the end of the rainy season. Nearly every town puts on a big show, with bazaars, public entertainments, fireworks and the release of paper hot-air balloons.

Ngan Wat Saket Wat Saket, Bangkok (first week of Nov). Probably Thailand's biggest temple fair, held around the Golden Mount, with all the usual festival trappings.

New Year's Eve Countdown Nationwide (Dec 31). Most cities and tourist destinations welcome in the new year with fireworks, often backed up by food festivals, beauty contests and outdoor performances.

Entertainment and sport

Bangkok is the best place to catch authentic performances of classical Thai dance, though more easily digestible tourist-oriented shows are staged in some of the big tourist centres as well as in Bangkok. The country's two main Thai boxing stadia are also in the capital, but you'll come across local matches in the provinces too.

Drama and dance

Drama pretty much equals **dance** in classical Thai theatre, and many of the traditional dance-dramas are based on the *Ramakien*, the Thai

version of the Hindu epic the *Ramayana*, an adventure tale of good versus evil which is taught in all the schools.

Of the three main genres of traditional Thai theatres, the most spectacular is **khon**, a stylized drama performed in masks and elaborate costumes by a troupe of highly trained classical dancers accompanied by a chorus and classical *phipat* orchestra.

Serious and refined, **lakhon** is derived from *khon* but is used to dramatize a greater range of stories. The form you're most likely to come across is *lakhon chatri*, which is performed at shrines like Bangkok's Erawan as entertainment for the spirits and a token of gratitude from worshippers. Dancers perform as an ensemble, wearing ornate costumes and accompanied by a *phipat* orchestra.

Likay is much more popular and light-hearted, with lots of comic interludes, bawdy jokes and panto-style over-the-top acting and singing, plus improvisations and topical satire. *Likay* troupes travel around the country doing shows at temple fairs and other events, often for free.

Nang thalung, or shadow plays (see p.280), are performed mainly in the far south, with two-dimensional puppets crafted from buffalo hide playing out scenes from popular dramas against a backlit screen, while the storyline is told through songs, chants and musical interludes.

Thai boxing

Thai boxing (*muay thai*) enjoys a following similar to football or baseball in the West: every province has a stadium and whenever the sport is shown on TV you can be sure that large noisy crowds will gather round the sets in streetside restaurants. The best place to see Thai boxing is at one of Bangkok's two main stadia, which between them hold bouts every night of the week (see p.141), but many tourist resorts also stage regular matches.

There's a strong spiritual and **ritualistic** dimension to *muay thai*, adding grace to an otherwise brutal sport. Each boxer enters the ring to the wailing music of a three-piece *phipat* orchestra, wearing the statutory red or blue shorts and, on his head, a sacred rope headband or *mongkhon*. Tied around his biceps are *phra jiat*, pieces of cloth that are often decorated with cabalistic symbols and may contain Buddhist tablets. The fighter then bows, first in the direction of his birthplace and then to the north, south, east and west, honouring both his teachers and the spirit of the ring. Next he performs a slow dance, claiming the audience's attention and demonstrating his prowess as a performer.

Any part of the body except the head may be used as an **offensive weapon** in *muay thai*, and all parts except the groin are fair targets. Kicks to the head are the blows that cause most knockouts. As the action hots up, so the orchestra speeds up its tempo and the betting in the audience becomes more frenetic. It can be a gruesome business, but it was far bloodier before modern boxing gloves were made compulsory in the 1930s, when the Queensbury Rules were adapted for *muay* – combatants used to wrap their fists with hemp impregnated with a face-lacerating dosage of ground glass.

A number of *muay thai* gyms and camps offer training **courses** for foreigners, including several in Bangkok, as well as Hua Hin, Ko Pha Ngan and Ko Yao Noi – see the relevant accounts for details.

Spas and traditional massage

With their focus on indulgent self-pampering, spas are usually associated with high-spending tourists, but the treatments on offer at Thailand's five-star hotels are often little different from those used by traditional medical practitioners, who have long held that massage and herbs are the best way to restore physical and mental well-being.

Thai massage (*nuad boran*) is based on the principle that many physical and emotional problems are caused by the blocking of vital energy channels within the body. The masseur uses his or her feet, heels, knees and elbows, as well as hands, to exert pressure on these channels, supplementing this acupressure-style technique by pulling and pushing the limbs into yogic stretches. This distinguishes Thai massage from most other massage styles, which are more concerned with tissue manipulation. One is supposed to emerge from a Thai massage feeling both relaxed and energized, and it is said that regular massages produce long-term benefits in muscles as well as stimulating the circulation and aiding natural detoxification.

Thais will visit a masseur for many conditions, including fevers, colds and muscle strain, but bodies that are not sick are also considered to benefit from the restorative powers of a massage, and nearly every hotel and guesthouse will be able to put you in touch with a **masseur**. On the more popular beaches, it can be hard to walk a few hundred metres without being offered a massage – something Thai tourists are just as enthusiastic about as foreigners. Thai masseurs do not traditionally use oils or lotions and the client is treated on a mat or mattress; you'll often be given a pair of loose-fitting trousers and perhaps a loose top to change into. English-speaking masseurs will often ask if there are any areas of your body that you would like them to concentrate on, or if you have any problem areas that you want them to avoid; if your masseur doesn't speak English, the simplest way to signal the latter is to point at the offending area while saying *mai sabai* ("not well"). If you're in pain during a massage, wincing usually does the trick, perhaps adding *jep* ("it hurts"); if your masseur is pressing too hard for your liking, say *bao bao na khrap/kha* ("gently please").

The best places for a basic massage are usually the government-accredited clinics and hospitals that are found in large towns all over the country. A session should ideally last at least one and a half hours and will cost from around B250. If you're a bit wary of submitting to the full works, try a **foot massage** first, which will apply the same techniques of acupressure and stretching to just your feet and lower legs. Most places also offer **herbal massages**, in which the masseur will knead you with a ball of herbs (*phrakop*) wrapped in a cloth and steam-heated; they're said to be particularly good for stiffness of the neck, shoulders and back.

The **science** behind Thai massage has its roots in Indian Ayurvedic medicine, which classifies each component of the body according to one of the four elements (earth, water, fire and air), and holds that balancing these elements within the body is crucial to good health. Many of the stretches and manipulations fundamental to Thai massage are thought to have derived from yogic practices introduced to Thailand from India by Buddhist missionaries in about the second century BC; Chinese acupuncture and reflexology have also had a strong influence. In the nineteenth century, King Rama III ordered a series of murals illustrating the principles of Thai massage to be painted around the courtyard of Bangkok's Wat Pho, and they are still in place today, along with statues of ascetics depicted in typical massage poses.

Wat Pho has been the leading school of Thai massage for hundreds of years, and it is possible to take courses there as well as to receive a massage (see p.85). Masseurs who trained at Wat Pho are considered to be the best in the country and masseurs all across Thailand advertise this as a credential, whether or not it is true. Many Thais consider blind masseurs to be especially sensitive practitioners.

All **spas** in Thailand feature traditional Thai massage and herbal therapies in their programmes, but most also offer dozens of other international treatments, including facials, aromatherapy, Swedish massage and various body wraps. Spa centres in upmarket hotels and resorts are usually open to non-guests but generally need to be booked in advance. Day-spas that are not attached to hotels are generally cheaper and are found in some of the bigger cities and resorts – some of these may not require reservations.

Meditation centres and retreats

Of the hundreds of meditation temples in Thailand, a few cater specifically for foreigners by holding meditation sessions and retreats in English. Novices as well as practised meditators are generally welcome at these wats, but absolute beginners might like to consider the regular retreats at Wat Suan Mokkh and Wat Khao Tham, which are conducted by supportive and experienced Thai and Western teachers and include talks and interviews on Buddhist teachings and practice. The meditation taught is mostly Vipassana, or "insight", which emphasizes the minute observation of internal sensations; the other main technique you'll come across is Samatha, which aims to calm the mind and develop concentration (these two techniques are not entirely separate, since you cannot have insight without some degree of concentration).

Longer **retreats** are for the serious-minded only. All the temples listed below welcome both male and female English-speakers, but strict segregation of the sexes is enforced and many places observe a vow of silence. Reading and writing are also discouraged, and you'll generally not be allowed to leave the retreat complex unless absolutely necessary, so try to bring whatever you'll need in with you. All retreats expect you to wear modest clothing, and some require you to wear white – check ahead whether there is a shop at the retreat complex or whether you are expected to bring this with you.

An average day at any one of these monasteries starts with a **wake-up call** at around 4am and includes several hours of **group meditation** and chanting, as well as time put aside for chores and personal reflection. However long their stay, visitors are usually expected to keep the eight main Buddhist precepts, the most restrictive of these being the abstention from food after midday and from alcohol, tobacco, drugs and sex at all times. Most wats ask for a minimal daily **donation** (around B200) to cover the costs of the simple accommodation and food.

Further details about many of the temples listed below – including how to get there – are given in the relevant sections in the Guide chapters. A useful **resource** is ⓦ dhammathai.org, which provides lots of general background, practical advice and details of meditation temples and centres around Thailand. In addition, ⓦ wanderingdhamma.org is a very interesting blog written by an American Ph.D. student, with some fascinating articles, information on English-speaking retreats in Thailand and lots of good links. Meanwhile, Little Bangkok Sangha (ⓦ littlebang.org) is a handy blog maintained by a British-born monk, Phra Pandit, which gives details of talks in Bangkok and retreats.

MEDITATION CENTRES AND RETREAT TEMPLES

In addition to those listed below, meditation centres and retreat temples are listed in the Guide chapters, including **Wat Khao Tham** on Ko Pha Ngan (see p.258), **Wat Mahathat** in Bangkok (see p.86), and **Wat Suan Mokkh** in Chaiya (see p.232) and on Ko Samui (see p.237).

House of Dhamma Insight Meditation Centre 26/9 Soi Lardprao 15, Chatuchak, Bangkok ☎ 02 511 0439, ⓦ houseofdhamma.com. Regular two-day courses in Vipassana, as well as day workshops in Metta (Loving Kindness) meditation. Courses in reiki and other subjects available.

World Fellowship of Buddhists (WFB) 616 Benjasiri Park, Soi Medhinivet off Soi 24, Thanon Sukhumvit, Bangkok ☎ 02 661 1284–7, ⓦ wfbhq.org. Headquarters of an influential worldwide organization of (mostly Theravada) Buddhists, founded in Sri Lanka in 1950, this is the main information centre for advice on English-speaking retreats in Thailand.

Outdoor activities

The vast majority of beach itineraries include a stint snorkelling or diving, and the big resorts of Pattaya, Phuket and Ko Samui offer dozens of other watersports as well. There is also a developing interest in more unusual outdoor activities, such as rock climbing and kayaking.

Diving and snorkelling

Clear, warm waters (averaging 28°C), prolific marine life and affordable prices make Thailand a very rewarding place for **diving** and **snorkelling**. Most islands and beach resorts have at least one dive centre that organizes trips to outlying islands, teaches novice divers and rents out equipment, and in the bigger resorts there are dozens to choose from. Check out our Underwater Thailand section (see p.20) for a guide to the country's spectacular marine life.

Thailand's three coasts are subject to different monsoon **seasons**, so you can dive all year round; the seasons run from November to April along the Andaman coast (though there is sometimes good diving here up until late Aug), and all year round on the Gulf and east coasts. Though every diver has their favourite reef, Thailand's **premier diving destinations** are generally considered to be Ko Similan, Richelieu Rock and Hin Muang and Hin Daeng – all of them off the Andaman coast. As an accessible base for diving, Ko Tao off the Gulf coast is hard to beat, with deep, clear inshore water and a wide variety of dive sites in very close proximity.

Whether you're snorkelling or diving, try to minimize your impact on the fragile reef structures by **not touching the reefs** and by asking your boatman not to anchor in the middle of one; **don't buy coral souvenirs**, as tourist demand only encourages local entrepreneurs to dynamite reefs.

Should you scrape your skin on coral, wash the wound thoroughly with boiled water, apply antiseptic and keep protected until healed. Wearing a T-shirt is a good idea when snorkelling to stop your back from getting sunburnt.

Diving

It's usually worth having a look at several **dive centres** before committing yourself to a trip or a course. Always verify the dive instructors' PADI (Professional Association of Diving Instructors) or equivalent accreditation and check to see if the dive shop is a member of PADI's International Resorts and Retailers Association (IRRA) as this guarantees a certain level of professionalism. You can view a list of IRRAs in Thailand at ⓦpadi.com.

We've highlighted IRRA dive shops that are accredited Five-Star centres, as these are considered by PADI to offer very high standards, but you

---

THAILAND'S TOP DIVING SPOTS

Ko Tao Boasting a dozen great spots in deep, clear water close to shore – at least some of which can be accessed all year round – "Turtle Island" has established itself as Southeast Asia's largest dive-training centre. See p.270

Ko Similan National park archipelago that's rated as one of the best and most varied diving destinations in the world. Prolific reefs dominate the east-facing coasts while the west is all granite boulders, caves and tunnels. Visibility extends to 30m and the cast of celebrity visitors includes white-tip sharks, barracuda, giant lobster, enormous tuna and whale sharks. See p.316

Ko Phi Phi Fringing reefs of hard and soft corals that descend to 35m, plus wrecks and varied marine life mean there's plenty here for both snorkellers and divers, all within easy reach of Phi Phi's hotels, nightlife and beautiful beaches. See p.372

Hin Daeng and Hin Muang Two spectacular, and challenging, reef walls off the Andaman coast that attract lots of reef fish and pelagics. Hin Muang, at well over 50m, is the deepest drop in Thailand and reliable for stingrays, manta rays, tuna, jacks, silvertip sharks and whale sharks. See p.339

Ko Lipe Around forty sites, most of them nearby in the undisturbed Ko Tarutao National Park, notable for their colourful diversity of topography (including wrecks), of corals, both hard and soft, and of species, including rare surgeonfish, sailfish and demon stingers. See p.416

Richelieu Rock The sunken pinnacle at Richelieu Rock is considered the country's premier dive site, famed for its manta rays and whale sharks. See p.339

should always consult other divers first if possible. Some dive operators do fake their PADI credentials. Avoid booking ahead over the internet without knowing anything else about the dive centre, and be wary of any operation offering extremely cheap courses: maintaining diving equipment is an expensive business in Thailand so any place offering unusually good rates will probably be cutting corners and compromising your safety. Ask to **meet your instructor** or dive leader, find out how many people there'll be in your group, check out the kind of instruction given (some courses are over-reliant on videos) and look over the equipment, checking the quality of the air in the tanks yourself and also ensuring there's an oxygen cylinder on board. Most divers prefer to travel to the dive site in a decent-sized **boat** equipped with a radio and emergency medical equipment rather than in a longtail. If this concerns you, ask the dive company about their boat before you sign up; firms that use longtails generally charge less.

Insurance should be included in the price of courses and introductory dives; for qualified divers, you're better off checking that your general travel insurance covers diving, though some diving shops can organize cover for you. There are **recompression chambers** in Pattaya, on Ko Samui and on Phuket and it's a good idea to check whether your dive centre is a member of one of these outfits, as recompression services are extremely expensive for anyone who's not.

There are a number of useful books available on diving in Thailand (see p.442).

THE MAIN DIVE RESORTS

THE EAST COAST
Ko Chang (see p.186)
Pattaya (see p.159)

THE GULF COAST
Ko Pha Ngan (see p.256)
Ko Samui (see p.237)
Ko Tao (see p.270)

THE ANDAMAN COAST
Ao Nang (see p.361)
Khao Lak (see p.314)
Ko Lanta (see p.387)
Ko Phi Phi (see p.372)
Phuket (see p.338)

THE DEEP SOUTH
Ko Lipe (see p.416)

Trips and courses

All dive centres run programmes of one-day **dive trips** (featuring two dives) and **night dives** for B1500–4500 (with reductions if you bring your own gear), and many of the Andaman-coast dive centres also do three- to seven-day **live-aboards** to the exceptional reefs off the remote Similan and Surin islands (from B11,900). Most dive centres can rent **underwater cameras** for about B1500 per day.

All dive centres offer a range of **courses** from beginner to advanced level, with equipment rental usually included in the cost; Ko Tao is now the largest, and most competitive, dive-training centre in Southeast Asia, with around fifty dive companies including plenty of PADI Five-Star centres. The most popular courses are the one-day **introductory** or resort dive (a pep talk and escorted shallow dive, open to anyone aged 10 or over), which costs anything from B2000 for a very local dive to B7000 for an all-inclusive day-trip to the Similan Islands; and the four-day **open-water course**, which entitles you to dive without an instructor (from B9800 on Ko Tao in high season). Kids' Bubblemaker courses, for children aged 8–9, cost around B2000.

Snorkelling

Boatmen and tour agents on most beaches offer **snorkelling** trips to nearby reefs and many dive operators welcome snorkellers to tag along for discounts of thirty percent or more; not all diving destinations are rewarding for snorkellers though, so check the relevant account in this book first. As far as snorkelling **equipment** goes, the most important thing is that you buy or rent a mask that fits. To check the fit, hold the mask against your face, then breathe in and remove your hands – if it falls off, it'll leak water. If you're buying equipment, you should be able to kit yourself out with a mask, snorkel and fins for about B1000, available from most dive centres. Few places rent fins, but a mask and snorkel set usually costs about B150 a day to rent, and if you're going on a snorkelling day-trip they are often included in the price.

National parks and wildlife observation

Thailand's hundred-plus **national parks**, which are administered by the National Park, Wildlife and Plant Conservation Department (W dnp .go.th), are generally the best places to **observe wildlife**. **Khao Sok** (see p.306) is southern Thailand's most popular inland park, while bird-watchers consider the coastal flats at **Khao Sam**

Roi Yot (see p.223) to be one of the country's primary observation spots. Many of southern Thailand's protected reserves are **marine parks**, including the archipelagos of **Ko Surin** (see p.303), **Ko Similan** (see p.316), **Ang Thong** (see p.253) and **Ko Tarutao** (see p.413).

All parks charge an **entrance fee**, which for foreigners is usually B200 (B100 for children), though some charge B100 and a few charge B400. Waymarked hiking **trails** in most parks are generally limited and rarely very challenging and decent park maps are hard to come by, so for serious national park treks you'll need to hire a guide and venture beyond the public routes. Nearly all parks provide **accommodation** and/or campsites (see p.38). Some national parks **close** for several weeks or months every year for conservation, safety or environmental reasons; dates are listed on the National Parks' website.

There's an introduction to Thailand's coastal environment and wildlife in "Contexts" (see p.437).

Rock climbing

The limestone karsts that pepper southern Thailand's Andaman coast make ideal playgrounds for **rock climbers**, and the sport has really taken off here in the past fifteen years. Most climbing is centred round **East Railay** and **Ton Sai** beaches on Laem Phra Nang in Krabi province (see p.364), where there are dozens of routes within easy walking distance of tourist bungalows, restaurants and beaches. **Offshore Deep Water Soloing** – climbing a rock face out at sea, with no ropes, partner or bolts and just the water to break your fall – is also huge round here. Several **climbing schools** at East Railay and Ton Sai provide instruction (from B1000/half-day), as well as guides and equipment rental (about B1300/day for two people). Ko Phi Phi (see p.372) also offers a few routes and a couple of climbing schools, as do Ko Tao (see p.273) and the quieter and potentially more interesting Ko Yao Noi (see p.348) and Ko Lao Liang (see p.412). For an introduction to climbing on Railay and elsewhere in south Thailand, see ⓦ railay.com, while *Rock Climbing in Thailand* and *King Climbers: Thailand Route Guide Book* are regularly updated guidebooks that concentrate on Railay, Ton Sai and the islands.

Sea kayaking

Sea kayaking is also centred around Thailand's Andaman coast, where the limestone outcrops, sea caves, *hongs* (hidden lagoons), mangrove swamps and picturesque shorelines of Ao Phang Nga in particular (see p.352) make for rewarding paddling. Kayaking day-trips around Ao Phang Nga can be arranged from any resort in Phuket, at Khao Lak, at all Krabi beaches and islands, and on Ko Yao Noi; multi-day kayaking expeditions are also possible. Over on Ko Samui, Blue Stars (see p.254) organize kayaking trips around the picturesque islands of the Ang Thong National Marine Park, while Kayak Chang (see p.184) offers half- to seven-day trips around Ko Chang. Many bungalows at other beach resorts have free kayaks or rent them out (from B100/hr) for casual, independent coastal exploration.

Travelling with children

Despite the relative lack of child-centred attractions in Thailand, there's plenty to appeal to families, both on the beach and inland, and Thais are famously welcoming to young visitors.

Of all the **beach resorts** in the country, two of the most family-friendly are the islands of Ko Samui and Ko Lanta. Both have plenty of on-the-beach accommodation for mid- and upper-range budgets, and lots of easy-going open-air shorefront restaurants so that adults can eat in relative peace while kids play within view. Both islands also offer many day-tripping activities, from elephant riding to snorkelling. Phuket is another family favourite, though shorefront accommodation here is at a premium; there are also scores of less mainstream alternatives. In many beach resorts older kids will be able to go kayaking or learn rock climbing, and many dive centres will teach the PADI children's scuba courses on request: the Bubblemaker programme is open to 8- and 9-year-olds and the Discover Scuba Diving day is designed for anyone 10 and over. **National parks** and their waterfalls and caves are good for days out, and there are lots of opportunities to go **elephant riding**. Bangkok has several attractions such as the Museum of Siam (see p.86).

Should you be in Thailand in January, your kids will be able to join in the free entertainments and activities staged all over the country on **National Children's Day** (Wan Dek), which is held on the second Saturday of January. They also get free entry to zoos that day, and free rides on public buses.

Hotels and transport

Many of the expensive **hotels** listed in this guide allow one or two under-12s to share their parents' room for free, as long as no extra bedding is required. It's often possible to cram two adults and two children into the double rooms in budget and mid-range hotels (as opposed to guesthouses), as beds in these places are usually big enough for two. An increasing number of guesthouses now offer three-person rooms, and may even provide special family accommodation. Decent cots are available free in the bigger hotels, and in some smaller ones (though cots in these places can be a bit grotty), and top and mid-range rooms often come with a small fridge. Many hotels can also provide a **babysitting** service.

Few museums or transport companies offer student reductions, but in some cases children get **discounts**. One of the more bizarre provisos is the State Railway's regulation that a child aged 3 to 12 qualifies for half-fare only if under 150cm tall; some stations have a measuring scale painted onto the ticket-hall wall. Most domestic airlines charge ten percent of the full fare for under-2s, and fifty percent for under-12s.

Other practicalities

Although most Thai babies don't wear them, **disposable nappies** (diapers) are sold at convenience stores, pharmacies and supermarkets in big resorts and sizeable towns; for stays on lonely islands, consider bringing some washable ones as back-up. A **changing mat** is another necessity as there are few public toilets in Thailand, let alone ones with baby facilities (though posh hotels are always a useful option). International brands of powdered milk are available throughout the country, and brand-name baby food is sold in big towns and resorts, though some parents find restaurant-cooked rice and bananas go down just as well. Thai women do not **breastfeed** in public.

For touring, child-carrier backpacks are ideal. Opinions are divided on whether or not it's worth bringing a **buggy** or three-wheeled **stroller**. Where they exist, Thailand's pavements are bumpy at best, and there's an almost total absence of ramps; sand is especially difficult for buggies, though less so for three-wheelers. Buggies and strollers do, however, come in handy for feeding and even bedding small children, as highchairs and cots are only provided in more upmarket restaurants and hotels. You can buy buggies fairly cheaply in most towns, but if you bring your own and then wish you hadn't, most hotels and guesthouses will keep it for you until you leave. Bring an appropriately sized **mosquito net** if necessary (see p.62) or buy one locally in any department store; a mini **sun tent** for the beach is also useful. Taxis and car-rental companies almost never provide baby **car seats**, and even if you bring your own you'll often find there are no seat belts to strap them in with. Most department stores have dedicated kids' sections selling everything from bottles and dummies. There are even several Mothercare outlets in Bangkok.

Hazards

Even more than their parents, children need protecting from the sun, unsafe drinking water, heat and unfamiliar **food**. Consider packing a jar of a favourite spread so that you can always rely on toast if all else fails to please. As with adults, you should be careful about unwashed fruit and salads and about dishes that have been left uncovered for a long time. As diarrhoea could be dangerous for a child, rehydration solutions (see p.64) are vital if your child goes down with it. Other significant **hazards** include thundering traffic; huge waves, strong currents and jellyfish; and the **sun** – not least because many beaches offer only limited shade, if at all. Sunhats, sunblock and waterproof suntan lotions are essential, and can be bought in the major resorts. You should also make sure, if possible, that your child is aware of the dangers of **rabies**; keep children away from **animals**, especially dogs and monkeys, and ask your medical advisor about rabies jabs.

INFORMATION AND ADVICE

Nancy Chandler's Family Travel ⓦ nancychandler.net /travelwkids.asp. Plenty of unusual ideas on Thai-style entertainment for kids, plus tips, links and Thailand-themed kids' books.

Thailand 4 Kids ⓦ thailand4kids.com. Lots of advice on the practicalities of family holidays in Thailand.

Travel essentials

Charities and volunteer projects

Reassured by the plethora of well-stocked shopping plazas, efficient services and apparent abundance in the rice fields, it is easy to forget that life is extremely hard for many people in Thailand. Countless **charities** work with Thailand's many poor and disadvantaged communities: listed below are a few that would welcome help in some way from visitors. The website of the *Bangkok Post* also carries an extensive list of charitable foundations and projects in Thailand at ⓦbangkokpost.com /outlookwecare. Longer-term placements and organized holidays that feature community-based programmes are also available (see p.65 and p.28).

Children's World Academy Kapong, near Khao Lak ☎ 087 271 2552, ⓦyaowawit.com. Set in quiet countryside on the Takua Pa–Phang Nga road, Yaowawit School was set up for tsunami orphans and socially disadvantaged children. It accepts donations, volunteer teachers and guests who wish to stay at its lodge, a hospitality training centre.

Human Development Foundation 100/11 Kae Ha Klong Toey 4, Thanon Damrongratthaphipat, Klong Toey, Bangkok ☎ 02 671 5313, ⓦmercycentre.org. Founded in 1973, Father Joe Maier's organization provides education and support for Bangkok's street kids and slum-dwellers, as well as for sea gypsies in the south. It now runs two dozen kindergartens in the slums, among many other projects. Contact the centre for information about donations, sponsoring and volunteering. *The Slaughterhouse: Stories from Bangkok's Klong Toey Slum* (see p.441) gives an eye-opening insight into this often invisible side of Thai life.

Koh Yao Children's Community Center Ko Yao Noi ⓦkoyao-ccc .com. Aims to improve the English-language and lifelong learning skills of islanders on Ko Yao Noi. Visitors, volunteers and donations welcome. See p.347.

Lifelong Learning Foundation (Thailand) ☎ 081 894 6936, ⓦtrangsea.com & ⓦlifelong-learning.org. Promoting nature conservation and the personal development of sea gypsies and other local people in Trang province, this nonprofit organization seeks donations, encourages partnerships with sympathetic overseas organizations, and especially welcomes the custom of tourists at its resorts at Ban Chao Mai (see p.405) and on Ko Mook (see p.409) and Ko Libong (see p.411), and on its award-winning tours.

The Students' Education Trust (SET) ⓦthaistudentcharity.org. High-school and further education in Thailand is a luxury that the poorest kids cannot afford so many are sent to live in temples instead. The SET helps such kids pursue their education and escape from the poverty trap.

Some of their stories are told in *Little Angels: The Real-Life Stories of Twelve Thai Novice Monks* (see p.441). SET welcomes donations.

Thai Child Development Foundation Pha To ⓦthaichilddevelopment.org. This small Thai–Dutch-run village project in Chumphon province helps educate, feed and look after needy local children. The foundation welcomes donations of materials and money, takes on volunteers, and has an ecotourism arm (see p.292).

Climate

There are three main **seasons** in most of Thailand: rainy, caused by the southwest monsoon (the least predictable, but roughly Nov–Oct); cool (Nov–Feb; felt most distinctly in the far north, but hardly at all in the south); and hot (March–May). The Gulf coast's climate is slightly different: it suffers less from the southwest monsoon, but is then hit by the northeast monsoon, making November its rainiest month.

Costs

Thailand can be a very cheap place to travel. At the bottom of the scale, you can manage on a **budget** of about B650 (£13/US$20) per day if you're willing to opt for basic accommodation, eat, drink and travel as the locals do, and stay away from the more expensive resorts like Phuket, Ko Samui and Ko Phi Phi – and you'd have to work hard to stick to this daily allowance in Bangkok. On this budget, you'll be spending around B200 for a dorm or shared room (more for a single room), around B200 on three meals (eating mainly at night markets and simple noodle shops, and eschewing beer), and the rest on travel (sticking to the cheaper buses and third-class trains where possible) and incidentals. With extras like air conditioning in rooms, taking the various forms of taxi rather than buses or shared

AVERAGE DAILY TEMPERATURES AND MONTHLY RAINFALL

	Jan	Feb	Mar	Apr	May	Jun	Jul	Aug	Sep	Oct	Nov	Dec
Bangkok												
Max temp (°C)	26	28	29	30	30	29	29	28	28	28	27	26
Rainfall (mm)	11	28	31	72	190	152	158	187	320	231	57	9
Pattaya												
Max temp (°C)	26	28	29	30	30	29	29	28	28	28	27	26
Rainfall (mm)	12	23	41	79	165	120	166	166	302	229	66	10
Ko Samui												
Max temp (°C)	26	26	28	29	29	28	28	28	28	27	26	25
Rainfall (mm)	38	8	12	63	186	113	143	123	209	260	302	98
Phuket												
Max temp (°C)	27	28	28	29	28	28	28	28	27	27	27	27
Rainfall (mm)	35	31	39	163	348	213	263	263	419	305	207	52

ADDRESSES IN THAILAND

Thai **addresses** can be immensely confusing, mainly because property is often numbered twice, first to show which real-estate lot it stands in, and then to distinguish where it is on that lot. Thus 154/7–10 Thanon Rajdamnoen means the building is on lot 154 and occupies numbers 7–10. However, neither of these numbers will necessarily help you to find a particular building on a long street; when asking for directions or talking to taxi drivers, it's best to be able to quote a nearby temple, big hotel or other landmark. There's an additional idiosyncrasy in the way Thai roads are sometimes named: in large cities a minor road running off a major road is often numbered as a soi ("lane" or "alley", though it may be a sizeable thoroughfare), rather than given its own street name. Thanon Sukhumvit, for example – Bangkok's longest – has minor roads numbered Soi 1 to Soi 103, with odd numbers on one side of the road and even on the other; so a Thanon Sukhumvit address could read something like 27/9–11 Soi 15, Thanon Sukhumvit, which would mean the property occupies numbers 9–11 on lot 27 on minor road number 15 running off Thanon Sukhumvit.

songthaews for cross-town journeys, and a meal and beer in a more touristy restaurant, a day's outlay would look more like B1000 (£20/US$30). Staying in well-equipped, mid-range hotels and eating in the more exclusive restaurants, you should be able to live very comfortably for around B2000 a day (£40/US$60).

Travellers soon get so used to the low cost of living in Thailand that they start **bargaining** at every available opportunity, much as Thai people do. Although it's expected practice for a lot of commercial transactions, particularly at markets and when hiring tuk-tuks and unmetered taxis (though not in supermarkets or department stores), bargaining is a delicate art that requires humour, tact and patience. If your price is way out of line, the vendor's vehement refusal should be enough to make you increase your offer: never forget that the few pennies or cents you're making such a fuss over will go a lot further in a Thai person's hands than in your own.

It's rare that foreigners can bargain a price down as low as a Thai could, anyway, while **two-tier pricing** has been made official at government-run sights, as a kind of informal tourist tax: at national parks, for example, foreigners pay up to B400 entry while Thais generally pay just B20. A number of privately owned tourist attractions follow a similar two-tier system, posting an inflated price in English for foreigners and a lower price in Thai for locals.

Big-spending shoppers who are departing via Suvarnabhumi, Hat Yai, Ko Samui, Krabi, Pattaya or Phuket airports can save some money by claiming a **Value Added Tax refund** (Ⓦrd.go.th/vrt), though it's a bit of a palaver for seven percent (the current rate of VAT). The total amount of your purchases (gems are excluded) from participating shops needs to be at least B5000 per person, with a minimum of B2000 per shop per day. You'll need to show your passport and fill in an application form (to which original tax invoices need to be attached) at the shop. At the relevant airport, you'll need to show your form and purchases to customs officers before checking in, then make your claim from VAT refund officers – from which fees of at least B100 are deducted.

Crime and personal safety

As long as you keep your wits about you, you shouldn't encounter much trouble in Thailand. **Pickpocketing** and **bag-snatching** are two of the main problems – not surprising considering that a huge percentage of the local population scrape by on under US$5 per day – but the most common cause for concern is the number of con-artists who dupe gullible tourists into parting with their cash. There are various Thai laws that tourists need to be aware of, particularly regarding passports, the age of consent and smoking in public.

Theft

To **prevent theft**, most travellers prefer to carry their valuables with them at all times, but it's often possible to use a locker in a hotel or guesthouse – the safest are those that require your own padlock, as there are occasional reports of valuables being stolen by hotel staff. **Padlock your luggage** when leaving it in hotel or guesthouse rooms, as well as when consigning it to storage or taking it on public transport. Padlocks also come in handy as extra security on your room, particularly on the doors of beachfront bamboo huts.

Theft from some long-distance **buses** is also a problem, with the majority of reported incidents taking place on the temptingly cheap overnight buses run by private companies direct from Bangkok's Thanon Khao San (as opposed to those that depart from the government bus stations) to destinations such as Surat Thani and southern beach resorts. The best solution is to go direct from the bus stations (see p.31).

Personal safety

On any bus, private or government, and on any train journey, never keep anything of value in luggage that is stored out of your sight and be wary of accepting food and drink from fellow passengers as it may be drugged. This might sound paranoid, but there have been enough **drug-muggings** for TAT to publish a specific warning about the problem. Drinks can also be spiked in bars and clubs; at full moon parties on Ko Pha Ngan this has led to sexual assaults against farang women, while prostitutes sometimes spike drinks so they can steal from their victim's room.

Violent crime against tourists is not common, but it does occur, and there have been several serious attacks on women travellers in recent years. However, bearing in mind that fourteen million foreigners visit Thailand every year, the statistical likelihood of becoming a victim is extremely small. **Obvious precautions** for travellers of either sex include locking accessible windows and doors at night – preferably with your own padlock (doors in many of the simpler guesthouses and beach bungalows are designed for this) – and not travelling alone at night in a taxi or tuk-tuk. Nor should you risk jumping into an unlicensed taxi at the airport in Bangkok at any time of day: there have been some very violent robberies in these, so take the well-marked licensed, metered taxis instead.

Among hazards to watch out for in the natural world, **riptides** claim a number of tourist lives every year, particularly off Phuket, Ko Chang (Trat), Hua Hin, Cha-am, Rayong, Pattaya and the Ko Samui archipelago during stormy periods of the monsoon season, so always pay attention to warning signs and red flags, and always ask locally if unsure.

Jellyfish can be a problem on any coast, especially just after a storm (see p.63).

Unfortunately, it is also necessary for female tourists to think twice about spending time alone with a **monk**, as not all men of the cloth uphold the Buddhist precepts and there have been rapes and murders committed by men wearing the saffron robes of the monkhood.

Though unpalatable and distressing, Thailand's high-profile **sex industry** is relatively unthreatening for Western women, with its energy focused exclusively on farang men; it's also quite easily avoided, being contained within certain pockets of the capital and a couple of beach resorts.

As for **harassment** from men, it's hard to generalize, but most Western women find it less of a problem in Thailand than they do back home. Outside the main tourist spots, you're more likely to be of interest as a foreigner rather than a woman and, if travelling alone, as an object of concern rather than of sexual aggression.

Regional issues

Because of the **violence in the deep south**, most Western governments are currently advising against travel to or through the border provinces of Songkhla, Yala, Pattani and Narathiwat, unless essential (see p.401). For up-to-the-minute advice on current political trouble-spots, consult your government's travel advisory (see box below).

Scams

Despite the best efforts of guidebook writers, TAT and the Thai tourist police, countless travellers to Thailand get scammed every year. Nearly all **scams** are easily avoided if you're on your guard against anyone who makes an unnatural effort to befriend you. We have outlined the main scams in the relevant sections of this guide, but con-artists are nothing if not creative, so if in doubt walk away at the earliest opportunity. The worst areas for scammers are the busy tourist centres, including many parts of Bangkok and the main beach resorts.

Many **tuk-tuk drivers** earn most of their living

GOVERNMENTAL TRAVEL ADVISORIES
Australian Department of Foreign Affairs ⓦ dfat.gov.au.
British Foreign & Commonwealth Office ⓦ fco.gov.uk.
Canadian Department of Foreign Affairs ⓦ international.gc.ca.
Irish Department of Foreign Affairs ⓦ foreignaffairs.gov.ie.
New Zealand Ministry of Foreign Affairs ⓦ mfat.govt.nz.
South African Department of Foreign Affairs ⓦ dfa.gov.za.
US State Department ⓦ state.gov.

REPORTING A CRIME OR EMERGENCY

In emergencies, contact the English-speaking **tourist police**, who maintain a 24-hour toll-free nationwide line (☎1155) and have offices in the main tourist centres; getting in touch with the tourist police first is invariably more efficient than directly contacting the local police, ambulance or fire service. The tourist police's job is to offer advice and tell you what to do next, but they do not file crime reports, which must be done at the nearest police station.

The British Embassy in Bangkok provides **advice** for British victims of crime in Thailand and also posts practical tips and a list of useful contacts on its website (☎02 305 8333, ⓦukinthailand.fco.gov.uk/en/help-for-british-nationals).

through securing **commissions** from tourist-oriented shops; this is especially true in Bangkok, where they will do their damnedest to get you to go to a gem shop (see below). The most common tactic is for drivers to pretend that the Grand Palace or other major sight you intended to visit is closed for the day (see p.78), and to then offer to take you on a round-city tour instead, perhaps even for free. The tour will invariably include a visit to a gem shop. The easiest way to avoid all this is to take a **metered taxi**; if you're fixed on taking a tuk-tuk, ignore any tuk-tuk that is parked up or loitering and be firm about where you want to go.

Self-styled **tourist guides**, **touts** and anyone else who might introduce themselves as **students** or **businesspeople** and offer to take you somewhere of interest, or invite you to meet their family, are often the first piece of bait in a well-honed chain of con-artists. If you bite, chances are you'll end up either at a gem shop or in a gambling den, or, at best, at a tour operator or hotel that you had not planned to patronize. This is not to say that you should never accept an invitation from a local person, but be extremely wary of doing so following a street encounter in Bangkok or the resorts. Tourist guides' ID cards are easily faked.

For many of these characters, the goal is to get you inside a dodgy **gem shop**, nearly all of which are located in Bangkok (see box, p.145), but the bottom line is that if you are not experienced at buying and trading in valuable gems you will definitely be ripped off, possibly even to the tune of several thousand dollars. Check the 2Bangkok website's account of a typical gem scam (ⓦ2bangkok.com/2bangkok-scams-sapphire.html) before you shell out any cash at all.

A less common but potentially more frightening scam involves a similar cast of warm-up artists leading tourists into a **gambling** game. The scammers invite their victim home on an innocent-sounding pretext, get out a pack of cards, and then set about fleecing the incomer in any number of subtle ways. Often this can be

especially scary as the venue is likely to be far from hotels or recognizable landmarks. You're unlikely to get any sympathy from police, as gambling is **illegal** in Thailand.

An increasing number of travel agents in tourist centres all over the country are trying to pass themselves off as official government tourist information offices, displaying nothing but "**TOURIST INFORMATION**" on their shop signs or calling themselves names like "T&T" (note that the actual TAT, the Tourism Authority of Thailand, does not book hotels or sell any kind of travel ticket). Fakers like this are more likely to sell you tickets for services that turn out to be sub-standard or even not to exist. A word of warning also about **jet skis** operators, who usually ask for a passport as guarantee, will often try to charge renters exorbitant amounts of money for any minor damage they claim to find on return.

Age restrictions and other laws

Thai law requires that tourists **carry their original passports** at all times, though sometimes it's more practical to carry a photocopy and keep the original locked in a safety deposit. The **age of consent** is 15, but the law allows anyone under the age of 18, or their parents, to file charges in retrospect even if they consented to sex at the time. It is against the law to have sex with a prostitute who is under 18. It is illegal for **under-18s** to buy cigarettes or to drive, and you must be 20 or over to **buy alcohol** or be allowed into a **bar or club** (ID checks are sometimes enforced in Bangkok). It is illegal for anyone to **gamble** in Thailand (though many do).

Smoking in public is widely prohibited. The ban covers all air-conditioned public buildings (including restaurants, bars and clubs) and air-conditioned trains, buses and planes and even extends to parks and the street; violators may be subject to a B2000 fine. Dropping cigarette butts, **littering** and spitting in public places can also earn you a B2000 fine. There are fines for **overstaying your visa** (see p.60), **working without a permit**,

not wearing a motorcycle helmet and violating other **traffic laws**.

Drugs

Drug-smuggling carries a maximum penalty in Thailand of death, and **dealing drugs** will get you anything from four years to life in a Thai prison; penalties depend on the drug and the amount involved. Travellers caught with even the smallest amount of drugs at airports and international borders are prosecuted for trafficking, and no one charged with trafficking offences gets bail. Heroin, amphetamines, LSD and ecstasy are classed as Category 1 drugs and carry the most severe penalties: even **possession** of Category 1 drugs for personal use can result in a **life sentence**. Away from international borders, most foreigners arrested in possession of small amounts of cannabis are released on bail, then fined and deported, but the law is complex and prison sentences are possible.

Despite occasional royal pardons, don't expect special treatment as a farang: you only need to read one of the first-hand accounts by foreign former prisoners (see p.441) or read the blogs at Ⓦthai prisonlife.com to get the picture. The **police** actively look for tourists doing drugs, reportedly searching people regularly and randomly on Thanon Khao San, for example. They have the power to order a urine test if they have reasonable grounds for suspicion, and even a positive result for marijuana consumption could lead to a year's imprisonment. Be wary also of **being shopped** by a farang or local dealer keen to earn a financial reward for a successful bust (there are setups at the Ko Pha Ngan full-moon parties, for example), or having substances slipped into your luggage (simple enough to perpetrate unless all fastenings are secured with padlocks).

If you are arrested, ask for your embassy to be contacted immediately (see p.145), which is your right under Thai law, and embassy staff will talk you through procedures; the website of the British Embassy in Thailand also posts useful information, including a list of English-speaking lawyers, at Ⓦukinthailand.fco.gov.uk/en/help-for-british-nationals. The British charity Prisoners Abroad (Ⓦprisonersabroad.org.uk) carries a detailed survival guide on its website, which outlines what to expect if arrested in Thailand, from the point of apprehension through trial and conviction to life in a Thai jail; if contacted, the charity may also be able to offer direct support to a British citizen facing imprisonment in a Thai jail.

Customs regulations

The **duty-free** allowance on entry to Thailand is 200 cigarettes (or 250g of tobacco) and a litre of spirits or wine.

To **export antiques** or newly cast **Buddha images** from Thailand, you need to have a licence granted by the Fine Arts Department (the export of antique Buddhas is forbidden). Licences can be obtained for example through the Office of Archeology and National Museums, 81/1 Thanon Si Ayutthaya (near the National Library), Bangkok (Ⓣ02 628 5032), or through the national museum in Phuket. Applications take at least three working days in Bangkok, generally more in the provinces, and need to be accompanied by the object itself, some evidence of its rightful possession, two postcard-sized colour photos of it, taken face-on and against a white background, and photocopies of the applicant's passport; furthermore, if the object is a Buddha image, the passport photocopies need to be certified by your embassy in Bangkok. Some antiques shops can organize all this for you.

Electricity

Mains **electricity** is supplied at 220 volts AC and is available at all but the most remote villages and basic beach huts. Where electricity is supplied by generators and/or solar power, for example on the smaller, less populated islands, it is often rationed to evenings only. If you're packing phone and camera chargers, a hair dryer, laptop or other appliance, you'll need to take a set of travel-plug adapters with you as several plug types are commonly in use, most usually with two round pins, but also with two flat-blade pins, and sometimes with both options.

Entry requirements

There are three main entry categories for visitors to Thailand; for all of them, under International Air Travel Association rules, your passport should be valid for at least six months. As visa requirements are subject to frequent change, you should always consult before departure a Thai embassy or consulate, a reliable travel agent, or the Thai Ministry of Foreign Affairs' website at Ⓦmfa.go.th/web/2637.php. For further, unofficial but usually reliable, details on all visa matters, go to Ⓦthaivisa.com and especially their various moderated forums.

Most Western passport holders (that includes citizens of the UK, Ireland, the US, Canada, Australia, New Zealand and South Africa) are allowed to enter the country for short **stays** without having to apply for a visa – officially termed the **tourist visa exemption**. You'll be granted a thirty-day stay at an international airport but only fifteen days at an overland border; the period of stay will be stamped into your passport by immigration officials upon entry. You're supposed to be able to somehow show proof of means of living while in the country (B10,000 per person, B20,000 per family), and in theory you may be put back on the next plane without it or sent back to get a sixty-day tourist visa from the nearest Thai embassy, but this is unheard of. You are also required to show proof of tickets to leave Thailand again within the allotted time. This is rarely checked by Thai immigration authorities, though there have been a few cases recently, mostly at the Cambodian border. However, if you have a one-way air ticket to Thailand and no evidence of onward travel arrangements, it's best to buy a tourist visa in advance: some airlines will stop you boarding the plane without one, as they would be liable for flying you back to your point of origin if you did happen to be stopped.

If you're fairly certain you may want to stay longer than fifteen/thirty days, then from the outset you should apply for a **sixty-day tourist visa** from a Thai embassy or consulate, accompanying your application – which generally takes several days to process – with your passport and one or two photos. The sixty-day visa currently costs, for example, £25 in the UK; multiple-entry versions are available, costing £25 per entry, which may be handy if you're going to be leaving and re-entering Thailand. Ordinary tourist visas are valid for three months, ie you must enter Thailand within three months of the visa being issued by the Thai embassy or consulate, while multiple-entry versions are valid for six months. Visa application forms can be downloaded from, for example, the Thai Ministry of Foreign Affairs' website.

Thai embassies also consider applications for **ninety-day non-immigrant visas** (£50, in the UK for example, for single entry, £125 multiple-entry) as long as you can offer a reason for your visit, such as study, business or visiting family/friends (there are different categories of non-immigrant visa for which different levels of proof are needed). As it can be a hassle to organize a ninety-day visa, it's generally easier to apply for a thirty-day extension to your sixty-day visa once inside Thai borders.

It's not a good idea to **overstay** your visa limits.

Once you're at the airport or the border, you'll have to pay a fine of B500 per day before you can leave Thailand. More importantly, however, if you're in the country with an expired visa and you get involved with police or immigration officials for any reason, however trivial, they are obliged to take you to court, possibly imprison you, and deport you.

Border runs, extensions and re-entry permits

Setting aside the caveats about proof of funds and onward tickets (see above), it's generally easy to get a new fifteen-day tourist visa exemption by hopping **across the border** into a neighbouring country and back. Such tourist visa exemptions can be **extended** within Thailand for a further seven days, sixty-day tourist visas for a further thirty days, at the discretion of immigration officials; extensions cost B1900 and are issued over the counter at immigration offices (*kaan khao muang*; ☎1111 for 24hr information in English, ⓦimmigration.go.th) in nearly every provincial capital – most offices ask for one or two photos as well, plus one or two photo-copies of the main pages of your passport including your Thai departure card, arrival stamp and visa. Many Khao San tour agents offer to get your visa extension for you, but beware: some are reportedly faking the stamps, which could get you into serious trouble. Immigration offices also issue **re-entry permits** (B1000 single re-entry, B3800 multiple) if you want to leave the country and come back again while maintaining the validity of your existing visa.

THAI EMBASSIES AND CONSULATES ABROAD

For a full listing of Thai diplomatic missions abroad, consult the Thai Ministry of Foreign Affairs' website at ⓦ mfa.go.th/web/2712.php; their other site, ⓦ thaiembassy.org, has links to the websites of most of the offices below.

Australia 111 Empire Circuit, Yarralumla, Canberra ACT 2600 ☎02/6206 0100; plus consulate at 131 Macquarrie St, Sydney, NSW 2000 ☎02/9241 2542–3.

Burma 94 Pyay Rd, Dagon Township, Rangoon ☎01/226721.

Cambodia 196 Preah Norodom Blvd, Sangkat Tonle Bassac, Khan Chamcar Mon, Phnom Penh ☎023/726306–10.

Canada 180 Island Park Drive, Ottawa, ON, K1Y 0A2 ☎613/722-4444; plus consulate at 1040 Burrard St, Vancouver, BC, V6Z 2R9 ☎604/687-1143.

Laos Vientiane: embassy at Avenue Kaysone Phomvihane, Saysettha District ☎021/214581–2, consular section at Unit 15 Bourichane Road, Ban Phone Si Nuan, Muang Si Sattanak ☎021/453916; plus consulate at Khanthabouly District, Savannakhet Province, PO Box 513 ☎041/212373.

Malaysia 206 Jalan Ampang, 50450 Kuala Lumpur ☎ 03/2148 8222; plus consulates at 4426 Jalan Pengkalan Chepa, 15400 Kota Bharu ☎ 09/748 2545; and 1 Jalan Tunku Abdul Rahman, 10350 Penang ☎ 04/226 9484.
New Zealand 110 Molesworth St, Thorndon, Wellington ☎ 04/476 8616.
Singapore 370 Orchard Road, Singapore 238870 ☎ 6737 2158.
South Africa 428 Pretorius/Hill St, Arcadia, Pretoria 0083 ☎ 012/342 5470.
UK & Ireland 29–30 Queens Gate, London SW7 5JB ☎ 020/7589 2944. Visa applications by post are not accepted here, but can be sent to various honorary consulates, including those in Hull (🅦 thaiconsul-uk .com) and Dublin (🅦 thaiconsulateireland.com).
US 1024 Wisconsin Ave NW, Suite 401, Washington, DC 20007 ☎ 202/944-3600; plus consulates at 700 North Rush St, Chicago, IL 60611 ☎ 312/664-3129; 611 North Larchmont Blvd, 2nd Floor, Los Angeles, CA 90004 ☎ 323/962-9574; and 351 E 52nd St, New York, NY 10022 ☎ 212/754-1770.
Vietnam 63–65 Hoang Dieu St, Hanoi ☎ 04/3823-5092–4; plus consulate at 77 Tran Quoc Thao St, District 3, Ho Chi Minh City ☎ 08/3932-7637–8.

Gay and lesbian Thailand

Buddhist tolerance and a national abhorrence of confrontation and victimization combine to make Thai society relatively tolerant of **homosexuality**, if not exactly positive about same-sex relationships. Most Thais are extremely private and discreet about being gay, generally pursuing a "don't ask, don't tell" understanding with their family. The majority of people are horrified by the idea of gay-bashing and generally regard it as unthinkable to spurn a child or relative for being gay.

Hardly any Thai celebrities are out, yet the predilections of several respected social, political and entertainment figures are widely known and accepted. There is no mention of homosexuality at all in Thai law, which means that the **age of consent** for gay sex is fifteen, the same as for heterosexuals. However, this also means that gay rights are not protected under Thai law.

Although excessively physical displays of affection are frowned upon for both heterosexuals and homosexuals, Western gay couples should get no hassle about being seen together in public – it's much more acceptable, and common, in fact, for friends of the same sex (gay or not) to walk hand-in-hand, than for heterosexual couples to do so.

Transvestites (known as *katoey* or "ladyboys") and **transsexuals** are also a lot more visible in Thailand than in the West. You'll find cross-dressers doing ordinary jobs, even in small upcountry towns, and there are a number of transvestites and transsexuals in the public eye too – including national volleyball stars and champion *muay thai* boxers. The government tourist office vigorously promotes the transvestite cabarets in Pattaya, Phuket and Bangkok, all of which are advertised as family entertainment. *Katoey* also regularly appear as characters in soap operas, TV comedies and films, where they are depicted as stereotyped but harmless figures of fun. Richard Totman's book *The Third Sex* offers an interesting insight into Thai *katoey*, their experiences in society and public attitudes towards them.

The scene

Thailand's gay scene is mainly focused on **mainstream venues** like karaoke bars, restaurants, massage parlours, gyms, saunas and escort agencies. For the sake of discretion, gay venues are usually intermingled with straight ones. Bangkok, Phuket and Pattaya have the biggest concentrations of farang-friendly gay bars and clubs. For a detailed guide to the gay and lesbian scene throughout the country, see the *Utopia Guide to Thailand* by John Goss, which can be ordered or downloaded as an e-book via 🅦 utopia-asia.com.

Thai **lesbians** generally eschew the word lesbian, which in Thailand is associated with male fantasies, instead referring to themselves as either *tom* (for tomboy) or *dee* (for lady). There are hardly any dedicated *tom-dee* venues in Thailand, but we've listed established ones where possible; unless otherwise specified, gay means male throughout this guide.

The farang-oriented gay **sex industry** is a tiny but highly visible part of Thailand's gay scene. With its tawdry floor shows and host services, it bears a dispiriting resemblance to the straight sex trade, and is similarly most active in Bangkok, Pattaya and Patong (on Phuket). Like their female counterparts in the heterosexual fleshpots, many of the boys working in the gay sex bars that dominate these districts are underage; note that anyone caught having sex with a prostitute below the age of 18 faces imprisonment. A significant number of gay prostitutes are gay by economic necessity rather than by inclination. As with the straight sex scene, we do not list commercial gay sex bars in the guide.

INFORMATION AND CONTACTS FOR GAY TRAVELLERS

Bangkok Lesbian 🅦 bangkoklesbian.com. Organized by foreign lesbians living in Thailand, Bangkok Lesbian hosts regular parties and posts general info and listings of the capital's lesbian-friendly hangouts on its website.

Dreaded Ned's ⓦ dreadedned.com. Guide to the scene in Thailand that's most useful for its what's-on listings.

Gay People in Thailand ⓦ thaivisa.com /forum/Gay-People -Thailand-f27.html. Popular forum for gay expats.

Utopia ⓦ utopia-asia.com and ⓦ utopia-asia.com/womthai.htm. Asia's best gay and lesbian website lists clubs, events, accommodation, tour operators and organizations for gays and lesbians and has useful links to other sites in Asia and the rest of the world.

Health

Although Thailand's climate, wildlife and cuisine present Western travellers with fewer health worries than in many Asian destinations, it's as well to know in advance what the risks might be, and what preventive or curative measures you should take.

For a start, there's no need to bring huge supplies of non-prescription medicines with you, as Thai **pharmacies** (*raan khai yaa*; typically open daily 8.30am–8pm) are well stocked with local and international branded medicaments, and of course they are generally much less expensive than at home. Nearly all pharmacies are run by trained English-speaking pharmacists, who are usually the best people to talk to if your symptoms aren't acute enough to warrant seeing a doctor. The British pharmacy chain, Boots, now has branches in many big cities (see ⓦ th.boots.com for locations). These are the best place to stock up on some Western products such as **tampons** (which Thai women do not use).

Hospital (*rong phayabaan*) cleanliness and efficiency vary, but generally hygiene and health-care standards are good and the ratio of medical staff to patients is considerably higher than in most parts of the West. As with head pharmacists, doctors speak English. Several Bangkok hospitals are highly regarded (see p.146), and all provincial capitals have at least one hospital: if you need to get to one, ask at your accommodation for advice on, and possibly transport to, the nearest or most suitable. In the event of a major health crisis, get someone to contact your embassy (see p.145) and insurance company – it may be best to get yourself transported to Bangkok or even home.

There have been outbreaks of **Avian Influenza** (**bird flu**) in domestic poultry and wild birds in Thailand (most recently in 2008) which have led to a small number of human fatalities, believed to have arisen through close contact with infected poultry. There has been no evidence of human-to-human transmission in Thailand, and the risk to humans is believed to be very low. However, as a precaution, you should avoid visiting live-animal markets and other places where you may come into close contact with birds, and ensure that poultry and egg dishes are thoroughly cooked.

Inoculations

There are no compulsory **inoculation** requirements for people travelling to Thailand from the West, but you should consult a doctor or other health professional, preferably at least four weeks in advance of your trip, for the latest information on recommended immunizations. In addition to making sure that your recommended immunizations for life in your home country are up to date, most doctors strongly advise vaccinations or boosters against tetanus, diphtheria, hepatitis A and, in many cases, typhoid, and in some cases they might also recommend protecting yourself against Japanese encephalitis, rabies and hepatitis B. There is currently no vaccine against malaria (see below). If you forget to have all your inoculations before leaving home, or don't leave yourself sufficient time, you can get them in Bangkok at, for example, the Thai Red Cross Society's Queen Saovabha Institute or Global Doctor (see p.146).

Mosquito-borne diseases

Mosquitoes in Thailand spread not only malaria, but also diseases such as dengue fever and the very similar chikungunya fever, especially during the rainy season. The main message, therefore, is to **avoid being bitten** by mosquitoes. You should smother yourself and your clothes in **mosquito repellent** containing the chemical compound DEET, reapplying regularly (shops, guesthouses and department stores all over Thailand stock it, but if you want the highest-strength repellent, or convenient roll-ons or sprays, do your shopping before you leave home). DEET is strong stuff, and if you have sensitive skin, a natural alternative is citronella (available in the UK as Mosi-guard), made from a blend of eucalyptus oils; the Thai version is made with lemon grass.

At night you should sleep either under a **mosquito net** sprayed with DEET or in a bedroom with **mosquito screens** across the windows (or in an enclosed a/c room). Accommodation in tourist spots nearly always provides screens or a net (check both for holes), but if you're planning to go way off the beaten track or want the security of having your own mosquito net just in case, wait until you get to Bangkok to buy one, where department stores sell them for much less than you'd pay in the West. Plug-in insecticide vaporizers, insect room sprays and mosquito coils – also widely available in

Thailand – help keep the insects at bay; electronic "buzzers" are useless.

Malaria

Thailand is **malarial**, with the disease being carried by mosquitoes that bite from dusk to dawn, but the risks involved vary across the country.

There is a significant risk of malaria, mainly in rural and forested areas, in a narrow strip along the **borders with Cambodia** (excluding Ko Chang), **Laos** and **Burma** (excluding, for example, resorts and road and rail routes along the Gulf coast). Discuss with your travel health adviser which anti-malarial drugs are currently likely to be effective in these areas, as prophylaxis advice can change from year to year.

Elsewhere in Thailand the risk of malaria is considered to be so low that anti-malarial tablets are not advised.

The **signs of malaria** are often similar to flu, but are very variable. The incubation period for malignant malaria, which can be fatal, is usually 7–28 days, but it can take up to a year for symptoms of the benign form to occur. The most important symptom is a raised temperature of at least 38°C beginning a week or more after the first potential exposure to malaria: if you suspect anything, go to a hospital or clinic immediately.

Dengue fever

Dengue fever, a debilitating and occasionally fatal viral disease that is particularly prevalent during and just after the rainy season, is on the increase throughout tropical Asia, and is endemic to many areas of Thailand, with over 115,000 reported cases in 2010. Unlike malaria, dengue fever is spread by mosquitoes that can bite during daylight hours, so you should also use mosquito repellent during the day. Symptoms include fever, headaches, fierce joint and muscle pain ("breakbone fever" is another name for dengue), and possibly a rash, and usually develop between five and eight days after being bitten.

There is no vaccine against dengue fever; the only treatment is lots of rest, liquids and paracetamol (or any other acetaminophen painkiller, not aspirin), though more serious cases may require hospitalization.

Rabies

Rabies is widespread in Thailand, mainly carried by dogs (between four and seven percent of stray dogs in Bangkok are reported to be rabid), but also cats and monkeys. It is transmitted by bites, scratches or even occasionally licks. Dogs are everywhere in Thailand and even if kept as pets they're often not very well cared for; hopefully their mangy appearance will discourage the urge to pat them, as you should steer well clear of them. Rabies is invariably fatal if the patient waits until symptoms begin, though modern vaccines and treatments are very effective and deaths are rare. The important thing is, if you are bitten, licked or scratched by an animal, to vigorously clean the wound with soap and disinfect it, preferably with something containing iodine, and to seek medical advice regarding treatment right away.

Other bites and stings

Thailand's seas are home to a few dangerous creatures that you should look out for, notably **jellyfish**, which tend to be washed towards the beach by rough seas during the monsoon season but can appear at any time of year. All manner of stinging and non-stinging jellyfish can be found in Thailand – as a general rule, those with the longest tentacles tend to have the worst stings – but reports of serious incidents are rare; ask around at your resort or at a local dive shop to see if there have been any sightings of venomous varieties. You also need to be wary of venomous **sea snakes**, **sea urchins** and a couple of less conspicuous species – **stingrays**, which often lie buried in the sand, and **stonefish**, whose potentially lethal venomous spikes are easily stepped on because the fish look like stones and lie motionless on the sea bed.

If **stung or bitten** you should always seek medical advice as soon as possible, but there are a few ways of alleviating the pain or administering your own first-aid in the meantime. If you're stung by a jellyfish, wash the affected area with salt water (not fresh water) and, if possible, with vinegar (failing that, ammonia, citrus fruit juice or even urine may do the trick), and try to remove the fragments of tentacles from the skin with a gloved hand, forceps, thick cloth or credit card. The best way to minimize the risk of stepping on the toxic spines of sea urchins, stingrays and stonefish is to wear thick-soled shoes, though these cannot provide total protection; sea urchin spikes should be removed after softening the skin with ointment, though some people recommend applying urine to help dissolve the spines; for stingray and stonefish stings, alleviate the pain by immersing the wound in hot water while awaiting help.

In the case of a **venomous snake bite**, don't try sucking out the venom or applying a tourniquet: wrap up and immobilize the bitten limb and try to stay still and calm until medical help arrives; all provincial hospitals in Thailand carry supplies of antivenins.

Some of Thailand's wilder, less developed beaches are plagued by **sandflies**, tiny, barely visible midges whose bites can trigger an allergic response, leaving big red weals and an unbearable itch, and possible infection if scratched too vigorously. Many islanders say that slathering yourself in (widely available) coconut oil is the best deterrent as sandflies apparently don't like the smell. Applying locally made camphor-based yellow oil (see p.176) quells the itch, but you may need to resort to antihistamines for the inflammation. **Leeches** aren't dangerous but can be a bother when walking in forested areas, especially during and just after the rainy season. The most effective way to get leeches off your skin is to burn them with a lighted cigarette, or douse them in salt; oily suntan lotion or insect repellent sometimes makes them lose their grip and fall off.

Worms and flukes

Worms can be picked up through the soles of your feet, so avoid going barefoot. They can also be ingested by eating undercooked meat, and liver **flukes** by eating raw or undercooked freshwater fish. Worms which cause schistosomiasis (bilharziasis) by attaching themselves to your bladder or intestines can be found in freshwater rivers and lakes. The risk of contracting this disease is low, but you should avoid swimming in most freshwater lakes.

Digestive problems

By far the most common travellers' complaint in Thailand, **digestive troubles** are often caused by contaminated food and water, or sometimes just by an overdose of unfamiliar foodstuffs (see p.39 and p.43).

Stomach trouble usually manifests itself as simple **diarrhoea**, which should clear up without medical treatment within three to seven days and is best combated by drinking lots of fluids. If this doesn't work, you're in danger of getting **dehydrated** and should take some kind of rehydration solution, either a commercial sachet of ORS (oral rehydration solution), sold in all Thai pharmacies, or a do-it-yourself version, which can be made by adding a handful of sugar and a pinch of salt to every litre of boiled or bottled water (soft drinks are not a viable alternative). If you can eat, avoid fatty foods.

Anti-diarrhoeal agents such as Imodium are useful for blocking you up on long bus journeys, but only attack the symptoms and may prolong infections; an antibiotic such as ciprofloxacin, however, can often reduce a typical attack of traveller's diarrhoea to one day. If the diarrhoea persists for a week or more, or if you have blood or mucus in your stools, or an accompanying fever, go to a doctor or hospital.

HIV and AIDS

HIV infection is widespread in Thailand, primarily because of the sex trade (see p.111). **Condoms** (*meechai*) are sold in pharmacies, convenience stores, department stores, hairdressers and even street markets. Due to rigorous screening methods, Thailand's medical blood supply is now considered safe from HIV/AIDS infection.

MEDICAL RESOURCES

Canadian Society for International Health ☎ 613/241-5785, ⓦ csih.org. Extensive list of travel health centres.

CDC ☎ 1-800/232 4636, ⓦ cdc.gov/travel. Official US government travel health site.

Hospital for Tropical Diseases Travel Clinic UK ⓦ thehtd.org.

International Society for Travel Medicine US ☎ 1-404/373-8282, ⓦ istm.org. Has a full list of travel health clinics.

MASTA (Medical Advisory Service for Travellers Abroad) UK ⓦ masta.org.

NHS Travel Health Website UK ⓦ fitfortravel.scot.nhs.uk.

The Travel Doctor – TMVC ☎ 1300/658 844, ⓦ tmvc.com.au. Lists travel clinics in Australia, New Zealand and South Africa.

Tropical Medical Bureau Ireland ☎ 1850/487 674, ⓦ tmb.ie.

Insurance

Most visitors to Thailand will need to take out **specialist travel insurance**, though you should check exactly what's covered. Insurers will generally not cover travel in Songkhla, Yala, Pattani and Narathiwat provinces in the deep south, as Western governments are currently advising against going to these areas unless it's essential (see p.401). Policies generally also exclude so-called **dangerous sports** unless an extra premium is paid: in Thailand this can mean such things as scuba diving, white-water rafting and trekking.

Internet

Internet access is very widespread and very cheap in Thailand. You'll find traveller-oriented **internet cafés** in every touristed town and resort in the country – there are at least twenty in the Banglamphu district of Bangkok, for example. In untouristed neighbourhoods throughout the country you can always check your email at the ubiquitous online games centres, favourite after-school haunts that are easily spotted from the piles

ROUGH GUIDES TRAVEL INSURANCE

Rough Guides has teamed up with WorldNomads.com to offer great travel insurance deals. Policies are available to residents of over 150 countries, with cover for a wide range of adventure sports, 24hr emergency assistance, high levels of medical and evacuation cover and a stream of travel safety information. Roughguides.com users can take advantage of their policies online 24/7, from anywhere in the world – even if you're already travelling. And since plans often change when you're on the road, you can extend your policy and even claim online. Roughguides.com users who buy travel insurance with WorldNomads.com can also leave a positive footprint and donate to a community development project. For more information go to ⓦ roughguides.com/shop.

of schoolboy pumps outside the door. Competition keeps prices low: upcountry you could expect to pay as little as B20 per hour, while rates in tourist centres average B1 per minute.

Increasing numbers of budget guesthouses and cheap hotels, especially in Bangkok, offer **wi-fi** in all or parts of their establishment; all upmarket hotels have it, though rates are sometimes astronomical. Plenty of cafés, restaurants, bars and other locations across the country provide wi-fi, which is usually free to customers. For a list of hot spots nationwide, try ⓦ jiwire.com; for free locations, go to ⓦ stickman weekly.com.

Laundry

Guesthouses and cheap hotels all over the country run low-cost, same-day **laundry** services, though in luxury hotels, it'll cost an arm and a leg. In some places you pay per item, in others you're charged by the kilo (generally around B30–50/kg); ironing is often included in the price.

Left luggage

Most major train stations have **left luggage** facilities, where bags can be stored for up to twenty days (around B30–80 per item per day); at bus stations you can usually persuade someone official to look after your stuff for a few hours. Many guesthouses and basic hotels also offer an inexpensive and reliable service, while upmarket hotels should be able to look after your luggage for free. There's also left luggage at Bangkok and Phuket international airports (B80–140/day).

Living in Thailand

The most common source of **employment** in Thailand is **teaching English**, especially in Bangkok. You can search for openings at schools all over Thailand on ⓦ ajarn.com, which also features extensive general advice on teaching and living in Thailand. Another useful resource is the excellent ⓦ thaivisa.com, whose scores of well-used forums focus on specific topics that range from employment in Thailand to legal issues and cultural and practical topics.

If you're a qualified **dive instructor**, you might be able to get seasonal work at one of the major resorts – in Phuket, Khao Lak and Ao Nang and on Ko Chang, Ko Phi Phi, Ko Lanta, Ko Samui and Ko Tao, for example. Guesthouse noticeboards occasionally carry adverts for more unusual jobs, such as playing extras in Thai movies. A tourist visa does not entitle you to work in Thailand, so, legally, you'll need to apply for a **work permit**.

STUDY, WORK AND VOLUNTEER PROGRAMMES

In addition to the programmes listed below, voluntary opportunities with smaller grassroots projects (see p.55) are available.

Council on International Educational Exchange (CIEE) US ☎ 1-207/553-4000, ⓦ ciee.org. Leading NGO that organizes paid year-long placements as English teachers in schools in Thailand.

Phuket English teachers ⓦ phukethasbeengoodtous.org. Welcomes short- and longer-term volunteers to teach and assist on its Practical English Language programme at schools on Phuket. The aim of the foundation is to improve kids' standards of English so that they can get the better-paid jobs in Phuket's tourist industry.

Starfish Ventures ⓦ starfishvolunteers.com. Paying volunteer and gap-year placements in Thailand in the areas of health, childcare, wildlife conservation, community development and teaching.

Volunteer Teaching in Thailand ⓦ volunteerteacherthailand .org. Continuing the good work begun by the thousands of volunteers who came to Khao Lak to help rebuild lives and homes following the 2004 tsunami, this organization teaches English to Khao Lak kids and adults to enhance their future prospects in the local tourist industry. Teaching experience is appreciated but not essential.

Mail

Overseas airmail usually takes around seven days from Bangkok, a little longer from the more isolated areas (it's worth asking at the post office about their express EMS services, which can cut this down to three days and aren't prohibitively expensive). **Post offices** in Thailand have recently been quite successfully privatized, and many now offer money-wiring facilities (in association with Western Union), parcel packing, long-distance bus tickets, amulets, whitening cream, you name it. They're generally open Monday to Friday 8.30am to 4.30pm, Saturday 9am to noon; some close Monday to Friday noon to 1pm and may stay open until 6pm, and a few open 9am to noon on Sundays and public holidays. Almost all main post offices across the country operate a **poste restante** service and will hold letters for one to three months. Mail should be addressed: *Name* (family name underlined or capitalized), Poste Restante, GPO, *Town or City*, Thailand. It will be filed by surname, though it's always wise to check under your first initial as well. The smaller post offices pay scant attention to who takes what, but in the busier GPOs you need to show your passport, pay B1 per letter or B2 per parcel received, and sign for them.

Post offices are the best places to buy **stamps**, though hotels and guesthouses often sell them too, usually charging an extra B1 per stamp. An airmail letter of under 10g costs B17 to send to Europe or Australia and B19 to North America; postcards and aerogrammes cost B15, regardless of where they're going. The **surface** rate for parcels to the UK is B950 for the first kg, then B175 per kg; to the US B550 for the first kg, then B140 per kg; and to Australia B650 for the first kg, then B110 per kg; the package should reach its destination in three months. The **airmail** rate for parcels to the UK is B900 for the first kg, then B380 per kg; to the US B950 for the first kg, then B500 per kg; and to Australia B750 for the first kg, then B350 per kg; the package should reach its destination in one or two weeks.

Maps

For most major destinations, the **maps** in this book should be all you need, though you may want to supplement them with larger-scale maps of Bangkok and the whole country. Bangkok bookshops are the best source of these; where appropriate, detailed local maps and their stockists are recommended throughout the Guide. If you want to buy a map before you get there, Rough Guides' 1:1,200,000 map of Thailand is a good option – and, since it's printed on special rip-proof paper, it won't tear. Reasonable alternatives include the 1:1,500,000 maps produced by Nelles and Bartholomew.

For **drivers**, the best atlas is *Thailand Deluxe Atlas* published by thinknet (Ⓦthinknet.co.th): at a scale of 1:550,000, it's bilingual and fairly regularly updated, but costs B550. It's available at most bookshops in Thailand where English-language material is sold. They also have a newer *Thailand Handy Atlas* at 1:1,000,000 for B270, and their mapping is available online at Ⓦmapguide thailand.com.

Money and banks

Thailand's unit of currency is the **baht** (abbreviated to "B"), divided into 100 satang – which are rarely seen these days. Coins come in B1 (silver), B2 (golden), B5 (silver) and B10 (mostly golden, encircled by a silver ring) denominations, notes in B20, B50, B100, B500 and B1000 denominations, inscribed with Western as well as Thai numerals, and generally increasing in size according to value.

At the time of writing, **exchange rates** were around B30 to US$1, B45 to €1 and B50 to £1. A good site for current exchange rates is Ⓦxe.com. Note that Thailand has no black market in foreign currency.

Banking hours are Monday to Friday from 8.30am to 3.30 or 4.30pm, but exchange kiosks in the main tourist centres are always open till at least 5pm, sometimes 10pm, and upmarket hotels change money (at poor rates) 24 hours a day. The Suvarnab-humi Airport exchange counters also operate 24 hours, while exchange kiosks at overseas airports with flights to Thailand usually keep Thai currency.

Sterling and US dollar **travellers' cheques** are accepted by banks and exchange booths in every sizeable Thai town, and most places also deal in a variety of other currencies; everyone offers better rates for cheques than for straight cash. Generally, a total of B33 in commission and duty is charged per cheque – though kiosks and hotels in isolated places may charge extra – so you'll save money if you deal in larger cheque denominations. Note that Scottish and Northern Irish sterling notes may not be accepted in some places.

American Express, Visa and MasterCard **credit and debit cards** are accepted at top hotels as well as in some posh restaurants, department stores, tourist shops and travel agents, but surcharging of up to seven percent is rife, and theft and forgery are major industries – try not to let the card out of your sight, always demand any carbon copies, and never leave cards in baggage storage. With a debit or credit card and personal identification number

(PIN), you can also withdraw cash from hundreds of 24-hour **ATMs** around the country. Almost every town now has at least one bank with an ATM that accepts overseas cards (all the banks marked on our maps throughout the Guide have ATMs), and there are a growing number of stand-alone ATMs in supermarkets. However, Thai banks now make a charge of B150 per ATM withdrawal (on top of whatever your bank at home will be charging you); to get around this, go into a bank with your card and passport instead and ask for a cash advance, or check out **ⓦ** aeon.co.th, the website of a Japanese bank that operates in Thailand, for locations of their ATMs – they don't charge for ATM withdrawals from foreign bank accounts, though there have been reports of people not receiving cash from Aeon ATMs but having their accounts debited.

Opening hours and public holidays

Most shops **open** long hours, usually Monday to Saturday from about 8am to 8pm, while department stores operate daily from around 10am to 9pm. Private office hours are generally Monday to Friday 8am to 5pm and Saturday 8am to noon, though in tourist areas these hours are longer, with weekends worked like any other day. Government offices work Monday to Friday 8.30am to noon and 1 to 4.30pm, and national museums tend to stick to these hours too, but some close on Mondays and Tuesdays rather than at weekends. Temples generally open their gates every day from dawn to dusk.

Many tourists only register **national holidays** because trains and buses suddenly get extraordinarily crowded: although government offices shut on these days, most shops and tourist-oriented businesses carry on regardless, and TAT branches continue to dispense information. (Bank holidays vary slightly from the government office holidays given below: banks close on May 1 and July 1, but not for the Royal Ploughing Ceremony nor for Khao Pansa.) Some national holidays are celebrated with theatrical festivals (see p.47). The only time an inconvenient number of shops, restaurants and hotels do close is during **Chinese New Year**, which, though not marked as an official national holiday, brings many businesses to a standstill for several days in late January or February. You'll notice it particularly in the south, where most service industries are Chinese-managed.

Thais use both the Western Gregorian **calendar** and a Buddhist calendar – the Buddha is said to have died (or entered Nirvana) in the year 543 BC,

so Thai dates start from that point: thus 2013 AD becomes 2556 BE (Buddhist Era).

NATIONAL HOLIDAYS

Jan 1 Western New Year's Day

Feb (day of full moon) Makha Puja. Commemorates the Buddha preaching to a spontaneously assembled crowd of 1250.

April 6 Chakri Day. The founding of the Chakri dynasty.

April (usually 13–15) Songkran. Thai New Year.

May 5 Coronation Day.

May (early in the month) Royal Ploughing Ceremony. Marks the start of the rice-planting season.

May (day of full moon) Visakha Puja. The holiest of all Buddhist holidays, which celebrates the birth, enlightenment and death of the Buddha.

July (day of full moon) Asanha Puja. The anniversary of the Buddha's first sermon.

July (day after Asanha Puja) Khao Pansa. The start of the annual three-month Buddhist rains retreat, when new monks are ordained.

Aug 12 Queen's birthday and Mothers' Day

Oct 23 Chulalongkorn Day. The anniversary of Rama V's death.

Dec 5 King's birthday and Fathers' Day. Also now celebrated as National Day (instead of Constitution Day).

Dec 10 Constitution Day

Dec 31 Western New Year's Eve

Phones

Most foreign **mobile-phone** networks have links with Thai networks but you might want to check on roaming rates, which are often exorbitant, before you leave home. To get round this, most travellers purchase a Thai pre-paid SIM card – 1-2-Call (**ⓦ** ais .co.th) is the biggest network with the best

---

INTERNATIONAL DIALLING CODES

Calling from abroad, the international **country code** for Thailand is **66**, after which you leave off the initial zero of the Thai number.

Calling from Thailand, you'll need the relevant country code (see p.68 for information on prefixes):

Australia 61
Canada 1
Ireland 353
New Zealand 64
South Africa 27
UK 44
US 1

For **international directory enquiries** and operator services, call **☎** 100.

coverage – for their mobile phone (*moe thoe*). Available for as little as B50 (sometimes free at airports, for example with True Move) and refillable at 7-Elevens around the country, they offer very cheap calls, both domestically and internationally (especially if you use low-cost international prefixes such as 1-2-Call's "005" or "009"). They also offer very cheap texting and are free of charge for all incoming calls; mobile internet and wi-fi packages are also generally available.

Even cheaper international calls – less than B1/minute to most countries – can be made with a Zay Hi **phonecard** (W zayhi.com), available in B300 and B500 denominations from post offices and branches of Family Mart. The cheapest option, of course, is to find a guesthouse or café with free wi-fi and **Skype** from your own device; Skype is also available on the computers in most internet cafés.

When **dialling** any number in Thailand, you must now always preface it with what used to be the area code, even when dialling from the same area. Where we've given several line numbers – eg ☎02 431 1802–9 – you can substitute the last digit, 2, with any digit between 3 and 9. For **directory enquiries** within Thailand, call ☎1133.

All mobile-phone numbers in Thailand have recently been changed from nine to ten digits, by adding the number "8" after the initial zero (you may still come across cards and brochures giving the old nine-digit number). Note also, however, that Thais tend to change mobile-phone providers – and therefore numbers – comparatively frequently, in search of a better deal.

One final local idiosyncrasy: Thai phone books list people by their first name, not their family name.

Photography

Most towns and all resorts have at least one **camera shop** where you will be able to get your digital pictures downloaded on to a CD for B100–150; the shops all have card readers. In tourist centres many internet cafés also offer CD-burning services, though if you want to email your pictures bringing your own cable will make life easier.

Time

Thailand is in the same time zone year-round, with no daylight savings period. It's five hours ahead of South Africa, seven hours ahead of GMT, twelve hours ahead of US Eastern Standard Time, three hours behind Australian Eastern Standard Time and five hours behind New Zealand Standard Time.

Tipping

It is usual to **tip** hotel bellboys and porters B20–40, and to round up taxi fares to the nearest B10. Most guides, drivers, masseurs, waiters and maids also depend on tips, and although some upmarket hotels and restaurants will add an automatic ten percent service charge to your bill, this is not always shared out.

Tourist information

The **Tourism Authority of Thailand**, or **TAT** (W tourismthailand.org), maintains offices in several cities abroad and has dozens of branches within Thailand (all open daily 8.30am–4.30pm, though a few close noon–1pm) plus counters at Suvarnabhumi International Airport. Regional offices should have up-to-date information on local festival dates and perhaps transport schedules, but none of them offers accommodation booking, and service can be variable. You can contact the TAT tourist assistance phoneline from anywhere in the country for free on ☎1672 (daily 8am–8pm). In Bangkok, the Bangkok Tourism Division is a better source of information on the capital (see p.122). In some smaller towns that don't qualify for a local TAT office, the information gap is filled by a **municipal tourist assistance office**, though at some of these you may find it hard to locate a fluent English-speaker.

TAT OFFICES ABROAD

Australia & New Zealand Suite 2002, Level 20, 56 Pitt St, Sydney, NSW 2000 ☎02/9247 7549, W thailand.net.au.
South Africa Contact the UK office.
UK & Ireland 1st Floor, 17–19 Cockspur St, London SW1Y 5BL ☎020/7925 2511, E info@tourismthailand.co.uk.
US & Canada 61 Broadway, Suite 2810, New York, NY 10006 ☎212/432-0433, E info@tatny.com; 611 North Larchmont Blvd, 1st Floor, Los Angeles, CA 90004 ☎323/461-9814, E tatla @tat.or.th.

Travellers with disabilities

Thailand makes few provisions for its disabled citizens and this obviously affects **travellers with disabilities**, but taxis, comfortable hotels and personal tour guides are all more affordable than in the West and most travellers with disabilities find

Thais only too happy to offer assistance where they can. Hiring a local tour guide to accompany you on a day's sightseeing is particularly recommended: government tour guides can be arranged through any TAT office.

Most **wheelchair-users** end up driving on the roads because it's too hard to negotiate the uneven pavements, which are high to allow for flooding and invariably lack dropped kerbs. Crossing the road can be a trial, particularly in Bangkok and other big cities, where it's usually a question of climbing steps up to a bridge rather than taking a ramped underpass. Few buses and trains have ramps, but in Bangkok some Skytrain stations and all subway stations have lifts.

Several **tour companies** in Thailand specialize in organizing trips featuring adapted facilities, accessible transport and escorts. The Bangkok-based Help and Care Travel Company (☏ 081 375 0792, ⓦ wheelchairtours.com) designs **accessible holidays** in Thailand for slow walkers and wheelchair-users, as well as offering airport transfers and personal assistants. Mermaid's Dive Centre in Pattaya (☏ 038 232219, ⓦ learn-in-asia.com /handicapped_diving.htm) runs International Association of Handicapped Divers programmes for **disabled divers** and instructors (see p.159).

Bangkok

VIEW OVER BANGKOK FROM THE SKY BAR

1

Bangkok

The headlong pace and flawed modernity of Bangkok match few people's visions of the capital of exotic Siam. Spiked with scores of high-rise buildings of concrete and glass, it's a vast flatness that holds an estimated population of eleven million, and feels even bigger. Yet under the shadow of the skyscrapers you'll find a heady mix of chaos and refinement, of frenetic markets, snail's-pace traffic jams and hushed golden temples, of dispiriting, zombie-like sex shows and early morning alms-giving ceremonies. Plenty of visitors enjoy the challenge of taking on the "Big Mango", but one way or another, the place is sure to get under your skin.

Most budget travellers head for the **Banglamphu** district, where if you're not careful you could end up watching DVDs all day long and selling your shoes when you run out of money. The district is far from having a monopoly on Bangkok accommodation, but it does have the advantage of being just a short walk from the major sights in the **Ratanakosin** area: the dazzling ostentation of the **Grand Palace** and **Wat Phra Kaeo**, lively and grandiose **Wat Pho** and the **National Museum**'s hoard of exquisite works of art. Once those cultural essentials have been seen, you can choose from a whole bevy of lesser sights, including **Wat Benjamabophit** (the "Marble Temple"), especially at festival time, and **Jim Thompson's House**, a small, personal museum of Thai design.

For livelier scenes, explore the dark alleys of **Chinatown**'s bazaars or head for the water: the great **Chao Phraya River**, which breaks up and adds zest to the city's landscape, is the backbone of a network of **canals** that remains fundamentally intact in the west-bank Thonburi district. Inevitably the waterways have earned Bangkok the title of "Venice of the East", a tag that seems all too apt when you're wading through flooded streets in the rainy season. Back on dry land, **shopping** varies from touristic outlets pushing silks, handicrafts and counterfeit watches, through home-grown boutiques selling street-wise fashions and stunning contemporary decor, to thronging local markets where half the fun is watching the crowds. Thailand's long calendar of festivals (see p.47) is one of the few things that has been largely decentralized away from the capital, but Bangkok offers the country's most varied **entertainment**, ranging from traditional dancing and the orchestrated bedlam of Thai boxing, through hip bars and clubs playing the latest imported sounds, to the farang-only sex bars of the notorious Patpong district, a tinseltown Babylon that's the tip of a dangerous iceberg. Even if the above doesn't appeal, you'll almost certainly pass through Bangkok once, if not several times – not only is it Thailand's

RAMAYANA MURALS, WAT PHRA KAEO

Highlights

❶ The Grand Palace The country's least-missable sight, incorporating its holiest and most dazzling temple, Wat Phra Kaeo. **See p.78**

❷ Wat Pho Admire the Reclining Buddha and the lavish architecture, and leave time for a relaxing massage. **See p.83**

❸ The National Museum The central repository of the country's artistic riches. **See p.86**

❹ The canals of Thonburi See the Bangkok of yesteryear on a touristy but memorable longtail-boat ride. **See p.101**

❺ Jim Thompson's House An elegant Thai design classic. **See p.107**

❻ Chatuchak Weekend Market Eight thousand stalls selling everything from triangular pillows to secondhand Levis. **See p.112**

❼ Thanon Khao San Legendary hangout for Southeast Asia backpackers; the place for cheap sleeps, baggy trousers and tall tales. **See p.122 & p.89**

❽ 63rd-floor sundowner Fine cocktails and jaw-dropping views, especially at sunset, at *The Sky Bar* and *Distil*. **See p.139**

❾ Thai boxing Nightly bouts at the national stadia, complete with live musical accompaniment and frenetic betting. **See p.141**

HIGHLIGHTS ARE MARKED ON THE MAP ON P.74

1

main port of entry, it's also the obvious place to sort out **onward travel**, with good deals on international air tickets, as well as a convenient menu of embassies for visas to neighbouring countries.

Ratanakosin

The only place to start your exploration of Bangkok is **Ratanakosin**, the royal island on the east bank of the Chao Phraya, where the city's most important and extravagant sights are. When Rama I developed Ratanakosin for his new capital in 1782, after the sacking of the former capital, Ayutthaya, by the Burmese and a temporary stay across the river in Thonburi, he paid tribute to its precursor by imitating Ayutthaya's layout and architecture – he even shipped the building materials downstream from the ruins of the old city. Like Ayutthaya, the new capital was sited for protection beside a river and turned into an artificial island by the construction of defensive canals, with a central **Grand Palace** and adjoining royal temple, **Wat Phra Kaeo**, fronted by an open cremation field, **Sanam Luang**; the Wang Na (Palace of the Second King), now the **National Museum**, was also built at this time. **Wat Pho**, which predates the capital's founding, was further embellished by Rama I's successors, who have consolidated Ratanakosin's pre-eminence by building several grand European-style palaces (now housing government institutions); Wat Mahathat, the most important centre of Buddhist learning in Southeast Asia; the National Theatre; the National Gallery; and Thammasat and Silpakorn universities.

Bangkok has expanded eastwards away from the river, leaving the Grand Palace a good 5km from the city's commercial heart, and the royal family have long since moved their residence to Dusit, but Ratanakosin remains the ceremonial centre of the whole kingdom – so much so that it feels as if it might sink into the boggy ground under the weight of its own mighty edifices. The heavy, stately feel is

HIGHLIGHTS
1. Grand Palace
2. The Wat Pho
3. The National Museum
4. The Canals of Thonburi
5. Jim Thompson's House
6. Chatuchak Weekend Market
7. Thanon Khao San
8. 63rd-floor sundowner
9. Thai boxing

BANGKOK DISTRICTS

1

ORIENTATION

Bangkok ("Krung Thep" in Thai) can be a tricky place to get your bearings as it's huge and ridiculously congested, with largely featureless modern buildings and no obvious centre. The boldest line on the map is the **Chao Phraya River**, which divides the city into Bangkok proper on the east bank, and **Thonburi**, part of Greater Bangkok, on the west (see map opposite).

The historical core of Bangkok proper, site of the **Ratanakosin**, cradled in a bend in the river. Three concentric canals radiate eastwards around Ratanakosin: the southern part of the area between the canals is the old-style trading enclave of **Chinatown** and Indian **Pahurat**, connected to the old palace by Thanon Charoen Krung (aka New Road); the northern part is characterized by old temples and the **Democracy Monument**, west of which is the backpackers' ghetto of **Banglamphu**. Beyond the canals to the north, **Dusit** is the site of many government buildings and the nineteenth-century Vimanmek Palace, and is linked to Ratanakosin by the three stately avenues, Thanon Rajdamnoen Nok, Thanon Rajdamnoen Klang and Thanon Rajdamnoen Nai.

"New" Bangkok begins to the east of the canals and beyond the main rail line and Hualamphong Station, and stretches as far as the eye can see to the east and north. The main business district is south of **Thanon Rama IV**, with the port of Khlong Toey at its eastern edge. The diverse area north of Thanon Rama IV includes the sprawling campus of Chulalongkorn University, huge shopping centres around **Siam Square** and a variety of other businesses. A couple of blocks northeast of Siam Square stands the tallest building in Bangkok, the 84-storey **Baiyoke II Tower**, whose golden spire makes a good point of reference. To the east lies the swish residential quarter of **Thanon Sukhumvit**.

lightened by traditional shophouses selling herbal medicines, pavement amulet-sellers and studenty canteens along the riverside road, **Thanon Maharat**; and by **Sanam Luang**, still used for cremations and royal ceremonies, but also functioning as a popular open park and the hub of the modern city's bus system. Despite containing several of the country's main sights, the area is busy enough in its own right not to have become a swarming tourist zone, and strikes a neat balance between liveliness and grandeur.

ARRIVAL AND DEPARTURE   RATANAKOSIN

Ratanakosin is within easy walking distance of Banglamphu, but is best approached from the river, via the **express-boat piers** (see p.118) of Tha Chang (the former bathing place of the royal elephants, which gives access to the Grand Palace) or Tha Thien (for Wat Pho). An extension of the subway line from Hualamphong is being built, with a new station at the Museum of Siam, five minutes' walk from Wat Pho, ten minutes from Tha Thien express-boat pier and fifteen minutes from the entrance to the Grand Palace.

CITY OF ANGELS

When **Rama I** was crowned in 1782, he gave his new capital a grand 43-syllable name to match his ambitious plans for the building of the city. Since then, 21 more syllables have been added. Krungthepmahanakhornbowornrattanakosinmahintarayutthayamahadilokpopnoppar atratchathaniburiromudomratchaniwetmahasathanamornpimanavatarnsathitsakkathattiyavis nukarprasit is certified by the *Guinness Book of Records* as the longest place-name in the world, roughly translating as "Great city of angels, the supreme repository of divine jewels, the great land unconquerable, the grand and prominent realm, the royal and delightful capital city full of nine noble gems, the highest royal dwelling and grand palace, the divine shelter and living place of the reincarnated spirits". Fortunately, all Thais refer to the city simply as **Krung Thep**, "City of Angels", though plenty can recite the full name at the drop of a hat. **Bangkok** – "Village of the Plum Olive" – was the name of the original village on the Thonburi side, where the French built a short-lived garrison in the 1660s; with remarkable persistence, it has remained in use by foreigners ever since.

1

CENTRAL BANGKOK

- ⓢ BTS Skytrain and station
- Ⓜ Subway and station
- Ⓐ Suvarnabhumi Airport Rail Link and station
- ☆ Khlong Saen Saeb boat stop

Southern Bus Terminal (Sai Tai) & Taling Chan

Nonthaburi

N

DUSIT

Vimanmek Palace
Parliament

National Library

Support Museum

Elephant Museum

Dusit Zoo

THANON RAJWITHI

THANON RAMA V

Suan Amporn

Rama V Statue

Chitrlada Palace

Royal Barge Museum

Khlong Bangkok Noi

BANGLAMPHU

Wat Benjamabophit

Royal Turf Club

RAMA VIII BRIDGE

Government House

Siriraj Hospital & Museums

Thonburi Train Station

THANON PHRANNOK

National Museum

KHAO SAN

RAJDAMNOEN

Sanam Luang

Democracy Monument

KLANG

Wat Rajnadda

Tha Phan Fah

Rajdamnoen Stadium

TAT ℹ

Bangkok Mission

LAN LUANG

Khlong Saen Saeb

RATANAKOSIN

Wat Rakhang

Wat Phra Kaeo

Grand Palace

Golden Mount

Wat Suthat

THANON BAMRUNG MUANG

THANON RAMA I

Chao Phraya River

Khlong Mon

THANON ARUN AMARIN

Wat Arun

THANON MAHARAT

Wat Pho

Chalermkrung Theatre

Pak Khlong Talat

CHAROEN KRUNG (NEW ROAD)

Wat Mangkon Kamalawat

Wat Kanlayanamit

Santa Cruz

Wat Prayoon

Wat Chakrawat

CHINATOWN

Wat Traimit

Hualamphong Station

Ⓜ Hua Lamphong

Khao Mor Cemetery

THANON SOMDET CHAO PHRAYA

THONBURI

River City

THANON SIPHRAYA

Wongwian Yai Train Station

THANON LAT YA

Taksin Monument

GPO

THANON SURIWONG

Wongwian Yai

THANON SILOM

ⓢ

Krung Thonburi

THANON KRUNG THONBURI

EXPRESSWAY

TAKSIN BRIDGE

Saphan Taksin

THANON SATHORN NUA
THANON SATHORN

ⓢ Central

Surasak

Krungthep Bridge

ACCOMMODATION	
ETZ Hostel	1
Sala Thai Daily Mansion	2

BAR	
Saxophone	1

1

Northern Bus Terminal (Mo Chit), Chatuchak Weekend Market & Don Muang Airport

CENTRAL CHAO PHRAYA EXPRESS-BOAT PIERS

N15	◁▲▷	Thewet *(all boats)*
N14		Rama VIII Bridge *(no flag)*
N13	▷	Phra Arthit *(no flag and orange flag)*
N12	◁▲▷	Phra Pinklao Bridge *(all boats)*
N11		Thonburi Railway Station *(no flag)*
N10	◁▲▷	Wang Lang *(all boats)*
N9	▲▷	Chang *(no flag, green flag and orange flag)*
N8	▷	Thien *(no flag and orange flag)*
N7		Ratchini *(no flag)*
N6	▷	Saphan Phut *(no flag and orange flag)*
N5	◁▲▷	Rachawongse *(all boats)*
N4	▶	Marine (Harbour) Department *(no flag and orange flag)*
N3	◁▲▷	Si Phraya *(all boats)*
N2		Wat Muang Kae *(no flag)*
N1	▷	Oriental *(no flag and orange flag)*
Central	◁▲▷	Sathorn *(all boats)*

▷ All-day	◁▲ Rush hour only (Mon–Fri)
Rush-hour no-flag boats stop at all piers (Mon–Fri)	

Samsen Station

Ari

EXPRESSWAY

THANON VOLANI

THANON YOTHIN

Sanam Pao

THANON RAJWITHI

THANON PHAHONYOTHIN

Phya Thai Palace

Victory Monument

Victory Monument

EXPRESSWAY

THANON RANGNAM

THANON RAJAPRAROP

THANON WIPHAWADI RANGSIT

TOLLWAY

THANON ASOKE DINDAENG

Rama IX (Phra Ram 9)

Phaya Thai

Phaya Thai

Suan Pakkad Palace Museum

Ratchaprarop

Baiyoke II Tower

Pratunam Market

THANON PHETCHABURI

Tha Saphan Hua Chang

Ratchathevi

Makkasan

Jim Thompson's House

THANON PHETCHABURI MAI

Phetchaburi

Tha Pratunam

Tha Witthayu

Bumrungrad

Tha Nana Nua

TAT HQ

Tha Asoke

National Stadium

Central Station (Siam)

Chit Lom

British Embassy

Suwannabhumi Airport

SIAM SQUARE

THANON PLOENCHIT

SUKHUMVIT (SOI NANA NUA)

SUKHUMVIT 3 (SOI NANA NUA)

SUKHUMVIT 13

SUKHUMVIT 15

SUKHUMVIT 23

THANON ASOK MONTRI (SOI 21)

Erawan Shrine

Phloen Chit

Ratchadamri

THANON HENRI DUNANT

Phloen Chit

Nana

Ban Kamthieng

THANON RATCHADAMRI

Chulalongkorn University

Royal Bangkok Sports Club

SOI LANGSUAN

THANON WITTHAYU (WIRELESS)

SOI RUAM RUDEE

SUKHUMVIT 2

SUKHUMVIT 4 (SOI NANA TAI)

Asok

Sukhumvit

THANON SUKHUMVIT

Queen Saovabha Institute

Sam Yan

SOI SARASIN

American Embassy

EXPRESSWAY

Emporium

Phrom Pong

Lumphini Park

Eastern Bus Terminal (Ekamai)

Bangkok Christian

Si Lom

THANON RAMA IV

Sala Daeng

SALA DAENG

CONVENT

THANON RATCHADAPISEK

Chong Nonsi

BNH

Lumphini

Lumphini Stadium

Lumphini Stadium

Goethe Institut

Khlong Toei

Queen Sirikit National Convention Centre (QSNCC)

SOI PHRA PINIT

SOI SUAN PHLU

M. R. Kukrit's Heritage Home

SOI NGAM DUPHLI

SRI BAMPHEN

SAPHAN KHU

0   500
metres

Wat Phra Kaeo and the Grand Palace

Thanon Na Phra Lan • Daily 8.30am–4pm, last admission 3.30pm (weapons museum, Phra Thinang Amarin Winichai and Dusit Maha Prasat interiors closed Sat & Sun) • B400, including a map and admission, within 7 days, to Dusit Park (see p.102) or Sanam Chandra Palace in Nakhon Pathom; 2hr personal audioguide B200, with passport or credit card as deposit • ⓦ palaces.thai.net

Hanging together in a precarious harmony of strangely beautiful colours and shapes, **Wat Phra Kaeo** is the apogee of Thai religious art and the holiest Buddhist site in the country, housing the most important image, the **Emerald Buddha**. Built as the private royal temple, Wat Phra Kaeo occupies the northeast corner of the huge **Grand Palace**, whose official opening in 1785 marked the founding of the new capital and the rebirth of the Thai nation after the Burmese invasion. Successive kings have all left their mark here, and the palace complex now covers 60 acres, though very little apart from the wat is open to tourists.

The only **entrance** to the complex in 2km of crenellated walls is the Gate of Glorious Victory in the middle of the north side, on Thanon Na Phra Lan. This brings you onto a driveway with a tantalizing view of the temple's glittering spires on the left and the dowdy buildings of the Offices of the Royal Household on the right: this is the powerhouse of the kingdom's ceremonial life, providing everything down to chairs and catering, even lending an urn when someone of rank dies. A textile museum under the auspices of the queen, which it's claimed will show how she invented a new Thai national dress in the 1960s, is scheduled to open among these buildings, but for now you'll have to content yourself with some crafts shopping at the Queen's Support Foundation (see p.142). Turn left at the end of the driveway for the ticket office and entrance turnstiles.

As this is Thailand's most sacred site, you have to **dress in smart clothes**: no vests or see-through clothes; men must wear full-length trousers, women trousers or over-the-knee skirts. Suitable garments can be borrowed from the office to the right just inside the Gate of Glorious Victory (same building as the Queen's Support Foundation shop; free, deposit of B200 per item).

Wat Phra Kaeo

It makes you laugh with delight to think that anything so fantastic could exist on this sombre earth.

W. Somerset Maugham, *The Gentlemen in the Parlour*

Entering the temple is like stepping onto a lavishly detailed stage set, from the immaculate flagstones right up to the gaudy roofs. Reinforcing the sense of unreality, the whole compound is surrounded by arcaded walls, decorated with extraordinary murals of scenes from the *Ramayana*. Although it receives hundreds of foreign sightseers and at least as many Thai pilgrims every day, the temple, which has no monks in residence, maintains an unnervingly sanitized look, as if it were built only yesterday.

The approach to the bot

Inside the entrance turnstiles, you're confronted by 6m-tall **yaksha**, gaudy demons from the *Ramayana*, who watch over the Emerald Buddha from every gate of the temple and ward off evil spirits; the king of the demons, green, ten-faced Totsagan (labelled

---

A WORD OF WARNING

When you're **heading for the Grand Palace or Wat Pho**, you may well be approached by someone, possibly pretending to be a student or an official, who will tell you that the sight is closed when it's not, or some other lies to try to lead you away from the entrance, because they want to lead you on a shopping trip for souvenirs, tailored clothes or, if you seem really gullible, gems (see p.145). The opening hours of the Grand Palace – but not Wat Pho – are indeed sometimes erratic because of state occasions, but you can check the details out on its website, ⓦ palaces.thai.net – and even if it's closed on the day you want to visit, that's no reason to throw yourself at the mercy of these shysters.

RATANAKOSIN

RESTAURANTS
Navy Club **1**
Rub Ar Roon **2**

N11 Tha Bangkok Noi

Bangkok Tourism (i)

THANON PHRA ARTHIT

PHRA PINKLAO BRIDGE

CHAO FA

RAJINEE

National Gallery

THANON CHAKRABONGSE

Banglamphu

National Theatre

RAJDAMNOEN KLANG

Democracy Monument

THONBURI

Tha Prachan

National Museum

N10 Tha Wang Lang (Siriraj)

Thammasat University

THANON PHRA CHAN

Royal Ratanakosin Hotel

Tha Maharat

THANON NA PHRA THAT

Sanam Luang

THANON RAJDAMNOEN NAI

Mae Toranee statue

Night Market

THANON ATSADANG

THANON RACHINI

Chao Phraya River

Wat Mahathat

N

Tha Chang N9

Silpakorn University Arts Centre

(i)

THANON NA PHRA LAN

Lak Muang

THANON LAKMUANG

THANON MAHARAT

Wat Phra Kaeo

THANON BAMRUNG MUANG

Wat Suthat

Grand Palace

THANON SANAM CHAI

THANON SARANROM

Wat Rajapradit

THANON RACHINI

THANON ATSADANG

Wat Rajabophit

Inner Palace

Khlong Lod

THANON FUANG NAKHON

THANON THAI WANG

Tha Thien N8

THANON CHAROEN KRUNG (NEW ROAD)

Pahurat & Chinatown

Wat Pho

SOI CHETUPHON

Wat Arun

Wat Pho Massage School

SOI SATTHAKAN

Museum of Siam

ACCOMMODATION
Arun Residence **3**
The Asadang **1**
Aurum: The River Place **4**
Chakrabongse Villas **5**
Sala Arun **2**

0 — 250
metres

N1 Express-boat pier

N7 Tha Ratchini

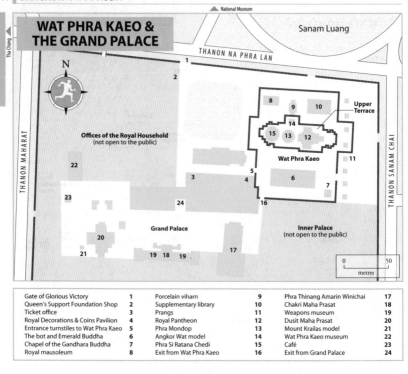

WAT PHRA KAEO &
THE GRAND PALACE

Gate of Glorious Victory	1	Porcelain viharn	9	Phra Thinang Amarin Winichai	17
Queen's Support Foundation Shop	2	Supplementary library	10	Chakri Maha Prasat	18
Ticket office	3	Prangs	11	Weapons museum	19
Royal Decorations & Coins Pavilion	4	Royal Pantheon	12	Dusit Maha Prasat	20
Entrance turnstiles to Wat Phra Kaeo	5	Phra Mondop	13	Mount Krailas model	21
The bot and Emerald Buddha	6	Angkor Wat model	14	Wat Phra Kaeo museum	22
Chapel of the Gandhara Buddha	7	Phra Si Ratana Chedi	15	Café	23
Royal mausoleum	8	Exit from Wat Phra Kaeo	16	Exit from Grand Palace	24

"Tosakanth") stands to the left of the entrance by the southwest corner of the golden Phra Si Ratana Chedi. Less threatening is the toothless old codger, cast in bronze and sitting on a plinth immediately inside the turnstiles by the back wall of the bot, who represents a Hindu **hermit** credited with inventing yoga and herbal medicine. In front of him is a large grinding stone where previously herbal practitioners could come to grind their ingredients – with enhanced powers, of course. Skirting around the bot, you'll reach its **main entrance** on the eastern side, in front of which stands a cluster of grey **statues**, which have a strong Chinese feel: next to Kuan Im, the Chinese *bodhisattva* of mercy shown holding a bottle of *amritsa* (sacred elixir), are a sturdy pillar topped by a lotus flower, which Bangkok's Chinese community presented to Rama IV during his 27 years as a monk, and two handsome cows which commemorate Rama I's birth in the Year of the Cow. Worshippers make their offerings to the Emerald Buddha at two small, stand-in Buddhas here, where they can look at the main image through the open doors of the bot without messing up its pristine interior with gold leaf, candle wax and joss-stick ash.

The bot and the Emerald Buddha

The **bot**, the largest building of the temple, is one of the few original structures left at Wat Phra Kaeo, though it has been augmented so often it looks like the work of a wildly inspired child. Eight *sema* stones mark the boundary of the consecrated area around the bot, each sheltering in a psychedelic fairy castle, joined by a low wall decorated with Chinese porcelain tiles, which depict delicate landscapes. The walls of the bot itself, sparkling with gilt and coloured glass, are supported by 112 golden garudas (birdmen) holding nagas, representing the god Indra saving the world by slaying the serpent-cloud that had swallowed up all the water. The symbolism reflects the king's traditional role as a rainmaker.

Of the bot's three doorways, the largest, in the middle, is reserved for the king himself. Inside, a 9m-high pedestal supports the tiny **Emerald Buddha**, a figure whose mystique draws pilgrims from all over Thailand – as well as politicians accused of corruption, who traditionally come here to publicly swear their innocence. Here especially you must act with respect, sitting with your feet pointing away from the Buddha. The spiritual power of the 60cm jadeite image derives from its legendary past. Reputed to have been created by the gods in India, it was discovered when lightning cracked open an ancient chedi in Chiang Rai in the early fifteenth century. The image was then moved around the north, dispensing miracles wherever it went, before being taken to Laos for two hundred years. As it was believed to bring great fortune to its possessor, the future Rama I snatched it back when he captured Vientiane in 1779, installing it at the heart of his new capital as a talisman for king and country.

Seated in the *Dhyana Mudra* (meditation), the Emerald Buddha has three **costumes**, one for each season: the crown and ornaments of an Ayutthayan king for the hot season; a gilt monastic robe for the rainy season, when the monks retreat into the temples; this is augmented with a full-length gold shawl in the cool season. To this day it's the job of the king himself to ceremonially change the Buddha's costumes – though in recent years, due to the present king's age, the Crown Prince has conducted proceedings. The Buddha was granted a new set of these three costumes in 1997: the old set is now in the Wat Phra Kaeo Museum (see p.83) while the two costumes of the new set that are not in use are on display among the blinding glitter of crowns and jewels in the Royal Decorations and Coins Pavilion, which lies between the ticket office and the entrance to Wat Phra Kaeo.

Among the paraphernalia in front of the pedestal sits the tiny, silver **Phra Chai Lang Chang** (Victory Buddha), which Rama I always carried into battle on the back of his elephant for luck and which still plays an important part in coronation ceremonies. Recently covered in gold, it occupies a prestigious spot dead centre, but is modestly obscured by a fan and by the umbrella of a larger gold Buddha in front. The tallest pair of a dozen standing Buddha images, all made of bronze but encased in gold and raising both hands to dispel fear, are at the front: Rama III dedicated the one on the Emerald Buddha's left to Rama I, the one on his right to Rama II, and Rama IV enshrined relics of the Buddha in their crowns.

The Royal Pantheon and minor buildings

On the north side of the bot, the eastern end of the **upper terrace** is taken up with the **Prasat Phra Thep Bidorn**, known as the **Royal Pantheon**, a splendid hash of styles. The pantheon has its roots in the Khmer concept of *devaraja*, or the divinity of kings: inside are bronze and gold statues, precisely life-size, of all the kings since Bangkok became the Thai capital. Constructed by Rama IV, the building is open only on special occasions, such as Chakri Day (April 6), when the dynasty is commemorated, and Coronation Day (May 5).

From here you get the best view of the **royal mausoleum**, the **porcelain viharn** and the **supplementary library** to the north (all of which are closed to tourists, though you can sometimes glimpse Thai Buddhists worshipping in the library) and, running along the east side of the temple, a row of eight bullet-like **prangs**, each of which has a different nasty ceramic colour. Described as "monstrous vegetables" by Somerset Maugham, they represent, from north to south, the Buddha, Buddhist scripture, the monkhood, the nunhood, the Buddhas who attained enlightenment but did not preach, previous emperors, the Buddha in his previous lives and the future Buddha.

The Phra Mondop and Phra Si Ratana Chedi

In the middle of the terrace, dressed in deep-green glass mosaics, the **Phra Mondop** was built by Rama I to house the *Tripitaka*, or Buddhist scripture, which the king had revised at Wat Mahathat in 1788, the previous version having been lost in the sack of

1

Ayutthaya. It's famous for the mother-of-pearl cabinet and solid-silver mats inside, but is never open. Four tiny **memorials** at each corner of the mondop show the symbols of each of the nine Chakri kings, from the ancient crown representing Rama I to the present king's discus, while the bronze statues surrounding the memorials portray each king's lucky white elephants, labelled by name and pedigree. A contribution of Rama IV, on the north side of the mondop, is a **scale model of Angkor Wat**, the prodigious Cambodian temple, which during his reign (1851–68) was under Thai rule (apparently, the king had wanted to shift a whole Khmer temple to Bangkok but, fortunately, was dissuaded by his officials). At the western end of the terrace, you can't miss the golden dazzle of the **Phra Si Ratana Chedi**, which Rama IV erected, in imitation of the famous bell-shaped chedis at Ayutthaya's Wat Phra Si Sanphet, to enshrine a piece of the Buddha's breastbone.

The murals

Extending for about a kilometre in the arcades that run inside the wat walls, the **murals of the Ramayana** depict every blow of this ancient story of the triumph of good over evil, using the vibrant buildings of the temple itself as backdrops, and setting them off against the subdued colours of richly detailed landscapes. Because of the damaging humidity, none of the original work of Rama I's time survives: maintenance is a never-ending process, so you'll always find an artist working on one of the scenes. The story is told in 178 panels, labelled and numbered in Thai only, starting in the middle of the northern side opposite the porcelain viharn: in the first episode, a hermit, while out ploughing, finds the baby Sita, the heroine, floating in a gold urn on a lotus leaf and brings her to the city. Panel 109 near the gate leading to the palace buildings shows the climax of the story, when Rama, the hero, kills the ten-headed demon Totsagan (Ravana), and the ladies of the enemy city weep at the demon's death. Panel 110 depicts his elaborate funeral procession, and in 113 you can see the funeral fair, with acrobats, sword-jugglers and tightrope-walkers. In between, Sita – Rama's wife – has to walk on fire to prove that she has been faithful during her fourteen years of imprisonment by Totsagan. If you haven't the stamina for the long walk round, you could sneak a look at the end of the story, to the left of the first panel, where Rama holds a victory parade and distributes thank-you gifts.

The palace buildings

The exit in the southwest corner of Wat Phra Kaeo brings you to the palace proper, a vast area of buildings and gardens, of which only the northern edge is on show to the public. Though the king now lives in the Chitrlada Palace in Dusit, the Grand Palace is still used for state receptions and official ceremonies, during which there is no public access to any part of the palace.

Phra Maha Monthien

Coming out of the temple compound, you'll first of all see to your right a beautiful Chinese gate covered in innumerable tiny porcelain tiles. Extending in a straight line behind the gate is the **Phra Maha Monthien**, which was the grand residential complex of earlier kings.

Only the **Phra Thinang Amarin Winichai**, the main audience hall at the front of the complex, is open to the public. The supreme court in the era of the absolute monarchy, it nowadays serves as the venue for ceremonies such as the king's birthday speech. Dominating the hall are two gleaming, intricately carved thrones that date from the reign of Rama I: a white umbrella with the full nine tiers owing to a king shelters the front seat, while the unusual *busbok* behind is topped with a spired roof and floats on a boat-shaped base. The rear buildings are still used for the most important part of the elaborate coronation ceremony, and each new king is supposed to spend a night there to show solidarity with his forefathers.

1

Chakri Maha Prasat

Next door you can admire the facade of the "farang with a Thai hat", as the **Chakri Maha Prasat** is nicknamed. Rama V, whose portrait you can see over its entrance, employed an English architect to design a purely Neoclassical residence, but other members of the royal family prevailed on the king to add the three Thai spires. This used to be the site of the elephant stables: the large red tethering posts are still there and the bronze elephants were installed as a reminder. The building displays the emblem of the Chakri dynasty on its gable, which has a trident (*ri*) coming out of a *chak*, a discus with a sharpened rim. The only part of the Chakri Maha Prasat open to the public is the ground-floor **weapons museum**, which houses a forgettable display of hooks, pikes and guns.

The Inner Palace

The **Inner Palace** (closed to the public), which used to be the king's harem, lies behind the gate on the left-hand side of the Chakri Maha Prasat. Vividly described in M.R. Kukrit Pramoj's novel *Si Phaendin*, the harem was a town in itself, with shops, law courts and an all-female police force for the huge population: as well as the current queens, the minor wives and their children (including pre-pubescent boys) and servants, this was home to the daughters and consorts of former kings, and the daughters of the aristocracy who attended the harem's finishing school. Today, the Inner Palace houses a school of cooking, fruit-carving and other domestic sciences for well-bred young Thais.

Dusit Maha Prasat

On the western side of the courtyard, the delicately proportioned **Dusit Maha Prasat**, an audience hall built by Rama I, epitomizes traditional Thai architecture. Outside, the soaring tiers of its red, gold and green roof culminate in a gilded *mongkut*, a spire shaped like the king's crown, which symbolizes the 33 Buddhist levels of perfection. Each tier of the roof bears a typical *chofa*, a slender, stylized bird's-head finial, and several *hang hong* (swans' tails), which represent three-headed nagas. Inside, you can still see the original throne, the **Phra Ratcha Banlang Pradap Muk**, a masterpiece of mother-of-pearl inlaid work. When a senior member of the royal family dies, the hall is used for the lying-in-state: the body, embalmed and seated in a huge sealed urn, is placed in the west transept, waiting up to two years for an auspicious day to be cremated.

The Wat Phra Kaeo Museum

In the nineteenth-century Royal Mint in front of the Dusit Maha Prasat – next to a small, basic **café** and an incongruous hair salon – the **Wat Phra Kaeo Museum** houses a mildly interesting collection of artefacts donated to the Emerald Buddha, along with architectural elements rescued from the Grand Palace grounds during restoration in the 1980s. Highlights include the bones of various kings' white elephants, and upstairs, the Emerald Buddha's original costumes and two useful scale models of the Grand Palace, one as it is now, the other as it was when first built. Also on the first floor stands the grey stone slab of the Manangasila Seat, where Ramkhamhaeng, the great thirteenth-century king of Sukhothai, is said to have sat and taught his subjects. It was discovered in 1833 by Rama IV during his monkhood and brought to Bangkok, where Rama VI used it as the throne for his coronation.

Wat Pho (Wat Phra Chetuphon)

Soi Chetuphon, to the south of the Grand Palace • Daily 8am–9pm • B50 • @ watpho.com

Where Wat Phra Kaeo may seem too perfect and shrink-wrapped for some, **Wat Pho** is lively and shambolic, a complex arrangement of lavish structures which jostle with

Visitors' entrances	1	Traditional Medicine Pavilions	5	Rama IV Chedi	9	European Pavilion	13
Entrances to Bot	2	Rama II Chedi	6	Chapel of the Reclining Buddha	10	Café	14
Bot	3	Phra Si Sanphet Chedi	7	Chinese Pavilion	11	Monks' Quarters	15
Massage Pavilions	4	Rama III Chedi	8	Library	12	Grand Palace	16

classrooms, basketball courts and a turtle pond. Busloads of tourists shuffle in and out of the **north entrance**, stopping only to gawp at the colossal Reclining Buddha, but you can avoid the worst of the crowds by using the **main entrance** on Soi Chetuphon to explore the huge compound.

Wat Pho is the oldest temple in Bangkok and older than the city itself, having been founded in the seventeenth century under the name Wat Photaram. Foreigners have stuck to the contraction of this old name, even though Rama I, after enlarging the temple, changed the name in 1801 to **Wat Phra Chetuphon**, which is how it is generally known to Thais. The temple had another major overhaul in 1832, when Rama III built the chapel of the Reclining Buddha, and turned the temple into a public centre of learning by decorating the walls and pillars with inscriptions and diagrams on subjects such as history, literature, animal husbandry and astrology. Dubbed Thailand's first university, the wat is still an important centre for traditional medicine, notably **Thai massage** (see box opposite), which is used against all kinds of illnesses, from backaches to viruses.

The eastern courtyard

The main entrance on Soi Chetuphon is one of a series of sixteen monumental gates around the main compound, each guarded by stone **giants**, many of them comic Westerners in wide-brimmed hats – ships that exported rice to China would bring these statues back as ballast.

The entrance brings you into the eastern half of the main complex, where a courtyard of structures radiates from the bot in a disorientating symmetry. To get to the bot, the principal congregation and ordination hall, turn right and cut through the two surrounding cloisters, which are lined with hundreds of Buddha images. The elegant **bot** has beautiful teak doors decorated with mother-of-pearl, showing stories from the *Ramayana* in minute detail. Look out also for the stone bas-reliefs around the base of the bot, which narrate the story of the capture and rescue of Sita from the *Ramayana* in 152 action-packed panels. The plush interior has a well-proportioned altar on which ten statues of disciples frame a graceful, Ayutthayan Buddha image containing the remains of Rama I, the founder of Bangkok (Rama IV placed them there so that the public could worship him at the same time as the Buddha).

1

Back outside the entrance to the double cloister, keep your eyes open for a miniature mountain covered in statues of naked men in tall hats who appear to be gesturing rudely: they are *rishis* (hermits), demonstrating various positions of healing massage. Skirting the southwestern corner of the cloisters, you'll come to two pavilions between the eastern and western courtyards, which display plaques inscribed with the precepts of traditional medicine, as well as anatomical pictures showing the different pressure points and the illnesses that can be cured by massaging them.

The western courtyard

Among the 99 chedis strewn about the grounds, the four **great chedis** in the western courtyard stand out as much for their covering of garish tiles as for their size. The central chedi is the oldest, erected by Rama I to hold the remains of the most sacred Buddha image of Ayutthaya, the Phra Si Sanphet. Later, Rama III built the chedi to the north for the ashes of Rama II and the chedi to the south to hold his own remains; Rama IV built the fourth, with bright blue tiles, though its purpose is uncertain.

In the northwest corner of the courtyard stands the chapel of the **Reclining Buddha**, a 45m-long gilded statue of plaster-covered brick which depicts the Buddha entering Nirvana, a common motif in Buddhist iconography. The chapel is only slightly bigger than the statue – you can't get far enough away to take in anything but a surreal close-up view of the beaming 5m smile. As for the feet, the vast black soles are beautifully inlaid with delicate mother-of-pearl showing the 108 *lakshanas*, or auspicious signs, which distinguish the true Buddha. Along one side of the statue are 108 bowls: putting a coin in each will bring you good luck and a long life.

TRADITIONAL MASSAGE AND SPAS IN BANGKOK

Thai massage sessions and courses are held most famously at Wat Pho, while luxurious and indulgent spa and massage treatments are available at many posh hotels across the city, as well as at the following stand-alone places.

Divana Massage and Spa 7 Soi 25, Thanon Sukhumvit ☎02 661 6784, ⍟divanaspa.com; map p.109. Delightful spa serving up Thai massages (B1150/100min), foot, aromatherapy and herbal massages, as well as facials and Ayurvedic treatments. Mon–Fri 11am–11pm, Sat & Sun 10am–11pm.

Nicolie Sun Square, a small shopping arcade on the south side of Thanon Silom between sois 21 and 23 ☎02 233 6957, ⍟nicolie-th.com; map p.110. Superb Thai (B1600/90min) and other massages, as well as facials and scrubs, in a soothing environment decorated with Asian objets d'art. Daily 11am–10pm.

Pian's Soi Susie Pub, which runs between the east end of Thanon Khao San and Thanon Ram Bhuttri ☎02 629 0924; map p.90. Uninvitingly clinical-looking but highly rated a/c massage centre, offering Thai massages (B200/hr) as well as foot, oil and herbal massages; you can also study Thai massage here. Daily 7.30am–12.30am.

Pimmalai Thanon Sukhumvit, 50m east of BTS On Nut, exit 1, between sois 81 and 83 ☎02 742 6452, ⍟pimmalai.com. In a nice old wooden house, Thai

massages (B250/1hr), plus foot, herbal and oil massages, body scrubs and facials. Daily 10am–10pm.

Ruen Nuad 42 Thanon Convent, near Thanon Sathon Nua ☎02 632 2662–3; map p.110. Excellent Thai massages (B350/1hr, B600/2hr), as well as aromatherapy and foot massages and a juice bar, in an a/c, characterful wooden house, down an alley opposite the BNH Hospital and behind *Naj* restaurant. Daily 10am–9pm.

Wat Pho (see p.83); map p.79. Excellent massages are available in two a/c buildings on the east side of Wat Pho's main compound; allow two hours for the full works (B420/hr; foot reflexology massage B420/hr). There are often long queues here, however, so you might be better off heading over to the massage centre's other premises just outside the temple, at 392/25–28 Soi Pen Phat 1, Thanon Maharat (the soi is unmarked but look for the *Coconut Palm* restaurant on the corner; daily 8am–6pm; ☎02 622 3533 or ☎02 622 3550–1, ⍟watpomassage.com). Here you can also enrol on a thirty-hour massage training course in English, over five days (B8500), and foot-massage courses for B6500. Daily 8am–7pm.

1

Museum of Siam (National Discovery Museum)

Thanon Sanam Chai • Tues–Sun 10am–6pm • B300, free after 4pm • ☎ 02 225 2777, ⓦ museumsiam.com

The high-tech and mostly bilingual **Museum of Siam** is an excellent, recently developed attraction that occupies the century-old, European-style, former Ministry of Commerce. It looks at what it is to be Thai, with lots of humorous short films and imaginative touches such as shadow-puppet cartoons and war video games. In addition, the museum stages playful temporary exhibitions, which in the past have let visitors have a go at rice-growing, and examine Thailand's enduring love affair with foreign commodities. Generally, it's great fun for adults and kids, and there's a nice little indoor-outdoor **café-restaurant** in the grounds run by the Black Canyon chain.

It all kicks off with the prehistory of Southeast Asia, or Suvarnabhumi (Land of Gold) as ancient documents refer to it, and the legendary arrival of Buddhism via missionaries sent by the great Indian emperor, Ashoka (Asoke). Much space is devoted to Ayutthaya, where we learn that during that kingdom's four-hundred-year history, there were no less than twenty outbreaks of war with the Burmese states, before the final annihilation in 1767. Beyond this, look out for a fascinating map of Thonburi, King Taksin's new capital between 1768 and 1782, as drawn by a Burmese spy. In the Bangkok period, there's coverage of the Chinese in Thailand and of early twentieth-century racialism, but next to nothing on the country's Muslims. Towards the end, under the banner of Westernization, visitors can wind up cartoon peep-shows and dress up in colonial-style uniform shirts.

Wat Mahathat

Main entrance on Thanon Maharat, plus a back entrance on Thanon Na Phra That on Sanam Luang

Eighteenth-century **Wat Mahathat** provides a welcome respite from the surrounding tourist hype, and a chance to engage with the eager monks studying at **Mahachulalongkorn Buddhist University** here. As the nation's centre for the Mahanikai monastic sect (where Rama IV spent many years as a monk before becoming king in 1851), and housing one of the two Buddhist universities in Bangkok, the wat buzzes with purpose. It's this activity, and the chance of interaction and participation, rather than any special architectural features, that make a visit so rewarding. The many university-attending monks at the wat are friendly and keen to practise their English, and are more than likely to approach you: diverting topics might range from the poetry of Dylan Thomas to English football results.

Vipassana Meditation Centre

Section Five, Wat Mahathat • Practice daily 7–10am, 1–4pm & 6–8pm, dhamma talk daily 8–9pm • Donations welcome • ☎ 02 222 6011 or 02 222 4981, ⓦ udomwid.org

At the wat's **Vipassana Meditation Centre**, sitting and walking meditation practice is available in English (there's now a competing "Meditation Study and Retreat Center", nearby in Section One of the wat, but this is less geared towards foreign meditators). Participants generally stay in the simple surroundings of the meditation building itself, and must wear white clothes (available to rent at the centre) and observe the eight main Buddhist precepts (see p.433).

The National Museum

Thanon Na Phra That, northwest corner of Sanam Luang • Wed–Sun 9am–4pm, some rooms may close at lunchtime; usually some rooms are closed for restoration, as advertised at the ticket office • B200 • ☎ 02 224 1333, ⓦ thailandmuseum.com

The **National Museum** houses a colossal hoard of Thailand's chief artistic riches, ranging from sculptural treasures in the north and south wings, through bizarre decorative objects in the older buildings, to outlandish funeral chariots and the exquisite Buddhaisawan chapel, as well as sometimes staging worthwhile temporary exhibitions.

INFORMATION

THE NATIONAL MUSEUM

Guided tours It's worth making time for the free guided tours in English on Wed & Thurs 9.30am, Sat 10am, by the National Museum Volunteers (who also organize interesting lectures and excursions; ⓦ museumvolunteersbkk.net): they're generally entertaining and their explication of the choicest exhibits provides a good introduction to Thai religion and culture.

Bookshop There's a well-stocked bookshop by the ticket office.

Eating Next to the bookshop is a pleasant a/c café, serving espressos, ice cream and a few lunch dishes, while the restaurant inside the museum grounds, by the funeral chariots building, dishes up decent, inexpensive Thai food.

History building

The first building you'll come to near the ticket office houses an overview of the authorised history of Thailand, including a small archeological gem: a black stone **inscription**, credited to King Ramkhamhaeng of Sukhothai, which became the first capital of the Thai nation (c.1278–99) under his rule. Discovered in 1833 by the future Rama IV, Mongkut, it's the oldest extant inscription using the Thai alphabet. This, combined with the description it records of prosperity and piety in Sukhothai's Golden Age, has made the stone a symbol of Thai nationhood. There's recently been much controversy over the stone's origins, arising from the suggestion that it was a fake made by Mongkut, but it seems most likely that it is indeed genuine, and was written partly as a kind of prospectus for Sukhothai, to attract traders and settlers to the underpopulated kingdom.

The main collection: southern building

At the back of the compound, two large modern buildings, flanking an old converted palace, house the museum's **main collection**, kicking off on the ground floor of the **southern building**. Look out here for some historic sculptures from the rest of Asia (S1), including one of the earliest representations of the Buddha, from Gandhara in modern-day Pakistan. Alexander the Great left a garrison at Gandhara, which explains why the image is in the style of Classical Greek sculpture: for example, the *ushnisha*, the supernatural bump on the top of the head, which symbolizes the Buddha's intellectual and spiritual power, is rationalized into a bun of thick, wavy hair.

Upstairs, the **prehistory** room (S6) displays axe heads and spear points from Ban Chiang in the northeast of Thailand, one of the earliest Bronze Age cultures ever discovered. Alongside are many roughly contemporaneous metal artefacts from Kanchanaburi province, as well as some excellent examples of the developments of Ban Chiang's famous pottery. In the adjacent **Dvaravati** room (S7; sixth to eleventh centuries), the pick of the stone and terracotta Buddhas is a small head in smooth, pink clay from Wat Phra Ngam, Nakhon Pathom, whose downcast eyes and faintly smiling full lips typify the serene look of this era. At the far end of the first floor, you can't miss a voluptuous Javanese statue of elephant-headed Ganesh, Hindu god of wisdom and the arts, which, being the symbol of the Fine Arts Department, is always freshly garlanded. As Ganesh is known as the clearer of obstacles, Hindus always worship him before other gods, so by tradition he has grown fat through getting first choice of the offerings – witness his trunk jammed into a bowl of food in this sculpture.

Room S9 next door contains the most famous piece of **Srivijaya** art (seventh to thirteenth centuries), a bronze Bodhisattva Padmapani found at Chaiya (according to Mahayana Buddhism, a *bodhisattva* is a saint who has postponed his passage into Nirvana to help ordinary believers gain enlightenment). With its pouting face and sinuous torso, this image has become the ubiquitous emblem of southern Thailand. The rough chronological order of the collection continues back downstairs with an exhibition of **Khmer** and **Lopburi** sculpture (seventh to fourteenth centuries), most notably some dynamic bronze statuettes and stone lintels. Look out for an elaborate lintel from Ku Suan Tang, Buriram (S3), which depicts Vishnu reclining on the dragon Ananta in the sea of eternity, dreaming up a new universe after the old one has been annihilated in the

1

Hindu cycle of creation and destruction. Out of his navel comes a lotus, and out of this emerges four-headed Brahma, who will put the dream into practice.

The main collection: northern building

The second half of the survey, in the northern building, begins upstairs with the **Sukhothai** collection (thirteenth to fifteenth centuries; N7–8), which features some typically elegant and sinuous Buddha images, as well as chunky bronzes of Hindu gods and a wide range of ceramics. The **Lanna** rooms (roughly thirteenth to sixteenth centuries; N5–6) include a miniature set of golden regalia, among them tiny umbrellas and a cute pair of filigree flip-flops, which would have been enshrined in a chedi. An ungainly but serene Buddha head, carved from grainy, pink sandstone, represents the **Ayutthaya** style of sculpture (fourteenth to eighteenth centuries; N9–10): the faintest incision of a moustache above the lips betrays the Khmer influences that came to Ayutthaya after its conquest of Angkor. A sumptuous scripture cabinet, showing a cityscape of old Ayutthaya, is a more unusual piece, one of a surviving handful of such carved and painted items of furniture.

Downstairs in the section on **Bangkok** or **Ratanakosin** art (eighteenth century onwards; N1), a stiffly realistic standing bronze brings you full circle. In his zeal for Western naturalism, Rama V had the statue made in the Gandhara style of the earliest Buddha image displayed in the first room of the museum.

The funeral chariots

To the east of the northern building, beyond the café on the left, stands a large garage where the fantastically elaborate **funeral chariots** of the royal family are stored. Pre-eminent among these is the Royal Chariot of Great Victory, built by Rama I in about 1789 for carrying the urn at his father's funeral. The 11m-high structure symbolizes heaven on Mount Meru, while the dragons and divinities around the sides – piled in five golden tiers to suggest the flames of the cremation – represent the mythological inhabitants of the mountain's forests. Each weighing around forty tonnes and requiring the pulling power of three hundred men, the teak chariots last had an outing in 2012, for the funeral of the only child of Rama VI, Princess Bejaratana.

Wang Na (Palace of the Second King)

The sprawling central building of the compound was originally part of the **Wang Na**, a huge palace stretching across Sanam Luang to Khlong Lod, which housed the "second king", appointed by the reigning monarch as his heir and deputy. When Rama V did away with the office in 1887, he turned the palace into a museum, which now contains a fascinating array of Thai objets d'art. As you enter (room 5), the display of sumptuous rare gold pieces behind heavy iron bars includes a well-preserved armlet taken from the ruined prang of fifteenth-century Wat Ratburana in Ayutthaya. In adjacent room 6, an intricately carved ivory seat turns out, with gruesome irony, to be a *howdah*, for use on an elephant's back. Among the masks worn by *khon* actors next door (room 7), look out especially for a fierce Hanuman, the white monkey-warrior in the *Ramayana* epic, gleaming with mother-of-pearl.

The huge and varied ceramic collection in room 8 includes some sophisticated pieces from Sukhothai, while the room behind (9) holds a riot of mother-of-pearl items, whose flaming rainbow of colours comes from the shell of the turbo snail from the Gulf of Thailand. It's also worth seeking out the display of richly decorated musical instruments in room 15.

The Buddhaisawan chapel

The second holiest image in Thailand, after the Emerald Buddha, is housed in the **Buddhaisawan chapel**, the vast hall in front of the eastern entrance to the Wang Na. Inside, the fine proportions of the hall, with its ornate coffered ceiling and lacquered window shutters, are enhanced by painted rows of divinities and converted demons, all turned to face the chubby, glowing **Phra Sihing Buddha**, which according to legend was magically created in Sri Lanka and sent to Sukhothai in the thirteenth century. Like the Emerald Buddha, the image was believed to bring good luck to its owner and was frequently snatched from one northern town to another, until Rama I brought it down from Chiang Mai in 1795 and installed it here in the second king's private chapel. Two other images (in Nakhon Si Thammarat and Chiang Mai) now claim to be the authentic Phra Sihing Buddha, but all three are in fact derived from a lost original – this one is in a fifteenth-century Sukhothai style. It's still much loved by ordinary people and at Thai New Year is carried out onto Sanam Luang, where worshippers sprinkle it with water as a merit-making gesture.

The careful detail and rich, soothing colours of the surrounding two-hundred-year-old **murals** are surprisingly well preserved; the bottom row between the windows narrates the life of the Buddha, beginning in the far right-hand corner with his parents' wedding.

Tamnak Daeng

On the south side of the Buddhaisawan chapel, the gaudily restored **Tamnak Daeng** (Red House) stands out, a large, airy Ayutthaya-style house made of rare golden teak, surmounted by a multi-tiered roof decorated with swan's-tail finials. Originally part of the private quarters of Princess Sri Sudarak, elder sister of Rama I, it was moved from the Grand Palace to the old palace in Thonburi for Queen Sri Suriyen, wife of Rama II; when her son became second king to Rama IV, he dismantled the edifice again and shipped it here to the Wang Na compound. Inside, it's furnished in the style of the early Bangkok period, with some of the beautiful objects that once belonged to Sri Suriyen, a huge, ornately carved box-bed, and the uncommon luxury of an indoor bathroom.

Banglamphu and the Democracy Monument area

Immediately north of Ratanakosin, **Banglamphu**'s most notorious attraction is **Thanon Khao San**, a tiny sliver of a road whose multiple guesthouses and buzzing, budget-minded nightlife have made it an unmissable way-station for travellers through Southeast Asia. There is plenty of cultural interest too, in a medley of idiosyncratic temples within a few blocks of nearby landmark **Democracy Monument**, and in the typical Bangkok neighbourhoods that connect them, many of which still feel charmingly old-fashioned.

ARRIVAL AND DEPARTURE   BANGLAMPHU

Banglamphu is served by plenty of **public transport**.

By boat Chao Phraya express-boat stops N13 (Phra Arthit), N14 (Rama VIII Bridge) and N15 (Thewet) are nearby (see p.118). Banglamphu is also served by public boats along Khlong Saen Saeb to and from their Phan Fah terminus, which are useful for Siam Square and the Skytrain.

By BTS In addition to connecting to the Skytrain via Khlong Saen Saeb boat, the other fast way to get on to the BTS system is to take a taxi from Banglamphu to BTS National Stadium.

By bus Dozens of useful buses serve Banglamphu (see boxes, p.92 and p.119).

Thanon Khao San

At the heart of Banglamphu is the legendary **Thanon Khao San**, almost a caricature of a travellers' centre, crammed with internet cafés and dodgy travel agents, the pavements

1

UTTHONG ROW

SAMSEN 12

THANON SRI AYUTTHAYA

THANON RATCHASIMA

THANON PHITSANULOK

THANON KRUNG KASEM

THANON SAMSEN

THANON PRACHA THIPATAI

Bus stop 1

THANON SRI AYUTTHAYA

THANON LUK LUANG

Khlong Krung Kasem

THEWET

SOI 2

SOI 1

National Library

Market

Market

SOI 14

SOI 16

School

THANON SAMSEN

Wat Indraviharn

THANON WISUT KASAT

Plant Market

SAMSEN 10

Wat Thawarad

Tha Thewet

RAMA VIII BRIDGE

Tha Saphan Rama VIII

SAMSEN 9

SAMSEN 7

SAMSEN 5

SAMSEN 3

SAMSEN 1

SAMSEN 8

SAMSEN 6

SAMSEN 4

SAMSEN 2

Velo Thailand

THANON SAMSEN

Khlong Banglamphu

Bus stop 3

Bus stop 2

Bangkok Clinic

Chao Phraya River

THONBURI

Phra Sumen Fortress

Santichaiprakan Park

THANON PHRA ARTHIT

Tha Phra Arthit

SOI CHANA

SONGKHRAM

Bus stop 2

Bus stop 3

Tha Phra Arthit Longtails

ACCOMMODATION

Bella Bella House	11
The Bhuthorn	21
Boonsiri Place	20
Buddy Lodge	17
Charoendee	
Boutique Hostel	15
Donna Guesthouse	18
KC Guest House	7
Khao San Palace Inn	14
Lamphu House	9
Lamphu Treehouse	13
Navalai River Resort	6
New Siam Riverside	8
New Siam 2	12
Old Bangkok Inn	19
Peachy Guest House	10
Phra Nakorn Norn Len	3
Praya Palazzo	2
Rajata Hotel	5
Sawatdee Guest House	4
Shambara	16
Tavee	1

RESTAURANTS & CAFÉS

Aquatini	5
Chote Chitr	14
Hemlock	12
Kai Yang Boran	9
Kaloang Home Kitchen	2
Krua Apsorn	1
Kway Jap Yuan	8
Khun Daeng	11
May Kaidee	9
May Kaidee 2	6
Padthai Thipamai	7
Popiang	8
Praya Palazzo	4
Roti Mataba	10

BARS & CLUBS

Ad Here the 13th	1
Bangkok Bar	3
Brick Bar	6
Café Democ	7
The Club	5
Club Culture	10
Hippie de Bar	4
Jazz Happens	2
Phra Nakorn	8
Taksura	9
Royal India	

SHOPS

Boots	4
Chang Torn	2
Lofty Bamboo	3
Shaman	1

BANGLAMPHU

Dusit

Rajdamnoen Stadium

TAT

RAJDAMNOEN NOK

NAKHORN SAWAN

LAN LUANG

King Prajadhipok (Rama VII) Museum

DAMRONG RAK

Tha Phan Fah

Khlong Saen Saeb

Golden Mount & Wat Saket

THANON BORIPHAT

THANON PHRA SUMEN

Queen's Gallery

Mahakhan Fort Community

Loha Prasat

Wat Rajnadda

THANON MAHACHAI

Khlong Ong Ang

RAJDAMNOEN KLANG

THANON PRACHA THIPATAI

THANON DINSO

Democracy Monument

City Hall

Sao Ching Cha

THANON BAMRUNG MUANG

Wat Suthat

THANON PHRA SUMEN

Ratchadamnoen P.O.

Bus stop 7

DAMNOEN KLANG NEUA

THANON DINSO

THANON MAHANNOP

Wat Bowoniwes

THANON TANAO

TROK SIN

TROK NAWA

Temple Supplies

SOI BOWONIWES

Lomprayah

THANON TANAO

SOI DAMNOEN KLANG TAI

THANON BOWONIWES

THANON TANI

Banglamphuthon P.O.

SOI SAM SEN

TROK KRASAPSIT

Night Market

Bus stop 4

THANON RAM BHUTTRI

Pian's

ETC

THANON KHAO SAN

DAMNOEN KLANG NEUA

RAJDAMNOEN KLANG

SOI DAMNOEN KLANG TAI

THANON TANAO

BUNSRI

THANON PHRAENG PHUTON

THANON KANLAYANA MAITRI

San Chao Poh Seua

Wat Chana Songkhram

SOI RAM BHUTTRI

Police Station

THANON CHAKRABONGSE

True

TROK MAYOM

Bus stop 6

THANON BURANASIT

Royal Ratanakosin Hotel

Night Market

THANON ATSADANG

Sor Vorapin's Gym

Olavi

National Gallery

CHAO FA

TROK MAYOM

TROK SA-KE

SOI RAM BHUTTRI

TROK RONG MAI

PHRA PINKLAO BRIDGE

RAJINEE

Bangkok Tourism

Bus stop 5

National Theatre

THANON NA PHRA THAT

Mae Toranee statue

Sanam Luang

THANON RAJDAMNOEN NAI

Lak Muang

THANON LAK MUANG

National Museum

Thammasat University

Wat Mahathat

N

BANGLAMPHU

Express-boat pier

Khlong Saen Saeb boat stop

0   200

metres

1

BANGLAMPHU'S BUS STOPS AND ROUTES

The main bus stops serving Banglamphu are on Thanon Rajdamnoen Klang: with nearly thirty westbound and eastbound routes, you can get just about anywhere in the city from here. But there are some other useful routes running out of Banglamphu that have different pick-up points in the area. To make things simpler, we've assigned numbers to these **bus stops**, though they are not numbered on the ground. Where there are two stops served by the same buses they share a number. Bus stops are marked on the Banglamphu map (see p.90).

BUS STOP 1: THANON KRUNG KASEM, NORTH SIDE

#53 (clockwise) to Hualamphong train station (buses start from here)

BUS STOP 2: THANON PHRA SUMEN, SOUTH SIDE, NEAR BANGLUMPOO PLACE HOTEL; AND THANON PHRA ARTHIT, EAST SIDE, NEAR HEMLOCK

#53 (anticlockwise) to the Grand Palace and Chinatown

BUS STOP 3: THANON PHRA ARTHIT, WEST SIDE, NEAR NEW SIAM RIVERSIDE; AND THANON PHRA SUMEN, NORTH SIDE, OPPOSITE BANGLUMPOO PLACE HOTEL

#3 & #9 to Chatuchak Weekend Market and Northern Bus Terminal
#53 (clockwise) to Hualamphong train station (change at Bus Stop 1, but same ticket)

BUS STOP 4: THANON CHAKRABONGSE, NEAR THE 7-ELEVEN

#3 to the Museum of Siam, Pak Khlong Talat and Wongwian Yai train station
#9 to Wat Pho, Pak Khlong Talat
#15 to Jim Thompson's House, Siam Square and Thanon Silom

BUS STOP 5: THANON RAJINEE (RACHINI), NEAR BANGKOK TOURISM INFORMATION CENTRE

#124 to Southern Bus Terminal

lined with cheap backpackers' fashions, racks of bootleg PlayStation games, tattooists and hair-braiders. It's a lively, high-energy base: great for shopping and making travel arrangements – though beware the innumerable Khao San scams (see p.57) – and a good place to meet other travellers. It's especially fun at night when young Thais from all over the city gather here to browse the clothes stalls, mingle with the crowds of foreigners and squash into the bars and clubs that have made Khao San a great place to party. Even if you're staying elsewhere, the Khao San area is a cultural curiosity in its own right, a unique and continually evolving expression of global youth culture fuelled by Thai entrepreneurship.

Democracy Monument

The megalithic yellowy wings of **Democracy Monument** (*Anu Sawari Pracha Tippatai*) loom provocatively over Rajdamnoen Klang, the avenue that connects the Grand Palace and the new royal district of Dusit, and have since their erection in 1939 acted as a focus for pro-democracy rallies. Conceived as a testimony to the ideals that fuelled the 1932 revolution and the changeover to a constitutional monarchy, the monument's positioning between the royal residences is significant, as are its dimensions, which allude to June 24, 2475 BE (1932 AD), the date the system was changed. In the decades since, Thailand's leaders have promulgated numerous interim charters and constitutions, the more repressive and regressive of which have been vigorously challenged in demonstrations on these very streets.

1

Thanon Bamrung Muang

Thanon Bamrung Muang, five minutes' walk south of Democracy Monument, is famous as the best place in Thailand to buy **Buddhist paraphernalia**, or *sanghapan*, and is well worth a browse. The road is lined with shops selling everything a good Buddhist might need, from household offertory tables to temple umbrellas and cellophane-wrapped Buddha images up to 2m tall. They also sell special alms packs for donating to monks, which typically come in saffron-coloured plastic buckets (used by monks for washing their robes, or themselves), and include such necessities as soap, toothpaste, soap powder, toilet roll, candles and incense.

Sao Ching Cha

Midway along Thanon Bamrung Muang, just in front of Wat Suthat

You can't miss the towering, red-painted teak posts of **Sao Ching Cha**, otherwise known as the **Giant Swing**. This strange contraption was once the focal point of a Brahmin ceremony to honour the Hindu god Shiva's annual visit to earth, in which teams of young men competed to swing up to a height of 25m and grab a suspended bag of gold with their teeth. The act of swinging probably symbolized the rising and setting of the sun, though legend also has it that Shiva and his consort Uma were banned from swinging in heaven because doing so caused cataclysmic floods on earth – prompting Shiva to demand that the practice be continued on earth to ensure moderate rains and bountiful harvests. Accidents were so common with the terrestrial version that it was outlawed in the 1930s.

Wat Suthat

Thanon Bamrung Muang • Daily 9am–4pm • B20

Were the Giant Swing still in operation, you'd get a fine view over adjacent **Wat Suthat** and its towering central viharn, Bangkok's tallest. This is one of Thailand's six most important temples, built in the early nineteenth century to house the 8m-high statue of the meditating **Phra Sri Sakyamuni Buddha**, which was brought all the way down from Sukhothai by river. It now sits on a glittering mosaic dais surrounded by surreal murals that depict the last 24 lives of the Buddha rather than the more usual ten. The encircling galleries contain 156 serenely posed Buddha images, making a nice contrast to the **Chinese statues** dotted around the temple courtyards, most of which were brought over from China during Rama I's reign, as ballast in rice boats; there are some fun character studies among them, including gormless Western sailors and pompous Chinese scholars.

Wat Rajnadda

5min walk east of Democracy Monument, at the point where Rajdamnoen Klang meets Thanon Mahachai • **Loha Prasat** daily 9am–5pm • Free

Among the assortment of religious buildings known collectively as **Wat Rajnadda**, the most striking is the multi-tiered, castle-like, early nineteenth-century **Loha Prasat**, or "Iron Monastery", whose 37 forbidding metal spires represent the 37 virtues necessary for attaining enlightenment. Modelled on a Sri Lankan monastery, its tiers are pierced by passageways running north–south and east–west – fifteen in each direction at ground level – with small meditation cells at each point of intersection.

Amulet market

In the southeast (Thanon Mahachai) corner of the temple compound, Bangkok's biggest **amulet market**, the **Wat Rajnadda Buddha Centre**, comprises at least a hundred stalls selling tiny Buddha images of all designs. Alongside these miniature charms are statues of Hindu deities, dolls and carved wooden phalluses, also bought to placate or ward off disgruntled spirits, as well as love potions and CDs of sacred music.

1

AMULETS

To invite good fortune, ward off malevolent spirits and gain protection from physical harm, many Thais wear or carry at least one **amulet** at all times. The most popular images are copies of sacred statues from famous wats, while others show revered monks, kings (Rama V is a favourite) or healers. On the reverse side, a yantra is often inscribed, a combination of letters and figures also designed to deflect evil, sometimes of a very specific nature: protecting your durian orchards from gales, for example, or your tuk-tuk from oncoming traffic. Individually hand-crafted or mass-produced, amulets can be made from bronze, clay, plaster or gold, and some even have sacred ingredients added, such as special herbs, or the ashes of burnt holy texts. But what really determines an amulet's efficacy is its history: where and by whom it was made, who or what it represents and who consecrated it. Stories of miracle cures and lucky escapes also prompt a rush on whatever amulet the survivor was wearing. Monks are often involved in the making of the images and are always called upon to consecrate them – the more charismatic the monk, the more powerful the amulet. Religious authorities take a relaxed view of the amulet industry, despite its anomalous and commercial functions, and proceeds contribute to wat funds and good causes.

The **belief in amulets** is thought to have originated in India, where tiny images were sold to pilgrims who visited the four holy sites associated with the Buddha's life. But not all amulets are Buddhist-related; there's a whole range of other enchanted objects to wear for protection, including tigers' teeth, rose quartz, tamarind seeds, coloured threads and miniature phalluses. Worn around the waist rather than the neck, the phallus amulets provide protection for the genitals as well as being associated with fertility, and are of Hindu origin.

For some people, amulets are not only a vital form of spiritual protection, but valuable **collectors' items** as well. Amulet-collecting mania is something akin to stamp collecting and there are at least half a dozen Thai magazines for collectors, which give histories of certain types, tips on distinguishing between genuine items and fakes, and personal accounts of particularly powerful amulet experiences. The most rewarding places to watch the collectors and browse the wares yourself are at Wat Rajnadda Buddha Centre (see opposite), probably the best place in Bangkok; along "Amulet Alley" on Trok Mahathat, between Wat Mahathat (see p.86) and the river, where streetside vendors will have cheaper examples; and at Chatuchak Weekend Market (see p.112). Prices start as low as B50 and rise into the thousands.

Wat Saket

Easiest access is along Thanon Boriphat (the specialist street for custom-carved wooden doors), 5min walk south from the khlong bridge and Phan Fah canal-boat stop at the eastern end of Rajdamnoen Klang

Beautifully illuminated at night, when it seems to float unsupported above the neighbourhood, the gleaming gold chedi of late eighteenth-century **Wat Saket** actually sits atop a structure known as the Golden Mount. Being outside the capital's city walls, the wat initially served as a crematorium and then a dumping ground for sixty thousand plague victims left to the vultures because they couldn't afford funeral pyres. There's no sign of this grim episode at modern-day Wat Saket of course, which is these days a smart, buzzing hive of religious activity at the base of the golden hilltop chedi. Wat Saket hosts an enormous annual **temple fair** in the first week of November, when the mount is illuminated with lanterns and the compound seethes with funfair rides and travelling theatre shows.

The Golden Mount

Daily 8am–5pm • B10

The **Golden Mount**, or **Phu Khao Tong**, dates back to the early nineteenth century, when Rama III commissioned a huge chedi to be constructed here, using building materials from the ruined fortresses and walls of the former capital, Ayutthaya. However, the ground proved too soft to support the chedi. The whole thing collapsed into a hill of rubble, but as Buddhist law states that a religious building can never be destroyed, however tumbledown, fifty years later Rama V simply crowned it with the more

1

sensibly sized chedi we see today, in which he placed some relics, believed by some to be the Buddha's teeth. These days the old rubbly base is picturesquely planted with shrubs and shady trees and dotted with gravestones and memorials. Winding stairways take you up to the chedi terrace and a fine view over Banglamphu and Ratanakosin landmarks, including the golden spires of the Grand Palace, the finely proportioned prangs of Wat Arun across the river beyond and, further upriver, the striking superstructure of the Rama VIII Bridge.

Chinatown

When the newly crowned Rama I decided to move his capital across to the east bank of the river in 1782, the Chinese community living on the proposed site of his palace was obliged to relocate downriver, to the **Sampeng** area. Two centuries on, **Chinatown** has grown into the country's largest Chinese district, a sprawl of narrow alleyways, temples and shophouses packed between Charoen Krung (New Road) and the river.

The **Chinese influence** on Thai culture and commerce has been significant ever since the first Chinese merchants gained a toehold in Ayutthaya in the fourteenth century. Following centuries of immigration and intermarriage, there is now some Chinese blood in almost every Thai citizen, including the king, and Chinese-Thai business interests play an enormous role in the Thai economy. This is played out at its most frantic in Chinatown, whose real estate is said to be among the most valuable in the country; there are over a hundred gold and jewellery shops along Thanon Yaowarat alone.

For the tourist, Chinatown is chiefly interesting for its **markets**, shophouses, open-fronted warehouses and remnants of colonial-style architecture, though it also harbours a few noteworthy **temples**. A meander through its most interesting neighbourhoods could easily soak up a whole day, allowing for frequent breaks from the thundering traffic and choking fumes. For the most authentic Chinatown experience, it's best to come during the week, as some shops and stalls shut at weekends; on weekdays they begin closing around 5pm, after which time the neighbourhood's other big draw – its **food** – takes centre stage.

GETTING THERE AND AROUND
CHINATOWN

Arrival The easiest way to reach Chinatown is either by subway to Hualamphong Station, or by Chao Phraya express boat to Tha Rachawongse (Rajawong; N5) at the southern end of Thanon Rajawong. A westward extension of the subway is being built, with new stations at Wat Mangkon Kamalawat and Pahurat. This part of the city is also well served by buses, with Hualamphong a useful and easily recognized place to disembark (see box, p.119). Be warned that buses and taxis may take an unexpectedly circuitous route due to the many and complex one-way systems in Chinatown.

Getting around Orientation in Chinatown can be tricky: the alleys (often known as trok rather than the more usual soi) are extremely narrow, their turn-offs and other road signs often obscured by mounds of merchandise and thronging crowds, and the longer ones can change their names several times. For a detailed tour of the alleys and markets, use *Nancy Chandler's Map of Bangkok* (see p.122); alternatively, ask for help at the BMA tourist information booth (Mon–Sat 9am–5pm) just northwest of the Chinese Arch at the beginning of Thanon Yaowarat, beside Soi 5.

Wat Traimit

Thanon Mittaphap Thai-China, just west of Hualamphong train and subway stations (exit 1) • Daily 8am–5pm, exhibitions closed Mon • Golden Buddha only B40, Golden Buddha and exhibitions B100 • ⓦ wattraimitr-withayaram.com

The obvious place to start a Chinatown tour is on its eastern perimeter, with **Wat Traimit** and its famous Golden Buddha. You can see the temple mondop's golden spire from quite a distance, a fitting beacon for the gleaming treasure housed on its third floor, the world's largest solid-gold Buddha. It's an apt attraction for a community so

HUALAMPHONG, CHINATOWN AND PAHURAT

N

THONBURI

Chao Phraya River

Ratchawat

Rattanakosin

- ─ (M) ─ ─ Subway and station

0	250
metres	

ACCOMMODATION
Baan Hualamphong	2
Shanghai Mansion	1

RESTAURANTS
Hua Seng Hong	2
Raan Khun Yaa	4
Royal India	1
T&K	3

Hualamphong Train Station

Wat Traimit

Chinese Arch

Wat Mangkon Kamalawat

Nakhon Kasem

Wat Ga Buang Kim

Wat Chakrawat

Merry King

Old Siam Plaza

Pahurat Market

Chalermkrung Theatre

Pak Khlong Talat

Rama 1 Statue

Memorial Bridge Night Bazaar

Tha Saphan Phut

Tha Rajawongse

Tha Saphan Phut

1

closely linked with the gold trade, even if the image has nothing to do with China's spiritual heritage. A recent attempt has been made to bridge this gap, with the installation of exhibitions of varying interest on the mondop's first and second floors, covering the history of Chinatown and of the iconic Buddha image.

The Golden Buddha

Over 3m tall and weighing five tonnes, the **Golden Buddha** gleams as if coated in liquid metal, seated on a white marble lotus-pad pedestal and surrounded by offerings of lotus flowers. It's a fine example of the curvaceous grace of Sukhothai art, slim-waisted and beautifully proportioned. Cast in the thirteenth century, the image was brought to Bangkok by Rama III, completely encased in stucco – a common ruse to conceal valuable statues from would-be thieves. The disguise was so good that no one guessed what was underneath until 1955 when the image was accidentally knocked in the process of being moved to Wat Traimit, and the stucco cracked to reveal a patch of gold. Just in time for Buddhism's 2500th anniversary, the discovery launched a country-wide craze for tapping away at plaster Buddhas in search of hidden precious metals, but Wat Traimit's is still the most valuable – it's valued, by weight alone, at over US$10 million.

The exhibitions

The exhibition on the making and history of the Golden Buddha, on the second floor of the mondop, is fairly missable, but the **Yaowarat Chinatown Heritage Centre** on the floor below is rather more compelling. Interesting though sanitized, its display boards trace the rapid expansion of the Chinese presence in Bangkok from the late eighteenth century, first as junk traders, later as labourers and tax farmers. Enhancing the story are a diorama of life on board a junk, lots of interesting photos from the late nineteenth century onwards and a fascinating scale model of Thanon Yaowarat in its 1950s heyday, when it was Bangkok's business and entertainment hub.

Sampeng Lane

From Wat Traimit, walk northwest from the big China Gate roundabout along Thanon Yaowarat, and make a left turn onto Thanon Songsawat to reach Sampeng Lane

Sampeng Lane (also signposted as Soi Wanit 1) is one of Chinatown's most enjoyable shopping alleys. Stretching southeast–northwest for about 1km, it's a great place to browse, unfurling itself like a serpentine department store and selling everything from Chinese silk pyjama pants to computer games at bargain-basement rates. Similar goods are more or less gathered in sections, so at the eastern end you'll find mostly cheap jewellery and hair accessories, for example, before passing through stalls specializing in ceramics, Chinese lanterns, then shoes, clothes (west of Thanon Rajawong) and, as you near Pahurat, fabrics, haberdashery and irresistibly girlie accessories.

Soi Issaranuphap

For a rather more sensual experience, take a right about halfway down Sampeng Lane, into **Soi Issaranuphap** (also signed along its course as Yaowarat Soi 11 then Soi 6, and later Charoen Krung sois 16 and 21). Packed with people from dawn till dusk, this long, dark alleyway, which also traverses Charoen Krung, is where you come in search of ginseng roots (essential for good health), quivering fish heads, cubes of cockroach-killer chalk and a gastronome's choice of dried mushrooms and brine-pickled vegetables. Alleys branch off to florid Chinese temples and tiny squares before Soi Issaranuphap finally ends at the Thanon Plaplachai intersection amid a flurry of shops specializing in paper **funeral art**. Believing that the deceased should be well provided for in their afterlife, Chinese people buy miniature paper replicas of necessities to be burned with the body: especially popular are houses, cars, suits of clothing and, of course, money.

Wat Mangkon Kamalawat

Best approached via its dramatic multi-tiered gateway 10m up Thanon Charoen Krung from the Soi Issaranuphap junction

If Soi Issaranuphap epitomizes age-old Chinatown commerce, then **Wat Mangkon Kamalawat** (also known as **Wat Leng Noei Yee** or, in English, "Dragon Flower Temple") stands as a fine example of the community's spiritual practices. It receives a constant stream of devotees, who come to leave offerings at the altars inside this important Mahayana Buddhist temple. As with the Theravada Buddhism espoused by the Thais, Mahayana Buddhism fuses with other ancient religious beliefs, notably Confucianism and Taoism, and the statues and shrines within Wat Mangkon cover the spectrum. As you pass through the secondary gateway, under the glazed ceramic gables topped with undulating Chinese dragons, you're greeted by a set of four outsize statues of bearded and rather forbidding sages, each symbolically clasping either a parasol, a pagoda, a snake's head or a mandolin. Beyond them, a series of Buddha images swathed in saffron netting occupies the next chamber, a lovely open-sided room of gold paintwork, red-lacquered wood, lattice lanterns and pictorial wall panels inlaid with mother-of-pearl. Elsewhere in the compound are booths selling devotional paraphernalia, a Chinese medicine stall and a fortune-teller.

Pak Khlong Talat

Pak Khlong Talat 24hr • **Memorial Bridge night bazaar** Tues–Sun roughly 8pm–midnight • Chao Phraya express boat to Tha Saphan Phut (N6)

A browse through the 24-hour flower and vegetable market, **Pak Khlong Talat**, is a fitting way to round off a day in Chinatown, though it's also a great place to come before dawn, when market gardeners from Thonburi and beyond boat and truck their freshly picked produce across the Chao Phraya ready for sale to shopkeepers, restaurateurs and hoteliers. The market has been operating from covered halls between the southern ends of Khlong Lod, Thanon Banmo, Thanon Chakraphet and the river bank since the nineteenth century and is the biggest wholesale market in the capital. The flower stalls, selling twenty different varieties of cut orchids and countless other tropical blooms, spill onto the streets along the riverfront as well and, though prices are lowest in the early morning, you can still get some good bargains in the afternoon. Most evenings, the riverside end of nearby Thanon Triphet and the area around the base of **Memorial Bridge** (Saphan Phut) hosts a huge **night bazaar** that's dominated by cheap and idiosyncratic fashions – and by throngs of teenage fashion victims.

Thonburi

For fifteen years between the fall of Ayutthaya in 1767 and the founding of Bangkok in 1782, the west-bank town of **Thonburi**, across the Chao Phraya from modern-day Bangkok, stood in as the Thai capital, under the rule of General Phraya Taksin. Its time in the spotlight was too brief for the building of the fine monuments and temples that graced earlier capitals at Sukhothai and Ayutthaya, but some of its centuries-old **canals**, which once transported everyone and everything, have endured; it is these and the ways of life that depend on them that constitute Thonburi's main attractions. In some quarters, life on this side of the river still revolves around these khlongs: vendors of food and household goods paddle their boats along the canals that crisscross the residential areas, and canalside factories use them to ferry their wares to the Chao Phraya River artery. Venture onto the backroads just three or four kilometres west of the river and you find yourself surrounded by market gardens and rural homes, with no hint of the throbbing metropolis across on the other bank. The most popular way to explore these old neighbourhoods is by **boat**, but joining a bicycle tour of the older neighbourhoods is also very rewarding (see p.118). Most boat trips also encompass

1

Thonburi's imposing riverside Temple of the Dawn, **Wat Arun**, and often the **Royal Barge Museum** as well, though both are easily visited by yourself.

ARRIVAL AND DEPARTURE   THONBURI

Getting to Thonburi is generally just a matter of crossing the river. Either use Phra Pinklao or Memorial/Phra Pokklao bridge, take a cross-river ferry, or hop on one of the express boats, which make several stops on the Thonburi bank.

Royal Barge Museum

Soi Wat Dusitaram, north bank of Khlong Bangkok Noi • Daily 9am–5pm • B100 • ⓦ thailandmuseum.com • Chao Phraya express boat to Tha Phra Pinklao (N12), or cross-river ferry from under Pinklao Bridge in Banglamphu to Tha Phra Pinklao, then walk up the road 100m and take the first left down Soi Wat Dusitaram; if coming by bus from the Bangkok side (#507, #509 and #511 all cross the river here), get off at the first stop on the Thonburi side, which is at the mouth of Soi Wat Dusitaram – signs from Soi Wat Dusitaram lead you through a jumble of walkways and stilt-houses to the museum (10min)

Since the Ayutthaya era, kings of Thailand have been conveyed along their country's waterways in royal barges. For centuries, these slender, exquisitely elegant, black-and-gold wooden vessels were used on all important royal outings, and even up until 1967 the current king would process down the Chao Phraya to Wat Arun in a flotilla of royal barges at least once a year, on the occasion of Kathin, the annual donation of robes by the laity to the temple at the end of the rainy season. But the boats, some of which are a hundred years old, are becoming quite frail, so **royal barge processions** are now held only every few years to mark special anniversaries. However, if your trip happens to coincide with one of these magnificent events, you shouldn't miss it (see ⓦtourismthailand.org). Fifty or more barges fill the width of the river and stretch for almost 1km, drifting slowly to the measured beat of a drum and the hypnotic strains of ancient boating hymns, chanted by over two thousand oarsmen dressed in luscious brocades.

The eight beautifully crafted vessels at the heart of the ceremony are housed in the **Royal Barge Museum**. Up to 50m long and intricately lacquered and gilded all over, they taper at the prow into imposing mythical figures after a design first used by the kings of Ayutthaya. Rama I had the boats copied and, when those fell into disrepair, Rama VI commissioned exact reconstructions, some of which are still in use today. The most important is *Sri Suphanahongse*, which bears the king and queen and is graced by a glittering 5m-high prow representing the golden swan Hamsa, mount of the Hindu god Brahma. In front of it floats *Anantanagaraj*, fronted by a magnificent seven-headed naga and bearing a Buddha image. The newest addition to the fleet is *Narai Song Suban*, which was commissioned by the current king for his golden jubilee in 1996; it is a copy of the mid-nineteenth-century original and is crowned with a black Vishnu (Narai) astride a garuda figurehead. A display of miniaturized royal barges at the back of the museum re-creates the exact formation of a traditional procession.

Wat Arun

Daily 8am–5pm • B50 • ⓦ watarun.org • Take the cross-river ferry from the pier adjacent to the Chao Phraya express-boat pier at Tha Thien

Almost directly across the river from Wat Pho rises the enormous, five-spired prang of **Wat Arun**, the Temple of Dawn, probably Bangkok's most memorable landmark and familiar as the silhouette used in the TAT logo. It looks particularly impressive from the river as you head downstream from the Grand Palace towards the *Oriental Hotel*, but is ornate enough to be well worth stopping off for a closer look.

A wat has occupied this site since the Ayutthaya period, but only in 1768 did it become known as the Temple of Dawn – when General Phraya Taksin reputedly reached his new capital at the break of day. The temple served as his royal chapel and housed the recaptured Emerald Buddha for several years until the image was moved to Wat Phra Kaeo in 1785. Despite losing its special status after the relocation, Wat Arun

1

EXPLORING THONBURI BY BOAT

The most popular way to explore the sights of Thonburi is by **boat**, taking in Wat Arun and the Royal Barge Museum, then continuing along Thonburi's network of small canals. The easiest option is to take a fixed-price trip from one of the piers on the Bangkok side of the Chao Phraya, most conveniently from Tha Chang near Wat Pho or the River City pier off Thanon Charoen Krung. You can also charter your own longtail from these piers and others such as Tha Phra Arthit in Banglamphu and Tha Sathorn, and from many five-star riverside hotels, but bear the prices listed below in mind when negotiating and be specific about your itinerary.

Many tours include visits to one of Thonburi's two main **floating markets**, both of which are heavily touristed and rather contrived. **Wat Sai** floating market is very small, very commercialized and worth avoiding; **Taling Chan** floating market is also fairly manufactured but more fun, though it only operates on Saturdays and Sundays (approx 9am–4pm). Taling Chan market is held on Khlong Chak Phra, in front of Taling Chan District Office, a couple of kilometres west of Thonburi train station, and can also be reached by taking bus #79 from Banglamphu. For a more authentic floating-market experience, consider heading just southwest of Bangkok to Amphawa, in Samut Songkhram province.

Arguably more photogenic, and certainly a lot more genuine, are the individual **floating vendors** who continue to paddle from house to house in Thonburi, touting anything from hot food to plastic buckets. You've a good chance of seeing some of them in action on almost any longtail boat tour on any day of the week, particularly in the morning.

Mitchaopaya Travel Service Tha Chang ☎02 623 6169, ⊛mitchaophraya.co.th. Offers trips of varying durations: in 1hr (B1000/boat, or B400/person if you can join in with other people), you'll go out along Khlong Bangkok Noi and back via Khlong Mon, passing Wat Arun and the Royal Barge Museum without stopping; in 90min (B1300), you'd have time to stop at either or you could do a longer route, coming back along Khlong Bangkok Yai; while in 2hr (B1500) you'll have time to go right down the back canals on the Thonburi side and visit an orchid farm. On Sat & Sun, the 90min and 2hr trips take in Taling Chan floating market.

Real Asia ☎02 665 6364, ⊛www.realasia.net. Runs guided full-day walking and boat tours of the Thonburi canals for B2000 per person, including lunch.

River City pier longtails ☎02 237 0077 ext 180. Private longtail trips for B1500 per boat for two people for 1hr.

Tha Phra Arthit longtails Pier in front of *The Phra Arthit River Lounge*, 200m south of the N13 Tha Phra Arthit express-boat pier, Banglamphu. An enjoyable 90min loop (B1200 per boat) via Khlong Bangkok Noi, Khlong Chak Phra and Khlong Bangkok Yai that takes in a variety of different khlong-side residences, temples and itinerant floating vendors, with the possibility of stopping at Taling Chan floating market at weekends. One- (B800 per boat) and two-hour (B1500) trips also possible.

Wan Fah River City Shopping Centre pier ☎02 622 7657–61, ⊛wanfahcruise.com. A 2hr cruise of the west-bank canals by a combination of ferry boat and converted rice barge. Daily 2.30pm; B800 per person.

continued to be revered, and its corncob prang was reconstructed and enlarged to its present height of 81m by Rama II and Rama III.

The prang that you see today is classic Ayutthayan style, built as a representation of Mount Meru, the home of the gods in Khmer cosmology. By climbing the two tiers of the square base that supports the **central prang**, you not only enjoy a good view of the river and beyond, but also get a chance to examine the tower's distinctive decorations. Both this main prang and the four minor ones that encircle it are studded all over with bits of broken porcelain, ceramic shards and tiny bowls that have been fashioned into an amazing array of polychromatic flowers. The statues of mythical *yaksha* demons and half-bird, half-human *kinnari* that support the different levels are similarly decorated. The crockery probably came from China, possibly from commercial shipments that were damaged at sea, and the overall effect is highly decorative and far more subtle than the dazzling glass mosaics that clad most wat buildings. On the first terrace, the mondops at each cardinal point contain statues of the Buddha at birth (north), in meditation (east),

1

preaching his first sermon (south) and entering Nirvana (west). The second platform surrounds the base of the prang proper, whose closed entranceways are guarded by four statues of the Hindu god Indra on his three-headed elephant Erawan. In the niches of the smaller prangs stand statues of Phra Pai, the god of the wind, on horseback.

Dusit

Connected to Ratanakosin via the boulevards of Rajdamnoen Klang and Rajdamnoen Nok, the spacious, leafy area known as **Dusit** has been a royal district since the reign of Rama V, King Chulalongkorn (1860–1910). The first Thai monarch to visit Europe, Rama V returned with radical plans for the modernization of his capital, the fruits of which are most visible in Dusit, notably at **Vimanmek Palace** and **Wat Benjamabophit**, the so-called "Marble Temple". Even now, **Rama V** still commands a loyal following, and the statue of him, helmeted and on horseback, which stands at the Thanon U-Thong Nai–Thanon Sri Ayutthaya crossroads, is presented with offerings every week and is also the focus of celebrations on Chulalongkorn Day (Oct 23). On December 2, Dusit is also the venue for the spectacular annual **Trooping the Colour**, when hundreds of magnificently uniformed Royal Guards demonstrate their allegiance to the king by parading around Suan Amporn, across the road from the Rama V statue.

Today, the Dusit area retains its European feel, and much of the country's decision-making goes on behind the high fences and impressive facades along its tree-lined avenues: the building that houses the National Parliament is here, as is Government House, and the king's official residence, Chitrlada Palace, occupies the eastern edge of the area. Normally a calm, stately district, in 2008 Dusit became the focus of the **mass anti-government protest** by the royalist PAD movement, whose thousands-strong mass of yellow-shirted supporters occupied Government House and part of Rajdamnoen Nok for three months, creating a heavily defended temporary village in this most refined of neighbourhoods.

By bus From Banglamphu, you can get to Dusit by taking the #70 (non-expressway) bus from Rajdamnoen Klang and getting off outside the Elephant Museum on Thanon U-Thong Nai, or the #56 from Thanon Phra Sumen and alighting at the corner of Thanon Ratchasima and Thanon Rajwithi, near the main entrance to Vimanmek Palace. From downtown Bangkok, easiest access is by bus from the Skytrain stop at Victory Monument; there are many services from here, including #28 and #108.

By boat Take the express boat to Tha Thewet and then walk.

Dusit Park

Main entrance on Thanon Rajwithi, with another ticket gate opposite Dusit Zoo on Thanon U-Thong Nai • Daily 9.30am–4pm, last admission 3.15pm • B100, or free with a Grand Palace ticket, which remains valid for one week • ⊕ vimanmek.com

The outstanding feature of what's known as **Dusit Park** is the breezy, elegant **Vimanmek Palace**, which was built by Rama V as a summer retreat on Ko Si Chang, from where it was transported here bit by bit in 1901. The ticket price also covers entry to a dozen other specialist collections in Dusit Park, which these days resembles a theme park, with piped muzak, cafés, souvenir shops and a huge coach park. Among these collections, which include antique textiles, photographs taken by the king, royal ceremonial paraphernalia and antique clocks, housed in handsome, pastel-painted, former royal residences, the most interesting are the Support Museum and Elephant Museum. Note that the same **dress rules** apply here as at the Grand Palace (see p.78).

Vimanmek Palace

Compulsory free guided tours every 30min, last tour 3.15pm

Built almost entirely of golden teak without a single nail, the coffee-coloured, L-shaped Vimanmek Palace is encircled by delicate latticework verandas that look

1

out onto well-kept lawns, flower gardens and lotus ponds. Not surprisingly, this "Celestial Residence" soon became Rama V's favourite palace, and he and his enormous retinue of officials, concubines and children stayed here for lengthy periods between 1902 and 1906. All of Vimanmek's 81 rooms were out of bounds to male visitors, except for the king's own apartments in the octagonal tower, which were entered by a separate staircase.

On display inside is Rama V's collection of **artefacts** from all over the world, including *bencharong* ceramics, European furniture and bejewelled Thai betel-nut sets. Considered progressive in his day, Rama V introduced many new-fangled ideas to Thailand: the country's first indoor bathroom is here, as is the earliest typewriter with Thai characters, and some of the first portrait paintings – portraiture had until then been seen as a way of stealing part of the sitter's soul.

The Support Museum
Immediately behind (to the east of) Vimanmek Palace

The **Support Museum** is housed in a very pretty hundred-year-old building, the Abhisek Dusit Throne Hall, which was formerly used for meetings and banquets. It showcases the exquisite handicrafts produced under Queen Sirikit's charity project, Support, which works to revitalize traditional Thai arts and crafts. Outstanding exhibits include a collection of handbags, baskets and pots woven from the *lipao* fern that grows wild in southern Thailand; jewellery and figurines inlaid with the iridescent wings of beetles; gold and silver nielloware; and lengths of intricately woven silk from the northeast.

Chang Ton Royal Elephant National Museum
Just behind (to the east of) the Support Museum, inside the Thanon U-Thong Nai entrance to Dusit Park • ⓦ thailandmuseum.com

These two whitewashed buildings once served as the stables for the king's white elephants. Now that the sacred pachyderms have been relocated, the stables have been turned into the **Royal Elephant National Museum**. Inside you'll find some interesting

---

THE ROYAL WHITE ELEPHANTS

In Thailand, the most revered of all elephants are the so-called **white elephants** – actually tawny brown albinos – which are considered so sacred that they all, whether wild or captive, belong to the king by law. Their special status originates from Buddhist mythology, which tells how the previously barren Queen Maya became pregnant with the future Buddha after dreaming one night that a white elephant had entered her womb. The thirteenth-century King Ramkhamhaeng of Sukhothai adopted the beast as a symbol of the great and the divine, decreeing that a Thai king's greatness should be measured by the number of white elephants he owns. The present king, Rama IX, has eleven, the largest royal collection to date.

Before an elephant can be granted official "white elephant" status, it has to pass a stringent assessment of its physical and behavioural **characteristics**. Key qualities include a paleness of seven crucial areas – eyes, nails, palate, hair, outer edges of the ears, tail and testicles – and an all-round genteel demeanour, manifested, for instance, in the way in which it cleans its food before eating, or in a tendency to sleep in a kneeling position. Tradition holds that an elaborate ceremony should take place every time a new white elephant is presented to the king: the animal is paraded with great pomp from its place of capture to Dusit, where it's anointed with holy water in front of an audience of priests and dignitaries, before being housed in the royal stables. Recently though, the king has called time on this exorbitantly expensive ritual, and only one of the royal white elephants is now kept inside the palace compound; the others live in less luxurious, rural accommodation.

The expression "white elephant" probably derives from the legend that the kings used to present certain troublesome noblemen with one of these exotic creatures. The animal required expensive attention but, being royal, could not be put to work in order to pay for its upkeep. The recipient thus went bust trying to keep it.

1

pieces of elephant paraphernalia, including sacred ropes, mahouts' amulets and magic formulae, as well as photos of the all-important ceremony in which a white elephant is granted royal status (see box, p.103).

Wat Benjamabophit

Corner of Thanon Sri Ayutthaya and Thanon Rama V: about 600m from Vimanmek's U-Thong Nai gate • Daily 8.30am–6pm • B20 • Bus #70 from Banglamphu to the crossroads in front of the Rama V statue, then walk east along Thanon Sri Ayutthaya

Wat Benjamabophit (aka Wat Ben) is a fascinating fusion of classical Thai and nineteenth-century European design, with the Carrara-marble walls of its bot – hence the tourist tag "**The Marble Temple**" – pierced by unusual stained-glass windows, neo-Gothic in style but depicting figures from Thai mythology. Rama V commissioned the temple in 1899, at a time when he was keen to show the major regional powers, Britain and France, that Thailand was *siwilai* (civilized), in order to baulk their usual excuse for colonizing. The temple's sema stones are a telling example of the compromises involved: they're usually prominent markers of the bot's sacred area, but here they're hard to spot, decorative and almost apologetic – look for the two small, stone lotus buds at the front of the bot on top of the white, Italianate balustrade. Inside the unusually cruciform bot, a fine replica of the highly revered Phra Buddha Chinnarat image of Phitsanulok presides over the small room containing some of Rama V's ashes. The courtyard behind the bot houses a gallery of Buddha images from all over Asia, set up by Rama V as an overview of different representations of the Buddha.

Wat Benjamabophit is one of the best temples in Bangkok to see religious **festivals** and rituals. Whereas monks elsewhere tend to go out on the streets every morning in search of alms, at the Marble Temple the ritual is reversed, and merit-makers come to them. Between about 5.30 and 7 or 7.30am, the monks line up on Thanon Nakhon Pathom, their bowls ready to receive donations of curry and rice, lotus buds, incense, even toilet paper and Coca-Cola; the demure row of saffron-robed monks is a sight that's well worth getting up early for. The evening candlelight processions around the bot during the Buddhist festivals of Makha Puja (in Feb) and Visakha Puja (in May) are among the most entrancing in the country.

Downtown Bangkok

Extending east from the main rail line and south to Thanon Sathorn and beyond, **downtown Bangkok** is central to the colossal expanse of Bangkok as a whole, but rather peripheral in a sightseer's perception of the city. In this modern high-rise area, you'll find the main shopping centres around **Siam Square**, though don't come looking for an elegant commercial piazza here: the "square" is in fact a grid of small streets, sheltering trendy fashion shops, cinemas and inexpensive restaurants. It lies to the southeast of **Pathumwan intersection**, the junction of Thanon Rama I (in Thai, "Thanon Phra Ram Neung") and Thanon Phrayathai, and the name is applied freely to the surrounding area. Further east, you'll find yet more shopping malls around the noisy and glittering **Erawan Shrine**, where Rama I becomes Thanon Ploenchit, an intersection known as **Ratchaprasong**. It was here that the opposition redshirts set up a fortified camp for several months in early 2010, before the Democrat government sent in the troops, leading to the deaths of 91 people. It's once more possible to stroll in peace here, using an elevated **walkway** that runs beneath the Skytrain lines but above the cracked pavements, noise and fumes of Thanon Rama I, all the way from the Siam Paragon shopping centre to the Erawan Shrine (further progress is blocked by Central and Chitlom Skytrain stations). East of Ratchaprasong, you pass under the expressway flyover and enter the farang hotel, shopping and entertainment quarter of **Thanon Sukhumvit**.

1

● **SHOPS**
D & O Shop — 7
Doi Tung by Mae Fah Luang — 3
Exotique Thai — 1
Gilles Caffier — 4
Lamont Contemporary — 8
Nandakwang — 5
Narai Phand — 11
NV Aranyik — 9
Panta — 2, 6
Thann Native — 10

● **RESTAURANTS & CAFÉS**
Aoi — 2
Din Tai Fung — 6
Gianni — 13
Greyhound Café — 8, 9
Home Kitchen — 18
Inter — 15
Jin-emon — 16
Mah Boon Krong food courts — 10
Midnight Kai Ton — 1
Polo Fried Chicken — 19
Royal India — 3
Sanguansri — 12
Som Tam (Nua) — 11
Taling Pling — 4, 7
Thang Long — 17
Vanilla Brasserie — 5
Vanilla Industry — 14

● **BAR**
Coco Walk — 1

■ **ACCOMMODATION**
A-One Inn — 3
Four Seasons — 5
Golden House — 6
Lub.d — 9
Luxx XL — 7
Swissôtel Nai Lert Park — 8
Ten Face — 1
Wendy House — 2
White Lodge — 4

— **S** — BTS Skytrain and station
☆ Khlong Saen Saeb boat stop

DOWNTOWN: AROUND SIAM SQUARE AND THANON PLOENCHIT

The area south of Thanon Rama I is dominated by Thailand's most prestigious centre of higher learning, Chulalongkorn University, and the green expanse of **Lumphini Park**. Thanon Rama IV (in Thai "Thanon Phra Ram Sii") then marks another change of character: downtown proper, centring around the high-rise, American-style boulevard of **Thanon Silom**, the heart of the financial district, extends from here to the river. Alongside the smoked-glass banks and offices, and opposite Convent Road, site of Bangkok's Carmelite nunnery, lies the dark heart of Bangkok nightlife, **Patpong**.

Surprisingly, among downtown's vast expanse of skyscraping concrete, the main attractions for visitors are three attractive museums housed in historic teak houses: **Jim Thompson's House**, **Ban Kamthieng** and the **Suan Pakkad Palace Museum**. The accounts of the sights below are arranged roughly north–south.

ARRIVAL AND DEPARTURE   DOWNTOWN

All of the sights reviewed here are within walking range of a **Skytrain** station; some are also served by the **subway**. Useful **buses** for getting to Ratanakosin include #508 and #25; further details of bus routes are given on p.119. If you're heading downtown from Banglamphu, allow at least an hour to get to any of the places mentioned here by bus. A much faster way to cross town is by public **boat** along Khlong Saen Saeb, beginning near Democracy Monument. Depending on the time of day, taking an **express boat** downriver from Banglamphu, and then changing onto the **Skytrain**, may even be quicker than catching the bus downtown.

Suan Pakkad Palace Museum

352–4 Thanon Sri Ayutthaya • Daily 9am–4pm • B100 • ☎ 02 246 1775–6 ext 229, ⓦ suanpakkad.com • 5min walk from BTS Phaya Thai

The **Suan Pakkad Palace Museum** stands on what was once a cabbage patch but is now one of the finest gardens in Bangkok. Most of this private collection of beautiful Thai objects from all periods is displayed in four groups of traditional wooden houses, which were transported to Bangkok from various parts of the country.

In House no. 8, as well as in the Ban Chiang Gallery in the modern Chumbhot-Pantip Center of Arts in the palace grounds, you'll find a very good collection of elegant, whorled pottery and bronze jewellery, which the former owner of Suan Pakkad Palace, Princess Chumbhot, excavated from tombs at Ban Chiang, the major Bronze Age settlement in the northeast. Scattered around the rest of the museum are some fine ceramics and attractive Thai and Khmer religious sculptures; an extensive collection of colourful papier-mâché *khon* masks; beautiful betel-nut sets; monks' elegant ceremonial fans; and some rich teak carvings, including a two-hundred-year-old temple door showing episodes from *Sang Thong*, a folk tale about a childless king and queen who discover a handsome son in a conch shell.

The Lacquer Pavilion

The highlight of Suan Pakkad is the renovated **Lacquer Pavilion**, across the reedy pond at the back of the grounds. Set on stilts, the pavilion is actually an amalgam of two eighteenth- or late seventeenth-century temple buildings, a *ho trai* (library) and a *ho khien* (writing room), one inside the other, which were found between Ayutthaya and Bang Pa-In. The interior walls are beautifully decorated with gilt on black lacquer: the upper panels depict the life of the Buddha while the lower ones show scenes from the *Ramayana*. Look out especially for the grisly details in the tableau on the back wall, showing the earth goddess drowning the evil forces of Mara. Underneath are depicted some European dandies on horseback, probably merchants, whose presence suggests that the work was executed before the fall of Ayutthaya in 1767. The carefully observed details of daily life and nature are skilful and lively, especially considering the restraints that the lacquering technique places on the artist, who has no opportunity for corrections or touching up.

Jim Thompson's House

Just off Siam Square at the north end of Soi Kasemsan 2, Thanon Rama I • Daily from 9am, viewing on frequent 30–40min guided tours in several languages, last tour 5pm • B100 • ☎ 02 216 7368, ⓦ jimthompsonhouse.com • BTS National Stadium, or via a canalside path from the Khlong Saen Saeb pier at Saphan Hua Chang

Jim Thompson's House is a kind of Ideal Home in elegant Thai style, and a peaceful refuge from downtown chaos. The house was the residence of the legendary American adventurer, entrepreneur, art collector and all-round character whose mysterious disappearance in the jungles of Malaysia in 1967 has made him even more of a legend among Thailand's farang community.

Apart from putting together this beautiful home, completed in 1959, Thompson's most concrete contribution was to turn traditional silk-weaving in Thailand from a dying art into the highly successful international industry it is today. The complex now includes a **shop** (closes 6pm), part of the Jim Thompson Thai Silk Company chain (see p.143).

Above the shop, the **Jim Thompson Center for the Arts** is a fascinating gallery that hosts both traditional and modern temporary exhibitions on textiles and the arts, such as royal maps of Siam in the nineteenth century or an interactive show that celebrated the hundredth anniversary of Thompson's birth and the vibrant evolution of Bangkok over the same period. There's also an excellent **bar-restaurant** (last food orders currently 6pm, though it may start to open in the evenings till 11pm), which serves a similar menu to *Jim Thompson's Saladaeng Café* (see p.135). Ignore any con-men at the entrance to the soi looking for mugs to escort on rip-off shopping trips, who'll tell you that the house is closed when it isn't.

The house

The grand, rambling **house** is in fact a combination of six teak houses, some from as far afield as Ayutthaya and most more than two hundred years old. Like all traditional houses, they were built in wall sections hung together without nails on a frame of wooden pillars, which made it easy to dismantle them, pile them onto a barge and float them to their new location. Although he had trained as an architect, Thompson had more difficulty in putting them back together again; in the end, he had to go back to Ayutthaya to hunt down a group of carpenters who still practised the old house-building methods. Thompson added a few unconventional touches of his own, incorporating the elaborately carved front wall of a Chinese pawnshop between the drawing room and the bedroom, and reversing the other walls in the drawing room so that their carvings faced into the room.

The impeccably tasteful **interior** has been left as it was during Jim Thompson's life, even down to the place settings on the dining table – Thompson entertained guests most nights and to that end designed the house like a stage set. Complementing the fine artefacts from throughout Southeast Asia is a stunning array of Thai arts and crafts, including one of the best collections of traditional Thai paintings in the world. Thompson picked up plenty of bargains from the Thieves' Quarter (Nakhon Kasem) in Chinatown, before collecting Thai art became fashionable and expensive. Other pieces were liberated from decay and destruction in upcountry temples, while many of the Buddha images were turned over by ploughs, especially around Ayutthaya. Some of the exhibits are very rare, such as a headless but elegant seventh-century Dvaravati Buddha and a seventeenth-century Ayutthayan teak Buddha.

After the guided tour, you're free to look again, at your leisure, at the former rice barn and gardener's and maid's houses in the small, jungly **garden**, which display some gorgeous traditional Thai paintings and drawings, as well as small-scale statues and Chinese ceramics.

1

Bangkok Art and Cultural Centre

Junction of Rama I and Phrayathai roads • Tues–Sun 10am–9pm • Free • ☎ 02 214 6630–1, ⊕ bacc.or.th • BTS National Stadium

A striking, white hunk of modernity, the prestigious **Bangkok Art and Cultural Centre** houses several galleries on its upper floors, connected by spiralling ramps like New York's Guggenheim, as well as several performance spaces. It hosts temporary shows by contemporary artists from Thailand and abroad across all media, from the visual arts to music and design, and there's usually something interesting on here – coming in from BTS National Stadium, there's a blackboard inside the entrance where the day's events and shows are chalked up in English.

The Erawan Shrine

Corner of Thanon Ploenchit and Thanon Rajdamri • 24hr • Free • BTS Chit Lom

For a glimpse of the variety and ubiquity of Thai religion, drop in on the **Erawan Shrine** (*Saan Phra Prom* in Thai). Remarkable as much for its setting as anything else, this shrine to Brahma, the ancient Hindu creation god, and Erawan, his elephant, squeezes in on one of the busiest and noisiest intersections in modern Bangkok. And it's not the only one: half a dozen other Hindu shrines are dotted around Ratchaphrasong intersection, most notably **Trimurti**, who combines the three main gods, Brahma, Vishnu and Shiva, on the opposite corner outside Central World Plaza. Modern Bangkokians see Trimurti as a sort of Cupid figure, and those looking for love bring red offerings.

The *Grand Hyatt Erawan Hotel*, towering over the Erawan Shrine, is the reason for its existence and its name. When a string of calamities held up the building of the original hotel in the 1950s, spirit doctors were called in, who instructed the owners to build a new home for the offended local spirits: the hotel was then finished without further mishap. Ill fortune struck the shrine itself, however, in early 2006, when a young, mentally disturbed, Muslim man smashed the Brahma statue to pieces with a hammer – and was then brutally beaten to death by an angry mob. An exact replica of the statue was quickly installed, incorporating the remains of the old statue to preserve the spirit of the deity.

Be prepared for sensory overload here: the main structure shines with lurid glass of all colours and the overcrowded precinct around it is almost buried under scented garlands and incense candles. You might also catch a group of traditional dancers performing here to the strains of a small classical orchestra – worshippers hire them to give thanks for a stroke of good fortune. To increase their future chances of such good fortune, visitors buy a bird or two from the flocks incarcerated in cages here; the bird-seller transfers the requested number of captives to a tiny hand-held cage, from which the customer duly liberates the animals, thereby accruing merit. People set on less abstract rewards will invest in a lottery ticket from one of the physically disabled sellers: they're thought to be the luckiest you can buy.

Ban Kamthieng (Kamthieng House)

131 Thanon Asok Montri (Soi 21), off Thanon Sukhumvit • Tues–Sat 9am–5pm • B100 • ⊕ siam-society.org • BTS Asok or Sukhumvit subway

Another reconstructed traditional Thai residence, **Ban Kamthieng** was moved in the 1960s from Chiang Mai to just off Thanon Sukhumvit and set up as an ethnological museum by the Siam Society. The delightful complex of polished teak buildings makes a pleasing oasis beneath the towering glass skyscrapers that dominate the rest of Sukhumvit. It differs from Suan Pakkad and Jim Thompson's House in being the home of a rural family, and the objects on display give a fair insight into country life for the well-heeled in northern Thailand.

The house was built on the banks of the Ping River in the mid-nineteenth century, and the ground-level display of farming tools and fish traps evokes the upcountry

THANON PHETCHABURI MAI

Phetchaburi Ⓜ

TAT ⓘ

Tha Nana Nua ☆

Tha Asoke ☆

Khlong Saen Saeb

Ⓢ — BTS Skytrain and station
Ⓜ - - Subway and station
☆ Khlong Saen Saeb boat stop

ACCOMMODATION	
Amari Boulevard	2
The Atlanta	4
The Eugenia	1
Imm Fusion	8
PS Guesthouse	5
Rex Hotel	7
Seven	6
Suk 11	3

Bumrungrad Hospital

Nana Square

Ploenchit Centre

Nana Entertainment Plaza

Pacific Place

Chuvit Garden

Sukhumvit Plaza

Times Square

Indian Embassy

Ban Kamthieng
Sukhumvit

Divana Spa

Washington Square Theatre

Chacrit Muay Thai Gym

Benjasiri Queen Sirikit Park

Phrom Pong

Emporium and Thailand Creative & Design Centre

Lake Rachada

BARS & CLUBS	
Bed Supperclub	2
Cheap Charlie's	3
Long Table	4
Q Bar	1
WTF	5

● SHOPS	
Asia Books	1
Dasa Book Cafe	4
The Shop @ TCDC	3
Thai Celadon	2

● RESTAURANTS & CAFÉS			
Aoi	11	Le Dalat Indochine	1
Baan Khanitha	3	Ramentei	10
Banya	5	Royal India	13
Beirut	4	Soul Food Mahanakorn	14
Bolan	16	Spring Summer Winter	8
Dosa King	7	Suk 11	6
Greyhound Café	12	Vientiane Kitchen	
Himali Cha-Cha	2, 9	(Khrua Vientiane)	15

THANON SUKHUMVIT

Queen Sirikit Convention Centre

Ⓜ Queen Sirikit Centre

0   250
metres

practice of fishing in flooded rice paddies to supplement the supply from the rivers. Upstairs, the main display focuses on the ritual life of a typical Lanna household, explaining the role of the spirits, the practice of making offerings, and the belief in talismans, magic shirts and male tattoos. The rectangular lintel above the door is a *hum yon*, carved in floral patterns that represent testicles and designed to ward off evil spirits. Walk along the open veranda to the authentically equipped kitchen to see a video lesson in making spicy frog soup, and to the granary to find an interesting exhibition on the ritual practices associated with rice farming. Elsewhere in the compound you'll find a tiny bookshop selling the Siam Society's and Silkworm's publications on Thailand, and a *Black Canyon* café.

Patpong

Concentrated into two lanes running between the eastern ends of Thanon Silom and Thanon Suriwong, the neon-lit go-go bars of the **Patpong** district loom like rides in a tawdry sexual Disneyland. In front of each bar, girls cajole passers-by with a lifeless sensuality while insistent touts proffer printed menus and photographs detailing the

DOWNTOWN: SOUTH OF THANON RAMA IV

● SHOPS
A Song Tailor	5
An Song Tailor	4
Boots	3
Golden Wool	7
Jewelry Trade Center (Silom Galleria)	8
Jim Thompson	2
Lambert	9
Khomapastr	1
The Legend	6

■ BARS & CLUBS
The Balcony	8
The Barbican	2
Disco Disco	10
DJ Station	6
GOD (Guys on Display)	5
JJ Park	9
O'Reilly's	11
The Sky Bar & Distil	12
Sphinx	4
Tapas Bar	7
Tawandang	13
German Brewery	3
Telephone Pub	1
Viva: The River	11

■ ACCOMMODATION
Baan Saladaeng	8
Lub.d	7
Luxx	6
New Road Guest House	2
Peninsula Bangkok	4
Rose Hotel	1
Sukhothai	9
Swan Hotel	5
Tarntawan Place Hotel	3

■ RESTAURANTS & CAFÉS
Aoi	11	Jim Thompson's	17
Baan Khanitha	18	Saladaeng Café	14
Beirut	19	Khrua Aroy Aroy	8
Celadon	12	Le Bouchon	9
Chai Karr	1	Mei Jiang	6
Dick's Café	16	Ramentei	3
Eat Me	9	Ruen Urai	15
Harmonique	5	Taling Pling	1
Himali Cha-Cha	4, 13	Tongue Thai	7
Home Cuisine	5		

Erawan Shrine · Soi Ngam Duphli · Lumphini Park · Royal Bangkok Sports Club

Chulalongkorn Hospital · CHULALONGKORN UNIVERSITY · Queen Saovabha Institute · Bangkok Christian Hospital · BNH Hospital

Canadian Embassy · Australian Embassy · Malaysian Embassy · Singapore Embassy · Burmese Embassy · Alliance Française · Ruen Nuad · Sala Daeng

Thaniya Plaza · Patpong 1 · Patpong 2 · Thai Airways · Chong Nonsi · Maha Uma Devi Temple · Silom Village · Assumption Cathedral · Oriental Hotel · Tha Wat Muang Kae · River City

Chao Phraya River · Saphan Taksin · Taksin Bridge · Thonburi · Tha Sathorn · Tha Oriental · Tha Si Phraya · Tha Krom Kan Khonsong · Thang Nam (Marine Dept)

Thanon Rajadamri · Thanon Henri Dunant · Silom · Saladaeng · Convent · Thanon Narathiwat Ratchanakharin · Thanon Si Phraya · Thanon Surawong · Thanon Silom · Thanon Sathorn Nua · Thanon Sathorn Tai · Thanon Charoen Krung (New Road) · Charoen Krung · Charoen Phanit · Expressway · Khlong Krung Kasem · Thanon Maha Nakhon · Soi Charoen Krung 45

Hualamphong Station · Wongwian Yai BTS Station · Sam Yan · Sam Square

S — BTS Skytrain and station
M — Subway and station
N1 — Express-boat pier

0 — 250 metres

THAILAND'S SEX INDUSTRY

Bangkok owes its reputation as the carnal capital of the world to a **sex industry** adept at peddling fantasies of cheap thrills on tap. More than a thousand sex-related businesses operate in the city, but the gaudy neon fleshpots of Patpong and Sukhumvit's Soi Nana and Soi Cowboy give a misleading impression of an activity that is deeply rooted in Thai culture: the overwhelming majority of Thailand's prostitutes of both sexes (estimated at anywhere between 200,000 and 700,000) work with Thai men, not farangs.

Prostitution and polygamy have long been intrinsic to the Thai way of life. Until Rama VI broke with the custom in 1910, Thai kings had always kept concubines, only a few of whom would be elevated to royal mothers. The practice was aped by the nobility and, from the early nineteenth century, by newly rich merchants keen to have lots of sons. Though the monarch is now monogamous, many men of all classes still keep **mistresses**, known as *mia noi* (minor wives), or have casual girlfriends (*gig*); the common view is that an official wife (*mia luang*) should be treated like the temple's main Buddha image – respected and elevated upon the altar – whereas the minor wife is like an amulet, to be taken along wherever you go. For less wealthy men, prostitution is a far cheaper option: at least two-fifths of sexually active Thai men are thought to visit brothels twice a month.

The **farang sex industry** is a relatively new development, having started during the Vietnam War, when the American military set up seven bases around Thailand. The GIs' appetite for "entertainment" attracted women from surrounding rural areas to cash in on the boom, and Bangkok joined the fray in 1967. By the mid-1970s, the GIs had left, but tourists replaced them, lured by advertising that diverted most of the traffic to Bangkok and Pattaya. Sex tourism has since grown to become an established part of the Thai economy and has spread to Phuket, Hat Yai, Ko Samui and Chiang Mai.

The majority of the women who work in the country's go-go bars and "bar-beers" (outdoor hostess bars) come from the poorest areas of north and northeast Thailand. **Economic refugees**, they're easily drawn into an industry in which they can make in a single night what it takes a month to earn in the rice fields. Many women opt for a couple of years in the sex bars to help pay off family debts and improve the living conditions of parents stuck in the poverty trap.

Many bar girls, and male prostitutes too, are looking for longer-term **relationships** with their farang customers, bringing a temporary respite from bar work and perhaps even a ticket out. A surprising number of one-night transactions do develop into some sort of holiday romance, with the young woman accompanying her farang "boyfriend" (often twice her age) around the country and maintaining contact after he's returned home. It's a common joke that some bar girls field half a dozen mobile phones so they can juggle all their various "sponsors". An entire sub-genre of novels and confessional memoirs (among them the classic *Hello, My Big Big Honey!: Letters to Bangkok Bar Girls and Their Revealing Interviews*) testifies to the role money plays in all this, and highlights the delusions common to both parties, not to mention the cross-cultural incomprehension.

Despite its ubiquity, prostitution has been **illegal** in Thailand since 1960, but sex-industry bosses easily circumvent the law by registering their establishments as clubs, karaoke bars or massage parlours, and making payoffs to the police and politicians. Sex workers, on the other hand, often endure exploitation and violence from pimps and customers rather than face fines and long rehabilitation sentences. Hardly surprising that many prefer to go freelance, working the clubs and bars in non-red-light zones such as Thanon Khao San. Life is made even more difficult because abortion is illegal in Thailand. The **anti-prostitution law**, however, does attempt to treat sex workers as victims rather than criminals and penalizes parents who sell their children. A high-profile voice in the struggle to improve the **rights of sex workers** is the Empower Foundation (Ⓦempowerfoundation.org), which not only organizes campaigns and runs education centres for bar workers but also manages its own bar in Chiang Mai.

Inevitably, **child prostitution** is a significant issue in Thailand, but NGOs such as ECPAT (Ⓦecpat.net) say numbers have declined over the last decade, due to zero-tolerance and awareness campaigns. The government has also strengthened legislation against hiring a prostitute under the age of 18, and anyone caught having sex with an under-15 is now charged with rape. The disadvantaged are still targeted by traffickers however, who "buy" children from desperately poor hill-tribe and other minority families and keep them as bonded slaves until the debt has been repaid.

1

degradations on show. Inside, bikini-clad women gyrate to Western music and play hostess to the (almost exclusively male) spectators; upstairs, live shows feature women who, to use Spalding Gray's phrase in *Swimming to Cambodia*, "do everything with their vaginas except have babies".

Patpong was no more than a sea of mud when the capital was founded on the marshy river bank to the west, but by the 1960s it had grown into a flash district of dance halls for rich Thais, owned by a Chinese millionaire godfather, educated at the London School of Economics and by the OSS (forerunner of the CIA), who gave his name to the area. In 1969, an American entrepreneur turned an existing teahouse into a luxurious nightclub to satisfy the tastes of soldiers on R&R trips from Vietnam, and so Patpong's transformation into a Western sex reservation began. At first, the area was rough and violent, but over the years it has wised up to the desires of the affluent farang, and now markets itself as a packaged concept of Oriental decadence.

The centre of the skin trade lies along the interconnected sois of **Patpong 1 and 2**, where lines of go-go bars share their patch with respectable restaurants, a 24-hour supermarket and an overabundance of pharmacies. Even the most demure tourists – of both sexes – turn out to do some shopping at the night market down the middle of Patpong 1, where hawkers sell fake watches, bags and designer T-shirts. By day, a relaxed hangover descends on the place. Farang men slump at the bars on Patpong 2, drinking and watching videos, unable to find anything else to do in the whole of Bangkok. Running parallel to the east, **Soi Thaniya** is Patpong's Japanese counterpart, lined with hostess bars and some good restaurants, while the focus of Bangkok's gay scene, **Silom 2** (ie Soi 2, Thanon Silom) and the more mixed **Silom 4**, flank Thaniya.

Chatuchak Weekend Market (JJ)

Occupies a huge patch of ground in the north of Bangkok, extending northwest from the corner of Phaholyothin and Kamphaeng Phet roads • Sat & Sun roughly 9am–6/7pm, though many stalls open earlier and some close later • Subway to Kamphaeng Phet or Chatuchak Park, BTS to Mochit; from Banglamphu, bus to BTS National Stadium or Ratchathewi, or the #159, #503 (non-expressway version) or #509 bus all the way from Rajdamnoen Klang (about 1hr)

With over eight thousand open-air stalls to peruse, and wares as diverse as Lao silk, Siamese kittens and designer lamps, the enormous **Chatuchak Weekend Market**, or **JJ** as it's usually abbreviated (from "Jatu Jak"), is Bangkok's most enjoyable – and exhausting – shopping experience. Kamphaeng Phet subway station exits right into the most interesting, southwestern, corner of the market, and a few very small electric trams circulate around the market's main inner road, transporting weary shoppers for free, though they always seem to be full.

Maps are posted at various points around the market, including in the subway stations; the best resource is *Nancy Chandler's Map of Bangkok*, which has a fabulously detailed and informatively annotated map of all the sections in the market. For specific help, you can ask at the **market office**, on the main inner ring road near Gate 1 off Thanon Kamphaeng Phet 2, which also has ATMs and currency exchange booths.

The market contains a controversial **wildlife** section that has long doubled as a clearing house for protected and endangered species such as gibbons, palm cockatoos and Indian pied hornbills, many of them smuggled in from Laos and Cambodia and sold to private animal collectors and foreign zoos. The illegal trade goes on beneath the counter, despite occasional crackdowns, but you're bound to come across fighting cocks around the back, miniature flying squirrels being fed milk through pipettes, and iridescent red-and-blue Siamese fighting fish, kept in individual jars and shielded from each other's aggressive stares by sheets of cardboard.

CLOCKWISE FROM TOP LEFT BANGKOK SKYLINE; LONGTAIL ON A THONBURI CANAL (P.99); JIM THOMPSON'S HOUSE (P.107); FABRIC STALL IN CHATUCHAK WEEKEND MARKET (ABOVE) >

1

Where to shop

Chatuchak is divided into 27 numbered **sections**, plus a dozen unnumbered ones, each of them more or less dedicated to a particular genre, for example household items, plants and secondhand books, and if you have several hours to spare, it's fun just to browse at whim. The market's primary customers are Bangkok residents in search of idiosyncratic fashions (try sections 5 and 6) and homewares (sections 2, 3, 4, 7 and 8), but Chatuchak also has plenty of collector- and tourist-oriented **stalls**; best buys include antique lacquerware, unusual sarongs, traditional cotton clothing and crafts from the north, silver jewellery, and ceramics, particularly the five-coloured *bencharong*. For handicrafts and traditional textiles, you should start with sections 22, 24, 25 and 26, which are all in a cluster at the southwest (Kamphaeng Phet subway) end of the market; sections A, B and C, behind the market's head office and information centre, are also full of interesting artefacts.

Foodies will want to check out **Talat Or Tor Khor** (OTK, the Agricultural Market Organization), a covered market that sells a fantastic array of fruit, veg and other produce from around the country, as well as prepared dishes to take away or to eat at the food court; it's on the south side of Thanon Kamphaeng Phet, next to Kamphaeng Phet subway station.

ARRIVAL AND DEPARTURE BANGKOK

Unless you arrive in Bangkok by train, be prepared for a long trip into the city centre. Suvarnabhumi Airport is 25km out and the three bus stations are not much closer in, though at least the Eastern Terminal is right beside a Skytrain stop.

BY PLANE

SUVARNABHUMI

Suvarnabhumi is Bangkok's main airport (coded "BKK" and pronounced "soo-wanna-poom"; ☎ 02 132 8888; ⒲ suvarnabhumiairport.com), situated 25km east of central Bangkok between highways 7 and 34. The large airport is well stocked with 24hr exchange booths, ATMs, places to eat, pharmacies and a post office. 24-hour information is available at the TAT desks at Gates 3 and 10 (☎ 02 134 0040–1) and there's a tourist police booth in the arrivals hall on Floor 2; there are 24hr left-luggage depots (B100/item/day) in arrivals and in the departures hall on Floor 4. Car-rental companies here include Avis and Budget (see p.34), though you'll have to pick your car up from the Public Transportation Centre (see below). There are a number of accommodation options near Suvarnabhumi (see p.129). When departing Bangkok, leave plenty of time to get to Suvarnabhumi, as getting there by bus, minibus or taxi can be severely hampered by traffic jams.

Public Transportation Centre Situated on the other side of the huge airport complex from the terminal building, the Public Transportation Centre is reached by a free, 10min ride on an "Express" shuttle bus from Gate 5 outside arrivals or Gate 5 outside departures – be sure not to confuse these with the much slower "Ordinary" shuttle buses, which ferry airport staff around the complex. However, because of the inconvenience involved, many long-distance buses now pick up and drop off at the terminal building.

Suvarnabhumi Airport Rail Link The high-speed rail link (SARL; ⒲ airportraillink.railway.co.th; daily 6am–midnight) from the basement of Suvarnabhumi is the quickest means of getting downtown. There's only one set of elevated tracks, ending at Phaya Thai station (an interchange with the Skytrain system, and served by a/c and non-a/c #59 and a/c #79 buses to Thanon Rajadamnoen Klang, for Banglamphu), but three services run on them: stopping, often crowded "City Line" services to Phaya Thai (every 12–20min; 24min; B45), via Makkasan, Ratchaprarop and four other stations; non-stop "Express" trains to Phaya Thai (every 30min; 17min; currently on promotion at B90 single, B150 return); and nonstop "Express" trains to Makkasan Station (every 40min; 15min; B150 single), which is inconveniently located although it's within walking distance of Phetchaburi subway station and served by a/c bus #556 to Thanon Rajadamnoen Klang (for Banglamphu) and the Southern Bus Terminal. Makkasan also offers a luggage check-in facility for most Thai Airways flights (3–12hr before departure).

Taxis Taxis to the centre are comfortable, air-conditioned and reasonably priced, although the driving can be hairy. Walk past the pricey taxis and limousines on offer within the baggage hall and arrivals hall, and ignore any tout who may offer a cheap ride in an unlicensed and unmetered vehicle, as newly arrived travellers are seen as easy prey for robbery and the cabs are untraceable. Licensed and metered public taxis are operated from clearly signposted and well-regulated counters, outside Floor 1's Gates 4 and 7. Including the B50 airport pick-up fee and around B70 tolls for the overhead expressways, a journey to Thanon Silom downtown, for example, should set you back around B300–350, depending on the traffic. Heading back to the airport, drivers will nearly always try to leave their meters off and agree an inflated price with you – say "*poet meter, dai mai* *khrap/kha?*" to get them to switch the meter on. If you leave the downtown areas before 7am or after 9pm you can get to the airport in half an hour, but at other times you should set off about an hour and a half before you have to check in.

City buses and minibuses The most economical way of getting into the city is by public a/c bus (B22–35) or pricier minibus from the Public Transportation Centre, but only the following routes are likely to be at all useful to visitors: #552 along Thanon Sukhumvit via On Nut (for the Skytrain), ending up at Khlong Toey; and #554 (also available from Gate 8, Floor 1 of the terminal building) and #555 to Don Muang and Rangsit. On departure, many travellers opt for one of the private minibus services to Suvarnabhumi (at least every 2hr; B130–150; at least 90min) organized through guesthouses and travel agents in Banglamphu and elsewhere around the city.

Long-distance buses From Gate 8, Floor 1 of the terminal building, there are long-distance buses to Pattaya and Aranyaprathet, and minibuses to Chanthaburi and Ko Chang. From the Public Transportation Centre, there are also long-distance buses to Rayong, Chanthaburi, Laem Ngop (for Ko Chang) and Trat.

Destinations: Chumphon (daily; 1hr); Ko Samui (20 daily; 1hr–1hr 30min); Krabi (15 daily; 1hr 20min); Nakhon Si Thammarat (4 daily; 1hr 5min); Phuket (30 daily; 1hr 20min); Surat Thani (5 daily; 1hr 15min); Trang (1–2 daily; 1hr 30min); Trat (3 daily; 1hr 5min).

DON MUANG

The old **Don Muang Airport** (coded "DMK"; ☎ 02 535 1253; ⊛ donmuangairportonline.com), 25km north of the city, is currently used only by Nok Air's domestic services (Orient Thai may also move back there from Suvarnabhumi). If you do wind up at Don Muang, the best way to get into the city centre is by licensed, metered taxi from the desk outside Arrivals (about B300–350, including B50 airport fee and expressway fees); depending on your destination in the city, you may save some time during rush hours by hopping out of the taxi at Mo Chit Skytrain station or Phahon Yothin subway station.

Destinations: Nakhon Si Thammarat (3 daily; 1hr 5min); Phuket (2 daily; 1hr 20min); Surat Thani (2 daily; 1hr 15min); Trang (2 daily; 1hr 30min).

BY TRAIN

Travelling to Bangkok by train from Malaysia and most parts of Thailand, you arrive at the main Hualamphong Station. A handful of slow, local trains on the Southern line, however, pull in at **Thonburi Station** (Bangkok Noi Station), a 15–20min walk from N11 and N10 express-boat piers.

HUALAMPHONG STATION

Hualamphong Station is centrally located at the edge of Chinatown and is on the subway line. The most useful of the city buses (see box, p.119) serving Hualamphong is the #159 (non-air-con), which runs west to Democracy Monument, Rajdamnoen Klang (for Banglamphu) and the Southern Bus Terminal, and east to MBK, Siam Square, Chatuchak and the Northern Bus Terminal. Station facilities include an exchange booth, several ATMs, an internet centre and a left-luggage office at the front of the main concourse (daily 4am–11pm; B30–100/day). The 24-hour State Railways (SRT) information booth in the main concourse, on the right, keeps English-language timetables. Between 8.30am and 4pm, advance tickets can be bought from the clearly signed Advance Booking counters #15–20 under the main departures board; at other times, check availability at the SRT information booth, then buy your ticket at any ticket counter (daily 4.30am–midnight). Train tickets can also be bought through almost any travel agent and through some hotels and guesthouses for a booking fee of about B50. "Basics" has more information on tickets and timetables (see p.32). The station area is fertile ground for con-artists, looking to prey on new arrivals. Anyone who comes up to you in or around the station concourse and offers help/information/transport or ticket-booking services is probably a scammer, however many official-looking ID tags are hanging round their neck. Hualamphong also nurtures plenty of dishonest tuk-tuk drivers – take a metered taxi or public transport instead.

Destinations: Aranyaprathet (2 daily; 5–6hr); Butterworth (Malaysia; daily; 21hr); Cha-am (5 daily; 3hr 10min–3hr 50min); Chumphon (12 daily; 7hr–9hr 30min); Hua Hin (14 daily; 4–5hr); Nakhon Si Thammarat (2 daily; 15–16hr); Pattaya (daily; 3hr 45min); Phetchaburi (13 daily; 2hr 45min–3hr 45min); Prachuap Khiri Khan (11 daily; 5–7hr); Pranburi (3 daily; 5hr 30min); Si Racha (daily; 3hr 15min); Surat Thani (10 daily; 9–12hr); Trang (2 daily; 15–16hr).

BY BUS

Bangkok's three main bus terminals, all of which have left-luggage facilities of some kind, are distributed around the outskirts of town. On departure, leave plenty of time to reach them, especially if setting off from Banglamphu, from where you should allow at least an hour and a half (outside rush hour) to get to the Eastern Bus Terminal, and a good hour to get to the Northern or Southern terminals. Seats on the most popular long-distance a/c bus services (such as to Krabi, Phuket and Surat Thani) should be reserved ahead of time, either at the relevant bus station or in any of the ways described in Basics (see p.30), as guesthouses may book you on to one of the dodgy tourist services (see p.116).

NORTHERN AND NORTHEASTERN BUS TERMINAL (MO CHIT)

All services from the north and northeast terminate at Bangkok's biggest bus station, the **Northern and**

1

Northeastern Bus Terminal (Mo Chit) on Thanon Kamphaeng Phet 2; some buses from the south and the east coast also use Mo Chit. The quickest way to get into the city centre from Mo Chit is to hop onto the Skytrain at Mo Chit Station on Thanon Phaholyothin, or the subway at the adjacent Chatuchak Park Station or at Kamphaeng Phet Station (at the bottom of Thanon Kamphaeng Phet 2), all of which are about a 15min walk from the bus terminal, and then change onto a city bus if necessary. Otherwise, it's a long bus or taxi ride into town: city buses from the Northern Bus Terminal include ordinary #159 to Siam Square, Hualamphong Station, Banglamphu and the Southern Bus Terminal; and ordinary and a/c #3, and a/c #509 and #512 to Banglamphu (see p.119).

Destinations Aranyaprathet (hourly; 4hr 30min); Chanthaburi (13 daily; 3–4hr); Pattaya (every 30min; 2–3hr); Rayong (every 30min; 2hr 30min–3hr 30min); Si Racha (every 30min; 2hr); Trat (5 daily; 4hr 30min).

EASTERN BUS TERMINAL (EKAMAI)

Most buses to and from east-coast destinations such as Pattaya, Ban Phe (for Ko Samet) and Trat (for Ko Chang) use the **Eastern Bus Terminal** (Ekamai) between sois 40 and 42 on Thanon Sukhumvit. This bus station is right beside the Ekamai Skytrain stop (see p.121), and is also served by lots of city buses, including a/c #511 to and from Banglamphu and the Southern Bus Terminals. Alternatively, you can use the Khlong Saen Saeb canal-boat service, which runs westwards almost as far as Banglamphu (see p.120); there's a pier called Tha Ekamai, at the northern end of Sukhumvit Soi 63, which is easiest reached from the bus station by taxi.

Destinations Ban Phe (for Ko Samet; 14 daily; 3hr–3hr 30min); Chanthaburi (hourly; 4–5hr); Laem Ngop (for Ko Chang; 3–4 daily; 5hr 15min); Pattaya (every 30min; 2hr 30min–3hr 30min); Rayong (every 40min; 2hr 30min–3hr); Si Racha (every 30min; 2–3hr); Trat (6 daily; 5–6hr).

SOUTHERN BUS TERMINAL (SATHAANII SAI TAI)

The huge, airport-like **Southern Bus Terminal**, or **Sathaanii Sai Tai**, handles transport to and from all points north of the capital, including Hua Hin, Chumphon (for Ko Tao), Surat Thani (for Ko Samui), Phuket and Krabi, as well as buses for destinations west of Bangkok. The terminal has recently been relocated to the junction of Thanon Borom Ratchonni and Thanon Phutthamonthon Sai 1 in Taling Chan, an interminable 11km west of the Chao Phraya River and Banglamphu, so access to and from city accommodation can take an age, even in a taxi. City buses serving Sathaanii Sai Tai include #124 for Banglamphu, #159 to Banglamphu, Hualamphong Station, Siam Square and the Northern Bus Terminal, #511 for Banglamphu, Thanon Sukhumvit and Ekamai, and #516 for Thewet and Banglamphu, but note that when arriving in

Bangkok most long-distance bus services make a more convenient stop before reaching the terminus (via a time-consuming U-turn), towards the eastern end of Thanon Borom Ratchonni, much nearer Phra Pinklao Bridge and the river; the majority of passengers get off here and it's highly recommended to do the same rather than continue to the terminal. The above-listed city buses all cross the river from this bus drop, as do many additional services, and this is also a faster and cheaper place to grab a taxi into town.

Destinations: Cha-am (roughly hourly; 2hr 45min–3hr 15min); Chumphon (roughly hourly; 7–9hr); Hat Yai (13 daily; 12hr); Hua Hin (every 40min; 3–4hr); Khao Lak (3 daily; 12hr); Ko Pha Ngan (2 daily; 14hr); Ko Samui (8 daily; 13hr); Krabi (12 daily; 12–14hr); Nakhon Si Thammarat (19 daily; 12hr); Phang Nga (8 daily; 12hr); Phetchaburi (4–7 daily; 2hr 15min); Phuket (30 daily; 12hr); Prachuap Khiri Khan (roughly hourly; 4–5hr); Pranburi (every 30min; 3hr 30min); Ranong (15 daily; 9hr); Satun (4 daily; 16hr); Surat Thani (10 daily; 10–12hr); Trang (11 daily; 12–14hr).

BY A/C MINIBUS

For short and medium-length journeys, a faster, more convenient alternative to traipsing out to the bus terminals is to make use of the licensed, **a/c minibus** services (*rot tuu*; see p.31) that depart from central downtown locations. Most services depart from the Victory Monument roundabout (*Anu Sawari*), which is easily reached via the Victory Monument Skytrain station. See the accounts of the relevant destinations for details.

BY TOURIST BUS

Many Bangkok tour operators sell tickets for **unlicensed budget tourist buses and minibuses** to popular long-distance destinations such as Surat Thani (for Ko Samui) and Krabi (for Ko Phi Phi), and to places closer at hand such as Ko Samet and Ko Chang. Their only advantage is convenience, as they mostly leave from the Khao San area in Banglamphu. Prices, however, can vary considerably but rarely work out cheaper than buses from the public terminals or licensed air-con minibuses. The big drawbacks, however, are the **lack of comfort** and **poor safety**, which particularly applies to the long-distance **overnight services**. It is standard practice for budget tour operators, especially those on Thanon Khao San, to assure you that overnight transport will be in a large, luxury VIP bus despite knowing it's actually a clapped-out old banger. **Security** on overnight tourist buses is a serious problem, and because they're run by unlicensed private companies there is no insurance against loss or theft of baggage: don't keep anything of value in luggage that's stored out of sight, even if it's padlocked, as luggage sometimes gets slashed and rifled in the roomy baggage compartment. In addition, passengers often find themselves dumped on the outskirts of their destination city, at the mercy of unscrupulous touts. Services to Ko Samet (B350 including boat transfer) and Ko Chang (B350 including boat) are usually by air-con minibus; these are usually cramped and can go scarily fast but luggage is generally secure. Bear in mind that Khao San tour operators open up and go bust all the time; never hand over any money until you see the ticket. One tourist company that is licensed and reliable is **Lomprayah**, who operate catamarans to Ko Tao, Ko Pha Ngan and Ko Samui and connecting buses from Banglamphu to Chumphon. They have an office at 154 Thanon Ram Buttri (☎ 02 629 2569–70, ⓦ lomprayah.com). Recommended travel agents are listed in the Directory (see p.147).

GETTING AROUND

Getting around can undoubtedly be a headache in a city where it's not unusual for residents to spend three hours getting to work. The main form of transport is **buses**, and once you've mastered the labyrinthine complexity of the route maps you'll be able to get to any part of the city, albeit slowly. Catching the various kinds of **taxi** is more expensive, and you'll still get held up by the daytime traffic jams. **Boats** are obviously more limited in their range, but they're regular and as cheap as buses, and you'll save a lot of time by using them whenever possible – a journey between Banglamphu and the GPO, for instance, will take around thirty minutes by water, half what it would usually take on land. The **Skytrain** and **subway** each have a similarly limited range but are also worth using whenever suitable for all or part of your journey; their networks roughly coincide with each other at the east end of Thanon Silom, at the corner of Soi Asoke and Thanon

1

Sukhumvit, and on Thanon Phaholyothin by Chatuchak Park (Mo Chit), while the Skytrain joins up with the Chao Phraya River express boats at the vital hub of Sathorn/Saphan Taksin (Taksin Bridge). At each Skytrain and subway station, you'll find a useful map of the immediate neighbourhood. Also under construction in the north of the city are the elevated metro lines known as the SRT Red Lines from Bang Sue, one of which will stop at Don Muang airport.

BY BUS

Bangkok has reputedly the world's largest bus network, on which operate three main types of bus service. On **ordinary** (non-a/c) buses, which are either red and white, blue and white, or small and green, fares range from B6.50 to B8.50; most routes operate from about 5am to 11pm, but some maintain a 24-hour service (see box opposite). **Air-conditioned** buses are either blue, orange or yellow (some are articulated) and charge between B12 and B36 according to distance travelled; most stop in the late evening, but a few of the more popular routes run 24-hour services. As buses can only go as fast as the car in front, which at the moment is averaging 4km per hr, you'll probably be spending a long time on each journey, so you'd be well advised to pay the extra for cool air – and the a/c buses are usually less crowded, too. For a comprehensive roundup of bus routes in the capital, buy a bus map (see below) or log onto the Bangkok Mass Transit Authority website (⊚ bmta .co.th), which gives details of all city-bus routes.

Maps To get around Bangkok on the cheap, you'll need to buy a bus map. Of the several available, the most useful and reliable are Bangkok Guide's *Bus Routes & Map*, which not only charts all major a/c and non-a/c bus routes but also carries detailed written itineraries of some two hundred routes; and Thinknet's more user-friendly

Bangkok Bus Guide, which also charts a/c and non-a/c buses, with close-up maps of Banglamphu and Victory Monument

BY BOAT

Bangkok was built as an amphibious city around a network of canals (*khlongs*) and the first streets were constructed only in the second half of the nineteenth century. Many canals remain on the Thonburi side of the river, but most of those on the Bangkok side have been turned into roads. The Chao Phraya River itself is still a major transport route for residents and non-residents alike, forming more of a link than a barrier between the two halves of the city.

EXPRESS BOATS

The Chao Phraya Express Boat Company operates the vital **express-boat** (*reua duan*; ⊚ chaophrayaexpressboat .com) services, using large water buses to plough up and down the river, between clearly signed piers (*tha*), which appear on all Bangkok maps. Tha Sathorn, which gives access to the Skytrain network, has been designated "Central Pier", with piers to the south of here numbered S1, S2, etc, those to the north N1, N2 and so on (see box, p.120 and map, p.76). Boats do not necessarily stop at every landing – they only pull in if people want to get on or off,

---

TOURS OF THE CITY

Unlikely as it sounds, the most popular organized **tours** in Bangkok for independent travellers are by bicycle, heading to the city's outer neighbourhoods and beyond; these are an excellent way to gain a different perspective on Thai life and offer a unique chance to see traditional communities close up. In addition to those listed below, other tour options include Thonburi canal tours (see p.101) and Chao Phraya Express tourist boats (see p.120).

ABC Amazing Bangkok Cyclist Tours and **Real Asia** 10/5–7 Soi Aree, Soi 26, Thanon Sukhumvit ☎ 02 665 6364, ⊚ realasia.net. ABC's are the most popular and longest-running bicycle tours, starting in the Sukhumvit area and taking you across the river to surprisingly rural khlong- and riverside communities (including a floating market at weekends); they also offer cycle-and-dine tours in the evening. Tours operate every day year-round, cover up to 30km depending on the itinerary, and need to be reserved in advance (B1000–2000 including bicycle). Part of the same company, Real Asia runs full-day canal and walking tours through Thonburi and leads outings by train to the historic fishing port of Samut Sakhon (both B2000, including lunch and boat trips).

Bangkok Bike Rides 14/1 Soi Promsi 2, Soi 39, Thanon Sukhumvit ☎ 02 712 5305, ⊚ bangkok bikerides.com or ⊚ spiceroads.com. Runs a programme of different day and half-day tours within Greater Bangkok (B1000–2650 per person, minimum two people), as well as to the floating markets and canalside neighbourhoods of Damnoen Saduak and Ayutthaya. Also offers multi-day trips out of the city.

Velo Thailand Soi 4, Thanon Samsen ☎ 02 628 8628, ⊚ velothailand.com. Runs half a dozen different bike tours of the capital out of its cycle shop on the edge of Banglamphu, including an after-dark tour (6–10pm; B1100) that takes in floodlit sights including Wat Pho, Wat Arun and the Pak Khlong Talat flower market.

1

USEFUL BUS ROUTES IN BANGKOK

In addition to those listed below, there are also bus routes from Suvarnabhumi Airport (see p.115). In Banglamphu, finding the right bus stop can sometimes be tricky (see p.92).

#3 (ordinary and a/c)
Northern Bus Terminal–Chatuchak Weekend Market–Thanon Phaholyothin–Thanon Samsen–Thanon Phra Arthit (for Banglamphu guesthouses)–Thanon Sanam Chai (for Museum of Siam)–Thanon Triphet–Memorial Bridge (for Pak Khlong Talat)–Taksin Monument (for Wongwian Yai) –Wat Suwan.

#15 (ordinary)
Thanon Ratchadaphisek–Krung Thep Bridge–Thanon Charoen Krung–Thanon Silom–Thanon Rajdamri–Siam Square–Thanon Lan Luang–Sanam Luang–Thanon Phra Arthit (for Banglamphu guesthouses).

#16 (ordinary and a/c)
Thanon Srinarong–Thanon Samsen–Thewet (for guesthouses)–Thanon Phitsanulok–Thanon Phrayathai–Siam Square–Thanon Suriwong.

#25 (ordinary and a/c, 24hr)
Pak Nam (for Ancient City buses)–Thanon Sukhumvit–Eastern Bus Terminal–Siam Square–Hualamphong Station–Thanon Yaowarat (for Chinatown)–Pahurat–Wat Pho–Tha Chang (for the Grand Palace); some #25 buses (ordinary only) only go as far as Hualamphong Station.

#53 circular (also anticlockwise; ordinary)
Thewet–Thanon Krung Kasem–Hualamphong Station–Thanon Yaowarat (for Chinatown)–Pahurat–Pak Khlong Talat–Thanon Maharat (for Wat Pho and the Grand Palace)–Sanam Luang (for National Museum)–Thanon Phra Arthit and Thanon Samsen (for Banglamphu guesthouses)–Thewet.

#56 circular (also clockwise; ordinary)
Thanon Phra Sumen–Wat Bowoniwes–Thanon Pracha Thipatai–Thanon Ratchasima (for Vimanmek Palace)–Thanon Rajwithi–Krung Thon Bridge–Thonburi–Phrapokklao Bridge–Thanon Chakraphet (for Chinatown)–Thanon Mahachai–Democracy Monument–Thanon Tanao (for Khao San guesthouses)–Thanon Phra Sumen.

#124 (ordinary)
Sanam Luang–Thanon Rajinee, near Information Centre (for Banglamphu guesthouses)–Phra Pinklao Bridge–Southern Bus Terminal–Mahidol University.

#159 (ordinary)
Southern Bus Terminal–Phra Pinklao Bridge–Democracy Monument–Hualamphong Station–MBK Shopping Centre–Thanon Ratchaprarop–Victory Monument–Chatuchak Weekend Market–Northern Bus Terminal.

#503 (a/c)
Sanam Luang–Democracy Monument (for Banglamphu guesthouses)–Thanon Rajdamnoen Nok (for TAT and boxing stadium)–Wat Benjamabophit–Thanon Sri Ayutthaya (for Thewet guesthouses)–Victory Monument–Chatuchak Weekend Market–Rangsit. Note, however, that during rush hours, some #503 buses take the expressway, missing out Chatuchak Weekend Market.

#508 (a/c)
Thanon Maharat–Grand Palace–Thanon Charoen Krung–Siam Square–Thanon Sukhumvit–Eastern Bus Terminal–Pak Nam (for Ancient City buses). Note, however, that during rush hours, some #508 buses take the expressway, missing out the Eastern Bus Terminal.

#509 (a/c)
Northern Bus Terminal–Chatuchak Weekend Market–Victory Monument–Thanon Rajwithi–Thanon Sawankhalok–Thanon Phitsanulok–Thanon Rajdamnoen Nok (for TAT and boxing stadium)–Democracy Monument–Thanon Rajdamnoen Klang (for Banglamphu guesthouses)–Phra Pinklao Bridge–Thonburi.

#511 (a/c, 24hr)
Southern Bus Terminal–Phra Pinklao Bridge (for Banglamphu guesthouses)–Democracy Monument–Thanon Lan Luang–Thanon Phetchaburi–Thanon Sukhumvit–Eastern Bus Terminal–Pak Nam (for Ancient City buses). Note, however, that between 4am and 11pm, some #511 buses take the expressway, missing out the Eastern Bus Terminal.

#512 (a/c)
Northern Bus Terminal–Chatuchak Weekend Market–Thanon Phetchaburi–Thanon Lan Luang–Democracy Monument (for Banglamphu guesthouses)–Sanam Luang–Tha Chang (for Grand Palace)–Pak Khlong Talat.

CENTRAL STOPS FOR THE CHAO PHRAYA EXPRESS BOATS

N15 Thewet (all express boats) – for Thewet guesthouses.
N14 Rama VIII Bridge (no flag) – for Samsen Soi 5.
N13 Phra Arthit (no flag and orange flag) – for Thanon Phra Arthit, Thanon Khao San and Banglamphu guesthouses.
N12 Phra Pinklao Bridge (all boats) – for Royal Barge Museum.
N11 Thonburi Railway Station (or Bangkok Noi; no flag).
N10 Wang Lang (aka Siriraj or Prannok; all boats).
N9 Chang (no flag, green flag and orange flag) – for the Grand Palace, Sanam Luang and the National Museum.
N8 Thien (no flag and orange flag) – for Wat Pho, and the cross-river ferry to Wat Arun.
N7 Ratchini (aka Rajinee; no flag).
N6 Saphan Phut (Memorial Bridge; no flag and orange flag) – for Pak Khlong Talat.
N5 Rachawongse (aka Rajawong; all boats) – for Chinatown.
N4 Harbour (Marine) Department (no flag and orange flag).
N3 Si Phraya (all boats) – walk north past the *Sheraton Royal Orchid Hotel* for River City shopping complex, head south for the GPO.
N2 Wat Muang Kae (no flag) – for the GPO.
N1 Oriental (no flag and orange flag) – for Thanon Silom.
Central Sathorn (all boats) – for the Skytrain and Thanon Sathorn.

and when they do stop, it's not for long – so when you want to get off, be ready at the back of the boat in good time for your pier. **No-flag**, local-line boats call at every pier between Wat Rajsingkorn, just upriver of Krung Thep Bridge, in the south, and Nonthaburi, 90min away to the north, but only operate during rush hour (Mon–Fri roughly 6.20–8am & 3–5.30pm, every 20–25min; B10–14). The only boats to run all day, every day are on the limited-stop **orange-flag** service (Nonthaburi to Wat Rajsingkorn in 1hr; roughly 6am–7pm, every 5–20min; B15). Other limited-stop services run during rush hour, flying either a **yellow flag** (Nonthaburi to Tha Sathorn or Rajburana, far downriver beyond Krung Thep Bridge, in about 50min; Mon–Fri roughly 6.15–8.30am & 3.30–8pm; B20–29) or a **green flag** (Pakkred to Tha Sathorn Mon–Fri 6.15–8.10am & 5–6pm, Tha Sathorn to Pakkred Mon–Fri 3.30–6.05pm; about 50min; B13–32). **Tickets** can be bought on board; don't discard your ticket until you're off the boat, as the staff at some piers impose a B1 fine on anyone disembarking without one.

TOURIST BOATS

The Chao Phraya Express Boat Company also runs **tourist boats**, distinguished by their light-blue flags, between Sathorn (every 30min; 9.30am–4pm) and Phra Arthit piers (every 30min; 10am–4.30pm). In between (in both directions), these boats call in at Oriental, Si Phraya, Rachawongse, Thien, Maharat (near Wat Mahathat and the Grand Palace) and Wang Lang. On-board guides provide running commentaries, and a one-day ticket for unlimited trips, which also allows you to use other express boats within the same route on the same day, costs B150;

one-way tickets are also available, costing, for example, B30 from Si Phraya to Thien.

CROSS-RIVER FERRIES

Smaller than express boats are the slow **cross-river ferries** (*reua kham fak*), which shuttle back and forth between the same two points. Found at or beside every express-boat stop and plenty of other piers in between, they are especially useful for exploring Thonburi. Fares are generally B3–4, payable at the entrance to the pier.

CANAL BOATS

Longtail boats (*reua hang yao*) ply the canals of Thonburi like commuter buses, stopping at designated shelters (fares are in line with those of express boats), and are available for individual rental here and on the river (see box, p.101). On the Bangkok side, **Khlong Saen Saeb** is well served by passenger boats, which run at least every 15min during daylight hours from the Phan Fah pier at the Golden Mount (handy for Banglamphu, Ratanakosin and Chinatown), and head way out east to Wat Sribunruang, with useful stops at Thanon Phrayathai, aka Saphan Hua Chang (for Jim Thompson's House and Ratchathevi Skytrain stop); Pratunam (for the Erawan Shrine); Thanon Witthayu (Wireless Road); and Soi Nana Nua (Soi 3), Thanon Asok Montri (Soi 21, for TAT headquarters and Phetchaburi subway stop), Soi Thonglo (Soi 55) and Soi Ekamai (Soi 63), all off Thanon Sukhumvit. This is your quickest and most interesting way of getting between the west and east parts of town, if you can stand the stench of the canal. You may have trouble actually locating the piers as few are signed in English and they all look very unassuming and rickety (see map, p.117); keep your eyes peeled for a plain wooden jetty – most jetties serve boats running in both directions. Once on the boat, state your destination to the conductor when he collects your fare, which will be between B10 and B24. Due to the construction of some low bridges, all passengers change onto a different boat at Tha Pratunam – just follow the crowd.

BY SKYTRAIN

Although its network is limited, the **BTS Skytrain**, or *rot fai faa* (W bts.co.th), provides a much faster alternative to the bus, and is clean, efficient and over-vigorously air-conditioned. There are only two Skytrain lines, which interconnect at Siam Square (Central Station). Both run every few minutes from around 6am to midnight, with fares of B15–55 per trip depending on distance travelled. You buy tickets from machines that accept only coins, but you can change notes at staffed counters. You'd really have to be motoring to justify buying a day pass at B120, while the various multi-trip cards are designed for long-distance commuters. The **Sukhumvit Line** runs from Mo Chit (stop N8) in the northern part of the city, via the interchange at Phayathai (N2) with the airport rail line, to Bearing (Soi 105, Thanon Sukhumvit; E14) in around 40min. The **Silom Line** runs from the National Stadium (W1) via Saphan Taksin (Taksin, or Sathorn, Bridge; S6), to link up with the full gamut of express boats on the Chao Phraya River (though there are plans to close down Saphan Taksin Station and build a moving walkway between the river and Surasak Station), to Wongwian Yai (S8) in Thonburi (a continuation to Bang Wa station on Thanon Phetkasem is being built).

BY SUBWAY

Bangkok's underground rail system, the **MRT subway** (or metro; in Thai, *rot fai tai din*; W bangkokmetro.co.th), has similar advantages to the Skytrain, though its current single line connects few places of interest for visitors. It runs every few minutes between around 6am and midnight from Hualamphong train station, via Silom (near Sala Daeng Skytrain station), Sukhumvit (near Asoke Skytrain) and Chatuchak Park (near Mo Chit Skytrain), to Bang Sue train station in the north of the city. Building work is under way to continue the line westwards from Hualamphong to Wat Mangkon Kamalawat in Chinatown, Pahurat, Thanon Sanam Chai in Ratanakosin, then across to Thonburi, the eventual plan being to complete a loop back to Bang Sue. Pay your fare (B15–B40) at a staffed counter or machine, where you'll receive a token to put through an entrance gate (the various day-passes and stored-value cards available are unlikely to be worthwhile for visitors).

BY TAXI

Bangkok **taxis** come in three forms, and are so plentiful that you rarely have to wait more than a couple of minutes

before spotting an empty one of any description. Neither tuk-tuks nor motorbike taxis have meters, so you should agree on a price before setting off, and expect to do a fair amount of haggling.

METERED TAXIS

For nearly all journeys, the best and most comfortable option is to flag down one of Bangkok's metered, a/c **taxi cabs**; look out for the "TAXI METER" sign on the roof, and a red light in the windscreen in front of the passenger seat, which means the cab is available for hire. Starting at B35, fares are displayed on a clearly visible meter that the driver should reset at the start of each trip (say "*poet meter, dai mai khrap/kha?*" to ask him to switch it on), and increase in stages on a combined distance/time formula; as an example, a medium-range journey from Thanon Ploenchit to Thanon Sathorn will cost around B50 at a quiet time of day. Try to have change with you as cabs tend not to carry a lot of money; tipping of up to ten percent is common, though occasionally a cabbie will round down the fare on the meter. If a driver tries to quote a flat fare rather than using the meter, let him go, and avoid the now-rare unmetered cabs (denoted by a "TAXI" sign on the roof). Getting a metered taxi in the middle of the afternoon when the cars return to base for a change of drivers can sometimes be a problem. If you want to book a metered taxi (B20–50 surcharge), try Siam Taxi Co-operative on ☎ 1661 or Taxi Radio on ☎ 1681.

TUK-TUKS

Somewhat less stable though typically Thai, **tuk-tuks** have very little to recommend them. These noisy, three-wheeled, open-sided buggies, which can carry three medium-sized passengers comfortably, fully expose you to the worst of Bangkok's pollution and weather. You'll have to bargain very hard to get a fare lower than the taxi-cab flagfall of B35; for a longer trip, for example from Thanon Convent to Siam Square, drivers will ask for as much as B200. Be aware, also, that tuk-tuk drivers tend to speak less English than taxi drivers – and there have been cases of robberies and attacks on women passengers late at night. During the day it's quite common for tuk-tuk drivers to try and **con** their passengers into visiting a jewellery, tailor's or expensive souvenir shop with them (see p.58).

MOTORBIKE TAXIS

Motorbike taxis generally congregate at the entrances to long sois – pick the riders out by their numbered, coloured vests – and charge from B10 for short trips down into the side streets. If you're short on time and have nerves of steel, it's also possible to charter them for hairy journeys out on the main roads (a short trip from Sanam Luang to Thanon Samsen will cost around B40). Crash helmets are compulsory on all main roads in the capital (traffic police

1

fine non-wearers on the spot), though they're rarely worn on trips down the sois.

CAR RENTAL

You'd be mad to rent a self-drive car for getting around Bangkok, especially as taxis are so cheap, but you may want to start a driving tour around the country here.

Avis 2/12 Thanon Witthayu (Wireless Road), Suvarnabhumi and Don Muang airports (☎ 02 251 1131–2, ⓦ avisthailand.com).

Budget 19/23 Building A, Royal City Avenue, Thanon Phetchaburi Mai, Suvarnabhumi Airport and Don Muang Airport (☎ 02 203 9222, ⓦ budget.co.th).

National 727 Thanon Srinakharin, Suvarnabhumi Airport and Don Muang Airport (☎ 02 722 8487, ⓦ nationalcarthailand.com).

INFORMATION

Bangkok Tourism Division The official source of information on the capital, whose main office is next to Phra Pinklao Bridge at 17/1 Thanon Phra Arthit in Banglamphu (Mon–Fri 8.30am–7pm, Sat & Sun 9am–5pm; ☎ 02 225 7612–4, ⓦ bangkoktourist.com). This is supported by about twenty strategically placed satellite booths around the capital (most daily 9am–5pm, though some closed Sun), including in front of the Grand Palace, at River City and Mah Boon Krong shopping centres, and in front of Banglamphu's Wat Chana Songkhram.

Tourism Authority of Thailand (**TAT**) For advice on destinations further afield, TAT maintains a Tourist Service Centre within walking distance of Banglamphu, at 4 Rajdamnoen Nok (daily 8.30am–4.30pm; ☎ 02 356 0650; freephone tourist assistance 8am–8pm ☎ 1672; ⓦ tourismthailand.org); it's a 20min stroll from Thanon Khao San, or a short ride in a/c bus #503. TAT also has booths at Suvarnabhumi Airport. Note, however, that the many other travel agents, shops and private offices across the capital displaying "TAT Tourist Information" signs or similar are not official Tourism Authority of Thailand information centres and will not be dispensing impartial advice (they may be licensed by TAT to run their business,

but that doesn't make them government information offices). The Tourism Authority of Thailand never uses the acronym TAT on its office-fronts or in its logo, and doesn't book hotels or sell transport tickets.

Listings Listings magazines rise and fall with confusing rapidity in Bangkok; the best of the current publications is the free, weekly *Bk Magazine* (ⓦ bk.asia-city.com) which comes out on Friday and gives a decent rundown of the art and drama scenes, live music and club nights for the week ahead. If you're interested in Bangkok's contemporary art scene, check out ⓦ bangkokartmap.com or pick up a copy of their free, monthly map for exhibition listings.

City maps For a personal guide to Bangkok's most interesting shops, markets, restaurants and backstreets, look for the famously idiosyncratic hand-drawn *Nancy Chandler's Map of Bangkok* and *Nancy Chandler's Map of Khao San and Old Bangkok*. Both carry a mass of annotated recommendations, are impressively accurate and regularly reissued; they're sold in most tourist areas, and copies and interim updates, as well as information about current events in Bangkok, are also available at ⓦ nancychandler.net. Maps are also available for Bangkok's bus routes (see p.118).

ACCOMMODATION

If your time in Bangkok is limited, you should think especially carefully about what you want to do in the city before deciding which part of town to stay in. Traffic jams are so appalling here that easy access to Skytrain, subway or river transport can be crucial. Advance reservations are recommended where possible during high season (Nov–Feb), though some guesthouses will only take cash deposits. For ultra-cheap double rooms under B400, your widest choice lies on and around **Banglamphu's** Thanon Khao San. The most inexpensive rooms here are no-frills crash-pads – small and often windowless, with thin walls and shared bathrooms – but Banglamphu also offers plenty of well-appointed mid-priced options with a/c and swimming pools. Other, far smaller and less interesting travellers' ghettoes that might be worth bearing in mind are the generally dingy **Soi Ngam Duphli**, off the south side of Thanon Rama IV, which nevertheless harbours a couple of decent shoestring options; and **Soi Kasemsan I**, which is very handily placed next to Siam Square and firmly occupies the moderate range, though with a few rooms for B500. Otherwise, the majority of the city's moderate and expensive rooms are scattered widely across the **downtown areas**, around Siam Square and Thanon Ploenchit, to the south of Thanon Rama IV and along **Thanon Sukhumvit**, and to a lesser extent in **Chinatown**. As well as easy access to transport links and shops, the downtown views from accommodation in these areas are a real plus, especially from the deluxe hotels that are scenically sited along the banks of the Chao Phraya River.

BANGLAMPHU

Nearly all backpackers head straight for Banglamphu, Bangkok's long-established travellers' ghetto just north of the Grand Palace, location of the cheapest accommodation,

the best traveller-oriented facilities and some of the most enjoyable bars and restaurants in the city. A growing number of Khao San guesthouses are reinventing themselves as good-value mini-hotels boasting chic decor, swimming pools, and even views from the windows, but the cheap sleeps are still there, particularly immediately west of Khao San, around the neighbourhood temple Wat Chana Songhkram, and along riverside Thanon Phra Arthit – where you'll also find some upscale places offering prime views over the Chao Phraya. About 10min walk north from Thanon Khao San, the handful of guesthouses scattered among the shophouses of the Thanon Samsen sois enjoy a more authentically Thai environment, while the Thewet area, a further 15min walk in the same direction or a 7min walk from the Thewet express-boat stop, is more local still. Heading south from Khao San, across multi-laned Rajdamnoen Klang, to the upscale guesthouses in the area immediately south of Democracy also puts you plumb in the middle of an interesting old neighbourhood, famous for its traditional shophouse restaurants. Theft is a problem in Banglamphu, particularly at the cheaper guesthouses, so don't leave anything valuable in your room and heed the guesthouses' notices about padlocks and safety lockers.

THANON KHAO SAN AND AROUND

Buddy Lodge 265 Thanon Khao San ☎02 629 4477, ⓦ buddylodge.com; map p.90. The most stylish hotel on Khao San and right in the thick of the action. The charming, colonial-style rooms are done out in cream, with louvred shutters, balconies, marble bathrooms, a/c and polished dark-wood floors, though they aren't as pristine as you might expect for the price. There's a beautiful rooftop pool, a spa, a gym, in-room wi-fi and several bars downstairs in the *Buddy Village* complex. Specify an upper-floor location away from Khao San to ensure a quieter night's sleep. Buffet breakfast included. $\overline{B2800}$

Charoendee Boutique Hostel 189 Thanon Khao San ☎02 629 1980, ⓦ charoendee.com; map p.90. Pleasantly surprising compound of pretty, colonial-style edifices with wooden shutters and latticework around a small, plant-strewn courtyard, hemmed in by a mess of surrounding buildings. Bedrooms are light and clean, bathrooms generally small but with hot showers. Good rates available for singles, which are fan-cooled and share bathrooms. Internet access, plus free coffee and toast for breakfast. At the bottom of a narrow alley, so quieter than many. Fan (shared bathroom) $\overline{B450}$, a/c (en-suite) $\overline{B650}$

Donna Guesthouse 75 Thanon Ratchadamnoen Klang ☎02 281 9374; map p.90. Down a tiny alley and hemmed in by other buildings, this friendly, bright, and very clean establishment occupies a cute, white, clapboard house opposite the west wall of Ratchadamnoen post office. Downstairs, the tile-floored, a/c rooms with en-suite cold showers are small but manageable, while upstairs, the seven wood-floored, fan rooms share three cold-water bathrooms. Fan $\overline{B250}$, a/c $\overline{B350}$

Khao San Palace Inn 139 Thanon Khao San ☎02 282

0578, ⓦ khaosanpalace.com; map p.90. Clean and well-appointed hotel, hung with appealing black-and-white photos of Bangkok, with a rooftop pool. Even the cheapest rooms have bathrooms, windows, a/c and satellite TV and are nicely tiled, making them good value, while some have panoramic views. $\overline{B720}$

Shambara 138 Thanon Khao San ☎02 282 7968, ⓦ shambarabangkok.com; map p.90. This calm little hideaway is set down a tiny soi at the eastern end of Khao San and has just nine simple but individually designed fan and a/c rooms, most with windows, sharing two shower rooms and two toilets. Good single rates. Very popular, especially with solo women travellers, so book well ahead. Fan $\overline{B450}$, a/c $\overline{B560}$

WEST: AROUND WAT CHANA SONGKHRAM, PHRA ARTHIT AND THE RIVER

Bella Bella House Soi Ram Bhuttri ☎02 629 3090; map p.90. Above an attractive, plant-strewn café, the pastel-coloured rooms here are no frills but well priced, and a few boast lovely views over Wat Chana Songkhram. The cheapest share cold-water bathrooms, a notch up gets you an en-suite hot shower, while the most expensive have a/c. In-room wi-fi available throughout. Shared bathroom $\overline{B300}$, en suite $\overline{B410}$, a/c $\overline{B490}$

KC Guest House 64 Trok Kai Chae, corner of Thanon Phra Sumen ☎02 282 0618, ⓦ kc64guesthouse.com; map p.90. Friendly, family-run guesthouse offering exceptionally clean, colourful rooms, either en suite (with hot water) or with shared, cold-water bathrooms. There's also a rooftop terrace and a decked eating area on the soi in front of 7-Eleven. Shared bathroom $\overline{B300}$, en suite $\overline{B420}$, a/c $\overline{B520}$

Lamphu House 75 Soi Ram Bhuttri ☎02 629 5861–2, ⓦ lamphuhouse.com; map p.90. With smart bamboo beds, coconut-wood clothes rails, and elegant rattan lamps in all the rooms, this travellers' hotel set round a quiet courtyard has a calm, modern feel. Cheapest fan rooms share facilities and have no outside view, while the triples and four-bed rooms are popular with families. Wi-fi is available throughout. Shared bathroom $\overline{B400}$, en suite $\overline{B520}$, a/c $\overline{B630}$

Navalai River Resort 45/1 Thanon Phra Arthit ☎02 280 9955, ⓦ navalai.com; map p.90. Style-conscious riverfront hotel, with an elegant rooftop pool, modishly furnished rooms, and river views from the most desirable. There's a/c, DVDs, bathtubs, private balconies and free wi-fi throughout, and the excellent riverside *Aquatini* restaurant is at ground level (see p.130). Buffet breakfast included. $\overline{B2900}$

★ **New Siam 2** 50 Trok Rong Mai ☎02 282 2795, ⓦ www.newsiam.net; map p.90. Very pleasant and well-run small hotel whose en-suite rooms with fan and cold shower or a/c and hot shower stand out for their

1

thoughtfully designed extras such as in-room safes, cable TV and drying rails on the balconies. Occupies a quiet but convenient location and has a small streetside pool. Popular with families, and triple rooms are also available. Fan B690, a/c B790

New Siam Riverside 21 Thanon Phra Arthit ☎02 629 3535, ⓦnewsiam.net; map p.90. Occupying a prime riverside spot, the latest in the *New Siam* empire offers well-designed, good-value rooms. Even the cheapest have a/c, full amenities and wi-fi, while the best of them boast fabulous river views from windows or private balconies. Also has a large riverside swimming pool and terrace restaurant. Breakfast included. B1390

Peachy Guest House 10 Thanon Phra Arthit ☎02 281 6471; map p.90. Popular, good-value, long-running Bangkok institution set round a small, late-night courtyard bar. Offers lots of clean, simple, wooden-floored rooms, most with shared bathrooms but some with a/c. Very good rates for singles. Fan and shared bathroom B200, a/c and shared bathroom B300, a/c en suite B400

★ **Praya Palazzo** 757/1 Soi 2, Thanon Somdet Phra Pinklao ☎02 883 2998, ⓦprayapalazzo.com; map p.90. A peaceful riverside sanctuary right opposite Banglamphu, this large, graceful, Italianate mansion has been lovingly restored by an architecture professor, with great attention to detail – right down to the wallpaper and lampshades – to give the feel of its 1920s origins. Twenty-first-century luxuries have been overlaid, of course, such as DVDs, free wi-fi and, in the bathrooms, big-head showers to go alongside the brass taps and swathes of coloured marble. There's a lovely pool in the garden and an excellent restaurant too (see p.130), where complimentary breakfast and afternoon tea are served; a spa is planned. Access is by the free hotel boat, which shuttles across to Phra Arthit express-boat pier (where a satellite hotel office operates in high season) and up to Tha Wasukri (for Dusit) on demand. Discounts for longer stays. B7900

NORTH: SAMSEN SOIS AND THEWET

Lamphu Treehouse 155 Saphan Wanchat, Thanon Phracha Thipatai ☎02 282 0991–2, ⓦlamphu treehotel.com; map p.90. Named after the *lamphu* trees that line the adjacent canal, this attractively turned-out guesthouse offers smart, a/c rooms, all with balconies and plenty of polished teakwood fittings, among other traditional Thai decorative elements. There's a pool, an inviting rooftop terrace, and wi-fi in the lobby. It's in a quiet neighbourhood but just a few minutes' walk from Democracy. Breakfast included. B1450

★ **Old Bangkok Inn** 609 Thanon Phra Sumen ☎02 629 1787, ⓦoldbangkokinn.com; map p.90. This chic little boutique guesthouse with an eco-friendly philosophy has just ten a/c rooms, each of them individually styled in dark wood, with antique northern Thai partitions, Burmese

doors, beds and ironwork lamps, plus elegant contemporary-accented bathrooms. All rooms have a PC with free internet access, and a DVD player. Some also have a tiny private garden. A 10min walk from Khao San. B3200

★ **Phra Nakorn Norn Len** 46 Thewet Soi 1, Thewet ☎02 628 8188, ⓦphranakorn-nornlen.com; map p.90. What was once a seedy short-time motel has been transformed into a bohemian haven with genuine eco-conscious and socially engaged sensibilities and a tangible fair-trade philosophy. Every one of the comfortable, though not luxurious, rooms has been hand-painted to a different retro Thai design, and each has a cute bathroom, balcony, free wi-fi and a/c. Public areas include a kids' play area and a washing machine and dryer; the rooftop enjoys unrivalled views of Wat Indraviharn's huge standing Buddha and is partly given over to growing organic veg for the restaurant. Mostly organic vegetarian breakfast included. B2400

★ **Rajata Hotel** 46 Soi 6, Thanon Samsen ☎02 628 8084, ⓦrajatahotel.com; map p.90. This traditional motel of large bedrooms and bathrooms around a quiet courtyard has been subtly transformed with retro furniture, hundreds of plants and a friendly welcome. All of the shining white, spotlessly clean accommodation has a/c and satellite TV; B200 extra gets you a hot shower, mini-bar and a complimentary breakfast in the courtyard café. Computers available, free wi-fi. B650

Sawatdee 71 Thanon Sri Ayutthaya (at Soi 16), Thewet ☎02 281 0757; map p.90. Cheap and basic, but friendlier than many in the Thewet area, this long-running old-style guesthouse offers no-frills fan rooms with partition walls. Shared bathroom B200, en suite B400

★ **Tavee** 83 Soi 14, Thanon Sri Ayutthaya, Thewet ☎02 280 1447; map p.90. Quiet, friendly guesthouse down a pedestrian alley behind *Sri Ayutthaya Guesthouse*. Beyond the stylish little café, with its chillout music, computers and free wi-fi, the fan rooms sport attractive wood floors and share chic hot-water bathrooms, while the en-suite a/c options are larger and enjoy a few more decorative touches. Fan B450, a/c B700

SOUTH: SOUTH OF DEMOCRACY

★ **The Bhuthorn** 96 Thanon Phraeng Phuthon, just off Thanon Kanlayana Maitri ☎02 622 2270, ⓦthebhuthorn.com; map p.90. The architect-owners have beautifully converted this hundred-year-old shophouse into a B&B. Behind the small lobby lie just three elegant rooms (including a junior suite with a mezzanine for B5000), fitted with Chinese, Thai and Western dark-wood antique furniture, chandeliers, *khon* masks and other *objets d'art*, as well as DVDs and additional modern comforts. Full breakfast (including daily Thai specials), afternoon tea and wi-fi included. B3600

Boonsiri Place 55 Thanon Buranasart ☎02 622 2189,

@boonsiriplace.com; map p.90. Run by two charming sisters, this mid-sized hotel is notable for its good value, environmentally-conscious policies and location in a lively, seedy old neighbourhood, just a 10min walk from the Grand Palace. Each of its 48 large a/c rooms (an extra B200 buys you considerably more space in a "Deluxe" room) is hung with a different painting commissioned from the late Thai traditional temple artist Chanok Chunchob. Wi-fi and computers available. Buffet breakfast included. B1400

RATANAKOSIN AND AROUND

Several small, upmarket hotels have recently opened on the west side of Ratanakosin, which put you in a peerless location, in a quiet, traditional, heavily Chinese neighbourhood of low-rise shophouses, overlooking the river and on the doorsteps of Wat Pho and the Grand Palace. The restaurants and nightlife of Banglamphu are within walking distance if you fancy a bit more of a buzz, while the sights of Thonburi and Chinatown, and Saphan Taksin are just a public boat ride away.

Arun Residence 36 Soi Pratu Nokyung, Thanon Maharat ☎02 221 9158, @arunresidence.com; map p.79. Stunning views of Wat Arun and charming, wooden-floored rooms and suites that mix traditional and contemporary Thai styles. Occupying an eccentrically converted shophouse (plumbing can sometimes be a problem), the hotel also has an attractive lounge with internet access, a rooftop bar and a good European and Thai restaurant, *The Deck*, where breakfast (included in the price) is served. B3500

The Asadang Thanon Atsadang, corner of Thanon Phraya Si ☎085 180 7100, @theasadang.com; map p.79. An early-twentieth-century neoclassical mansion on Ratanakosin's doorstep, this very upscale B&B is perhaps a little truer to Thai roots than its sister, *The Bhuthorn* (see opposite), showcasing antique Thai furniture, carved lintels and attractive local fabrics; it's certainly airier and more spacious, with white wooden walls throughout. If you can manage the narrow, steep spiral staircase (and the higher rate, B4500), plump for the cute roof-top "Ratchabopit" overlooking the eponymous temple, which boasts a rocking chair, full-length windows and a plant-strewn private terrace. Free wi-fi throughout. Full breakfast (including daily Thai specials) included. B3600

Aurum: The River Place 394/27–29 Soi Pansook, Thanon Maharat ☎02 622 2248, @aurum-bangkok .com; map p.79. Modelled on a French townhouse, with wooden shutters and wrought-iron balconies, this spruce, four-storey hotel is set back very slightly from the river and four of the rooms are "City View" only, but the other eight offer at least partial views of the water. Splashed with colourful Thai fabrics and sporting heavily varnished wooden floors, the well-equipped rooms are a little on the small side, apart from those on the top floor. There's free

wi-fi and a daytime riverside café, *Vivi The Coffee Place*, where complimentary breakfast is served. B3700

Chakrabongse Villas 396 Thanon Maharat ☎02 222 1290, @thaivillas.com; map p.79. Upmarket riverside accommodation with a difference: nine tranquil rooms, suites and villas beautifully furnished in a choice of Thai, Chinese and Moroccan styles, set in the luxuriant gardens of hundred-year-old Chakrabongse House overlooking Wat Arun. All have a/c, free wi-fi and cable TV, and there's a small, attractive swimming pool and a riverfront pavilion for relaxing or dining (if ordered in advance). Canoes and bicycles available for guests. B5850

Sala Arun 47 Soi Tha Thien, Thanon Maharat ☎02 622 2932–3, @salaarun.com; map p.79. Sister property to *Arun Residence*, also on the river, two blocks up. The six teak-floored rooms (and one suite) feature objets d'art from the owners' worldwide travels, DVDs, iPod docks and free wi-fi, while complimentary breakfast is served in the boldly coloured ground-floor café, which has computers and a small terrace with armchairs facing Wat Arun. All bedrooms come with balconies and all are the same price, so it's best to avoid city-view "Krungthep" and "Sukhothai". B3500

CHINATOWN AND HUALAMPHONG STATION AREA

Set between the Ratanakosin sights and downtown, Chinatown (Sampeng) is among the most frantic and fume-choked parts of Bangkok – and there's quite some competition. If you're in the mood, however, it's got plenty of interest, sees barely any Western overnighters, and is also very handy for Hualamphong Station, which is on the subway system.

Baan Hualamphong 336/20 Soi Chalong Krung ☎02 639 8054, @baanhualampong.com; map p.96. Just 5min from Hualamphong, this stylish wooden guesthouse is the most welcoming of several similar places in the soi, with a traveller-friendly vibe. There are big, bright, twin rooms plus five-person dorms, but most bedrooms share bathrooms. Has kitchen, internet and laundry facilities, inviting lounging areas and a left-luggage service, and is open 24hr. Very good single rates. Dorm B220, fan double B520, a/c double B720

★ **Shanghai Mansion** 479 Thanon Yaowarat, next to Scala shark's fin restaurant ☎02 221 2121, @shanghaimansion.com; map p.96. The most design-conscious accommodation in Chinatown has embraced the modern Chinoiserie look with gusto. It's not actually an historic mansion, but has been purpose-built on the site of a former Beijing opera house, with most bedrooms (and their windows and private terraces) facing onto an appealing, four-storey atrium, and thus cosily isolated from the Chinatown frenzy. Rooms are prettily done out in silks, lacquer-look furniture and lanterns, featuring a lot of

1

sumptuous reds and purples, as well as a/c, hot showers and free wi-fi. Breakfast included. B2500

SIAM SQUARE, THANON PLOENCHIT AND NORTHERN DOWNTOWN

Siam Square and nearby Thanon Ploenchit are as central as Bangkok gets: all the accommodation listed here is within walking distance of a Skytrain or subway station. On hand are the city's best shopping possibilities – notably the phalanx of malls along Thanon Rama I – and a wide choice of Thai and international restaurants and food courts. There's no ultra-cheap accommodation around here, but a few scaled-up guesthouses complement the expensive hotels. Concentrated in their own small "ghetto" on Soi Kasemsan 1, which runs north off Thanon Rama I, between the Bangkok Art and Cultural Centre and Jim Thompson's House, these offer typical travellers' facilities and basic hotel comforts – a/c and en-suite hot-water bathrooms – at moderate prices; the Khlong Saen Saeb canal-boat pier, Tha Saphan Hua Chang (easily accessed via Thanon Phrayathai), is especially handy for heading west to the Golden Mount and beyond to Ratanakosin.

A-One Inn 25/13 Soi Kasemsan 1, Thanon Rama I ☎02 215 3029 or ☎02 216 4770, ⊕aoneinn.com; map p.105. The original upmarket guesthouse, and still justifiably popular, with a 24hr internet café, wi-fi and a reliable left-luggage room. All bedrooms have fridges and satellite TV and come in a variety of sizes, including triples; discounts for longer stays. B970

★ Four Seasons 155 Thanon Rajdamri ☎02 126 8866, ⊕fourseasons.com; map p.105. The stately home of Bangkok's top hotels, formerly the *Regent*. Afternoon tea is still served in the monumental lobby, which is adorned with magnificent, vibrant eighteenth-century-style murals depicting the Thai cosmology, and flanked by acclaimed Thai, Italian and Japanese restaurants, a steakhouse and an opulent spa by MSpa. The large and luxurious rooms are decorated in warm Thai colours and dark wood, and there's an excellent concierge service. Discounts for longer stays. B8030

Golden House 1025/5–9 Thanon Ploenchit ☎02 252 9535–7, ⊕goldenhousebangkok.com; map p.105. A very clean and welcoming small hotel in a peerless location, down a short soi by Chit Lom BTS. The plain but attractive, parquet-floored bedrooms are equipped with a/c, hot water, cable TV, free wi-fi and mini-bar – ask for one of the larger front rooms with bay windows, which leave just enough space for a couple of armchairs. Breakfast included. Long-term discounts available. B1650

Lub.d 925/9 Thanon Rama I ☎02 612 4999, ⊕lubd .com; map p.105. New branch of the hip, well-run Silom hostel (see opposite), with similar style and facilities (including women-only dorms). It's right on Thanon Rama I, under BTS National Stadium, so handy for just about

everything but rather noisy. Dorm B550, double with shared bathroom B1400, en-suite double B1900

Luxx XL 82/8 Soi Lang Suan ☎02 684 1111, ⊕staywithluxx.com/xl; map p.105. Quietly set back behind *Thang Long* restaurant, this hip boutique hotel (younger, but bigger, brother of the original Silom *Luxx*) shelters large, balconied "Studio" rooms in a seductive contemporary style, all red wood and grey stone. As well as a 13m, infinity-edge, slate pool, all kinds of thoughtful extras are on offer: bicycles for use in nearby Lumphini Park; an honesty bar; and in the rooms, DVD players (with iPod and iPhone connections) and free wi-fi. Discounts for longer stays. B2600

★ Swissôtel Nai Lert Park 2 Thanon Witthayu ☎02 253 0123, ⊕swissotel.com; map p.105. This welcoming, low-rise hotel is distinguished by its lushly beautiful gardens, overlooked by many of the chic and spacious, balconied bedrooms; set into the grounds are a landscaped swimming pool, tennis courts, squash court and popular spa and health club. Good deli-café, cool bar and fine Japanese, French and Chinese restaurants. B4000

Ten Face 81 Soi 2, Soi Ruam Rudee ☎02 695 4242, ⊕tenfacebangkok.com; map p.105. The name comes from Totsagan, the ten-faced demon of the *Ramakien* (see p.451); this place ingeniously combines sleek, contemporary design with striking artworks inspired by the national myth, without being gimmicky. All the rooms are spacious suites with espresso machines, free wi-fi, SIM cards and iPods, some with small kitchens; ask for a room at the back if you're worried about noise from the nearby expressway. There's a fusion restaurant, fitness centre, long, narrow "dipping" pool and shuttle service to Ploen Chit Skytrain, plus a special concierge, who DJs in the ultra-hip *Sita Bar* and dispenses the lowdown on Bangkok parties and happenings. B3200

Wendy House 36/2 Soi Kasemsan 1, Thanon Rama I ☎02 214 1149, ⊕wendyguesthouse.com; map p.105. Friendly and well-run guesthouse, with smart, clean and comfortable rooms, all with fridge, cable TV and free wi-fi. There are internet terminals in the ground-floor café, where breakfast (included in the price) is served. Reliable luggage storage, and long-stay discounts available. B1100

White Lodge 36/8 Soi Kasemsan 1, Thanon Rama I ☎02 216 8867 or ☎02 215 3041, ☎02 216 8228; map p.105. Cheapest guesthouse on the soi, and not always the cleanest, with plain white cubicles and a lively, welcoming atmosphere – the best rooms, bright and quiet, are on the upper floors. B500

DOWNTOWN: SOUTH OF THANON RAMA IV

South of Thanon Rama IV, the area sometimes known as Bangrak contains a full cross section of accommodation. Tucked away at its eastern edge, there are a few cheap

1

places that are worth recommending in the small travellers' ghetto of Soi Ngam Duphli and adjacent Soi Sri Bamphen and Soi Saphan Khu. The neighbourhood is often traffic-clogged and occasionally seedy, but is close to Lumphini Park and subway station and handy for Suvarnabhumi Airport. As well as a fair scattering of medium-range places, the arc between Thanon Rama IV and the river also lays claim to the capital's biggest selection of top hotels, which are among the most opulent in the world. Traversed by the Skytrain, this area is especially good for eating and for gay and straight nightlife, mostly near the east end of Thanon Silom (around which several gay-friendly hotels are scattered). Staying by the river itself in the atmospheric area around Thanon Charoen Krung, also known as New Road, has the added advantage of easy access to express boats.

★ **Anantara Riverside** 257 Thanon Charoennakorn ☎02 476 0022, ⓦanantara.com; map p.117. A luxury retreat from the frenetic city centre, well to the south on the Thonburi bank, but connected to Taksin Bridge (for the Skytrain and Chao Phraya express boats), 15min away, by hotel ferries every 20min. Arrayed around a highly appealing, landscaped swimming pool, the tranquil, riverside gardens are filled with birdsong, while the stylish and spacious bedrooms come with varnished hardwood floors and balconies. There's a fitness centre, tennis courts, kids' club, a branch of the classy Mandara Spas, and among a wide choice of eateries, a good Japanese teppanyaki house. B5900

Baan Saladaeng 69/2 Soi 3, Thanon Saladaeng ☎02 636 3038, ⓦbaansaladaeng.com; map p.110. On a tiny, central alley, this chic designer guesthouse offers eleven individually styled and priced rooms, such as the Pop Art Mania Room and the Moroccan Suite, some with bathtubs and balconies and one with its bath on the balcony. A/c, rain showers, mini-bars, cable TV, comfy beds and free wi-fi throughout. No children. Breakfast included. B1000

ETZ Hostel 5/3 Soi Ngam Duphli ☎02 286 9424, ⓦetzhostel.com; map p.76. Above a branch of the recommended ETC travel agent, and very handy for Lumphini subway and Thanon Rama IV, though consequently a little noisy. Helpful and very clean, the hostel sports a playful contemporary decor in primary colours, a popular roof terrace and a large, attractive lounge with free computers. The a/c dorms share hot showers and fit four to twelve people, or you could upgrade to a bright white double with large, en-suite, hot-water bathroom. Breakfast and luggage storage are available; free wi-fi throughout. Dorm B200, double B900

Lub.d 4 Thanon Decho ☎02 634 7999, ⓦlubd.com; map p.110. Meaning "sleep well" (*lap dii*), this buzzing, upmarket hostel has a/c and hot water throughout and an industrial feel to its stylishly lit decor. This crisp modernity extends to the bedrooms, among which the dorms (some

women-only) and the bunk-bedded "Railway" private rooms share large bathroom areas, while the top-of-the-range en-suite doubles boast TVs. The hostel lays on some interesting activities and tours, and there's free wi-fi throughout, a popular bar and café, washing machines, free storage facilities and free internet terminals, but no kitchen. Dorm B350, "Railway" B1100, double B1500

Luxx 6/11 Thanon Decho ☎02 635 8800, ⓦstaywithluxx.com; map p.110. Welcoming boutique hotel offering a good dose of contemporary style at reasonable prices. Decorated in white, grey and natural teak, the rooms feature DVD players, free wi-fi and cute wooden baths surmounted by rain showers. Discounts for longer stays. Breakfast included. B2200

★ **New Road Guest House** 1216/1 Thanon Charoen Krung, between sois 34 and 36 ☎02 630 9371, ⓦvisitbeyond.com/Thailand; map p.110. Thai headquarters of Danish backpacker tour operator, Visit Beyond, offering a wide choice of accommodation around a courtyard off New Road, as well as a helpful service centre and travel agent, and interesting Thailand tours. There are fan and a/c dorms, as well as "Backpacker" fan rooms with mini-bars and well-equipped, hot-water bathrooms; a/c rooms sport attractive wooden floors, Thai decorative touches and cable TV. Guests can hang out in the restaurant, the sociable bar with pool table or the DVD room; computers, free wi-fi and free baggage storage are available. Dorm B160, fan double B450, a/c double B900

★ **Peninsula Bangkok** 333 Thanon Charoennakorn ☎02 861 2888, ⓦpeninsula.com; map p.110. On the Thonburi bank, with shuttle boats down to Taksin Bridge station. Superb top-class hotel: service is flawless, the ultra-luxurious decor stylishly blends traditional Western and Asian design, and every room has a panoramic view of the Chao Phraya. The lovely riverside gardens shelter a three-tiered pool, a beautiful spa run by ESPA, a fitness centre and tennis courts. B12,500

Rose 118 Thanon Suriwong ☎02 266 8268–72, ⓦrosehotelbkk.com; map p.110. Set back from the main road but very handy for the city's nightlife, this 30-year-old hotel has been cleverly refurbished: the compact rooms (all with bathtubs and wi-fi) now boast a simple but stylish, modernist look, in keeping with the age of the place. The ground-floor public rooms, where breakfast (included in the price) is served, are more elegant again, and there's a beautiful swimming pool (with a small gym and dry saunas) at the back. B2150

★ **Sala Thai Daily Mansion** 15 Soi Saphan Khu ☎02 287 1436; map p.76. The last and best of several budget guesthouses on this quiet, narrow alleyway off Soi Saphan Khu, near Soi Sri Bamphen. A clean and efficiently run place, with bright, cheerful rooms with wall fans, sharing hot-water bathrooms, and a large, leafy roof garden. Decent rates for single rooms. Fan B400, a/c B600

1

★ **Sukhothai** 13/3 Thanon Sathorn Tai ☎ 02 344 8888, ⊛ sukhothai.com; map p.110. The most elegant of Bangkok's top hotels, its decor inspired by the walled city of Sukhothai, offers low-rise accommodation, as well as a beautiful garden spa, all coolly furnished in silks, teak and granite. Service is of the highest standard and the architecture makes the most of the views of the surrounding six acres of gardens, lotus ponds and pools dotted with statuary. There's also a health club, 25m infinity pool, squash and tennis courts, and excellent restaurants including *Celadon* (see p.134). `B9180`

Swan 31 Soi 36, Thanon Charoen Krung ☎ 02 235 9271–3, ⊛ swanhotelbkk.com; map p.110. Next to the stately residence of the French ambassador, this good-value, well-run and welcoming Chinese hotel has successfully upgraded, with regular renovations, to keep up with the times. Arrayed around a 15m pool, the rooms are bright, clean and spacious (though bathrooms in the standard rooms are small), with a/c, hot water, cable TV, mini-bars and armchairs; some have balconies with armchairs. Computers and wi-fi available. Breakfast included. `B1500`

Tarntawan Place Hotel 119/5–10 Thanon Suriwong ☎ 02 238 2620, ⊛ tarntawan.com; map p.110. Set back from the main road, a pretty, flower-strewn lobby announces this welcoming and well-run, gay-friendly hotel. The decent-sized, well-equipped rooms are gracefully furnished in natural colours, with free wi-fi. Guests also receive free breakfast, as well as reduced-price entry to a gym and swimming pool on Soi Thaniya. Discounts for longer stays. `B2900`

THANON SUKHUMVIT

Thanon Sukhumvit is Bangkok's longest road – it keeps going east all the way to Cambodia – but for such an important artery it's far too narrow for the volume of traffic that needs to use it, and is further hemmed in by the overhead Skytrain line that runs above it. Packed with high-rise hotels and office blocks, an impressive array of specialist restaurants (from Lebanese to Lao), and stall after stall selling cheap souvenirs and T-shirts, it's a lively place that attracts a high proportion of single male tourists to its enclaves of girlie bars on Soi Nana Tai and Soi Cowboy. But for the most part it's not a seedy area, and is home to many expats and middle-class Thais. The majority of overnighters are business travellers, though Sukhumvit also has several very good mid-priced guesthouses. Even at the west end of Sukhumvit, many of the sois are refreshingly quiet, even leafy; transport down the longer sois is provided by motorbike-taxi (*mohtoesai*) drivers who wait at the soi's mouth, clad in numbered waistcoats. Hotels further east are quite convenient for Suvarnabhumi Airport but far from the main shopping and eating hubs. Odd-numbered sois run off the north side of Thanon

Sukhumvit, even-numbered off the south side; many of the sois are long enough to have sub-sois running off them, which usually have their own names.

Amari Boulevard Soi 5 ☎ 02 255 2930, ⊛ amari.com; map p.109. At this long-running but modernized four-star tourist hotel, it's worth paying a little extra for a deluxe room to enjoy fine views of the Bangkok skyline and have a bit more space and a DVD player. The attractive sixth-floor rooftop swimming pool and garden terrace becomes the Thai-food restaurant *Season* in the evenings. Substantial discounts in low season. `B3800`

The Atlanta At the far southern end of Soi 2 ☎ 02 252 1650, ⊛ theatlantahotelbangkok.com; map p.109. A Bangkok institution, this classic, five-storey budget hotel was built in 1952 around a famously photogenic Art Deco-style lobby and continues to emphasize an old-fashioned hospitality. It offers some of the cheapest accommodation on Sukhumvit: rooms are plain and simple, though they are all en suite and some have a/c and hot water; many have small balconies. There's a swimming pool and kids' pool in the garden, wi-fi and internet access, a good restaurant and a free left-luggage facility. Fan `B700`, a/c `B800`

The Eugenia 267 Soi 31 ☎ 02 259 9017, ⊛ theeugenia .com; map p.109. This cosy little Relais & Chateaux hideaway of just twelve rooms in a late nineteenth-century mansion re-creates an ambience of old-fashioned Indochinese charm with four-poster beds, freestanding copper bathtubs, mellow colour schemes and a bijou courtyard pool. It's a good 15min walk from BTS Phrom Pong but free hotel transport is offered from here. Discounts for stays of two nights or more. `B6800`

Imm Fusion 1594/50 Thanon Sukhumvit, 30m walk west along Thanon Sukhumvit from BTS On Nut, exit 2, beyond Soi 50 ☎ 02 331 5555, ⊛ immhotel.com; map p.109. Step through the entrance of this attractively themed hotel and you could be in Morocco, with its rich earthy colours, wrought ironwork, pretty tiles and plenty of Moorish arches. Rooms are comfortable and equally tasteful, and come with a/c, hot showers, TV, free wi-fi and breakfast. There's a gorgeous indoor pool, spa and restaurant, and the staff are charming. `B1530`

★ **PS Guesthouse** 26/1 Soi 8 ☎ 02 255 2309, ⊕ psguesthouse@hotmail.com; map p.109. This small, calm, friendly guesthouse offers huge, airy and very well-equipped rooms, each with a/c, hot showers, TV, safety box, fridge, free tea and coffee, and refreshingly green, plant-screened balconies. Pay a little extra for in-room kitchen facilities. Complimentary wi-fi throughout. `B900`

Rex Hotel Between sois 32 and 34 (opposite Soi 49), about 300m west from BTS Thong Lo, exit 2 ☎ 02 259 0106–15, ⊛ rexhotelbangkok.com; map p.109. The best-value accommodation close to the Eastern Bus Terminal (one stop on the BTS), this old-fashioned but attractively refurbished hotel is comfortable and run with an old-world graciousness. A rooftop pool and a restaurant complement the spacious a/c rooms, and rates include breakfast. **B1150**

Seven 3/15 Soi Sawasdee 1, off Soi 31 ☎02 662 0951, ⓦsleepatseven.com; map p.109. A personable welcome and plenty of local advice awaits once you head down the quiet alley to this super-stylish B&B. Bold, cartoon-like murals, as well as DVDs, iPod docks, big-head showers and balconies, enhance the six rooms, which are priced according to size. All include a good, free, continental breakfast, wi-fi, local calls and the loan of a local mobile phone. **B3000**

Suk 11 Behind the 7-Eleven store at 1/33 Soi 11 ☎02 253 5927, ⓦsuk11.com; map p.109. One of the most unusual little hotels in Bangkok, this is also the most backpacker-orientated guesthouse in the area. The interior of the apparently ordinary apartment-style building has been transformed to resemble a village of traditional wooden houses, accessed by a dimly lit plankway that winds past a variety of guest rooms, terraces and lounging areas. The rooms themselves are simple but comfortable, all with a/c, and some are en suite; all showers are hot. It's well run and thoughtfully appointed, provides free breakfast, has pay wi-fi (in the lobby), computers and

washing machines, and stores left luggage (B20/day). Good rates for singles; triples and family rooms also available. Shared bathroom **B749**, en suite **B963**

SUVARNABHUMI AIRPORT

Novotel Suvarnabhumi ☎02 131 1111, ⓦnovotel .com. The official airport hotel, set within the complex and a 10min walk from arrivals via a walkway in the basement (or catch the shuttle bus from outside arrivals Gate 4). Offering smart, contemporary rooms with marble bathrooms, Thai, Japanese, Cantonese and international restaurants, a swimming pool and fitness centre, the *Novotel* operates on a 24hr basis – you can check in at any time, and check out 24hr later. **B6000**

Queens Garden Resort 5min drive from the airport complex, to the north near Highway 7 ☎02 172 6114, ⓦqueensgardenresort.net. Hot water, a/c, mini-bar and satellite TV in all of the plain bedrooms, which include triples and connecting rooms. Facilities include a restaurant, beer garden, pool table, computers and wi-fi. 24-hour pick-ups (B150 each way per room) are available, but a regular metered taxi from the airport will be cheaper, even with the B50 airport tax. **B1000**

EATING

As you'd expect, nowhere in Thailand can compete with Bangkok's diversity when it comes to food: it boasts an astonishing fifty thousand places to eat, almost one for every hundred citizens. Although prices are generally higher here than in the provinces, it's still easy to dine well on a budget. For **Thai** food, the best gourmet restaurants in the country operate from the downtown districts, proffering wonderful royal, traditional and regional cuisines that definitely merit a visit. At the lower end of the price scale, one-dish meals from around the country are rustled up at the **food courts** of shopping centres and department stores, as well as at **night markets** and **street stalls**, which are so numerous in Bangkok that we can only flag the most promising areas. For the non-Thai cuisines, Chinatown naturally rates as the most authentic district for pure **Chinese** food; likewise neighbouring Pahurat, the capital's Indian enclave, is best for unadulterated **Indian** dishes, while there's a sprinkling of Indian and (mostly southern Thai) **Muslim** restaurants around Silom's Maha Uma Devi Temple and nearby Thanon Charoen Krung. Sukhumvit's Soi 3 is a hub for **Middle Eastern** cafés, complete with hookah pipes at the outdoor tables; good, comparatively cheap **Japanese** restaurants are concentrated on Soi Thaniya, at the east end of Thanon Silom; and there's a **t** enclave in Sukhumvit Plaza, at the corner of Soi 12. In the more expensive restaurants listed below you may have to pay a ten percent **service charge** and seven percent VAT.

BANGLAMPHU AND THE DEMOCRACY MONUMENT AREA

Copycat entrepreneurship means that Khao San is stacked full of backpacker restaurants serving near-identical Western and (mostly) watered-down Thai food; there's even a lane, one block east, parallel to Thanon Tanao (behind *Burger King*), that's dominated by vegetarian cafés, following a trend started by *May Kaidee*. Hot-food stalls selling very cheap night-market snacks operate until the early hours. Things are more varied down on Thanon Phra Arthit, with its arty little café-restaurants favoured by Thammasat University students, while the riverside places, on Phra Arthit and further north off Thanon Samsen and in Thewet, tend to be best for seafood with a view. For the real old-fashioned Thai taste

though, browse southern Thanon Tanao, where traditional shophouses have been selling specialist sweets and savouries for generations.

AROUND KHAO SAN

★ **May Kaidee** East off Thanon Tanao ⓦmaykaidee .com; map p.90. Simple, neighbourhood Thai vegetarian restaurant, with two outlets on opposite sides of the soi, that still serves some of the best veggie food in Banglamphu despite having spawned several competitors on the same alley. Come for Western breakfasts or try the tasty green curry, the Vietnamese-style veggie spring rolls or the sticky black–rice pudding with mango or banana. Most dishes B60–70. All-you-can-eat buffet party with Thai dancing on Sat nights (B120). Daily 9am–10pm.

1

THAI COOKERY CLASSES IN BANGKOK
As well as the places listed below, nearly all the luxury hotels in Bangkok offer cookery classes.

Baipai 8/91 Soi 54, Thanon Ngam Wongwan ☎ 02 561 1404, ⓦ baipai.com. Thorough, four-hour classes in a quiet, suburban house in northern Bangkok. B2200, including transfers from central hotels. Closed Sun.

Blue Elephant 233 Thanon Sathorn Tai (BTS Surasak) ☎ 02 673 9353–4, ⓦ blueelephant.com. In a grand, century-old building, courses that range from B3300 for a half-day to a five-day private course for professional chefs for B90,000.

Helping Hands Klong Toey ⓦ cookingwithpoo .com. Set up with the help of a Christian charity, a chance to experience the slums of Klong Toey and spend a morning learning to cook. B1200, including a market tour and free transfers from next to Phrom Pong BTS station. Closed Sun.

May Kaidee 33 Thanon Samsen ☎ 089 137 3173, ⓦ maykaidee.com. Banglamphu's famous vegetarian cook shares her culinary expertise at the Samsen branch of her restaurant chain for B1200 per half-day, including making raw food dishes and a market visit. Also available are shorter "cooking parties" for B600 and special classes such as fruit carving for B1500.

Thai House 22km from central Bangkok in Bangmuang ☎ 02 903 9611 or ☎ 02 997 5161, ⓦ thaihouse.co.th. Set in a rural part of Nonthaburi province, one- (B3800) to three-day (B16,650) cooking courses, all including transfers from downtown, the latter including vegetable and fruit-carving, all meals and home-stay accommodation in traditional wooden houses.

Popiang 43 Soi Ram Bhuttri; map p.90. Popular, friendly place for cheap seafood: mussels cost just B80 per plate, squid B100, or you can get a large helping of seafood noodles for B110. Eat in the low-rent restaurant area or on the street beneath the temple wall. Daily 7am–1am.

Royal India Rambuttri Village complex, 95 Soi Ram Bhuttri ☎ 02 282 6688; map p.90. Branch of the famous Pahurat restaurant (see p.132), by a carp pond in a pleasant courtyard. Daily 6am–midnight.

PHRA ARTHIT AREA
Aquatini *Navalai River Resort*, 45/1 Thanon Phra Arthit ☎ 02 280 9955; map p.90. Occupying a nice wooden deck in a perfect breezy riverfront spot beside the express-boat pier (even better after sunset when the boats stop running), this hotel restaurant does exceptionally good mid-priced Thai food. Seafood's a speciality: the deep-fried ruby fish served with cashew nuts and bell peppers is very good, and their tangy coconut-milk *tom kha kai* soup is especially delicious. Most seafood mains B200–300. Daily 6.30am–1am.

★ **Hemlock** 56 Thanon Phra Arthit ☎ 02 282 7507; map p.90. Small, stylish, a/c restaurant that's very popular with students and young Thai couples. Offers a long and interesting menu of unusual Thai dishes, including banana-flower salad (B95) and several kinds of *laap*. The traditional *miang* starters (shiny green wild tea leaves filled with chopped vegetables, fish, prawn or meat) are also very tasty, and there's a good vegetarian selection. Worth reserving a table on Friday and Saturday nights. Mon–Sat 4–11pm.

Kway Jap Yuan Khun Daeng Thanon Phra Arthit ☎ 085 246 0111; map p.90. This basic, bustling canteen does a roaring trade with Thammasat University students,

who come for the delicious *kway jap yuan*, noodle soup similar to Vietnamese *pho* but a little starchier – go for the version with egg (B40–50) and a baguette (B29) and you're set up for the day. Find it in an historic shophouse, unmistakably painted white and green – colours which the flamboyant owner often sports himself. Mon–Sat 11am–10pm.

★ **Praya Palazzo** 757/1 Soi 2, Thanon Somdet Phra Pinklao ☎ 02 883 2998, ⓦ prayapalazzo.com; map p.90. Superb royal Thai cuisine, using hard-to-find recipes that came out of Rama V's palace. Complex flavours come together in perfect harmony, in roast shrimp dip with crispy catfish, spicy beef soup with shrimp paste, and pork with young aubergines, yellow chilli paste and sour sauce (all B350). Or make the most of the boat ride and the historic architecture of this small garden hotel by coming for afternoon tea (B800), which features delicious Thai sweets alongside sandwiches and scones. Call to make a booking and arrange a free pick-up from Tha Phra Arthit express-boat pier. Daily 11.30am–2pm, 2.30–5pm & 6–9.30pm.

Roti Mataba 136 Thanon Phra Arthit ☎ 02 282 2119; map p.90. Famous 70-year-old outlet for the ever-popular fried Indian breads, or *rotis*, served here in lots of sweet and savoury varieties, including with vegetable and meat curries (from B51), stuffed with meat and veg (*mataba*), and with bananas and condensed milk (from B15); biryanis (*khao mok*) are also on offer. Choose between pavement tables and a basic upstairs a/c room. Tues–Thurs 10am–9pm, Fri–Sun 10am–9.30pm.

THANON SAMSEN AND THE WET
Kaloang Home Kitchen Beside the river at the far western end of Thanon Sri Ayutthaya ☎ 02 281 9228;

OPPOSITE WAT ARUN AT SUNSET (P.100) >

1

map p.90. Flamboyant service and excellent seafood attracts an almost exclusively Thai clientele to this open-air, no-frills, bare-wood restaurant that perches on stilts over the river. Dishes well worth sampling include the fried rolled shrimps served with a sweet dip and any of the host of Thai salads; there's a selection of traditional desserts to finish (you) off with. Most mains are B100–150, more for crab, shrimp and some fishes. Daily 11am–10pm.

Krua Apsorn Thanon Samsen, opposite Thanon Uthong Nok on the southwestern edge of Dusit ☎02 668 8788, ⓦkruaapsorn.com; map p.90. Very good, spicy and authentic food and a genteel welcome make this unpretentious, a/c restaurant popular with the area's civil servants – as well as the royalty whom they serve. Try the green fish-ball curry (B100) or the yellow curry with river prawns and lotus shoots (B110), both recommended by the leading Thai restaurant guide, and put the fire in your mouth out with home-made coconut sorbet. Mon–Sat 10.30am–7.30pm.

May Kaidee 2 33 Thanon Samsen, between the khlong and Soi 1 ⓦmaykaidee.com; map p.90. A/c branch of Banglamphu's best-loved Thai veggie restaurant (see p.129), which also runs vegetarian cookery classes (see p.130). Daily 9am–10pm.

SOUTH: THANON TANAO AND THANON MAHACHAI

Chote Chitr 146 Thanon Phraeng Phuton ☎02 221 4082; map p.90. The word's out about this unreconstructed, 80-year-old, shophouse restaurant of just half-a-dozen tables – it's been featured in the *New York Times* and the *FT*. However, the wide-ranging menu of Thai dishes (most about B100) in large, homely portions is still excellent. The formidable owner will explain what's good today, perhaps a deep-fried whitefish with mango salad (B200). Shame about the pet dogs running around the tables, though. Mon–Sat 11am–9pm.

Kai Yang Boran 474–476 Thanon Tanao, immediately to the south of the Chao Poh Seua Chinese shrine; map p.90. Locally famous grilled chicken (B180 for a small bird) and *som tam* (from B40) restaurant (with a/c), wallpapered with photos of celebrities who have eaten here. *Nam tok* with roast pork and several kinds of *laap* round out the northeastern menu. Daily 8am–9pm.

Padthai Thipsamai 313 Thanon Mahachai (no English sign), near Wat Rajnadda ☎02 221 6280, ⓦthipsamai .com; map p.90. The most famous *phat thai* in Bangkok, flash-fried by the same husband-and-wife team since 1966. The "special" option is huge, comes with especially juicy prawns, and is wrapped in a translucent, paper-thin omelette. Best washed down with fresh coconut juice. Daily except alternate Wed, from 5.30pm until late.

RATANAKOSIN

The places reviewed below are especially handy for sightseers, but there are also plenty of street stalls around Tha Chang and a load of simple, studenty restaurants off the north end of Thanon Maharat near Thammasat University, as well as a decent restaurant at *Arun Residence* and a daytime café at *Aurum* (see p.125).

Navy Club Tha Chang ☎02 222 0081; map p.79. Walk on by the prominent but overpriced *Navy Club 77 Café* on the corner of Na Phra Lan and Maharat roads, to find this place just beyond an ATM on the south side of the express-boat pier, announced by an English sign and a navy guard (don't be put off – anyone can eat here, even farangs). The decor's deeply institutionalized but the real draw is the shaded terrace built over the river, where you can enjoy tasty dried prawn and lemon-grass salad (B120) and other marine delights. Mon–Fri 11am–2pm & 4–10pm, Sat & Sun 11am–10pm.

Rub Ar Roon Opposite Wat Pho at 310–2 Thanon Maharat ☎02 622 2312; map p.79. Among many open-fronted, century-old shophouses on this stretch, this cosy, congenial café used to be a dispensary and still has its original teak cabinets. The Thai food is varied and very reasonably priced, and there are sandwiches (B75–85), espressos, Thai herbal teas and fruit shakes. Daily 8am–6pm.

CHINATOWN AND PAHURAT

Much of the fun of Chinatown dining is in the browsing of the night-time hot-food stalls that open up all along Thanon Yaowarat, around the mouth of Soi Issaranuphap (Yaowarat Soi 11) and along Soi Phadungdao (Soi Texas); wherever there's a crowd you'll be sure of good food. Pan Siam's *Good Eats: Chinatown* map, available from major bookshops, is also a great resource for the weirder local specialities.

Hua Seng Hong 371 Thanon Yaowarat ☎02 222 7053, ⓦhuasenghong.co.th; map p.96. Vibrant, ever-popular, few-frills restaurant, with an open kitchen out front alongside a stall that does a brisk, all-day trade in dim sum. Dishes from around B100, less for noodle soup, more for delicacies such as braised geese's feet. Daily 9am–1am.

Raan Khun Yaa Wat Traimit; map p.96. Just to the right inside the temple's Thanon Mittaphap entrance, this basic, very traditional restaurant, now in its third generation of operation, is especially famous for its delicious and cheap *kaeng khiaw wan neua* (green beef curry; B35), on a menu that otherwise changes daily. Mon–Sat 6am–1pm.

Royal India Just off Thanon Chakraphet at 392/1 ☎02 221 6565; map p.96. Great dhal, perfect parathas and famously good North Indian curries (from around B100), served in a dark little café in the heart of Bangkok's most Punjabi of neighbourhoods to an almost exclusively South Asian clientele. Daily 10am–10pm.

YELLOW-FLAG HEAVEN FOR VEGGIES

Every autumn, for nine days during the ninth lunar month (between late Sept and Nov), Thailand's Chinese community goes on a **meat-free** diet to mark the onset of the Vegetarian Festival (Ngan Kin Jeh), a sort of Taoist version of Lent. Though the Chinese citizens of Bangkok don't go in for skewering themselves like their compatriots in Trang and Phuket (see p.325), they do celebrate the Vegetarian Festival with gusto: some people choose to wear only white for the duration, all the temples throng with activity, and nearly every restaurant and foodstall in Chinatown turns vegetarian for the period, flying small yellow flags to show that they are upholding the tradition and participating in what's essentially a nightly veggie food jamboree. For vegetarian tourists this is a great time to be in town – just look for the yellow flag and you can be sure all dishes will be one hundred percent vegan. Soya substitutes are a popular feature on the vegetarian Chinese menu, so don't be surprised to find pink prawn-shaped objects floating in your noodle soup or unappetizingly realistic slices of fake duck. Many hotel restaurants also get in on the act during the Vegetarian Festival, running special veggie promotions for a week or two.

T&K (Toi & Kid's Seafood) 49 Soi Phadungdao, corner of Thanon Yaowarat; map p.96. Known for their barbecued seafood, with everything from prawns (from B150 a serving) to oysters (B40 each) on offer. Eat at streetside tables or inside with a/c. Daily 4.30pm–2am.

SIAM SQUARE, THANON PLOENCHIT AND NORTHERN DOWNTOWN

In this area, there are also branches of *Taling Pling* (see p.135), on the ground floor of Siam Paragon (☎02 129 4353; daily 11am–10pm) and Floor 3, Central World (☎02 613 1360–1; daily 11am–9.30pm); *Royal India* (see p.132; basement; ☎02 610 7667; daily 10am–10pm) and *Aoi* (see p.134; ground floor; ☎02 129 4348–50; Mon–Fri 11.30am–2.30pm & 5.30–10.30pm, Sat & Sun 11am–10.30pm), both in Siam Paragon; and *Greyhound Café* (see p.136), in the Siam Centre (☎02 658 1129; daily 10am–9pm) and in Central Chidlom department store on Thanon Ploenchit (☎02 255 6964; daily 10am–9pm).

Din Tai Fung Floor 7, Central World ☎02 646 1282, ⓦdintaifung.com.sg; map p.105. Among Central World's fifty-odd restaurants, this attractive and efficient all-day dim sum place stands out, not least because its Hong Kong branch has a Michelin star. Its superb speciality is steamed pork dumplings with clear broth inside each one (B145), but other dishes such as spring rolls with duck and spring onion (B160) are also very tasty. Sit at the big windows overlooking Ratchaprasong or watching the chefs beavering away in the open kitchen. Daily 11am–9pm.

Gianni 34/1 Soi Tonson, Thanon Ploenchit ☎02 252 1619, ⓦgiannibkk.com; map p.105. Probably Bangkok's best independent Italian restaurant, offering a sophisticated blend of traditional and modern in both its decor and food, with main courses starting at around B350. Twice-weekly shipments of artisan ingredients from the old country are used in dishes such as lobster and artichoke risotto and squid-ink spaghetti with clams, prawns and

asparagus. Daily 11.30am–2pm & 6–10pm.

★ **Home Kitchen (Khrua Nai Baan)** 94 Soi Lang Suan ☎02 253 1888, ⓦkhruanaibaan.com; map p.105. Like an upcountry restaurant in the heart of the city, this congenial, unpretentious spot offers a choice between a/c and outdoor tables behind a huge open kitchen. On the inexpensive Thai and Chinese picture menu, you're bound to find something delicious, including dozens of soups – try the *kaeng som*, with shrimp and mixed vegetables, for B150 – six kinds of *laap* and a huge array of seafood. Success has spawned a smarter new branch with the same menu, in an attractive villa just two doors away. Daily 8am–midnight.

Inter 432/1–2 Soi 9, Siam Square; map p.105. Honest, efficient Thai restaurant that's popular with students and shoppers, serving good one-dish meals from B55, as well as curries, soups, salads and seafood, in a no-frills, fluorescent-lit canteen atmosphere. Daily 10am–10pm.

Jin-emon Ground floor, MBK Shopping Centre, near the Pathumwan Princess Hotel ☎02 626 0151; map p.105. Multiculturalism's gone mad at this welcoming Japanese spaghetti house, but the results are very tasty (mains around B100–150). Some of the sauces are frankly weird but they all come on delicious, high-quality pasta, and there are good-value set menus of extras (drinks, garlic bread, salads and the like). Leave room, or – more likely – come back for "big toast", a loaf of bread scooped out and filled with ice cream. Daily 10am–10pm.

Mah Boon Krong Shopping Centre Corner of Rama I and Phrayathai roads; map p.105. Two decent food-courts at the north end of MBK: the long-running area on Floor 6, operating on a coupon system, is a good introduction to Thai food, with English names and pictures of a huge variety of tasty, cheap one-dish meals from all over the country displayed at the various stalls, as well as fresh juices and a wide range of desserts; the upmarket version on Floor 5 is an international affair, spanning India,

Italy, Vietnam, China and Japan, plus vegetarian food at *Tamarind Café* and good moussaka at *Olive*. Floor 6 daily 10am–8.30pm, Floor 5 daily 10am–10pm.

Midnight Kai Ton Unmarked soi between Soi 30 and Soi 32, Thanon Phetchaburi; map p.105. Famous, late-night, anti-hangover refuge that serves just one dish: delicious *khao man kai*, boiled chicken breast with broth, dipping sauces and rice that's been cooked in chicken stock. It'll set you back just B30–40, more if you ask for liver and other innards (*khreuang nai*, literally "the inner workings"). More choice is offered by the string of other popular foodstalls between here and the corner of Phetchaburi and Rajdamri roads. Daily 7pm–4.30am.

Polo Fried Chicken (Kai Thawt Jay Kee Soi Polo) Soi Polo, Thanon Witthayu ☎02 655 8489; map p.105. On the access road to the snobby polo club, this is Bangkok's most famous purveyor of the ultimate Thai peasant dish, fried chicken. All manner of northeastern dishes, including fish, sausages and loads of salads, fill out the menu, but it would be wrong to come to this basic, a/c restaurant and not have the classic combo of finger-licking chicken (B80 for a half), *som tam* and sticky rice. Daily 7am–10pm.

Sanguansri 59/1 Thanon Witthayu (no English sign, but the house number's in Arabic numerals) ☎02 251 9378; map p.105. The rest of the street may be a multi-storey building site but this low-rise, canteen-like old-timer, run by a friendly bunch of middle-aged women, clings on. And where else around here can you lunch on a sweet, thick and toothsome *kaeng matsaman* for B60? It goes well with *kung pla*, a tasty, fresh prawn and lemon-grass salad that can be spiced to order. Mon–Sat 10am–3pm.

Som Tam (Nua) 392/14 Soi 5, Siam Square ☎02 251 4880; map p.105. This basic but lively modern restaurant on a pedestrian alley is a great place to get to know the full range of Thai spicy salads. The house *som tam*, with pork crackling and sausage, goes well with the very tasty deep-fried chicken (B90), or there's northeastern *laap* and *nam tok*, and central Thai *yam* by the dozen. Daily 10.45am–9.30pm.

Thang Long 82/5 Soi Lang Suan ☎02 251 3504, ⊕thanglongsince1987.com; map p.105. Excellent Vietnamese food, such as whole, deep-fried, lemon-grass fish (B275), in this stylish, minimalist and popular restaurant. Eat in the front garden, which is all black stone and ornamental plants, or inside where these motifs are complemented with red wood and brown leather. Daily 11am–2pm & 5–11pm.

Vanilla Brasserie Ground floor, Siam Paragon shopping centre ☎02 610 9383; and *Vanilla Industry*, Soi 11, Siam Square ☎02 658 4720, ⊕vanillaindustry .com; map p.105. Two sophisticated shrines to Western gourmet delights that combine restaurant, patisserie, crêperie, glacier and chocolatier (and in Siam Square, a

cooking school). On offer are delicious parma ham and mascarpone crêpes (B390), salads and other main courses, spot-on desserts, and excellent teas and coffees. Both daily 10am–10pm.

DOWNTOWN: SOUTH OF THANON RAMA IV

Several popular groupings of street stalls are worth noting here: the top end of Thanon Convent, just off Thanon Silom; away to the west opposite the Maha Uma Devi Temple, Silom Soi 20; and the late-night noodle soup stalls on the east end of Thanon Suriwong. In this area, there are also branches of *Baan Khanitha* (see opposite) at 69 Thanon Sathorn Tai, at the corner of Soi Suan Phlu (☎02 675 4200–1; daily 11am–11pm); and *Beirut* (see p.136), in the Silom 64 building, set back off Thanon Silom behind *Sabushi*, opposite the Silom Complex (☎02 266 7150–1; daily 10am–9pm).

★ **Aoi** 132/10–11 Soi 6, Thanon Silom ☎02 235 2321–2, ⊕aoi-bkk.com; map p.110. The best place in town for a Japanese blowout, justifiably popular with the expat community. Excellent authentic food and elegant decor. Good-value lunch bento boxes (from B350) available and a superb sushi bar. Daily 11.30am–2.30pm & 5.30/6pm–10.30/11pm.

★ **Celadon** Sukhothai Hotel, 13/3 Thanon Sathorn Tai ☎02 344 8888; map p.110. Consistently rated as one of the best hotel restaurants in Bangkok and a favourite with locals, serving outstanding traditional and contemporary Thai food – try the banana-flower salad and the red curry with chicken rolls and salted egg – in an elegant setting surrounded by lotus ponds. Daily noon–3pm & 6.30–11pm.

Chai Karr 312/3 Thanon Silom, opposite Holiday Inn ☎02 233 2549; map p.110. Folksy, traditional-style wooden decor is the welcoming setting for a wide variety of well-prepared, modestly priced Thai and Chinese dishes, followed by home-made coconut ice cream and freshly ground coffee. Mon–Sat 11.30am–10pm.

Eat Me 1/6 Soi Phiphat 2, Thanon Convent ☎02 238 0931, ⊕eatmerestaurant.com; map p.110. Justly fashionable art gallery and restaurant in a striking, white, modernist building, with changing exhibitions on the walls and a temptingly relaxing balcony. The eclectic, far-reaching menu features such mains as Tasmanian salmon with salsa verde (B690), and the lemon-grass *crème brûlée* is not to be missed. Daily 3pm–1am.

Harmonique 22 Soi 34, Thanon Charoen Krung, on the lane between Wat Muang Kae express-boat pier and the GPO ☎02 237 8175; map p.110. A relaxing, welcoming, moderately priced restaurant that's well worth a trip: tables are scattered throughout several converted shophouses, decorated with antiques and bric-a-brac, and a quiet, leafy courtyard, and the Thai food is varied and excellent – among the seafood specialities, try the crab (B180) or red shrimp (B85) curries. Mon–Sat 11am–10pm.

Himali Cha-Cha 1229/11 Soi 47/1, Thanon Charoen Krung, south of GPO ☎02 235 1569, ⊛himalichacha .com; map p.110. Fine, moderately priced North Indian restaurant, founded by a character who was chef to numerous Indian ambassadors, and now run by his son. Tasty chicken tikka masala (B195) and a good vegetarian selection, with a homely atmosphere and attentive service. There's also a branch down a short alley off the north end of Thanon Convent (☎02 238 1478; same hours), opposite *Molly Malone's* Irish pub. Daily 11am–3.30pm & 6–10.30pm.

Home Cuisine Islamic Restaurant 186 Soi 36, Thanon Charoen Krung ☎02 234 7911; map p.110. The short, cheap menu of Indian and southern Thai dishes here has proved popular enough to warrant a refurbishment in green and white, with comfy booths, pot plants and a few outdoor tables overlooking the colonial-style French embassy. The *khao mok kai* (B85), a typical hybrid version of a chicken biryani, served with aubergine curry, is delicious. Mon–Sat 11am–10pm, Sun 6–10pm.

Jim Thompson's Saladaeng Café 120/1 Soi 1, Thanon Saladaeng ☎02 266 9167, ⊛saladaengcafe.com; map p.110. A civilized, reasonably priced haven with tables in the elegantly informal a/c interior or out in the leafy garden. The Thai food stretches to one or two unusual dishes such as grilled pork neck with garlic and tamarind dip (B180), and there's pasta, salads and a few other Western dishes. The array of desserts is mouthwatering, rounded off by good coffee and a wide choice of teas. Daily 11am–11pm.

★ **Khrua Aroy Aroy** 3/1 Thanon Pan ☎02 635 2365; map p.110. Aptly named "Delicious, Delicious Kitchen", this simple shophouse restaurant stands out for its choice of cheap, tasty, well-prepared dishes from all around the kingdom, notably *khao soi*, *kaeng matsaman* and *khanom jiin*. Daily 7am–about 8pm, or earlier if the food runs out.

Le Bouchon 37/17 Patpong 2, near Thanon Suriwong ☎02 234 9109; map p.110. Cosy bar-bistro that's much frequented by the city's French expats, offering home-cooking such as lamb shank in a white bean sauce (B580); booking is strongly recommended. Mon–Sat noon–3pm & 6.30–11pm.

Mei Jiang Peninsula Hotel, 333 Thanon Charoennakorn ☎02 861 2888, ⊛peninsula.com; map p.110. Probably Bangkok's best Chinese restaurant, with beautiful views of the hotel's riverside gardens, and very attentive and graceful staff. Cantonese specialities include delicious teas, lobster rolls, smoked duck with tea and excellent lunchtime dim sum such as crystal prawn dumplings, starting at around B100 a dish. Daily 11.30am–2.30pm & 6–10.30pm.

★ **Ramentei** 23/8–9 Soi Thaniya ☎02 234 8082; map p.110. Excellent Japanese noodle café, bright, clean and welcoming, under the same ownership as *Aoi* (see opposite). The open kitchen turns out especially good, huge bowls of miso ramen, which goes very well with the gyoza dumplings. Most dishes B150–200. Daily 11am–2am.

Ruen Urai Rose Hotel, 118 Thanon Suriwong ☎02 266 8268–72, ⊛ruen-urai.com; map p.110. Set back behind the hotel, this peaceful, hundred-year-old, traditional house, with fine balcony tables overlooking the beautiful hotel pool, comes as a welcome surprise in this full-on downtown area. The varied Thai food is of a high quality (though you can forget the house wine): try the *tom khlong talay* (B250) and don't be misled by the name, which means "seafood canal soup" – it's a delicious, refined, spicy and sour soup from the northeast, with tamarind juice and herbs. Daily noon–11pm.

★ **Taling Pling** 60 Thanon Pan ☎02 234 4872; see map p.110. One of the best Thai restaurants in the city outside of the big hotels, specializing in classic dishes from the four corners of the kingdom. The house deep-fried fish salad (B135) is delicious and refreshing, while the toothsome, deeply flavoured green beef curry (B145) with roti is recommended by the leading Thai restaurant guides. The atmosphere's convivial and relaxing, too. Daily 11am–10pm.

★ **Tongue Thai** 18–20 Soi 38, Thanon Charoen Krung, in front of the Oriental Place shopping mall ☎02 630 9918–9; see map p.110. Very high standards of food and cleanliness, with charming, unpretentious service, in a hundred-year-old shophouse elegantly decorated with Thai and Chinese antiques. Veggies are very well catered for with delicious dishes such as tofu in black bean sauce and deep-fried banana-flower and corn cakes, while carnivores should try the fantastic beef curry (*panaeng neua*; B170). Daily 11am–2pm & 5.30–10.30pm.

THANON SUKHUMVIT

In this area, there are also branches of Japanese *Aoi* (see opposite; Floor 4; ☎02 664 8590; daily 11/11.30am–2.30/3pm & 5/5.30–10.30pm) and *Royal India* (see p.132; Floor 5; ☎081 633 0737; daily 10am–10pm), both in the Emporium shopping centre; *Ramentei* Japanese noodle café on Soi 33/1 (see above; ☎02 662 0050; daily 11am–midnight); and the North Indian *Himali Cha-Cha* (see above), on Soi 31 (☎02 259 6677) and at the mouth of Soi 3/1 (☎02 655 6223; both daily 11am–3.30pm & 6–10.30pm). For street food, check out the night market at the mouth of Soi 38 (BTS Thong Lo).

Baan Khanitha 36/1 Soi 23 ☎02 258 4128, ⊛baan -khanitha.com; map p.109. The big attraction at this long-running favourite haunt of Sukhumvit expats is the setting in a traditional Thai house. The food is upmarket Thai and fairly pricey, and includes lots of fiery salads

1

(*yam*), and a good range of *tom yam* soups, green curries and seafood curries. Most mains cost B200–500. Daily 11am–11pm.

Banya 12 Soi 7 ☎ 02 251 6468; map p.109. The decor in this white villa is unexceptional, but it stands out on this section of Sukhumvit because it's spacious (with outdoor tables at the front), quiet and low-rise and offers good, reasonably priced Thai food. Try the spicy green chicken curry with roti (B130) or the zesty Thai mushroom salad with prawns, squid and minced pork (B120). Daily noon–10pm.

★ **Beirut** Basement, Ploenchit Centre, at the mouth of Soi 2 ☎ 02 656 7377; map p.109. It's worth crossing the road from Bangkok's main Middle Eastern ghetto (Soi 3 and Soi 3/1) for the top-notch Lebanese food in this comfortable, a/c restaurant. Among dozens of salads and stuffed breads, the superb *motabel* (*baba ganoush*) is fluffy and smoky, while the falafels are suitably moist inside and crunchy out. These are best sampled on a B280 set menu, which gets you three dishes plus pitta bread. Good baklava, too. Daily 10am–10pm.

★ **Bolan** 42 Soi Pichai Rongnarong, Soi 26 ☎ 02 260 2962, ⓦ bolan.co.th; map p.109. Meticulous and hugely successful attempt to produce authentic traditional food in all its complexity – while upholding the "Slow Food" philosophy – that'll give you a lipsmacking education in Thai cuisine. Delights on the seasonal menu might include duck jungle curry with green banana (B580) and clear soup of jackfruit seed and chicken (B250), or let the chefs design a harmonious "Bolan Balance" menu for you (B1680). In a garden villa with especially attractive veranda tables, 15min walk from Phrom Pong BTS behind *Four Wings Hotel*. Tues–Sun 6pm–late.

Dosa King Soi 11/1, with a back entrance on Soi 11 ☎ 02 651 1700, ⓦ dosaking.net; map p.109. Usually busy with expat Indian diners, this vegetarian Indian restaurant serves good food from both north and south, including over a dozen different *dosa* (southern pancake) dishes, tandooris and the like. It's an alcohol-free zone so you'll have to make do with sweet lassi instead. Most dishes B100–200. Daily 11am–11pm.

Greyhound Café Floor 2, Emporium shopping centre ☎ 02 664 8663, ⓦ greyhoundcafe.co.th; map p.109. Next to a branch of the hip, Thai fashion outlet that owns it, this café clothes itself head-to-toe in black and white industrial chic, including the blackboards advertising regular specials and the shining tablecloths and napkins. The menu is mostly comfort food, such as tasty and well-prepared egg and bacon fried rice with pork soup (B150), plus a few more ambitious, fusion main courses, and some wicked Western and Thai desserts. Daily 11am–10pm.

Le Dalat Indochine 57 Soi 23 (Soi Prasanmitr) ☎ 02 259 9593, ⓦ ledalatbkk.com; map p.109. There's Indochinese romance aplenty at this delightful, re-created

Vietnamese brick mansion decked out with pot plants, plenty of photos and eclectic curiosities. The extensive, high-class Vietnamese menu features favourites such as a *goi ca* salad of aromatic herbs and raw fish (B260) and *chao tom* shrimp sticks on sugar cane (B360). Good-value lunchtime sets. Daily 11.30am–2.30pm & 5.30–10pm.

Soul Food Mahanakorn 56/10 Soi 55 (Soi Thong Lo, Exit 3 from BTS Thong Lo, then it's 100m up the soi on the right) ☎ 02 714 7708, ⓦ soulfoodmahanakorn .com; map p.109. If you already have your favourite stall for *som tam* or *laap*, this is not for you, but if not, this trim, welcoming, American–Thai bistro makes a great introduction to street food from around Thailand, using top-quality ingredients. The beef *khao soi* (curried noodle soup; B180) is thick, creamy and toothsome, and the *som tam* (B140) can be spiced to order. Daily blackboard specials, and a huge selection of creative cocktails. Daily 5.30pm–midnight.

Spring Summer Winter 199 Soi Promsri 1, about 15min walk from BTS Phrom Pong, 700m north up Soi 39 then 350m east along Soi Promsri 1 ☎ 02 392 2747, ⓦ springnsummer.com; map p.109. A fashionable three-in-one experience occupying a pair of chic modernist buildings set round a grassy lawn in a residential soi. *Spring* (dishes from around B300) serves delicious fusion cuisine (Thai with strong influences from Japan and India), with an emphasis on seafood, in dishes such as scrumptiously tangy pomelo and wingbean salad, and fried rice with seared salmon and avocado; *Summer* indulges chocoholics with all manner of treats from frozen tiramisu to cheesecakes and chocolate hotpots; and *Winter* sets up a bar on the lawn in between, with food from *Spring* and *Summer*, and lounging cushions. Spring daily 11.30am–2.30am & 6–11pm; Summer daily noon–midnight; Winter 7pm–midnight, weather permitting.

Suk 11 Soi 11 ☎ 02 253 5468, ⓦ suk11.com; map p.109. Part of the idiosyncratic *Suk 11* guesthouse (see p.129), with which it shares a traffic-free sub-soi, this restaurant also re-creates an atmosphere of old-fashioned village Thailand, with its wooden building, lamplight and plentiful foliage. The food is good, authentic, mid-priced Thai (mostly B100–200), with plenty of spicy *yam* salads, delicious chicken *laap*, tasty *phanaeng* curry plus cocktails and imported wines by the glass. It all adds up to a special occasion ambience, but without the pretension or high prices of its better-known competitors. Daily 3.30–11pm.

★ **Vientiane Kitchen (Khrua Vientiane)** 8 Soi 36, about 50m south off Thanon Sukhumvit ☎ 02 258 6171, ⓦ vientianekitchen.com; map p.109. Just a 3min walk west then south from BTS Thong Lo (Exit 2) and you're transported into a little piece of Isaan, where the menu's stocked full of northeastern delicacies, a live band sets the mood with heart-felt, sometimes overamplified folk songs, and there are even performances by a troupe of traditional dancers (daily at 8pm). The Lao- and Isaan-accented menu (mostly B100–300) includes vegetable soup with ants' eggs, spicy-fried frog, jackfruit curry and snakehead fish (from B300), plus there's a decent range of veggie options

such as *som tam* and sweet and sour dishes, and Thai desserts. With its airy, barn-like interior and mixed clientele of Thais and expats, it's a very enjoyable dining experience. Daily noon–midnight.

DRINKING AND NIGHTLIFE

For many of Bangkok's male visitors, nightfall is the signal to hit the city's sex bars, most notoriously in the area off the east end of Thanon Silom known as Patpong (see p.109). Fortunately, Bangkok's **nightlife** has thoroughly grown up in the past ten years to leave these neon sumps behind, and now offers everything from microbreweries and vertiginous, roof-top cocktail bars to fiercely chic clubs and dance bars, hosting top-class DJs. The high-concept bars of Sukhumvit and the lively, teeming venues of Banglamphu, in particular, pull in the style-conscious cream of Thai youth and are tempting an increasing number of travellers to stuff their party gear into their rucksacks. During the cool season (Nov–Feb), an evening out at one of the seasonal **beer gardens** is a pleasant way of soaking up the urban atmosphere (and the traffic fumes). You'll find them in hotel forecourts or sprawled in front of dozens of shopping centres all over the city, most notably Central World Plaza. Among the city's **club nights**, look out for the interesting regular events organized by Zudrangma Record Store (ⓦzudrangmarecords.com) at venues such as *Cosmic Café* (see p.138), which mix up dance music from all around Thailand and from all over the world. Getting back to your lodgings should be no problem in the small hours: many bus routes run a (reduced) service throughout the night, and tuk-tuks and taxis are always at hand – though it's probably best for unaccompanied women to avoid using tuk-tuks late at night.

BANGLAMPHU

The travellers' enclave of Banglamphu takes on a new personality after dark, when its hub, Thanon Khao San, becomes a "walking street", closed to all traffic but open to almost any kind of makeshift stall, selling everything from fried bananas and buckets of "very strong" cocktails to share, to bargain fashions and one-off artworks. Young Thais crowd the area to browse and snack before piling in to Banglamphu's more stylish bars and indie live-music clubs, most of which are free to enter (though some ask you to show ID first).

Ad Here the 13th (Blues Bar) 13 Thanon Samsen, opposite Soi 2; map p.90. Relaxed, little neighbourhood live-music joint with sociable seats out on the pavement, where musos congregate nightly to listen to Thai and expat blues and jazz bands (from about 9.30pm onwards). Well-priced beer and plenty of cocktails. Daily 6pm–midnight.

Bangkok Bar 100 Thanon Ram Bhuttri ☎02 281 2899, ⓦbkkbar.com; map p.90. By far the most ambitious and best of several live-music places on this street, whose Thai indie-rock bands and DJs – including occasional big-name

appearances – are popular with young locals. In a multi-tiered bar-restaurant around a fountain courtyard, the stage is on the first floor but can also be viewed from the second-floor balconies. B100 including one drink. Daily 6pm–3am.

Brick Bar Buddy Village complex, 265 Thanon Khao San ⓦbrickbarkhaosan.com; map p.90. Massive red-brick vault of a live-music bar whose regular roster of reggae, ska, soul and blues bands, and occasional one-off appearances, are hugely popular with Thai twenty-somethings and teens. Big, sociable tables are set right under the stage and there's food too. The biggest nights are Fridays and Saturdays when there's a B150 entry charge, which includes one free drink. Daily 7pm–1.30am.

Café Democ 78 Thanon Rajdamnoen Klang ⓦcafe-democ.com; map p.90. Fashionable, dark and dinky bar in a turret-like building that overlooks Democracy Monument from its huge windows and is spread over one and a half cosy floors, with extra seating on the semicircular mezzanine. Almost-nightly sessions from Thai and international DJs, sometimes as a warm-up for nearby *Club*

OPENING HOURS AND ID CHECKS

Most bars and clubs in Bangkok are meant to **close** at 1am, while those at the east end of Silom and on Royal City Avenue can stay open until 2am. In previous years, there have been regular "social order" clampdowns by the police, strictly enforcing these closing times, conducting occasional urine tests for drugs on bar customers, and setting up widespread ID checks to curb under-age drinking (you have to be 20 or over to drink in bars and clubs). However, at the time of writing, things were much more chilled, with many bars and clubs staying open into the wee hours on busy nights and ID checks in only a few places. It's hard to predict how the situation might develop, but you'll soon get an idea of how the wind is blowing when you arrive in Bangkok – and there's little harm in taking a copy of your passport out with you, just in case.

1

Culture (see below), plus occasional gigs by up-and-coming Thai bands. By day, it's a relaxed café. Daily 11am/noon–2am.

The Club 123 Thanon Khao San ☎02 629 1010, ⓦ.theclubkhaosan.com; map p.90. High ceilings, an elevated, central DJ station spinning electronic dance music, and state-of-the-art lighting draw a sophisticated young Thai and international crowd. B100 including one drink. Daily 10pm–3am.

Club Culture Unmarked soi just off the south side of Thanon Rajdamnoen Klang, southeast of Democracy Monument ☎089 497 8422, ⓦ club-culture-bkk.com; map p.90. Popular with both Thai and expat hipsters, this converted four-storey shophouse with three separate rooms hosts an assortment of international and local DJs playing house music of all hues, plus techno, electronica, drum'n'bass, as well as live indie bands, depending on the night. Admission depends on what's on but is usually at least B150 including one drink. Wed–Sat 10pm–late.

★ **Hippie de Bar** 46 Thanon Khao San ☎02 629 3508; map p.90. Inviting courtyard bar set away from the main fray, surrounded by graffitied walls, TV screens and its own-brand fashion boutique. Attracts a mixed studenty/arty/hip-hop society, mostly Thai crowd, to drink cheapish beer at its wrought-iron tables and park benches. Indoors is totally given over to kitsch, with plastic armchairs, Donny Osmond posters and ancient TVs. Sun–Thurs 4pm–2am, Fri & Sat 4pm–3am.

Jazz Happens Thanon Phra Arthit ☎02 282 9934, ⓦ facebook.com/jazzhappens; map map p.90. Typical Phra Arthit bar, full of students, with just one small room and a few sociable pavement tables, but what sets this place apart is that some of the students are from Silpakorn University's Faculty of Jazz, playing here in a self-styled jazz commune. Tuck into a decent selection of well-priced cocktails and a short menu of drinking food while you're listening. Daily 7pm–midnight.

Phra Nakorn 58/2 Soi Damnoen Klang Tai ☎02 622 0282; map p.90. Styles itself as "a hangout place for art lovers", and it successfully pulls in the capital's artists and art students, who can admire the floodlit view of the Golden Mount from the rooftop terrace, play pool on the second floor or browse one of the regular exhibitions on the first floor. Daily 6pm–1am.

★ **Taksura** Thanon Tanao ☎02 622 0708; map p.90. This run-down but cinematically lit, hundred-year-old mansion, its wooden shutters flung wide open, is set back but visible from Tanao down a very short alley. Behind the large, sheltered garden, the interior is your archetypal students' common room, with a hodge-podge of retro chairs, indie music on the CD player and reasonably priced drink and food. Daily 5pm–1am.

SIAM SQUARE, THANON PLOENCHIT AND NORTHERN DOWNTOWN

Downtown, Siam Square has much less to offer after dark than Thanon Silom, further south. Out to the northeast, running south off Thanon Rama IX, lies RCA (Royal City Avenue), an officially sanctioned "nightlife zone" that's allowed to stay open until 2am. It's lined mostly with warehouse-like clubs that have a reputation as meat markets, but if there's something interesting on at *Cosmic Café*, it's worth the taxi ride out here.

Coco Walk Thanon Phrayathai; map p.105. It would be hard not to enjoy yourself at this covered parade of loosely interchangeable but buzzing, good-time bars, right beside Ratchathevi BTS. Popular with local students, they variously offer pool tables, live musicians, DJs and cover bands, but all have reasonably priced beer and drinking food. Daily roughly 6pm–1am.

Cosmic Café Block C, Royal City Avenue (RCA) ☎081 304 6907; map, p.117. The look's nothing special, just several floors of bars and a large outdoor terrace, but this place stands out for its imaginative programming, ranging from poetry and art installations to live indie bands and DJs playing anything from ska to *mor lam*. Roughly daily 7pm–2am.

Saxophone 3/8 Victory Monument (southeast corner), just off Thanon Phrayathai ☎02 246 5472, ⓦ saxophonepub.com; map p.76. Lively, easy-going, spacious venue with decent Thai and Western food and a diverse roster of bands – mostly jazz (Mon–Thurs & Sun) and blues (Fri & Sat), plus acoustic guitar, funk, rock and reggae – which attracts a good mix of Thais and foreigners. Daily 6pm–2am.

SOUTHERN DOWNTOWN: SOUTH OF THANON RAMA IV

Most of the action here happens around the east end of Thanon Silom, though a few bars further west lay on great views of the river or the vast cityscape. If, among all the choice of nightlife around Silom, you do end up in one of Patpong's sex shows, watch out for hyper-inflated bar bills and other cons – plenty of customers get ripped off in some way, and stories of menacing bouncers are legion.

The Barbican 9/4–5 Soi Thaniya, east end of Thanon Silom ☎02 233 4141–2, ⓦ greatbritishpub.com; map p.110. Stylishly modern fortress-like decor to match the name: dark woods, metal and undressed stone. With Guinness on tap and a long menu of imported beers, it could almost be a smart City of London pub – until you look out of the windows onto the soi's incongruous Japanese hostess bars. Good food, and happy hours daily 4–7pm. Daily 11am–1am.

O'Reilly's Corner of Silom and Thaniya roads ☎02 632 7515; map p.110. Welcoming Irish bar that's especially good for watching TV sport. Guinness and Kilkenny bitter on draught, multifarious drinks offers including 4–7pm happy hours, popular food and varied live music Tues, Thurs & Fri evenings. Daily 10am–1am.

★ **The Sky Bar & Distil** Floor 63, State Tower, 1055 Thanon Silom, corner of Thanon Charoen Krung ☎02 624 9555; map p.110. Thrill-seekers and view addicts shouldn't miss forking out for an alfresco drink here, 275m above the city's pavements – come around 6pm to enjoy the stunning panoramas in both the light and the dark. It's standing-only at *The Sky Bar*, a circular restaurant-bar on the edge of the building with almost 360° views, but for the sunset itself, you're better off on the outside terrace of *Distil* on the other side of the building (where bookings are accepted), which has a wider choice of drinks, charming service and huge couches to recline on. Daily 5/6pm–1am.

Tapas Bar Soi 4, Thanon Silom ☎02 234 4737; map p.110. Vaguely Spanish-oriented, pricey bar (but no tapas) with Moorish-style decor, whose outside tables are probably the best spot for checking out the comings and goings on this pedestrianized, partly gay soi. In the multi-roomed interior, which stretches up to a third-floor roof terrace, the music is mostly house. Admission pricing policy changes regularly but is currently Fri & Sat B200 including one drink, Sun–Thurs free. Daily 7pm–2am.

★ **Tawandang German Brewery** 462/61 Thanon Rama III ☎02 678 1114–6; map p.110. A taxi-ride south of Chong Nonsi BTS down Thanon Narathiwat Ratchanakharin – and best to book a table in advance – this vast all-rounder is well worth the effort. Under a huge dome, up to 1600 revellers enjoy good food, great micro-brewed German beer and a mercurial, hugely entertaining cabaret, featuring Fong Naam, who blend Thai classical and popular with Western styles of music, as well as magic shows, ballet, hip-hop and dancing. Daily 5pm–1am.

Viva: The River Ground floor, River City shopping centre ☎02 639 6305; map p.110. Recently opened bar, with a lovely terrace on the river and a gnarly interior decor of hide-bound chairs and ships' winches. On offer are some serious cocktails, good coffees and smoothies, as well as breakfasts and comfort food (till midnight) such as gourmet hot dogs, pizzas and salads; chilled DJs play every night, plus occasional live music. Daily 8am–1am.

THANON SUKHUMVIT

A night out on Thanon Sukhumvit could be subsumed by the girlie bars and hostess-run bar-beers (open-sided drinking halls with huge circular bars) on sois Nana and Cowboy, but there's plenty of style on

Sukhumvit too, especially in the rooftop bars and enjoyably trendy clubs.

★ **Bed Supperclub** 26 Soi 11 ☎02 651 3537, ⓦbedsupperclub.com; map p.109. Worth visiting for the futuristic visuals alone, this seductively curvaceous space-pod bar is still the top nightspot in this trendy soi. Inside, the all-white interior is dimly lit and surprisingly cosy, with deep couches inviting drinkers to recline around the edges of the upstairs gallery, getting a good view of the downstairs bar and DJ. The vibe is always welcoming and a lot less pretentious than you might expect; some nights are themed, with regular promotions and international guest DJs. The starker restaurant section serves a global fusion menu, accompanied by lounge DJs and contemporary shows of music, dance and performance art (closed Mon; Fri & Sat set four-course menu). ID required; admission depends on what's on, but is typically B600 including two drinks after 10pm. Bar daily 8pm–2am.

Cheap Charlie's Soi 11; map p.109. Idiosyncratic, long-running, low-tech, open-air bar that's famous for its cheap beer and customers' hall-of-fame gallery. It now offers the luxury of plastic tables and chairs, on a quiet, pedestrianized side-alley. Mon–Sat 5.30pm–midnight.

Long Table Column Tower, 48 Soi 16 ☎02 302 2557–9, ⓦlongtablebangkok.com; map p.109. This achingly fashionable 25th-floor restaurant is named for its 25m-long communal centrepiece table, which seats seventy and serves contemporary Thai cuisine. But the real attraction is the sleek, Shanghai-style open-sided balcony bar whose "long-tail" cocktails give you ample time to lounge glamorously on the leather sofas and soak up the wraparound panoramas across downtown skyscrapers. Daily 5pm–2am.

Q Bar 34 Soi 11 ☎02 252 3274, ⓦqbarbangkok.com; map p.109. Very dark, very trendy, New York-style bar-club occupying two floors and a terrace. Famous for its wide choice of chilled vodkas, and for its music from local and international DJs, *Q Bar* appeals to a mixed crowd of fashionable people, particularly on Fri and Sat nights. Admission price depends on who's on but count on B500 including two free drinks (currently free Mon & Tues); don't turn up in shorts, singlets or sandals if you're male. ID required. Daily 8pm–late.

WTF 7 Soi 51 ☎02 662 6246, ⓦwtfbangkok.com; map p.109. Small, hip, Spanish-influenced bar-café and art gallery, which hosts occasional poetry nights, left-field DJs and gigs. Adorned with luridly coloured Thai film posters and a great soundtrack, it offers tapas (from B70), pizzas and a tempting variety of cocktails and wines. It's 5min walk west of BTS Thong Lo, 100m up Soi 51, near the mouth of a small sub-soi on the left. Tues–Sun 7pm–12.30am.

1

GAY BANGKOK

The bars, clubs and café-restaurants listed here, located around the east end of Thanon Silom and especially in the narrow alleys of Soi 2 and Soi 4, are the most notable of Bangkok's **gay nightlife** venues. More general background on gay life in Thailand, plus contacts and sources of information, most of them concentrated in Bangkok, can be found in Basics (see p.61). Advice on opening hours and on carrying ID is given in Drinking and Nightlife (see p.137).

The Balcony Soi 4, Thanon Silom ☎02 235 5891, ⓦ balconypub.com; map p.110. Unpretentious, fun place with plenty of outdoor seats for people-watching, welcoming staff, reasonably priced drinks, upstairs karaoke and decent Thai and Western food. Happy hour till 8pm. Daily 5.30pm–2am.

Dick's Café Duangthawee Plaza, 894/7–8 Soi Pratuchai, Thanon Suriwong ☎02 637 0078, ⓦ dickscafe.com; map p.110. Elegant day-and-night café-bar-restaurant, with a *Casablanca* theme to the decor (styling itself on Rick's Café Americain). On a traffic-free soi of go-go bars off the north side of Suriwong, it's ideal for drinking, eating decent Thai and Western food or just chilling out. Daily 10.30am–2am.

Disco Disco Soi 2, Thanon Silom; map p.110. Small, pared-down bar-disco with a minimalist, retro feel, playing good dance music to a fun young crowd. Daily 10.30pm–3am.

DJ Station Soi 2, Thanon Silom ☎02 266 4029, ⓦ dj-station.com; map p.110. Highly fashionable but unpretentious three-storey club, packed at weekends, attracting a mix of Thais and farangs; popular cabaret show nightly at 11.30pm. B100 including one drink (B200 including two drinks Fri & Sat). Daily 10.30pm–3am.

GOD (Guys on Display) 60/18–21 Soi 2/1, Thanon Silom, in a small pedestrianized alley between Soi Thaniya and Soi 2 ☎02 632 8033; map p.110. Large, busy club with go-go dancers, somewhat more Thai-oriented and with later hours than *DJ Station*. B150 including one drink. *Diamond* next door is a smart bar-restaurant that's open till 2am. Daily roughly midnight–6am.

JJ Park 8/3 Soi 2, Thanon Silom ☎02 235 1227; map p.110. Classy, Thai-oriented bar, for relaxed socializing rather than raving, with nightly singers and cabaret acts, and a chill-out annexe, *Club Café*, next door. Daily 10.30pm–3am.

Sphinx 98–104 Soi 4, Thanon Silom ☎02 234 7249, ⓦ sphinxpub.com; map p.110. Plush decor with a vaguely Egyptian theme, terrace seating and very good Thai and Western food attract a sophisticated crowd to this ground-floor bar and restaurant; karaoke upstairs at *Pharaoh's* on Fri & Sat. Daily 6pm–1am.

Telephone Pub 114/11–13 Soi 4, Thanon Silom ☎02 234 3279, ⓦ telephonepub.com; map p.110. Bangkok's first Western-style gay bar when it opened in 1987, this cruisy, dimly lit eating and drinking venue has a terrace on the alley, telephones on the tables inside for making new friends and karaoke upstairs. Daily 6pm–2am.

ENTERTAINMENT

On the cultural front, the most accessible of the capital's performing arts is **Thai dancing**, particularly when served up in bite-size portions in tourist shows. **Thai boxing** is also well worth watching: the raucous live experience at either of Bangkok's two main national stadia far outshines the TV coverage.

CULTURE SHOWS AND PERFORMING ARTS

Because of the language barrier, most Thai theatre is inaccessible to foreigners and so, with a few exceptions, the best way to experience the traditional performing arts is at shows designed for tourists, most notably at Siam Niramit. Many tourist restaurants offer low-tech versions of the Siam Niramit experience, in the form of nightly culture shows – usually a hotchpotch of Thai dancing and classical music, with a martial-arts demonstration thrown in; it's always worth calling ahead to reserve, especially if you want a vegetarian version of the set menu. You can, however, witness Thai dancing being performed for its original ritual purpose, usually several times a day, at the Lak Muang Shrine behind the Grand Palace (see map, p.79) and the Erawan Shrine on the corner of Thanon Ploenchit (see p.108). Look out also for the Joe Louis Theatre (ⓦ joelouistheatre.com), an excellent traditional puppet

theatre company who are set to take up residence in 2013 at Asiatique (ⓦ thaiasiatique.com), a new shopping centre on Thanon Charoen Krung, about 2km south of Saphan Taksin on the east bank of the river. For background on Thai classical dance and traditional theatre, see p.48. Meanwhile, more glitzy and occasionally ribald entertainment is the order of the day at the capital's ladyboy cabaret shows.

National Theatre Sanam Luang, Ratanakosin ☎02 224 1342; map p.79. Roughly weekly shows of traditional performing arts such as *khon*, plus twice-monthly medley shows of music, dancing and *lakhon* (classical dance-drama) for tourists and other beginners (usually the first and last Fri of the month at 5pm; B60–100), as well as outdoor shows of classical music and dancing on dry-season weekends. However, it's difficult to get information about what's on in English – try the nearby Bangkok Tourism Division (see p.122).

New Calypso Cabaret Asia Hotel, on the west side of Ratchathevi Skytrain station at 296 Thanon Phrayathai ☎ 02 216 8937, ⓦ calypsocabaret.com; but planning to move to Asiatique shopping centre on Thanon Charoen Krung (ⓦ thaiasiatique.com), about 2km south of Saphan Taksin. A bevy of luscious transvestites don glamorous outfits and perform over-the-top song-and-dance routines. B1200, or B900 if booked online three days ahead. Daily 8.15pm & 9.45pm.

Chalermkrung Theatre (Sala Chalermkrung) 66 Thanon Charoen Krung, on the intersection with Thanon Triphet in Pahurat, next to Old Siam Plaza ☎ 02 224 4499, ⓦ salachalermkrung.com or ⓦ thaiticketmajor .com; map p.96. Mainstream traditional and contemporary theatre, plus regular *khon* performances with English subtitles. Thurs & Fri 7.30pm; from B800.

Siam Niramit 19 Thanon Tiam Ruammit, 5min walk (or a free shuttle ride from Exit 1) from Thailand Cultural Centre subway, following signs for the South Korean embassy ☎ 02 649 9222, ⓦ siamniramit.com; map p.117. Unashamedly tourist-oriented but the easiest place to get a glimpse of the variety and spectacle intrinsic to traditional Thai theatre. The 80min show presents a history of regional Thailand's culture and beliefs in a high-tech spectacular of fantastic costumes and huge chorus numbers, enlivened by acrobatics and flashy special effects. The complex also includes crafts outlets and a buffet restaurant (dinner plus show B1850). Tickets (from B1500) can be bought on the spot, online or through most travel agents. Daily 8pm.

Thailand Cultural Centre Thanon Ratchadapisek ☎ 02 247 0028, ⓦ thaiticketmajor.com; Thailand Cultural Centre subway; map p.117. All-purpose venue, under the control of the Ministry of Culture, that hosts mainstream classical concerts, traditional and contemporary theatre, and visiting international dance and theatre shows.

THAI BOXING

The violence of the average **Thai boxing** match (see p.48) may be off-putting to some, but spending a couple of hours at one of Bangkok's two main stadia can be immensely entertaining, not least for the enthusiasm of the spectators and the ritualistic aspects of the fights. Seats for foreigners cost B1000–2000 (cheaper, standing tickets are reserved for Thais), though at Rajdamnoen the view from the B1000 section is partially obscured. Sessions usually feature ten bouts, each consisting of five three-minute rounds with two-minute rests in between each round, so if you're not a big fan it may be worth turning up an hour late, as the better fights tend to happen later in the billing. To engage in a little *muay thai* yourself, visit one of several gyms around Bangkok that offer classes to foreigners.

Chacrit Muay Thai School Next to Washington Square Theatre on Sukhumvit, between sois 22 and 24 ☎ 02 260 5816, ⓦ chacritmuaythaischool.com; map p.109. Drop-in sessions B800/hr; longer courses available. Closed Sun.

Lumphini Stadium Thanon Rama IV, next to Lumphini subway ☎ 02 251 4303, ⓦ muaythailumpini.com; map p.76. Tues & Fri 6.30pm, Sat 4pm & 8.15pm.

Rajdamnoen Stadium Next to the TAT office on Thanon Rajdamnoen Nok ☎ 02 281 4205; map p.76. Mon, Wed, Thurs & Sun 6.30pm.

Sor Vorapin's Gym 13 Trok Kasap, off Thanon Chakrabongse in Banglamphu ☎ 02 282 3551, ⓦ thaiboxings.com; map p.90. Holds *muay thai* classes twice daily (B500 per session). Sor Vorapin also offers extended training and a homestay at a second gym in Thonburi (B6500 all-in for 1 week) – see the website for details.

SHOPPING

Bangkok has a good reputation for shopping, particularly for antiques, gems, contemporary interior design and fashions, where the range and quality are streets ahead of other Thai cities; silk and handicrafts are good buys too. As always, watch out for **fakes**: cut glass masquerading as precious stones, old, damaged goods being passed off as antiques, counterfeit designer clothes and accessories, pirated CDs and DVDs, even mocked-up international driver's licences (though Thai travel agents and other organizations aren't that easily fooled). Bangkok also has the best English-language bookshops in the country. Downtown is full of smart, multistorey **shopping plazas** like Siam Centre, Siam Paragon and Central World on Thanon Rama I and Emporium on Thanon Sukhumvit, which is where you'll find the majority of the city's fashion stores, as well as designer lifestyle goods and bookshops. The plazas tend to be pleasantly air-conditioned and thronging with trendy young Thais, but don't hold much interest for tourists unless you happen to be looking for a new outfit. Shopping centres, department stores and tourist-oriented shops in the city keep late **hours**, opening daily at 10 or 11am and closing at about 9pm; many small, upmarket boutiques, for example along Thanon Charoen Krung and Thanon Silom, close on Sundays, one or two even on Saturdays. Monday is meant to be no-street-vendor day throughout Bangkok, a chance for the pavements to get cleaned and for pedestrians to finally see where they're going, but plenty of stalls manage to flout the rule.

MARKETS

For travellers, spectating, not shopping, is apt to be the main draw of Bangkok's neighbourhood markets – notably the bazaars of Chinatown and the blooms and scents of Pak Khlong Talat, the flower and vegetable market just west of Memorial Bridge (see p.99). The massive Chatuchak

1

SHOPPING FOR EVERYDAY STUFF

You're most likely to find useful everyday items in one of the city's numerous **department stores**: seven-storey Central Chidlom on Thanon Ploenchit (daily 10am–10pm), which boasts handy services like watch-, garment- and shoe-repair booths as well as a huge product selection (including large sizes), is probably the city's best. For **children's stuff**, Central Chidlom also has a branch of Mothercare, as do the Emporium and Siam Paragon shopping centres. Meanwhile, the British chain of **pharmacies**, Boots the Chemist, has scores of branches across the city, including on Thanon Khao San, in Siam Paragon, in Central World, in Emporium and a late-night branch at the Thanon Suriwong end of Patpong 1.

The best place to buy anything to do with **mobile phones** (see p.67) is the scores of small booths on the third floor of Mah Boon Krong (MBK) Shopping Centre at the Rama I/Phrayathai intersection. For **computer** hardware and genuine and pirated software, as well as digital cameras, Panthip Plaza, at 604/3 Thanon Phetchaburi, is the best place; it's slightly off the main shopping routes, but handy for Khlong Saen Saeb boat stop Tha Pratunam, or a longer walk from BTS Ratchathevi. Mac-heads are catered for here, including authorized resellers, and there are dozens of repair and secondhand booths, especially towards the back of the shopping centre and on the upper floors.

Weekend Market is an exception, being both a tourist attraction and a marvellous shopping experience (see p.112). With the chief exception of Chatuchak, most markets operate daily from dawn till early afternoon; early morning is often the best time to go to beat the heat and crowds.

HANDICRAFTS, TEXTILES AND CONTEMPORARY DESIGN

Samples of nearly all regionally produced handicrafts end up in Bangkok, so the selection is phenomenal. Many of the shopping plazas have at least one classy handicraft outlet, and competition keeps prices in the city at upcountry levels, with the main exception of household objects – particularly wickerware and tin bowls and basins – which get palmed off relatively expensively in Bangkok. Several places on and around Thanon Khao San sell reasonably priced triangular "axe" pillows (*mawn khwaan*) in traditional fabrics, which make fantastic souvenirs but are heavy to post home; some places sell unstuffed versions which are simple to mail home, but a pain to fill when you return. The cheapest outlet for traditional northern and northeastern textiles is Chatuchak Weekend Market (see p.112), where you'll also be able to nose out some interesting handicrafts. Most Thai silk, which is noted for its thickness and sheen, comes from the northeast and the north. However, there is a decent range of outlets in the capital, including many branches of Jim Thompson (see opposite). Bangkok is also rapidly establishing a reputation for its contemporary interior design, fusing minimalist Western ideals with traditional Thai and other Asian craft elements. The best places to sample this, as detailed in the reviews below, are on Floor 4 of the Siam Discovery Centre and Floor 4 of the Siam Paragon shopping centre, both on Thanon Rama I, and Floor 3 of the Gaysorn Plaza on Thanon Ploenchit.

BANGLAMPHU AND RATANAKOSIN

Lofty Bamboo Buddy Hotel shopping complex, 265 Thanon Khao San ⓦloftybamboo.com; map p.90. Fair-trade outlet for Thai crafts, accessories and jewellery, including silver made by Karen people from north and west Thailand and recycled textile products from tsunami-affected communities in Phang Nga. Daily 10.30am–7.30pm.

Queen's Support Foundation Grand Palace (on the right just inside the Gate of Glorious Victory); map p.80. Not-for-profit shop that's especially good for beautiful, top-quality *yan lipao*, traditional basketware made from delicately woven fern stems. Under renovation at the time of writing, but should have reopened by the time you read this.

DOWNTOWN: AROUND SIAM SQUARE AND THANON PLOENCHIT

D & O Shop Floor 3, Gaysorn Plaza ⓦdandoshop .com; map p.105. A dozen enterprising local designers have formed the Design and Objects Association to showcase their diverse contemporary wares here: vases, lamps, tableware, jewellery, bags, stationery. Daily 10am–8pm.

Doi Tung by Mae Fah Luang Floor 4, Siam Discovery Centre ⓦdoitung.org; map p.105. Part of the late Princess Mother's development project based at Doi Tung, selling very striking and attractive cotton and linen in warm colours, made up into clothes, cushion covers, rugs and so on, as well as rustic ceramics. Mon–Thurs 11am–8pm, Fri–Sun 11am–9pm.

Exotique Thai Floor 4, Siam Paragon; map p.105. A collection of small outlets from around the city and the country – including silk-makers and designers from Chiang Mai – that makes a good, upmarket one-stop shop, much more interesting than Narai Phand (see below). There's everything from jewellery, through celadons, to beauty products, with a focus on contemporary adaptations of traditional crafts. Daily 10am–10pm.

Gilles Caffier Floor 4, Siam Discovery Centre ⓦ gillescaffier.com; map p.105. Cushion covers and other items made from leather and hides, plus some frankly uncategorizable, but therefore very striking, objets d'art, from a French designer based in Nakhon Pathom, who has spent time in Japan but takes his influences from around the world. Daily 10am–8pm.

Lamont Contemporary Floor 3, Gaysorn Plaza ⓦ lamont-design.com; map p.105. Beautiful lacquerware bowls, vases and boxes, as well as bronze, glass, crystal and ceramic objects, all in imaginative contemporary styles. Lamont also have a pan-Asian antique and repro shop opposite, and branches in the *Sukhothai* (both contemporary and antique lines), *Oriental* (mostly antiques) and *Four Seasons* (mostly contemporary) hotels. All daily 10am–8pm.

Nandakwang Floor 4, Siam Discovery Centre ☏ 02 658 0407; map p.105. Outlet of a famous cotton company from Pasang in northern Lamphun province, whose main draws are cushion covers (including axe cushions) and bags in sumptuous colours, often featuring floral motifs. Daily 10am–9pm.

Narai Phand Ground floor, President Tower Arcade, just east of Gaysorn Plaza, Thanon Ploenchit ⓦ naraiphand.com; map p.105. This souvenir centre was set up to ensure the preservation of traditional crafts and to maintain standards of quality, as a joint venture with the Ministry of Industry in the 1930s, and has a duly institutional feel, though it makes a reasonable one-stop shop for last-minute presents. It offers a huge assortment of reasonably priced goods from all over the country, including silk and cotton, *khon* masks, *bencharong*, celadon, woodcarving, silver, *yan lipao* basketware and axe cushions. Daily 10am–8pm.

NV Aranyik Floor 3, Gaysorn Plaza ⓦ nv-aranyik.com; map p.105. A good place to buy that chunky, elegant Thai-style cutlery you may have been eating your dinner with in Bangkok's posher restaurants, with both traditional and contemporary handmade designs; plus lovely, handmade stainless-steel bowls. Daily 10am–8pm.

Panta Floor 4, Siam Discovery Centre, and Floor 4, Siam Paragon ⓦ pantathailand.net; map p.105. Modern design store that stands out for its experimental furniture, including way-out-there cushions and other items made of woven rattan, wood and dried water-hyacinth stalks. Discovery daily 10am–9pm; Paragon daily noon–8/9pm.

Thann Native Floor 3, Gaysorn Plaza ⓦ thann.info; map p.105. Striking contemporary rugs, cushion covers and other furnishings, plus famous spa and beauty products (with a high-concept modern spa next door). Daily 10am–8pm.

DOWNTOWN: SOUTH OF THANON RAMA IV

Jim Thompson 9 Thanon Suriwong, corner of Thanon Rama IV; branches at the Jim Thompson House Museum (see p.107), Suvarnabhumi Airport and many department stores, malls and hotels around the city; ⓦ jimthompson.com; map p.110. A good place to start looking for traditional Thai fabric, or at least to get an idea of what's out there. Stocks silk, linen and cotton by the metre and ready-made items from shirts to cushion covers, which are well designed and of good quality, but pricey. They also have a home-furnishings section and a good dressmaking service. A couple of hundred metres along Thanon Suriwong from the main branch, at no. 149/4–6, a Jim Thompson Factory Sales Outlet (daily 9am–6pm) sells remnant home-furnishing fabrics and home accessories at knock-down prices (if you're really keen on a bargain, they have a much larger factory outlet way out east of the centre on Soi 93, Thanon Sukhumvit; daily 9am–6pm). Daily 9am–9pm.

Khomapastr 56–58 Thanon Naret, between Suriwong and Si Phraya ⓦ khomapastrfabrics.com; map p.110. Branch of the famous Hua Hin cotton shop (see p.221). Mon–Sat 9am–5.30pm.

The Legend Floor 3, Thaniya Plaza, corner of Soi Thaniya and Thanon Silom ☏ 02 231 2170; map p.110. Stocks a small selection of well-made Thai handicrafts, from wood and wickerware to pretty fabrics and celadon and other ceramics, at reasonable prices. Daily 11am–8pm.

THANON SUKHUMVIT

The Shop @ TCDC Thailand Creative and Design Centre, Floor 6, Emporium, Thanon Sukhumvit, between sois 22 and 24 ⓦ tcdc.or.th; map p.109. The retail outlet at Bangkok's design centre sells innovative products dreamt up by local creatives, mostly fairly funky stocking-fillers, bags and household items, with just a whiff of kitsch. Tues–Sun 10.30am–9pm.

Thai Celadon Soi 16 (Thanon Ratchadapisek) ⓦ thaiceladon.thailand.com; map p.109. Classic celadon stoneware made in Chiang Mai without commercial dyes or clays and glazed with the archetypal blues and greens that were invented by the Chinese to emulate the colour of precious jade. Mainly crockery, vases and lamps, plus some figurines. Daily 9am–5pm.

TAILORED CLOTHES

Inexpensive tailoring shops crowd Silom, Sukhumvit and Khao San roads, but the best single area to head for is the short stretch of Thanon Charoen Krung between the GPO and Thanon Silom (near the Chao Phraya express-boat stops at Tha Oriental and Tha Wat Muang Kae, or 15min

1

walk from Surasak Skytrain station), where most of the recommended tailors below are. It's generally advisable to avoid tailors in tourist areas such as Thanon Khao San, shopping malls and Thanon Sukhumvit's Soi Nana and Soi 11, although if you're lucky it's still possible to come up trumps here. Prices vary widely depending on material and the tailor's skill. As a very rough guide, for labour alone expect to pay B5000–6000 for a two-piece suit, though some tailors will charge rather more (check whether or not the price you're quoted includes the lining). For middling material, expect to pay about B3000–5000, or anything up to B20,000 for top-class cloth. Special deals offering two suits, two shirts, two ties and a kimono for US$99 should be left well alone.

A Song Tailor 8 Trok Chartered Bank, just round the corner from Tongue Thai restaurant off Thanon Charoen Krung, near the Oriental Hotel ☎02 630 9708; map p.110. Friendly, helpful small shop that's a good first port of call if you're on a budget. Men's and women's suits and shirts; ideally three to four days with two fittings, but can turn work around in two days. Mon–Sat 10am–7.30pm, Sun 8–10am.

Ah Song Tailor 1203 Thanon Charoen Krung, opposite Soi 36 ☎02 233 7574; map p.110. Younger brother of the above (neither of them should be confused with the nearby Ah Sun Tailor), a meticulous tailor who takes pride in his work. Men's and women's suits and shirts in around four days, with two fittings. Mon–Sat 10am–7pm.

Chang Torn 95 Thanon Tanao ☎02 282 9390; map p.90. Well-regarded, traditional tailor in Banglamphu, who prefers ten days to make a suit. Mon–Sat 10am–5pm.

Golden Wool 1340–2 Thanon Charoen Krung ☎02 233 0149, ⓦgolden-wool.com; map p.110. Larger operation than all of the above, which can turn around decent work for men and women in two days, though prices are slightly on the high side. Mon–Sat 9am–8pm.

FASHIONS

Thanon Khao San is lined with stalls selling low-priced fashions: the tie-dyed vests, baggy cotton fisherman's trousers and embroidered blouses are all aimed at backpackers, but they're supplemented by cheap contemporary fashions that appeal to urban Thai trendies as well. Downtown, the most famous area for low-cost, low-quality casual clothes is the warren-like Pratunam Market and surrounding malls such as Platinum Fashion Mall around the junction of Phetchaburi and Ratchaprarop roads (see map, p.105), but for the best and latest trends from Thai designers, you should check out the shops in Siam Square and across the road in the more upmarket Siam Centre. Prices vary considerably: street gear in Siam Square is undoubtedly inexpensive (and look out for outlet stores such as Jaspal's in Emporium), while genuine Western brand names are generally competitive but not

breathtakingly cheaper than at home; larger sizes can be hard to find.

Central World Ratchaprasong Intersection, corner of Rama I and Rajdamri ⓦcentralworld.co.th; map p.105. This shopping centre – recently refurbished after it was torched during the suppression of the red-shirt street protests in 2010 – is so huge that it defies easy classification, but you'll find plenty of Thai and international fashions on its lower floors and in the attached Zen department store at its southern end. Daily 10am–9/10pm.

Emporium Thanon Sukhumvit, between sois 22 and 24 ⓦemporiumthailand.com; map p.109. Enormous and rather glamorous shopping plaza, with its own department store and a good range of fashion outlets, from exclusive designer wear to trendy high-street gear. Genuine brand-name shops include Prada, Chanel, Louis Vuitton, as well as established local labels such as Soda and Jaspal. Daily 10am–8/10pm.

Gaysorn Plaza Thanon Ploenchit ⓦgaysorn.com; map p.105. The most chic of the city's shopping plazas: in among Prada, Emporio Armani and Louis Vuitton, a few Thai names have made it onto the second floor, notably Fly Now, which mounts dramatic displays of women's party and formal gear, alongside more casual wear, and Myth, a gathering of seven cutting-edge local designers for men and women in one store. Daily 10am–8pm.

Mah Boon Krong (MBK) At the Rama I/Phrayathai intersection ⓦmbk-center.co.th; map p.105. Vivacious, labyrinthine shopping centre which most closely resembles a traditional Thai market that's been rammed into a huge mall. It houses hundreds of small, mostly fairly inexpensive outlets, including plenty of high-street fashion shops. Daily 10am–8/9pm.

Siam Centre Thanon Rama I ⓦsiamcenter.co.th; map p.105. Particularly good for hip local labels, many of which have made the step up from the booths of Siam Square across the road – look out for Greyhound, Jaspal and Theatre – as well as international names like FCUK and Quiksilver. Daily 10am–9pm.

Siam Square map p.105. Worth poking around the alleys here, especially near what's styled as the area's "Centerpoint" between sois 3 and 4. All manner of inexpensive boutiques, some little more than booths, sell colourful street-gear to the capital's fashionable students and teenagers.

BOOKS

English-language bookshops in Bangkok are always well stocked with everything to do with Thailand, and most carry fiction classics and popular paperbacks as well. The capital's secondhand bookshops are not cheap, but you can usually part-exchange your unwanted titles.

Asia Books Branches include on Thanon Sukhumvit between sois 15 and 19 (see map p.109), in Times

GEM SCAMS

Gem scams are so common in Bangkok that TAT has published a brochure about it and there are several websites on the subject, including the very informative ⓦ 2bangkok.com/2bangkok -scams-sapphire.html, which describes typical scams in detail. Never buy anything through a tout or from any shop recommended by a "government official"/"student"/"businessperson"/ tuk-tuk driver who just happens to engage you in conversation on the street, and note that there are no government jewellery shops, despite any information you may be given to the contrary, and no special government promotions or sales on gems.

The basic **scam** is to charge a lot more than what the gem is worth based on its carat weight – at the very least, get it **tested** on the spot, ask for a written guarantee and receipt. Don't even consider **buying gems in bulk** to sell at a supposedly vast profit elsewhere: many a gullible traveller has invested thousands of dollars on a handful of worthless multicoloured stones, believing the vendor's reassurance that the goods will fetch at least a hundred percent more when resold at home.

If you're determined to buy precious stones, check that the shop is a member of the **Thai Gem and Jewelry Traders Association**, by visiting their website which has a directory of members (ⓦ thaigemjewelry.or.th). To be doubly sure, you may want to seek out shops that also belong to the TGJTA's **Jewel Fest Club** (ⓦ jewelfest .com), which guarantees quality and will offer refunds; see their website for a directory of members.

Square between sois 12 and 14, and in Emporium between sois 22 and 24; in Peninsula Plaza and in Central World, both on Thanon Rajdamri; in Siam Discovery Centre and Siam Paragon, both on Thanon Rama I; and in Thaniya Plaza on Soi Thaniya off Thanon Silom ⓦ asiabooks.com. English-language bookshop (and publishing house) that's especially recommended for its books on Asia – everything from guidebooks to cookery books, novels to art (the Sukhumvit 15–19 branch has the very best Asian selection). Also stocks bestselling novels and coffee-table books.

Dasa Book Cafe Between sois 26 and 28, Thanon Sukhumvit ⓦ dasabookcafe.com; map p.109. Bangkok's best secondhand bookshop, Dasa is appealingly calm and intelligently, and alphabetically, categorized, with sections on everything from Asia to chick lit, health to gay and lesbian interest. Browse its stock online, or enjoy coffee and cakes in situ. Daily 10am–8pm.

Shaman Books 71 Thanon Khao San, Banglamphu; map p.90. Well-stocked secondhand bookshop where all books are logged on the computer. Lots of books on Asia (travel, fiction, politics and history) as well as a decent range of novels and general-interest books. Daily 10am–11pm.

JEWELLERY AND GEMS

Bangkok boasts the country's best gem and jewellery shops, and some of the finest lapidaries in the world, making this *the* place to buy cut and uncut stones such as rubies, blue sapphires and diamonds. However, countless gem-buying tourists get badly ripped off, so be extremely wary.

Asian Institute of Gemological Sciences 48th floor, Jewelry Trade Center, 919/539 Thanon Silom ☎ 02 267 4325, ⓦ aigsthailand.com; map p.110. Independent professional advice and precious stones certification from its laboratory. Also runs reputable courses, such as a five-day (15hr) introduction to gems and gemology (US$280).

Jewelry Trade Center (Silom Galleria) West end of Thanon Silom ⓦ silomgalleria.net; map p.110. Dozens of members of the Thai Gem and Jewelry Traders Association have outlets in this shopping mall (and on the surrounding streets). Mon–Sat roughly 10.30am–6pm.

Lambert Floor 4, Silom Shanghai Building, Soi 17, 807–9 Thanon Silom ☎ 02 236 4343, ⓦ lambertgems .com; map p.110. Thoroughly reputable, thirty-year-old, American-owned outlet, offering a full service: loose stones and pearls, including collectors' stones, ready-made pieces, cutting, design, redesign and repairs. Mon–Fri 9am–5pm, Sat 9am–4pm.

DIRECTORY

Embassies and consulates Australia, 37 Thanon Sathorn Tai ☎ 02 344 6300, ⓦ thailand.embassy.gov.au; Burma (Myanmar), 132 Thanon Sathorn Nua ☎ 02 234 4789; Cambodia, 518/4 Thanon Pracha Uthit (Soi Ramkamhaeng 39) ☎ 02 957 5851–2; Canada, 15th floor, Abdulrahim Place, 990 Thanon Rama IV ☎ 02 636 0540, ⓦ thailand.gc.ca; China, 57 Thanon Rajadapisek ☎ 02 245 7033 or 02 245 7036; India, 46 Sukhumvit Soi 23 ☎ 02 258 0300–6, ⓦ indianembassy.in.th; Indonesia, 600–602 Thanon Phetchaburi ☎ 02 252 3135–9; Ireland (honorary consul), Room 407, Thaniya Building, 62 Thanon Silom ☎ 02 632 6720, ⓦ irelandinthailand.com; Laos, 502/1–3

1

Soi Sahakarnpramoon, Thanon Pracha Uthit ☎02 539 6667–8 ext 106, ⓦbkklaoembassy.com; Malaysia, 35 Thanon Sathorn Tai ☎02 629 6800; New Zealand, 14th Floor, M Thai Tower, All Seasons Place, 87 Thanon Witthayu ☎02 254 2530; Singapore, 129 Thanon Sathorn Tai ☎02 286 2111; South Africa, Floor 12A, M Thai Tower, All Seasons Place, 87 Thanon Witthayu ☎02 659 2900, ⓦsaembbangkok.com; UK, 14 Thanon Witthayu ☎02 305 8333; US, 120 Thanon Witthayu ☎02 205 4000; Vietnam, 83/1 Thanon Witthayu ☎02 650 8979.

Emergencies For English-speaking help in any emergency, call the tourist police on their free 24hr phoneline ☎1155. The tourist police headquarters is on the eastern edge of town at 2107 Bangkok Tower, Thanon Phetchaburi Mai (east of the Wat Mai Chong Lom stop on the Saen Saeb canal-boat service and well to the east of Phetchaburi subway station; ☎02 308 0333), or drop in at the more convenient Chana Songkhram Police Station at the west end of Thanon Khao San in Banglamphu (☎02 282 2323). In the evenings, you'll also find tourist police at the Silom end of Patpong 1.

Exchange The Suvarnabhumi Airport exchange desks and those in the upmarket hotels are open 24hr, while many other exchange booths stay open till 8pm or later, especially along Khao San, Sukhumvit and Silom roads and in the major shopping malls. You can also withdraw cash from hundreds of ATMs around the city and at the airports.

Hospitals, clinics and dentists Most expats rate the private Bumrungrad International Hospital, 33 Sukhumvit Soi 3 (☎02 667 1000, emergency ☎02 667 2999, ⓦbumrungrad.com), as the best and most comfortable in the city, followed by the BNH (Bangkok Nursing Home) Hospital, 9 Thanon Convent (☎02 686 2700, emergency ☎02 632 1000, ⓦbnhhospital.com); and the Bangkok Hospital Medical Centre, 2 Soi Soonvijai 7, Thanon Phetchaburi Mai (☎02 310 3000, emergency ☎1719, ⓦbangkokhospital.com). You can get vaccinations and malaria advice, as well as rabies advice and treatment, at the Thai Red Cross Society's Queen Saovabha Memorial Institute (QSMI) and Snake Farm on the corner of Thanon Rama IV and Thanon Henri Dunant (Mon–Fri 8.30am–4.30pm, Sat 8.30am–noon; ☎02 252 0161–4 ext 125 or 132, ⓦsaovabha.com). Among general clinics, there's one in Banglamphu in the Rambuttri Village complex on Soi Rambuttri run by the Bangkok Hospital (☎02 629 5260; daily 10am–8pm), and Global Doctor, Ground Floor, Holiday Inn Hotel, 981 Thanon Silom (corner of Thanon Surasak; ☎02 236 8442–4, ⓦglobaldoctorclinic .com), is recommended. For dental problems, try the Bumrungrad Hospital's dental department on ☎02 667 2300; the Dental Hospital, 88/88 Sukhumvit Soi 49 (☎02 260 5000–15, ⓦdentalhospitalbangkok.com); or Siam Family Dental Clinic, 292/6 Siam Square Soi 4 (☎081 987 7700, ⓦsiamfamilydental.com).

Immigration office North of the centre off Thanon Wiphawadi Rangsit at Floor 2, B Building, Government Complex, Soi 7, Thanon Chaengwattana (Mon–Fri 8.30am–noon & 1–4.30pm; ☎02 141 9889, ⓦbangkok .immigration.go.th, which includes a map); see p.60 for information on visa extensions. Be very wary of any Khao San tour agents who offer to organize a visa extension for you: some are reportedly faking the relevant stamps and this has caused problems at immigration.

Internet access Most hotels, an increasing number of guesthouses and a few restaurants and bars offer wi-fi, usually free to customers, sometimes for a fee. For a list of hot spots, try ⓦjiwire.com; for free locations, go to ⓦstickmanweekly.com. Banglamphu is packed with places offering internet access, in particular along Thanon Khao San, where competition keeps prices very low; to surf in a/c style, head for *True*, off the western end of Thanon Khao San (daily 9.30am–11pm). The Ratchadamnoen Post Office on Banglamphu's Soi Damnoen Klang Neua (daily 10am–10pm) has cheap public internet booths. Downtown, the TAT office on the north side of Thanon Ploenchit near Central Chidlom offers cheap surfing (daily 8am–9pm), while the flagship branch of *True* on Floor 3 of Siam Paragon shopping centre, Thanon Rama I, is only a little more expensive and offers wi-fi. Elsewhere in the downtown area, during the day, there are several, rather noisy, places on Floor 7 of the MBK Shopping Centre (Zone D, towards the *Pathumwan Princess Hotel*). There's also an internet centre in the public telephone office on Thanon Charoen Krung (see opposite) and on Floor 3 of the Emporium shopping centre on Thanon Sukhumvit (roughly daily 8am–8pm).

Laundry Nearly all guesthouses and hotels offer same-day laundry services (about B35/kg at a guesthouse, much more at a hotel), or there are several self-service laundries on and around Thanon Khao San.

Left luggage At Suvarnabhumi Airport (B100/day); Don Muang Airport (B75/day); Hualamphong train station (B30–100/day); the bus terminals and most hotels and guesthouses.

Post offices The GPO is at 1160 Thanon Charoen Krung (postcode 10501), near Wat Muang Kae express-boat pier and walkable from Si Phraya pier. Poste restante, which is kept for two months, can be collected here. This and most other services at the GPO are open Mon–Fri 8am–8pm, Sat & Sun 8am–1pm; the parcel-packing service, however, operates Mon–Fri 8am–5pm, Sat 9am–noon. If you're staying on or near Thanon Khao San in Banglamphu, it's more convenient to use the local postal, packing and poste restante services at either Ratchadamnoen Post Office, Soi Damnoen Klang Neua, Bangkok 10200 (Mon–Fri 8am–5pm, Sat 9am–noon); or Banglamphubon PO, Soi Sibsam Hang, Bangkok 10203 (daily 8am–5pm). On Thanon Sukhumvit, use Nana PO, between sois 4 and 6,

Thanon Sukhumvit, Bangkok 10112 (Mon–Fri 8.30am–6pm, Sat, Sun & hols 9am–5pm).

Telephones It's best to buy a Thai SIM card for both international and domestic calls (see p.67), but otherwise there are international cardphones dotted around the city, including at the CAT office in the compound of the GPO on Thanon Charoen Krung (see opposite; Mon–Fri 8am–8pm, Sat & Sun 8am–4pm) which also offers a fax service and a free collect-call service. Many internet cafés have facilities for making cheap or free international calls over the internet.

Travel agents If buying onward international air tickets, be warned that there are many dodgy, transient travel agents in Bangkok, particularly on and around Thanon Khao San, which is known for its shady operators who display fake TAT licences, issue false tickets and flee with travellers' money overnight. The best advice is to use one of the tried and tested agents listed here. Never hand over any money until you've been given the ticket and checked it carefully. Asian Trails, 9th Floor, SG Tower, 161/1 Soi Mahadlek Luang 3, Thanon Rajdamri (☎02 626 2000, ⓦasiantrails.net), sells flights, does interesting Thailand tours and runs scheduled and private transfers to many coastal destinations from Bangkok hotels and the airport; Educational Travel Centre (ETC) sells air and bus tickets, Thailand tours and day-trips, and has offices inside the *Royal Ratanakosin Hotel*, 2 Thanon Rajdamnoen Klang, Banglamphu (☎02 224 0043, ⓦetc.co.th), at 180 Thanon Khao San, Banglamphu (☎02 629 1885), and at 5/3 Soi Ngam Duphli (underneath *ETZ Hostel*), off Thanon Rama IV (☎02 286 9424); *New Road Guest House* (see p.127) is a reliable agent for train, bus and minibus tickets, as well as their own unusual tours; Olavi Travel sells air tickets and budget transport within Thailand and is opposite the west end of Thanon Khao San at 53 Thanon Chakrabongse, Banglamphu (☎02 629 4711–3, ⓦolavi.com); and the Bangkok branch of the worldwide STA Travel is a reliable outlet for cheap international flights and local tours: 14th Floor, Wall Street Tower, 33 Thanon Suriwong (☎02 236 0262, ⓦstatravel.co.th).

The east coast

KO KOOD

The east coast

Just a few hours' drive from the capital, the east-coast resorts attract a mixed crowd of weekending Bangkokians and sybaritic tourists. Transport connections are good and, for overlanders, there are several Cambodian border crossings within reach. Beautiful beaches aren't the whole picture, however, as the east coast is also crucial to Thailand's industrial economy, its natural gas fields and deep-sea ports having spawned massive development along the first 200km of coastline, an area dubbed the Eastern Seaboard. The initial landscape of refineries and depots shouldn't deter you though, as offshore it's an entirely different story, with beaches as glorious as more celebrated southern retreats and enough peaceful havens to make it worth packing your hammock.

The first worthwhile stop comes 100km east of Bangkok at the town of **Si Racha**, which is the point of access for tiny **Ko Si Chang**, whose dramatically rugged coastlines and low-key atmosphere make it a restful retreat. In complete contrast, nearby **Pattaya** is Thailand's number one package-tour destination, its customers predominantly middle-aged European men enticed by the resort's sex-market reputation and undeterred by its lacklustre beach. Things soon look up, though, as the coast veers sharply eastwards towards Ban Phe, revealing the island of **Ko Samet**, the prettiest of the beach resorts within comfortable bus-ride range of Bangkok.

East of Ban Phe, the landscape becomes lusher and hillier around **Chanthaburi**, the dynamo of Thailand's gem trade and one of only two eastern provincial capitals worth visiting. The other is **Trat**, 68km further along the highway, and an important hub both for transport into **Cambodia** via Hat Lek – one of this region's two main border points, the other being Aranyaprathet (see box, p.153) – and for the forty islands of the Ko Chang archipelago. The most popular of this island group is large, forested **Ko Chang** itself, whose lovely, fine beaches have made it Thailand's latest resort destination. A host of smaller, less-developed islands fill the sea between Ko Chang and the Cambodian coast, most notably temptingly diverse **Ko Mak** and **Ko Kood**.

Highway 3 extends almost the entire length of the east coast, beginning in Bangkok as Thanon Sukhumvit, and known as such when it cuts through towns, and hundreds of **buses** ply the route, connecting all major mainland destinations. It's also possible to travel between the east coast and the northeast and north without doubling back through the capital: the most direct routes into **Isaan** start from Pattaya, Rayong and Chanthaburi. Bangkok's Suvarnabhumi Airport is less than 50km from Si

HAT KHLONG PHRAO, KO CHANG

Highlights

❶ Ko Samet This pretty little island, fringed with a dozen or so beaches of fine, dazzlingly white sand, is easy to get to and offers a wide choice of accommodation, though it's suffering a little for its popularity these days. **See p.166**

❷ Trat Welcoming guesthouses and restaurants and an atmospheric old quarter make for a worthwhile stopover on the way to the islands or Cambodia. **See p.176**

❸ Ko Chang Head for Lonely Beach if you're in the mood to party, or to Hat Khlong Phrao,

Ao Bang Bao or Hat Khlong Gloi for progressively more tranquil scenes. **See p.180**

❹ Ko Mak Lovely, lazy, palm-filled island with peaceful white-sand beaches, a welcoming atmosphere and some stylish accommodation. **See p.194**

❺ Ko Kood The real beauty of the east, with some great beaches, Thailand's fourth-largest island is untamed and as yet largely undeveloped. **See p.198**

HIGHLIGHTS ARE MARKED ON THE MAP ON P.152

Racha, and there are two domestic **airports** along the east coast itself: at U-Tapao naval base, southeast of Pattaya, and just west of Trat. Though a rail line connects Bangkok with Si Racha and Pattaya, it is served by just one slow **train** a day in each direction; a branch line makes two journeys a day to Aranyaprathet near the Cambodian border.

Si Racha

The eastbound journey out of Bangkok is not at all scenic, dominated initially by traffic-choked suburban sprawl and then by the industrial landscape of the petrochemical and shipping industries that power Thailand's Eastern Seaboard. The

HIGHLIGHTS
1. Ko Samet
2. Trat
3. Ko Chang
4. Ko Mak
5. Ko Kood

GULF OF THAILAND

0   50
kilometres

THE EAST COAST

CROSSING THE CAMBODIAN BORDER VIA ARANYAPRATHET

The most commonly used overland crossing into **Cambodia** from Thailand is at **Poipet**, which lies just across the border from the Thai town of **Aranyaprathet**, 210km due east of Bangkok. It's best to arm yourself in advance with an e-visa for Cambodia (see p.29) and to make the journey by regular public transport, but it's also possible to buy a package all the way through to Siem Reap and to get a thirty-day visa on arrival at the border, though both of the latter options are more likely to open you up to possible **scams**, including a fake "Cambodian Consulate" in Aranyaprathet and rip-off currency exchange (it's not compulsory to buy riel before entering Cambodia, despite what some touts may say). For further details, see ⓦthaivisa.com for its visa-run forum; and ⓦtalesofasia.com/cambodia-overland.htm for a very detailed description of the crossing and for advice on onward transport into Cambodia. Once you've walked across the border and entered Cambodia, it's about two hours in a taxi or bus to reach Siem Reap, 150km away. If you have the deep misfortune of getting stuck in dusty, dirty Aranyaprathet, where local transport comes in the form of tuk-tuks, try the comfortable fan and a/c rooms at *Inter Hotel* at 108/7 Thanon Chatasingh (☏037 231291, ⓦourweb.info/interhotel; fan B300, a/c B550).

From **Bangkok**, you can travel to Aranyaprathet Station, 4km from the border post, by **train** (2 daily; 6hr); you'll need to catch the 5.55am if you want to get across the border the same day. Return trains depart Aranyaprathet at 6.35am and 1.35pm (5hr 25min–6hr). Alternatively, take a **bus** from Bangkok's Northern (Mo Chit) Bus Terminal to Aranyaprathet (at least hourly; 4hr 30min), or a faster, more expensive a/c minibus from Victory Monument. To reach Aranyaprathet from east-coast towns, the easiest route is to take a bus from Chanthaburi to the town of **Sa Kaew**, 130km to the northeast, and then change to one of the frequent buses for the 55km ride east to Aranyaprathet or the new, direct public buses to Siem Reap.

It's also possible to buy a **through ticket to Siem Reap** from Trat and Ko Chang, or from Thanon Khao San in Bangkok (B200–600), but this option is dogged by scams (including a visa "service charge", described in detail at ⓦtalesofasia.com/cambodia-overland-bkksr-package .htm and on the forum at ⓦthaivisa.com), takes much longer than doing it independently, and nearly always uses clapped-out buses or even pick-ups on the Cambodian side, despite the promised "luxury bus".

first major population centre is the provincial capital of **Chonburi**, whose only notable attraction is its annual October bout of buffalo-racing. Twenty kilometres on, you reach the fast-growing town of **SI RACHA**, a prosperous residential and administrative hub for the Eastern Seaboard's industries and home to a sizeable population of expat families. The town is best known though as the source of *nam phrik Si Racha*, the chilli-laced ketchup found on every kitchen table in Thailand, and as the departure point for the island of **Ko Si Chang** (see p.154). Si Racha's only sight is the Sino–Thai "island temple" of **Wat Ko Loy**, a gaudy hexagon presided over by a statue of the Chinese Goddess of Mercy, Kuan Im, and located on an islet at the end of a 1500m causeway, adjacent to the pier for boats to Ko Si Chang.

ARRIVAL AND DEPARTURE   SI RACHA

BY BUS

Frequent buses pass through Si Racha on their journeys between Bangkok's Eastern (Ekamai) and Northern (Mo Chit) terminals, and Pattaya and Trat further east. They all drop off and pick up near the huge Robinsons/Pacific Park shopping centre on Thanon Sukhumvit in the town centre.

First-class terminal Fast, first-class, dedicated Si Racha–Bangkok buses have their own small terminal a couple of hundred metres south of Robinsons, on the east side of Thanon Sukhumvit, set back slightly from the road next to

Tops supermarket; from here, there are also a/c minibuses to Suvarnabhumi Airport.

Destinations Bangkok (Eastern/Northern bus terminals; every 30min; 1hr 30min–2hr 30min); Chanthaburi (6 daily; 3hr 30min); Pattaya (every 20min; 30min); Trat (6 daily; 5hr).

BY TRAIN

Though a rail line connects Bangkok with Pattaya and Sattahip via Si Racha, it is served by just one slow, third-class, often late, train a day in each direction. The

train station is on the far eastern edge of town, a tuk-tuk ride from the pier for Ko Si Chang.
Destinations Bangkok (daily; 3hr 30min); Pattaya (daily; 30min).

BY BOAT
Ko Si Chang pier, known as Tha Wat Ko Loy, is 2.5km from

Robinsons shopping centre; a motorbike taxi or tuk-tuk will drive you there for B30–50 or, if walking, take any road west towards the sea as far as Thanon Chermchompon (also spelt Jermjompol), then head north up Chermchompon until you reach the junction for the Ko Si Chang pier and Wat Ko Loy. Boats run to Ko Si Chang between 7am and 8pm.
Destinations Ko Si Chang (hourly; 40–50min).

ACCOMMODATION AND EATING

For **eating**, Thanon Si Racha Nakhon 3 is a good place to browse, lined with restaurants and night-time foodstalls, or there's an official night market by the day market and clocktower further south down Thanon Chermchompon.

City Hotel 6/126 Thanon Sukhumvit ☎038 322700, ⓦcitysriracha.com. This high-rise, 200-room hotel, 300m south of Pacific Place, offers smart a/c digs with wi-fi throughout, as well as a gym, a spa, a tennis court, Japanese and international restaurants and a pool. B2825
Sri Wattana Soi Sri Wattana, directly across Thanon

Chermchompon from Thanon Si Racha Nakhon 3, about 500m south of the pier junction ☎038 311037. Very simple, cabin-like en-suite fan rooms, built on a jetty jutting out over the atmospheric but sometimes smelly waterfront, with a pleasant sea-view terrace. B200

Ko Si Chang

The unhurried pace and absence of consumer pressures make small, dry, rocky **KO SI CHANG** an engaging place to get away from it all for a day or two. Unlike most other east-coast destinations, it offers no real beach life – it's a populous, working island with a deep-sea port, rather than a tropical idyll – and there's little to do here but explore the craggy coastline by kayak or ramble up and down its steep, scrubby contours on foot or by motorbike. The island is famous as the location of one of Rama V's summer palaces, a few parts of which have been restored, and of a popular Chinese pilgrimage temple, as well as for its rare white squirrels, which live in the wooded patches inland.

Rama V's Palace

Hat Tha Wang • Tues–Sun 9am–5pm • Free

The most famous sight on the island is **Rama V's Palace**, which occupies a large chunk of gently sloping land midway down the east coast, behind pebbly **Hat Tha Wang**. It's an enjoyable place to explore and can be reached on foot from *Tiew Pai Park Resort* in about half an hour. Shortly before reaching the palace ruins, you'll pass the small and less than riveting **Cholatassathan Museum**, established by the resident Aquatic Resources Research Institute to provide an introduction to the coral and marine life around Ko Si Chang.

Built in the 1890s as a sort of health resort for sickly royals, the palace (also known as **Phra Judhadhut Ratchathan**) formed the heart of an extensive complex comprising

KO SI CHANG FESTIVALS

Ko Si Chang celebrates three particularly interesting festivals. **Songkhran** is marked from April 17 to 19 with sandcastle-building, greasy-pole-climbing and an exorcism ritual for any islanders who have suffered unpleasant deaths over the previous year. At **Visakha Puja**, the full-moon day in May when Buddha's birth, death and enlightenment are honoured, islanders process to the old palace with hand-crafted Chinese lanterns. And on September 20, Ko Si Chang honours its royal patron **King Chulalongkorn**'s birthday with a *son et lumière* in the palace grounds and a beauty contest staged entirely in costumes from the Chulalongkorn era.

homes for royal advisers, chalets for convalescents, quarters for royal concubines and administrative buildings. By the turn of the twentieth century, however, Rama V (King Chulalongkorn) had lost interest in his island project and so in 1901 his golden teak palace was moved piece by piece to Bangkok, and reconstructed there as Vimanmek Palace; its foundations are still visible just south of the palace's Saphan Asadang pier. Following recent renovations, the elegant design of the palace grounds is apparent once more. They fan out around an elaborate labyrinth of fifty interlinked ponds and a maze of stone steps and balustrades that still cling to the shallow hillside. Close to the shore, four of the original Western-style **villas** have been reconstructed to house displays, of varying interest, on Chulalongkorn's relationship with Ko Si Chang; one of them also doubles as a weekend coffee shop. Inland, signs direct you up the hillside to the palace's unusual whitewashed shrine, **Wat Asadang**, whose circular walls are punctuated with Gothic stained-glass windows and surmounted by a chedi.

Hat Tham Pang and Ko Khang Khao

The main beach on the west coast, and the most popular one on the island, is **Hat Tham Pang**. It's a tiny patch of sand, backed by shoulder-to-shoulder umbrellas and deckchairs belonging to the basic beach restaurants; you can rent snorkels and kayaks here too. The best **snorkelling** spots are further south, around the tiny islands off Ko Si Chang's southern tip, particularly off the north coast of **Ko Khang Khao**, forty minutes by kayak from Hat Tham Pang.

Wat Tham Yai Prik

Accessible via a fork off Thanon Asadang opposite *Tiew Pai* (10min walk)

The **Wat Tham Yai Prik** temple and meditation centre is open to interested visitors and meditators. Unusually, nuns as well as monks here wear brown (rather than white) and everyone participates in the upkeep of the monastery: you can see some of the fruits of their labour in the extensive roadside orchard. Just west of the wat lies the pretty, rocky cove known as **Hat Tham** or **Hat Sai**, which is only really swimmable at low tide.

Khao Khat

On the northwest trajectory of the ring road, you'll pass beneath the gaze of a huge yellow Buddha before reaching the rocky northwest headland of **Khao Khat**, a few hundred metres further on. The uninterrupted panorama of open sea makes this a classic sunset spot, and there's a path along the cliffside.

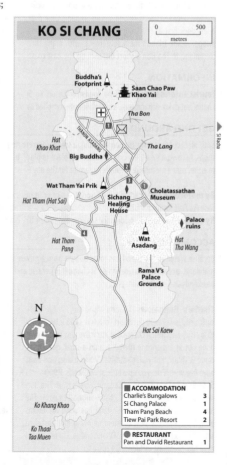

KO SI CHANG

0 — 500 metres

Buddha's Footprint
Saan Chao Paw Khao Yai
Tha Bon
THANON ASADANG
Hat Khao Khat
Tha Lang
Si Racha
Big Buddha
Wat Tham Yai Prik
Sichang Healing House
Cholatassathan Museum
Hat Tham (Hat Sai)
Palace ruins
Hat Tham Pang
Wat Asadang
Hat Tha Wang
Rama V's Palace Grounds
N
Hat Sai Kaew
Ko Khang Khao
Ko Thaai Taa Muen

■ ACCOMMODATION	
Charlie's Bungalows	3
Si Chang Palace	1
Tham Pang Beach	4
Tiew Pai Park Resort	2

● RESTAURANT	
Pan and David Restaurant	1

Saan Chao Paw Khao Yai

The showy, multi-tiered Chinese temple of **Saan Chao Paw Khao Yai** (Shrine of the Father Spirit of the Great Hill) is stationed at the top of a steep flight of steps and commands a good view of the harbour and the mainland coast. Established here long before Rama V arrived on the island, the shrine was dedicated by Chinese seamen who saw a strange light coming out of one of the **caves** behind the modern-day temple. The caves, now full of religious statues and related paraphernalia, are visited by boatloads of Chinese pilgrims, particularly over Chinese New Year. Continue on up the cliffside to reach the small pagoda built for Rama V and enshrining a **Buddha's Footprint**. Two very long, very steep flights of stairs give access to the footprint: the easternmost one starts at the main waterfront entrance to the Chinese temple and takes you past a cluster of monks' meditation cells, while the westerly one rises further west along the ring road and offers the finest lookouts.

ARRIVAL AND DEPARTURE   KO SI CHANG

By boat Ferries to Ko Si Chang leave from Tha Wat Ko Loy in Si Racha (see p.154) from 7am to 8pm (B40), wending their way past the congestion of international cargo boats and Thai supply barges that anchor in the protected channel between the mainland and Ko Si Chang. On arrival, boats dock first at Tha Lang (also signed as Tateawavong Bridge) in the island's main settlement, with many then continuing to Tha Bon a short distance up the east coast.

Motorized samlor drivers meet the boats and charge B40 to most accommodation, or B80 to Hat Tham Pang; as they are paid commission by some hotels and restaurants, be wary of any opinionated remarks. Boats to the mainland leave Tha Lang between 6am and 7pm; the same boats depart Tha Bon 15min earlier.

Destinations Si Racha (hourly; 40–50min).

INFORMATION

Tourist information There's no tourist office on Ko Si Chang, but ⓦ ko-sichang.com, a useful website compiled by

David at *Pan and David Restaurant* (see opposite), offers detailed coverage of the island.

GETTING AROUND

Both piers connect with Thanon Asadang, a small, concrete ring road on which you'll find the market, a bank and many shops. In town it's easy enough to walk from place to place, but to really enjoy what Ko Si Chang has to offer you'll need to either rent a motorbike or charter a samlor for the day.

By motorbike Bikes can be rented from the pier or from *Tiew Pai Park Resort* for B250.

By samlor The island's trademark samlors are driven by

distinctive, elongated 1200cc motorbikes and virtually monopolize the roads, as there are barely any private cars; a tour of the island will set you back around B250.

ACCOMMODATION

Because water on the island has to be bought from a private desalination company at six times the price it costs on the mainland, **accommodation** on Ko Si Chang is expensive and disappointingly poor value. Booking ahead is advisable for weekends and public holidays.

Charlie's Bungalows Thanon Asadang, 2min walk south of Tiew Pai Park Resort in town ⓣ085 191 3863, ⓦ kohsichang.net. A dozen or so attractive new bungalows, done out in a maritime theme around a small garden; all come with a/c, hot water, satellite TV and fridge, and most have free wi-fi. Prices go up a little at weekends. **B900**

Si Chang Palace Thanon Asadang, across from Tha Bon in town ⓣ038 216276–9, ⓦ sichangpalace.com. The most upmarket place on the island has good a/c rooms with balconies, the best of them enjoying fine eastward sea views; all have hot water, TV and fridge. There's a pool here too. Breakfast included. **B1200**

Tham Pang Beach Hat Tham Pang ⓣ038 216179, ⓦ tampangbeachresort.com. The busiest west-coast accommodation, whose twenty fairly rudimentary concrete bungalows – all with bathroom, fans and TVs, some with sea views – are stacked in tiers up the cliffside behind Ko Si Chang's only beach. There's a restaurant plus beach equipment for rent. Reservations essential for weekends. **B550**

Tiew Pai Park Resort Thanon Asadang, in town near Tha Lang ⓣ038 216084, ⓦ tiewpai.net. Very central and cheaper than the competition, this is most backpackers' first choice. Bungalows and rooms are crammed around a

2

scruffy garden across the road from the restaurant and many are pretty basic; the best value are the en-suite fan bungalows, some of which have TV and fridge, and there are also some cheap single rooms with shared bathrooms. Fan B400, a/c B700

EATING

★ **Pan and David Restaurant** Thanon Asadang, 200m before the entrance to the old palace grounds ☎ 038 216075, ⓦ ko-sichang.com. The only restaurant of note on the island, run by a sociable and well-informed American expat and his Thai wife. The long and delicious menu includes authentically fiery Thai salads, tasty home-made fettuccine (B235 with bolognese sauce), fillet steak, Thai curries (around B160), and home-made fresh strawberry ice cream. Daily except Wed roughly 10am–9.30pm, opens earlier Sat & Sun.

DIRECTORY

Massage The charming little Sichang Healing House (☎ 038 216467; daily except Wed 9am–6pm), west off Thanon Asadang on the way to the old palace, offers Thai massage (B500 for 90min) and herbal treatments, as well as five-day massage courses (B6000), at its cute little garden retreat. There's a small branch on Hat Tham Pang too.

Pattaya

With its streets full of high-rise hotels and hustlers on every corner, **PATTAYA** is the epitome of exploitative tourism gone mad, but most of Pattaya's two million annual visitors don't mind that the place looks like the Costa del Sol bathed in smog because what they are here for is sex. The city swarms with male and female **prostitutes**, spiced up by Thailand's largest population of transvestites (*katoey*), and plane-loads of Western men flock here to enjoy their services in the rash of hostess bar-beers, go-go clubs and massage parlours for which "Patpong-on-Sea" is notorious. The signs trumpeting "Viagra for Sale" say it all. Pattaya also has the largest **gay scene** in Thailand, with several exclusively gay hotels and an entire zone devoted to gay sex bars.

Pattaya's evolution into sin city began with the Vietnam War, when it got fat on selling sex to American servicemen. When the soldiers and sailors left in the mid-1970s, Western tourists were lured in to fill their places, and ex-servicemen soon returned to run the sort of joints they had once blown their dollars in. These days, at least half the bars and restaurants in Pattaya are Western-run. More recently, there has been an influx of criminal gangs from Germany, Russia and Japan, who reportedly find Pattaya a convenient centre for running their rackets in passport and credit-card fraud, as well as child pornography and prostitution; expat murders are a regular news item in the *Pattaya Mail*.

Local tourism authorities are trying hard to improve Pattaya's **image**, and with surprising success have begun enticing families and older couples with a catalogue of more wholesome entertainments such as theme parks, golf courses, shopping plazas and year-round diving. Russian holidaymakers seem particularly keen and Cyrillic script is now much in evidence around the resort. A recent flush of more sophisticated boutique hotels and restaurants is also starting to bring in a younger Thai crowd, which has brightened the picture a little. But in truth the beach here is far from pristine – way outshone by Ko Samet just along the coast – so after-hours "entertainment" is still the primary inducement.

Pattaya Beach

At the heart of this ever-expanding adult playground is 4km-long **Pattaya Beach**, the noisiest, most unsightly zone of the resort, crowded with yachts and tour boats and fringed by a sliver of sand and a paved beachfront walkway. The densest glut of hotels, restaurants, bars, fast-food joints, souvenir shops and tour operators is halfway down Pattaya Beach Road (also signed as Pattaya Saineung), in **Central Pattaya** (Pattaya Klang), between sois 6 and 13, but after dark the action moves to the neon zone south of Soi 13/2. Here, in **South Pattaya**, and specifically along ultra-sleazy **Walking Street**, sex is peddled in hundreds of go-go bars, discos, massage parlours and open-sided bar-beers. The gay district is also here, in the lanes

2

PATTAYA BEACH

ACCOMMODATION	
Areca Lodge	8
Centara Nova Hotel	5
The Cottage	3
Diana Dragon Apartment	7
Dusit Thani Pattaya	2
Ice Inn	6
Pattaya Marriott	9
Sandalay Resort	4
Woodlands Hotel and Resort	1

RESTAURANTS & CAFÉS	
Ali Baba	5
Italia	6
Khao Suay	3
Ko Khun Pon Yang Kham	1
Mantra	2
PIC Kitchen	4

BARS & CLUBS	
The Blues Factory	5
Heineken Beer Garden	1
Hopf Brew House	4
Jazz Pit	2
Minus Five Ice Bar	3

SHOPS	
Asia Books	1
Thais4Life	2

0 — 500 metres

N

Naklua Bay & Sanctuary of Truth

Bangkok Airways

DOLPHIN CIRCLE — NORTH PATTAYA ROAD (PATTAYA NEUA)

Tiffany's

Amari Orchid Hotel

Central Centre

International Hospital

Alcazar

Thai Massage School — SOI YODSAK

Pattaya Bay

Hard Rock Hotel

Montien

Tops Supermarket

TOT

CENTRAL PATTAYA ROAD (PATTAYA KLANG)

Police

Pattaya Memorial Hospital

Central Festival Centre

Mike Shopping Mall

SOI SAISONG 11

SOI SAISONG 13

The Avenue

17/1 (SOI YAMATO)

13/2 (SOI POST OFFICE)

CAT

Royal Garden Plaza

Samet Island Tour

PATTAYA-LAND

Songthaews to Naklua

Boats to Ko Larn

WALKING STREET

Songthaews to Jomtien

A/C minibuses to Bangkok

SOI BUAKAOW

SOI YENSABAI

SOUTH PATTAYA ROAD (PATTAYA TAI)

Pattaya 35 Group

Tourist Police

TAT

SEE 'JOMTIEN BEACH & BUDDHA HILL' MAP FOR CONTINUATION

Jomtien Beach

First-class Bus Station & Thanon Sukhumvit

Naklua, Northeast Bus Stations & Train Station

ACTIVITIES IN PATTAYA

DIVING AND SNORKELLING

Though Pattaya's reefs are far less spectacular than those along the Andaman Coast, they can be dived year-round, and underwater visibility is consistent. Most **dive trips** focus on the group of "outer islands" about 25km from shore, which include Ko Rin, Ko Man Wichai and Ko Klung Badaan, where you have a reasonable chance of seeing barracuda, moray eels and blue-spotted stingrays. There are also three rewarding wreck dives in the Samae San/Sattahip area. Be careful when choosing a dive operator as there are plenty of charlatans around. All tour agents sell **snorkelling** trips to nearby islands, the majority of them going to the reefs and beaches of **Ko Larn**. You can also make your own way to Ko Larn by public boat from the Bali Hai pier at the far southern end of Walking Street (roughly hourly; 45min; B30).

Mermaid's Dive Centre Thanon Tabphaya in Jomtien, plus 3 branches around the resort ☎038 303333, ⓦmermaiddive.com. One of the most reputable dive shops in Pattaya, a PADI Five-Star Career Development Centre. It charges B3000 for two dives, with accompanying snorkellers paying B1000, and B14,000 for the four-day Openwater course.

WATERSPORTS

Beachfront stalls in Pattaya and Jomtien offer **waterskiing**, **parasailing** and **jet-skiing**, but you should avoid the last-mentioned: the jet-ski jockeys are notorious for finding scratches on the machine at the end of the rental and trying to charge an exorbitant amount in damages.

Amara Watersports Blue Lagoon Watersports Club, Soi 14 Naa Jomtien, at the far south end of Jomtien Beach ☎038 233276, ⓦamarawatersports.com. Windsurfing courses, rental and sales, as well as paddleboards, catamarans and kayaks.

Kiteboarding Asia Blue Lagoon Watersports Club, Soi 14 Naa Jomtien, at the far south end of Jomtien Beach ☎085 134 9588, ⓦkiteboardingasia.com. Kitesurfing courses, rental and sales.

MASSAGE

Thai Massage Development School Soi Yodsak, Central Pattaya ☎038 414115–6, ⓦtmdmassage.com. In among the full-body soaps and "full-service" massage joints, you'll find this traditional place, where you can have a proper Thai massage (B300/60min), or a herbal compress, oil or foot massage; it also offers two-week massage training courses.

COOKING CLASSES

Happy Home Soi 14, off the north side of Central Pattaya Rd, out towards Pattaya 3 Rd ☎084 417 5258, ⓦhappyhome-thaicookingschool.com. Morning (including a market visit) and afternoon classes, with vegetarian versions of all dishes available, and including a weekly dessert class. B1000 including a recipe booklet.

known as **Pattayaland** sois 1, 2 and 3 (or **Boyz Town**), but actually signed as sois 13/3, 13/4 and 13/5.

Jomtien Beach and Buddha Hill

South around the headland from South Pattaya, **Jomtien Beach** (sometimes spelt Chom Tian) is also fronted by enormous high-rises, many of them condominiums. Though the atmosphere here is not as frantic as in Pattaya, Jomtien also flounders under an excess of bar-beers and shops flogging tacky souvenirs and, like its neighbour, is forever under construction. The nicest stretch of sand is shady **Dongtan Beach**, beyond the northern end of Jomtien Beach Road, which is also Pattaya's main gay beach, though used by all. The bulge of land behind Dongtan Beach, separating Jomtien from South Pattaya, is Khao Phra Tamnak, variously translated as **Buddha Hill** or **Pattaya Hill**, site of several posh hotels and the Pattaya Park waterpark and funfair.

Underwater World

Thanon Sukhumvit, just south of the Thep Prasit junction near Tesco Lotus, behind Jomtien Beach • Daily 9am–6pm • B500 • Ⓦ underwaterworldpattaya.com

If you've been disappointed with local reef life, the small and expensive but rather beautiful aquarium at **Underwater World** might make up for it, with its trio of long fibreglass tunnels that transport you through shallow rockpools to the ocean floor. There are touch pools and masses of reef fish, as well as a long roster of feeding times, detailed on the website.

Sanctuary of Truth (Wang Boran)

Off the west end of Soi 12, Thanon Naklua, close to the Garden Sea View hotel, beyond the north end of Pattaya Beach • Daily 8am–6pm • B500 • Ⓦ sanctuaryoftruth.com • From Central Pattaya take a Naklua-bound songthaew as far as Soi 12, then a motorbike taxi

The hugely ambitious **Sanctuary of Truth**, or **Wang Boran**, stands in a dramatic seaside spot behind imposing crenellated walls. Conceived by the man behind the Muang Boran Ancient City complex near Bangkok, it's a majestic 105m-high temple-palace built entirely of wood and designed to evoke the great ancient Khmer sanctuaries of Angkor. Though begun in 1981, it is still a work-in-progress, its external walls covered in a growing gallery of beautiful, symbolic woodcarvings inspired by Cambodian, Chinese, Thai and Indian mythologies.

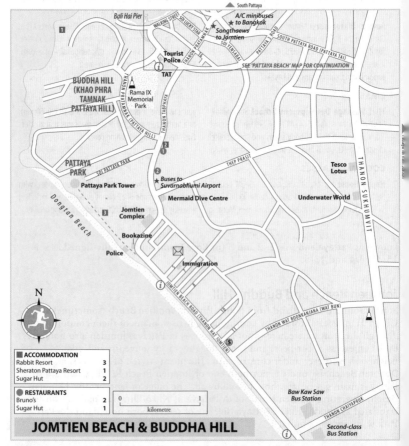

■ ACCOMMODATION	
Rabbit Resort	3
Sheraton Pattaya Resort	1
Sugar Hut	2

● RESTAURANTS	
Bruno's	2
Sugar Hut	1

JOMTIEN BEACH & BUDDHA HILL

ARRIVAL AND DEPARTURE

BY PLANE

Pattaya's **U-Tapao Airport** (☎ 038 245599) is inconveniently located at the naval base near Sattahip, about 25km south of the resort, from where a taxi will cost you about B800, so you're probably better off using Bangkok's Suvarnabhumi Airport (see p.115). The Bangkok Airways office is at Fairtex Arcade, North Pattaya Rd (☎ 038 412382).

Destinations Ko Samui (1–2 daily; 1hr); Phuket (1 daily; 1hr 35min).

BY BUS

All first-class and VIP Bangkok buses, and some airport buses, arrive at and depart from the bus station on North Pattaya Rd. Slower second-class buses and some airport buses use the station on Thanon Chaiyapruk in Jomtien, and there are also airport buses from a terminal on Thanon Tabphaya in Jomtien. It's also possible to get to Pattaya direct from Isaan and the north: Nakorn Chai buses to and from Chiang Mai, Chiang Rai, Khorat and Ubon use a terminus on Thanon Sukhumvit, across from the Central Pattaya Rd intersection (☎ 038 424871); other Isaan buses can be found at two terminals on the opposite side of Thanon Sukhumvit and at the first-class bus station on North Pattaya Rd. Coming by bus from Si Racha, Rayong or Trat you'll probably get dropped on Thanon Sukhumvit, the resort's eastern limit, from where songthaews will ferry you into town. If heading on to these towns, you need to pick up your bus from one of the drops on Thanon Sukhumvit (easiest at the junctions with North, Central and South Pattaya roads).

Destinations Bangkok (Eastern/Northern bus terminals; every 30min; 2hr 30min–4hr); Bangkok (Southern Bus Terminal; roughly hourly; 3hr 30min); Bangkok (Suvarna-bhumi Airport, Floor 1 of the terminal; 7 daily; 2hr); Chanthaburi (6 daily; 3hr); Chiang Mai (8 daily; 12–14hr); Chiang Rai (2 daily; 15–17hr); Khorat (4 daily; 5hr); Rayong (every 30min; 1hr 30min); Si Racha (every 20min; 30min); Trat (6 daily; 4hr 30min); Ubon Ratchathani (6 daily; 10–12hr).

BY AIR-CONDITIONED MINIBUS

You can catch an a/c minibus to Bangkok's Victory Monument for B100 from several spots, including the east end of Central Pattaya Rd near Foodland and South Pattaya Rd in front of the Family Mart near Krung Thai Bank. Any hotel can arrange a ticket on a shared a/c minibus to Suvarnabhumi Airport for around B250/person (or about B800/car for a metered taxi). There are also tourist minibus services to Ko Samet and Ko Chang (tickets can also be booked through most tour agents): Samet Island Tour on Soi Yamato (☎ 038 427277, ⓦ malibu-samet.com) to the Ban Phe pier (for Ko Samet; B250); and Pattaya 35 Group opposite Big C on South Pattaya Rd (☎ 038 423447) to Ko Chang (B400 including ferry), via Ban Phe and Chanthaburi.

BY TRAIN

Pattaya is on a branch of the eastern rail line, and there's one slow train a day in each direction between the resort and Bangkok. Pattaya has two stations, both off the east side of Thanon Sukhumvit: the main one is about 500m north of the Central Pattaya Rd intersection, while Pattaya Tai Station is in South Pattaya near the Thanon Thep Prasit junction.

Destinations Bangkok (daily; 4hr); Si Racha (daily; 30min).

INFORMATION

Tourist information There are municipal tourist service booths (daily roughly 8.30am–4pm) on the beach at the mouth of Walking Street, at City Hall on North Pattaya Rd, at the north end of Jomtien Beach Rd and opposite Thanon Chaiyapruk on Jomtien Beach. The TAT office is inconveniently located at 609 Thanon Pratamnak between South Pattaya and Jomtien (daily 8.30am–4.30pm; ☎ 038 428750, ⓔ tatchon@tat.or.th).

Newspapers The weekly *Pattaya Mail* (ⓦ pattayamail .com) is one of several local newspapers that fills readers in on the often lurid goings-on.

GETTING AROUND

By songthaew Public songthaews – known locally as baht buses, and also available to charter – circulate continuously around the resort from dawn until at least 11pm. Most follow a standard anticlockwise route up Pattaya 2 Rd as far as North Pattaya Rd and back down Pattaya Beach Rd, for a fixed fee of B10/person; others run along the main east–west arteries of North, Central and South Pattaya roads. Songthaews to Jomtien start from next to the school on the south side of the junction of Pattaya 2 Rd and South Pattaya Rd and cost B10–20. Songthaews to Naklua, beyond north Pattaya, start from the north side of the same junction and head up Pattaya 2 Rd (also B10–20).

By motorbike Motorbike rental is available everywhere from B200/day, but beware of faulty vehicles, and of scams – sometimes rented bikes get stolen by touts keen to keep the customer's deposit, so you may want to use your own lock.

By car Avis car rental (ⓦ avisthailand.com) has an office inside the *Dusit Resort* (☎ 038 361627); many of the motorbike touts also rent out jeeps for about B1200/day.

ACCOMMODATION

The quietest and least sleazy end of town to stay in is **North Pattaya**, between Central Pattaya Road and North Pattaya Road (Thanon Hat Pattaya Neua). There's no travellers' scene in Pattaya and hotels offering doubles under B450 outside low season are almost impossible to find; the cheapest alternatives are often rooms above the bars on sois 6, 13/2, 13/3 and 13/4.

PATTAYA BEACH

Areca Lodge 198/21 Soi Saisong 13 (aka Soi Diana Inn), Central Pattaya ☎038 410123, ⓦarecalodge.com; map p.158. An unusually stylish place for Pattaya, with pleasantly furnished a/c rooms in three wings built around two swimming pools, most of them with balconies, all with hot showers, mini-bars, TV and wi-fi. Buffet breakfast included. B1850

Centara Nova Hotel Soi 12 (aka Soi A.R. or Soi Sukrudee), Central Pattaya Rd ☎038 725999, ⓦcentarahotelsresorts.com; map p.158. Central, quiet and welcoming boutique hotel, done out in a plush contemporary style that features a lot of burnished gold. There's a large, attractive pool fed by an artificial waterfall, a spa that uses Dead Sea mud and salt, a fitness centre and free computers and wi-fi. Breakfast included. B4500

The Cottage Off Pattaya 2 Rd, North Pattaya ☎038 425650, ⓦthecottagepattaya.com; map p.158. Good-value, simply furnished semi-detached brick bungalows, all with a/c, hot water, TV and fridge, pleasantly set among tall trees within a mature tropical garden away from the main road but opposite the Central Centre. Facilities include two small swimming pools and wi-fi in most rooms. B1000

Diana Dragon Apartment 198/16 Soi Saisong 13 (aka Soi Diana Inn), Central Pattaya ☎038 423928, ⓦdianapattaya.co.th; map p.158. This long-running Pattaya institution has some of the cheapest doubles in town, and they're good value considering the competition: huge and quite light, with wi-fi available, plus use of the pool at *Diana Inn*, 100m away. Fan B450, a/c B750

Dusit Thani Pattaya 240/2 Pattaya Beach Rd, North Pattaya ☎038 425611, ⓦdusit.com; map p.158. In the less sleazy part of town, this luxury Thai chain hotel is one of only a few Beach Rd hotels to be actually on the beach (the others are at the southern end). Sea-view rooms are worth paying extra for as the impressive panoramas take in the whole bay. Also on offer are two swimming pools, a spa and tennis courts, as well as good-value transfers from their hotel on Thanon Silom in Bangkok. B5300

Ice Inn Corner of Saisong 12 and Pattaya 2 Rd, Central Pattaya ☎038 720671, ⓦiceinnpattaya.com; map p.158. Cheap fan-cooled singles and reasonably priced a/c doubles in this small thirty-room hotel behind a handicrafts shop a few metres from the busier bar-beer sois. Rooms are simple but are all en suite. B790

Pattaya Marriott 218 Pattaya Beach Rd, Central Pattaya ☎038 412120, ⓦmarriotthotels.com; map p.158. Located in the heart of the resort (attached to the Royal Garden Plaza shopping centre), and across the road from the beach, this international chain hotel is both very central and refreshingly calm, not least because it's designed around a huge swimming pool and tropical garden full of palms. Not surprisingly it's the first choice for anyone in Pattaya on business, with wi-fi available (at a price) throughout. Rooms are capacious and comfortable and have either pool- or sea view. Facilities include two restaurants, a fitness centre and kids' yoga. B6900

Sandalay Resort Between sois 1 and 2, Pattaya Beach Rd, North Pattaya ☎038 422660, ⓦsandalayresort.com; map p.158. This hundred-room hotel with swimming pool is in the quieter northern part of town just across the road from the beach. It has contemporary-styled, well-designed, though quite small, standard a/c rooms plus impressively large deluxe versions. Both options are available with sea view and tiny balcony at extra cost, but all have free wi-fi. Good discounts often available. Breakfast included. B2900

Woodlands Hotel and Resort 164 Thanon Pattaya-Naklua, North Pattaya ☎038 421707, ⓦwoodland-resort.com; map p.158. A quiet, unpretentious and welcoming family-friendly garden resort 100m north of the Dolphin Circle roundabout, 400m from a scruffy but quiet thread of beach. The elegant, a/c rooms are in two storeys set round the pools and garden; the most expensive have direct access to the pool from ground-floor balconies. Broadband throughout. B2100

JOMTIEN AND BUDDHA HILL

★ **Rabbit Resort** Dongtan beachfront, Jomtien ☎038 303303, ⓦrabbitresort.com; map p.160. Beautiful place that's the most appealing option in Jomtien, and located on the nicest stretch of beach, the predominantly but not exclusively gay Dongtan Beach. Most accommodation is in teakwood cottages that are elegantly furnished with Thai fabrics and antiques and have garden-style bathrooms; there are also some "forest rooms" in a two-storey block. All are set around a tropical garden and pool just metres off the beach. Breakfast included. Rooms B4900, cottages B5900

Sheraton Pattaya Resort 437 Thanon Pratamnak (Cliff Rd), South Pattaya ☎038 259888, ⓦstarwoodhotels.com; map p.160. Pattaya's best hotel is smaller and more intimate than most in its class and offers five-star rooms and private pavilions, all with balconies, rain showers, DVD players and wi-fi, for which you pay extra. The beautiful series of freeform swimming pools and the spa are set within lush gardens — compensating for the minuscule private beach — though it's built on a hill so be prepared for lots of steps. You'll need transport to get to the shops and restaurants of downtown Pattaya. B6800

Sugar Hut 391/18 Thanon Tabphaya, midway between South Pattaya and Jomtien ☎ 038 251686, ⓦ sugar-hut .com; map p.160. The most characterful accommodation in Pattaya comprises a charming collection of Ayutthaya-style traditional wooden bungalows set in a fabulously profuse garden with three swimming pools. The bungalows are in tropical-chic style, with low beds, open-roofed shower rooms, mosquito nets and private verandas. You'll need your own transport as it's nowhere near the restaurants, shops or sea. B4000

EATING

In among the innumerable low-grade Western cafés that dominate Pattaya's **restaurant scene** are a few much classier joints serving good, sophisticated cuisine – at top-end prices. For the cheapest, most authentic Thai food, just head for the nearest of Pattaya's myriad building sites and you'll find street stalls catering to the construction-site workers.

PATTAYA BEACH

Ali Baba 1/13–14 Central Pattaya Rd ☎ 038 361620; map p.158. Look beyond the name and the wonderfully kitsch decor and waiters' uniforms, and you'll find some very good Indian food, which keeps many of Pattaya's visitors from the subcontinent happy. There's an authentically long menu of vegetarian dishes, featuring plenty of cheese, some interesting starters with okra, and the butter chicken's a real winner (B215). Daily 11am–midnight.

Italia Walking St, South Pattaya; map p.158. This very Italian café is an incongruously swish little haven with outdoor tables for watching the sleazy cabaret show that is Walking Street. Delicious home-made ice creams (B95 for 2 scoops), espressos, Sambuca and the like. Daily 9am–4am.

Khao Suay Ground Floor, Central Centre, Pattaya 2 Rd, North Pattaya; map p.158. A long menu of good modern Thai food (most mains about B110) draws Thai families to this tiny café inside the shopping centre. The varied options include *kaeng tai pla* (southern Thai fish stomach curry) and *nam prik pla thuu* (chilli relish with mackerel). Daily 11am–9.45pm.

★ **Ko Khun Pon Yang Kham** North Pattaya Rd, at Soi 6 ☎ 038 420571, ⓦ ko-khun.com; map p.158. This garden restaurant offers Thailand's equivalent of wagyu beef, from pampered Pon Yang Kham cows that are bred (from French, Swiss and Thai breeds) and reared in Isaan. It's served northeastern-style too, so no chips or mustard, but it goes well with *som tam*, and the red wine is decent (B90/glass). B135 for a small but delicious portion of sirloin on a sizzling hot plate. Daily 5.30pm–midnight.

★ **Mantra** Amari Orchid Hotel, Beach Rd, North Pattaya ☎ 038 429591, ⓦ mantra-pattaya.com; map p.158. Setting the standard unexpectedly high for Pattaya, this large, beautifully designed bar-restaurant creates an ambience somewhere between a contemporary Shanghai hotel and a maharaja's palace. Downstairs there's an open-plan view of the seven different, equally eclectic kitchens specializing in Japanese, Chinese, Indian, Mediterranean and Western food, grills and seafood. A meal might begin with avocado sushi (B410), supplemented with bite-sized Peking duck (B240), continue with coq au vin (B380), and end with lemon grass and pandanus crème brûlée. The walk-in wine cellar keeps over 160 imported wines. Daily 5pm–1am, Sun brunch 11am–3pm.

PIC Kitchen Soi 5, North Pattaya ☎ 038 428374, ⓦ pic-kitchen.com; map p.158. One of Pattaya's top traditional Thai restaurants, set in a stylish series of teak buildings with the option of Thai-style cushion seating. Elegantly presented curries, lots of different seafood platters, spicy salads and some vegetarian dishes. Mains from B160. Daily 11am–2pm & 5–10.30pm.

JOMTIEN BEACH

Bruno's 306/63 Chateau Dale Plaza, Thanon Tabphaya, Jomtien ☎ 038 364600–1, ⓦ brunos-pattaya.com; map p.160. A local institution that's a favourite with expats celebrating special occasions. The food is upmarket, expensive, European – Provençal-style rack of lamb, sirloin steak, dark-chocolate mousse – and there's a cellar of some 150 wines. Main dishes from B250. Daily noon–2.30pm & 6pm–late.

Sugar Hut 391/18 Thanon Tabphaya, Jomtien; map p.160. Attached to the charming hotel of the same name (see above), this restaurant gives you the chance to soak up the ambience and enjoy the tropical gardens without shelling out for a bungalow (though the food's not cheap either). Meals are served in an open-sided *sala* and the menu is mainly classy Thai; recommendations include roast duck in red curry. Daily 7am–midnight.

DRINKING AND NIGHTLIFE

Pattaya's **nightlife** revolves around sex (see box, p.164). It is, however, just about possible to have a night out without getting entangled in sleaze, at one of the growing number of hostess-free **bars** listed below, a few of which are surprisingly style-conscious. However you choose to spend your evening, be warned that Pattaya is notorious for transvestite **pickpockets**, who target drunk men walking home in the early hours: while one "distracts" the victim from the front, the other extracts the wallet from behind.

2

PATTAYA'S SEX INDUSTRY

Of the thousand-plus bars in Pattaya, the vast majority are staffed by women and men whose aim is to get bought for the night – depending on whom you believe, there are between six thousand and twenty thousand Thais (and quite a few Russians) working in Pattaya's **sex industry**; most depressing of all is that this workforce includes children as young as 10, despite fairly frequent high-profile paedophile arrests. The vast majority of Pattaya's bars are open-air **"bar-beers"**, which group themselves in neon clusters all over North, Central and South Pattaya so that there's barely a 500m stretch of road without its rowdy enclave. The setup is the same in all of them: from mid-afternoon the punters – usually lone males – sit on stools around a brashly lit circular bar, behind which the hostesses keep the drinks, bawdy chat and well-worn jokes flowing.

Drinks are a lot more expensive in the bouncer-guarded **go-go bars** on Walking Street in South Pattaya, where near-naked hostesses serve the beer and live sex shows keep the boozers hooked through the night. The scene follows much the same pattern as in Patpong, Nana and Soi Cowboy in Bangkok, with the women dancing on a small stage in the hope they might be bought for the night – or the week. Go-go dancers, shower shows and striptease are also the mainstays of the **gay scene**, centred on Pattayaland Soi 3 (Soi 13/5), South Pattaya.

The Blues Factory Soi Lucky Star, Walking St, South Pattaya ⓦthebluesfactorypattaya.com; map p.158. Considered to be the best live-music venue in Pattaya, with sets most nights (Tues–Sat) from the famously charismatic rock guitarist Lam Morrison and his band, and (except on Tues & Wed) from the house blues band as well. Daily 8.30pm–late.

Heineken Beer Garden Central Centre, Pattaya 2 Rd, North Pattaya; map p.158. Outdoor tables, draught Heineken and live music nightly (from about 8pm) from Thai singers and bands, doing mostly Thai pop and country. Also serves a full menu of Thai food (dishes from about B120), with Isaan and seafood specialities. Daily 5pm–2am.

Hopf Brew House Pattaya Beach Rd, between sois 13/1 (Yamato) and 13/2 (Post Office), Central Pattaya; map p.158. Cavernous and very popular a/c beer hall that brews its own Pilsener and wheat beer, serves generous wood-fired pizzas and other Italian dishes, and stages live music nightly. Attracts a youngish crowd, including vacationing couples. Daily 2pm–1/2am.

Jazz Pit Soi 5, North Pattaya ⓦjazzpitpub.com; map p.158. Nightly live jazz (from 8pm) in the cosy lounge-bar adjacent to the *PIC Kitchen* restaurant, and occasional high-profile celeb jamming sessions. Daily 7pm–midnight.

Minus Five Ice Bar Amari Nova Suites, Soi 12 (Soi Sukrudee), Central Pattaya Rd ☎038 426768, ⓦminus5pattaya.com; map p.158. Your chance to literally chill out at this cube of a bar sculpted entirely from ice, right down to the draught beer kegs on the ice-cold counter. For B500 you get lent a winter coat and mittens and are given 20min to down as many vodka shots as you can, then it's back out into the warmth of the trendy Bangkok-style bar adjacent. Daily 6pm–late.

ENTERTAINMENT

CINEMAS

There are several English-language screenings a day at the multiplexes.

Major Cineplex The Avenue shopping centre, Pattaya 2 Rd, Central Pattaya ⓦmajorcineplex.com.

SF Cinema City Central Festival Centre, Pattaya Beach Rd, Central Pattaya ⓦsfcinemacity.com.

TRANSVESTITE CABARETS

Tour groups – and families – constitute the main audience at Pattaya's *katoey* **cabarets**. Glamorous and highly professional, each theatre has a troupe of sixty or more transvestites who run through twenty musical-style numbers in fishnets and crinolines, ball gowns and leathers, against ever more lavish stage sets. Any tour agent can organize tickets.

Alcazar Opposite Soi 4 on Pattaya 2 Rd in North Pattaya ⓦalcazarpattaya.com. Daily 6.30pm, 8pm & 9.30pm. B600

Tiffany's North of Soi 1 on Pattaya 2 Rd in North Pattaya ⓦtiffany-show.co.th. Daily 6pm, 7.30pm & 9pm. B500. Also hosts an annual international *katoey* beauty pageant over 5 days in early Nov, Miss International Queen (ⓦmissinternationalqueen.com).

SHOPPING

Asia Books Floor 3, Central Festival Centre, between Pattaya Beach and Pattaya 2 roads. Good selection of English-language books. Daily 11am–11pm.

Thais4Life 504 Soi Yensabai Condotel, off Soi 17 (Soi

VC), South Pattaya ⓦthais4life.com. One of Pattaya's best secondhand bookshops, this charity sells all its books for B80 and donates profits to medical and other needy projects including Baan Jing Jai orphanage. Mon–Sat noon–6pm.

DIRECTORY

Emergencies For all emergencies, call the tourist police on ☎1155 (free, 24hr) or contact them at their office beside TAT on Buddha Hill, between South Pattaya and Jomtien; in the evenings, they also set up a post at the north end of Walking Street.
Hospitals and dentists The best-equipped hospital is the private Bangkok-Pattaya Hospital (☎1719 or ☎038 259999, ⓦbangkokpattayahospital.com) on Thanon Sukhumvit, about 400m north of the intersection with North Pattaya Rd, which also has dental services.
Immigration office Soi 5, off Jomtien Beach Rd, Jomtien (Mon–Fri 8.30am–4.30pm; ☎038 252750).

Ban Phe

The small coastal town of **BAN PHE**, which lies 17km east of Rayong, its provincial capital, and about 200km from Bangkok, is the port for Ko Samet. Several piers for Samet boats compete for attention here, along with minimarkets, internet centres and tour desks selling onward bus tickets and private transfers. Ban Phe's main street runs from west to east behind the seafront, passing in turn the Chok Krisda pier and the nearby Taruaphe pier, before petering out a few hundred metres later at the municipal pier, Tha Reua Tessaban.

ARRIVAL AND DEPARTURE   BAN PHE

When the time comes to leave Ko Samet, you can book tickets for any of the followng direct buses and minibuses from Ban Phe at tour agencies on the island.

BY BUS
There are direct a/c buses operated by Cherdchai between Bangkok's Eastern (Ekamai) Bus Terminal and Ban Phe; on departure from Ban Phe, you can easily find them near the municipal pier. Coming by bus from Chanthaburi or Trat, you'll be dropped at a T-junction on Highway 3, from where a songthaew or motorbike taxi will take you the remaining 5km to the Ban Phe piers. Rayong has a wider choice of buses, including services to Chiang Mai and Isaan; the Ban Phe piers are served by frequent songthaews (about 30min) from Rayong bus station.
Destinations Bangkok (14 daily; 3hr); Chanthaburi (from Highway 3; 6 daily; 1hr 30min); Trat (from Highway 3; 6 daily; 3hr).

BY AIR-CONDITIONED MINIBUS
A/c minibuses run between many locations in Bangkok, including Thanon Khao San (about 4hr; B250), Victory Monument (about 3hr 30min; B200) and Suvarnabhumi Airport (about 3hr; B500), and Ban Phe. There are also services from Pattaya (see p.161) and Ko Chang (see p.183). On departure, you'll find numerous a/c minibus companies in Ban Phe, including some at the municipal pier and in the two sois opposite Taruaphe (including Pattaya and Ko Chang services); a frequent Victory Monument service 200m west of the municipal pier; and the helpful RMT at the front of the Chok Krisda pier (☎086 344 4026), which serves all three bus terminals in Bangkok, as well as Victory Monument.

BY BOAT
Frequent boats run from Ban Phe to Ko Samet, leaving from various piers – Tha Reua Tessaban has the widest choice. Details are given in our Ko Samet coverage (see p.169).

ACCOMMODATION

Christie's Prominent green building opposite the Taruaphe pier ☎089 834 9103, ⓦchristiesbanphe .com. If you get stuck in Ban Phe, this is a good choice for accommodation, offering homely, attractive rooms, some on the back away from the main road, all with a/c, hot water, TV, fridge and free wi-fi. Downstairs is a restaurant and Irish bar, which organizes visa runs to Cambodia and trips to Siam Reap, and next door is a secondhand bookshop. **B600**

DIRECTORY

Tourist police At the municipal pier ☎038 651669 or ☎1155.

Ko Samet

B200 national park admission fee

Blessed with the softest, squeakiest sand within weekending distance of Bangkok, the tiny island of **KO SAMET**, which measures just 6km from top to toe, is a favourite escape for Thais, expats and tourists. Its fourteen small but dazzlingly white beaches are breathtakingly beautiful, lapped by pale blue water and in places still shaded by coconut palms and occasional white-flowered cajeput (*samet*) trees, which gave the

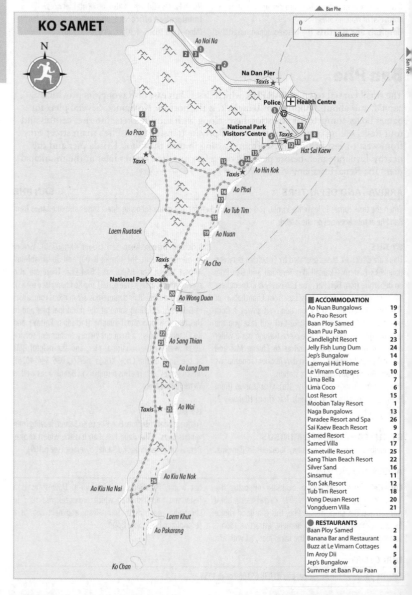

KO SAMET

N

Ban Phe

0   1
kilometre

Ban Phe

Ao Noi Na

Na Dan Pier
Taxis ★

Police
@ + Health Centre

National Park
Visitors' Centre
Taxis ★

Ao Prao

Taxis ★

Hat Sai Kaew

Ao Hin Kok
Taxis ★

Ao Phai

Ao Tub Tim

Laem Ruataek

Ao Nuan

Taxis ★

Ao Cho

National Park Booth

Ao Wong Duan

Ao Sang Thian

Ao Lung Dum

Taxis ★ Ao Wai

Ao Kiu Na Nok

Ao Kiu Na Nai

Laem Khut

Ao Pakarang

Ko Chan

■ ACCOMMODATION	
Ao Nuan Bungalows	19
Ao Prao Resort	5
Baan Ploy Samed	4
Baan Puu Paan	3
Candlelight Resort	23
Jelly Fish Lung Dum	24
Jep's Bungalow	14
Laemyai Hut Home	8
Le Vimarn Cottages	10
Lima Bella	7
Lima Coco	6
Lost Resort	15
Mooban Talay Resort	1
Naga Bungalows	13
Paradee Resort and Spa	26
Sai Kaew Beach Resort	9
Samed Resort	2
Samed Villa	17
Sametville Resort	25
Sang Thian Beach Resort	22
Silver Sand	16
Sinsamut	11
Ton Sak Resort	12
Tub Tim Resort	18
Vong Deuan Resort	20
Vongduern Villa	21

● RESTAURANTS	
Baan Ploy Samed	2
Banana Bar and Restaurant	3
Buzz at Le Vimarn Cottages	4
Im Aroy Dii	5
Jep's Bungalow	6
Summer at Baan Puu Paan	1

WATERSPORTS AND BOAT TRIPS ON SAMET

Samet has no decent coral reefs of its own, so you'll have to take a boat trip to the islands of Ko Kudi and Ko Thalu, off the northeast coast, to get good **snorkelling** (around B700 from most beaches) or **diving**. From the main beaches you can also organize **boat trips** around Samet itself (around B500), rent kayaks and jet skis and arrange banana boat rides and parasailing.

Samed Resorts Diving Centre Ao Prao ☎038 and B17,000 for the four-day PADI Openwater course.
644100–3, ⓦ samedresorts.com. B3500 for two dives

2

island its name and which are used to build boats. But they are also crowded – although on weekdays there's a lot more room to breathe and relax – and developed to full capacity with over fifty sprawling, albeit low-rise, bungalow developments, a disfiguring number of which pay scant attention to landscaping and rubbish disposal. It's a sobering state of affairs considering that much of the island's coastline has been protected as part of the Khao Laem Ya – Mu Ko Samet **national park** since 1981; all visitors to Ko Samet are required to pay the standard national park fee on arrival, and most hoteliers also pay rent to park authorities, but there's little evidence that this income has been used to improve the island's infrastructure.

Samet's best **beaches** are along the **east coast**, where you'll find nearly all the bungalow resorts, though there's one rather exclusive beach on the otherwise largely inaccessible west coast, and the north-coast shoreline retains a pleasingly village ambience. Most islanders and many resort staff live in the northeast, near the island's main pier, in the ramshackle, badly drained village of **Na Dan**, which has small shops and cheap foodstalls as well as Samet's only school, health centre and wat. Na Dan's high street, which runs from the pier down to Hat Sai Kaew, and its other small roads, are paved, as is the road along the north coast to Ao Noi Na. However, from Hat Sai Kaew south, there's only one poorly maintained dirt road (with a branch west to Ao Prao) that runs down the island's forested central ridge, and much of the **interior** is dense jungle, home to hornbills, gibbons and spectacular butterflies. The evergreen vegetation belies the fact that there are no rivers on this unusually dry island, which gets only scant rainfall in an average year. Lack of rain is another plus point for tourists, though it means water is a precious and expensive commodity as it has to be trucked in from the mainland.

The most backpacker-oriented beaches are east-coast **Ao Hin Kok**, **Ao Phai** and **Ao Tub Tim**, with Ao Hin Kok and Ao Phai both quite lively in the evenings; the travellers' vibe at nearby **Ao Nuan** is more alternative, with **Ao Sang Thian** and north-coast **Ao Noi Na** also worth investigating. **Hat Sai Kaew** and **Ao Wong Duan** are the biggest centres on the east coast, dominated by upper-scale accommodation aimed at families, package tourists and Bangkok trendies. Samet's super-deluxe accommodation is on west-coast **Ao Phrao** and southern beauty **Ao Kiu**.

Shops and stalls in Na Dan (which has a pharmacy) and on all the main beaches sell basic travellers' necessities. Many bungalows have **safety deposits** and it's worth making use of them: theft is an issue on Samet and there are occasional instances of drinks being spiked by freelance bar-girls and punters waking next day without their valuables.

Hat Sai Kaew and Na Dan

From **NA DAN** pier, a ten-minute walk south along the paved high street brings you to **HAT SAI KAEW**, or Diamond Beach, named for its long and extraordinarily beautiful stretch of luxuriant sand, so soft and clean it squeaks underfoot – a result, apparently, of its unusually high silicon content. Unsurprisingly, it's the busiest beach on Samet, its shorefront packed with bungalows, restaurants, beachwear stalls, deckchairs and parasols, though the northern end is slightly more peaceful.

Ao Hin Kok

Separated from Hat Sai Kaew by a low promontory on which sits a mermaid statue (a reference to the early nineteenth-century poem, *Phra Abhai Mani*, by famous local poet Sunthorn Phu), **AO HIN KOK** is much smaller than its neighbour, and has more of a travellers' vibe. Just three sets of bungalows overlook the petite white-sand beach from the slope on the far side of the dirt road, and you can walk here from Na Dan in about fifteen minutes.

Ao Phai

Narrow but sparkling little **AO PHAI**, around the next headland from Ao Hin Kok, is Samet's party beach, where the shoreside *Silver Sand* bar and disco is known for its late-night dance music (with a strong gay presence at weekends). Not everyone has to join in though, as the bungalows on the fringes of the bay are far enough away for a good night's sleep. There's a minimarket and travel agent on the beach, and you can walk to Na Dan pier in twenty minutes.

Ao Tub Tim

Also known as Ao Pudsa, **AO TUB TIM** is another cute white-sand bay sandwiched between rocky points, partly shaded with palms and backed by a wooded slope. It has just two bungalow operations and is only a short stroll from Ao Phai and the other beaches further north, and a half-hour hike from Na Dan pier.

Ao Nuan

Clamber up over the headland from Ao Tub Tim (which gives you a fine panorama over Hat Sai Kaew) to reach Samet's smallest and most laidback beach, the secluded **AO NUAN**, effectively the private domain of *Ao Nuan Bungalows* (see p.171). Because it's some way off the main track, the beach gets hardly any through-traffic and feels quiet and private. Although not brilliant for swimming, the rocky shore reveals a good patch of sand when the tide withdraws; the more consistent beach at Ao Tub Tim is only five minutes' walk to the north, and **Ao Cho**, which has some coral, is a five-minute walk south along the footpath.

Ao Wong Duan

The horseshoe bay of **AO WONG DUAN**, a ten-minute walk round the next-but-one point from Ao Nuan, is Samet's second most popular beach after Hat Sai Kaew. Though it's not as pretty and suffers even more from hordes of day-trippers, it does offer some attractive upmarket accommodation; most guests are either package tourists, Pattaya overnighters, or weekending Bangkokians so shoestring travellers aren't well catered for. Although the beach is fairly long and broad, the central shorefront is almost lost under a knot of tiny bars (many with irresistibly comfy armchairs) and tourist shops, and the main stretch of beach all but disappears at high tide. Facilities include minimarkets, ATMs and internet access.

Ao Sang Thian (Candlelight Beach) and Ao Lung Dum

A favourite with Thai students, who relish the beauty of its slightly wild setting, **AO SANG THIAN** ("Candlelight Beach") and contiguous Ao Lung Dum display almost none of the commerce of Wong Duan, a couple of minutes' walk over the hill, though the scenic shorefront is fronted by an unbroken line of bungalows. The narrow, white-sand coastline is dotted with wave-smoothed rocks and partitioned by larger outcrops that create several distinct bays; as it curves outwards to the south you get a great view of the island's east coast. At its southern end, Ao Sang Thian becomes **AO LUNG DUM**, and the various little bungalow outfits fringing the shore here are pretty similar.

Ao Wai

A fifteen-minute walk along the coast path from Lung Dum brings you to **AO WAI**, a very pretty white-sand bay, partially shaded and a good size considering it supports just one (large) **bungalow** operation, *Sametville Resort*, which also spills across on to neighbouring little Ao Hin Kleang.

Ao Kiu

Over an hour's walk south of Ao Sang Thian, via a track that begins behind *Vong Deuan Resort* on Ao Wong Duan and can be joined at the southern end of Ao Thian, the gorgeous little twin bays of **AO KIU** – Ao Kiu Na Nok on the east coast and Ao Kiu Na Nai on the west – are separated by just a few hundred metres of land. Both beaches are the domain of Samet's most exclusive hotel, the *Paradee Resort and Spa* (see p.172).

Ao Prao (Paradise Bay)

Across on the upper west coast, the rugged, rocky coastline only softens into beach once, at **AO PRAO**, also known as Paradise Bay, on the northwestern stretch, some 4km north of Ao Kiu Na Nai. This is Samet's most upmarket beach, dominated by two expensively elegant resorts, plus one slightly more affordable option, and nothing else to lower the tone. If you're only visiting for the day, the most direct route from the east-coast beaches is via the inland track from behind *Sea Breeze* on Ao Phai, which takes about twenty minutes on foot. If staying on Ao Prao, your hotel will arrange boat transfers.

Ao Noi Na

West of Na Dan, the island's north coast – known simply as **AO NOI NA** even though it's not strictly a single bay – has a refreshingly normal village feel compared to the rest of Samet. There are an increasing number of places to stay along the narrow coastal road here, offering serene views across the water to the mainland hills behind Ban Phe, and just one white-sand beach of note at the far western end. Though this beach has been hogged by the luxurious *Mooban Talay Resort*, it's not private and you can walk there from Na Dan pier in about twenty-five minutes, passing a couple of good **restaurants** (see p.173) en route.

ARRIVAL AND DEPARTURE   **KO SAMET**

The port of departure for Ko Samet is **Ban Phe** (see p.165). If you want to book your onward travel while on Ko Samet, CP Travel on Hat Sai Kaew (☎ 038 644136), in the beach-access arcade near the National Park office, sells **bus** and **minibus** as well as domestic and international **air tickets**; it also has a few new and secondhand books.

BY BOAT

RESORT BOATS

If you're staying in any of Samet's mid-range or expensive accommodation, ask the resort about boats when you book: many establishments have their own big boats or speedboats to ferry you direct from Ban Phe on reasonably priced shared transfers (usually at set times). Such transfers may be free, but a few resorts make their paid transfers compulsory. You might also want to look into the packages offered by many resorts, which is how most Thais travel to Ko Samet: as well as boats and accommodation, these might include things like dinners and massages.

2

PUBLIC BOATS
There are half a dozen competing piers in Ban Phe, offering a bewildering variety of speedboats and bigger, slower but much cheaper wooden boats; prices on the latter to Samet's main pier, Na Dan, are fixed (B50 one way; 40min). Watch out for rip-off touts in Ban Phe who try to sell boat tickets at inflated prices or falsely claim that visitors to Ko Samet have to buy a return boat ticket. The first boat from Ko Samet back to Ban Phe leaves Na Dan pier at 7am, and in theory there's then an hourly service across to Ban Phe until 6pm, but if you have a plane to catch you should allow for boat no-shows and delays.

Tha Reua Tessaban The municipal pier at the east end of Ban Phe has a rather chaotic market hall of a dozen or so private booths which offer the widest choice of speedboats, as well as wooden boats (in high season, hourly to Na Dan, plus three daily to Ao Wong Duan for B80).

Chok Krisda About 500m west of Tha Reua Tessaban, this helpful pier (☎081 862 4067, �🌐ck-pier.com) offers speedboats (B1300/boat to Na Dan) as well as wooden boats hourly to Na Dan (8am–6pm), Ao Noi Na (2 daily; about 40min; B60) and Ao Wong Duan (2 daily, 3 daily in the opposite direction; about 1hr 15min; B70).

GETTING AROUND

The best way to get up and down the island is by walking along the east-coast beaches and the mostly well-marked paths that connect them. Samet's principal inland road is a rough, deeply rutted and alternately dusty/muddy dirt track that runs north–south and gives access to all the main beaches.

By songthaew Fleets of green songthaews wait for fares at the Na Dan pier and half-a-dozen other stands around the island, as marked on our map; they will also pick up from accommodation if you get staff to phone them. Rates are fixed and high. You'll generally be charged for chartering the whole vehicle (potentially up to B350 to go from Na Dan pier to Ao Sang Thian). Only if there's a large group of people travelling, for example

when boats dock at Na Dan, will you get the "shared" rates (B20–40/person).

By motorbike or ATV You need to be very confident to negotiate the mud and potholes on a motorbike (from B300/day), which is why it's become fashionable to rent a lumbering four-wheeled ATV instead (from B1200/day); both are available for rent at Na Dan pier and on most beaches.

ACCOMMODATION

The trend across the island is upmarket and in high season you'll be hard pressed to secure an en-suite **bungalow** for under B800, though a few no-frills B300 huts do remain. All beaches get packed on weekends and national holidays, when booking ahead is advisable, though, unusually for Thailand, walk-in guests are often offered the best rates. Many bungalow managers raise their **prices** by sixty percent during peak periods and sometimes on weekends as well: the rates quoted here are typical weekday high-season rates.

HAT SAI KAEW AND NA DAN
Much of the accommodation on Hat Sai Kaew is crammed uncomfortably close together and prices are high. Cheap rooms are sometimes available above the shops and restaurants on the Na Dan road.

Laemyai Hut Home North end of Hat Sai Kaew ☎038 644282, �🌐laemyai.com. The fan bungalows here are the best of the cheapest options on this beach, not least because they're dotted widely around a shaded, sandy, plant-filled garden in one of the prettiest spots, under the Laem Yai headland at the quieter northern end. Fan bungalows are simple but en suite and colourfully painted; a/c versions, some with hot showers, are also available. Fan B800, a/c B1200

Lima Bella Na Dan ☎038 644222, ⛏limasamed.com. This little garden haven occupies a quiet heliconia-filled plot with its own pretty swimming pool, on the semicircular road that arcs round behind and to the east of Na Dan high street. Its 26 design-conscious a/c rooms all have hot water, fridges, TVs and daybeds; some have separate mezzanine

bedrooms or living areas and many have bathtubs. The ambience is more intimate and private than most hotels on Samet and it's popular with families. Free wi-fi in the lobby; breakfast included. B3730

Sai Kaew Beach Resort Hat Sai Kaew ☎038 644197, ⛏samedresorts.com. This popular and highly efficient resort has over 150 a/c rooms with hot water, TV and fridge, most of them in distinctive and thoughtfully designed bungalows in bright primary colours. The cheaper "deluxe" cottages and rooms occupy their own grassy area with a separate swimming pool, in front of a pretty but minute little patch of sandy shoreline; they have garden bathrooms and the cottages have private decks. "Premier" rooms are more urban and hotel-like. B6200

Sinsamut Hat Sai Kaew ☎038 644134, ⛏sinsamut -kohsamed.com. Initial appearances aren't encouraging here, with various types of rooms stuffed into cheek-by-jowl little blocks behind the restaurant midway down the beach, but most are pleasant inside, with bright, colourful, contemporary decor, and some have outdoor space. The quirky fan-cooled "*katom*" bungalows, set around a grassy little roof garden, enjoy the best outlook. Free wi-fi throughout. Fan B800, a/c B1500

Ton Sak Resort Hat Sai Kaew ☎038 644314, ⓦtonsak .com. The timbered cabins here are packed very close together, but the surrounding borders of shrubs add a little privacy, and few are more than 100m from the water. Interiors are comfortable if a little old-fashioned, and have a/c and modern hot-water bathrooms. Breakfast included. B3300

AO HIN KOK

Jep's Bungalow Ao Hin Kok ☎038 644112–3. A spread of options in unremarkable wooden chalets and concrete bungalows, ranged up the shady, terraced, sandy-soiled garden: fan-cooled with shared or en-suite bathrooms, or a/c with hot water, TV and breakfast included. It has internet access (computers and wi-fi, both payable), a tour desk and a good restaurant (see p.173). Fan and shared bathroom B300, fan en-suite B500, a/c B1200

Naga Bungalows Ao Hin Kok ☎087 958 6206. Long-running, somewhat jaded resort, with a beachfront bar, a Thai boxing ring, a secondhand bookshop, a bakery, currency exchange, internet access and some of the cheapest accommodation on Ko Samet: simple bamboo and wood huts stacked in tiers up the slope, with decks, mosquito nets and shared bathrooms, as well as pricier concrete a/c rooms with their own adjacent cold-water bathroom. The compound's a bit scrappy, but the rooms are reasonably well maintained. Fan B400, a/c B600

AO PHAI

Lost Resort Ao Phai, on the main track to Wong Duan and Ao Prao ☎038 644041–2, ⓦthelostresort.net. A short way inland from *Sea Breeze*, this two-storey block sits peacefully among the hornbills and fruit bats in a grove of tall trees. The ten rooms here can be fan or a/c and are of a good standard and well priced. Fan B600, a/c B800

Samed Villa South end of Ao Phai ☎038 644094, ⓦsamedvilla.com. The huge rooms and villa-style bungalows at this Swiss-owned resort are packed into a fairly small area along the rocks at the southern end of the bay (good views from the front row) and up the slope behind the restaurant. Interiors are luxurious and well furnished and especially good for families; they all have a/c, hot water, TV, free wi-fi and fridges. Buffet breakfast included. B1600

Silver Sand Middle of Ao Phai ☎038 644300–1, ⓦsilversandresort.samet.i8.com. This party hub has a spread of well-turned-out rooms, including whitewashed, a/c chalets ranged around a pretty garden; they all come with safety boxes, verandas and good modern hot-water bathrooms, and some have polished wooden floors. Fan B800, a/c B1200

AO TUB TIM

★ **Tub Tim Resort** Ao Tub Tim ☎038 644025–9, ⓦtubtimresort.com. The most popular place to stay here is a sprawling, well-run resort with over a hundred handsome chalet-style wooden bungalows of various sizes and designs, all with classy modern furnishings and outdoor space, plus a good restaurant. Fan B600, fan and hot shower B1000, a/c (breakfast included) B1500

AO NUAN

Ao Nuan Bungalows Ao Nuan ☎087 142 7512. The octagonal restaurant and simple, idiosyncratic huts here hark back to a mellower, old-school island vibe, entirely removed from the commercialism of the other beaches (though room rates are definitely modern-day). The nine sturdy timber huts are each built to a slightly different design and dotted across the tree-covered slope that drops down to the bay, with a few hanging right over the beach. Sharing bathrooms, the cheapest are large but spartan, with just a platform bed and a mosquito net; the most expensive now boast a/c and hot water. Fan B800, a/c B1500

AO WONG DUAN

Vong Deuan Resort Middle of Ao Wong Duan ☎038 651777, ⓦvongdeuan.com. Ideally located in the middle of the beach, with attractive a/c bungalows in various designs set around a pretty tropical garden, including nice white cottages with thatched roofs, contemporary styled interiors and garden bathrooms (with hot showers). Service is efficient, attentive and hotel-like, which makes it a favourite with older guests. Breakfast included. B2000

Vongduern Villa Southern Ao Wong Duan ☎038 652300, ⓦvongduernvilla.com. Occupying a big, shady chunk of the bay's southern end, this resort features over fifty rooms of various types and standards, all of them design-conscious and a/c. "Standard" rooms are whitewashed timber huts built on stilts, with picture windows, decks and modern furnishings; while "Deluxe" means more minimalist versions kitted out with dark-wood floors, Japanese-style platform beds and DVD players. There's also an attractive restaurant deck jutting out over the water, a coffee bar and kayaks and snorkelling equipment for rent. Standard B1200, deluxe B1800

AO SANG THIAN

Candlelight Resort Ao Sang Thian ☎089 247 9597. Very nice wooden bungalows with lots of light and air strung out in a long line, each one facing the water. Most are fan-cooled, with hot showers and TVs; the resort's a/c options are either in these wooden bungalows or in large, very clean concrete rooms with small bathrooms behind the restaurant. Fan B800, a/c B1200

2

2

Sang Thian Beach Resort Towards Ao Sang Thian's northern end ☎038 644255, ⓦsangthianbeachresort .com. This complex comprising a minimart, an ATM, a massage centre and expansive, waterfront restaurant areas (with free wi-fi) is somewhat institutional, and the welcome lacks the human touch, too. However, the resort boasts tasteful a/c timber chalets built up the cliffside on a series of decks and steps – the decor is navy-and-white maritime chic. There's hot water, TVs and fridges, and views, mostly encompassing the sea, are pretty. It also has much less interesting compact brick bungalows and concrete rooms up the eastern slope. B2000

AO LUNG DUM

Jelly Fish Lung Dum Ao Lung Dum ☎081 458 8430 or ☎081 652 8056. Friendly spot under the bougainvillaea with a decent waterside restaurant. Most of the twenty bungalows with hot showers are right on the rocky shore, practically overhanging the water; a few cheaper rooms and bungalows at the back are also available. Fan B800, a/c B1000

AO WAI

Sametville Resort Ao Wai ☎038 651681–2, ⓦsametvilleresort.com. At this sizeable resort with a large pool, bungalows in all categories vary in quality, but you've plenty to choose from – including some cute converted boats – unless you come at the weekend, when it tends to fill up with Thai groups. Also on offer are rental motorbikes, snorkelling equipment and Thai massage. Fan B1100, a/c B1700

AO KIU

Paradee Resort and Spa Ao Kiu ☎038 644104–7, ⓦsamedresorts.com. Top of the range on Samet, a very luxurious five-star resort where each of the forty villas stretches over more than 100 square metres and most have their own small private pools. There's also an infinity-edged main pool, a spa and fitness centre, plus lots of nice little extras like DVD players, free wi-fi, free kayaks and snorkelling equipment. B17,000

AO PRAO (PARADISE BAY)

Ao Prao Resort Ao Prao ☎038 644101, ⓦsamedresorts .com. Fifty luxurious wooden chalets and rooms set in a mature tropical garden that slopes down to the beach, all with a/c, TVs and mini-bars. There's an infinity pool, a dive centre, windsurfing and kayaking, among lots of watersports, and a picturesquely sited restaurant with a live band most evenings in high season. The resort runs a shuttle boat from Ban Phe three times a day (B250). B7700

Le Vimarn Cottages Ao Prao ☎038 644104, ⓦsamedresorts.com. The most indulgent resort on this beach comprises charming, gorgeously furnished cottages,

a delightful spa and an infinity pool. Its *Buzz* restaurant (see opposite) is highly regarded. B10,700

Lima Coco Ao Prao ☎038 644068, ⓦlimasamed.com. The youngest, trendiest and cheapest choice on the beach, with a Bangkok contemporary chic look and lots of white walls, brightly coloured cushions, day beds and decks. Rooms are built close together in layers up the side of the hill, so that most have some kind of a sea view. Free wi-fi; kayaks, snorkels and sunbeds for rent. Breakfast included. B4400

AO NOI NA

Baan Ploy Samed (Ploy Sea) Ao Noi Na ☎02 438 9771–2, ⓦsamedresorts.com. Striking, brown contemporary building with an orange infinity pool, where bedrooms done out in dark wood and orange come with a/c, rain showers, TV and fridge. Pricier options come with a sea-view deck, while the most expensive rooms are in stilted wooden houses, 50m out in the sea. Breakfast and boat transfers included. B5500

★ **Baan Puu Paan** Ao Noi Na ☎081 172 4486, ✉lizziecj@hotmail.com or ✉baanpuupaan@hotmail .com. Less than 15min walk from Na Dan, this chilled-out boutique guesthouse offers three beautiful en-suite bungalows built on stilts in the sea. They're all furnished with cushions and lamps, and prices stay the same year-round and at weekends; the pick of them is large and fan-cooled, with cheery maritime decor and a huge deck offering unparalleled views. Guests can either swim off the jetty or from the tiny beaches to either side, and there's a pool table and free wi-fi throughout. Fan B1200, a/c B1500

Mooban Talay Resort Northwestern Ao Noi Na ☎081 838 8682, ⓦmoobantalay.com. At the far northwest end of the beach is one of the classiest resorts on the island, a secluded haven at the end of the road, set under the trees on a gorgeous, quiet white-sand beach. Accommodation is in large, attractive a/c bungalows, all with platform beds, garden bathrooms, wi-fi and outdoor seating: the priciest, seafront ones have enormous decks, and there's a beachside pool and a spa. Boat transfers and breakfast included. B6800

Samed Resort Ao Noi Na ☎038 644334 or ☎081 427 9571, ⓦsamed-resort.net. British-managed set of a dozen bungalows, occupying a wide sandy grove just across the road from a tiny, almost private beach; though the beach is a bit scruffy it has shade, with hammocks, and good swimming. Bungalows range from small, en-suite concrete affairs with hammocks to large cottages with nice mezzanine beds, a/c, TV and hot showers; interiors in all are modern and cheery. In busy periods, you can also rent tents here (B300 for two including bedding). The shoreside restaurant, and its lively bar, has a pool table and table tennis. Free wi-fi throughout. Discounts for longer stays. Fan B500, a/c B1000

EATING AND DRINKING

Most visitors to Ko Samet just eat at their resorts, and in truth there are few restaurants worth making an effort to get to.

HAT SAI KAEW AND NA DAN

Banana Bar and Restaurant Na Dan high street, not far from the police station. Tiny establishment serving tastily authentic yellow, green and red curries (B80), as well as *tom yam* and spicy salads. Daily 9am–11.30pm.

Im Aroy Dii Na Dan high street, 10m from the National Park box on Hat Sai Kaew, on the left-hand side of the road (no English sign). There's not much to this basic but clean and bright restaurant, but its name, meaning "Full, Delicious, Good", says it all: tasty, cheap dishes on rice (from B50), as well as more interesting options such as squid with salted egg and chicken with cashew nuts (both B120). Fruit shakes and a cheery chef-owner, too. Daily early–9pm.

AO HIN KOK

★ **Jep's Bungalow** Ao Hin Kok ✆038 644112, ⊛jepbungalow.com. Popular all-rounder serving a great menu of authentic Thai dishes (including popular *som tam* sets for B150), seafood, Indian (with chicken tikka for B120 and plenty of veggie dishes), Japanese, Italian and Mexican food at its tables on the sand, set under trees strung with fairylights and given extra

atmosphere by mellow music. Also does cappuccino and cakes. Daily 7am–12.30am.

AO PRAO (PARADISE BAY)

Buzz at Le Vimarn Cottages Ao Prao ✆038 644104, ⊛samedresorts.com. Very refined restaurant serving highly regarded, highly priced Thai food, including a wide choice of salads, dips and curries (from B260), in its chic modern dining room and upstairs terrace. The attached Italian restaurant, *O*, is just overpriced.

AO NOI NA

Baan Ploy Samed Ao Noi Na ✆038 644188–9. Seafood restaurant in a group of wooden houses on stilts, 50m out in the sea – a boatman will come over and pick you up. Rock lobster is a speciality (B1500/kg), but there are also more manageable dishes such as shrimp green curry (B200). Daily 10am–10pm.

Summer at Baan Puu Paan Ao Noi Na ✆081 172 4486. Stunningly sited eating area at the end of a jetty, where you can tuck into all kinds of tasty global dishes, from fish tikka (B320) to pasta and risotto. There's also a Moroccan-styled roadside bar-restaurant. Daily 8am–10pm or later.

DIRECTORY

Banks There are ATMs at the Na Dan pier-head, beside the Hat Sai Kaew national park office, on Ao Wong Duan and Ao Sang Thian; the bigger bungalows also change money.
Emergencies Ko Samet's health centre and police station (✆038 644111) are on Na Dan high street, but for anything serious you should go to the Bangkok-Rayong hospital in

Rayong (✆038 921999, ⊛rayonghospital.com).
Internet There are internet centres around the National Park office on the Na Dan high street, a couple of which have wi-fi, and on almost every beach.
Post office At *Naga Bungalows* on Ao Hin Kok.

Chanthaburi

For over five hundred years, the seams of rock rich in sapphires and rubies that streak the hills of eastern Thailand have drawn prospectors and traders of all nationalities to the provincial capital of **CHANTHABURI**, 80km east of Ban Phe. Many of these hopefuls established permanent homes in the town, particularly the Shans from Burma, the Chinese and the Cambodians. Though the veins of precious stones have now been all but exhausted, Chanthaburi's reputation as a gem centre has continued to thrive and this is still one of the most famous places in Thailand to trade in gems (most of them now imported from Sri Lanka and elsewhere), not least because Chanthaburi is as respected a cutting centre as Bangkok, and Thai lapidaries are considered among the most skilled – and affordable – in the world. Chanthaburi is also an exceptionally fertile province, renowned for its abundance of orchards, particularly durian, rambutan and mangosteen, which are celebrated with an annual **fruit festival** in the town, held in May or June.

The town is made for low-key exploration, without being particularly compelling. Similarly, the Chanthaburi coastline is barely developed for tourism, though it's popular with Thai visitors for its quiet, shady beaches. However, even if you're not

CHANTHABURI

ACCOMMODATION
Kasemsarn Hotel — 1
The River Guest House — 2

RESTAURANT
Chanthorn Pochana — 1

planning a visit to Chanthaburi, you may find yourself stranded here for a couple of hours between **buses**, as this is a major transit point for east-coast services (including most Rayong–Trat buses) and a handy terminus for buses to and from the northeast.

Thanon Rim Nam

Chanthaburi's most interesting neighbourhoods are close to the **river**, particularly along **Thanon Rim Nam**, with its mix of pastel-painted, colonial-style housefronts and traditional wooden shophouses, many displaying finely carved latticework. This district is home to a large Catholic Vietnamese community, most of whom fled here in waves following religious persecution between the eighteenth century and the late 1970s. The earliest refugees constructed what is now, following several revamps, Thailand's largest cathedral, the **Church of the Immaculate Conception**, located across the footbridge from the southern end of Thanon Rim Nam.

The gem dealers' quarter

West of the bridge, the **gem dealers' quarter** begins, centred around Trok Kachang and Thanon Sri Chan (the latter signed in English as "Gem Street") and packed with dozens of gem shops. Most lie empty during the week, but on Fridays, Saturdays and

CROSSING TO CAMBODIA VIA CHANTHABURI PROVINCE

Most foreigners use the Aranyaprathet–Poipet crossing to get into **Cambodia** (see p.153), with access possible by bus via Chanthaburi. There are also two less used crossings in Chanthaburi province, giving access to the Cambodian town of Pailin, just east of the border. Daung Lem Border Crossing at **Ban Laem** is 88km northeast of Chanthaburi (not served by public transport) and the Phsa Prom border crossing is at **Ban Pakkard** (aka Chong Phakkat), 72km northeast of Chanthaburi. There's a minibus service in the morning from Chanthaburi (just south across the bridge from *The River Guest House*) to Ban Pakkard (1hr; B150). It's best to arm yourself in advance with an e-visa for Cambodia, but it's also possible to get a thirty-day visa on arrival at the border; if entering Thailand via this route you'll probably be obliged to show proof of onward travel from Thailand.

Sunday mornings they come alive as local dealers arrive to sift through mounds of tiny coloured stones and classify them for resale to the hundreds of buyers who drive down from Bangkok.

Taksin Park

West of the gem quarter and market, the landscaped **Taksin Park** is the town's recreation area and memorial to King Taksin of Thonburi, the general who reunited Thailand between 1767 and 1782 after the sacking of Ayutthaya by the Burmese. Chanthaburi was the last Burmese bastion on the east coast – when Taksin took the town he effectively regained control of the whole country. The park's heroic bronze statue of Taksin is featured on the back of the B20 note.

ARRIVAL AND DEPARTURE   CHANTHABURI TOWN

By bus Chanthaburi bus station (☎039 311299) is on Thanon Saritdidech, about 750m northwest of the town centre and market. Seven daily buses make the scenic Chanthaburi–Sa Kaew–Khorat journey in both directions – Sa Kaew is a useful interchange for buses to Aranyaprathet and Cambodia (see box, p.153).

Destinations Bangkok (Eastern Bus Terminal; at least hourly; 4–5hr); Bangkok (Northern Bus Terminal; 13 daily; 3–4hr); Bangkok (Suvarnabhumi Airport; 5 daily; 3hr); Khorat (7 daily; 6hr); Laem Ngop (for Ko Chang; 3 daily; 1hr); Phitsanulok (daily; 11hr); Rayong (8 daily; 2hr); Sa Kaew (for Aranyaprathet; 10 daily; 3hr); Trat (hourly; 1hr 30min).

ACCOMMODATION

Kasemsarn Hotel 98/1 Thanon Benchama-Rachutit ☎039 312340, ⓦkasemsarnhotel.net. Unexpectedly contemporary hotel, whose comfortable a/c rooms, with hot showers, fridges and TVs, are built round a central atrium and done out in whitewash and dark wood; they all have free wi-fi and there are free computers and a smart coffee shop downstairs. B800
The River Guesthouse 3/5–8 Thanon Sri Chan ☎039 328211. Traveller-oriented outfit on the edge of the gems quarter, with a riverside terrace next to the road bridge where breakfast is served. Its cheapest rooms are tiny and windowless and share cold-water bathrooms; the better fan and a/c en-suite rooms have narrow beds and TVs, and some boast river-view balconies and hot showers. Computers and free wi-fi throughout. Fan B150, en-suite fan B250, a/c B400

EATING

Foodstalls in the market and along the riverside sois sell Vietnamese spring rolls (*cha gio*) with sweet sauce. Locally made Chanthaburi rice noodles (*sen Chan*) are popularly used in *phat thai* throughout Thailand, but in Chanthaburi they're also crucial to the local beef noodle soup, *kway tiaw neua liang*, whose dark broth is flavoured with pungent herbs and spices, including the cardamom that the Chanthaburi mountains are famous for.

Chanthorn Phochana 102/5–8 Thanon Benchama-Rachutit. By far the best of the town's restaurants is this spot a few metres up the road from the *Kasemsarn Hotel*, for which Thai foodies make a beeline. As well as selling Chanthaburi delicacies as souvenirs, it serves regional dishes such as *lon puu* (a kind of salad dip with crab; B100) and *kway tiaw neua liang*, and a delicious range of spicy *yam* salads, Thai curries and stir-fries, many of them using local herbs and vegetables. Daily 8.30am–9pm.

Coastal Chanthaburi

The barely developed **coastline** to the west of Chanthaburi is very pretty, popular with Thai visitors for its empty beaches and shady casuarina trees and worth exploring if you have your own transport.

Hat Khung Wiman and Ao Khung Kraben

Just off Route 3399, about 30km southwest of Chanthaburi, or 80km east of Ban Phe, **HAT KHUNG WIMAN** is a quiet, shady, bronze-sand beach and has two nice places to stay. A couple of kilometres southeast of here and you're at the lip of **AO KHUNG KRABEN**, a deep, lagoon-like scoop of a bay that's occasionally visited by dugongs and is edged by dense mangrove forest. A wide swathe of this mangrove swamp is protected under a royal conservation project and crossed by a km-long boardwalk; you can also rent kayaks in the cool season to follow a signed riverine trail. Access is via Laem Sadet on the southern curve of the bay.

KKB (Khung Kraben Bay) Aquarium

Across the road from the mangrove project on Laem Sadet's beach road • Tues–Fri 8.30am–4.30pm, Sat & Sun 8.30am–5.30pm • Free • ⓦ aquariumthailand.com

The impressively stocked **KKB Aquarium** is a royal initiative and displays a multicoloured variety of reef fish, some sea horses and a few larger marine creatures, with informative English signage.

ACCOMMODATION   **KHUNG WIMAN**

Al Medina Beach House Hat Khung Wiman ⓣ 039 417105, ⓦ almedinabeach.com. Nine very chic, Moroccan-inspired rooms, all with a/c, hot water and DVD players, some with rain showers and bathtubs. Bicycles, kayaks and wi-fi available. Breakfast included. B4550

★ **Faasai Resort** Khung Wiman ⓣ 039 417404, ⓦ faasai.com. This New Zealand–Thai owned, environmentally conscious resort is an ideal base from which to explore the coast. Its comfortable, family-friendly, a/c bungalows sit in a tropical garden with views to the Cardamom mountains on the Cambodian border and there's a swimming pool, wi-fi and Wat Pho-trained massage therapists on site. Very unusually, the resort also has its own private little wetland conservation area, where you can sit bird-watching, swim in the natural spring pool or kayak along the rivulet. Hat Khung Wiman is 10min walk away and *Faasai* rents bicycles, motorbikes and cars and organizes interesting local tours. B1700

Trat

The small and pleasantly unhurried provincial capital of **TRAT**, 68km southeast of Chanthaburi, is the perfect place to stock up on essentials, extend your visa, or simply take a break before striking out again. Most travellers who find themselves here are heading either for Ko Chang, via the nearby port at **Laem Ngop**, for the outer islands, or for Cambodia, via the border at **Hat Lek**, 91km southeast of town. But Trat itself has its own distinctive, if understated, old-Thailand charm and there are lots of welcoming guesthouses to tempt you into staying longer.

YELLOW OIL

Trat is famous across Thailand for the **yellow herbal oil** mixture, *yaa luang*, invented by one of its residents, Mae Ang Ki, and used by Thais to treat many ailments: sniff it for travel sickness and blocked sinuses, or rub it on to relieve mosquito and sandfly bites, ease stomach cramps, or sterilize wounds. Ingredients include camphor and aloe vera. It's well worth investing in a lip-gloss-sized bottle of the stuff before heading off to the sandfly-plagued islands; you can buy it for about B70 and upwards at Trat market and at nearby Tratosphere bookshop. There are now several imitations, but Mae Ang Ki's original product (ⓦ somthawinyellowoil.com) has a tree logo to signify that it's made by royal appointment.

TRAT

■ ACCOMMODATION	
Ban Jaidee	1
Basar Garden	3
Residang House	4
Rimklong Boutique Hotel	2

● RESTAURANTS	
Cool Corner	2
Kluarimklong	3
Raan Ahaan Mangsawirat	1

● SHOP	
Tratosphere	1

2

Though there are no real sights in Trat, the historic neighbourhood down by Khlong Trat, where you'll find most of the guesthouses and traveller-oriented restaurants, is full of old wooden shophouses and narrow, atmospheric sois. The covered market in the heart of town is another fun place to wander. Out-of-town attractions that make enjoyable focuses for a leisurely cycle ride (ask at *Cool Corner* restaurant for detailed directions and other recommended routes) include the mangrove forest to the southeast near Dan Khao, and the ornate seventeenth-century **Wat Buppharam**, 2km west of Trat Department Store, and the nearby lake.

Mangrove forest

Slightly further afield, in the **mangrove forest** near Dan Khao, 5.5km southeast of town, a boardwalk with informative English signs takes you through the swamp; after dark it's a good place to see twinkling fireflies too. The boardwalk access is currently unsigned in English, but head for Dan Kao and after about 5.4km you'll pass dolphin statues on your left; the track to the mangroves is about 100m further on, on the right (if you get to the estuary and road's end you've gone about 500m too far).

ARRIVAL AND DEPARTURE   TRAT

BY PLANE
Tiny **Trat airport** (☏ 039 525767–8), served by Bangkok

Airways, is about 16km from the Ko Chang piers at Laem Ngop. There's an airport shuttle minibus direct to Ko Chang hotels for B470/person, including ferry ticket (B700 by speedboat). However, Bangkok Airways keeps the cost of shared a/c minibuses to Trat town extortionately high at B500/person, for a ride of less than 30min (though at least you'll be dropped off at your hotel).

Destinations Bangkok (3 daily; 50min); Ko Samui (4 weekly; 1hr 15min); Phuket (4 weekly; 3hr).

BY BUS

All buses terminate at the bus station, 1.5km northeast of central Trat on Highway 318, from where songthaews shuttle passengers into the town centre (B20, or B60 if chartered) or on to the departure points for the islands (see below). A/c minibuses to Bangkok's Victory Monument leave from the 7-Eleven just off Thanon Vivatthana, on the north side of town; there are also minibuses to Hat Lek from the bus station (see box below).

Destinations Bangkok (Eastern Bus Terminal; 6 daily; 4hr 30min–6hr); Bangkok (Northern Bus Terminal; 6 daily; 4hr 30min); Bangkok (Suvarnabhumi Airport; 6 daily; 4hr 10min); Chanthaburi (hourly; 1hr 30min); Pattaya (6 daily; 4hr 30min); Rayong (6 daily; 3hr 30min); Si Racha (6 daily; 5hr).

BY BOAT

Details of boat services to Ko Chang, Ko Mak and Ko Kood are given in the relevant accounts. If you book your boat ticket through your guesthouse in Trat, you should be able to arrange pick-up (usually free) from the guesthouse.

VIA LAEM NGOP

All ferries to Ko Chang and some services to Ko Mak leave from one of three piers to the west of the small port town of Laem Ngop, 17km southwest of Trat (see map, p.182): Tha Thammachat and Tha Centrepoint for the Ko

Chang car ferries, and Tha Kromaluang (Naval Monument Pier) for Ko Mak. These piers are served by songthaew share-taxis from Trat's bus station and by songthaew and a/c minibus share-taxis from Thanon Sukhumvit in the town centre, costing B50/person or B250–300 if chartered; if sharing, allow 60–90min before your boat leaves for the share-taxi to fill up and get you to the pier. There's also plenty of long-distance transport direct to Laem Ngop, bypassing Trat town: a/c buses from Bangkok (5hr 15min–6hr), either from the Eastern (Ekamai) Bus Terminal, via Suvarnabhumi Airport and Chanthaburi (3–4 daily), or from Thanon Khao San and Hualamphong Station (2 daily); and a/c minibuses from Bangkok's Victory Monument, Northern and Eastern bus terminals, Suvarnabhumi Airport and Thanon Khao San.

VIA TRAT–SALAK PET SONGTHAEW

If you're going to the east coast of Ko Chang you can take a direct songthaew to Salak Pet (B150, including car ferry) from the temple compound behind *KFC* and Trat Department Store in Trat.

VIA LAEM SOK

Some boats to Ko Mak and nearly all boats to Ko Kood depart from Laem Sok, 30km south of Trat; boat tickets bought in Trat should include free transfers to Laem Sok, but there's also a Laem Sok songthaew service (30–60min) that leaves from the town centre (see map, p.177).

VIA BAN DAN KAO

A few boats to the outer islands depart from Ban Dan Kao, on the river estuary 6km northeast of Trat town; again, your boat ticket should include free transfers to Dan Kao, but otherwise you'll have to charter a songthaew from Trat market.

CROSSING THE CAMBODIAN BORDER VIA HAT LEK

Many travellers use the **Hat Lek–Koh Kong border crossing** for overland travel into Cambodia. It's best to arm yourself in advance with an **e-visa** for Cambodia (see p.29) and to make the journey by regular public transport, but it's also possible to buy a package all the way through to Sihanoukville and Phnom Penh (B750–1000 through travel agents in Trat) and to get a thirty-day visa on arrival at the border, though both of the latter options are more likely to open you up to possible **scams** (see p.153). For a comprehensive guide to the crossing and to the various transport options – and scams – on both sides of the border, see ⓦtalesofasia.com/cambodia-overland.htm and the ⓦthaivisa.com forum.

The only way to get to **Hat Lek** under your own steam is by minibus from Trat bus station, 91km northwest (roughly every 45min; 1hr–1hr 30min; B120). Hat Lek (on the Thai side) and Koh Kong (in Cambodia) are on opposite sides of the Dong Tong River estuary, but a bridge connects the two banks. Once through immigration, taxis ferry you into **Koh Kong** town for onward transport to Sihanoukville and Phnom Penh or for guesthouses should you arrive too late for connections (mid-afternoon onwards). **Vans, buses and share-taxis** to Phnom Penh and Sihanoukville take around 4–5hr.

INFORMATION

Tourist information The Trat and Ko Chang TAT office (daily 8.30am–4.30pm; ☎039 597259, ✉tattrat@tat.or.th) is out in Laem Ngop, but any guesthouse will help you out with information on transport to the islands or into Cambodia. Alternatively, drop by the Tratosphere bookshop at 23 Soi Kluarimklong (☎039 523200) for tips on Trat and the islands from the knowledgeable French owner, have a look at his website, ⓦtratmap.com, or visit *Cool Corner* restaurant for a browse through the travellers' comment books.

ACCOMMODATION

Most **guesthouses** in Trat are small and friendly and are well used to fielding travellers' queries about the islands and Cambodia. All those listed here are within 10min walk of the covered market.

★ **Ban Jaidee** 67 Thanon Chaimongkon ☎039 520678 or ☎083 589 0839, ✉maneesita@hotmail.com. Very calm, inviting and rather stylish guesthouse with a pleasant seating area downstairs and just nine simple bedrooms. The nicest rooms are in the original building and have polished wood floors, though those in the modern extension are further from the traffic noise. All rooms share hot-water bathrooms. Free wi-fi. B200

Basar Garden 87 Thanon Thoncharoen ☎039 523247 or ☎087 402 4620. Decent-sized en-suite rooms in a lovely, atmospheric old wooden house at the greener end of town. Curtains and drapes made from faded batik sarongs add to the faintly bohemian ambience and all rooms have fans and mosquito nets. Free wi-fi and free bicycles. B250

Residang House 87/1–2 Thanon Thoncharoen ☎039 530103, ⓦtrat-guesthouse.com. Comfortably appointed, good-value three-storey German–Thai-managed guesthouse. Rooms are large, light and clean and all have windows, thick mattresses, hot-water bathrooms and wi-fi; there are family rooms too. Internet access downstairs. Fan B300, a/c B500

★ **Rimklong Boutique Hotel** 194 Thanon Lak Muang ☎039 523388, ✉soirimklong@hotmail.co.th. The four ground-floor rooms (plus one apartment) at this friendly, popular hotel are done out in a crisp contemporary style and well-equipped: a/c, hot water, cable TV, fridge and free wi-fi. Those on the side offer a bit more privacy than the two whose doors open right onto Thanon Lak Muang. The café in reception boasts a serious espresso machine, but you'll have to bring in your own food from outside for breakfast. B800

EATING

Two of the best and cheapest **places to eat** in Trat are at the covered day market on Thanon Sukhumvit, and the night market (roughly 5–10pm), between Soi Vichidanya and Soi Kasemsan, east of Thanon Sukhumvit.

★ **Cool Corner** 49–51 Thanon Thoncharoen. Run single-handedly by a local writer/artist, this place has lots of personality, both in its cute hand-painted decor and in its traveller-oriented menu of real coffee, Indian chai, veggie specials, quality breakfasts and great Thai food (including chicken and cashew nuts for B90). A good place to while away an hour or three, listening to the mellow music and perusing the travellers' comment books. Daily roughly 7am–10pm, sometimes closing in the afternoon.

Kluarimklong Soi Kluarimklong. More Bangkok than Trat in its style and menu, this unexpectedly classy little place, under the same ownership as the nearby *Rimklong* Boutique Hotel, has both an indoor and a courtyard dining area. It serves delicious, upmarket Thai food, including steamed *haw mok thalay* seafood curry with coconut (B80) and lots of spicy *yam* salads and *tom yam* soups. Daily 11am–10pm.

Raan Ahaan Mangsawirat No English sign, but follow the soi near Ban Jaidee, off Thanon Chaimongkon. Typical no-frills, very cheap Thai vegetarian place, where you choose two portions of veggie curry, stir-fry or stew from the trays laid out in the display cabinet, and pay about B30 including rice. Open early morning until about 1/2pm.

SHOPPING

Tratosphere 23 Soi Kluarimklong ☎039 523200. This French–Thai place is a cut above most secondhand bookshops and a very good source of local information; you can also buy curios from all over Thailand here, as well as Mae Ang Ki yellow oil. Daily, variable hours.

DIRECTORY

Emergencies Call the tourist police, who have a base at Laem Ngop, on ☎1155 (free, 24hr).

Hospital The best hospital is the private Bangkok–Trat Hospital (☎039 532735 or freephone ☎1719, ⓦbangkoktrathospital.com), part of the Bangkok Hospital group, which has emergency facilities; it's on the Sukhumvit

Highway, 1km north of Trat Department Store.
Immigration office Located in Laem Ngop, 100m west of the TAT office (Mon–Fri 8.30am–4.30pm; ☎ 039 597261).
Travel agencies Book international and domestic flights

at Koh Chang TT Travel on Thanon Sukhumvit (☎ 039 531420; closed Sun); they also book accommodation on the islands, arrange taxis to Trat airport and transport to Cambodia, and provide local information.

Ko Chang

2

Edged with a chain of long, mostly white-sand beaches and dominated by a broad central spine of jungle-clad hills that rises sharply to over 700m, **KO CHANG** is developing fast but still feels green. It's Thailand's second-largest island, after Phuket, but unlike its bigger sister has no villages or tourist facilities within its steeply contoured and densely forested **interior**, just a few rivers, waterfalls and hiking trails that come under the auspices of the Mu Ko Chang National Park. Some of its marine environment is also protected, as the national park extends to over forty other islands in the Ko Chang archipelago. Ko Chang's own coast, however, has seen major development over the past decade, and the island is now well established as a mainstream destination, crowded with package tourists and the overspill from Pattaya, and suffering the inevitable inflated prices and inappropriate architecture. That said, it's still possible to find accommodation to suit most budgets and though the beaches may be busy they're undeniably handsome, with plenty of inviting places to swim, stroll, or snooze under a palm tree.

At 30km north to south, Ko Chang has plenty of coast to explore. The western **beaches** are the prettiest and the most congested, with **White Sand Beach** (**Hat Sai Khao**) drawing the biggest crowds to its mainly upmarket and increasingly overpriced mid-range accommodation; smaller **Hat Kai Bae** is also busy. Most backpackers opt for so-called **Lonely Beach** (officially **Hat Tha Nam**), with its roadside village of travellers' accommodation and famous beachfront party scene; those in search of quiet choose the more laidback **Hat Khlong Phrao**, a long and lovely sweep of sand that caters to most pockets, or **Bang Bao**, which has a village on a jetty with fine views, and its quiet neighbouring beach, **Hat Khlong Gloi**. Every beach has **currency exchange** and most have **ATMs**, along with minimarkets, tour agents, dive shops, internet access, clothes stalls and souvenir shops. White Sand Beach and Hat Kai Bae have the densest concentrations of facilities.

During **peak season**, accommodation on every beach tends to fill up very quickly, so it's worth booking ahead. The island gets a lot quieter (and cheaper) from June to October, when heavy downpours and fierce storms can make life miserable, though sunny days are common too; be especially careful of riptides on all the beaches during the monsoon season.

Sandflies can be a problem on the southern beaches (see p.64); watch out also for **jellyfish**, which plague the west coast in April and May, and for **snakes**, including surprisingly common cobras, sunbathing on the overgrown paths into the interior. The other hazard is **theft** from rooms and bungalows: use your own padlock on bags (and doors where possible) or, better still, make use of hotel safety boxes. After a local eradication programme, Ko Chang is no longer considered to be a malaria-risk area by health authorities in the US and the UK.

ARRIVAL AND DEPARTURE   KO CHANG

Access to Ko Chang from the **mainland** is by boat from the Laem Ngop coast, 17km southwest of Trat; details of transport to and from Laem Ngop are given on p.178. On arrival, tickets on tourist buses and minibuses to Ko Chang will often include the ferry crossing and transport to your hotel. During high season there are also boats to Ko Chang from Ko Mak and Ko Kood. On Ko Chang, **songthaew share-taxis** meet boats at the Tha Dan Kao and Ao Saparot ferry piers and transport passengers to west-coast beaches (B50 to White Sand Beach, 25min; B100 to Lonely Beach, 1hr; B150 to Bang Bao, 1hr 15min). On departure, either wait for a songthaew on the main road or ask your accommodation to book one for you (for a small extra fee, usually B20). If you're heading to Ko Chang's east coast, you can make use of the songthaew through-service from central Trat (see p.178).

CLOCKWISE FROM TOP LEFT KO MAK (P.194); KO SAMET (P.166); KO SI CHANG (P.154) >

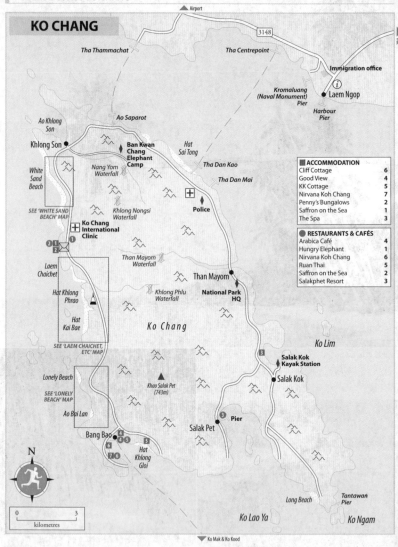

KO CHANG

Airport
3148
Trat

Tha Thammachat
Tha Centrepoint
Immigration office
Kromaluang (Naval Monument) Pier
Laem Ngop
Harbour Pier

Ao Khlong Son
Ao Saparot
Khlong Son
Hat Sai Tong
Ban Kwan Chang Elephant Camp
Tha Dan Kao
White Sand Beach
Nang Yom Waterfall
Tha Dan Mai

SEE 'WHITE SAND BEACH' MAP
Khlong Nongsi Waterfall
Police

Ko Chang International Clinic

Laem Chaichet
Than Mayom Waterfall
Than Mayom
Hat Khlong Phrao
Khlong Phlu Waterfall
National Park HQ
Hat Kai Bae
Ko Chang
Ko Lim

SEE 'LAEM CHAICHET, ETC' MAP
Salak Kok Kayak Station
Salak Kok

Lonely Beach
Khao Salak Pet (743m)
SEE 'LONELY BEACH' MAP
Ao Bai Lan
Pier
Salak Pet

N
Bang Bao
Hat Khlong Gloi

0   3
kilometres

Long Beach
Tantawan Pier
Ko Lao Ya
Ko Chang
Ko Ngam

Ko Mak & Ko Kood

■ ACCOMMODATION	
Cliff Cottage	6
Good View	4
KK Cottage	5
Nirvana Koh Chang	7
Penny's Bungalows	2
Saffron on the Sea	1
The Spa	3

● RESTAURANTS & CAFÉS	
Arabica Café	4
Hungry Elephant	1
Nirvana Koh Chang	6
Ruan Thai	5
Saffron on the Sea	2
Salakphet Resort	3

BY BOAT AND PLANE

Bangkok Airways runs a shuttle bus service from Ko Chang beaches via the ferry and on to Trat Airport (B470/person, or B700 by speedboat; see p.177); contact the office in central Hat Sai Khao on ☎ 039 551654.

BY BOAT VIA LAEM NGOP

The main Laem Ngop–Ko Chang boat services are operated by two different car ferry companies from two different piers. Fares are competitive and change frequently: expect to pay B80–120/person one way, and about B200 for a vehicle, though deals on the latter vary considerably.

Centrepoint Ferry (☎ 039 538196) runs from Tha Centrepoint, 3km west of Laem Ngop, to Tha Dan Kao; and the more popular Ferry Ko Chang (☎ 039 518588 or ☎ 039 555188) runs from Tha Thammachat, 9km west of Laem Ngop, to Ao Saparot.

Destinations Tha Thammachat–Ao Saparot (25min); Tha Centrepoint–Tha Dan Kao (45min). Departures 6/6.30am–6/7pm, hourly in high season, every 2hr rest of year.

BY BOAT AND BUS FROM KO CHANG

Every tour agency on Ko Chang offers all manner of bus and a/c minibus packages (including ferries) from the island to other popular tourist destinations – we've listed the key ones. Most (it's worth checking) will include pick-up from your hotel either by songthaew, if you're going by big bus from the mainland ports, or by the minibus itself, which will then board the ferry and take you all the way through.

Destinations Bangkok (big bus to Khao San Rd B300, not including songthaew to the ferry; minibus to Khao San Rd B650; minibus to Sukhumvit Rd hotels B800; about 5hr); Bangkok Suvarnabhumi Airport (big bus B450; minibus B800; about 5hr); Ban Phe (for Ko Samet, minibus B600; about 3hr 30min); Pattaya (minibus B600; about 4hr 30min); Cambodia (minibus to Siem Reap, changing at the border, B600; about 10hr).

BY BOAT VIA KO MAK AND KO KOOD

In high season, Bang Bao Boat (☎ 087 054 4300, ⓦ bangbaoboat.com) runs wooden boats from Bang Bao on Ko Chang to *Koh Mak Resort* on Ao Suan Yai on Koh Mak, as well as speedboats to *Koh Mak Resort* and on to the west coast of Ko Kood. Prices include transfers to or from the west coast of Ko Chang. Several other companies run similar high-season inter-island speedboats (for the same prices), including Kai Bae and Leelawadee, who sail from Hat Kai Bae on Ko Chang, via *Makathanee Resort* on Ao Kao on Ko Mak, to the west coast of Ko Kood. Tour agencies on Ko Chang, as well as guesthouses on Ko Mak and Ko Kood, will have current details.

Bang Bao Boat destinations Wooden boat Ko Chang–Ko Mak (roughly Sept–June daily; 1hr 30min–2hr; B400); speedboat Ko Chang–Ko Mak (roughly Sept–June 2 daily; 1hr; B550), then Ko Mak–Ko Kood (about 1hr; B400 – Ko Chang to Ko Kood B900).

GETTING AROUND

By songthaew A paved road runs nearly all the way round the island connecting all the beaches, served by plentiful, white songthaew share-taxis. They tend to charge according to how many passengers they have as well as the distance travelled (usually B50–150/person), but sometimes, especially on more remote beaches, you might have to wait until they fill up with enough passengers or the driver will ask you to charter the whole vehicle.

By motorbike or car You can rent motorbikes (from B250) and cars (from B1000) on every beach, but the road is notoriously dangerous, with precipitously steep hills punctuated by sharp, unexpected hairpins, and many reckless, often drunk drivers, so think twice if you're an inexperienced motorcyclist – accidents happen every day and fatalities are frequent.

By mountain bike Available opposite Ko Chang Gym in the VJ Plaza complex in Laem Chaichet (B250/day).

INFORMATION

Tourist information The widely distributed detailed free maps and quarterly Ko Chang guides published by Whitesands Publications (ⓦ koh-chang-guide.com) are a handy source of information, and the website provides an accommodation-booking service, but for more intelligent insights and opinionated advice, check out ⓦ iamkoh chang.com, compiled by a Ko Chang resident.

DIRECTORY

Clinic The private 24hr Ko Chang International Clinic (☎ 1719 or ☎ 039 532735, ⓦ bangkoktrathospital.com) is located beyond the south end of White Sand Beach, 1km south of *Plaloma Resort*; it has emergency ambulances and a dental service, and will transfer seriously ill patients to its parent Bangkok–Trat Hospital in Trat.

Post office On the main road beyond the southern end of White Sand Beach (Mon–Fri 10am–noon & 1–6pm, Sat 10am–1pm).

Tourist police At the north end of Hat Khlong Phrao (☎ 1155).

Travel agent A good, helpful agent – for flights, hotel bookings, day-trips, onward transport, car and bike rental, as well as overseas calls and internet access – is Koh Chang Adventure Travel on Hat Sai Khao, between Bangkok Airways and Soi Kert Manee (☎ 039 551389 or ☎ 089 247 6834).

White Sand Beach (Hat Sai Khao)

Framed by a band of fine white sand at low tide, a fringe of casuarinas and palm trees and a backdrop of forested hills, **Hat Sai Khao**, more commonly referred to as **White Sand Beach**, is, at 2.5km long, the island's longest beach and its most commercial, with scores of mid-range and upmarket hotel and bungalow operations packed together along the shore, plus dozens of shops, travel agents, bars and restaurants lining the inland side of the road. The vibe is much more laidback and traveller-oriented at the far quieter

2

KO CHANG ACTIVITIES

Tour agents on every beach or at your accommodation should be able to sell you tickets for most of the **activities** described below. There are **spas** at Ao Bai Lan (see p.192) and Ao Salak Kok (see p.193); you can also **snorkel** and **dive** in the archipelago (see p.186).

ELEPHANT CAMPS

Ko Chang or "Elephant Island" is named for its hilly profile rather than its indigenous pachyderms, but there are several **elephant camps** on the island that have brought in their own lumbering forest dwellers so that tourists can ride and help bathe them.

Ban Kwan Chang (Khlong Son) Elephant Camp East of Khlong Son village ☎081 919 3995 (not to be confused with Baan Chang Thai in Khlong Phrao). Based in a quiet, forested area in the north of the island, this is the camp with the best reputation. It was set up by the man behind the Asian Elephant Foundation and is staffed by Suay mahouts and their elephants from Ban Ta Klang village in northeast Thailand, which has for centuries been a centre for working elephants. In the morning, visitors can either do a 40min elephant ride through adjacent plantations (B500) or extend the ride to an hour and bathe and feed the animals as well (B900); in the afternoon, 35min rides cost B450. Return transport from your accommodation is included. You could extend your trip to this part of the island by making the easy 300m walk to tiny Nang Yom falls, 500m beyond the camp, though Khlong Phlu falls in Khlong Phrao are more satisfying (see p.187).

KAYAKING

Kayak Chang At Amari Emerald Cove Resort, Hat Khlong Phrao ☎087 673 1923, ⓦ kayakchang.com. Well-organized, safety-conscious, British-run company offering half- (B1500) and full-day (B2100) local trips and expeditions around the archipelago of up to 7 days, as well as kayaking lessons and rental. Return transport from your accommodation is included.

YOGA

Baan Zen Hat Khlong Phrao ☎086 530 9354, ⓦ baanzen.com. Private, 90min yoga classes (B900) and short courses (from B5500 for 3 days), as well as reiki courses.

COOKING CLASSES

KaTi Culinary Cooking School Hat Khlong Phrao ☎039 557252, ⓦ kati-culinary.com. The amiable chef who runs the recommended *KaTi* restaurant teaches well-regarded cooking classes (Mon–Sat; B1200, including recipe book and transfers as far as White Sand Beach and Hat Kai Bae).

northern end of the beach, however, beyond *KC Grande*, and this is where the most budget-priced accommodation squeezes in, some of it pleasingly characterful and nearly all of it enjoying its own sea view. An extra bonus is that the road is well out of earshot up here, and there's hardly any passing pedestrian traffic. There are some low-key beach **bars** up there too, and more along the shorefront in the central beach area – all of them quite different in feel from the rash of brash, Pattaya-style bar-beers inland from *Plaloma Cliff Resort* in southern Hat Sai Khao. Wherever you stay on Hat Sai Khao, be careful when swimming as the **currents** are very strong and there's no lifeguard service.

ACCOMMODATION

WHITE SAND BEACH

Arunee Resort Just across the road from White Sand Beach ☎039 551075, ✉aruneeresorttour@hotmail .com; map opposite. Built in a partitioned wooden row-house, the sixteen small, very simple terraced rooms here all have a small veranda, mattress, fan and tiny en-suite bathroom and are a good price for central Hat Sai Khao. The friendly owner has a tour desk and internet shop out front. **B500**

Cookies Hotel White Sand Beach ☎081 861 4227, ⓦ cookieskohchang.com; map opposite. If you want hotel-style facilities at affordable prices this is a good option, right in the middle of the beach. Rooms are in two locations, with the far less interesting site being across the road, with only shops and traffic to look at through the picture windows. Better to pay B500 extra and go for a ground-floor, sea-view "superior" room, set round the shorefront swimming pool. Rooms are large and comfortable and all have a/c, hot water, TV, fridge and a veranda. **B2000**

KC Grande Resort White Sand Beach ☎039 551199, ⓦkckohchang.com; map right. The largest and priciest hotel on the beach is able to charge top dollar because it spreads over a huge area of the northern shorefront. Accommodation ranges from rows of a/c bungalows set in landscaped gardens fronting the beach to more expensive rooms, some with sea views, in the three-storey hotel block. Facilities are good and include a pool, a spa, free wi-fi and a bar with live bands in the evening. Breakfast included. B4500

Maylamean Bungalows White Sand Beach ☎082 257 6271; map right. In the cluster of funky, north-beach cliffside shanty bungalows, this stands out both for its colourful paintwork and because its en-suite rooms and wooden huts, while also built on stilts steeply up the cliffside, are larger and a bit more private than many of its neighbours. B450, with hot shower B800

Penny's Bungalows Beyond the south end of White Sand Beach, down a lane behind the post office ☎039 551122, ⓦpenny-thailand.com; map p.182. Welcoming, helpful, German-run place on what's sometimes called Pearl Beach (Hat Khai Mook). On a compact, flowery plot around a lovely little pool with a kids' pool and jacuzzi, the well-maintained bungalows and hotel-style rooms all have a/c, hot water, TV, fridge and a few decorative touches; the smaller, cheaper ones are near the sea. The free wi-fi in the restaurant reaches some of the rooms. B1200

★ **Saffron on the Sea** Beyond the south end of White Sand Beach, three doors north of Penny's (see above) ☎039 551253, ⓔkochangsaffron onthesea@yahoo.com; map p.182. In a lovely, lush garden behind a very good restaurant (see p.187) are seven attractive, homely rooms with a/c, hot water, TV and fridge; cheaper rooms have no sea view. Management is friendly and there's free wi-fi in the restaurant, free kayaks and snorkels. B1600

Star Beach White Sand Beach ☎087 558 4085; map right. Basic, cheerily painted plywood huts cling limpet-like to the rock-face here, just above the sand on the quiet, northern stretch of the beach. Rooms are very simple but are all en suite (some with hot showers) and enjoy high-level sea views and breezes. B500

White Sand Beach Resort White Sand Beach ☎081 863 7737, ⓦwhitesandbeachresort.net; map right. Spread across a long, attractive stretch of uncommercialized beach at the far north end of the beach, *White Sand* offers a big range of nicely spaced bungalows, many of them lapping up uninterrupted sea views. Interiors are fairly

WHITE SAND BEACH (HAT SAI KHAO)

N

■ ACCOMMODATION	
Arunee Resort	5
Cookies Hotel	6, 7
KC Grande Resort	4
Maylamean Bungalows	2
Star Beach	3
White Sand Beach Resort	1

● RESTAURANTS	
15 Palms	2
Norng Bua Seafood	3
Pen's	1
The Spa	4

■ BARS	
Oodie's Place	1
Sabay Bar	2

Police box

7- Eleven

Pharmacy

BB Divers

Bangkok Airways

Koh Chang Adventure Travel

SOI KERT MANEE

Scuba Zone

V- Mart

Chang Kao Plaza

Ploloma Cliff Resort

0 — 500
metres

Ko Chang International Clinic, Post Office & Pearl Beach ▼

Ao Saparot & Tha Dan Kao

simple, but have a/c, wooden floors, hot showers, TVs, fridges and a faintly contemporary style. For a proper peaceful beach vibe and a little bit of affordable comfort, within 10min walk of resort facilities, this is a good option considering the competition. If arriving by songthaew, get off at the 7-Eleven beside *KC Grande* and phone for transport. B1500

2

DIVING AND SNORKELLING IN THE KO CHANG ARCHIPELAGO

Because there's just one main tide a day in the inner Gulf, the **reefs** of the Ko Chang archipelago are much less colourful and varied than Andaman coast dive sites, and they can get very crowded, but they're rewarding enough to make a day-trip worthwhile. The main **dive and snorkel sites** are west of Ko Mak, in the national marine park around **Ko Rang** and its satellite islets. These range from beginners' reefs with lots of hard corals and anemones at depths of 4–6m, frequented by plenty of reef fish – including a resident ten-thousand-strong shoal of yellow fusiliers – and the occasional moray eel, to the more challenging 25m dive at the Pinnacles. There are also some technical wreck dives of Japanese boats from World War II and even some centuries-old Chinese trading ships. The coral around Ko Yuak, off Ko Chang's Hat Kai Bae, is mostly dead, though some operators still sell trips there.

DIVE SHOPS ON KO CHANG

The biggest concentration of **dive shops** is on Ko Chang, though there are also some on Ko Mak and Ko Kood (see relevant accounts for details). All dive shops on Ko Chang will organize pick-ups from any beach.

Waves permitting, Ko Chang operators run trips year-round, though during the **monsoon season** (June–Sept), visibility can be poor. **Prices** for local dive trips, with two tanks, are about B2700–B2900, or from B850 for accompanying **snorkellers**. Dive courses cost about B14,500 for the four-day Openwater, and B4500 for the one-day Discover Scuba introduction.

BB Divers Offices at Lonely Beach, Hat Khlong Phrao and White Sand Beach, main office in Bang Bao ☎ 086 155 6212 or ☎ 039 558040–1, ⓦ bbdivers .com. Belgian-run, environmentally minded PADI Five-Star IDC centre and certified Reef Check Facility which uses fishing boats (with sun decks) rather than speedboats. Accommodation is available at *Barrio Bonito* on Lonely Beach (see p.190).

Scuba Zone Offices at White Sand Beach, Hat Kai Bae and Lonely Beach ☎ 039 619035, ⓦ scuba -kohchang.com. British-run PADI Five-Star centre, which also offers technical and wreck diving.

SNORKELLING

From about November to May, several companies run dedicated **snorkelling trips** to reefs and islands around Ko Chang, Ko Wai and Ko Rang. Tickets are sold by tour agents on every beach and prices range from B600 to B1500, depending on the size of the boat (some take as many as a hundred people in high season) and the number of islands visited. In general the more islands "featured" (sailed past), the less time there is for snorkelling, though nearly all the actual snorkelling happens around **Ko Rang**.

EATING AND DRINKING

15 Palms White Sand Beach ☎ 039 551095, ⓦ 15palms.com; map p.185. One of the most popular of the row of restaurants that set their tables out on the sand, partly because of its nightly high-season fireshows and transvestite shows on Tues & Sat. There's a fresh seafood barbecue every night (B350), plus Thai, Italian and Mexican à la carte, washed down by imported beers and lots of cocktails. Free wi-fi. Daily 8am–1am.

Hungry Elephant Beyond the south end of the beach, just north of and across the road from the post office; map p.182. The French and Thai food at this unassuming roadside place has a good reputation with local expats. The Thai chef trained at the French Embassy in Bangkok and does toothsome steaks – au poivre, chateaubriand and crème cognac – mostly for about B300. Daily roughly 10/11am–10pm.

Norng Bua Seafood On the main road, White Sand Beach; map p.185. Popular, bustling basic restaurant, serving noodle soups, fried noodles and fried rice with seafood (B45); other seafood dishes start at B100. Daily 7am–10pm.

Oodie's Place On the main road, White Sand Beach; map p.185. Ko Chang's most famous live-music venue, with live blues, rock, reggae and r'n'b played most nights, plus Thai food (from B80), pizzas (from B200) and French food (from B300). Daily 4pm–1am.

Pen's White Sand Beach; map p.185. Tiny beach restaurant in the northern bungalow cluster that serves exceptionally good home-style Thai food at fairly cheap prices (B80–100 for curries), as well as Western breakfasts. Daily 8.30am–9.30pm.

Sabay Bar White Sand Beach ⓦ sabaybarkohchang .com; map p.185. One of Ko Chang's longest-running institutions, where you can choose to sit in the chic a/c bar and watch the nightly live sets from the in-house cover band, or lounge on mats and cushions on the sand and listen in via the outdoor speakers. You pay for the pleasure, however, as drinks are pricey. Also stages fire-juggling shows on the beach and full-moon parties. Daily 6pm–2am.

Saffron on the Sea Beyond the south end of the beach, behind the post office three doors north of Penny's (see p.185) ☎ 039 551253; map p.182. On a pretty seafront deck, this restaurant is highly recommended for its Thai food, which doesn't stray too far from the usual suspects, such as green curry (B180) and

nam tok pork salad (B150); also serves baguettes and pastas. Daily roughly 7.30am–9.30pm.

The Spa On the main road, White Sand Beach; map p.185. Welcoming, environmentally friendly outreach restaurant of *The Spa Resort* (see p.194). Food is mostly vegetarian, and organic where possible, and includes a delicious "ginger nuts" stir-fry (B140), very good omelettes, seafood, breakfasts and Mexican dishes. There are lots of health drinks and good espressos. Daily 10am–10pm.

Laem Chaichet and Hat Khlong Phrao

Four kilometres south of Hat Sai Khao, the scenic, rocky cape at **LAEM CHAICHET** curves round into sweeping, casuarina-fringed **HAT KHLONG PHRAO**, one of Ko Chang's nicest beaches, not least because it has yet to see the clutter and claustrophobic development of its neighbours. For the moment at least, most of the restaurants, bars and shops are way off the beach, along the roadside, with the shorefront left mainly to a decent spread of accommodation. Laem Chaichet protects an inlet and tiny harbour and offers beautiful views south across the bay and inland to the densely forested mountains. To the south, Hat Khlong Phrao begins with a nice 1km-long run of beach that's interrupted by a wide khlong, whose estuary is the site of some characterful stilt homes and seafood restaurants. You can rent a kayak from almost anywhere along the beach to explore the estuary, and after dark you could paddle upriver to see the fireflies twinkling in the khlongside *lamphu* trees. Beyond the estuary, the long southern beach is partly shaded by casuarinas and backed in places by a huge coconut grove that screens the shore from the road; it's quite a hike to the roadside shops and restaurants from here though, at least 1km along a rutted track.

Both Chaichet and Khlong Phrao have roadside tourist villages with **ATMs**, minimarkets, tour agents, dive centres, internet access, shops and restaurants. The **tourist police** have a post here, and from the southern end of Khlong Phrao it's only a few hundred metres south to the start of the Kai Bae tourist village amenities.

Khlong Phlu Falls
2km east off the main road • B200

Upstream from Hat Khlong Phrao, the khlong that divides the beach in two tumbles into Ko Chang's most famous cascade, **Khlong Phlu Falls** (Nam Tok Khlong Phlu). Signs lead you inland to a car park and some hot-food stalls, where you pay your national park entry fee and walk the last five minutes to the 25m-high waterfall (best in the rainy season) that plunges into an invitingly clear pool defined by a ring of smooth rocks.

ACCOMMODATION	LAEM CHAICHET AND HAT KHLONG PHRAO

Amari Emerald Cove Resort Hat Khlong Phrao ☎ 039 552000, ⓦ amari.com; map p.188. Top-of-the-scale hotel from the reliable Thai chain, occupying a lovely, tranquil spot on the southern beach, complete with its own palm-shaded sandy terrace, spa and huge seafront swimming pool with a palatial jacuzzi. The rooms, in low-rise three-storey blocks set around the pool, tropical garden and lagoons, are in luxurious style, with wooden floors and balconies. B4980

Baan Rim Nam Hat Khlong Phrao ☎ 087 005 8575, ⓦ iamkohchang.com; map p.188. Peaceful, scenic and unusual, this converted fishing family's house is built on stilts over the wide, attractive khlong at the end of a

walkway through the mangroves. Run by the British author of the best Ko Chang website, it has just five comfortable a/c rooms with good hot-water bathrooms and free wi-fi, plus decks for soaking up views of the khlongside village, but no restaurant. You can borrow kayaks and it's a couple of minutes' walk to the beach, or 20min to the main Khlong Phrao facilities. B800

Barali Beach Resort Hat Khlong Phrao ☎ 039 557238, ⓦ baralikohchang.com; map p.188. One of the more elegant spots on the southern beach, with tastefully designed, Balinese-style rooms (some with their own plunge pools), furnished with four-poster beds, sunken

2

White Sand Beach, Post Office & Ko Chang International Clinic

VJ Plaza
← Ko Chang Gym

Ko Chang Plaza

Police

Laem Chaichet

Hat Khlong Phrao

Tourist Police

Wat
Khlong Phrao

BB Divers

Baan Zen

Hat Kai Bae

Scuba Zone

ACCOMMODATION

Amari Emerald Cove Resort	6
Baan Rim Nam	2
Barali Beach Resort	5
Koh Chang Paradise Resort	1
KP Huts	4
Porn Bungalow	8
Sea View Resort and Spa	9
Siam Cottage	7
Tiger Hut	3

RESTAURANTS & CAFÉS

KaTi	1
Papa's Bakery & Deli	3
Tonsai	2

**LAEM CHAICHET,
HAT KHLONG PHRAO
AND HAT KAI BAE**

N

0	approx.	500
	metres	

Lonely Beach

baths and lots of polished wood, and set around a beachfront infinity-edge swimming pool and a spa. B4330
Koh Chang Paradise Resort Laem Chaichet ☎039 551100–1, ⓦkohchangparadise.com; map opposite. The biggest and most popular place to stay on the Chaichet end of the beach occupies a huge area between the road and the shore so offers easy access to the beach as well as shops and restaurants. Its generously designed concrete bungalows have French windows and comfortable, hotel-style, a/c interiors. Some have private plunge pools and there's also a central swimming pool and a spa. B4425
KP Huts Hat Khlong Phrao ☎084 077 5995, ⓔkp_huts 2599@hotmail.com; map opposite. Though the fifty timber huts here are very simple for the price, they are attractively scattered through the broad, grassy shoreside coconut grove (about 1.5km from roadside amenities) with

plenty of sea views. Even some of the cheapest options (with shared bathrooms) are right on the shore, and a few are raised high on stilts for an extra-seductive panorama; all of the en-suite huts have hot showers and some are designed for families. Internet access. Shared bathroom B400, en suite B700
Tiger Hut Hat Khlong Phrao ☎084 109 9660; map opposite. One of the few budget-minded, old-school travellers' beach bungalows left on Ko Chang, occupying a sandy beachfront garden just south of the khlong and about 2km down a track from the main road. The woven-bamboo and clapboard huts have simple interiors with mosquito nets over the beds and decent-sized bathrooms, and there's a restaurant deck and bar with pool table. Shared bathroom B300, en suite B600

EATING AND DRINKING

KaTi On the main road, Hat Khlong Phrao ☎039 557252; map opposite. Restaurant and cookery school (see p.184) serving very tasty Thai food, slightly adapted for Western tastes, including lots of seafood, *matsaman* chicken curry (B150) and *laap* beef salad (B120), plus delicious home-made ice creams and Thai desserts. Mon–Sat 11am–3pm & 6–10pm, Sun 6–10pm.

Tonsai On the main road, Hat Khlong Phrao; map opposite. The atmosphere at this welcoming, civilized restaurant is pleasingly mellow, and the menu includes *matsaman* curries (B150), some interesting Thai dips and relishes, pastas, lots of vegetarian options and at least fifty cocktails. Mon 5–10pm, Tues–Sun 11.30am–10pm.

Hat Kai Bae

Narrow, pretty little **HAT KAI BAE** presents a classic picture of white sand, pale blue water and overhanging palms, but in places the shorefront is very slender indeed – and filled with bungalows – and the beach can disappear entirely at high tide. The beach is bisected by a khlong and rocky point, with most of the accommodation to the south. Seaward views from the southernmost end take in the tiny island of Ko Man Nai, whose sandy shores are easily reached by kayak, half an hour offshore from *Porn's Bungalows*. Kai Bae's roadside tourist village is busy and stretches a couple of kilometres. It's got plenty of shops, bars and restaurants, as well as ATMs, currency exchange, dive shops and internet access.

ACCOMMODATION **HAT KAI BAE**

Porn Bungalow Off the access road to Sea View, Hat Kai Bae ☎080 613 9266 or ☎089 099 8757, ⓦpornsbungalows-kohchang.com; map opposite. The most famous of the dwindling number of budget accommodation options on Hat Kai Bae has scores of fan bungalows in various styles, well spaced out under the trees along a huge expanse of the shorefront. The cheapest are concrete huts at the back at the south end; the most luxurious are spacious wooden cabins with hot showers and wraparound decks. Porn's has two reception areas, at its northernmost and southernmost ends, and a two-storey restaurant, with a bar, wi-fi and pool table, in the middle. Also has kayaks for paddling to offshore Ko Man Nai. Fan and cold shower B600, fan and hot shower B800
Sea View Resort and Spa Hat Kai Bae ☎081 830

7529, ⓦseaviewkohchang.com; map opposite. Swanky and huge beachfront hotel set in lawns and tropical flower gardens, which stretch around the steep headland at the south end of the beach and up to a lighthouse by the main road, which shelters view-filled tables belonging to their *Lighthouse Restaurant*. A cable car joins up the resort's two swimming pools, pretty spa and its large, light and airy a/c rooms and cottages. B3000
Siam Cottage Hat Kai Bae ☎089 153 6664; map opposite. With cheerily painted interiors, fans, partly outdoor bathrooms and decks, the 36 wooden bungalows here face each other across a narrow but well-watered, flowery lot that runs down to the sea. There's a cute restaurant and internet access, as well as kayaks for rent. Fan B500, a/c B800

2

LONELY BEACH & AO BAI LAN

■ **ACCOMMODATION**
Barrio Bonito	7
Easy House	6
Nature Beach	1
Siam Hut	2
The Sunflower	3
Sunset Hut	4
Warapura Resort	5

Siam Beach

Lonely Beach

Minimart

@

Scuba Zone

@

BB Divers

● **RESTAURANTS**
Barrio Bonito	3
Krua Sai Ngam	
(Sign Ngam Kitchen)	1
The Sunflower	2

N

Ao Bai Lan

Bailan Herbal Sauna

Mercure Resort

Treetop Adventure Park

0 — 300
metres

Hat Kai Bae

Bang Bao

EATING AND DRINKING

Papa's Bakery & Deli On the main road, Hat Kai Bae; map p.188. Hot pretzels, pizzas, croissants, baguettes and cakes emerge from this friendly German bakery, as well as the bread for some very tasty sandwiches (around B100). If you're sitting in, you can also tuck into pastas and good espressos; to take away, there are imported cheeses and salamis, too. Internet access. Daily 8am–7pm.

Lonely Beach (Hat Tha Nam)

Hat Tha Nam – dubbed **LONELY BEACH** before it became Ko Chang's top place to party – is small and lively, with a shorefront that's occupied by increasingly expensive accommodation and a hinterland village, ten minutes' walk away, that's the most traveller-oriented on the island. It's at Lonely Beach, overlooking the rocks immediately south of the strand, and along the sandy sois that run inland to the main road, that backpackers feel most at home, in little bungalows and guesthouses squashed any old how beneath the remaining trees, with every other shop-shack offering tattoos or internet access. Despite the creeping concrete, creatively designed little wood and bamboo bar-restaurants abound, some of them offering chilled, low-key escapes from the loud dance music, all-night parties and buckets of vodka Red Bull that the beachfront places are notorious for.

Day and (especially) night, you should be extremely careful when swimming off Lonely Beach, particularly around *Siam Beach* at the northern end, as the steep shelf and dangerous current result in a sobering number of **drownings** every year, particularly during the monsoon season; do your swimming further south and don't go out at all when the waves are high. Also be careful with your belongings – many a drunken night sees cameras, phones and wallets pilfered unnoticed.

Among the roadside shops you'll find an **ATM**, dive centres, tour agents and motorbike rental and repair.

ACCOMMODATION

Barrio Bonito On the main road, towards the south end of Lonely Beach ☎ 080 092 8208, ⊛ barrio bonitokohchang.com; map above. Behind this excellent bar-restaurant (see opposite), the garden shelters some cute, colourful, single-storey rooms, all

LONELY BEACH

with bathrooms and armchairs, though they're quite small and tightly packed. There's wi-fi in the restaurant, where good breakfasts are served, and a tiny swimming pool at the front. Fan and cold shower <u>B350</u>, fan and hot shower <u>B500</u>

Easy House Inland, up a side road opposite Kachapura Resort, Lonely Beach ☎089 116 8191, ✉hippeehappy @yahoo.com; map opposite. Laidback place built around polished, dark-wood platforms, with free wi-fi. The old-style bungalows, decorated with murals and equipped with mosquito nets, fans and en-suite bathrooms, are quite crowded together, but quiet and cheap. B500

Nature Beach Central Lonely Beach ☎039 558027 or ☎081 803 8933; map opposite. Responsible for Lonely Beach's party reputation, this place's rooms, bar-restaurant (with built-in DJ station) and the beach out front are all hugely popular. It occupies a prime location in the middle of the strand and is at the heart of the action (so if you prefer a quiet night's sleep head elsewhere). All 65 of its shady, closely set bungalows have been recently upgraded, ranging from attractive, polished-concrete en-suite abodes with verandas at the back by the road, through fan-cooled log cabins, some with hot showers, further forward, to large a/c bungalows at the front with hot water and a bit of chic. There's a tour desk, internet access and wi-fi (both payable). Fan B500, fan and hot shower B700, a/c B1500

Siam Hut Central Lonely Beach ☎086 609 7772, ⓦsiamhutkohchang.com; map opposite. The cheapest place to stay right on the beach, this classic traveller's rest has evening barbecues and movies, a dive school, a tattoo parlour, recycling bins, kayaks for rent and a 24hr kitchen (with wi-fi). Accommodation consists of rows and rows of primitive, split-bamboo huts – eighty in total – all en suite (some with hot showers) and with little else but plank floors, mattresses and mozzie nets. Fan B380, a/c B520

The Sunflower Lonely Beach, inland on Soi Sunset ☎084 017 9960, ⓦthe-sunflower.com; map opposite.

Run by a genial German and his Thai family, the two-dozen bungalows here are set under palm and banana trees 200m or so from the roadside village and equidistant from the rocky coast at *Sunset Hut*, a 5min walk south of the sandy beach. Choose between bamboo or wooden fan bungalows with mosquito nets and open-roofed bathrooms, and concrete bungalows with a/c and hot showers; all have good thick mattresses and are kept very clean. The restaurant is good (see below) and has wi-fi. Fan B300, a/c B700

Sunset Hut Lonely Beach, 5min walk south beyond Siam Hut, on the rocks ☎089 245 4626; map opposite. The concrete en-suite bungalows here have hot showers, proper beds and big windows; some have perfect, private, over-sea decks too. There are also some big a/c bungalows, but all are tightly packed together in rows running parallel to the shore. The seafront deck-restaurant and bar holds occasional parties. Though you can only swim here at high tide, it's a short walk to the sandy beach and just 400m inland to roadside shops and restaurants. The builders were in for refurbishment at the time of research, so prices will probably go up once they've finished. Fan B300, a/c B500

Warapura Resort Lonely Beach, 2min walk south beyond Sunset Hut, on the rocks ☎083 987 4777, ⓦwarapuraresort.com; map opposite. Welcoming place with a good dose of Bangkok chic in its twenty gleaming-white, balconied rooms and villas, a few of which are on the seafront; all have large bathrooms with hot rain showers, a/c, mini-bars, TVs and DVD players. "Cozy Seaview" rooms are especially stylish, with dark-wood furniture and a large indoor sitting area (B2200 including breakfast). Good-sized, attractive pool and free wi-fi throughout. B1400

EATING AND DRINKING

The most intense **partying** on Ko Chang happens down on the beach here, usually at *Nature Beach*, which kicks off most high-season nights with seafood barbecues, live music and fire-juggling shows; there's also a big beach party at *Siam Hut* on Friday nights.

★ **Barrio Bonito** On the main road, towards the south end of Lonely Beach ☎080 092 8208, ⓦbarriobonitokohchang.com; map opposite. Mexican-run bar-restaurant serving excellent, authentic food such as nachos with minced beef (B200) as well as some more unusual dishes, washed down with Corona and lots of tequila cocktails. It's a very congenial haven, with lots of places to chill in the landscaped garden, free wi-fi and Latin sounds all the way. Daily 8am–10pm.

Krua Sai Ngam (Sign Ngam Kitchen) On the main road, central Lonely Beach; map opposite. Popular, basic, authentic Isaan restaurant, which even does *som tam* with crab and *pla ra* (fermented fish sauce) – an acquired taste but very northeastern (on the menu as "Som Tam

E-sarn"; B40). Also offers catfish and snakehead fish in various soups, curries and salads (try the *yam plaa duk foo*; B120), grilled chicken and simple dishes on rice (B40). No English sign, but look for the corrugated-iron roof and the seafood displayed on ice at the front, directly opposite Soi Sunset. Daily noon–11.30pm.

The Sunflower Lonely Beach, inland on Soi Sunset ☎084 017 9960, ⓦthe-sunflower.com; map opposite. Friendly, laidback guesthouse restaurant dishing up very generous set breakfasts (B150), authentically spicy Thai curries (B50), a wide choice of pricier Western food and German beer. Flop on to the axe cushions and soak up the cool sounds or watch a movie. Free wi-fi. Daily 8am–3pm & 5–10pm.

Ao Bai Lan

A fifteen-minute walk along the road and over the hill from the southern end of Lonely Beach village will bring you to **AO BAI LAN**, which hasn't got much of a beach to speak of, but is the site of two of Ko Chang's most interesting attractions, the **Treetop Adventure Park** and the **Bailan Herbal Sauna**.

Treetop Adventure Park

South end of Ao Bai Lan • Daily 9am–5pm • B950/half-day, including transport from the west coast • ☎ 084 310 7600, ⓦ treetopadventurepark.com

If you're happy with heights and like a physical challenge, make an afternoon of it at **Treetop Adventure Park**, an enjoyable and professionally managed jungle activity centre where you get to swing through the trees on a series of trapezes, flying foxes, aerial skateboards, rope ladders and webs. Everyone gets a full safety harness and gloves and starts off with a training session before tackling the two adventure courses (or the special kids' one), which take around two hours in all, though there's no limit to repeat attempts.

Bailan Herbal Sauna

On the main road, Ao Bai Lan • Daily 3–9pm • Sauna B200, treatments from B50, massages B300/hr • ☎ 039 558077, ⓦ bailan-kohchang.com

Bailan Herbal Sauna is the perfect place to tease out any sore muscles. This charming, creatively designed US–Thai-run herbal steam sauna is an alternative little sanctuary of adobe buildings with glass-bottle windows, secluded within a patch of roadside forest. There's a sociable communal sauna, home-made DIY herbal treatments using fresh herbs from their own garden (kaffir lime for hair, white-mud for face and turmeric for skin), and massages are also available, along with fresh juices and herbal teas.

Bang Bao

Almost at the end of the west-coast road, the southern harbour village of **BANG BAO**, much of it built on stilts off a 1km-long central jetty, is the departure point for boat trips and transfers to the outer islands and is also an increasingly popular place to stay. Though it has no beach of its own, you're within a short motorbike ride of both little-developed Hat Khlong Gloi, 2km to the east, and Lonely Beach, 5km up the coast. It's possible to stay on the jetty itself and tuck into seafood at one of its famous restaurants, but you'll probably have to fight your way through vanloads of day-trippers, who clog the narrow path along the jetty as they linger over the trinket shops, clothes stalls and dive shops.

ACCOMMODATION   BANG BAO

Cliff Cottage West side of Ao Bang Bao, next to Nirvana ☎ 085 904 6706, ⓦ cliff-cottage.com; map p.182. British-run resort with a nice deck restaurant on the west-facing cove, and kayaks and snorkels for rent. Basic, thatched, bare-wood huts with decent mattresses, mosquito nets and good sunset views sit up on a small, dusty, shady rise; there's also a rowhouse of fan and a/c rooms, all with hot showers, facing in on Bang Bao bay. Smarter wooden bungalows for families are planned. Fan hut B400, fan room B700, a/c B900

Good View Bang Bao jetty ☎ 087 927 1357 or ☎ 089 108 0429, ⓦ goodviewbangbao.wordpress.com; map p.182. As the name says, the views from this guesthouse, built over the water halfway down the east side of the jetty, are good, though not great, taking in the shoreline opposite. Lovely, clean, bright, large, wooden-floored bedrooms come with huge hot-water bathrooms, big balconies and a/c – it's

worth paying B200 extra for an upstairs room. There's a very large, attractive ground-floor deck with a book corner, and free wi-fi throughout. B800

★ **Nirvana Koh Chang** West side of Ao Bang Bao ☎ 039 558061–4, ⓦ nirvanakohchang.com; map p.182. Secluded on a narrow neck of land across the bay to the west of the village, this boutique resort is a relaxed and lushly landscaped retreat with two pools and access to good snorkelling in the bay behind (free equipment available); there's no real beach but Nirvana runs free boats over to Hat Khlong Goi twice a day. Also on offer are cooking classes, free kayaks and free wi-fi throughout. Accommodation is in a wide range of chic, Balinese-accented rooms and villas, some with direct sea views, and there's an attractive restaurant too (see opposite). Good à la carte breakfast included. B2000

EATING AND DRINKING

Arabica Café Opposite 7-Eleven, just before the start of Bang Bao jetty; map p.182. Good espressos (B40), pancakes, sandwiches and Western breakfasts, in a leafy little café with cute fountains. Daily 8am–9pm.

Nirvana Koh Chang West side of Ao Bang Bao ☎039 558061–4, ⓦnirvanakohchang.com; map p.182. Even if you're not staying you can come and eat at the dramatically sited *Tantra* restaurant, built on stilts in the bay, or drink at the panoramic, sunset-facing *Sun Deck*, which is reached by a cliffside boardwalk and hosts soothing live music most days – or both. Creatively furnished with woodcarvings from the Indonesian archipelago, the restaurant serves a menu of contemporary

Thai and French food (including imported artisan cheeses), as well as tasty fusion dishes created by the French chef, such as beef tournedos in panaeng sauce (B350). Very good wine list. Free transfers from anywhere on the west coast of Ko Chang. Sun Deck daily 5–7pm; Tantra daily 6–10pm.

Ruan Thai Bang Bao jetty ☎089 833 5117; map p.182. The best of several neighbouring restaurants, with a deck built on stilts off the west side of the jetty and fresh seafood awaiting its fate in tanks at the front. The fried rice stuffed with prawns is very good (B50), or you could upgrade to salads, curries and squid dishes (B100); most other seafood dishes are B200. Daily 9am–10pm.

Hat Khlong Gloi

The nearest swimmable beach to Bang Bao is long, sandy **Hat Khlong Gloi**, 2km east of the village and not far short of the end of the tarmac. It's backed by a lagoon and a long stretch of beach-scrub, but has great views from its small beach cafés and deckchairs. If you're coming by motorcycle, park up at the west end of the beach and walk, as the paved access road then takes a steep, tortuous route around the back of the beach.

ACCOMMODATION   HAT KHLONG GLOI

KK Cottage 100m from the west end of Hat Khlong Gloi ☎039 558169, ⓦfacebook.com/klongkloicottage; map p.182. Friendly, popular spot on a nice stretch of beach, with deckchairs and umbrellas and great views of the bay

and the offshore islands. The rather scruffy compound has small, thatched, fan-cooled, en-suite bungalows at the back, concrete ones at the front. B500

The east coast

The beaches along the mangrove-fringed **east coast** are less inviting than those in the west, but this side of Ko Chang is much less developed and makes for a fun day-trip; it's about 35km from Khlong Son in the north to Salak Pet in the south.

Than Mayom

South of the piers at Ao Saparot and Tha Dan Kao, the east-coast road runs through long swathes of rubber and palm plantations, with jungle-clad hills to the west and bronze-coloured beaches to the east, passing the national park office and bungalows at **Than Mayom**, where signs direct you inland to Than Mayom falls, a 45-minute uphill hike away.

Salak Kok

On the western side of Ao Salak Kok, *The Spa* (see p.194) is a wellness and detox retreat that's open to day visitors for food or treatments. Fork left at the junction just south of *The Spa* to reach the southern edge of the bay and its small fishing settlement, **SALAK KOK**, site of the award-winning Salak Kok Kayak Station run by the Koh Chang Discovery Club, a community tourism venture that offers **kayak rental** along a marked route through the mangroves (B100/hr). From Salak Kok, continue down to the tip of the southeastern headland to reach **Hat Sai Yao**, or **LONG BEACH**, the prettiest white-sand beach on this coast, which is good for swimming and has some coral close to shore.

Salak Pet

Most day-trippers turn right not left just after *The Spa* and head instead for the little fishing port of **SALAK PET** on the south coast, which is served by daily songthaews all the way from Trat town (see p.178). Still a fairly quiet spot, Salak Pet is best known for its excellent **seafood restaurant**, *Salakphet Resort*.

ACCOMMODATION AND EATING   THE EAST COAST

★ **Salakphet Resort** Salak Pet ☎081 429 9983, ⓦkohchangsalakphet.com; map p.182. The bayside dining deck here offers fine views and seafood so good that people travel all the way from Trat just for lunch; crabs are a speciality – particularly stir-fried with black pepper, or with curry powder – but it's all fresh so the possibilities are infinite. Daily 8am–8pm.

The Spa Ao Salak Kok ☎039 553091, ⓦthespakohchang .com; map p.182. Beautifully designed wellness and detox retreat that's upmarket but reasonably priced; it also has branches on Ko Samui and in Chiang Mai. Its a/c accommodation is set in a lovely mature tropical garden that runs down to the mangrove-ringed bay of western Ao Salak Kok and has a good restaurant. Breakfast included. Day visitors are welcome for massage (B500/1hr, B700/90min), herbal saunas and facials and to eat at its restaurant. B1800

Ko Mak

Small, slow-paced, peaceful **KO MAK** (sometimes spelt "Maak") makes an idyllic, low-key alternative to Ko Chang, 20km to the northwest. Measuring just sixteen square kilometres, it's home to little more than four hundred people, divided into five main clans, who work together to keep the island free of hostess bars, jet skis, banana boats and the like, and on initiatives such as mountain-bike trails. A couple of narrow concrete roads traverse the island, which is dominated by coconut and rubber plantations; elsewhere a network of red-earth tracks cuts through the trees. Ko Mak is shaped like a star, with fine white-sand beaches along the northwest coast at **Ao Suan Yai** and the southwest coast at **Ao Kao**, where most of the island's (predominantly mid-range and upper-bracket) tourist accommodation is concentrated; the principal village, **Ban Ao Nid**, is on the southeast coast and there's another village at **Ban Laem Son** on the east coast. The main beaches are just about within walking distance of each other, and other parts of the island are also fairly

BARS
Monkey Bar	2
Talay Bar	1

RESTAURANTS & CAFÉS
Beach Café	3
Food Art Hut	2
Food Garden	1
Ko Mak Seafood	4

ACCOMMODATION
Ao Kao White Sand Beach Resort	9
Baan Koh Mak	6
Bamboo Hideaway Resort	4
Goodtime	5
Holiday Beach Resort	3
Island Hut	8
Koh Mak Resort	2
Lazy Day	10
Monkey Island	7
Suchanaree Resort	1

KO MAK

ACTIVITIES ON KO MAK

The mediocre reefs of Ko Rang (see p.186), part of the Ko Chang National Marine Park, are less than an hour's boat ride west of Ko Mak and are the island's main **diving and snorkelling** destination; they're the main focus of Ko Chang dive and snorkel boats too, so you won't be alone. You can also join a **cookery class**.

Koh Mak Divers On the Ao Kao road just east of Island Hut ☎ 083 297 7724, ⓦ kohmakdivers.com. British-run PADI centre that charges B2400 for two fun dives, B3500 for the beginners' one-day Discover Scuba Diving course and B750 for snorkellers; transfers from your accommodation included.

Smile Koh Mak Next to Koh Mak Seafood restaurant at Ban Ao Nid ☎ 081 901 9972, ⓦ smilekohmak.com. 4hr cookery classes (B1200, including a recipe book),

with vegetarian options available. Also offers fruit and vegetable carving courses over 2 days (6hr). Transfers from your accommodation included.

Totti On the Ao Kao road opposite the Makathanee Resort ☎ 081 916 6536 or book through your accommodation. Snorkelling day-trips in a wooden boat to the national marine park. B750, including transfers from your accommodation and lunch box.

---

easy to explore on foot, or by mountain bike, motorbike or kayak – the best way to discover the empty undeveloped beaches hidden along the north and eastern coasts. The **reefs** of Ko Rang are also less than an hour's boat ride away so snorkelling and diving trips are quite popular. There is as yet no major commercial development on the island and **no bank or ATM**, but bungalows on both beaches will change money. There's a small clinic off the Ao Nid road, though for anything serious a speedboat will whisk you back to the mainland.

During the **rainy season** (early June–Sept), choppy seas mean that boat services to Ko Mak are much reduced. Most Ko Mak accommodation stays open – and offers tempting discounts – but the smaller places often don't bother to staff their restaurants. Islanders say that it can be very pleasant during this "green season", though you may be unlucky and hit a relentlessly wet few days.

Ao Kao

Ko Mak's longest and nicest beach is **AO KAO** on the southwest coast, a pretty arc of sand overhung with stooping palm trees and backed in places by mangroves. The beach is divided towards its southern end by a low rocky outcrop that's straddled by *Ao Kao White Sand Beach Resort*, with *Lazy Day Resort* occupying the strand beyond, while the long western beach is shared by a dozen other sets of bungalows, most of them around the pier at the *Makathanee Resort*. The roadside inland from the main accommodation area is where you'll find most of the restaurants and bars: if you're walking from the southern end, by far the easiest access is via the beach, tides permitting.

Ao Suan Yai and around

Long, curvy **AO SUAN YAI** is not quite as pretty a beach as Ao Kao and only has a couple of resorts, but the sand is fine and the outlook is beautiful, with Ko Chang's hilly profile filling the horizon and Ko Kham and other islets in between. You'll need a bicycle or motorbike to access the variety of restaurants on the Ao Kao road.

ARRIVAL AND DEPARTURE   **KO MAK**

As the island gets more popular, **boat services** from the mainland and the other islands are increasing: check ⓦ kohmak .com for current routes and schedules. Boats arrive at one of Ko Mak's three **piers** – at *Koh Mak Resort* on Ao Suan Yai, at the *Makathanee Resort* on Ao Kao or at Ao Nid – and are always met by a modest welcoming committee of accommodation staff offering free transport; similarly, if you book a room in advance, ask your resort for a free pick-up. When it comes to moving on, all hotels keep current boat schedules and can sell you a ticket.

2

VIA LAEM SOK

A new catamaran service sails to Ao Nid on Ko Mak from Laem Sok pier, 30km south of Trat (☎086 972 4918, ⓦkohmakcatamaran.com; daily, 1hr 30min; B350 including transfer to/from Trat bus station or downtown market); it's likely that this service will run in the off-season, too. Some of the Laem Sok–Ko Kood high-season speedboats will call in at Ao Nid if they have enough customers (see p.201).

VIA LAEM NGOP

A year-round slow boat runs from the Kromaluang (Naval Monument) pier in Laem Ngop, some 20km southwest of Trat (3 weekly, 3hr; B300). From approximately October to

May, Panan's speedboats also operate from this pier to *Ko Mak Resort* on Ao Suan Yai (2 daily, 45min–1hr; B450); the second of these is at 4pm, handy if you're arriving from Bangkok. A/c minibuses to Laem Ngop from Bangkok, for example, will sometimes only go as far as the Thammachat or Centrepoint Ko Chang piers, however – check exactly which piers are served when you buy your minibus ticket, or you may be able to pay the driver a little extra to go on to Kromaluang.

VIA KO CHANG OR KO KOOD

Boats run between Ko Chang, Ko Mak and Ko Kood in high season (see p.183).

INFORMATION

Tourist information The best one-stop shop for information about Ko Mak, accommodation bookings and all kinds of transport is the helpful, farang-run Info Point at *Koh Mak Resort* on Ao Suan Yai (Oct–March daily 8.30am–8pm; ☎085 665 3794, ⓔkohmakinfopoint @yahoo.com). As well as boat and bus tickets, it offers

currency exchange, Visa cash advances, internet access, motorbike, mountain bike and kayak rental, activities bookings and postal services. There's also a travel agent at *Makathanee Resort* (☎081 870 6287), by the pier on Ao Kao, which offers internet access. ⓦkohmak.com is a useful, fairly comprehensive website about the island.

GETTING AROUND

The island has hardly any traffic, and most visitors rent a mountain bike or motorbike. Apparently it's possible to walk, wade and swim around the entire perimeter in 10hr.

By taxi ☎089 752 5292 or ☎089 833 4474. B50/person, minimum charge/vehicle B100; B100/person after 10pm.
By mountain bike or motorbike These (respectively B150/day and B300–350/day) can be rented through accommodation or from *Ko Mak Resort*'s Info Point; otherwise, *Food Art Hut* on Ao Kao (see opposite) has a particularly wide choice of bicycles, including kids' bikes.

The island has some long and potentially interesting signed mountain-bike routes – discreet concrete posts enigmatically carved with route numbers A1–C7 – but the explanatory map for navigating them is currently out of print: you should be able to pick them up if you simply go exploring.

ACCOMMODATION

AO KAO

Ao Kao White Sand Beach Resort Ao Kao ☎039 501005, ⓦaokaoresort.com. This welcoming, efficiently managed and lively set of upmarket bungalows occupies an attractive garden fronting the prettiest part of the beach. Its twenty large, comfortable, attractive timber bungalows come with a/c, hot showers and DVD players and most have direct sea views. There are lots of activities, including live bands on Saturday nights, giant chess in the bar, a kids' trampoline, massage, free internet and wi-fi and kayaks and motorbikes for rent. Breakfast included. **B2500**
★ **Baan Koh Mak** Near the pier on Ao Kao ☎089 895 7592, ⓦbaan-koh-mak.com. Arrayed around a clipped lawn, the eighteen bungalows at this chic and welcoming resort are modern, bright and comfortable, cutely done out in white, green and polished concrete, with a/c, hot water, small bedrooms and decent-sized bathrooms; verandas sport

either swings or bamboo hammocks. There's a very good restaurant here too (with computers and free wi-fi). **B1400**
Goodtime Ao Kao ☎039 501000, ⓦgoodtime-resort .com. Luxurious, tasteful, Thai-style rooms and villas, all with a/c, hot water, TV, fridge, DVD player, wi-fi and use of a pool. They're located on higher ground inland from Ao Kao's *Makathanee Resort*, around 15min walk from the beach. Room **B2600**, villa **B4400**
Holiday Beach Resort Ao Kao ☎086 751 7668, ⓦholidaykohmak.com. Friendly, well-maintained place, strewn with flowers, facing a large, beachside lawn with deckchairs and tables. White clapboard is the architectural style of choice here, either in cute cottages with cold showers and mosquito nets in the second row, or in large, attractive, hot-water bungalows at the front. Computers and free wi-fi in the restaurant, and kayaks, mountain bikes and motorbikes for rent. Breakfast included. Fan **B800**, a/c **B1300**

Island Hut Ao Kao ☎087 139 5537. This family-run little place has the best-value and most idyllically sited accommodation on the beach, though not always the friendliest welcome. The two-dozen en-suite rough-hewn timber huts are more artfully designed than they might appear: most have cheery stripey doors and idiosyncratic driftwood artwork; all have fans, hanging space and their own deckchairs on decks or on private sandy porches. Price depends on proximity to the narrow but pretty shore: the most expensive are at the water's edge. B250

Lazy Day Ao Kao ☎081 882 4002, ⓦkohmaklazyday .com. Civilized spot on a huge beachside lawn strewn with flowers and trees. As well as a/c, hot showers and mini-bars (but no TVs, to preserve the quiet), the spacious, bright, mostly beachfront bungalows sport polished concrete floors, shining white walls and French windows out onto their balconies. Free wi-fi and kayaks; bikes and motorbikes to rent. Breakfast included. B2250

★ **Monkey Island** Ao Kao ☎081 447 8448, ⓦmonkeyislandkohmak.com. There's a big range of quality, contemporary-styled bungalows here, all in timber and thatch, and a laidback, hippy-ish vibe. Top-end "Gorilla" seafront villas are huge, with a/c, hot water and the possibility of connecting villas; the large a/c "Chimpanzee" bungalows are also good, while some of the small "Ape" and "Baboon" options share bathrooms. There's a kids' swimming pool, plus free wi-fi and internet access. Fan and shared bathroom B350, fan en-suite B600, a/c (including breakfast) B1300

AO SUAN YAI AND AROUND

Bamboo Hideaway Resort A couple of kilometres southeast of Ao Suan Yai, accessed via tracks through the rubber plantations ☎039 501085, ⓦbamboo hideaway.com. An idiosyncratic haven, built almost entirely from lengths of polished bamboo. Its comfortable a/c rooms all have mosquito nets on the beds, hammocks and hot showers, and are connected by a raised bamboo walkway. Although the south coast is just a couple of minutes' walk downhill, Ao Suan Yai has the nearest decent beach. There's an attractive swimming pool on site, as well as a good restaurant. Breakfast included. B2200

★ **Koh Mak Resort** Ao Suan Yai ☎039 501013, ⓦkohmakresort.com. With no less than 1km of shoreline to play with, nearly all of the bungalows here are beachfront (including the "Standard" fan options with hot showers) and enjoy lovely panoramas from their verandas. Among a huge range of accommodation, the most interesting are the very modern, design-conscious rooms and villas – all polished concrete, stacked slate walls, huge picture windows and rain showers, some with private little walled gardens, some with jacuzzis on their rooftop verandas. There's an infinity-edged swimming pool and similarly chic pool bar here too, two restaurants and the jack-of-all-trades Info Point (see opposite). Free wi-fi in all rooms. Breakfast included. Fan B1500, a/c B1800

Suchanaree Resort Ao Suan Yai ☎081 983 2629, ⓔSuchanaree_Tour @hotmail.com. Right next door to *Koh Mak Resort*, but couldn't be more different: it's an intimate, friendly little place in a lush garden, set by a khlong with tables and deckchairs on the shady, beachfront lawn. The small, basic but good-quality, shaggy-thatched wooden bungalows all have fan, mozzie nets and bathrooms. B550

EATING AND DRINKING

AO KAO

★ **Beach Café** At Baan Ko Mak, Ao Kao. Coolly done out in black, white and orange with some nice sofas, this restaurant serves exceptionally delicious Thai food, including good *tom kha* soups and great *phanaeng* curries (both B90). Daily 8am–10pm.

Food Art Hut Opposite Monkey Island, Ao Kao. Idiosyncratic all-rounder, offering ice cream, desserts, cakes and espressos, as well as Thai dishes and simple, passable Western food such as spaghetti bolognese (B99), breakfasts, pizzas and sandwiches, washed down with German wheat beer. Daily 8am–3pm & 5–9pm.

Food Garden Opposite Monkey Island, Ao Kao. This popular, cheap and enjoyable garden restaurant serves *phat thai*, various spicy salads and *matsaman* curries (B80), as well as breakfasts and seafood barbecues in the evening. Daily 8am–10pm.

Monkey Bar Monkey Island, Ao Kao. Live music nightly, including jamming sessions, at this bar built around the beachfront trees. Daily 8pm–midnight.

Talay Bar On the beach in front of Beach Café at Baan Ko Mak, Ao Kao. Tables on the sand – with a fire show at 8pm – and great margaritas (B150) plus a long list of other cocktails. Mellow music and evening barbecues. Evenings till late.

BAN AO NID

Ko Mak Seafood Just north of Ao Nid pier ☎089 833 4474. Built out into the sea on stilts, with views of the bay and, apparently, of Cambodia on a clear day, this restaurant is mostly true to its name, serving *phat thai* with fresh prawns (B90) and more complex dishes such as tasty squid with salted eggs (B200). (Don't get your hopes up about the advertised Ko Mak Museum next door, though – it's just a collection of old things in an old house.) Free transfers, free wi-fi. Daily 10.30am–9.30pm.

2

Ko Kood

The fourth-largest island in Thailand, forested **KO KOOD** (also spelt Ko Kut and Ko Kud) is still a wild and largely uncommercialized island. Though it's known for its sparkling white sand and exceptionally clear turquoise water, particularly along the west coast, Ko Kood is as much a nature-lover's destination as a beach-bum's. Swathes of its shoreline are fringed by scrub and mangrove rather than broad sandy beaches and those parts of the island not still covered in virgin tropical rainforest are filled with palm groves and rubber plantations. Most of the 25km-long island is penetrated only by sandy tracks and, in places, by navigable khlongs, if at all. All of this makes Ko Kood a surprisingly pleasant place to explore on foot (or kayak), especially as the cool season brings refreshing breezes most days. The interior is also graced with several waterfalls, the most famous of which is Nam Tok Khlong Chao, inland from Ao Khlong Chao and the focus of occasional day-trips from Ko Chang and Ko Mak.

Because of its lack of roads, Ko Kood has to date been the almost exclusive province of package-tourists, but things are becoming much easier for independent travellers, with a choice of scheduled boat services from the mainland, as well as from Ko Chang and Ko Mak, and the emergence of some budget-minded guesthouses. The island is still pretty much a **one-season destination**, though, as rough seas mean that nearly all the boat services only operate from November through May. An increasing number of places are staying open year-round, however, and offer tempting discounts to those willing to chance the rains and the off-season quiet. There is some **malaria** on the island so be especially assiduous with repellent and nets if you are not taking prophylactics; there's a malaria-testing station in Ban Khlong Hin Dam.

Most of Ko Kood's fifteen hundred residents make their living from fishing and growing coconut palms and rubber trees. Many have Khmer blood in them, as the island population mushroomed at the turn of the twentieth century when Thais and Cambodians resident in nearby Cambodian territory fled French control.

The main settlements are **Ban Khlong Hin Dam**, just inland from the main Nam Leuk (Hin Dam) pier, **Ban Khlong Mat**, a natural harbour-inlet a few kilometres further north up the coast, the stilted fishing village of **Ban Ao Salat** across on the northeast coast and the fishing community of **Ban Ao Yai** on the southeast coast. On the southwest coast, several of the main beaches also have small villages. Of these, the obvious choices for budget travellers are **Ao Khlong Chao** and **Ao Ngamkho**, which both have a choice of accommodation and eating options and are within walking distance of each other; **Ao Bang Bao** also has cheapish bungalows and is the longer and arguably better beach but has no village and is more isolated. Seclusion is the thing on all the other west-coast beaches, most of which are the province of just one or two upmarket resorts.

DIVING AND SNORKELLING OFF KO KOOD

Ko Kood's three **dive operators** charge around B3000 for two dives, with **snorkellers** paying B1000, and B14,500 for the four-day Openwater Diver course. You might prefer to opt for a local Ko Kood dive as the usual sites around Ko Rang (see p.186) are always packed with dive boats from Ko Chang and Ko Mak.

BB Divers Opposite Away Resort at the north end of Ao Khlong Chao ☎082 220 6002, ⊛bbdivers.com.

Koh Kood Divers Next to Siam Beach Resort at Ao Bang Bao ☎085 698 4122, ⊛kohkooddivers.com.

Paradise Divers Headquarters at Ko Kood Beach Resort at Ao Khlong Mat, with another desk at Happy Days on Ao Ngamkho ☎087 144 5945, ⊛kohkood -paradisedivers.com.

2

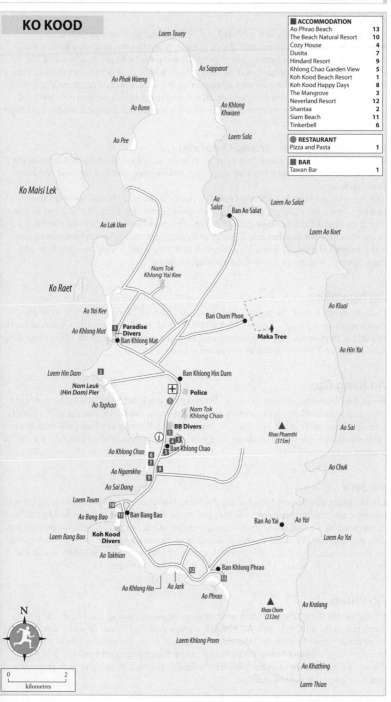

KO KOOD

ACCOMMODATION	
Ao Phrao Beach	13
The Beach Natural Resort	10
Cozy House	4
Dusita	7
Hindard Resort	9
Khlong Chao Garden View	5
Koh Kood Beach Resort	1
Koh Kood Happy Days	8
The Mangrove	3
Neverland Resort	12
Shantaa	2
Siam Beach	11
Tinkerbell	6

RESTAURANT	
Pizza and Pasta	1

BAR	
Tawan Bar	1

Laem Touey

Ao Sapparot

Ao Phak Waeng

Ao Bonn

Ao Khlong
Khwaen

Ao Pee

Laem Sala

Ko Maisi Lek

Ao
Salat

Laem Ao Salat

Ban Ao Salat

Ao Lak Uan

Laem Ao Koet

Nam Tok
Khlong Yai Kee

Ko Raet

Ao Yai Kee

Ao Kluai

Ban Chum Phon

Ao Khlong Mat

**Paradise
Divers**
Ban Khlong Mat

Maka Tree

Ao Hin Yai

Laem Hin Dam

Ban Khlong Hin Dam

Nam Leuk
(Hin Dam) Pier

Police

Ao Taphao

Nam Tok
Khlong Chao

BB Divers

Ao Sai

Khao Phaenthi
(315m)

Ban Khlong Chao

Ao Khlong Chao

Ao Chuk

Ao Ngamkho

Ao Sai Dang

Laem Toum

Ban Bang Bao

Ao Bang Bao

**Koh Kood
Divers**

Ban Ao Yai

Ao Yai

Laem Bang Bao

Laem Ao Yai

Ao Takhian

Ban Khlong Phrao

Ao Khlong Hin

Ao Jark

Ao Phrao

Khao Chom
(232m)

Ao Kralang

Laem Khlong Prom

Ao Khathing

N

Ao Khathing

Laem Thian

0   2
kilometres

Ao Khlong Chao

About 5km south of the main Nam Leuk (Hin Dam) pier on the west coast, **AO KHLONG CHAO** (pronounced "Jao") is a fun place to stay, boasting both a small sandy beach – no great beauty but a perfectly pleasant "village" beach – and the pretty 2km-long mangrove-lined Khlong Chao, which runs down from the famous Khlong Chao Falls. Close by and upstream of the road-bridge that spans the khlong, just 300m from the palm-fringed beach, is a cluster of little guesthouses, some of them built partially on stilts over the river, which offer the cheapest accommodation on the island.

Nam Tok Khlong Chao (Khlong Chao Falls)

30min walk from Ao Khlong Chao, or kayak 20min upriver from the Khlong Chao bridge to the jetty near the falls, then walk for 10min; you can drive to within 500m of the falls, following the signs from near Khlong Chao Garden View Resort, south of the Khlong Chao bridge

The three-tiered **Nam Tok Khlong Chao** is a pretty if not exceptional waterfall that tumbles down into a large, refreshing pool that's perfect for a dip; it's quietest in the mornings, before the package groups arrive. The track continues beyond the falls through jungle for another few kilometres before terminating at a rubber plantation – if you walk the whole thing it's a pleasant and very quiet four-hour trip there and back, though watch out for snakes, especially cobras.

Ao Ngamkho

Having climbed over the point at the south end of Ao Khlong Chao, the road dips down again to the tiny village at **AO NGAMKHO** and its beach, actually a series of pretty, miniature bays either side of a khlong and between rocky points, with quite rewarding snorkelling and plenty of fish at its southern end.

Ao Bang Bao

From Ao Ngamkho, follow signs for *The Beach* to reach **AO BANG BAO**, about twenty minutes' walk further south (15min west off the main road). This is one of Ko Kood's prettiest beaches, fronted by a longish sweep of bleach-white sand and deliciously clear turquoise water, plus the inevitable fringe of coconut palms, and embraced by a pair of protective promontories.

Ao Jark

On the main southbound road at the Ao Bang Bao turn-off, a 35-minute walk through coconut and rubber plantations brings you to **Ao Khlong Hin**, a wild little bay that's dominated by a small coconut-processing centre and is not really great for swimming. Ten minutes further along the road, which hugs the coast so close here it gets washed by the waves at high tide, remote and breathtakingly lovely little **AO JARK** sits at the mouth of a wide, serene khlong and feels secluded and private.

Ao Phrao

Continue for 2km (about 20min walk) along the pretty coastal road from Ao Jark to reach the most southerly bay, **AO PHRAO**, a long, stunning beach of white sand backed by densely planted palms and the slopes of Khao Chom. Behind Ao Phrao, the tiny fishing village of **Ban Khlong Phrao** occupies the mangrove-lined banks of Khlong Phrao (which extends another kilometre inland). There's a clinic here as well as a few small shops and hot-food stalls.

Ao Yai

A 5km track that's very steep and rough in places connects Ban Khlong Phrao with **Ban Ao Yai**, the southeast coast's main if rather lacklustre fishing village, built entirely on stilts and jetties around the shoreline of a natural harbour. Its main visitors are the crews of anchored fishing boats from Thailand and Cambodia, who come here for drink, supplies, karaoke and the rest.

Ban Khlong Hin Dam and around

The bays of northern Ko Kood, beyond Ao Khlong Chao, are even more thinly populated than the southwest coast, with just a few resorts. Inland is the island's administrative centre, **Ban Khlong Hin Dam**, 3.5km north of Ao Khlong Chao, site of a few shops, the hospital, police station, school and principal island temple. Ko Kood's main west-coast pier is a couple of kilometres to the west, at **Nam Leuk (Laem Hin Dam)**.

About 5km north of Ban Khlong Hin Dam, the small but appealing three-tiered waterfall **Nam Tok Khlong Yai Kee** is basically a miniature version of the famous Nam Tok Khlong Chao and rushes down into a good-sized pool that's ideal for swimming. It's accessible via a five-minute path that's very steep in places, but there are ropes at the crucial points.

Ban Ao Salat and around

The road northeast from Ban Khlong Hin Dam ends after 9km at the tiny stilt village, fishing community and port of **Ban Ao Salat**. Several of the wooden houses strung out along the jetty-promenade serve food and this is a great place for a fresh-seafood lunch, especially crab.

East off this road, in the mature rainforest near Ban Chum Phon, is a locally famous **five-hundred-year-old maka tree** (*Bridelia insulana*), known to islanders as the *ton maai yai*, that's an impressive 35m or more in height and drips with lianas and epiphytes. A kilometre-long path through rubber trees and rainforest will get you there, but you'll need to go with a local to stay on the right track.

ARRIVAL AND DEPARTURE   KO KOOD

BY BOAT

All boat tickets to Ko Kood from the mainland should include transfers to the pier from Trat, though it's worth double-checking. Mainland and Ko Chang speedboats will drop off at and pick up from most of the west-coast accommodation. All Ko Kood hotels keep current timetables and sell tickets.

FERRIES FROM THE MAINLAND

In all but the worst weather, Ninmungkorn (☎086 126 7860) runs a year-round boat service to Ko Kood from the Trat mainland, departing from Laem Sok, about 30km south of Trat, occasionally calling at Ao Nid on Ko Mak, and terminating at Ao Salat on the island's northeast coast (1–2 daily; about 1hr 30min; B350 including transfers on Ko Kood). Ninmungkorn now has high-season competition from the recently inaugurated Ko Kood Express, which sails from Laem Sok to Nam Leuk pier on Ko Kood's west coast (☎039 501150; 1 daily, though this may increase to 2; 1hr 30min–2hr; B350).

SPEEDBOATS FROM THE MAINLAND

There are also several different companies offering high-season speedboat services between the Trat mainland and Ko Kood's western piers and beaches; these are faster and more expensive (up to 4 daily; about 1hr; B600) but can be wet and uncomfortable in all but the flattest seas. Schedules and mainland departure points vary – the usual piers are Laem Sok and Dan Kao, 6km northeast of central Trat – and are best checked with Trat guesthouses or travel agents, the TAT office in Laem Ngop, or guest-houses on Ko Kood.

VIA KO CHANG AND KO MAK

Boats run between Ko Chang, Ko Mak and Ko Kood in high season (see p.183). Speedboats from the mainland to Ko Kood will go via Ao Nid on Ko Mak if there are enough takers (B350, either from Laem Sok or Ko Kood).

INFORMATION

Tourist information There's a municipal tourist information office on Ao Khlong Chao, just north of the bridge over the khlong, on the west side of the road (daily 8.30am–6pm).

GETTING AROUND

Exploring the island on foot is both feasible and fun, and south of Ao Khlong Chao much of the route is shady. From Ao Khlong Chao to Ao Bang Bao takes about 40min; from Ao Bang Bao to Ao Jark is about 1hr, then another 20min to Ao Phrao.

By songthaew These can be chartered for around B1000/day.

By motorbike You can rent motorbikes through most guesthouses and resorts (from B250/day), but be warned that the mostly concrete west-coast road is narrow and steep, and badly rutted in places.

By mountain bike The number of hills may also deter you from getting around by mountain bike – they're available at *Happy Days* on Ao Ngamkho (B150/day) and through some other resorts.

ACCOMMODATION

Ko Kood now offers the whole spectrum of accommodation, from cheap crashpads to swanky villas, though nearly all of the budget resorts are inland from the beaches.

AO KHLONG CHAO

Cozy House On the south bank of the khlong, Ao Khlong Chao ☎089 094 3650, ⓦkohkoodcozy.com. Has the cheapest rooms in Khlong Chao (with shared bathrooms), in an extended stilt house centred round a lovely breezy communal khlong-side deck. The pricier rooms and bungalows are not such good value but the home-cooked food is exceptional, especially the fish. Lots of facilities for backpackers, including computers, rental kayaks and motorbikes, petanque and volleyball. B250

Khlong Chao Garden View Ao Khlong Chao ☎087 908 3593. Away from the khlong, this friendly place is set on a lawn dotted with ornamental trees beside the road 50m south of the bridge, and about 100m inland from the sea. Choose between basic, fan-cooled huts with small bathrooms, and larger a/c bungalows with TVs. There's good food at the popular garden restaurant too, especially the *phanaeng* curries. Fan B400, a/c B1000

★ **The Mangrove** On the south bank of the khlong, Ao Khlong Chao ☎085 279 0278, ⓦkohkood -mangrove.com. The best of the khlong-side options, with nice views of the water and sturdy wooden bungalows spaced around a well-tended lawn, dotted with pretty plants and trees. Interiors are modern and well furnished with TV and hot water. Free kayaks and motorbikes for rent. Fan B800, a/c B1500

Tinkerbell Ao Khlong Chao ☎081 813 0058, ⓦtinkerbellresort.com. Stylishly designed and land-scaped resort at the south end of the beach, which offers a difficult choice. For the same price (including breakfast), you can plump for either a bright, pastel-coloured villa with a/c, hot rain shower, fridge, TV, DVD player and large balcony hard on the beach, or an equally attractive two-storey house in the second row, with a plunge pool and a separate large living room and toilet upstairs. There's a small swimming pool fed by an artificial waterfall, and free wi-fi throughout. B6900

AO NGAMKHO

Dusita Ao Ngamkho ☎081 420 4861, ⓦdusitakohkood .com. Directly on the shore, just south of the khlong, this small, friendly outfit offers plainly outfitted fan and a/c wooden cabins, some with nice pebbledash outdoor bathrooms, that all enjoy beautiful sea views and some shade among the sparse coconut grove hung with hammocks. Fan B900, a/c B1400

Hindard Resort Ao Ngamkho ☎081 762 9519, @rungdech@hotmail.com. The large, comfortable, hot-water wooden chalets here, some with outdoor bathrooms, sit on a flower-strewn slope atop the little rocky point at the southern end of the bay, with panoramic sea views and easy access to swimming and snorkelling among the coral off the point. Massage and free wi-fi, snorkels and kayaks. Fan B1200, a/c B1500

Koh Kood Happy Days Ao Ngamkho ☎087 144 5945 or ☎086 018 6012; ⓦkohkood-happydays.com. This backpacker-oriented resort, beside the road, 200m from the northern section of the beach, offers ten en-suite fan and a/c rooms in a little guesthouse block, all with wooden floors, pretty furnishings and a shared veranda. There's also motorbike and mountain-bike rental and internet access, plus a dive shop, a sociable bar and restaurant and a general store next door. Fan B450, a/c B800

AO BANG BAO

The Beach Natural Resort Ao Bang Bao ☎086 009 9420, ⓦthebeachkohkood.com. Though it doesn't actually sit on the nicest part of the beach, but behind a rocky area towards the northern end, this resort's diverse, thatched Balinese-style bungalows are tastefully furnished and have garden bathrooms; they're grouped quite closely together so most only offer sea glimpses. All have hot showers and some have a/c (6pm–7.30am only). Facilities include computers and free wi-fi, kayaks, bicycles and motorbikes. Breakfast included. Fan B1400, a/c B2200

Siam Beach Ao Bang Bao ☏ 081 899 6200, ⓦ siam beachkohkood.net. This resort occupies almost all of the best part of the beach, sprawling across an extensive area, and is popular with budget travellers, though it's more isolated than similarly priced options on Ao Ngamkho and Ao Khlong Chao. Its big, no-frills huts and bungalows on the seafront nearly all enjoy uninterrupted bay views. Some of the newer a/c rooms are in a less idyllic spot close to a khlong and back from the shore a bit, but they're cheaper than the beachside a/c options and have hot showers. The restaurant cooks up regular seafood barbecues and there's internet access, motorbike and kayak rental. Breakfast included. Fan B1200, a/c and hot showers B1500, a/c and cold showers B1800

AO JARK

Neverland Resort Ao Jark ☏ 081 762 6254, ⓦ neverlandresort.com. The only accommodation on this beach is set among the palms between the limpid blue sea and the calm green khlong. It offers comfortable, balconied, log-clad a/c bungalows, some with hot showers, in a pretty garden, as well as fully equipped two-person tents (B500), kayaks and snorkels. Breakfast included. B1600

AO PHRAO

Ao Phrao Beach Ao Phrao ☏ 081 429 7145, ⓦ kokut .com. Mainly but not exclusively package-oriented clusters of thatched and more expensive concrete a/c bungalows, all with hot showers and TVs; facilities include internet, free wi-fi, free kayaks and a karaoke room. Breakfast included. B3600

AROUND BAN KHLONG HIN DAM

★ **Koh Kood Beach Resort** Ao Khlong Mat, about 2km northwest of Ban Khlong Hin Dam ☏ 081 908 8966, ⓦ visitbeyond.com. This excellent Danish-run resort is set in loads of space on a sweeping, grassy slope above a lovely pool and a nice stretch of sandy beach. Rooms are of two types, all with a/c, outdoor hot showers, mini-bars, TVs, DVD players and sea views from their generous decks: high-roofed, thatched Balinese-style bungalows and slightly more expensive "Thai Twin Houses", very suitable for families, in which two rooms share a jacuzzi. Motorbikes, mountain bikes, snorkels and kayaks are available, as well as computers and wi-fi in the restaurant. Breakfast included. B3500

Shantaa North end of Ao Taphao, about 2km west of Ban Khlong Hin Dam ☏ 081 817 9648, ⓦ shantaa kohkood.com. On a landscaped grassy rise, these nicely decorated villas have a/c and hot rain showers in attractive indoor-outdoor bathrooms. There's not much of a beach but plenty of decks with sunloungers. Computers and wi-fi available in the restaurant. Breakfast included. B4500

EATING AND DRINKING

There are very few eating and drinking options away from the resorts, but a couple might tempt you to make a detour.

Pizza and Pasta South side of Ban Khlong Hin Dam ☏ 083 297 2860, ⓦ pizzanpasta.info. Genial Italian–Thai roadside restaurant serving a mean bolognese with home-made tagliatelle (B250), pizzas (B220), a few salads, espressos and pastries for breakfast. Also does a delivery service. Daily 8.30am–9pm.

Tawan Bar Ao Khlong Chao. Small roadside bar run by a friendly musician, with live music every night. Daily 3pm–2am.

DIRECTORY

Exchange There's no bank on Ko Kood, but you can change money at the bigger resorts.

Hospital Ban Khlong Hin Dam (☏ 039 521852).

Internet access In the tourist information centre on Ao Khlong Chao and at most resorts.

Pharmacy The shop across from the hospital in Ban Khlong Hin Dam has a small pharmacy section and sells antihistamine tablets for bites from sandflies (see p.64), which can be legion on Ko Kood.

Police Ban Khlong Hin Dam (☏ 039 521745).

Postal agent In the shop next to *Happy Days* on Ao Ngamkho.

Southern Thailand: the Gulf coast

KO SAMSAO, ANG THONG MARINE PARK

Southern Thailand: the Gulf coast

Southern Thailand's gently undulating Gulf coast is famed above all for the Samui archipelago, three small, idyllic islands lying off the most prominent hump of the coastline. This is the country's most popular seaside venue for independent travellers, and a lazy stay in a beachfront bungalow is so seductive a prospect that most people overlook the attractions of the mainland, where the sheltered sandy beaches and warm clear water rival the top sunspots in most countries. Added to that you'll find scenery dominated by forested mountains that rise abruptly behind the coastal strip, and a sprinkling of fascinating historic sights.

3

The crumbling temples of ancient **Phetchaburi** are the first historic sight you'll meet heading south out of Bangkok and fully justify a break in your journey. Beyond, the stretch of coast around **Cha-am** and **Hua Hin** is popular with weekending Thais escaping the capital and is crammed with condos, high-rise hotels and bars, not to mention a large population of foreign tourists. Far quieter and preferable are the beaches further south: the sophisticated little resort of **Pak Nam Pran**; golden-sand **Hat Phu Noi**, which is also the best base for exploring the karsts and caves of **Khao Sam Roi Yot National Park**; the welcoming town of **Prachuap Khiri Khan**, fronted by a lovely bay and flanked by an equally appealing beach; and laidback, lightly developed **Ban Krud**.

Of the islands, **Ko Samui** is by far the most naturally beautiful, with its long white-sand beaches and arching fringes of palm trees. The island's beauty has not gone unnoticed by tourist developers of course, and its varied spread of accommodation these days draws as many package tourists and second-homers as backpackers. In recent years the next island out, **Ko Pha Ngan**, has drawn increasing numbers of independent travellers away from its neighbour: its accommodation is generally simpler and cheaper than Ko Samui's, and it offers a few stunning beaches with a more laidback atmosphere. The island's southeastern headland, **Hat Rin**, has no fewer than three white-sand beaches to choose from, but now provides all the amenities the demanding backpacker could want, not to mention its notorious full moon parties. The furthest inhabited island of the archipelago, **Ko Tao**, has taken off as a **scuba-diving** centre, but despite a growing nightlife and restaurant scene, still has the feel of a small, rugged and isolated outcrop.

Tucked away beneath the islands, **Nakhon Si Thammarat**, the cultural capital of the south, is well worth a short detour from the main routes through the centre of the peninsula – it's a sophisticated city of grand old temples, delicious cuisine and distinctive handicrafts. With its small but significant Muslim population, and machine-gun dialect, Nakhon begins the transition into Thailand's deep south.

SHADOW PUPPETS, NAKHON SI THAMMARAT

Highlights

❶ Phetchaburi Charming historic town, boasting several fine old working temples, as well as delicious traditional desserts. **See p.209**

❷ Pak Nam Pran Chic, artfully designed boutique hotels on a long, sandy beach, a popular weekend escape for design-conscious Bangkokians. **See p.222**

❸ Ang Thong National Marine Park A dramatic, unspoilt group of over forty remote islands, accessible on boat-trips from Ko Samui or Ko Pha Ngan. **See p.253**

❹ Full moon at Hat Rin, Ko Pha Ngan Party on, and on… **See p.260**

❺ Ao Thong Nai Pan on Ko Pha Ngan Beautiful, secluded bay with good accommodation. **See p.264**

❻ A boat-trip round Ko Tao Satisfying exploration and great snorkelling, especially off the unique causeway beaches of Ko Nang Yuan. **See p.267**

❼ Nakhon Si Thammarat Historic holy sites, intriguing shadow puppets, great-value accommodation and excellent cuisine. **See p.276**

❽ Krung Ching waterfall Walk past giant ferns and screeching monkeys to reach this spectacular drop. **See p.283**

HIGHLIGHTS ARE MARKED ON THE MAP ON P.208

SOUTHERN THAILAND: THE GULF COAST

BANGKOK

Ratchaburi

Samut Songkhram

35

3

3

KAENG KRACHAN NATIONAL PARK

Phetchaburi

1

Cha-am

Pattaya

3

3

37

Hua Hin

2

Pala-u Falls

Pranburi

Pak Nam Pran
Hat Phu Noi

KHAO SAM ROI YOT NATIONAL PARK

Kuiburi

Prachuap Khiri Khan

B U R M A

Wang Duan

Ban Krud

Bang Saphan Yai
Suan Luang

GULF OF THAILAND

4

Thung Wua Laen

Chumphon

41

Hat Sai Ri
Ao Thung Makham

6 *Ko Tao*

Ranong

4006

Lang Suan

ANG THONG NATIONAL MARINE PARK

5

Ko Pha Ngan

3

4

ANDAMAN SEA

4

Wat Suan Mokkh

Chaiya

Ko Samui

Don Sak

Khanom

Surat Thani

KHAO SOK NATIONAL PARK

Phunphin

401

Sichon

401

44

8 *Krung Ching*

Phang Nga

41

Khao Luang
(1835m)

7

Nakhon Si Thammarat

403

Krabi

Thung Song

Ron Phibun

408

403

41

Phuket

Trang

4

Phatthalung

0	50

kilometres

N

HIGHLIGHTS
1 Phetchaburi
2 Pak Nam Pran
3 Ang Thong National Marine Park
4 Full moon at Hat Rin, Ko Pha Ngan
5 Ao Thong Nai Pan on Ko Pha Ngan
6 A boat-trip around Ko Tao
7 Nakhon Si Thammarat
8 Krung Ching waterfall

The Gulf coast has a slightly different **climate** from the Andaman coast and much of the rest of Thailand, being hit heavily by the northeast monsoon's rains, especially in November, when it's best to avoid this part of the country altogether. Most times during the rest of the year should see pleasant, if changeable, weather, with some effects of the southwest monsoon felt between May and October. Late December to April is the driest period, and is therefore the region's high season, which also includes July and August.

ARRIVAL AND GETTING AROUND   THE GULF COAST

The main arteries through this region are highways 4 (also known as the Phetkasem Highway, or usually Thanon Phetkasem when passing through towns) and 41, served by plentiful buses.

By plane The main airports in this region are on Ko Samui, at Surat Thani and Nakhon Si Thammarat, the latter two providing, in combination with buses and boats, cheaper but slower competition for getting to the islands.

By train The railway from Bangkok connects all the mainland towns, including a branch line to Nakhon; nearly all services depart from Hualamphong Station, but a few slow trains use Thonburi Station. You can also head south from Kanchanaburi by train, changing at Ban Pong or Nakhon Pathom.

By boat Daily boats run to all three main islands from two jumping-off points: Surat Thani, 650km from Bangkok, is close to Ko Samui and is generally more convenient for Ko Pha Ngan too, but if you're heading from Bangkok to Pha Ngan you might want to consider Chumphon, which is certainly the main port for Ko Tao.

3

Phetchaburi

Straddling the Phet River about 120km south of Bangkok, the provincial capital of **PHETCHABURI** (sometimes "Phetburi") has been settled ever since the eleventh century, when the Khmers ruled the region, but only really got going six hundred years later, when it flourished as a trading post between the Andaman Sea ports and Ayutthaya. Despite periodic incursions from the Burmese, the town gained a reputation as a cultural centre – as the ornamentation of its older temples testifies – and after the new capital was established in Bangkok it became a favourite country retreat of Rama IV, who had a hilltop palace, **Phra Nakhon Khiri**, built here in the 1850s. Modern Phetchaburi is known for its limes and rose apples but its main claim to fame is as one of Thailand's finest sweet-making centres, the essential ingredient for its assortment of *khanom* being the sugar extracted from the sweet-sapped palms that cover the province. This being very much a cottage industry, today's downtown Phetchaburi has lost relatively little of the ambience that so attracted Rama IV: the central riverside area is hemmed in by historic wats in varying states of disrepair, along with plenty of traditional wooden shophouses. The town's top three temples, described below, can be seen on a leisurely two-hour circular walk beginning from Chomrut Bridge, while Phetchaburi's other significant sight, the palace-museum at Phra Nakhon Khiri, is on a hill about 1km west of the bridge.

Despite the attractions of its old quarter, Phetchaburi gets few overnight visitors as most people see it on a day-trip from Bangkok, Hua Hin or Cha-am. It's also possible to combine a day in Phetchaburi with an early-morning expedition from Bangkok to the floating markets of Damnoen Saduak, 40km north; budget tour operators in Bangkok's Thanon Khao San area offer this option as a day-trip package for about B600 per person. The town sees more overnighters during the **Phra Nakhon Khiri Fair**, spread over at least five days in February, which features parades in historic costumes, cooking demonstrations and traditional entertainments such as *likay* and *lakhon*.

Wat Yai Suwannaram

Thanon Phongsuriya, about 700m east of Chomrut Bridge

Of all Phetchaburi's temples, the most attractive is the still-functioning seventeenth-century **Wat Yai Suwannaram**. The temple's fine old teak **sala** has elaborately carved doors, bearing a gash reputedly inflicted by the Burmese in 1760 as they plundered their way towards Ayutthaya. Across from the *sala* and hidden behind high, whitewashed walls stands the windowless Ayutthaya-style bot. The bot compound overlooks a pond, in the middle of which stands a small but well-preserved scripture library, or **ho trai**: such structures were built on stilts over water to prevent ants and other insects destroying the precious documents. Enter the walled compound from the south and make a clockwise tour of the cloisters filled with Buddha statues before entering the bot itself via the eastern doorway (if the door is locked, one of the monks will get the key for you). The **bot** is supported by intricately patterned red and gold pillars and contains a remarkable, if rather faded, set of murals, depicting Indra, Brahma and other lower-ranking divinities ranged in five rows of ascending importance. Once you've admired the interior, walk to the back of the bot, passing behind the central cluster of Buddha images, to find another Buddha image seated against the back wall: climb the steps in front of this statue to get a close-up of the left foot, which for some reason was cast with six toes.

Wat Kamphaeng Laeng

Thanon Phra Song, a 15min walk east and then south of Wat Yai

The five tumbledown prangs of **Wat Kamphaeng Laeng** mark out Phetchaburi as the likely southernmost outpost of the Khmer empire. Built probably in the thirteenth century to honour the Hindu deity Shiva and set out in a cruciform arrangement facing east, the laterite corncob-style prangs were later adapted for Buddhist use, as can be seen from the two that now house Buddha images. There has been some attempt to restore a few of the carvings and false balustraded windows, but these days

PHETCHABURI

Tham Khao Luang

Train Station

3173

Prachomklao Hospital

Buses to Bangkok

CAT

Night Market

A/C minibuses to Ratchaburi & Bangkok

THANON RAJWITHI

Police Station

Raan Khanom Waan Mee Pin

Wat Trailok

Khao Wang

Cable car

Wat Chisa In

Buses to Cha-am & Hua Hin

THANON PHONGSURIYA

Phra Nakhon Khiri

Chomrut Bridge

Wat Yai Suwannaram

Baw Khaw Saw Bus Terminal

THANON CHISA-IN

Wat Uthai Photharam

Khao Bandai-it

THANON PHETKASEM

Wat Mahathat

THANON PHRA SONG

Wat Kamphaeng Laeng

THANON BANDAI-IT

Wat Phra Song

Phetcharat Hospital

THANON SURIPHAN

TOT

4

Wat Lat

THANON RAJDAMNOEN

THANON DAMNOEN KASEM

THANON PHANICHAREON

Wat Chi Phrakut

THANON THA HIN

ACCOMMODATION
Rabieng Rimnum Guest House — 3
Royal Diamond — 1
Sabai Dee Resort — 2

N

Clock Tower

RESTAURANT
Rabieng Rimnum Guest House — 1

Wat Ko Kaew Sutharam

0 — 500 metres

Bangkok

Phet River

THANON MATAYAWONG

THANON PHOKARONG

Cha-am & Hua Hin

worshippers congregate in the modern whitewashed wat behind these shrines, leaving the atmospheric and appealingly quaint collection of decaying prangs and casuarina topiary to chickens, stray dogs and the occasional tourist.

Wat Mahathat

Thanon Damnoen Kasem

Heading west along Thanon Phra Song from Wat Kamphaeng Laeng, across the river you can see the prangs of Phetchaburi's most fully restored and important temple, **Wat Mahathat**, long before you reach them. Boasting the "Mahathat" title only since 1954 – when the requisite Buddha relics were donated by the king – it was probably founded in the fourteenth century, but suffered badly at the hands of the Burmese. The five landmark prangs at its heart are adorned with stucco figures of mythical creatures, though these are nothing compared with those on the roofs of the main viharn and the bot. Instead of tapering off into the usual serpentine *chofa*, the gables are studded with miniature *thep* and *deva* figures (angels and gods), which add an almost mischievous vitality to the place. In a similar vein, a couple of gold-embossed crocodiles snarl above the entrance to the bot, and a caricature carving of a bespectacled man rubs shoulders with mythical giants in a relief around the base of the gold Buddha, housed in a separate mondop nearby.

Khao Wang

Dominating Phetchaburi's western outskirts stands Rama IV's palace, a stew of mid-nineteenth-century Thai and European styles scattered over the crest of the hill known as **Khao Wang** ("Palace Hill"). During his day, the royal entourage would struggle its way up the steep brick path to the summit, but now there's a **cable car** (daily 8.30am–4.30pm; B40 return) which starts from the western flank of the hill off Highway 4; there's also a path up the eastern flank, starting near Thanon Rajwithi. If you do walk up the hill, be warned that hundreds of quite aggressive monkeys hang out at its base and on the path to the top.

Up top, the wooded hill is littered with wats, prangs, chedis, whitewashed gazebos and lots more, in an ill-assorted combination of architectural idioms – the prang-topped viharn, washed all over in burnt sienna, is particularly ungainly. Whenever the king came on an excursion here, he stayed in the airy summer house, **Phra Nakhon Khiri** (daily 9am–4pm; B150), with its Mediterranean-style shutters and verandas. Now a museum, it houses a moderately interesting collection of ceramics, furniture and other artefacts given to the royal family by foreign friends. Besides being cool and breezy, Khao Wang also proved to be a good stargazing spot, so Rama IV, a keen astronomer (see p.226), had an open-sided, glass-domed observatory built close to his sleeping quarters.

ARRIVAL AND DEPARTURE
PHETCHABURI

BY TRAIN
Phetchaburi station is on the north side of the town centre.

Destinations Bangkok (Hualamphong Station 10 daily, Thonburi Station 3 daily; 2hr 45min–3hr 45min); Chumphon (10 daily; 4hr–6hr 30min); Hat Yai (4 daily; 11hr 30min–13hr 30min); Hua Hin (12 daily; 1hr); Nakhon Pathom (13 daily; 1hr 30min–2hr); Nakhon Si Thammarat (2 daily; 12–13hr); Prachuap Khiri Khan (11 daily; 2–3hr); Ratchaburi (13 daily; 40min–1hr); Surat Thani (8 daily; 6hr 45min–9hr); Trang (2 daily; 13hr).

BY BUS
Phetchaburi is served mostly by through-buses on their way to or from Bangkok – all services between the capital and southern Thailand have to pass through the town on Highway 4.

Through-buses There's a small Baw Khaw Saw terminal on the east side of Highway 4 (Thanon Phetkasem), which is where southbound through-buses will set you down or pick you up. Northbound through-buses on their way to Bangkok stop on the opposite side of the highway: ask to get off at "Sii Yaek Phetcharat", the crossroads of Highway 4 and Thanon Bandai-It by Phetcharat Hospital – otherwise you might be put off at the Big C Department Store about 5km south of town. Songthaews and motorbike taxis run between Highway 4 and the town centre.

From/to Cha-am and Hua Hin Non-a/c buses from and to Cha-am and Hua Hin use the small terminal in the town centre, less than a 10min walk from Chomrut Bridge.

From/to Bangkok The terminal for dedicated Phetchaburi–Bangkok a/c buses is about a 10min walk from Chomrut Bridge, just off Thanon Rajwithi. Note that if you're coming here from Kanchanaburi, you can avoid Bangkok by heading for Ratchaburi, where you can catch a bus, a/c minibus or train to Phetchaburi.

Destinations Bangkok (4–7 daily; 2hr 15min); Cha-am (every 30min; 1hr 20min); Hua Hin (every 30min; 1hr 50min).

BY MINIBUS

Several companies offer licensed a/c minibuses to Victory Monument in Bangkok, including one just east of the night market and the river (marked on our map) that also covers Ratchaburi.

GETTING AROUND

By samlor or songthaew Shared songthaews circulate round the town, but to see the major temples in a day and have sufficient energy left for climbing Khao Wang, you might want to hire a samlor or a songthaew for a couple of hours, at about B100/hr.

By bicycle or motorbike You can rent bicycles (B120/day) and motorbikes (B250–350/day) from *Rabieng Rimnum Guest House*.

INFORMATION AND TOURS

Rabieng Rimnum Guest House There's no TAT office in town, but *Rabieng Rimnum Guest House* (see below) is a good source of local information. It also offers internet access and organizes day-trips and overnight visits to Kaeng Krachan National Park for bird-watching and hiking from November to July.

ACCOMMODATION

Rabieng Rimnum (Rim Nam) Guest House 1 Thanon Chisa-in, on the southwest corner of Chomrut Bridge ☎ 032 425707 or 089 919 7446, ⓦ rabiengrimnum .com. Occupying a century-old house next to the Phet River and, less appealingly, a noisy main road, this popular, central guesthouse offers nine simple rooms with shared, cold-water bathrooms, lots of local information and the best restaurant in town. Excellent rates for singles. B240
Royal Diamond Soi Sam Chao Phet, in a grid of small streets just off the Phetkasem Highway ☎ 032 411061–70, ⓦ royaldiamondhotel.com. On the northwest side of Khao Wang, this welcoming place is Phetchaburi's best upmarket option. The large, comfortable a/c rooms with hot water, TVs, fridges and free wi-fi are fairly well insulated from the noise of the highway (though not necessarily from the live bands in the hotel's own beer garden). Very modest breakfast included. B800
Sabai Dee Resort Thanon Khong Kacheng ☎ 086 344 4418. Your best budget option if *Rabieng Rimnum* across the street is full. All sharing cold-water bathrooms, accommodation is either in very simple bamboo bunga-lows with mosquito nets in a small garden by the river, or in slightly more expensive, large, white rooms with polished wooden floors in the main building. B250

EATING

As well as for *khanom*, Phetchaburi is famous for savoury **khao jae**: originally a Mon dish designed to cool you down in the hot season, it consists of rice in chilled, flower-scented water served with delicate, fried side dishes, such as shredded Chinese radish and balls of shrimp paste, dried fish and palm sugar. It's available at the day market until sold out, usually around 3pm.

PHETCHABURI'S *KHANOM*

Almost half the shops in Phetchaburi stock the town's famous **khanom** (sweet snacks), as do many of the souvenir stalls crowding the base of Khao Wang and vendors at the day market on Thanon Matayawong. The most well-known local speciality is *maw kaeng* (best sampled from Raan Khanom Waan Mee Pin on the west side of Thanon Matayawong, just north of Phongsuriya), a baked sweet egg custard made with mung beans and coconut and sometimes flavoured with lotus seeds, durian or taro. Other Phetchaburi classics to look out for include *khanom taan*, small, steamed, saffron-coloured cakes made with local palm sugar, coconut and rice flour, and wrapped in banana-leaf cases; and *thong yot*, orange balls of palm sugar and baked egg yolk.

Rabieng Rimnum Guest House 1 Thanon Chisa-in, on the southwest corner of Chomrut Bridge ☏ 032 425707 or 089 919 7446, ⓦ rabiengrimnum.com. The town's best restaurant, an airy, wooden house with riverside tables attached to the guesthouse of the same name. It offers a long and interesting menu of inexpensive Thai dishes, from banana-blossom salad (B70) to the tasty Phetchaburi speciality, sugar-palm fruit curry with prawns (B75), and is deservedly popular with local diners. Daily 7.30am–midnight.

Cha-am and around

Forever in the shadow of its more famous neighbour, Hua Hin, 25km to the south, the resort of **CHA-AM** is nevertheless very popular with Thais on short breaks, and it sports one or two package-holiday high-rises and Western-style restaurants for Europeans, too. Mostly, though, it's weekending families and partying student groups from Bangkok who eat and drink at the rows of umbrella-shaded tables and deckchairs on the sand, or brave the sea on banana boats or rubber tyres, the women clad modestly in T-shirts and shorts rather than bikinis. The long, straight beach here is pleasantly shaded, though rather gritty and very narrow at high tide, and the water is perfectly swimmable, if not pristine. During the week the pace of life in Cha-am is slow, and it's easy to find a solitary spot under the thick canopy of casuarinas, particularly at the northerly end of the beach, but that's rarely possible at weekends, when prices shoot up and traffic thickens considerably.

Cha-am has a functional pocket of development around Thanon Phetkasem (Highway 4), close to the junction with Thanon Narathip, the main access road to the beach, 1km to the east. However, the 3km seaside promenade of Thanon Ruamchit is where you'll find most of the hotels, restaurants, a small police station (corner of Thanon Narathip), several internet shops and a few other tourist-oriented businesses; Thanon Ruamchit's sois are numbered according to whether they're north or south of Thanon Narathip.

Phra Ratchaniwet Marukhathaiyawan

10km south of Cha-am, off the road to Hua Hin, Highway 4 • Daily except Wed 8.30am–4.30pm • Grounds B30, palace B30; English guidebook B80 • Best accessed by private transport, but Cha-am–Hua Hin buses (roughly every 30min) stop within 2km of the palace at the sign for Rama VI Camp – just follow the road through the army compound

Set in beautiful grounds, the lustrous seaside palace of Rama VI, **Phra Ratchaniwet Marukhathaiyawan** (aka Mrigadayavan Palace), is rarely visited by foreigners, though it sees plenty of Thai visitors. Designed by an Italian architect, Ercole Manfredi, in a Westernized Thai style, and completed in 1924, the entire, 400m-long complex of sixteen golden teak pavilions and connecting walkways is raised off the ground on over a thousand concrete columns, with a niche for water at the base of each to keep out ants. It's often referred to as "the palace of love and hope" as Rama VI first visited with his pregnant queen, who later miscarried (and was subsequently demoted to royal consort), but it was abandoned to the corrosive sea air after the king's death in 1925. Restoration work began in the 1970s, and today most of the structure looks as it once did, a stylish composition of verandas and latticework painted in shades of cream and light blue, with an emphasis on cool simplicity. The spacious open hall in the north wing, hung with chandeliers and encircled by a first-floor balcony, was used as a meeting room and as a theatre for the king to perform in his own plays. The king stayed in the central group of buildings, with the best sea view and a 50m-long elevated walkway to his private bathing pavilion, while the south wing contained the apartments of the royal consorts, with its own bathing pavilion connected by a walkway.

3

ARRIVAL AND DEPARTURE
CHA-AM

By train The station, a few blocks west of the main Phetkasem–Narathip junction, is served by a handful of trains a day, from either Hualamphong or Thonburi stations in Bangkok.

Destinations Bangkok (5 daily; 3hr 30min–4hr 30min); Chumphon (3 daily; 5–7hr); Hat Yai (1 daily; 13hr 30min); Hua Hin (5 daily; 30min); Prachuap Khiri Khan (4 daily; 2hr).

By bus Through-buses and local services from and to Hua Hin and Phetchaburi stop on Highway 4, close to the junction with Thanon Narathip, the main road running east

to the beach. Bangkok–Cha-am a/c buses use the depot at the little plaza off the beachfront Thanon Ruamchit, just south of Thanon Narathip.

Destinations Bangkok (roughly hourly; 2hr 45min–3hr 15min); Hua Hin (roughly every 30min; 35min); Phetchaburi (every 20–30min; 50min–1hr 20min).

By minibus If you're heading for Bangkok, you could catch one of the frequent Hua Hin–Victory Monument a/c minibuses, operated by several companies: either go to one of the companies' pavement desks at the Phetchaburi–Narathip junction, or phone ahead to book (see p.217).

GETTING AROUND

By bicycle or motorbike A number of shops along the beachfront road, Thanon Ruamchit, rent motorbikes as well

as bicycles, tandems and even three- and four-person bikes.

INFORMATION

Tourist information The local TAT office (daily 8.30am–4.30pm; ☎ 032 471005–6, ✉ tatphet @tat.or.th), which provides information about the whole of

Phetchaburi province, is on Highway 4 (west side), about 1km south of Thanon Narathip.

ACCOMMODATION

There are no obvious backpacker-oriented places in Cha-am; instead you'll find mainly small, mid-range hotels and guesthouses, concentrated on Thanon Ruamchit and the adjoining sois, and upmarket, out-of-town resorts, many on the road down to Hua Hin (see p.218). Many Cha-am hotels put their prices up on Saturdays, over bank-holiday weekends and during school holidays (mid-March to mid-May and Oct).

Golden Beach Cha-am Hotel Just south of Soi Cha-am North 8 at 208/14 Thanon Ruamchit ☎ 032 433833, ⓦ goldenbeachchaam.com. Good-value twenty-storey hotel with a full-height atrium, a swimming pool, gym and internet access, set back from the promenade. The nicely appointed rooms have a/c, hot water, mini-bars and TVs, as well as balconies, most with sea views. `B2000`

Hôtel de la Paix 6km north of central Cha-am ☎ 032 709555, ⓦ hoteldelapaixhh.com. Sleek designer hideaway featuring a triumphal, white-marble staircase up to the lobby and a huge reflective pool as its centrepiece. The accommodation blocks have a striking cubic look but are very comfortable for all that, while creative, beautifully presented food is served at the breezy restaurant, *Clouds Loft*. There are two swimming pools (plus seven villas with private pools), a spa and an events centre offering cooking

classes, kayaking and mountain-biking. `B9700`

Nana House North of Soi Cha-am North 10 towards the canal ☎ 032 433632, ⓦ nanahouse.net. Wide range of well-kept accommodation with a/c, hot water and wi-fi, including two-bedroom houses (B4000). The bright, pretty, tiled rooms in the purple building down the quieter side alley are better value than the swankier affairs in the main building on the front. Breakfast included. `B900`

Nirandorn 3 Just south of the Narathip junction on Thanon Ruamchit ☎ 032 470300. Clean, well-maintained hotel rooms and a few tightly packed, motel-style bungalows, decorated in crisp, modern whites and browns, with sofas, safes, a/c, TVs, fridges and hot water; all rooms in the hotel block are sea-facing, sporting balconies and deckchairs. There's also a small, attractive swimming pool. Rooms `B700`, bungalows `B800`

EATING AND DRINKING

The choice of **restaurants** in Cha-am is not a patch on the range you get in Hua Hin, but there should be enough Thai-style seafood to keep you satisfied, including at the dozens of deckchair-and-umbrella places on the beach.

Krua Medsai North end of the beach, just after the canal ☎ 032 430196. A very Thai institution, this huge, open-sided, thatched pavilion sits on the beach, with *luk thung* on the sound system, views down to Hua Hin and nice breezes off the sea. People flock here for the very good

seafood, simply grilled or in dishes such as delicious *hoy jor*, crabmeat, minced pork and water chestnuts wrapped in tofu skin (B80). Daily 10am–10pm.

O-Zone Thanon Ruamchit, north of Soi Cha-am North 7 ☎ 032 470897. Popular bar-restaurant whose attractions include mellow live folk music early evening (about 7–8.15pm), followed by bands playing Thai and Western pop (about 9.15pm–12.30am), and a menu that encompasses a few Western dishes such as pizza and steak, one-plate Thai dishes and more complex offerings such as crispy fried catfish salad (B150). Daily 5/6pm–12.30/1am.

Poom North of Soi Cha-am North 6 at 274/1 Thanon Ruamchit ☎ 032 471036. Welcoming, no-frills restaurant which serves a good selection of seafood dishes on its sea-view terrace – try the shrimps with garlic (B250) or crab with black pepper (B300–400, according to weight). Daily 10am–midnight.

Hua Hin

Thailand's oldest beach resort, **HUA HIN** used to be little more than an overgrown fishing village with one exceptionally grand hotel, but the arrival of mass tourism, high-rise hotels and farang-managed hostess bars has made a serious dent in its once idiosyncratic charm. With the far superior beaches of Ko Samui, Krabi and Ko Samet so close at hand, there's little to draw the dedicated sunseeker here. The town's most distinctive attractions are its squid-pier restaurants and guesthouses on Thanon Naretdamri, characterful spots to stay or enjoy fine seafood, while at the other end of the scale the former *Railway Hotel* (now the *Centara Grand*) provides all the atmosphere you can afford. In addition, the town makes a convenient base for day-trips to Khao Sam Roi Yot National Park to the south and Pala-u Falls in Kaeng Krachan National Park to the west. If none of that appeals, you might consider stopping by for Hua Hin's well-respected **jazz festival** in August (ⓦhuahinjazz.com) or for the rather more unusual **elephant polo tournament**, held every September (ⓦanantaraelephantpolo.com).

3

Brief history

The **royal family** were Hua Hin's main visitors at the start of the twentieth century, but the place became more widely popular in the 1920s, when the opening of the Bangkok–Malaysia rail line made short excursions to the beach much more viable. The Victorian-style *Railway Hotel* was opened in 1922, originally as a necessary overnight stop on the three-day journey to Malaysia. At the same time Rama VI commissioned the nine-hole Royal Hua Hin Golf Course (now 18 holes; ☎032 512475) to the west of the station, and in 1926 Rama VII had his own summer palace, Klai Klangwon ("Far from Worries"), erected at the northern end of the beach. It was here, ironically, that Rama VII was staying in 1932 when the coup was launched in Bangkok against the system of absolute monarchy. The current king has made many visits here too, which means that the navy is on constant guard duty in the resort and the police are also on their best behaviour; consequently both Thais and expats consider Hua Hin an especially safe place to live and do business – hence the number of farang-oriented real-estate agencies in the area.

The central shorefront

The prettiest part of Hua Hin's 5km-long **beach** is the patch in front of and to the south of the *Centara Grand*, where the sand is at its softest and whitest. North of here the shore is crowded with tables and chairs belonging to a string of small restaurant shacks, beyond which the beach ends at a Chinese temple atop a flight of steps running down to Thanon Naretdamri. The coast to the north of the pagoda is dominated by the jetties and terraces of the squid-pier guesthouses and seafood restaurants, the hub of the original fishing village, which dates back to the early nineteenth century.

South to Khao Takiab

6km south of the town centre • Green songthaews run to Khao Takiab every 20min or so from central Thanon Sa Song

South of the *Centara Grand*, holiday homes and high-rise condos overshadow nearly the whole run of beach down to the promontory known as Khao Takiab (Chopstick Hill), but during the week it's fairly quiet along here, with just a few widely spaced food stalls along the broad, squeakily soft beach. **Khao Takiab** itself is a wooded outcrop surmounted by a temple and home to a troupe of monkeys; the road to the top is guarded by a tall, golden, standing Buddha and affords good coastal views.

ARRIVAL AND DEPARTURE   **HUA HIN**

There are currently no scheduled services to Hua Hin Airport.

BY TRAIN

All services between the south and Bangkok (mostly using Hualamphong, with a few stopping trains serving Thonburi station) stop at Hua Hin's photogenic 1920s station, a 10min walk west of the seafront.

Destinations Bangkok (14 daily; 3hr 30min–5hr); Butterworth (Malaysia; 1 daily; 17hr 30min); Chumphon (13 daily; 3hr 30min–5hr 20min); Hat Yai (5 daily; 10hr 30min–12hr 30min); Nakhon Si Thammarat (2 daily; 12hr); Prachuap Khiri Khan (11 daily; 1hr 30min); Surat Thani (11 daily; 5hr 40min–8hr); Trang (2 daily; 12hr).

BY BUS

Baw Khaw Saw terminal Most government and private buses use the main Baw Khaw Saw terminal, which is well to the south of the centre, between Thanon Phetkasem

sois 96 and 98, though some services will drop you off at the central clocktower (Wat Hua Hin) on their way in. Non-a/c Cha-am and Phetchaburi buses from the Baw Khaw Saw pick up at a spot just north of the junction of Thanon Phetkasem and Thanon Chomsin.

Destinations Bangkok (at least hourly; 4hr); Cha-am (roughly every 30min; 35min); Chiang Mai (3 daily; 12hr); Chumphon (hourly in the morning, fewer in the afternoon; 3hr 30min–4hr 30min); Hat Yai (4 daily; 10hr); Krabi (3 daily; 9hr); Phetchaburi (every 20–30min; 1hr 15min–1hr 50min); Phuket (3 daily; 9hr); Prachuap Khiri Khan (roughly hourly; 1hr 30min–2hr); Pranburi (hourly; 30min); Surat Thani (2 daily; 7hr).

From/to Bangkok First-class a/c buses (every 40min; 3hr) to Bangkok's Southern Bus Terminal, stopping only at Phetchaburi, leave from beside the *Sri Phetkasem* hotel on

EXCURSIONS AND ACTIVITIES AROUND HUA HIN

A popular day-trip from Hua Hin is 63km west to the fifteen-tiered **Pala-u Waterfall**, situated close to the Burmese border and within **Kaeng Krachan National Park** (B200; ⓦdnp.go.th). Though the falls themselves are hardly exceptional, the route there takes you through lush, hilly landscape and past innumerable pineapple plantations. There's no public transport to the falls, but every tour operator features them in its programme. To get there under your own steam, follow the signs from the west end of Thanon Chomsin along Highway 3218. Once inside the park you'll see hundreds of butterflies and may also catch sight of monitor lizards and six species of hornbills. A slippery and occasionally steep path follows the river through the fairly dense jungle up to the falls, passing the (numbered) tiers en route to the remote fifteenth level, though most people opt to stop at the third level, which has the first pool of any decent depth (full of fish but not that clear) and is a half-hour walk from the car park.

Hua Hin also offers excursions to Khao Sam Roi Yot National Park, Phetchaburi and Amphawa floating market, not to mention the old summer palace of Phra Ratchaniwet Marukhathaiyawan just to the north (see p.213). In addition, a number of **activities** are available, such as cycling and kiteboarding.

TOUR OPERATORS

Hua Hin Adventure Tour 69/8 Thanon Naebkehat ☎032 530314, ⓦhuahinadventuretour.com. A huge range of tours, including Pala-u Falls (from B1800/person), a boat trip in Kaeng Krachan National Park (from B2200) and Khao Sam Roi Yot National Park (from B1700, kayaking on Khao Daeng canal B400 extra), plus Thai cooking classes.

Hua Hin Bike Tours 4/34 Soi 96/1, Thanon Phetkasem ☎081 173 4469, ⓦhuahinbiketours .com. A variety of guided half-day (B1500) and day rides (from B2500 including lunch), including transfers, as well as rental from B375/day.

Kiteboarding Asia ☎081 591 4593, ⓦkiteboarding asia.com. Kiteboarding courses and rental from three shops, including a spot off the end of Soi 75/1, about 2.5km south of the Sofitel (B4000 for a one-day course, B11,000 for three days; best conditions from Feb to mid-May).

Mermaid Cruises ☎032 632223 or ☎084 800 7400, ⓦhuahincruises.com. Eco-friendly trips on the Pran River to the south of Hua Hin (B1950/person, including lunch and transfers), using quiet electric-powered longtails that allow you to get close to the wildlife, including 3m-long monitor lizards, egrets, ospreys, wild peacocks and six species of kingfisher. Kayaking day-trips on the river are also offered (B1150, including packed lunch). Among several sea cruises, Mermaid also run full-day trips on a big boat down to Khao Sam Roi Yot (B1950, including lunch; park admission fee B200 extra).

Western Tours 11 Thanon Damnern Kasem ☎032 533304, ⓦwesterntourshuahin.com. Weekly roster of day-trips to Khao Sam Roi Yot National Park (B1700/person, kayaking on Khao Daeng canal B500 extra), Pala-u Falls (B1700, elephant riding B500 extra), Phetchaburi (B1500), Amphawa Floating Market (B2400) and a snorkelling tour (B2700).

Thanon Sa Song – these are much faster than the second-class a/c services from the Baw Khaw Saw and clocktower.
To the islands Lomprayah (☎032 533739, ⓦlomprayah .com; book at their office on Soi Kanjanomai) runs a twice-daily bus and catamaran service, beginning in Bangkok and picking up at Hua Hin's clocktower (daily at 8.30am and 11.30pm) to Ko Tao (B1000), Ko Pha Ngan (B1300) and Ko Samui (B1400), via Chumphon.

BY MINIBUS

Several private companies run a/c minibuses to and from Bangkok's Victory Monument (departing when full, usually around every 30min; 2hr 30min), including Piya 666 Tour on Thanon Naebkehat, south of Thanon Chomsin (☎081 571 0071; in Cha-am ☎082 249 2882; in Bangkok ☎084 464 6586), who have their base in Bangkok at Century Plaza, on the corner of Thanon Phrayathai and Thanon Rangnam, on the south side of the monument.

GETTING AROUND

By taxi service Hua Hin's taxi services include plentiful motorcycle taxis, samlors and pricy tuk-tuks.
By songthaew Green songthaews operate a fixed route from the airport, 6km north of town, via Thanon Sa Song to Khao Takiab in the south.

By car or motorbike Car rental outlets include Avis, on the north side of town at 15/112 Thanon Phetkasem, near Soi 29 (☎032 547523, ⓦavisthailand.com). Among the transport touts who rent out mopeds for B200/day (B150/day for two days or more) on Thanon Damnern

Kasem, try Khun Dennapa (☎081 942 5615, ⱳden
-carrental.com), who hangs out on the pavement on the

north side of the street in front of the *Sirin Hotel*, near
7-Eleven.

INFORMATION

Tourist information The TAT office is on Thanon
Phetkasem, just north of Thanon Chomsin (daily 8.30am–
4.30pm; ☎032 513885). There's also a municipal tourist
information office (Mon–Fri 8.30am–4.30pm; ☎032
511047, ext 100) in the local government buildings on the
corner of Thanon Damnern Kasem and Thanon Phetkasem,

with a satellite office just up Phetkasem at the clocktower
(Mon–Fri 8.30am–4.30pm, Sat & Sun 9am–5pm).
Publications and websites Among Hua Hin's many
English-language publications and maps, the *Hua Hin
Pocket Guide*, a free, monthly booklet, is worth looking out
for, while ⱳhuahinafterdark.com is a useful website.

ACCOMMODATION

A night or two at the former *Railway Hotel* (now the *Centara Grand*) is reason in itself to visit Hua Hin, but there are plenty
of other **places to stay**. The most unusual **guesthouses** are those built on the **squid piers** on Thanon Naretdamri,
north of the pagoda, with rooms strung out along wooden jetties so you can hear, feel – and smell, especially at low tide
– the sea beneath you, even if you can't afford a room with an actual sea view. Room rates at many places can drop
significantly from Mondays to Thursdays, so don't be afraid to ask for a discount.

All Nations 10 Thanon Dechanuchit ☎032 512747,
ⱳallnationshuahin.com. A range of comfortable rooms
in varying sizes with free wi-fi and balconies, a few with
distant sea views. A/c rooms have hot showers, TVs and
fridges and are priced according to size; bathrooms with
hot water are shared between two fan rooms. Also has a
roof terrace. Fan **B350**, a/c **B600**

Anantara 5km north of central Hua Hin on Thanon
Phetkasem ☎032 520250, ⱳanantara.com. Set in
effusive, beautifully designed tropical gardens, this is a
lovely resort-style idyll, just out of town (with a regular
shuttle service). Accommodation is in eight-room Thai-
style pavilions, whose stylishly appointed rooms use plenty
of red wood. The hotel has very good Italian, Thai and grill
restaurants, two pools, a gorgeous spa, a kids' club, two
tennis courts and its own stretch of beach, with kayaks
available. **B8200**

Baan Somboon 13/4 Thanon Damnern Kasem ☎032
511538 or 032 533638, ✉baansomboon@gmail.com.
Down a quiet but very central soi, this guesthouse divides
between a lovely, old-fashioned house with polished
teak floors, decorated with a melange of Thai antiques,
woodcarvings and Western "old master" prints, and a small
annexe. Spruce, homely rooms come with small, hot-water
bathrooms, fridges, TVs and either fan or a/c, and there's a
small garden crammed with plants, songbirds and a fish

tank. Continental breakfast included. **B950**

★ **Centara Grand** 1 Thanon Damnern Kasem ☎032
512021–38, ⱳcentarahotelsresorts.com. The original
Thai "destination hotel", the main building is a classic of
colonial-style architecture, boasting high ceilings, polished
wood panelling, period furniture, wide sea-view balconies
and a huge, landscaped garden full of topiary animals.
Across the road, lush gardens shelter gorgeous, all-white
clapboard villas, most with their own small marble pools,
some with large outdoor jacuzzis. With a total of four
swimming pools, a spa, tennis courts, a kids' club, snooker
and a giant chessboard, you need never leave the grounds.
You can even tuck into afternoon tea at *The Museum*, the
original lobby, which now displays hotel memorabilia.
Rooms **B7600**, villas **B11,700**

Chomsin Hotel 130/4 Thanon Chomsin ☎032
515348–9, ⱳchomsinhuahin.com. Handsome, cream-
coloured small hotel with a pleasant welcome, offering
smart, bright, compact rooms in neutral colours with a
few decorative touches and plenty of amenities: a/c, hot
showers, cable TV, mini-bars, safes and free wi-fi (plus
computers in the lobby). **B1000**

Dusit Resort Hua Hin 9km north of Hua Hin on
Thanon Phetkasem ☎032 520009, ⱳdusit.com. One
of the most luxurious spots on this stretch of coast, with
large, elegant rooms set around a tropical garden and

SOI 67 GUESTHOUSES

About fifteen minutes' walk south down the beach from the *Centara Grand*, or 2km by road down
Thanon Phetkasem, there's a little knot of accommodation on Soi 67. Here, facing each other
across the short, narrow soi about 100m back from the beach, are a dozen little guesthouses,
mainly Scandinavian–Thai run, which share a swimming pool; none comprises more than twenty
rooms and most charge about B900. They're very popular with older European couples, many of
whom return for several months every winter, so booking is essential.

FROM TOP KHAO WANG, PHETCHABURI (P.211); HAT SAI REE, KO TAO (P.272) >

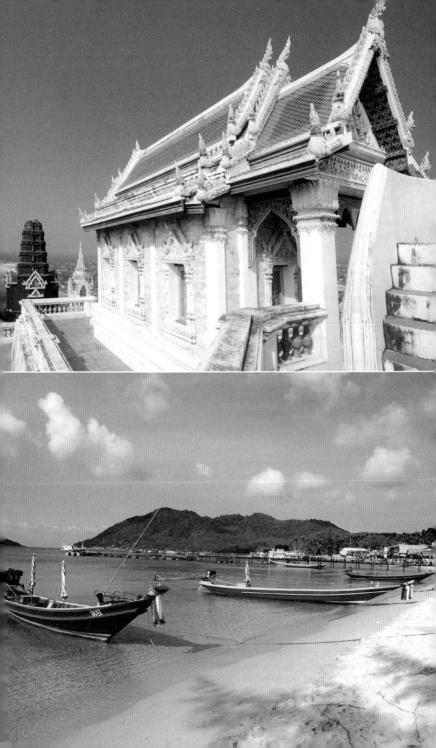

lotus-filled lagoon. Facilities include four restaurants, a huge swimming pool with children's pool and a separate saltwater pool, a spa, fitness centre, watersports, horse-riding, tennis and squash courts and an Avis car rental desk. B7000

Fu-Lay Guest House and Hotel 110/1 Thanon Naretdamri, guesthouse ☎032 513145, ⓦfulayhuahin .net; hotel ☎032 513670, ⓦfulayhuahin.com. *Fu-Lay* is in two halves, with guesthouse rooms strung along a jetty and balconied, a/c hotel accommodation in a low-rise block across the street. The jetty guesthouse is the most stylish of its kind in Hua Hin, offering attractively appointed a/c rooms with nice hot-water bathrooms, plus some cheap en-suite fan rooms (some with hot water) and a breezy seating area set right over the water. Fan B430, a/c B980

Hilton Hua Hin 33 Thanon Naretdamri ☎032 538999, ⓦhuahin.hilton.com. Set bang in the centre of Hua Hin's beachfront, the *Hilton's* high-rise profile disfigures the local skyline, but the facilities are extensive and the views excellent. There's a large, inviting lagoon-like swimming pool right on the seafront, a spa, a kids' club, a panoramic rooftop Chinese restaurant and an impressive indoor-outdoor water garden in the lobby. All three hundred rooms are large and comfortable and have sea-view balconies. B7300

Jinning Beach Hotel East end of Soi 67, off Thanon Phetkasem ☎032 532597, ⓦjinningbeachhotel.com. Typical Soi 67 guesthouse under welcoming Danish–Thai management, with seventeen a/c rooms in seven different sizes, some with verandas, and all with hot water, TV and fridge. B800

Mod 116 Thanon Naretdamri ☎032 512296. A friendly little jetty guesthouse that's recently been renovated. Rooms are all shining white, with small but attractive bathrooms, and come with either fan and cold water or a/c and hot; all have cable TV and free wi-fi. There's a nice, breezy, covered sea-view terrace at the end. Fan B600, a/c B800

Pattana Guest Home 52 Thanon Naretdamri ☎032 513393, ⓔhuahinpattana@hotmail.com. Small, comfortable rooms with character, in an appealingly traditional, teak former fisherman's house, with a flower-strewn courtyard, quietly located at the end of a small soi. Some rooms have private, cold-water bathrooms, some have balconies. Shared bathroom B300, en-suite B400

Tong Mee House 1 Soi Raumpown, Thanon Naebkehat ☎032 530725, ⓔtongmeehuahin@hotmail.com. In a modern, five-storey block on a quiet soi, this friendly guesthouse offers great value: small but neat rooms come with a/c, hot water, wi-fi, fridges, TVs and small balconies, and there's a computer and books to borrow in the lobby. B550

Veranda Lodge Soi 67, Thanon Phetkasem ☎032 533678, ⓦverandalodge.com. Chic boutique hotel set in its own beachfront garden. Deluxe rooms have a contemporary look (lime green, pink or china-blue walls) and petite balconies; most of the various suites and bungalows have separate living rooms and small kitchen areas, and all have balconies. A/c, wi-fi, cable TV, DVD players and mini-bars throughout, and there's a small pool fed by a waterfall and a seafront terrace restaurant. Breakfast included. B2900

EATING AND DRINKING

Hua Hin is renowned for its **seafood**, and some of the best places to enjoy the local catch are the seafront and squid-pier restaurants along Thanon Naretdamri. Fish also features heavily at the large and lively **night market**, which sets up at sunset along Soi 72 (the western end of Thanon Dechanuchit). The biggest concentration of **bars** is in the network of sois between the *Hilton Hotel* and Wat Hua Hin, particularly along Soi Bintabat, Soi Kanjanomai and Thanon Poonsuk; most of these places are so-called "bar-beers", with lots of seating round the bar and hostesses dispensing beer and flirtation through the night.

★ **Baan Itsara** 7 Thanon Naebkehat, north of Soi 51 ☎032 530574. Excellent seafood in a traditional lime-green wooden house with simple tables on a seaside terrace. The speciality here is sweet basil sauce – which comes out something like pesto – with, for example, squid (B180) or king prawns (B420), but the grilled mackerel and the seafood *laap* with land-lotus leaves are also very good. Daily 10.30am–10pm.

Chao Lay 15 Thanon Naretdamri. Hua Hin's most famous jetty restaurant is deservedly popular, serving up high-quality seafood, including rock lobster, blue crab, scallops, cottonfish, mixed seafood hot plates and specialities such as mackerel curry soufflé (*haw mok*). Most main dishes cost B150–200. Daily 10am–10pm.

Cool Breeze 62 Thanon Naretdamri ☎032 531062. Either in the nice little garden at the back or amid the fresh, leafy decor inside, you can tuck into some very tasty tapas (including plenty of vegetarian options) at this new bar-café, which imports many of its ingredients from Spain. Interesting weekly specials might include scallops with Serrano ham (B225), or you can get a set of twelve tapas for B425. Also does baguettes, paella and other seafood and meat mains. Happy hour till 7pm includes 3-for-2 tapas and 2-for-1 sangria. Daily 11am–11pm.

Hagi Centara Grand, corner of Damnern Kasem and Naretdamri rds ☎032 512021–38. Tasty, authentic sushi (sets from B480), including delicious, hand-rolled *temaki* with crispy salmon skin and cucumber, tempura and *teppanyaki* grills at this elegant and welcoming Japanese restaurant. Pick your spot in the Zen-style garden, adorned with black slate, bamboo plants and a rocky pond, or in the a/c section with its sushi counter. Daily 5–11pm.

Pa Jeua Thanon Naretdamri, opposite the Hilton Hua Hin. Famous roadside stall that sells Thailand's favourite dessert, delicious *khao niaw mamuang* (fresh mango with sticky rice and coconut milk), for B60. Daily 9am–3pm.

Som Moo Joom (Jek Pia) 51/6 Thanon Dechanuchit (corner of Thanon Naebkehat); no English sign. Exceptionally good seafood at very cheap prices has made this bare-bones evening restaurant extremely popular with

Thai holiday-makers. The trademark dish, *moo joom*, is a clear soup in which you cook your own pork (or shrimp/ squid), but the menu also covers the range of standard seafood dishes. From 6am to 1pm, several popular stalls take over the space, offering coffee, seafood, satay and noodle soup with seafood. Daily 5–8pm.

Youyen (Hua Hin Balcony) Thanon Naebkehat, near Soi 5 ☎032 531191–2. At the lovely terrace seating by the sea here, you can enjoy an excellent variety of authentic Thai food – try the delicious stir-fried shrimp with green sauce, green peppercorns, crispy garlic and sweet basil (B280). Daily 11am to roughly 9pm.

ENTERTAINMENT

Sasi Dinner Theatre Near the Hyatt Regency, about 4km south of the Centara Grand ☎032 512488 or ☎081 880 4004, ☻sasi-restaurant.com. The Sasi Dinner Theatre was closed for renovation at the time of writing, but usually stages a performance of classical Thai dance, plus traditional fighting and contemporary ballet, every night (about B750 including set dinner and transfer).

Thai Boxing Garden Off Thanon Poonsuk ☎032 515269. Tuesdays and Saturdays are fight nights at the *Thai Boxing Garden* with programmes starting at 9pm and featuring five different fights (B400–600); it's owned by local *muay thai* champion Khun Chop, who also runs Thai boxing classes every day by appointment (B400/hr).

SHOPPING

Bookazine Near the corner of Damnern Kasem and Naretdamri rds ☎032 516512. Small outlet in a supermarket for English books, magazines and newspapers. Daily 8am–11pm.

Cicada Market Suan Sri, Thanon Takiab (near the Hyatt Regency, about 4km south of the Centara Grand), ☻cicadamarket.net. Modelled on Chiang Mai's walking streets, this weekend market features jewellery, cute accessories, lots of T-shirts and other clothes, art galleries and, of course, plenty of food, plus regular performances of all kinds in the amphitheatre. Fri & Sat 4–11pm, Sun 4–10pm.

Hua Hin International Colonnade Mall, corner of Phetkasem and Damnern Kasem rds. Decent selection of secondhand books. Daily 10am–9pm.

Khomapastr 218 Thanon Phetkasem ☎032 511250, ☻khomapastrfabrics.com. Famous outlet for *pha kiaw* (or

pha khomapastr), brightly coloured, hand-printed cotton with lovely, swirling *kannok* patterns, usually with strong elements of gold – Khomapastr's founder, himself a prince, was inspired to start the business when rummaging through trunks of nineteenth-century royal clothing at Bangkok's National Museum in the 1940s. You can buy the cloth by the piece or metre, or made up into skirts, shirts, cushion covers and bags. Mon–Sat 9am–7pm, Sun 9am–5pm.

Plearn Wan Thanon Phetkasem, between sois 38 and 40 ☻plearnwan.com. Curious exercise in nostalgia and commercialism – the name "Enjoy the Past" says it all – that's been a raging success with Thais from all over the country. It's essentially a shopping mall, but in vintage wooden style, selling retro everything: *luk krung* CDs, old-fashioned toys, traditional coffee and desserts, ukuleles… Mon–Thurs 10am–10pm, Fri 10am–midnight, Sat 9am–midnight, Sun 9am–10pm.

DIRECTORY

Banks and exchange There are currency-exchange counters all over the resort, especially on Thanon Damnern Kasem and Thanon Naretdamri; most of the main bank branches with ATMs are on Thanon Phetkasem.

Hospital Bangkok Hospital, 888 Thanon Phetkasem, south of the centre near Soi 94 (☎032 616800).

Immigration office On the canal road, left off Soi 10, Thanon Phetkasem, about 5km northwest of the town centre (Mon–Fri 8.30am–4.30pm; ☎032 526556).

Internet access Dozens of outlets, including the pricy but comfortable *World News*, owned by the *Hilton* on Thanon Naretdamri (daily 8am–10.30pm), where the good coffees,

juices and snacks might tempt you to part with more of your baht.

Meditation English-medium classes in sitting and walking meditation, with talks on Buddhism, at Wat Khao Santi, just off Soi 91, Thanon Phetkasem (Wed 8.30–11.30am; free, donations welcome; ☻meditationinhuahin.org).

Pharmacy Several in the resort, including the helpful and well-stocked Medihouse (daily 9.30am–11pm), opposite the *Hilton* on Thanon Naretdamri.

Thai language Classes and private lessons at TLC, 83/14 Wongchomsin Building, Thanon Phetkasem (near Soi 63/1; ☎032 533428, ☻thailanguagecentre.org).

Tourist police For all emergencies, call the tourist police on the free, 24hr phoneline (☎ 1155), or contact them at their office opposite the *Centara Grand* at the beachfront end of Thanon Damnern Kasem (☎ 032 516219).

Travel agency Reliable Western Tours (see p.217) sells international and domestic air tickets, as well as bus tickets to southern Thailand.

Pak Nam Pran

The stretch of coast between Hua Hin and Chumphon barely registers on most foreign tourists' radar, but many better-off Bangkokians have favourite beaches in this area, the nicest of which is sophisticated **PAK NAM PRAN** (aka Pranburi). Just 30km or so south of Hua Hin, Pak Nam Pran used to cater only for families who owned beach villas here, but in the past few years the shorefront homes have been joined by a growing number of enticing, if pricey, boutique hotels, and signs are there's more development to come. For now, facilities consist of just a few minimarkets, car-rental outlets and independent bars and restaurants, especially around the *Evason* hotel towards the northern end of the beach, plus the possibility of organizing day-trips to nearby Khao Sam Roi Yot National Park through hotel staff; there's also kiteboarding through Kiteboarding Asia, about 1km south of the *Evason* (☎ 089 743 5564, ⓦkiteboardingasia.com).

As along much of the Gulf coast, the **beach** itself, also known as Hat Naresuan, is not exceptional (it has hardly any shade and is suffering from erosion in parts), but it is long, with fine sand, and nearly always empty, and you're quite likely to see dolphins playing within sight of the shore. The strand stretches south from Pak Nam Pran town at the mouth of the Pran River – which is known for its colourful fishing boats, specializing in squid – for around 7km to Khao Kalok headland and the tiny Thao Kosa Forest Park.

ARRIVAL AND DEPARTURE
PAK NAM PRAN

Easiest access is via the town of **Pranburi**, which straddles Highway 4 some 23km south of Hua Hin. There's no public transport from Pranburi to Pak Nam Pran beach, 10km or so away, but hotels can arrange transfers and any Pranburi songthaew driver will taxi you there. Pranburi's main crossroads (Highway 4 and Thanon Ratbamrung) is 2km south of Tesco Lotus at Talat Chaikaew – if making your own way, the easiest route is to turn east off Highway 4 here and take minor road 3168 down to the sea, picking up the relevant sign for your hotel.

FROM/TO PRANBURI

By train Pranburi's quaint old station is 4km east of the Highway 4 crossroads (Talat Chaikaew) towards the beach, off the north side of Route 3168.

Destinations Bangkok (Hualamphong 1 daily, Thonburi 2 daily; 5hr–5hr 30min); Chumphon (2 daily; 4hr 30min); Hat Yai (1 daily; 12hr 30min); Prachuap Khiri Khan (3 daily; 1hr).

By bus As well as many through services to and from the south, Pranburi is served by a/c buses from Bangkok's

Southern Bus Terminal, which drop passengers close by the main Highway 4 crossroads at Talat Chaikaew.

Destinations Bangkok (first-class: hourly, 3hr; second-class, stopping at Hua Hin: every 30min, 4hr); Hua Hin (every 30min; 30min).

By minibus A/c minibuses from Bangkok's Victory Monument (☎ 085 403 6113) generally stop at the Tesco Lotus supermarket on Highway 4 opposite Pranburi's City Hall, but you could ask the driver to take you to your beach hotel for a little extra money.

ACCOMMODATION

Pak Nam Pran's charming **accommodation** is its biggest draw: for once, "boutique" is the appropriate term, as many of the hotels here offer a dozen or fewer rooms. With influences ranging from Greece to the South Pacific, from Morocco to Scandinavia, the style tends to be more arty than five-star, though you will certainly be comfortable. Some hotels aren't suitable for kids owing to their multiple levels and unfenced flights of steps. Breakfast is generally included in the price of the room. During weekends in high season (Nov–May), hoteliers routinely put their prices up and you'll need to book ahead. The following are spread over a 2km stretch of the beachfront road, starting about 4km south of Pak Nam Pran town.

★ **Aleenta** Central Pak Nam Pran beach ☎ 032 618333, ⓦ aleenta.com. This stunningly designed hotel, divided between the Main Wing and the Frangipani Wing, 500m down the beach, offers gorgeous circular, thatched bungalows and very tasteful villa-style rooms, most with uninterrupted sea views, decks and plunge pools. The feel is modernist chic, with elegantly understated local furnishings and huge windows, and iPods and wi-fi capability rather than TVs. There's a small rooftop pool and spa; yoga, t'ai chi and cooking classes are available. **B7100**

Baan Panali Southern Pak Nam Pran beach, 200m south of Huaplee ☎ 086 051 2333 or ☎ 081 844 2484, ⓦ baan-panali.com. Not as striking as some of the beach's other offerings, but much cheaper and stylish enough: a cream-painted, adobe-style block with large, colourful, tiled rooms and a cute little swimming pool on its beachfront terrace. All but one room face the sea with a terrace or balcony, and all have a/c, hot showers, TVs and fridges. **B2000**

Evason Northern Pak Nam Pran beach ☎ 032 632111, ⓦ sixsenses.com/evason. The biggest and best-known hotel in Pak Nam Pran, but as accommodation is screened by graceful gardens, the feel is quite private and small-scale. Rooms are attractively cool and contemporary, with big balconies and DVD players; for extra privacy, you could check into a super-luxe private-pool villa, a favourite choice of Thai film stars. Facilities include a huge pool, a spa, two restaurants, tennis courts and a kids' club with its own pool. **B5700**

★ **Huaplee Lazy Beach** Central Pak Nam Pran beach ☎ 032 630554–5, ⓦ huapleelazybeach.com. This exceptionally cute collection of seven idiosyncratic white-cube beachfront rooms and one suite around a pretty lawn is the work of the architect-interior designer owners. It's a characterful place of whimsical, marine-themed interiors done out with white-painted wood floors, blue-and-white colour schemes and funky shell and driftwood decor. The rooms are airy and bright but all have a/c, as well as fridges and TVs (no hot water); some have fantastic sea-view terraces. **B3300**

Jamsawang Resort Northern Pak Nam Pran beach ☎ 032 570050, ⓦ jamsawang.com. One of the cheapest places to stay in the area, run by a friendly family. Dotted around a neatly trimmed garden across the road from the beach, all bungalows have a/c, hot water, fridge and TV; a few ("Thai-style") are comfortable if not especially sophisticated pale-blue concrete affairs, but most are pricier (from B2000), more stylishly furnished, yellow-painted "Bali-style" bungalows, with garden bathrooms. **B1400**

EATING

Krua Jaew On the edge of Pak Nam Pran town, about 2km north of the Evason ☎ 032 631302. The best of several neighbouring seafront restaurants, offering an enormous, mid-priced menu of 120 mostly fish and seafood dishes, including excellent crab curry (B300), seafood curry soufflé (*haw mok thalay*, on the menu as "steamed seafood with spicy and coconut milk"; B120) and the local speciality, deep-fried dried squid (*pla meuk det diaw*; B150). Unsigned in English, but it's the first restaurant you'll come to heading up the beach road into Pak Nam Pran, with its kitchen and most of its tables on the left-hand side, and a few tables towards the beach on the right. Daily 9am–9pm.

Krua Sawatdikan Khao Kalok On the south side of Khao Kalok's rocky outcrop at the far southern end of Pak Nam Pran beach, about 1km from Baan Panali ☎ 086 701 8597 (unsigned in English). This simple shorefront restaurant has an extensive menu of very good seafood dishes (mostly B80–150) and great views of Khao Sam Roi Yot from its beach tables under the casuarinas; mosquitoes are a problem here though, so take repellent. Daily 10am–8pm.

Khao Sam Roi Yot National Park

National park entry fee B200 • ☎ 032 821568, ⓦ dnp.go.th

With a name that translates as "The Mountain with Three Hundred Peaks", **KHAO SAM ROI YOT NATIONAL PARK**, with its northern entrance 28km south of Pak Nam Pran beach or 63km from Hua Hin, encompasses a small but varied, mosquito-ridden coastal zone of just 98 square kilometres. The dramatic limestone crags after which it is named are the dominant feature, looming 600m above the Gulf waters and the forested interior, but perhaps more significant are the mud flats and freshwater marsh which attract and provide a breeding ground for thousands of migratory birds. **Bird-watching** at Thung Khao Sam Roi Yot swamp is a major draw, but the famously photogenic Phraya Nakhon Khiri cave is the focus of most day-trips, while a few decent trails and a couple of secluded beaches provide added interest.

Orientation in the park is fairly straightforward. One main inland road runs roughly north–south through it from the R3168 (the road from Pranburi's main junction to Pak Nam Pran), passing, in order: the 2km side road to **Hat Phu Noi**, a quiet, golden-sand beach that offers several resort alternatives to the park's accommodation and the chance to see dolphins in the cool season; the northern park checkpoint, 4km further on; the turn-offs for Ban Bang Pu (the jumping-off point for Tham Phraya Nakhon), Ban Khung Tanot (for Tham Sai) and Hat Sam Phraya (all to the east); then going over Khao Daeng canal, before looping westwards around the main massif, past the **park headquarters** (where park brochures and maps are available) and the southern checkpoint (14km from the northern checkpoint), to Highway 4 at kilometre-stone 286.5.

Tham Phraya Nakhon

B300 return per boat from Wat Bang Pu

Khao Sam Roi Yot's most visited attraction is the **Tham Phraya Nakhon** cave system, hidden high up on a cliffside above **Hat Laem Sala**, an unremarkable sandy bay with a national park visitor centre that's inaccessible to vehicles. The usual way to get to Hat Laem Sala is by a five-minute boat ride from the knot of food stalls behind Wat Bang Pu on the edge of **Ban Bang Pu** fishing village (6km from the northern checkpoint). It's also possible to walk over the headland from behind Wat Bang Pu to Hat Laem Sala, along a signed, but at times steep, 500m trail. From Hat Laem Sala, another taxing though shaded trail runs up the hillside to Tham Phraya Nakhon in around thirty minutes.

The huge twin **caves** are filled with stalactites and stalagmites and wreathed in lianas and gnarly trees, but their most dramatic features are the partially collapsed roofs, which allow the sunlight to stream in and illuminate the interiors, in particular beaming down on the famous royal pavilion, Phra Thi Nang Khua Kharunhad, which was built in the second cave in 1890 in honour of Rama V.

Tham Sai

A three-hour trek south from Tham Phraya Nakhon brings you to **Tham Sai**, a thoroughly dark and dank limestone cave, complete with stalactites, stalagmites and petrified waterfalls; lamps and torches are available here for B60. The trek offers some fine coastal views, but a shorter alternative is the twenty-minute trail from **Ban Khung Tanot** village (accessible by road, 8km on from the Ban Bang Pu turn-off).

Khao Daeng and around

Canal cruise B400 for up to 6 people, kayaks B500 • ☎ 089 903 1619

The next turning off the main road will take you down to **Hat Sam Phraya**, a quiet, kilometre-long beach with a national park visitor centre, while a little further on the road crosses mangrove-fringed **Khao Daeng canal**. From beside Wat Khao Daeng, on the west side of the main road here, you can charter a boat for a one-hour cruise that's best in the early morning or the late afternoon; kayaks are available at the same spot.

A couple of kilometres on, you can scramble up **Khao Daeng** itself, a 157m-high outcrop that offers good summit views over the coast, via a thirty-minute trail that begins near the park headquarters. The park's two official **nature trails** also begin close to the headquarters – the thirty-minute "Horseshoe Trail" takes in the forest habitats of monkeys, squirrels and songbirds, while the 45-minute "Mangrove Trail" leads through the swampy domiciles of monitor lizards and egrets, with the chance of encountering long-tailed (crab-eating) macaques.

Thung Khao Sam Roi Yot

Accessed not from the main park road, but by turning east off Highway 4, 200m north of kilometre-stone 276, and continuing for 9km • Punts B150 per person • ☏ 081 486 1842

The park hosts up to three hundred species of **birds** and between September and November the mud flats are thick with migratory flocks from Siberia, China and northern Europe. To the west of Khao Sam Roi Yot lies Thailand's largest freshwater marsh, **Thung Khao Sam Roi Yot** (aka Beung Bua), near the village of Rong Jai (Rong Che). This is an excellent place for observing waders and songbirds, and is one of only two places in the country where the **purple heron** breeds; punts are available here for one- to two-hour bird-watching excursions.

ARRIVAL AND GETTING AROUND KHAO SAM ROI YOT

Like most of Thailand's national parks, Khao Sam Roi Yot is hard to explore without your own **transport**, and its sights are spread too far apart to walk between.

By motorbike or car Motorbikes can be rented in Hua Hin (which also has car rental), as well as at *Dolphin Bay Resort* or Prachuap Khiri Khan.

With a tour The park can be visited on a one-day tour from Hua Hin, including cycling tours with Hua Hin Bike Tours (see p.217), Pak Nam Pran or *Dolphin Bay Resort*.

ACCOMMODATION AND EATING

Given the limitations of the park accommodation, many people prefer to stay a few kilometres to the north at the long, pleasingly shaded beach of Hat Phu Noi.

IN THE PARK
National Park accommodation ☏032 821568, ⓦdnp.go.th. Accommodation is at headquarters, at Hat Sam Phraya, a beach between Khao Daeng canal and Ban Khung Tanot, at Hat Laem Sala and at Thung Khao Sam Roi Yot; all four sites have restaurants. At Hat Laem Sala it's a choice between camping, at B150–225 per tent, or staying in one of the national park bungalows with hot showers (for 6–9 people); at Sam Phraya and Thung Khao Sam Roi Yot it's camping only; and at the headquarters it's bungalows only (for 5–6 people). Bungalows must be booked ahead through the National Parks office in Bangkok (see p.39). Hat Laem Sala B̲1̲6̲0̲0̲, HQ B̲1̲2̲0̲0̲

HAT PHU NOI
Brassiere Beach Bottom end of Hat Phu Noi ☏032 630555, ⓦbrassierebeach.com. Under the same architect owners as *Huaplee* at Pak Nam Pran (see p.223), *Brassiere Beach* gets its name from the two conical Nom

Sao ("Breast") islands offshore and the mainland spirit house where fishermen leave bras for good luck, and contains rooms with playful monikers like "La Perla". That may sound a bit naff to some, but the hotel itself is the height of quirky chic, airy and light-filled, with a mostly white-and-blue colour scheme. Some rooms have their own small jacuzzi and pool or an outdoor bathroom, and kayaks and bicycles are available. Breakfast included. B̲3̲8̲0̲0̲
Dolphin Bay Northern end of the beach ☏032 559333, ⓦdolphinbayresort.com. Eco-conscious, family-friendly resort offering comfortable a/c rooms, bungalows, apartments and villas with fridges, hot water and TVs, large children's and adults' pools set in an attractive, palm-fringed lawn, plus a kids' playground and internet access and wi-fi. Pick-ups from Pranburi (B250) can be arranged and there's plenty of things to do once you're here: half-day tours of the park (B700 for a car with driver), boat trips to local islands, plus kayak, motorbike and bicycle rental. B̲1̲5̲9̲0̲

Prachuap Khiri Khan and around

Despite lacking any must-see attractions, the tiny, unfrequented provincial capital of **PRACHUAP KHIRI KHAN**, 67km south of Pranburi, makes a pleasant place to break any journey up or down the coast. Its greatest asset is its setting: a huge, palm-fringed, half-moon bay, dotted with colourful fishing boats and tipped by a rocky outcrop at the north end and by a small group of jungly islands to the south – the waterfront promenade in the town centre is great for a seafood lunch with a view. There's a lovely **beach** in the next bay to the south, Ao Manao, and generally Prachuap is a fine spot to settle into small-town Thai life.

The town is contained in a small grid of streets that runs just 250m east to west, between the sea and the train station – with Highway 4 beyond the railway tracks – and around 1km north to south, from the Khao Chong Krajok hill at the northern end to the Wing 5 air-force base in the south. **Orientation** couldn't be simpler: the major road across from the station to the pier is Thanon Kongkiat, and there are four main north–south roads: Thanon Phitak Chat near the station, Thanon Salacheep, Thanon Susuek and the seafront road, Thanon Chai Thalay.

Khao Chong Krajok

The monkey-infested hill of **Khao Chong Krajok** is Prachuap's main sight: if you climb the 417 steps from Thanon Salacheep to the golden-spired chedi at the summit you get a great perspective on the scalloped coast below and west to the mountainous Burmese border, just 12km away.

Ao Manao

Inside Wing 5 air-force base (you usually need to sign in at the base checkpoint) • Head south down Thanon Salacheep (or down the promenade and turn right) to reach the checkpoint and continue for 2km through the base to the beach • Tuk-tuk to the beach around B60

At the far southern end of town, the long sandy beach at **Ao Manao** is the best place in the area for swimming and sunbathing. On weekdays you're likely to have the sand almost to yourself, but it's a very popular spot with Thai families on weekends when the stalls at the beachfront food centre do a roaring trade in the locally famous *som tam puu* (spicy papaya salad with fresh crab), which you can eat at the deckchairs and tables under the trees on the beach. You can walk to the north end of the bay to the base of an outcrop known as Khao Lommuak, where a memorial commemorates the skirmish that took place here between Thai and Japanese forces in World War II.

King Mongkut Memorial Park of Science and Technology

12km south of town, on the beach at Wa Ko (Waghor) • Daily 9am–4pm, fish-feeding at 11am & 2pm (subject to change) • Aquarium B20 • ☎ 032 661104 • To get there, turn east off Highway 4 at kilometre-stone 335, or go through Ao Manao air-force base, bearing left along the coast all the way

The main feature of the **King Mongkut Memorial Park of Science and Technology** (also signed as Phra Chomklao Science Park) is the extensive and well-stocked **Waghor Aquarium**. Highlights include an underwater tunnel, touch pools and fish-feeding, and there are display boards and labels for most of the fish in English. It's nothing like as slick as Siam Ocean World in Bangkok, but then again it's less than a tenth of the price. About 500m south along the beach road, the park also contains an astronomy museum that's decidedly low-tech but with enough labels in English to maintain interest.

The park is thought to mark the spot where **Rama IV**, known as the father of Thai science, came to observe a solar eclipse on August 18, 1868. Having predicted the eclipse's exact course, King Mongkut decided to publicize science among his subjects by mounting a large expedition, aiming specifically to quash their centuries-old fear that the sun was periodically swallowed by the dragon Rahoo, and more generally to rattle traditional notions of astrology and cosmology. To this end, he invited scientists all the way from France and the British governor of Singapore, and himself turned up with fifty elephants and all his court, including the astrologers – who, as the leader of the French expedition noted, "could hardly be blamed if they did not display much enthusiasm for the whole project". Unfortunately, both the king and his 15-year-old son contracted malaria at Waghor; Mongkut passed away in Bangkok on October 1, but Chulalongkorn survived to become Thailand's most venerated king, Rama V.

ARRIVAL AND DEPARTURE

BY TRAIN

Nearly all services on the Southern Line from Bangkok stop at the train station, which is just on the west side of the centre, at the western end of Thanon Kongkiat.

Destinations Bangkok (11 daily; 5–7hr); Chumphon (11 daily; 2hr–3hr 30min); Hat Yai (4 daily; 9–11hr); Nakhon Si Thammarat (2 daily; 10hr 30min); Surat Thani (8 daily; 4hr 30min–6hr); Trang (1 daily; 11hr).

BY BUS OR MINIBUS

Prachuap doesn't have a proper bus station, and the number of dedicated services to and from the town centre is dwindling, with many people either heading out to Highway 4 to flag down a through-bus, or catching an a/c minibus.

Buses from/to Bangkok Pudtan Tour, on Thanon Phitak Chat just south of Thanon Kongkiat, runs a "first-class" a/c service to Bangkok's Southern Terminal, which stops at Pranburi and Phetchaburi, but takes the Hua Hin bypass, Highway 37. Further north just off Thanon Phitak Chat, there's a sometimes unreliable, "second-class" a/c service

to Bangkok, which stops frequently, including in central Hua Hin.

A/c minibuses from/to Bangkok Several companies offer a/c minibuses to Bangkok, including Monsiri Travel on Thanon Phitak Chat north of Thanon Kongkiat (☎089 005 5139), whose services run either to Victory Monument or to the Southern and Northern Bus Terminals, stopping at Pranburi and Phetchaburi on the way.

Buses to the south There's a daily non-a/c bus to Chumphon from Thanon Phitak Chat but for the fastest services to the south you need to wait on Highway 4 at the Highway Police office, about 1km north of the access road into town, for the a/c buses that whizz down from Bangkok; several southbound services pick up passengers here between 8.30am and 11.30am (and many more around midnight).

Destinations Bangkok (roughly hourly; 4–5hr); Chumphon (1 daily; 3hr); Hua Hin (2–3 daily; 1hr 30min–2hr); Phetchaburi (roughly hourly; 3hr–3hr 30min); Pranburi (roughly hourly; 1hr–1hr 30min).

INFORMATION AND GETTING AROUND

Tourist information There's a small tourist information office (daily 8.30am–4.30pm, occasionally closing noon–1pm for lunch; ☎032 611491), where town maps are available, at the far northern end of town in a compound of provincial offices; it's on the ground floor of a modern, white building facing the beachfront road.

Bicycle and motorbike rental Bicycles (B70/day) and motorbikes (B250/day) can be rented from *Sun Beach Guesthouse*.

Kayak rental You can rent a kayak from Kayak Adventures, on the seafront next to the *Hadthong Hotel*.

ACCOMMODATION

Faa Chom Khleun Ao Manao ☎032 661088–9, ⓦaomanao.com. If you don't mind cosying up to the Thai military, this spruce, wi-fi-enabled air-force hotel on the Wing 5 base puts you right on the beach. All rooms have sea-view balconies, a/c, hot water, TV and fridge, and there's a large swimming pool. No English sign. B900

Hadthong Hotel 21 Thanon Susuek, but also with an entrance just south of the pier on the beachfront road ☎032 601050–5, ⓦhadthong.com. Well-run spot with comfortable rooms, many sporting balconies and great sea views, all with wi-fi, fridges, a/c, hot water and TVs – plus a 15m swimming pool, internet room and snooker club. Breakfast included. B950

Maggie's Home-stay 5 Soi Tampramuk 4, between Salacheep and Susuek rds, just south of Thanon Kongkiat ☎032 604216 or 087 597 9720, ⓔmaggies .homestay@gmail.com. Welcoming spot behind a pretty front garden, with hammocks and salas for chilling out

under the trees. The diverse rooms are either in a bright and airy, traditional wooden house with polished floors and shared hot-water bathrooms or, less attractively, in the outhouses at the back, though some of these are en-suite (cold showers). There's wi-fi throughout, and bikes and motorbikes for rent. Good rates for singles. Fan B260, a/c B500

★ **Sun Beach Guesthouse** 160 Thanon Chai Thalay, 500m or so down the promenade from the pier ☎032 604770, ⓦsunbeach-guesthouse.com. Run by a welcoming and helpful Thai–German couple, this palatial guesthouse is done out like a Mediterranean villa, with Corinthian columns and smart tiling everywhere. The bright, comfortable, sky-blue rooms come with a/c, hot water, fridges, TVs, free wi-fi and balconies, with prices varying according to the quality of the sea view. There's a seductive pool and whirlpool, and internet access. B700

EATING AND DRINKING

Prachuap's famously good seafood is most cheaply sampled at the town's lively and varied main **night market**, which sets up shop in the empty lot around the junction of Thanon Kongkiat and Thanon Phitak Chat.

Ma-prow Thanon Chai Thalay, south of the Hadthong Hotel. Mellow, rustic, airy restaurant, which serves tasty squid with salted eggs (B150) and deep-fried sea bass fillet with tamarind and peanut sauce (B180), as well as a few Western dishes such as fish'n'chips. Daily 11am–11pm.

★ **Plern Smud** South of the pier at 44 Thanon Chai Thalay, alongside the Hadthong Hotel ☎032 611115 (English-language sign at the Thanon Susuek entrance only, not on the beachfront road). The town's best restaurant has a pleasant, spacious courtyard facing the sea, and serves delicious pan-fried oysters, tasty crab claws (B150) and excellent *kaeng pa pla say* (fish jungle curry; B100) on its seafood-dominated menu. Daily 10am–9.30pm.

Rome Beer (MC Club House) Thanon Chai Thalay, just south of Ma-prow. Excellent spot for a waterside drink, hung with motorcycle memorabilia and home to some of the friendliest bikers you're ever likely to meet. Daily 4.30pm–late.

DIRECTORY

ATMs and exchange On Thanon Salacheep and Thanon Phitak Chat, including on the latter at Krung Thai Bank, which opens daily.

Internet access Many places on Thanon Salacheep.

Post office Directly behind the *Hadthong Hotel* on Thanon Susuek (Mon–Fri 8.30am–4.30pm, Sat & Sun 9am–noon).

Ban Krud

Graced with a tranquil, 5km sweep of white sand, pale-blue sea and swaying casuarinas, **BAN KRUD**, 70km south of Prachuap, supports a dozen or so fairly upmarket bungalow outfits and seafood restaurants along the central stretch of its shorefront road. About 1km inland from the main T-junction at the beach, the small, traditional village, which now includes several ATMs, clusters around the train station. At the beach's northern end are a colourful fishing village, which hosts a Thursday afternoon market, and a panoramic headland beyond, **Khao Thongchai**, that's dominated by the 14m-high Phra Phut Kitti Sirichai Buddha image and its sparkling modern temple, **Wat Phra Mahathat Phraphat**. Crowned with nine golden chedis, the temple displays an impressive fusion of traditional and contemporary features, including a series of charming modern stained-glass windows depicting Buddhist stories; reach it via a 1.5km-long road that spirals up from the beachfront. Other than a visit to the temple and possibly a snorkelling trip to Ko Thalu (B350/person through, for example, *Sala Thai Resort*), the main pastime in Ban Krud is sitting under the trees and enjoying a long seafood lunch or dinner.

ARRIVAL AND DEPARTURE   BAN KRUD

By train Most services on the Southern Line from Bangkok stop at Ban Krud's tiny train station, where you should be able to find a motorbike taxi (with sidecar).

Destinations Bangkok (3 daily; 5hr 30min–7hr 30min); Chumphon (6 daily; 2hr); Hat Yai (2 daily; 8hr 30min–10hr 30min); Nakhon Si Thammarat (1 daily; 10hr); Surat Thani (5 daily; 4hr–5hr 30min); Trang (1 daily; 10hr).

By bus Most southbound buses drop passengers on Highway 4, from where motorbike-and-sidecar taxis cover the 8km down to the beach; just two Bangkok–Bang Saphan a/c buses a day stop at Ban Krud itself.

ACCOMMODATION

★ **Bayview** North of the headland and the ramshackle youth hostel, 4km from Sala Thai on Hat Tangsai ☎032 695566–7, ⌨bayviewbeachresort.com. Very welcoming and relaxed spot with a swimming pool, a kids' pool and a lovely area for deckchairs under the beachside casuarinas. All the well-spaced, diverse bungalows boast a/c, fridges, TVs and hot water, and there's an excellent restaurant, internet access and wi-fi, free bicycles, and kayaks, cars and motorbikes to rent. Prices rise a little at weekends. Breakfast included. **B1300**

Sala Thai About 1km north of the central beachfront T-junction ☎032 695181, ⌨salathaibeachresort.com. Friendly resort, whose cutesy wooden bungalows with a/c, hot water and TV are spread around a spacious, pretty garden with lots of shady trees, just across the road from the beach; it also has a few very basic bamboo bungalows with fans, mosquito nets and shared bathrooms, as well as a popular burger bar. Bikes and motorbikes for rent. Fan **B250**, a/c from **B600**

Chumphon

South Thailand officially starts at **CHUMPHON**, where the main highway splits into west- and east-coast branches, and inevitably the provincial capital saddles itself with the title "gateway to the south". Most tourists take this tag literally and use the town as nothing more than a transport interchange between the Bangkok train and boats to **Ko Tao**, **Pha Ngan and Samui**, so the town is well equipped to serve these passers-through, offering clued-up travel agents, efficient transport links and plenty of internet cafés. In truth, there's little call for exploring the fairly average beaches, islands and reefs around town when the varied and attractive strands of Ko Tao are just a short hop away, while the Chumphon National Museum is little short of pitiful.

ARRIVAL AND DEPARTURE
CHUMPHON

BY PLANE

Solar Air (☎02 535 2455–6, in Chumphon ☎081 902 9466, ⓦsolarair.co.th) has recently launched a daily service from Bangkok, with discounted through-tickets with Lomprayah to Ko Tao and Pha Ngan available. If you haven't got a through-ticket, a taxi to town from Chumphon airport, which is 40km to the north, will cost around B700.

BY TRAIN

Chumphon train station is on the northwest edge of town, less than ten minutes' walk from most guesthouses and hotels.

Destinations Bangkok (12 daily; 7hr–9hr 30min); Butterworth (Malaysia; 1 daily; 14hr); Hat Yai (6 daily; 7hr–8hr 30min); Nakhon Si Thammarat (2 daily; 7hr); Surat Thani (11 daily; 2hr 5min–4hr); Trang (2 daily; 7hr).

BY BUS OR MINIBUS

Government bus station The government bus station is 11km south of town on Highway 4, connected to the centre by songthaews (B50/person) and motorbike taxis (B100), though long-distance services will sometimes drop in town; two Bangkok a/c buses a day drop off and pick up on Thanon Tawee Sinka, west of TAT.

Private bus and minibus services There are several private a/c bus and minibus services that depart from various locations (see map below), including minibuses to Ranong and Surat Thani; Suwanathee buses to Bangkok; and Chokeanan Tour buses to Bangkok and Hat Yai – some Rungkit buses to Phuket, via Ranong and Khao Lak, start from the same spot, though some use the government bus station. Agents such as *Suda* and *Fame* (see p.230) can

CHUMPHON

Train Station

Police Station

Night Market

THANON KROMLUANG

A/c minibuses to Surat Thani

Ocean Department Store

Chumphon Hospital

Bangkok bus stop

TAT

TOT

SOI SALA DAENG 6

SOI DAENG SALA 4

Cinema

SOI SALA DAENG 3

A/C minibuses to Ranong

Farang Bar

THANON SALA DAENG

THANON PRACHA UTHIT

Chokeanan Tour buses

THANON PARAMIN MANKA

THANON THA TAPAO

Virasin Hospital

Suwanathee buses

Khlong Tha Tapao

Wat Suphannimit

◼ ACCOMMODATION	
Chumphon Guest House	1
Fame	2
Novotel	5
Paradorn	3
Suda Guest House	4

⬤ RESTAURANTS & CAFÉS	
Ahaan Jeh	2
Boom	5
Fame	3
Green Kitchen	4
Papa	1

Highway 4 & Bus station

also fix you up with minibuses to Krabi, Ko Lanta and Phetchaburi.

Destinations Bangkok (roughly hourly; 7–9hr); Hat Yai (4 daily; 7hr 30min); Hua Hin (hourly; 3hr 30min–4hr 30min); Khao Lak (4 daily; 5hr); Phuket (4 daily; 7hr); Prachuap Khiri Khan (6 daily; 2–3hr); Ranong (4 daily; 2–3hr); Surat Thani (roughly hourly; 3hr 30min).

BY BOAT

There are several different boat services from Chumphon to Ko Tao, Pha Ngan and Samui, tickets for all of which are sold by travel agents and guesthouses in town. Of these, the Songserm Express is the most likely to be cancelled if the weather is very bad. The fast Seatran service between Chumphon and Ko Tao has recently been suspended, but may resurface.

GETTING TO THE PIER

Lomprayah and Songserm tickets include transport to the pier from town, with pick-ups available even from guest-houses and from the station, including off the overnight train from Bangkok that arrives around 4am. The car ferry and the less comfortable midnight boat do pick-ups from town guesthouses at around 10pm (B50/person); however, these boats (and their pick-ups) sometimes leave an hour or two early, because of tides and the weather.

BOATS AND SERVICES

Lomprayah Catamaran Office at the train station ☎ 077 558212–3, ⓦ lomprayah.com. Daily 7am & 1pm, from Ao Thung Makham Noi, 27km south of Chumphon; 1hr 45min to Ko Tao (B600); around 3hr 30min to Ko Pha Ngan (B1000); around 4hr to Maenam, Ko Samui (B1100).

Songserm Express Office at the train station ☎ 077 506205, ⓦ songserm-expressboat.com. Daily 7am, from Pak Nam, about 20km south of Chumphon; 2hr 30min to Ko Tao (B450); around 4hr 30min to Ko Pha Ngan (B750).

Car ferry ☎ 077 580030. Mon–Sat 11pm, from Tha Yang, about 15km south of Chumphon; 6hr; B300, including blankets and pillows in an a/c room (the Ko Jaroen 2 that runs from Tha Yang on Mon, Wed & Fri also has dorm-style bunk beds for B400).

Midnight boat ☎ 077 553052. Daily midnight, from Tha Yang, about 15km south of Chumphon; 6hr; B200.

INFORMATION AND TOURS

Tourist information The TAT office is down a short soi at 111 Thanon Tawee Sinka (daily 8.30am–4.30pm; ☎ 077 501831, ⓔ tatchumphon@tat.or.th), offering free internet access.

Suda Guest House Thanon Sala Daeng Soi 3 (aka Soi Bangkok Bank), 30m off Thanon Tha Tapao ☎ 077 504366 or ☎ 085 571 2229. The best source of information and fixer in town, offering a personal, unbiased service, is Suda at her eponymous guesthouse. As well as tickets to Ko Tao, Suda offers discounted dive packages; bus, minibus and train tickets; twice-daily visa runs via Ranong to Burma (from B650, excluding B500 for Burmese visa); motorbike (B150–200/day) and car (B1000–1300/day) rental; internet access; packages to Ko Chang (Ranong) and Ko Phayam; and jungle treks and rafting at Pha To near Ranong.

Other tour agencies Among the bigger multipurpose travel agents, avoid if you can busy *Farang Bar*, which resembles a human meat-processing factory, in favour of *Fame* (see below), which offers much the same transport services as Suda.

ACCOMMODATION

Chumphon Guest House (Kae House) Soi 1, Thanon Kromluang ☎ 077 502900, ⓦ facebook.com/Sunisa Jet. Sociable, laidback place with 24hr check-in, hosted by the effervescent Kae, on a quiet, residential soi with a pleasant outdoor bar-restaurant. Motorcycle rental, boat tickets, free wi-fi and computers, and informal cooking classes and day-trips around Chumphon. Accommodation ranges from small rooms out front, one of which has an en-suite cold-water bathroom, to rooms in the main wooden house sharing hot showers. Shared bathroom `B150`, en-suite `B250`

Fame 188/20–21 Thanon Sala Daeng ☎ 077 571077, ⓦ chumphon-kohtao.com. Above the restaurant and tour agency of the same name, this place has ten good-sized and very clean rooms with mattresses on the floor, fans and hot water in either shared or en-suite bathrooms; computers and free wi-fi. Shared bathroom `B150`, en-suite `B250`

Novotel 15km southeast near Pak Nam ☎ 077 529529, ⓦ novotel-chumphon.com. This low-rise luxury hotel on Paradornpab beach, done out in an unobtrusive Thai contemporary style, features spacious rooms with balconies and lots of dark wood, two restaurants (international and northeastern Thai), two swimming pools, a spa, fitness centre, golf course and kids' club. `B2240`

Paradorn Hotel 180/12 Thanon Sala Daeng ☎ 077 511598 or 077 511500, ⓦ chumphon-paradorn.com. The best value of the town's mid-range hotels, a shining, white block where all rooms have a/c, hot water, fridge, TV and free wi-fi. Not on a main road, so should be quiet. There's an espresso bar too. `B360`

★ **Suda Guest House** Thanon Sala Daeng Soi 3 (aka Soi Bangkok Bank), 30m off Thanon Tha Tapao ☎ 077 504366 or 085 571 2229. Chumphon's most welcoming homestay, offering clean, well-maintained rooms, most with shared hot-water bathrooms, in the owner's modern house. Plenty of information available, B20 showers for passers-through and much more (see opposite). Phone for free transport from train or bus station. Suda plans to install wi-fi and to open an all-en-suite extension. Good reductions for singles. Fan and shared bathroom B̲2̲0̲0̲, en-suite B̲4̲0̲0̲, a/c and shared bathroom B̲3̲5̲0̲, en-suite B̲5̲0̲0̲

EATING AND DRINKING

The cheapest place to eat is the **night market**, which sets up along both sides of Thanon Kromluang and is an enjoyable place to munch your way through a selection of fried noodles, barbecued chicken and sticky, coconut-laced sweets.

Ahaan Jeh Right next to Fame on Thanon Sala Daeng. Tiny place offering a ready-cooked buffet of Thai–Chinese vegetarian food at B20 per serving – get there early, as most dishes are finished before closing time. Daily 7am to about 3pm.

Boom (The Bakery Café) Thanon Tha Tapao ☎077 511523. A bakery with a few pavement tables for watching the world go by, serving good espressos, tasty brownies and other Western and Thai cakes. Mon–Sat 8am–7pm.

Fame 188/20–21 Thanon Sala Daeng ☎077 571077. Travellers' restaurant specializing in Italian food, including pizzas, as well as Indian dhal, loads of sandwiches using home-baked bread, and huge American (B140) and veggie

(B110–120) breakfasts; free wi-fi. Daily 5am–9.30pm.

Green Kitchen Off Thanon Suksumer ☎077 571731. Good, authentic Vietnamese cuisine such as grilled beef in betel leaves (B50) and fresh spring rolls (B60), plus Thai food and some European dishes. Daily 10am–10pm.

Papa Across from the train station on Thanon Kromluang ☎077 504504. One of the liveliest places to eat dinner, this huge restaurant – mostly open-air, but with an a/c room – has an extensive menu of fresh seafood, Thai salads such as wingbean salad (B80) and Chinese dishes, plus a few Western standards. Also puts on live music every evening, and has as an attached nightclub, *Papa 2000*. Daily noon–2/3am.

Chaiya

About 140km south of Chumphon, **CHAIYA** is thought to have been the capital of southern Thailand under the Srivijayan civilization, which fanned out from Sumatra between the eighth and thirteenth centuries. Today there's little to mark the passing of Srivijaya, but this small, sleepy town has gained new fame as the site of **Wat Suan Mokkh**, a progressively minded temple whose meditation retreats account for the bulk of Chaiya's foreign visitors (most Thais only stop to buy the famous local salted eggs). Unless you're interested in one of the retreats, the town is best visited on a day-trip, either as a break in the journey south, or as an excursion from Surat Thani.

Wat Phra Boromathat

Western side of town, on the access road from Highway 41

The main sight in Chaiya is **Wat Phra Boromathat**, where the ninth-century chedi – one of very few surviving examples of Srivijayan architecture – is said to contain relics of the Buddha himself. Hidden away behind the viharn in a pretty, red-tiled cloister, the chedi looks like an oversized wedding cake surrounded by an ornamental moat. Its unusual square tiers are spiked with smaller chedis and decorated with gilt, in a style similar to the temples of central Java.

National Museum

On the eastern side of the temple • Wed–Sun 9am–4pm • B30 • ⓦ thailandmuseum.com

The **National Museum** is a bit of a disappointment. Although the Srivijaya period produced some of Thailand's finest sculpture, much of it discovered at Chaiya, the best pieces have been carted off to the National Museum in Bangkok. Replicas have been left in their stead, which are shown alongside fragments of some original statues, two intricately worked 2000-year-old bronze drums, found at Chaiya and Ko Samui, and various examples of Thai handicrafts. The best remaining pieces are a calm and elegant sixth- to seventh-century stone image of the Buddha meditating from

Wat Phra Boromathat, and an equally serene head of a Buddha image, Ayutthayan-style in pink sandstone, from Wat Kaeo.

Wat Kaeo

On the south side of town

Heading towards the centre of Chaiya from Wat Phra Boromathat, you can reach this imposing ninth- or tenth-century brick chedi by taking the first paved road on the right, which brings you first to the restored base of the chedi at Wat Long, and then after 1km to **Wat Kaeo**, enclosed by a thick ring of trees. Here you can poke around the murky antechambers of the chedi, three of which house images of the Buddha subduing Mara.

Wat Suan Mokkh

6km south of Chaiya on Highway 41 • Ⓦ suanmokkh.org • All buses between Surat Thani and Chumphon stop near the wat

The forest temple of **Wat Suan Mokkh** (Garden of Liberation) was founded by the abbot of Wat Phra Boromathat, **Buddhadasa Bhikkhu**, southern Thailand's most revered monk until his death in 1993 at the age of 87. His radical, back-to-basics philosophy, encompassing Christian, Zen and Taoist influences, lives on and continues to draw Thais from all over the country to the temple, as well as hundreds of foreigners. It's not necessary to sign up for one of the wat's **retreats** to enjoy the temple, however – you can simply drop by for a quiet stroll through the wooded grounds.

The unusual layout of the wat is centred on the Golden Hill: scrambling up between trees and monks' huts, past the cremation site of Buddhadasa Bhikkhu, you'll reach a hushed clearing on top of the hill, which is the temple's holiest meeting place, a simple open-air platform decorated with images of the Buddha and the Wheel of Law. At the base of the hill, the outer walls of the Spiritual Theatre are lined with bas-reliefs, replicas of originals in India, which depict scenes from the life of the Buddha. Inside, every centimetre is covered with colourful didactic painting, executed by resident monks and visitors in a jumble of realistic and surrealistic styles.

MEDITATION RETREATS AT SUAN MOKKH

Meditation retreats are led by Western and Thai teachers over the first ten days of every month at the International Dharma Heritage (Ⓦ suanmokkh-idh.org), a purpose-built compound 1km from the main temple at Wat Suan Mokkh. Large numbers of foreign travellers, both novices and experienced meditators, turn up for the retreats, which are intended as a challenging exercise in mental development – it's not an opportunity to relax and live at low cost for a few days. Conditions imitate the rigorous lifestyle of a *bhikkhu* (monk) as far as possible, each day beginning before dawn with meditation according to the Anapanasati method, which aims to achieve mindfulness by focusing on the breathing process. Although talks are given on Dharma (the doctrines of the Buddha – as interpreted by Buddhadasa Bhikkhu) and meditation technique, most of each day is spent practising Anapanasati in solitude. To aid concentration, participants maintain a rule of silence, broken only by daily chanting sessions, although supervisors are sometimes available for individual interviews if there are any questions or problems. Men and women are segregated into separate dormitory blocks and, like monks, are expected to help out with chores.

PRACTICALITIES

Turn up at Wat Suan Mokkh as early as possible (by 3pm at the latest) on the last day of the month to register (you can stay in Suan Mokkh the night before registration for free). The busiest period for the retreats is December–April, especially February and March. The fee is B2000 per person, which includes two vegetarian meals a day and accommodation in simple cells. Participants are required to hand in their mobile phones and are not allowed to leave the premises during the retreat – bring any supplies you think you might need (though there is a small, basic shop on site).

ARRIVAL AND DEPARTURE   CHAIYA

By train The town lies on the main Southern Rail Line, served by trains (mostly overnight) from and to Bangkok (9 daily; 8–11hr).

By bus Chaiya is 3km east of Highway 41, the main road down this section of the Gulf coast: buses running between Chumphon and Surat Thani will drop off (or pick up) on the highway, from where you can catch a motorbike taxi or blue songthaew into town.

By minibus or songthaew From Surat Thani's Talat Kaset II bus station, hourly a/c minibuses and more frequent but slower songthaews take around an hour to reach Chaiya town centre.

Surat Thani

Uninspiring **SURAT THANI** ("City of the Good People"), 60km south of Chaiya, is generally worth visiting only as a jumping-off point for the Samui archipelago. Strung along the south bank of the Tapi River, with a busy port for rubber and coconuts near the river mouth, the town is experiencing rapid economic growth and paralyzing traffic jams. It might be worth a stay, however, when the Chak Phra Festival (see box, p.234) is on, or as a base for seeing the nearby historic town of Chaiya.

3

ARRIVAL AND DEPARTURE   SURAT THANI

Surat's best **travel agency** is the reliable Phantip, in front of Talat Kaset I at 293/6–8 Thanon Taladmai (☎ 077 272230 or ☎ 077 272906), where among many other things you can book train and plane tickets. Be aware that there have been many reports of overcharging and **scams** by unregistered agents and touts selling tickets for minibus and bus services out of Surat, especially involving any kind of combination ticket, including those heading for Khao Sok National Park, Phuket, Krabi and Malaysia. To avoid this, either go direct to the relevant a/c minibus office at Talat Kaset II bus station (local offices are generally on the west side of the station, long-distance ones on the east side, and they all have to be authorized by the provincial office), or buy a bus ticket direct from the station, or walk the short distance to Phantip Travel.

ACCOMMODATION
Ban Don	1
Roi Koh (100 Islands)	3
Wangtai Hotel	2

RESTAURANTS & CAFÉS
Ban Don	2
Milano	1
Vegetarian restaurant	3

SURAT THANI

THE CHAK PHRA FESTIVAL

At the start of the eleventh lunar month (usually in October) the people of Surat Thani celebrate the end of Buddhist Lent with the **Chak Phra Festival** (Pulling the Buddha), which symbolizes the Buddha's return to earth after a monsoon season spent preaching to his mother in heaven. On the Tapi River, tugboats pull the town's principal Buddha image on a raft decorated with huge nagas, while on land sleigh-like floats bearing Buddha images and colourful flags and parasols are hauled across the countryside and through the streets. As the monks have been confined to their monasteries for three months, the end of Lent is also the time to give them generous offerings in the *kathin* ceremony, of which Surat Thani has its own version, called Thot Pha Pa, when the offerings are hung on tree branches planted in front of the houses before dawn. Longboat races, between teams from all over the south, are also held during the festival.

BY PLANE

Arriving by air from Bangkok (currently Air Asia 2 daily, Nok Air 3 daily, Thai Airways 2 daily; 1hr 15min) or Kuala Lumpur (Air Asia 3 weekly; 1hr 35min), you can take a B100 minibus through Phantip or from the *Wangtai Hotel* for the 27km journey south from the airport (☎077 441230–1) into Surat Thani, or a combination ticket to Ko Samui (B350) or Ko Pha Ngan (B550). Budget (☎077 441166) has an outlet at the airport for car rental. If you're flying out of Surat, you can most easily catch the airport minibus from town at the Phantip office. Thai Airways have an office in town at 3/27–28 Thanon Karoonrat, off Thanon Chonkasem (☎077 272610).

BY TRAIN

Arriving by train means arriving at Phunphin, 13km to the west, from where buses run into Surat Thani, via the Baw Khaw Saw bus terminal, at least every forty minutes (more frequently in the early morning) between around 5.30am and 7pm, while share-taxis (based in Surat at Talat Kaset II) charge around B200 to charter the whole car into town. It's also possible to buy through-tickets to Ko Samui and Ko Pha Ngan from the train station, including a connecting bus to the relevant pier. Buses heading out of Surat to Phang Nga and Phuket make a stop at Phunphin train station.
Destinations Bangkok (10 daily; 9–12hr); Butterworth (Malaysia; 1 daily; 10hr 30min); Hat Yai (7 daily; 4hr 30min–6hr); Nakhon Si Thammarat (2 daily; 4hr 30min); Trang (2 daily; 4hr 30min).

BY BUS

Buses use three different locations, two of which are on Thanon Taladmai in the centre of town: Talat Kaset I on the north side of the road (Phunphin, non-a/c Nakhon Si Thammarat services and other local buses) and opposite at Talat Kaset II (most long-distance buses, including those for Krabi, Phuket, Hat Yai and Ranong, and Nakhon Si Thammarat a/c services). The Baw Khaw Saw terminal, 2km southwest of the centre on the road towards Phunphin, handles mostly Bangkok services. If you're heading for Krabi, there are roughly hourly non-a/c buses from Talat Kaset II

and faster hourly a/c buses through Phantip (as well as a/c minibuses).
Destinations Bangkok (Southern Terminal; 10 daily; 10–12hr); Chumphon (roughly hourly; 3hr 30min); Hat Yai (10 daily; 5hr–5hr 30min); Khao Sok (10 daily; 2hr 30min); Krabi (hourly; 3–4hr); Nakhon Si Thammarat (21 daily; 2hr 10min–2hr 40min); Phang Nga (5 daily; 3hr 30min); Phuket (8 daily; 5hr); Phunphin (at least every 40min; 40min); Ranong (10 daily; 4–5hr).

BY MINIBUS OR SHARE-TAXI

A/c minibuses (to Chumphon, Ranong, Ratchabrapa Dam, Khao Sok, Phang Nga, Phuket, Krabi, Trang, Hat Yai and Nakhon Si Thammarat) and a dwindling number of share-taxis congregate around Talat Kaset II bus station, on the south side of Thanon Taladmai.

BOAT OPERATORS IN SURAT

Details of boats to Ko Samui, Ko Pha Ngan and Ko Tao, most of which leave from Don Sak pier, 68km east of Surat, are given in the account of each island – see p.238, 256 and p.269. Phunphin and the bus stations are teeming with touts, with transport waiting to escort you to their employer's boat service to the islands – they're generally reliable, but make sure you don't get talked onto the wrong boat. If you manage to avoid getting hustled, you can buy tickets from Phantip or direct from the boat operators.
Lomprayah Thanon Taladmai, corner of Thanon Amphoe, just east of Taksin Hospital ☎077 288732–3, ⓦlomprayah.com. Catamarans to Samui and Pha Ngan, with their own connecting buses to Don Sak and connections on to Ko Tao.
Phangan Tour Thanon Taladmai ☎077 205799. Handles buses to Don Sak for the Raja vehicle ferries to Ko Pha Ngan.
Samui Tour Thanon Sri Surat ☎077 282352. Handles buses to Ko Samui and Ko Pha Ngan via the Raja vehicle ferries from Don Sak.
Seatran In the petrol station on Thanon Taladmai opposite Wat Thammabucha ☎077 275060–2,

ⓦseatranferry.com. Vehicle ferries to Samui (with their own connecting buses), from Don Sak.

Night boats The night boats to Samui, Pha Ngan and Tao, which are barely glorified cargo boats, line up during the day at Ban Don Pier in the centre of Surat; it's just a question of turning up and buying a ticket.

GETTING AROUND

By share-songthaew Small share-songthaews buzz around town, charging around B15–20/person.

INFORMATION

Tourist information TAT's office is at the western end of town at 5 Thanon Taladmai (daily 8.30am–noon & 1–4.30pm; ☎077 288817–9 or ☎077 282352, ⓔtatsurat @tat.or.th).

ACCOMMODATION

A lot of **accommodation** in Surat Thani is noisy, grotty and overpriced, but there are a few notable exceptions.

Ban Don Hotel Above a restaurant at 268/2 Thanon Namuang. ☎077 272167. Most of the very clean rooms here, with en-suite cold-water bathrooms, TV and fans or a/c, are set back from the noise of the main road. Fan **B300**, a/c **B450**

Roi Koh (100 Islands) On the southern bypass near the tourist police and opposite Tesco Lotus ☎077 201150–8, ⓦroikoh.com. Though out of the centre, this place offers attractive, comfortable rooms with a/c, hot water, TVs and mini-bars, a small spa and a decent-sized pool set in a lush garden with a waterfall. Breakfast included. **B770**

Wangtai Hotel 1 Thanon Taladmai, on the western side of the centre by the TAT office ☎077 283020–5, ⓦwangtaisurat.com. Surat Thani's best upmarket option, and surprisingly good value, with over two hundred large, smart rooms with wi-fi around a good-sized swimming pool. **B790**

EATING

Besides the restaurants listed below, there's a large **night market** between Thanon Si Chaiya and Thanon Ban Don, which displays an eye-catching range of dishes; a smaller offshoot by Ban Don pier offers less choice but is handy if you're taking a night boat.

Ban Don Restaurant 268/2 Thanon Namuang. Basic, bustling restaurant with plain, marble-topped tables, which serves large portions of tasty, inexpensive Thai and Chinese food – mostly noodle and rice dishes, such as *khao man kai* (B35), but also green curry and *tom yam*. Daily 6am–11pm.

Milano Near the night-boat piers on Thanon Ban Don. This place has an authentic oven turning out very tasty and reasonably priced pizzas, though its home-made pasta is not so successful. Also serves other Western main courses, Mexican dishes, sandwiches, breakfasts and espresso coffee. Daily 10am–11pm.

Vegetarian restaurant One block east of Talat Kaset II bus station on Thanon Tha Thong. Wide selection of cheap and delicious curries and other tray food for B25/ plate. Look for the yellow flags outside and a sign saying "vegetarian food". Daily 7am till about 3.30pm.

DIRECTORY

Internet access Boss, just west of the post office on Thanon Taladmai (daily 9am–midnight).

Tourist police On the southern bypass near the junction with Thanon Srivichai, the westward continuation of Thanon Taladmai (☎1155 or 077 405575).

Ko Samui

A million visitors a year, ranging from globetrotting backpackers to suitcase-toting fortnighters, come to southern Thailand just for the beautiful beaches of **KO SAMUI**, 80km from Surat. At 15km across and down, Samui is generally large enough to cope with this diversity – except during the rush at Christmas and New Year – and the paradisal sands and clear blue seas have to a surprising extent kept their good looks, enhanced by a thick fringe of palm trees that gives a harvest of more than two million coconuts each month. However, development behind the beaches – which has brought the islanders far greater prosperity than the crop could ever provide – speeds along in a messy, haphazard fashion with little concern for the environment. At least there's a local bylaw limiting new construction to the height of a coconut palm (usually about three storeys), though this has not deterred either the luxury hotel groups or the real-estate developers who have recently been throwing up estates of second homes for Thais and foreigners.

For most visitors, the days are spent indulging in a few watersports or just lying on the beach waiting for the next drinks-seller, hair-braider or masseur to come along. For something more active, you should not miss the almost supernatural beauty of the **Ang Thong National Marine Park** (see p.253), which comprises many of the eighty islands in the Samui archipelago. Otherwise, a day-trip by rented car or motorbike on the 50km round-island road, perhaps making time for a meal at the excellent *Ban Hua Thanon Seafood* on the south coast, will throw up plenty more fine beaches.

The island's most appealing strand, **Chaweng**, has seen the heaviest, most crowded development and is now the most expensive place to stay, though it does offer by far the best range of amenities and nightlife, ranging from tawdry bar-beers to hip nightclubs. Its slightly smaller neighbour, **Lamai**, lags a little behind in terms of looks and top-end development, but retains large pockets of backpacker bungalow resorts. The other favourite for backpackers is **Maenam**, which, though less attractive again, is markedly quiet, with plenty of room to breathe between the beach and the round-island road. Adjacent **Bophut** is similar in appearance, but generally more sophisticated, with a cluster of boutique resorts, fine restaurants and a distinct Mediterranean feel in

KO SAMUI ACTIVITIES

Samui has around a dozen scuba-diving companies, offering trips for divers and snorkellers and courses throughout the year, and there's a recompression chamber at Bangrak (☎077 427427, ⍵sssnetwork.com). Most trips for experienced divers, however, head for the waters around Ko Tao (see p.270); a day's outing costs around B4000–5500, but of course if you can make your own way to Ko Tao, you'll save money. Also on offer are plenty of spas, as well as meditation retreats, island tours, ziplines, go-karting, kiteboarding and cooking classes.

DIVE OPERATORS

Easy Divers Head office opposite Sandsea Resort, Lamai ☎077 413373, ⍵easydivers-thailand.com. PADI Five-Star dive centre, with several branches around the island.

Planet Scuba Head office next to the Seatran pier on Bangrak ☎077 413050, ⍵planetscuba.net. PADI Five-Star dive centre, with several branches.

SPAS

Eranda Far north end of Chaweng ☎077 422666, ⍵erandaspa.com. Set on a waterfall- and flower-splashed hillside with a plunge pool, offering plenty of style (2hr Thai massage B1900).

Peace Tropical Spa On Route 4169 near the centre of Bophut beach ☎077 430199, ⍵peacetropicalspa .com. Half a dozen types of massage, including a 1hr 30min Thai massage for B1500, as well as body and facial treatments.

The Spa Resort Lamai ☎077 230855, ⍵thespa resorts.net. Everything from Thai massage (B447/hr) for non-guests, to residential fasting programmes

(from B21,000 for 8 days). Also on offer are body and facial wraps, and yoga, meditation and raw-food culinary classes, as well as in-house accommodation, either on the beach or in the hills above Lamai.

Tamarind Springs Lamai ☎077 230571, ⍵tamarindsprings.com. Set in a beautiful, secluded coconut grove just off the main road. A session in their herbal steam room, set between boulders by a waterfall-fed plunge pool, and a 2hr 30min Thai massage, for example, costs B5500; massage training courses are also available.

OTHER ACTIVITIES

Canopy Adventures ☎077 414150–1 or ☎087 046 7307, ⍵canopyadventuresthailand.com. A series of ziplines between treehouses and past waterfalls in the hills 4km above Maenam (2–3hr; B1750, including transfers).

Kiteboarding Asia ☎081 591 4592, ⍵kiteboarding asia.com. Instruction in kiteboarding (B4000 for one day), either from the beach south of Ban Hua Thanon or from Nathon, depending on the time of year, as well as rentals.

Mr Ung's Magical Safari Tours ☎077 230114, ⍵ungsafari.com. Day-trips that traverse the rough tracks of the mountainous interior to some spectacular viewpoints, as well as taking in Hin Yay Hin Ta, the Big Buddha and monkey and elephant shows (from B1400, including lunch).

Samui Go-kart Route 4169 1km west of Bophut

village ☎077 425097. Offers everyone the chance to let off steam without becoming another accident statistic on the roads of Samui (daily 9am–8/9pm; from B600/10min, including free transfers).

Samui Institute of Thai Culinary Arts (SITCA) Soi Colibri, opposite Centara Grand Resort in Chaweng ☎077 413172, ⍵sitca.net. This highly recommended outfit runs 3hr cookery classes in the morning and afternoon (B1950), plus six- and twelve-day courses and fruit-carving classes. Closed Sun.

Wat Suan Mokkh meditation retreats ⍵dipa bhavan.org. Wat Suan Mokkh (see p.232) offers retreats from the 20th to the 27th of each month at Dipabhavan, a hermitage in the hills above Lamai (full details on the website); pick-ups are laid on from *Utopia Resort*, north of the central crossroads in Lamai.

3

its congenial beachfront village. **Choeng Mon**, set apart in Samui's northeast corner, offers something different again: the small, part-sandy, part-rocky bay is tranquil and pretty, the seafront between the handful of upmarket hotels is comparatively undeveloped, and Chaweng's nightlife is within easy striking distance.

No particular **season** is best for coming to Ko Samui (see also p.55). The northeast monsoon blows heaviest in November, but can bring rain at any time between October and January, and sometimes causes high waves and strong currents, especially on the east coast. January is often breezy, March and April are very hot, and between

May and October the southwest monsoon blows onto Samui's west coast and causes some rain. **Festivals** include a week-long jazz festival in September (ⓦsamuijazzfestival .com) and a six-day sailing regatta in May/June, with lots of attendant parties and festivities (ⓦsamuiregatta.com). At the lower end of Samui's **accommodation** scale, there are very few bungalows left for under B400, while at the most upmarket places you can pay well over B4000 for the highest international standards. The prices listed are based on high-season rates, but out of season (roughly April–June, Oct & Nov) dramatic reductions are possible.

ARRIVAL AND DEPARTURE   KO SAMUI

BY PLANE

Flights to Samui Airport, in the northeastern tip of the island, are among the most expensive in Thailand, so you might want to consider flying from Bangkok to Surat Thani (see p.233) or Nakhon Si Thammarat (see p.276), nearby on the mainland; Nok Air, for example, offers good-value through-tickets via either of these airports, including flight, bus and boat to Samui.

Airlines You can get to Ko Samui direct from Suvarnabhumi Airport with Thai Airways (2 daily; in Bangkok ☎ 02 356 1111), or with Bangkok Airways (about 20 daily; in Bangkok ☎ 02 265 5555, at Samui airport ☎ 077 428555), which also operates flights from Chiang Mai, Hong Kong, Krabi, Pattaya, Phuket, Singapore and Trat. Berjaya Airlines currently operates a twice-weekly service from Kuala Lumpur, while Firefly runs daily from KL.

Airport facilities As well as bars and restaurants, the terminals have currency-exchange facilities and ATMs, a post office with international telephones and several car rental outlets including Avis (☎084 700 8161, ⓦavisthailand.com).

Minibus transfers A/c minibuses meet incoming flights (and connect with departures, bookable through your accommodation), charging B120 to Chaweng for example. Destinations Bangkok (20 daily; 1hr–1hr 30min); Chiang Mai (2 weekly; 2hr 30min–3hr 30min); Hong Kong (1 daily; 3hr 30min); Krabi (1 daily; 50min); Kuala Lumpur, Malaysia (1–2 daily; 2hr); Pattaya (U-Tapao; 1–2 daily; 1hr); Phuket (2–5 daily; 50min); Singapore (1 daily; 2hr); Trat (4 weekly; 1hr 20min).

BY BOAT AND BUS

The most obvious route for getting to Ko Samui by boat (45min–1hr 30min) is from Don Sak, 68km east of Surat Thani (see p.234); catching a boat from Chumphon is generally more expensive and leaves you a long time on the sometimes choppy sea. There are also boats from Ko Samui to Ko Pha Ngan (see p.256) and to Ko Tao (see p.269); all offer the same service in the return direction.

FROM SURAT THANI

Don Sak to Na Thon From Don Sak, hourly Seatran vehicle ferries (on Ko Samui ☎077 426000–2) and

twice-daily Lomprayah catamarans (on Samui ☎077 950028) run to the island capital, Na Thon, all with their own connecting buses from Surat.

Don Sak to Lipa Noi and Na Thon Raja vehicle ferries run hourly between Don Sak and Lipa Noi, 8km south of Na Thon (on Samui ☎077 415230–3); every two hours to coincide with alternate boats, Samui Tour (on Samui ☎077 421092) runs buses from Surat or Phunphin via the ferry, and on to Na Thon.

Surat Thani to Na Thon The night boat leaves Ban Don pier in Surat Thani itself for Na Thon at 11pm every night; tickets are sold at the pier on the day of departure.

Fares and journey times Seatran and Samui Tour charge B250 to get to Samui from Surat, B280 from Phunphin train station, including a connecting bus; total journey time from Surat is around 3hr. Lomprayah charge B450 from Surat (special offers sometimes available; total journey time 2hr 15min), B500 from Phunphin, including a connecting bus. The night boat takes 6hr and costs B250.

LONG-DISTANCE SERVICES

Ko Samui's government bus terminal (Baw Khaw Saw) is on Thanon Taweeratpakdee towards the north end of Na Thon (☎077 421125 or ☎077 420765). It handles bus-and-boat services (via Don Sak and Lipa Noi), for example from Bangkok's Southern Terminal (mostly overnight; some also stopping at Mo Chit bus terminal), which cost from B540 on a basic a/c bus to B940 on a VIP bus – these are far preferable to the cheap deals offered by dodgy travel agents on Thanon Khao San, as the vehicles used on the latter services are often substandard and many thefts have been reported. The Baw Khaw Saw also sells through-tickets to Nakhon Si Thammarat, which involve catching the ferry to Don Sak, then changing on to an a/c minibus. Destinations Bangkok (8 daily; 13hr); Hat Yai (2 daily; 7hr); Krabi (1 daily; 7hr); Phuket (1 daily; 8hr).

BY BOAT AND TRAIN FROM BANGKOK

At Hualamphong Station, you can buy a discounted through-ticket to Samui with the State Railway – B698, for example, in a second-class a/c bunk, upper tier, to Phunphin station, plus B350 for your bus and Lomprayah catamaran to Na Thon from there.

GETTING AROUND

BY SONGTHAEW

Songthaews, which congregate at the car park near the southerly pier in Na Thon, cover a variety of set routes during the daytime, either heading off clockwise or anticlockwise on Route 4169, to serve all the beaches; destinations are marked in English and fares range from B50 to Maenam to B60 to Chaweng or Lamai. In the evening, they tend to operate more like taxis and you'll have to negotiate a fare to get them to take you exactly where you want to go.

BY TAXI

Ko Samui sports dozens of a/c taxis. Although they all have meters, you'd be wasting your breath trying to persuade any driver to use his; instead, you're looking at a flat fare of

around B300 from Na Thon to Maenam, B500 to Chaweng, for example. You'll also see one or two motorbike taxis buzzing about the island, which charge from B30 for a local drop, up to B250 from Na Thon to Chaweng.

BY MOTORBIKE OR CAR

You can rent a motorbike for around B200 in Na Thon and on the main beaches. Dozens are killed on Samui's roads each year, so proceed with great caution, and wear a helmet – apart from any other consideration you can be landed with an on-the-spot B500 fine by police for not wearing one. In addition, thieves have been snatching bags from the front baskets of moving motorbikes on Samui, so keep yours on your person – or think about upgrading to a four-wheel drive, from around B800 a day.

INFORMATION

Tourist information TAT runs a small but helpful office (daily 8.30am–noon & 1–4.30pm; ☎ 077 420504 or ☎ 077 420720, ✉ tatsamui@tat.or.th), tucked away on an unnamed side road in Na Thon (north of the pier and inland from the post office). Here, and at many other places around Samui, you can pick up Siam Map Company's

detailed map of the island.

Tourist police The tourist police are on the Route 4169 ring road between Bophut and Chaweng, north of Big C supermarket on the same side of the road (☎ 1155 or ☎ 077 430016).

Na Thon

The island capital, **NA THON**, at the top of the long western coast, is a frenetic half-built town which most travellers use only as a service station before hitting the sand: although most of the main beaches now have post offices, currency-exchange facilities, ATMs, supermarkets, travel agents and clinics, the biggest concentration of amenities is here. The town's layout is simple: the three piers come to land at the promenade, Thanon Chonvithi, which is paralleled first by narrow Thanon Ang Thong, then by Thanon Taweeratpakdee, aka Route 4169, the round-island road; the main cross-street is Thanon Na Amphoe, by the central pier. If you're driving yourself, note that there's a one-way system in the centre of town: south on Taweeratpakdee, north on Chonvithi.

ACCOMMODATION   NA THON

Nathon Residence Thanon Taweeratpakdee next to Siam City (Thanachart) Bank ☎ 077 236081, ✉ nathon -res@windowslive.com. If you really need a place to stay in Na Thon, this is your best bet, a friendly, well-run

establishment with plain but spotless tiled rooms with a/c, cable TV, free wi-fi, fridges and en-suite bathrooms, some with hot water – ask for a quiet room at the back. Computers available for guest use. **B500**

EATING AND DRINKING

Several stalls and small cafés purvey inexpensive Thai food around the market on Thanon Taweeratpakdee and on Thanon Chonvithi (including a lively night market by the piers).

About Art & Craft Thanon Chonvithi, opposite the southerly pier, a few doors up from Siam Commercial Bank. The tiny frontage here reveals a dim crafts shop and café, serving good, mostly vegetarian food and dozens of juices and smoothies. There are some interesting veggie versions of Thai dishes, such as *laap* with tofu, or try the

burritos with avocado (B160). Mon–Sat 8am–5pm.

Coffee Island Corner of Thanon Chonvithi and Thanon Na Amphoe ☎ 077 420153. Inexpensive and justifiably popular, especially for breakfast; also serves sandwiches (tuna B80), pancakes and pizzas, as well as Thai food and a wide variety of coffees. Free wi-fi. Daily 6.30am–late.

DIRECTORY

Bookshop Nathon Book Store on Thanon Na Amphoe (Mon–Sat 9am–6pm or later; ☎077 420332) is a good, helpful secondhand place, with some new titles.

Hospital The state hospital (☎077 421230–2) is 3km south of town off Route 4169.

Immigration office Located 2km south of town down Route 4169 (Mon–Fri 8.30am–4.30pm; ☎077 421069).

Post office Towards the northern end of the promenade, just north of the central pier (Mon–Fri 8.30am–4.30pm, Sat & Sun 9am–noon), with poste restante and packing services. International telephones upstairs (Mon–Fri 8.30am–4pm).

Travel agent The reliable Phantip, for everything from international flight tickets to local bus and train tickets, is on Thanon Taweeratpakdee, north of Thanon Na Amphoe (☎077 421221–2).

Maenam

MAENAM, 13km from Na Thon in the middle of the north coast, is Samui's most popular beach for budget travellers. Its exposed 4km-long bay is not the island's prettiest, being more of a broad dent in the coastline, and the sloping, white-sand beach is relatively narrow and slightly coarse by Samui's high standards. But Maenam features many of the cheapest bungalows on the island, unspoilt views of fishing boats and Ko Pha Ngan, and good swimming. Despite the recent opening of some upmarket developments on the shoreline and a golf course in the hills behind, this is still the quietest and most laidback of the major beaches. Though now heavily built up with multistorey concrete shophouses (including several banks) and rows of small bars, the main road is set back far from the sea, connected to the beachside bungalows by an intricate maze of minor roads through the trees. At the midpoint of the bay, **Ban Maenam** is centred on a low-key road down to the fishing pier, which is flanked by cafés, internet shops, travel agents, dive shops, secondhand bookshops and small boutiques. On Thursday evenings this becomes a pleasant **walking street** (modelled on Chiang Mai's walking streets), with performances of traditional music and dance. On offer are lots of cheap clothes and some souvenirs, everything from bras to ukeleles, but what's most tempting is the panoply of food, both savoury and sweet, that locals cook up to sell.

ACCOMMODATION   MAENAM

As well as several luxury resorts, Maenam has around thirty inexpensive and moderately priced bungalow complexes, most offering a spread of accommodation; the cheapest of these are at the far eastern end of the bay and offer the possibility of walking round to Bophut beach if you fancy a change of scene.

★ **Four Seasons Resort** About 5km west of Maenam near Laem Yai ☎077 243000, ⓦfourseasons.com. The top hotel in the Maenam area, this ultra-luxury spot has its own small beach and enjoys lovely views of Ko Pha Ngan and the setting sun. Each of the large, beautiful villas, designed for indoor-outdoor living in a subtle, modern but natural style, using brown and marine colours, has its own infinity-edge swimming pool; the resort lays on a wide range of activities, from spa treatments to sailing and Thai cooking classes. B24,500

Harry's At the far western end, near Wat Na Phra Larn ☎077 425447, ⓦharrys-samui.com. Popular, well-run place, set back about 100m from the beach amid a secluded and shady tropical garden. The public areas feature strong elements of traditional Thai architecture, though not the bungalows, which are nevertheless clean and spacious, with a/c, hot water, TV, fridge and safe. Free internet access and a decent-sized swimming pool and jacuzzi. B1000

Lolita On the east side of Santiburi Resort ☎077 425134, ⓔlolitakohsamui@yahoo.com. Quiet, friendly and efficiently run resort in a beautiful, grassy garden on a long stretch of beach. A wide variety of large, wood and concrete bungalows, all with hot showers, cluster around a kitsch, circular bar-restaurant adorned with pink Corinthian columns, and come in just two price categories: at the back, with fans, or with a/c and fridges on the beach. Fan B800, a/c B1700

Maenam Resort 500m west of the village, just beyond Santiburi Resort ☎077 247287, ⓦmaenamresort.com. A welcoming, tranquil resort (no TVs) in tidy, shady grounds, with an especially long stretch of beach. The large bungalows, with verandas, hot water, fridges, wi-fi and a/c, offer good-value comfort. B1600

Maenam Villa At the far eastern end of the bay, next to SR (see p.242 for directions) ☎077 425501, ⓔmaenamvilla@hotmail.com. Friendly spot on a spacious triangular plot with kayaks available. Choose between clean, bright, older bungalows with verandas and

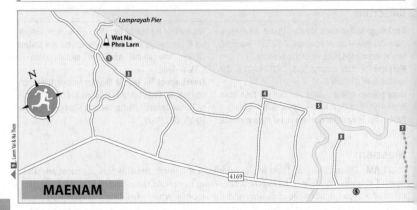

MAENAM

cold showers, and large, concrete, open-plan villas with a/c, hot water and small terraces. Fan B500, a/c B1200

Moonhut On the east side of the village ☎077 425247, Ⓦ moonhutsamui.com. Welcoming English-run place on a large, sandy, shady plot, with a lively restaurant and beach bar, wi-fi and colourful, substantial and very clean bungalows; all have verandas, mosquito screens, wall fans and en-suite bathrooms, and some have hot water and a/c. Kayaking, waterskiing and wakeboarding available. Fan B550, a/c B1100

Santiburi Resort 500m west of the village ☎077 425031, Ⓦ santiburi.com. German-run, top-end hotel in beautifully landscaped grounds spread around a huge freshwater swimming pool and stream. Accommodation is mostly in Thai-style villas, inspired by Rama IV's summer palace at Phetchaburi, each with a large bathroom and separate sitting area, furnished in luxurious traditional style; some also have a private outdoor plunge pool. Facilities include watersports on the private stretch of beach, tennis courts, squash court, gym and golf course,

a kids' club and a spa. B23,900

Shangrilah West of Maenam Resort, served by the same access road ☎077 425189. In this huge compound that sprawls onto the nicest, widest stretch of sand along Maenam, the main area of shoulder-to-shoulder bungalows sports beautiful flowers, trees and carefully tended topiary. All rooms are well maintained and en-suite, with verandas, ceiling fans and sturdy furniture; some fan rooms at the front boast hot showers, which are also provided in all of the large, a/c rooms. The restaurant serves good Thai food. Fan B400, with hot water B800, a/c B1200

SR At the far eastern end of the bay ☎077 427529–30, Ⓔ sr_bungalow@hotmail.com. A quiet, welcoming, good-value place, set in a narrow flower garden, with a very good restaurant and wi-fi. Accommodation is in large, smart, concrete bungalows with verandas and chairs, a/c, hot showers, TVs and fridges. To get there, either walk along the beach, or turn off Route 4169 at Family Mart and continue through the grounds of *W Hotel*. B700

EATING AND DRINKING

Angela's Bakery Opposite the police station on the main through-road to the east of the pier ☎077 427396. American-style, a/c diner, with a few shady tables out front, offering great breakfasts (French toast B80) and a wide choice of sandwiches, salads, soups and Western main courses, as well as cakes and apple pie. Mon–Sat 8.30am–4pm, Sun 8.30am–2pm.

Ko Seng On the road parallel to and just east of the pier road ☎077 425365. This locally famous seafood restaurant, simply decorated apart from the chunky wooden tables and chairs, has featured on national TV.

Buy your fish and seafood according to weight, or plump for dishes such as *kaeng som plaa* (B150), a thin fish curry with tamarind paste. Daily 10am–10pm.

Sunshine Gourmet At the west end of the bay, signposted on a lane that runs east from Wat Na Phra Larn. Popular, clean and friendly spot that does a bit of everything, from cappuccino, through own-baked pies (B150 for steak and kidney), sandwiches and cakes, to international, especially German, main courses, seafood and other Thai dishes. Daily noon–9pm.

Bophut

The next bay east is **BOPHUT**, which has a similar look to Maenam but shows a marked difference in atmosphere and facilities, with a noticeable Mediterranean influence. The

ACCOMMODATION		RESTAURANTS & CAFÉS	
Four Seasons Resort	9	Angela's Bakery	3
Harry's	3	Ko Seng	2
Lolita	7	Sunshine Gourmet	1
Maenam Resort	5		
Maenam Villa	2		
Moonhut	6		
Santiburi Resort	8		
Shangrilah	4		
SR	1		

3

quiet, 2km-long beach attracts a mix of young and old travellers, as well as families, and **Ban Bophut**, now tagged "**Fisherman's Village**", at the east end of the bay, is well geared to meet their needs, with a sprinkling of boutique hotels and banks, ATMs, scuba-diving outlets, travel agents, internet cafés and minimarts. While through traffic sticks to Route 4169 to Chaweng and Route 4171 towards the airport, development of the village has been reasonably sensitive, preserving many of its old wooden shophouses on the two narrow, largely car-free streets that meet at a T-junction by the pier. At night, in sharp contrast to Chaweng's frenetic beach road, it's a fine place for a promenade, with a concentration of good upmarket restaurants and low-key farang-run bars; on Friday evenings, the village hosts a **walking street**, very similar to Maenam's Thursday affair (see p.241). The nicest part of the beach itself is at the west end of the bay, towards *Zazen* resort, but again the sand is slightly coarse by Samui's standards. Kayaks, sailing and windsurfing are available, for example, near the centre of the beach at *Bandara Resort*, next to *Anantara*.

ACCOMMODATION   BOPHUT

There's very little inexpensive accommodation left among Bophut's twenty or so resorts. Most establishments are well spaced out along the length of the beach, though a handful of small, comfortable hotels cluster together in Ban Bophut.

Anantara West of the village on the main road ☎077 428300, ⱳanantara.com. Luxury hotel with attentive service in the style of an opulent oriental palace. Blocks of balconied rooms are arrayed round lush gardens, ponds, an attractive swimming pool and a central bar and restaurant, offering contemporary Italian cuisine with Asian influences. There's also a very attractive spa, a kids' club and a huge range of activities, from yoga and Thai cooking classes to tennis and watersports. **B9100**

Hansar At the west end of the village ☎077 245511, ⱳhansarsamui.com. You'll be surprised how spacious this hotel feels, with its long beachfront and just 74 low-rise rooms (all with huge shower areas and sea views from their big balconies), set around gardens and a pool. The stylish decor is a riot of geometry in brown and beige – unvarnished wood, bamboo, marble and granite – and there's a spa, gym and luxury restaurant, *H Bistro*, with ingredients flown in from around the world. **B9500**

Juzz'a Pizza 2 East of the village T-junction ☎077

245663. Above a good restaurant (see p.244), four small but smart rooms, well equipped with comfy beds, a/c, hot showers, fridges and cable TV. Two rooms look onto the road, while the other two have beachside terraces with great views. **B800**

The Lodge Towards the western end of the village ☎077 425337, ⱳlodgesamui.com. Small, two-storey, beachfront hotel with immaculately clean and tastefully decorated modern rooms, all with balconies looking over the water, and boasting a/c, ceiling fan, mini-bar, satellite TV, plus spacious bathrooms with tubs to soak in. There's a seafront bar downstairs where you can get breakfast. **B1930**

Samui Ley West of the village T-junction ☎077 245647, ⱳsamuiley.com. Kitsch and very cute small hotel, with a strong Thai pop aesthetic, sporting floral prints, retro posters and bright pastel colours everywhere. The large rooms have free wi-fi and antique TVs that actually work, as well as a/c, hot showers, sofas and beachfront balconies. Downstairs are a boutique with free computers for guests' use and a terrace café on the beach. **B2700**

The Waterfront East of the village T-junction ☎077 427165, ⓦthewaterfrontbophut.com. English-run boutique hotel, sociable and family-friendly, with a small swimming pool in a grassy garden. All of the simply but tastefully decorated rooms and bungalows have a/c, hot water, mini-bars, safes, cable TV, DVD players and views of the sea. Free pick-ups, wi-fi, internet access and babysitting; breakfast included in the price. **B3045**

Zazen At the far west end of the beach ☎077 425085, ⓦsamuizazen.com. Stylish bungalows and villas clustered round a cute pool and kids' pool, furnished with Thai and other Asian objets d'art, as well as satellite TV, DVD, free wi-fi and mini-bar (plus iPod docks in some); all sport a tropical-style open-air bathroom with rain shower. Other facilities at this eco-friendly resort include a spa, a fine restaurant that hosts Thai dancing Thurs and Sun, cooking classes, kayaks, windsurfers, table tennis, pétanque and the like. **B7150**

EATING AND DRINKING

Happy Elephant West of the village T-junction ☎077 245347. This long-standing restaurant offers a good choice of mostly Thai food, including a few less mainstream dishes such as pork *nam tok* (B220) and lots of seafood, which is displayed out front and priced by weight. Service is friendly and there's an attractive beachside terrace. Daily 11am–10pm.

Juzz'a Pizza 2 East of the village T-junction ☎077 245663. Friendly, small, elegant restaurant with a beachside terrace, serving excellent, authentic pizzas (around B250), with vegetarian and seafood options, as well as pastas, sandwiches and Thai and Western main courses. Daily noon–10pm.

Ristorante alla Baia Just west of the village T-junction ☎077 245566. Run by an Italian who is passionate about his food and has come up with a well-designed menu of standard but authentic dishes, such as *scaloppine al vino bianco* (pork or chicken fillets in white wine; B290). Also on offer are pizzas, home-made pasta

and seafood, with the catch of the day displayed outside. With white tablecloths, flowers on every table, lots of wrought iron and a terrace on the beach, you could almost be overlooking the Adriatic. Daily 11am–10.30pm.

Samui French Bakery 200m south of the village T-junction, towards Route 4169. The real deal: delicious croissants, breads, quiches (B70) and patisserie such as *tarte aux pommes* (B70), to go with espresso coffee. Also offers sandwiches and salads. Daily 7.30am–5pm.

The Shack Grill West of the village T-junction ☎077 246041 or 087 264 6994, ⓦtheshackgrillsamui.com. Small, pricey spot, run by an ebullient New Yorker, and focused on the large, open grill at the front of the restaurant: here all manner of local seafood and imported meats, such as Wagyu beef and New Zealand lamb, are cooked to your liking. Good cold meat platters with mozzarella (B465), delicious apple pie and decent house wine. Daily 6–11pm.

Bangrak

Beyond the sharp headland with its sweep of coral reefs lies **BANGRAK**, sometimes called **Big Buddha Beach** after the colossus that gazes sternly down on the sun worshippers from its island in the bay. The beach is no great shakes, especially during the northeast monsoon, when the sea retreats and leaves a slippery mud flat, and generally it's hard to recommend staying here, as the resorts are squeezed together in a narrow, noisy strip between busy Route 4171 and the shore, underneath the airport flight path.

The **Big Buddha** (*Phra Yai*) is certainly big and works hard at being a tourist attraction, but is no beauty. A short causeway at the eastern end of the bay leads across to a messy clump of souvenir shops and foodstalls in front of the temple, catering to day-tripping Thais as well as foreigners. Ceremonial dragon-steps then bring you up to the covered terrace around the Big Buddha, from where there's a fine view of the sweeping north coast. Look out for the B10 rice-dispensing machine, which allows you symbolically to give alms to the monks at any time of the day.

Choeng Mon

After Bangrak comes the high-kicking boot of Samui's **northeastern cape**, with its small, rocky coves overlooking Ko Pha Ngan and connected by sandy lanes. Songthaews run along Route 4171 to the largest and most beautiful bay, **Choeng Mon**, whose white sandy beach is lined with casuarina trees that provide shade for the bungalows and upmarket resorts. Choeng Mon is now popular enough to support small supermarkets, travel agents and a bank, but on the whole it remains relatively uncommercialized and laidback.

ACCOMMODATION   CHOENG MON

Boat House Hotel Central Choeng Mon ☎077 425041–52, ⓦimperialhotels.com. Named after the two-storey rice barges that have been converted into suites in the grounds, the *Boat House* also offers good-value luxury rooms with balconies in more prosaic modern buildings, often filled by package tours. As well as a beachside boat-shaped pool, there's a garden pool, a spa, a fitness room, a kids' club, free wi-fi, kayaks and windsurfers. B4000

Island View Tucked in on the east side of the Boat House Hotel ☎077 245031, ⓦislandviewsamui.com. Smart, good-value rooms and chalets with a/c, hot water, TV and fridge, in a lively compound that crams in a supermarket, a small bookshop and a beachfront bar, as well as a massage *sala* and kayaks on the beach. Rooms B1000, bungalows B1200

Kirati Resort 100m east of Island View ☎081 881 2703, ⓦkiratisamui.com. All the accommodation here has a/c, hot water, free wi-fi, a balcony and a fridge. Choose between a variety of spacious chalets with nice decorative touches in the jungly garden, and bright, new rooms in a hotel-style block, with granite-tiled floors, dark-wood

sofas and smart, modern bathrooms. Bungalows B1000, rooms B2200

Ô Soleil West of the Boat House Hotel ☎077 425232, ✉buisseretjean@yahoo.fr Lovely, orderly, Belgian-run place in a pretty, tranquil garden dotted with ponds. Among the well-built, clean bungalows, the cheapest are fan-cooled, with cold showers, at the back, while the a/c offerings, all with hot showers, fridges and TVs, are priced according to size. New, more luxurious bungalows are being built and prices may go up. Fan B400, a/c B600

★ **Tongsai Bay** North side of Choeng Mon ☎077 245480, ⓦtongsaibay.co.th. Easy-going, environmentally aware establishment with excellent service. The luxurious rooms, red-tiled cottages and palatial villas (some with their own pool) command beautiful views over the huge, picturesque grounds, the private beach and two swimming pools. In addition they all sport second bathtubs on their secluded open-air terraces, and some also have outdoor, four-poster beds with mosquito nets if you want to sleep under the stars. There's also an array of very fine restaurants and a delightful spa. B9300

Chaweng

For looks alone, none of the other beaches can match **CHAWENG**, with its broad, gently sloping strip of white sand sandwiched between the limpid blue sea and a line of palm trees. Such beauty has not escaped attention of course, which means, on the plus side, that Chaweng can provide just about anything the active beach bum demands, from thumping nightlife to ubiquitous and diverse watersports. The negative angle is that the new developments are ever more cramped and expensive, while building work behind the palm trees and repairs to the over-commercialized main beach road are always in progress.

North Chaweng

The 6km bay is framed between the small island of Ko Matlang at the north end and the 300m-high headland above Coral Cove in the south. From **Ko Matlang**, where the waters provide some decent snorkelling, an often exposed coral reef slices southwest across to the mainland, marking out a shallow lagoon and **North Chaweng**. This S-shaped part of the beach is comparatively peaceful, though it has some ugly pockets of development; at low tide it becomes a wide, inviting playground, and from October to January the reef shelters it from the northeast winds. Here, on the beach by the *Chaweng Regent*, Samui Ocean Sports (☎081 940 1999, ⓦsailing-in-samui.com) rents windsurfers and kayaks, as well as offering sailing lessons, trips and charters.

Central Chaweng and Chaweng Noi

South of the reef, the idyllic shoreline of **Central Chaweng** stretches for 2km in a dead-straight line, the ugly, traffic-clogged and seemingly endless strip of amenities on the parallel main drag largely concealed behind the tree line and the resorts. Around a low promontory is **Chaweng Noi**, a little curving beach in a rocky bay, which is comparatively quiet in its northern part, away from the road. Well inland of Central Chaweng, the round-island road, Route 4169, passes through the original village of **Ban Chaweng**.

Coral Cove

South of Chaweng, the road climbs past **Coral Cove**, a tiny, isolated beach of coarse sand hemmed in by high rocks, with some good coral for snorkelling. It's well worth making the trip to the *Beverly Hills Café*, at the tip of the headland dividing Chaweng from Lamai, for a jaw-dropping view over Chaweng and Choeng Mon to the peaks of Ko Pha Ngan (and for some good, moderately priced food, notably seafood).

ACCOMMODATION   CHAWENG

Over fifty **bungalow resorts** and **hotels** at Chaweng are squeezed into thin strips running back from the beachfront at right angles. The cheapest digs here are generally little more than functional, while more and more expensive places are sprouting up all the time, offering sumptuous accommodation at top-whack prices.

NORTH CHAWENG

Amari Palm Reef North Chaweng ⊕077 422015–8, ⓦamari.com. Congenial, eco-friendly luxury hotel that's unpretentious and good value. Spacious accommodation,

stretching back across the road from the beach and all with DVD players, includes family-friendly duplexes, and there are two elegant restaurants, including *Prego* (see p.248), a full-service spa, a gym, two free-form swimming pools

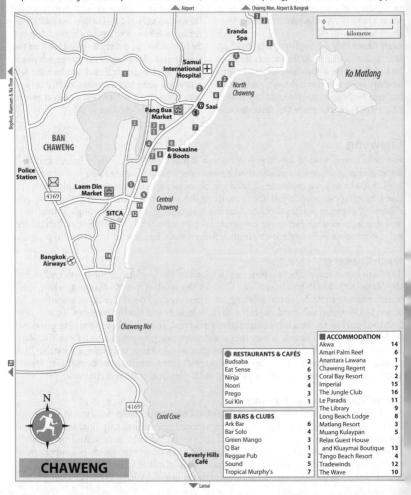

CHAWENG

RESTAURANTS & CAFÉS

Budsaba	2
Eat Sense	6
Ninja	5
Noori	4
Prego	3
Suí Kin	1

BARS & CLUBS

Ark Bar	6
Bar Solo	4
Green Mango	3
Q Bar	1
Reggae Pub	2
Sound	5
Tropical Murphy's	7

ACCOMMODATION

Akwa	14
Amari Palm Reef	6
Anantara Lawana	1
Chaweng Regent	7
Coral Bay Resort	2
Imperial	15
The Jungle Club	16
Le Paradis	11
The Library	9
Long Beach Lodge	8
Matlang Resort	3
Muang Kulaypan	5
Relax Guest House	
and Kluaymai Boutique	13
Tango Beach Resort	4
Tradewinds	12
The Wave	10

and a kids' pool. Various discounts and packages available on their website. B5320

Anantara Lawana North Chaweng ☎077 960333, ⓦanantara.com. The design of this luxury hotel was inspired by Chinese merchants' houses in Thailand in the last century, which gives a pleasing retro feel to the rooms, most of which have outdoor bathrooms. Much of the accommodation is in two-storey houses, in which the ground-floor room has a plunge pool and the first-floor room a terrace; other villas either have their own pools or share semi-private ones. There's also a main, semicircular pool, of course, down by the beach, as well as an excellent spa and a very good restaurant, *Tree Tops*, where you eat in romantic, open-sided treehouses. B9500

Chaweng Regent At the bottom end of North Chaweng ☎077 230391–400, ⓦchawengregent.com. Reliable, well-run, luxury place offering elegant bungalows and low-rise rooms with private terraces and all mod cons, around lotus ponds, two pools, a fitness centre, sauna and spa. B6100

★ **Coral Bay Resort** At the far north end of North Chaweng ☎077 234555, ⓦcoralbay.net. A charming, eco-friendly vision of how Chaweng might have developed – if only there'd been more space. In quiet, delightful, ten-acre gardens with over 500 species of plants, the huge, thatched villas have been thoughtfully and tastefully designed with local woods, bamboo and coconut; all have extensive verandas, waterfall showers, free broadband and DVD/CD/MP3 players (movies available from the library). There's an attractive pool, a spa and a good beachside bar-restaurant; kayaks and snorkels available. B6850

Matlang Resort At the far north end of North Chaweng ☎077 230468–9. Tranquil, friendly place on the beach with nice views of Ko Matlang, though getting ever more tightly squeezed by the surrounding luxury resorts. Choose between old-style thatched, wooden bungalows with verandas, mosquito screens and hot showers, and brightly painted, new rooms with a/c. Fan B500, a/c B1000

Muang Kulaypan North Chaweng ☎077 230849–50, ⓦkulaypan.com. Chaweng's original boutique hotel is arrayed around a large, immaculate garden with a black-tiled swimming pool and an excellent beachside restaurant (see p.248). Stylish rooms – each with their own private balcony or garden – combine contemporary design with traditional Thai-style comforts. Breakfast included. B4500

Tango Beach Resort North Chaweng ☎077 422470, ⓦtangobeachsamui.com. This helpful and welcoming place has a modern Thai style that sets it apart from most of Samui's farang-oriented hotels: a variety of cutesy, colourful, well-equipped rooms are separated by a small, shady pool (and kids' pool) and a wooden boardwalk that runs down to the beach, where kayaks are available. Breakfast included. B2650

CENTRAL CHAWENG

★ **Akwa** Towards the south end of Central Chaweng ☎084 660 0551, ⓦakwaguesthouse.com. Cute, homely, brightly coloured rooms all decorated with cartoon murals and well equipped with a/c, hot water, mini-bars, TVs, DVD players (with DVDs to borrow) and free wi-fi. "Deluxe" are bigger than "Standard", and there are penthouses and a garden apartment. Not on the beach but close to it, and guests get free access to the pool at *Seascape Resort*, opposite. B500

Le Paradis Central Chaweng ☎077 239041–3, ⓦleparadisresort.com. Set in lush gardens, this place was partly under renovation at the time of writing but offers very stylish contemporary villas hung with large, colourful paintings and equipped with open-air bathrooms with large baths, large balconies, a/c, cable TV, DVD players, safes and free wi-fi. Attractive beachside swimming pool and health spa. B6300

The Library Central Chaweng ☎077 422767–8, ⓦthelibrary.name. High-concept design hotel, based around a library of books, DVDs and CDs with computer terminals. The idea is continued in the rooms, which all sport iMacs (with free wi-fi) and DVD players, and have a sleek, cubic theme; they're divided into suites (downstairs) and studios with balconies (upstairs). There's a blood-red swimming pool, a fitness centre and a beachfront terrace restaurant, *The Page*. Studios B15,800, suites B18,000

Long Beach Lodge Towards the north end of Central Chaweng ☎077 422162, ⓦlongbeachsamui.com. An unusually spacious and shady, sandy compound. All the orderly, clean bungalows and rooms are a decent size and have hot water, fridge, TV and a/c. Service is friendly, and breakfast is included in the price. From B1200

Relax Guest House and Kluaymai Boutique Soi Colibri, a small lane at the south end of Central Chaweng, opposite the landmark Centara Grand Beach Resort ☎077 413836, ✉sombatsamui@hotmail.com. Functional crashpads, but well maintained and good value for the facilities: either fan and hot water or a/c, hot water, fridge and TV (wi-fi available in the office). Or you could upgrade to the "boutique" rooms next door, under the same management, with DVD players, in-room wi-fi and a touch of decor. Fan B300, a/c B500, "boutique" B800

Tradewinds Central Chaweng ☎077 414294, ⓦtradewinds-samui.com. A cheerful, well-run place of characterful bungalows and rooms (all with a/c, hot water, mini-bar, cable TV, wi-fi and balcony) with plenty of room to breathe in colourful tropical gardens. The resort specializes in sailing, with its own catamarans (instruction available), as well as offering kayaking, snorkelling and croquet. Breakfast included. B2500

The Wave Central Chaweng ☎077 230803, ⓦthewavesamui.com. One of the cheapest guesthouses on Chaweng, this helpful, English-run place is not on the

3

beach, but above a popular bar-restaurant on the main road. Most of the rooms have fans and share cold-water bathrooms, while the a/c offerings, including a top-floor duplex with a rooftop terrace, feature hot showers, TVs, fridges and free wi-fi. All kinds of advice and tours available, as well as a huge library. Fan $\underline{B400}$, a/c $\underline{B850}$

CHAWENG NOI

Imperial Chaweng Noi ☎077 422020–36, ⊛imperial hotels.com. The longest-established luxury hotel on Samui is a grand but lively establishment with a Mediterranean feel, set in sloping, landscaped gardens; features include two pools (one sea water, one fresh with a jacuzzi),

a spa, a tennis court and classes such as Thai cookery and fruit carving. $\underline{B7800}$

★ **The Jungle Club** 2km up a steep, partly paved road from Chaweng Noi ☎081 894 2327, ⊛jungleclub samui.com. Breezy, French–Thai antidote to Chaweng's commercial clutter: a huge, grassy, shady plot with a small pool on the edge of the slope to catch the towering views of Ko Pha Ngan and beyond. A chic bar-restaurant has been built into the rocks, while the accommodation – all thatched, with mosquito nets and fans – includes wooden huts with cold showers and concrete bungalows with hot water and DVD players. Free pick-ups twice a day. $\underline{B800}$, with hot shower from $\underline{B1800}$

EATING

Chaweng offers all manner of foreign **cuisines**, from French to Russian, much of it of dubious quality. Among all this, it's quite hard to find good, reasonably priced Thai food – as well as the places recommended below, it's worth exploring the cheap and cheerful foodstalls, popular with local workers, at either **Laem Din night market**, on the middle road between Central Chaweng and Highway 4169, or Pang Bua market (roughly 6am–midnight) on the Ban Chaweng road, which includes a famous stall for *khao niaw mamuang* (mango with sticky rice).

Budsaba Restaurant At the Muang Kulaypan Hotel ☎077 230849–50. This charming, upmarket beachfront restaurant fully justifies the journey up to North Chaweng: you get to recline in your own seaside *sala* or open-sided hut on stilts while tucking into excellent Thai dishes such as pomelo salad (B180). Daily 7am–10.30pm.

Eat Sense Central Chaweng, next to Charlie's Huts ☎077 414242, ⊛eatsensesamui.com. Spacious, relaxing, mostly open-air restaurant on the beachfront, serving expensive but delicious Thai and international food, using only organic vegetables – try the deep-fried prawns with cashew nuts and tamarind sauce. Daily 11am–midnight.

Ninja Opposite Burirasa Resort in Central Chaweng. Popular, well-run, very basic and cheap restaurant, serving simple Thai favourites such as *tom yam* (B55), *som tam* and *phat thai*, as well as crêpes, breakfasts and other Western food. Open 24hr.

Noori Opposite Chaweng Buri Resort towards the north end of Central Chaweng ☎077 413108, ⊛noori indiasamui.com. Superior Indian food in relatively basic

surroundings, including all the old favourites such as chicken tikka masala (B210), as well as plenty of seafood and vegetarian options. Also has a branch further south on Central Chaweng, past the *Centara Grand Resort*, and offers Indian cooking classes. Daily 11.30am–11.30pm.

★ **Prego** Amari Palm Reef, North Chaweng ☎077 422015–8. Excellent, chic, open-sided restaurant that would stand on its own two feet in Milan, the head chef's home town. The varied menu of contemporary Italian dishes includes good *antipasti*, pizzas, handmade pastas and top-notch risottos, and there's a very good selection of wines. Booking advised in high season. Daily 11.30am–midnight.

Sui Kin The Akyra Resort, North Chaweng ☎077 915100, ⊛theakyra.com. Very good, open-air restaurant overlooking this Japanese-style resort that features a lot of dark wood in its attractive decor. The *unagi* sushi (eel; B280) and the tuna and scallop tartare (B250) are both very tasty, or you could opt for teppanyaki, tempura, grilled fish or contemporary sushi (mostly California rolls). Daily noon–10.30pm.

DRINKING AND NIGHTLIFE

Avoiding the raucous hostess bars and English theme pubs on the main through road, the best place to **drink** is on the beach: at night dozens of resorts and dedicated bars lay out candlelit tables with axe cushions for reclining on the sand, especially towards the north end of Central Chaweng and on North Chaweng.

Ark Bar North end of Central Chaweng ☎077 961333, ⊛ark-bar.com. Hosts very popular beach parties, with international and Thai house DJs, live music, fire shows and a free barbecue. Parties Wed & Fri from 2pm until well into the night.

Bar Solo North end of Central Chaweng, on the main road just north of Green Mango ⊛barsolosamui.com.

One of the bars of the moment, whose black-and-white industrial look is matched by the hardcore techno on the sound system. Diversions include a pool table and shisha pipes, and there's a happy hour till 8pm. Look out for its regular beach parties at Hat Plai Laem, in the northeast corner of the island. Daily 2pm–3am.

Green Mango North end of Central Chaweng.

Long-standing dance venue, in a huge shed that combines an industrial look with that of a tropical greenhouse. Now with its own alley, Soi Green Mango, lined with other vibrant bars and clubs. Daily 10pm–3am.

Q Bar North off the Ban Chaweng road ☎077 962420, ⓦqbarsamui.com. Sleek, futuristic decor, great views over the lake from high on its north shore and cutting-edge music from local and international DJs, at this branch of the famous Bangkok bar-club. Daily 6pm–late.

Reggae Pub Inland from Central Chaweng across the lake ⓦreggaepubsamui.com. Chaweng's oldest nightclub is a venerable Samui institution – with a memorabilia shop to prove it. It does time now as an unpretentious, good-time,

party venue, with plenty of drinking games, pool tables, big-screen sports and live reggae bands every night, plus occacional big-name concerts. Daily 6pm–3am.

Sound Next soi south of Green Mango. With its smart front bar and large garden club at the back, this is where people stagger on to when other places close. Daily 11pm–6am.

Tropical Murphy's Opposite McDonald's in Central Chaweng. One theme pub that is worth singling out: with draught Guinness, Magners and Kilkenny, a huge range of big-screen sports, quiz nights, live music, free wi-fi and decent food, *Murphy's* has turned itself into a popular landmark and meeting place. Daily 8am–2am.

DIRECTORY

Airlines Bangkok Airways, south end of Ban Chaweng on Route 4169 ☎077 601300.

Bookshops There are several branches of Bookazine, most conveniently next to *Tropical Murphy's* on the beach road in Central Chaweng (daily 10am–10pm), selling English-language books, newspapers and magazines. In North Chaweng, on the east side of the beach road at the T-junction with the Ban Chaweng road, Saai is good for secondhand books (daily 9am–11pm).

Hospital The private Samui International Hospital in North Chaweng (☎077 230781–2, ⓦsih.co.th) provides

24hr ambulance and emergency services, house calls, a dental clinic and travel inoculations.

Internet access Dozens of outlets, including at Saai bookshop (see above).

Pharmacy Boots has a convenient branch in the middle of Central Chaweng, just up the road from *Tropical Murphy's* pub.

Walking street Very similar to Maenam's (see p.241), on Wed evenings near the beach, between *Long Beach Lodge* and *Ninja*.

Lamai

LAMAI is like a second city to Chaweng's capital, not quite as developed and much less frenetic, while lacking the latter's wide range of chic hotels, restaurants and nightclubs. Development is concentrated into a farang toytown of tawdry open-air hostess bars and Western restaurants that has grown up behind the centre of the beach, interspersed with supermarkets, clinics, banks, ATMs, internet cafés, dive shops and travel agents. Running roughly north to south for 4km, the white, palm-fringed beach itself is still a picture, and generally quieter than Chaweng, with far less in the way of watersports – it's quite easy to get away from it all by staying at the peaceful extremities of the bay, where the backpackers' resorts are preferable to Chaweng's functional guesthouses. At the northern end, the spur of land that hooks eastward into the sea is perhaps the prettiest spot and is beginning to attract some upmarket development: it has more rocks than sand, but the shallow sea behind the coral reef is protected from the high seas of November, December and January.

The original village of **Ban Lamai**, set well back on Route 4169, remains surprisingly aloof, and its wat contains a small museum of ceramics, agricultural tools and other everyday objects. Most visitors get more of a buzz from **Hin Yay** (Grandmother Rock) and **Hin Ta** (Grandfather Rock), small rock formations on the bay's southern promontory, which never fail to raise a giggle with their resemblance to the male and female sexual organs.

ACCOMMODATION   LAMAI

Lamai's **accommodation** is generally less cramped and slightly better value than Chaweng's, though it presents far fewer choices at the top end of the market. The far southern end of the bay towards the Grandparent Rocks has the tightest concentration of budget bungalows.

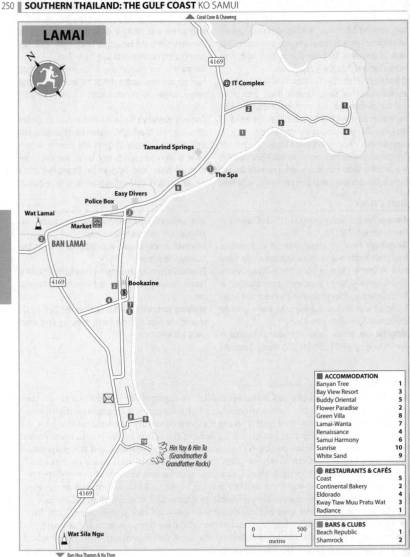

▲ Coral Cove & Chaweng

LAMAI

@ IT Complex

Tamarind Springs

The Spa

Easy Divers
Police Box

Wat Lamai
Market
BAN LAMAI

Bookazine

Hin Yay & Hin Ta
(Grandmother &
Grandfather Rocks)

Wat Sila Ngu

▼ Ban Hua Thanon & Na Thon

■ ACCOMMODATION	
Banyan Tree	1
Bay View Resort	3
Buddy Oriental	5
Flower Paradise	2
Green Villa	8
Lamai-Wanta	7
Renaissance	4
Samui Harmony	6
Sunrise	10
White Sand	9

● RESTAURANTS & CAFÉS	
Coast	5
Continental Bakery	2
Eldorado	4
Kway Tiaw Muu Pratu Wat	3
Radiance	1

0 ——— 500
metres

■ BARS & CLUBS	
Beach Republic	1
Shamrock	2

Banyan Tree On the bay's northern headland ☏ 077 915333, ⓦ banyantree.com. Occupying a steep-sided, landscaped valley, with towering views of Chaweng from the lobby bar, *Banyan Tree* provides the height of luxury in its beautiful, stilted pool villas: lofty living rooms, walk-in wardrobes, possibly the biggest big-head showers in Thailand and lots of extra touches such as iPod docks. Electric buggies will ferry you down to the spa, the main swimming pool, kids' pool and private cove with a good stretch of beach, where plenty of watersports are on offer. B34,800

Bay View Resort On the bay's northern headland ☏ 077 458778–9, ⓦ bayviewsamui.com. Neat, stylish bungalows with verandas, mini-bars, wi-fi and hot-water bathrooms in an extensive, flower-bedecked compound; the poshest come with a/c and cable TV. Offers a friendly, German–Thai welcome, kayaking, internet access and great sunset views of the beach from the attractive restaurant. Fan B1500, a/c B1900

Buddy Oriental East of Ban Lamai ☏ 077 458560–5, ⓦ buddysamui.com. Welcoming branch of the Khao San Rd hotel, in "colonial" style: four-poster beds with mosquito nets, wooden blinds and bathrooms tiled with black and white marble. The bedrooms and one swimming pool are set well back from the road beyond an avenue of shops, while on the beach side of the road are another pool, a restaurant and bar. Other facilities include a spa, a large kids' club, free wi-fi and computers for guest use. B6000

Flower Paradise On the bay's northern headland ☎077 418059 or 089 288 8362, ⍟samuiroestiland .com. Just a short walk from the beach, a friendly, well-run German–Swiss place in a small but beautiful garden. All the attractive, well-tended bungalows of varying sizes have verandas and hot water, and there's a good restaurant, *Röstiland* (closed Mon) – specializing in the eponymous hash browns – which also offers free wi-fi. Fan B350, a/c B650

Green Villa On the access road to White Sand, at the far southern end of the bay ☎077 424296, ⍟greenvilla@hotmail.com. Though set back from the beach towards the main road, this resort enjoys a spacious garden among palm trees, and a small swimming pool. Clean, simple, en-suite, wooden bungalows with fans (some with hot water) or grand, a/c villas with TVs, fridges, hot-water bathtubs and open-air showers. Fan B450, with hot water B550, a/c B2000

Lamai-Wanta East of the central crossroads ☎077 424550, ⍟lamaiwanta.com. Welcoming, well-placed hotel with a seductive beachfront swimming pool and a good restaurant (see below). Set around trim lawns, the large, plain rooms are decorated in white, beige and dark wood in a minimalist Thai style, while the bungalows (which feature DVD players) are a little more elegant; all have a/c, TVs, mini-bars, safes, wi-fi and hot water. Discounts for longer stays. Breakfast included. Rooms B2650, villas B4100

Renaissance On the bay's northern headland ☎077 429300, ⍟marriott.com. In a fine position with access to two beaches, this luxury Marriott resort presents a stark choice: long, lofty villas, each with its own plunge pool, in lush, frog-filled gardens, or far cheaper rooms at the back with balconies and outdoor jacuzzis. There's an enticing, many-tiered beachside pool, a spa, tapas bar, and a roster of activities including Thai massage and towel-folding classes. Rooms B8850, villas B16,500

Samui Harmony South of Buddy Oriental Hotel ☎077 458120, ⍟samuiharmony@hotmail.com. Tightly packed between the road, canal and beach, but friendly, well tended and shaded by lush vegetation, with a café, travel agency (with computers for guest use) and free wi-fi throughout. You've got three choices: small, neat, en-suite, wooden huts, with either fan and cold shower (though these may be upgraded to hot soon), or a/c, hot water, TV and fridge, or larger a/c affairs on the beach. Fan B500, a/c B800

Sunrise On the Hin Yay Hin Ta access road ☎077 424433, ⍟sunrisebungalow.com. Welcoming and clued-up establishment on the far southern end of the beach. In a quiet, shady garden amid coconut palms, choose between clean fan rooms with cold or hot showers and larger a/c bungalows with hot water, some with cable TV and fridge. Free wi-fi, a decent restaurant, books to borrow, a gym and, in high season, a small spa. Fan B550, with hot water B800, a/c B1200

White Sand At the far southern end of the bay ☎077 424298. Long-established and laidback place in a large, shady, sandy compound, which attracts plenty of long-term travellers. It offers simple, old-style, fan-cooled huts, either with mosquito nets and shared bathrooms or en suite with mosquito screens on the windows, as well as concrete bungalows with hot water, TV and a/c, and three attractive bamboo cottages on the beach that get the best of the sea breezes (cold showers and no a/c). Fan B150, en-suite B300, a/c B600

EATING AND DRINKING

There are far fewer eating options on Lamai than on Chaweng to tempt you away from your guesthouse kitchen. Besides the **restaurants** recommended below, there's a **market** of cheap takeaway foodstalls and simple restaurants inland just off Highway 4169 (east of Tesco Lotus supermarket) that's popular with locals for lunch and dinner (closes around 8 or 9pm). Apart from a few bar-restaurants on the beach near *Lamai-Wanta*, Lamai's **nightlife** is all within spitting distance of the central crossroads.

Beach Republic On the bay's northern headland ☎077 458100, ⍟beachrepublic.com. Although it features accommodation and a spa, this hip beach club is best known for its restaurant and bar, arrayed around two pools and a jacuzzi, with plenty of loungers and day-beds and fine views of the bay. Among sandwiches, global tapas, pasta and pizza, the very good beer-battered fish and chips (B380) stand out. Weekly events currently include "Soulful Saturdays" with a DJ (1–6pm) and Sunday brunch (11.30am–3.30pm), with a DJ until 6pm. Restaurant daily 10.30am–10.30pm.

Coast Lamai-Wanta Hotel, east of the central crossroads ☎077 424550. Hip, open-sided restaurant by the hotel pool and beach, minimalist but mellow, with a menu that's half Thai, including tasty *kaeng matsaman kai* (B160), and half international, with some touches of Asian fusion. Daily 6.30am–9pm.

Continental Bakery North of the central crossroads, near Highway 4169. Friendly, Swiss-run place serving good breads, cakes, sandwiches and espressos, as well as all-day breakfasts ranging from French and American to Belgian (with pork steak, apparently). Daily 6am–3pm, possibly later in high season.

Eldorado Just west of the central crossroads. Highly recommended friendly, good-value Swedish restaurant, serving a few Thai favourites, salads, steaks, pizzas and other international main courses, plus one or two indigenous specialities such as Swedish meatballs (B190). Daily 8am–10.30pm.

Kway Tiaw Muu Pratu Wat Highway 4169, Ban Lamai. A locals' favourite, this basic restaurant serves very tasty noodle soup with pork, spare ribs or seafood, or a combination of all three (B35–65). There's no English sign, but it's right beside the entrance to Wat Lamai, with a white-on-red Thai sign. Daily 9am–7pm.

Radiance The Spa Resort, at the far north end of the beach. Excellent, casual beachside restaurant, serving a huge range of vegetarian Thai and international (including Mexican) dishes, plus raw and vegan food, as well as plenty of meat and marine offerings. The veggie "ginger nuts" stir-fry (B100) and som tam with spicy Thai sausage (B70) are excellent. A long menu of juices, smoothies and shakes includes a delicious lime juice with honey. Daily 7am–10pm.

Shamrock North of the central crossroads. Popular, friendly Irish bar with pool tables and TV sports, which hosts lively cover bands every evening and keeps Guinness, Magners cider and Kilkenny bitter on draught. Happy hour till 8pm. Daily 10am–2am.

The south and west coasts

Lacking the long, attractive beaches of the more famous resorts, the **south and west coasts** have much less to offer in the way of accommodation, though there are one or two interesting spots that are worth heading for on a round-island tour. If you happen to be here in November, the west coast's flat, unexceptional beaches might make a calm alternative when the northeast winds buffet the other side of the island.

Samui Butterfly Garden
Off Route 4170, about 3km south of Ban Hua Thanon, opposite Centara Villas • Daily 8.30am–5.30pm • B200

On a net-covered, rocky hillside with fine views of the sea, the **Samui Butterfly Garden** is opposite (and owned by) *Centara Villas*. The entrance fee is a bit steep, but it allows you to wander among artificial waterfalls and lush vegetation, surrounded by dozens of brilliantly coloured lepidopterans.

Ko Taen and Ko Mad Sum
The two small islands of **Ko Taen** and **Ko Mad Sum**, a short way off the south coast, offer some of Samui's best snorkelling. TK Tour in Ban Thongkrut (☎077 334052–3, ⓦtktoursamui.com) covers both on a five-hour boat trip, costing B1100 per person (B1300 with kayaking), including pick-up from your accommodation, snorkelling equipment and lunch on the long beach of Ko Mad Sum.

Na Muang Falls
About 5km inland of **Ban Hua Thanon**, near **Ban Thurian**, the **Na Muang Falls** make a popular outing as they're not far off the round-island road (each of the two main falls has its own signposted kilometre-long paved access road off Route 4169). The lower fall splashes and sprays down a 20m wall of rock into a large pool, while Na Muang 2, upstream, is a more spectacular, shaded cascade that requires a bit of foot-slogging from the car park (about 15min uphill).

Ko Si Ko Ha
At **Ban Taling Ngam**, on the west coast, the *Five Islands Gallery Café* (☎077 415359, ⓦthefiveislands.com) lays on half-day **boat trips** in luxury longtails to see the caves of **Ko Si Ko Ha**, the heavily guarded islands just offshore where sea gypsies gather swifts' nests for bird's-nest soup (see p.376). With time for snorkelling and swimming, the trip is rounded off by a varied Thai lunch or dinner at *Five Islands* beachside restaurant; the package costs from B6600 for two people including transfers from your accommodation.

EATING   **BAN HUA THANON**

★ **Ban Hua Thanon Seafood** Highway 4169, Ban Hua Thanon ☎077 418355. Justly famous restaurant, recommended in all the Thai food guides, in a Muslim fishing village just south of Lamai. A world away from Samui's slick resort restaurants, this rustic wooden shophouse with lovely outdoor tables on the water keeps its reasonably priced fish (about B100/100g) in tanks at the front. Recommended dishes include baked green mussels with lemon grass and excellent crispy, shredded prawn with mango salad. Daily 10am–10pm.

Ang Thong National Marine Park

Closed Nov • Park entry fee B200 (usually included in price of tour) • Park headquarters ☎077 280222 or ☎077 286025, ⓦ dnp.go.th

Even if you don't get your buns off the beach for the rest of your stay on Samui or Pha Ngan, it's worth taking at least a day out to visit the beautiful **Ang Thong National Marine Park**, a lush, dense group of 42 small islands strewn like a dragon's teeth over the deep-blue Gulf of Thailand, 30km or so west of Samui. Once a haven for pirate junks, then a Royal Thai Navy training base, the islands and their coral reefs, white-sand beaches and virgin rainforest are now preserved under the aegis of the National Parks Department. Erosion of the soft limestone has dug caves and chiselled out fantastic shapes that are variously said to resemble seals, a rhinoceros, a Buddha image and even the temple complex at Angkor.

The surrounding waters are home to dolphins, wary of humans because local fishermen catch them for their meat, and *pla thu* (short-bodied mackerel), part of the national staple diet, which gather in huge numbers between February and April to spawn around the islands. On land, long-tailed macaques, leopard cats, wild pigs, sea otters, squirrels, monitor lizards and pythons are found, as well as dusky langurs, which, because they have no natural enemies here, are unusually friendly and easy to spot. Around forty bird species have had confirmed sightings, including the white-rumped shama, noted for its singing, the brahminy kite, black baza, little heron, Eurasian woodcock, several species of pigeon, kingfisher and wagtail, as well as common and hill mynah; in addition, island caves shelter swiftlets, whose homes are stolen for bird's nest soup (see p.376).

Ko Wua Talab

The largest landmass in the group is **Ko Wua Talab** (Sleeping Cow Island) where the park headquarters shelter in a hollow behind the small beach. From there it's a steep 430m **climb** (about 1hr return; bring walking sandals or shoes) to the island's peak to gawp at the panorama, which is especially fine at sunrise and sunset: in the distance, Ko Samui, Ko Pha Ngan and the mainland; nearer at hand, the jagged edges of the surrounding archipelago; and below the peak, a secret cove on the western side and an almost sheer drop to the clear blue sea to the east. Another climb from the beach, only 200m but even harder going (allow 40min return), leads to **Tham Buabok**, a cave set high in the cliff-face. Some of the stalactites and stalagmites are said to resemble lotuses, hence the cave's appellation, "Waving Lotus". If you're visiting in September, look out for the white, violet-dotted petals of **lady's slipper orchids**, which grow on the rocks and cliffs.

Ko Mae Ko

The park's name, Ang Thong ("Golden Bowl"), comes from a landlocked saltwater lake, 250m in diameter, on **Ko Mae Ko** to the north of Ko Wua Talab, which was the inspiration for the setting of the bestselling novel and film, *The Beach*. A well-made path (allow 30min return) leads from the beach through natural rock tunnels to the rim of the cliff wall that encircles the lake, affording another stunning view of the archipelago and the shallow, blue-green water far below, which is connected to the sea by a natural underground tunnel.

ARRIVAL AND DEPARTURE ANG THONG

There are no scheduled boats to Ang Thong, only organized **day-trips**, which can be booked through your accommodation or a travel agent. If you do want to stay, you can go over on a boat-trip ticket – it's valid for a return on a later day.

FROM KO SAMUI

Blue Stars North end of Central Chaweng, next soi south of Soi Green Mango ☎077 413231, ⍟bluestars .info. If you want to make the most of the park's beautiful scenery of strange rock formations and hidden caves, take a dedicated kayaking trip with Blue Stars. For a one-day trip, taking in the lake at Ko Mae Ko and kayaking and snorkelling among the islands in the northern part of the park, they charge B2200, including pick-up from your accommodation and boat over to the park, buffet lunch and snorkelling gear.

Highway Opposite the southerly pier, near Siam Commercial Bank, on Thanon Chonwithi, Na Thon ☎077 421290 or ☎081 843 1533, ⍟highseatour.com. The main operator, whose big boats leave Na Thon every day at 8.30am, returning at 4.30–5pm. In between, there's a two-hour stop to explore Ko Wua Talab (just enough time to visit the viewpoint, the cave and have a quick swim, so don't dally), lunch on the boat, some cruising through the archipelago, a visit to the viewpoint over the lake on Ko Mae Ko and a snorkelling stop. Tickets cost B1300/person (or B1850 with kayaking), including pick-up from your accommodation.

Lomprayah Maenam ☎077 427765–6, ⍟lomprayah .com One of several companies in Maenam, Bangrak and Bophut offering speedboat day-trips to Ang Thong (B2200).

FROM KO PHA NGAN

Similar day-trips to those from Samui are available on Pha Ngan, costing B1800 or B2000 with kayaking.

Orion ☎081 999 2000, ⍟www,phanganboattrips .com. Day-trips in a wooden cruiser.

Safari Boat ☎077 238232, ⍟safariboat.info. Day-trips to Ang Thong by speedboat.

Seaflower Bungalows Ao Chaophao (see p.266). Organizes occasional two-day, one-night boat treks into the park, which involve snorkelling, caving, catching your own seafood, and sleeping in tents or hammocks on the beach (B3500/person, including food and soft drinks; minimum eight people).

FROM KO TAO

Davy Jones' Locker ☎077 456604, ⍟davyjoneslocker .asia. This dive company attached to *Silver Sands Resort* (see p.273) occasionally runs overnight trips to Ang Thong (B4500/person, B6000 including diving).

INFORMATION AND GETTING AROUND

Tourist information In the past, the marine park has operated a satellite information office near the middle pier in Na Thon, Samui, which may reopen.

Boat rental For getting around the archipelago from Ko Wua Talab, it's possible to charter a motorboat from marine park staff; the best snorkelling is off Ko Thai Plao.

ACCOMMODATION AND EATING

National park bungalows At park headquarters on Ko Wua Talab ☎077 280222 or 077 286025, ⍟dnp .go.th. Simple two- to eight-berth bungalows and a restaurant. B500

Camping At park headquarters on Ko Wua Talab and on Ko Samsao. Two-person tents can be rented for around B200 a night from headquarters.

Ko Pha Ngan

In recent years, backpackers have tended to move over to Ko Samui's fun-loving little sibling, **KO PHA NGAN**, 20km to the north, which still has a comparatively simple atmosphere, mostly because the poor road system is an impediment to the developers. With a dense jungle covering its inland mountains and rugged granite outcrops along the coast, Pha Ngan lacks the huge, gently sweeping beaches for which Samui is famous, but it does have plenty of coral to explore and some beautiful, sheltered bays. If you're seeking total isolation, trek out to **Hat Khuat** (**Bottle Beach**) on the north coast or the half-dozen pristine beaches on the east coast; **Thong Nai Pan**, at the top of the east coast, is not quite as remote, and offers a decent range of amenities and accommodation; while on the long neck of land at the southeast corner, **Hat Rin**, a pilgrimage site for ravers, is a thoroughly commercialized backpackers' resort in a gorgeous setting.

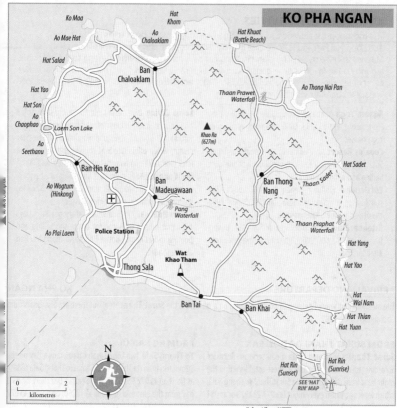

KO PHA NGAN

Ko Maa
Ao Mae Hat
Hat Salad
Hat Yao
Hat Son
Ao Chaophao
Ao Seethanu
Laem Son Lake
Ban Hin Kong
Ao Wogtum (Hinkong)
Ao Plai Laem
Police Station
Thong Sala
Hat Khom
Ao Chaloaklam
Ban Chaloaklam
Hat Khuat (Bottle Beach)
Thaan Prawet Waterfall
Khao Ra (627m)
Ao Thong Nai Pan
Ban Madeuawaan
Pang Waterfall
Ban Thong Nang
Thaan Sadet
Hat Sadet
Thaan Praphat Waterfall
Hat Yang
Hat Yao
Wat Khao Tham
Ban Tai
Ban Khai
Hat Wai Nam
Hat Thian
Hat Yuan
N
Hat Rin (Sunset)
Hat Rin (Sunrise)
SEE 'HAT RIN' MAP
0   2
kilometres
Ko Samui (Bangrak) ▼

3

Much of Pha Ngan's development has plonked itself on the south and west sides along the only coastal roads on the island, which fan out from **Thong Sala**, the capital. The long, straight south coast is lined with bungalows, especially around **Ban Tai** and **Ban Khai**, to take the overspill from nearby Hat Rin, but it's hard to recommend staying here, as the beaches are mediocre by Thai standards, and the coral reef that hugs the length of the shoreline gets in the way of swimming. The west coast, however, offers several handsome sandy bays with great sunset views, notably **Hat Yao** and **Hat Salad**.

Pha Ngan's **bungalows** all now have running water and electricity, and plenty of places offer air conditioning, though there are only a handful of real luxury hotels. The three hundred-plus resorts generally have more space to spread out than on Ko Samui, and the cost of living is lower. The **prices** given on the following pages are standard for most of the year (though on Hat Rin they vary with the phases of the moon), but in slack periods you'll be offered discounts (possible, roughly, in May, June, Oct & Nov), and at the very busiest times (especially Dec & Jan) Pha Ngan's bungalow owners are canny enough to raise the stakes. **Nightlife** is concentrated at Hat Rin, climaxing every month in a wild **full moon party** on the beach; a couple of smaller outdoor parties have now got in on the act: the **Half Moon Festival** (twice monthly, about a week before and after the full moon; ⓦhalfmoonfestival.com) and the monthly **Black Moon Party** (ⓦblackmoon-culture.com), both at Ban Tai on the south coast.

KO PHA NGAN ACTIVITIES

The most popular activities on Ko Pha Ngan are round-island **boat trips** from Hat Rin, Ao Thong Nai Pan and Hat Yao (see the relevant accounts) and trips to Ang Thong National Marine Park (see p.254). The island isn't a great base for **scuba diving**: getting to the best sites around Ko Tao involves time-consuming and expensive voyages, and there aren't as many dive companies here as on Ko Samui or Ko Tao. Other **activities** include learning to cook Thai food, yoga, kiteboarding, windsurfing and sailing.

Agama Yoga North of Thong Sala at Ao Wogtum (Hin Kong) ☎089 233 0217, ⊛agamayoga.com. Yoga classes.

Cookies Resort Ao Plai Laem, just north of Thong Sala ☎083 181 7125, ⊛cookies-phangan.com. Sailing and windsurfing.

Cuttlebone Holiday Beach Resort, about 2km southeast of Thong Sala ☎081 940 1902, ⊛cuttlebone.net. Kiteboarding.

Kiteboarding Asia Opposite Milky Bay Resort, Ban Tai ☎080 600 0573, ⊛kiteboardingasia.com. Kiteboarding.

Lotus Diving Dive resort on Ao Chaloaklam (plus an office at Backpackers Information Centre in Hat Rin) ☎077 374142, ⊛lotusdiving.net. PADI Five-Star centre, which offers frequent courses and trips to Sail Rock (see p.271), halfway between Pha Ngan and Tao.

My Wok and Me East end of Thong Sala, at the start of the road out towards Ban Tai ☎077 377846, ⊛mywokandme.com. Cooking classes.

Safari Boat ☎077 238232, ⊛safariboat.info. Day-trips that take in an elephant camp, snorkelling and boating to Hat Khom, Bottle Beach, Ao Thong Nai Pan and Hat Sadet.

ARRIVAL AND DEPARTURE

KO PHA NGAN

The most obvious way of getting to Ko Pha Ngan is on a boat from the **Surat Thani** area, but there are also boats from Chumphon (see p.230).

FROM SURAT THANI OR DON SAK

Surat Thani to Thong Sala Boat services fluctuate according to demand, but the longest-established is the night boat from Ban Don pier in Surat Thani to Thong Sala, which leaves at 11pm every night (☎077 284928 or ☎081 326 8973; 7hr; B450); in the opposite direction, the night boat departs from Thong Sala at 10pm. Tickets are available from the pier on the day of departure, but note that occasionally these boats don't depart, if they haven't got enough takers to make it worth their while.

Don Sak to Thong Sala There are five Raja vehicle ferries a day (on Pha Ngan ☎077 377452–3), which charge B400, including bus transport to the pier from Surat Thani, with a total journey time of around 4–5hr. In addition, there are two Lomprayah catamarans a day (on Pha Ngan ☎077 238411–2, ⊛lomprayah.com), charging B550, with a total journey time from Surat of about 3hr.

FROM BANGKOK

Bus and train packages From Bangkok bus and train packages similar to those for getting to Ko Samui are available (see p.238), notably government buses from the Southern Terminal (first-class a/c 1 daily B800; VIP 1 daily B1100; 12–14hr). Leaving Pha Ngan, you can catch these buses from the Raja Ferry pier in Thong Sala (☎077 238507 or ☎077 238762).

FROM KO SAMUI

To Thong Sala Two Lomprayah catamarans a day do the 30min trip from Na Thon on Ko Samui to Thong Sala (B300; at Na Thon ☎077 950028). Two Seatran Discovery boats a day from the east end of Bangrak (B250; on Samui ☎077 246086–8, Pha Ngan ☎077 238679; ⊛seatranferry.com) and two Lomprayah catamarans from Maenam (B300; at Maenam ☎077 427765–6) call in at Thong Sala after 30min, on their way to Ko Tao.

To Hat Rin and the east coast From the centre of Bangrak, the *Haad Rin Queen* crosses four times a day to Hat Rin in under an hour (times have remained fairly constant over the years: from Bangrak 10.30am, 1pm, 4pm & 6.30pm, from Hat Rin 9.30am, 11.40am, 2.30pm & 5.30pm; B200; on Samui ☎077 484668, on Pha Ngan ☎077 375113). If there are enough takers and the weather's good enough – generally reliable between roughly mid-Jan and late Oct – one small boat a day crosses from the pier in Ban Maenam at noon to Hat Rin (B250), before sailing up Ko Pha Ngan's east coast, via Hat Sadet and anywhere else upon demand, to Thong Nai Pan (B350).

FROM KO TAO

There are boats from Ko Tao to Ko Pha Ngan (see p.269); all offer the same service in the return direction.

MEDITATION RETREATS AT WAT KHAO THAM

On a quiet hillside above Ban Tai, 4km from Thong Sala on the south coast, **Wat Khao Tham** holds ten-day **meditation retreats** most months of the year (B5000/person to cover food; ⓦ watkowtahm.org). The American and Australian teachers emphasize compassionate understanding as the basis of mental development. Space is limited (retreats are especially heavily subscribed Dec–March), so it's best to pre-register either in person or in writing; go to the website for full details of rules and requirements and the schedule of retreats.

INFORMATION

Tourist information There's no TAT office on Ko Pha Ngan, but a free, widely available booklet, *Phangan Info*, provides regularly updated information about the island, and has a good website, ⓦ phangan.info, on which you can book accommodation. Affiliated to this is the website of Hat Rin's travel agency, ⓦ backpackersthailand.com, which is also a good source of information.

Maps The best map for serious exploration of the island is Visid Hongsombud's *Guide Map of Koh Pha-ngan and Koh Tao* (B120), though it's hard to find.

Thong Sala

Like the capital of Samui, **THONG SALA** is a port of entrance and little more, where the incoming ferries, especially around noon, are met by touts sent to escort travellers to bungalows elsewhere on the island. Songthaews and jeeps to the rest of the island congregate by the pier heads, while the main street that runs inland from the Raja Ferry pier shelters a dusty row of banks, supermarkets, travel agents and scuba-diving outfits, with a popular night market on the north side of the road.

GETTING AROUND

By motorbike or jeep Motorbikes (B150–200/day) and jeeps (B800–1000/day) can be rented from many places on the main road to the piers. Take care on Pha Ngan's often steep and rough roads.

ACCOMMODATION AND EATING

Nira's South along the waterfront from the main street, opposite the Seatran pier. Very pleasant branch of the famous Hat Rin café (see p.262) offering "quick meals to catch the boat": all-day breakfasts, espressos, bakery goods such as quiche lorraine (B65), deli sandwiches and Thai and Western main courses. Free computer for customers' use. Daily 7am–7pm.

Pha Ngan Chai Hotel By the piers, Thong Sala ⓣ 077 238109. If you really need to stay in Thong Sala, head for this incongruous white high-rise overshadowing the piers, which makes a fair stab at international-standard features for visiting businesspeople and government officials, with a/c, hot water, TVs, fridges and, in some rooms, sea-view balconies, as well as a pool, free wi-fi and internet access. Breakfast included. B1000

DIRECTORY

Hospital The island's basic main hospital (ⓣ 077 377034 or 077 375103) lies 3km north of town, on the inland road towards Mae Hat. There's also a 24hr emergency rescue service, staffed by volunteers (ⓣ 077 377500).
Police The main station is 2km up the Ban Chaloaklam road (ⓣ 077 377114), and there's a tourist police office at the main pier in Thong Sala (ⓣ 1155).
Post office About 500m southeast of the piers on the old main street (Mon–Fri 8.30am–noon & 1–4.30pm, Sat 9am–noon).

Pang (Phaeng) Waterfall

Than Sadet–Ko Pha Ngan National Park, 4km northeast of Thong Sala off the road to Chaloaklam • Free admission • Take a Chaloaklam-bound songthaew as far as Ban Madeuawaan, from where it's a 1km signposted walk east

From most places on the island, it's fairly easy to get to the grandiosely termed Than Sadet–Ko Pha Ngan National Park, which contains **Pang (Phaeng) Waterfall**, Pha Ngan's biggest drop. The park headquarters and a simple canteen are northeast of Thong Sala off the main road to Chaloaklam. From here, the main fall – bouncing down in stages over the hard, grey stone – is a steep 250m walk up a forest path. The trail then continues for 300m to a stunning viewpoint overlooking the south and west of the island.

Hat Rin

HAT RIN is firmly established as the major party venue in Southeast Asia, especially in the peak seasons of August, December and January, but it's most famous for its year-round **full moon parties** – something like *Apocalypse Now* without the war. Hat Rin's compact geography is ideally suited to an intense party town: it occupies the flat neck of Pha Ngan's southeast headland, which is so narrow that the resort comprises two back-to-back beaches, joined by transverse roads at the north and south ends. The eastern beach, usually referred to as **Sunrise**, or Hat Rin Nok (Outer Hat Rin), is what originally drew visitors here, a classic curve of fine white sand between two rocky

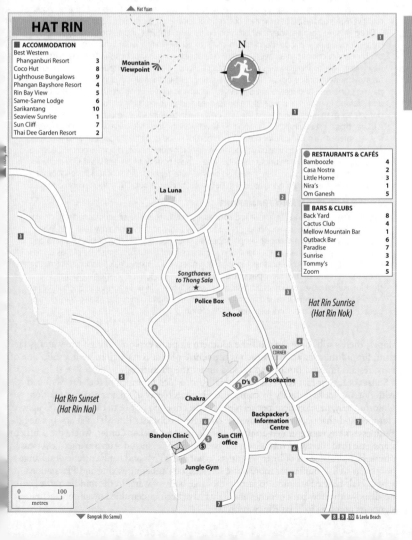

HAT RIN

■ ACCOMMODATION

Best Western Phanganburi Resort	3
Coco Hut	8
Lighthouse Bungalows	9
Phangan Bayshore Resort	4
Rin Bay View	5
Same-Same Lodge	6
Sarikantang	10
Seaview Sunrise	1
Sun Cliff	7
Thai Dee Garden Resort	2

● RESTAURANTS & CAFÉS

Bamboozle	4
Casa Nostra	2
Little Home	3
Nira's	1
Om Ganesh	5

■ BARS & CLUBS

Back Yard	8
Cactus Club	4
Mellow Mountain Bar	1
Outback Bar	6
Paradise	7
Sunrise	3
Tommy's	2
Zoom	5

Hat Yuan

Mountain Viewpoint

N

La Luna

Songthaews to Thong Sala

Police Box

School

Hat Rin Sunrise (Hat Rin Nok)

CHICKEN CORNER

D's

Bookazine

Chakra

Hat Rin Sunset (Hat Rin Nai)

Backpacker's Information Centre

Bandon Clinic

Sun Cliff office

Jungle Gym

0   100
metres

Bangrak (Ko Samui)

& Leela Beach

FULL MOON PARTIES: A SURVIVOR'S GUIDE

Even if you're not the type to coat yourself in day-glo and dance till dawn, a **full moon party** at Hat Rin is certainly a sight to see, and the atmosphere created by thousands of folk mashing it up on a beautiful, moon-bathed beach, lit up by fireworks and fire-jugglers, is quite a buzz. If you're planning to get in on the action, first of all you'll need to check exactly when the party is: when the full moon coincides with an important **Buddhist festival**, the party is moved one night away to avoid a clash; check out ✪fullmoon.phangan.info for details. There's also a big party at Hat Rin on Christmas Day, and a massive one on New Year's Eve. An **admission fee** to the parties of B100 is now charged.

On full moon night, *Paradise*, at the very southern end of Sunrise, styles itself as the main party **venue**, sometimes bringing in big-name international DJs. However, the mayhem spreads along most of Sunrise, fuelled by hastily erected drinks stalls and around a dozen major **sound systems** – listen out for psy-trance and driving techno at *Zoom*, and tech house at *Tommy's* and funky house and drum'n'bass at *Sunrise* further up the beach. Next day, as the beach party winds down, *Back Yard* kicks off its afterparty at around eleven in the morning, with the best of the previous night's DJs; it's up the hill behind the south end of Sunrise off the path to Leela Beach.

Drug-related horror stories are common currency in Hat Rin, and some of them are even true: dodgy Ecstasy, *ya baa* (Burmese-manufactured methamphetamines) and all manner of other concoctions put an average of two farangs a month into hospital for psychiatric treatment. The local authorities have started clamping down on the trade in earnest, setting up a permanent police box at Hat Rin, instigating regular roadblocks and bungalow searches, paying bungalow and restaurant owners to inform on travellers whom they've sold drugs to, and drafting in scores of police (both uniformed and plain-clothes) on full moon nights. It doesn't seem to have dampened the fun, only made travellers a lot more circumspect.

Other **tips** for surviving the full moon are mostly common sense: leave your valuables in your resort's safe – it's a bad night for bungalow break-ins – and don't take a bag out with you; keep an eye on your drink to make sure it's not spiked; watch out for broken bottles on the beach; and do not go swimming while under the influence – there have been several deaths by drowning at previous full moon parties. There have also been several reports of sexual assaults on women and of unprovoked, late-night gang attacks in Hat Rin, especially around full moon night.

ACCOMMODATION AND TRANSPORT

Hat Rin now has around five thousand **rooms** – some of them hastily converted into dorms at party time – but on full moon nights up to thirty thousand revellers may turn up. Unless you're prepared to forget about sleep altogether, you should arrive several days early to bag a room, as many resort owners specify a minimum stay of five nights (in some places up to nine nights, especially during the August, December and January peak seasons). Alternatively, hitch up with one of the many **party boats** (about B700 return per person) organized through guesthouses and restaurants on Ko Samui, especially at Bangrak and Bophut, which usually leave between 9pm and midnight and return around dawn; there's also transport by boat or car from all the other beaches on Pha Ngan.

slopes; there's still some coral off the southern slope to explore, though the water is far from limpid these days. This beach is the centre of Hat Rin's action, with a solid line of bars, restaurants and bungalows tucked under the palm trees.

Sunset beach, or Hat Rin Nai (Inner Hat Rin), which for much of the year is littered with flotsam, looks ordinary by comparison but has plenty of quieter accommodation. Unfortunately, development between the beaches does no justice to the setting: it's ugly, cramped and chaotic, with new low-rise concrete shophouses thrown up at any old angle. Businesses here, concentrated around what's known as **Chicken Corner**, where the southern transverse road meets the road along the back of Sunrise, include supermarkets, overseas phone facilities, dozens of internet outlets, plenty of ATMs and bank currency-exchange booths, as well as outlets for more outré services such as bikini waxing and Playstation rental. Half-hearted attempts to tart up the large body of water in the middle of the headland with a few park benches and lights have been undermined by all-too-accurate signposts pointing to "Hat Rin Swamp".

HAT RIN ACTIVITIES

Many places on Hat Rin, including the Backpackers Information Centre (see below), book one-day **boat trips** up the east coast and back, typically charging B800 (including simple lunch and snorkelling equipment) and taking in Mae Hat, Thong Nai Pan, Bottle Beach and Thaan Sadet. Back on dry land, Chakra, in an alley off the southern transverse (☎087 283 4365), does good **massages** and runs massage courses, while Jungle Gym near the pier (☎077 375115) offers **Thai boxing** classes, a steam room and **yoga**.

ARRIVAL AND DEPARTURE   HAT RIN

By songthaew or minibus Songthaews (B100 during the day, more at night) and a/c minibuses (B150) run between Thong Sala and Hat Rin.

By boat The easiest approach to Hat Rin, if you're coming from Ko Samui, or even Surat Thani, is on the boat from Bangrak on Samui's north coast (see p.256): four boats a day cross to the pier on Sunset beach in under an hour.

GETTING AROUND

By jeep or motorbike Plenty of places on Hat Rin rent jeeps (about B1000/day) and motorbikes (from B150/day). There have been lots of reports, however, of travellers being charged exorbitant amounts if they bring the vehicle back with even the most minor damage – at the very least, check the vehicle over very carefully before renting. *Sun*

Cliff (see p.262), who have an office just off the southern transverse, is a reliable place for motorbikes, and won't try this scam. The section of road between Hat Rin and Ban Khai is paved but winding and precipitous – take care if you're driving yourself.

INFORMATION AND TOURS

★ **Backpackers Information Centre** The excellent, English-Thai Backpackers Information Centre, based to the south of Chicken Corner (daily 10am–10pm; ☎077 375535, ⓦbackpackersthailand.com), is a reliable, helpful and clued-up full-service travel agency, with a website that's very useful not just for Pha Ngan but for the whole of Thailand, including lots of advice and mini-package tours.

They can book tours and other activities on Ko Pha Ngan and through-tickets from Hat Rin to all the tourist centres in southern Thailand, as well as to Kuala Lumpur and Singapore. They also act as agents for Ko Pha Ngan's Lotus Diving and Ko Tao's Crystal Diving (with discounted deals available for advance bookings).

ACCOMMODATION

Staying on **Sunrise** is often expensive and noisy, though you should have more luck towards the north end of the beach. On **Sunset**, the twenty or more resorts are squeezed together in orderly rows, and are especially quiet and inexpensive between April and June and in October. Many visitors choose to stay on the **headland** to the south of the main beaches, especially at white-sand, palm-fringed **Leela Beach** on the west side of the promontory, which is a twenty-minute walk along a well-signposted route from Chicken Corner. At any of the places out here your bungalow is likely to have more peace and space and better views, leaving you a torchlit walk to the night-time action.

Best Western Phanganburi Resort Towards the north end of Sunset beach ☎077 375481, ⓦbestwesternphanganburi.com. Welcoming, luxury complex that encompasses three hotel blocks, dozens of bungalows, a spa, a gym and two very attractive pools in its extensive, beachside grounds. Decorated in a simple but smart Thai style, all the rooms have a/c, hot water, fridge, safety box, free wi-fi and satellite TV. Breakfast included. B2400

Coco Hut Leela Beach ☎077 375369, ⓦcocohut.com. On a clean, quiet stretch of beach, this lively, efficiently run place is smart and attractive, with some traditional southern Thai elements in the architecture. On offer is a

wide variety of upscale accommodation, from wooden bungalows with a/c, hot showers, fridges, TVs and DVDs, to beachfront villas with outdoor jacuzzis, as well as an attractive pool, an adobe-style spa and free wi-fi at the restaurant. Breakfast included. B2600

Lighthouse Bungalows On the far southwestern tip of the headland ☎077 375075, ⓦlighthousebungalows.com. At this friendly haven, fan-cooled wooden and concrete en-suite bungalows, sturdily built to withstand the wind and backed by trail-filled jungle, are priced according to size and comfort; all have good-sized balconies with hammocks. The restaurant food is varied and tasty. Phone for a boat pick-up from Sunset pier or

Thong Sala, or do the 30min walk from Chicken Corner, the last section along a wooden walkway over the rocky shoreline. **B600**

Phangan Bayshore Resort In the middle of Sunrise ☏077 375227, ⊛phanganbayshore.com. Hat Rin's first upmarket resort, a well-ordered, slightly institutional place, boasting 80m of beachfront. There's a large, kidney-shaped pool and a wide variety of close-knit bungalows and rooms with a/c, hot water, TV and fridge, on a green lawn shaded with palms. Minimum stay 3 nights. **B1680**

Rin Bay View Near the pier on Sunset ☏077 375188. A good-value, friendly option in a tightly squeezed central location, occupying a narrow strip of land by the beach, ornamented with flowers and trees. The a/c bungalows and rooms with mosquito screens, hot showers, TVs, fridges and balconies are a decent size and generally well maintained and clean. **B1000**

Same-Same Lodge Above Sunrise at the start of the road to Leela Beach ☏077 375200, ⊛same-same.com. Sociable Danish-run spot with free wi-fi set above a popular, often raucous, bar-restaurant. The clean, colourful and decent-sized rooms come with fan and cold showers or a/c and hot water. Fan **B550**, a/c **B850**

Sarikantang Leela Beach ☏077 375055–6, ⊛sarikantang.com. Boutique resort with two swimming pools, a beachside spa and a good measure of style. Accommodation ranges from bungalows with a/c, TVs, fridges, verandas and hot-water bathrooms to villas with DVD players, separate living rooms and outdoor

jacuzzis. Internet room, free wi-fi and free kayaks. Breakfast included. **B1700**

Seaview Sunrise Northern end of Sunrise ☏077 375160, ⊛seaviewsunrise.com. On a big plot of shady, flower-strewn land at the quieter end of the beach, this clean, friendly, orderly old-timer with a good restaurant offers a total of forty bungalows and rooms. Those on the beachfront are all fan-cooled, with cheaper versions available further back, with or without hot showers. The a/c offerings all have hot water, TV and fridge. Fan **B400**, a/c **B1000**

Sun Cliff High up on the tree-lined slope above the south end of Sunset ☏077 375134 or ☏077 375463, ⊕rsvnsuncliff@hotmail.com. Friendly, spacious place with great views of the south coast and Ko Samui, especially from its heart-shaped pool by the restaurant. Among a wide range of bungalows that are a bit rough around the edges, you'll find some quirky architectural features such as rock-built bathrooms and fountains; some have huge decks for partying. A/c rooms all have hot showers, fridges and TVs. Fan **B300**, fan and hot shower **B500**, a/c **B600**

Thai Dee Garden Resort Northern transverse ☏089 770 2290, ⊕thaidee-@hotmail.com. Pleasant staff and a range of smart concrete and white clapboard bungalows, on a broad, grassy slope strewn with trees and plants and set back from the road. Choose either fan and cold water or a/c and hot. One of the last places to fill at full moon; discounts for stays of two nights or more possible at other times. Free wi-fi at reception. Fan **B300**, a/c **B890**

EATING

Bamboozle Off the southern transverse, near Sunset pier ☏085 471 4211. Among a wide variety of tasty Mexican food here, the chicken fajitas with all the trimmings (B250) are especially good. Also offers pizzas and a short menu of tapas. Daily 10am–late.

★**Casa Nostra** On the southern transverse ☏086 267 8445. Excellent, tiny Italian café-restaurant which prepares great pastas – try the spaghetti bolognese (B180) – pizzas, espresso coffee, salads and plenty of other dishes for vegetarians, such as home-made cannelloni with ricotta and spinach, and a chocolate mousse to die for. Daily 1–11.30pm.

Little Home On the southern transverse. This well-organized, basic restaurant is your best bet for cheap

Thai food in Hat Rin, serving staples such as chicken and cashew nuts (B80) and green, red and yellow curries, plus Western breakfasts. Daily 11am–11pm.

Nira's Near Chicken Corner. Justly popular restaurant and bakery. Around the clock it offers great croissants – sweet and savoury – cakes, sandwiches and coffees; during the busy part of the day, it operates as a restaurant, serving up good breakfasts, burgers and other basic hot meals. Free wi-fi. Bakery 24hr; restaurant daily 8am–8pm.

Om Ganesh On the southern transverse near the pier ☏086 063 2903. Relaxing Indian restaurant with good thalis (from B150), biryanis, plenty of veggie dishes and breads, and cheerful service. Free deliveries. Daily 8am–11pm.

NIGHTLIFE

Cactus Club South end of Sunrise. Open-air dance hall that pumps out mostly radio-friendly dance music onto low-slung candlelit tables and mats on the beach. Evenings till late.

Mellow Mountain Bar North end of Sunrise. Made for chilling, this trippy hangout occupies a great position

up in the rocks, with peerless views of the beach. Evenings till late.

Outback Bar On the southern transverse. Lively British-run meeting place with free pool tables, big-screen sports, free wi-fi, draught Carlsberg and well-received steak pies and the like. Daily 10am–late.

DIRECTORY

Bookshops Bookazine (daily 11am–8pm), on the southern transverse, carries a decent line of new fiction and travel books, as well as magazines and newspapers, while D's (daily 9am–10pm), on a new, little-used road that runs parallel to and north of the southern transverse, is good for secondhand books and has a café.

Clinic Bandon International Hospital, a large private hospital on Ko Samui, runs a clinic on the southern transverse near the pier (☎ 077 375471–2).

Hat Yuan, Hat Thian and Hat Sadet

North of Hat Rin, there are no roads along the rocky, exposed east coast, which stretches as far as **Ao Thong Nai Pan**, the only substantial centre of development. First up are the adjoining small, sandy bays of **HAT YUAN** and **HAT THIAN**, which have established a reputation as a quieter alternative to Hat Rin. A rough track has recently been bulldozed from Ban Khai, and the bays now sport about a dozen bungalow outfits between them.

Steep, remote **HAT SADET**, about 8km as the crow flies from Hat Rin, has a handful of bungalow operations, sited here because of their proximity to **Thaan Sadet**, a boulder-strewn brook that runs out into the sea. The spot was popularized by various kings of Thailand – Rama V visited no less than fourteen times – who came here to walk, swim and vandalize the huge boulders by carving their initials on them; the river water is now considered sacred and is transported to Bangkok for important royal ceremonies. A rough track runs through the woods above and parallel to Thaan Sadet to connect with the road from Thong Sala to Ao Thong Nai Pan.

If you're feeling intrepid, you could try hiking along this stretch of coast, which in theory is paralleled by a steep, 15km trail (as marked on Visid Hongsombud's map – see p.258), though it's reported to be overgrown in many places. With decent navigational skills, the leg between Hat Rin, starting from near *Laluna Bungalows*, and Hat Yuan should certainly be manageable (about 2hr), aided by green dot and white arrow markers.

ARRIVAL AND DEPARTURE   HAT YUAN, HAT THIAN, HAT SADET

By boat A daily, seasonal boat runs via the east coast beaches from Hat Rin to Thong Nai Pan, having started its voyage across at Maenam on Ko Samui (see p.256).

Otherwise there are ample longtails at Hat Rin that will take you up the coast – around B150/person to Hat Yuan, for example.

ACCOMMODATION

HAT YUAN

Barcelona ☎ 077 375113. Good, relaxing budget choice, with great views and well-built accommodation, mostly in white, stilted bungalows running up the hillside from the beach, the best of them (B700) with large verandas and hot showers. Shared bathrooms B200, en-suite B300

Centara Pariya Resort ☎ 081 737 3883, ⓦ centara hotelsresorts.com. The most luxurious resort in the vicinity of Hat Rin comprises forty spacious villas, some with their own private jacuzzi pool, all with rain showers, bathtubs and large verandas; a/c and hot water are available from 6pm to 10am. There's a free-form pool and a kids' pool and a spa, as well as plenty of watersports and wi-fi. Access is by speed boat, either from Hat Rin or from Bophut on Samui. B4600

HAT THIAN

The Sanctuary ☎ 081 271 3614, ⓦ thesanctuary thailand.com. The main operation on Hat Thian offers a

huge range of basic and luxury en-suite bungalows and family houses, as well as dorm accommodation (B200–300), kayaking and good vegetarian meals, seafood and home-made bread and cakes. It also hosts courses in yoga, meditation and many new-age subjects, and provides two kinds of treatment: the spa does massage, facials and beauty treatments, while the wellness centre goes in for fasting and cleansing. B450

HAT SADET

Mai Pen Rai ☎ 081 999 2000, ⓦ thansadet.com. Best of the bungalows on Hat Sadet, this welcoming spot has a wide variety of attractive accommodation with airy bathrooms, fans and hammocks (some with big upstairs terraces), either on the beach at the stream mouth or scattered around the rocks for good views. A jeep taxi leaves Thong Sala pier for the resort every day at 1pm (B200). B500

3

Ao Thong Nai Pan

AO THONG NAI PAN is a beautiful, semicircular bay backed by steep, green hills, which looks as if it's been bitten out of the island's northeast corner by a gap-toothed giant, leaving a tall hump of land (occupied by *Panviman Resort*) dividing the bay into two parts: **Thong Nai Pan Noi** to the north, **Thong Nai Pan Yai** to the south. With lovely, fine, white sand, the longer, more indented Thong Nai Pan Yai has marginally the better beach, but both halves of the bay are sheltered and deep enough for swimming. A bumpy road, only partly paved, winds its way for 13km over the steep mountains from Ban Tai on the south coast to Thong Nai Pan, but once you get here you'll find most of the basic amenities you'll need: internet shops, travel agents, dive outfits, ATMs and a tiny post office (on Thong Nai Pan Yai).

ARRIVAL AND DEPARTURE   AO THONG NAI PAN

By jeep Jeeps connect with incoming and outgoing boats at Thong Sala every day (B200/person).
By boat One seasonal boat a day runs via the east coast

beaches from Hat Rin to Thong Nai Pan, having started its voyage across at Maenam on Ko Samui (see p.256).

TOURS

Boat tours Day-trips taking in Ao Mae Hat, Hat Khuat (Bottle Beach) and Thaan Sadet can be arranged through

Baan Panburi Village (see below), for example (B600/person, minimum 8 people).

ACCOMMODATION

★ **Anantara Rasananda** Thong Nai Pan Noi ☎077 239555, ⓦanantara.com. Congenial and chic luxury hideaway, with speedboat transfers from Samui. Accommodation is in 60 spacious, contemporary villas and suites, all with their own plunge pool, most with outdoor bathrooms. There's also a main, infinity-edge swimming pool, which forms the central hub of the resort, along with the sociable bar and excellent restaurant. The very good spa stretches up the hillside behind, with a steam room built into the rocks. Other activities include kayaking, cooking and massage classes. B16,500
Baan Panburi Village Southern end of Thong Nai Pan Yai ☎077 238599 or 077 445075, ⓦbaanpanburivillage .com. Two rows of well-designed bungalows with verandas and deckchairs run down a slope dotted with wicker hammocks, either side of a small, artificial waterfall.

Choose between old-style, thatched, wood-and-bamboo huts with mosquito nets, fans and cold showers, and large, wooden, a/c affairs with hot water and tiled floors. Free kayaks. Fan B600, a/c B1300
★ **Dolphin** Southern end of Thong Nai Pan Yai ⓔkimgiet@hotmail.com (no phone bookings). Popular, tranquil spot, overgrown with lush vegetation and with lots of comfortable *salas* and hammocks to recline in. The 26 large, very clean, en-suite bungalows come with either fans (some with hot water for B800) or a/c and hot showers; the latter include big family affairs and family rooms (both B2500) with silk cushions and other nice decorative touches. Also has an appealing clothes and crafts boutique, Karma, on the main road in Thong Nai Pan Yai. Fan B600, a/c B1500

EATING

Dolphin Southern end of Thong Nai Pan Yai. Good, mellow beachfront restaurant serving Western breakfasts, great coffee, lasagne (B220) and other pastas, salads,

sandwiches and Thai food, plus tapas in the evening. Daily 8.30am–4.30pm & 6.30pm–late.

The north coast

The largest indent on the **north coast**, Ao Chaloaklam, has long been a famous R&R spot for fishermen from all over the Gulf of Thailand, with sometimes as many as a hundred trawlers littering the broad and sheltered bay. As a tourist destination, it has little to recommend it – save that its village, **Ban Chaloaklam**, can easily be reached from Thong Sala, 10km away, by songthaew (B150) along a paved road – but the small, quiet beaches to the east, Hat Khom and Hat Khuat, have much more to offer.

Hat Khom

Dramatically tucked in under Ao Chaloaklam's eastern headland is the tiny cove of **HAT KHOM**. Linked to the outside world by a partly paved road, it offers a handful of simple bungalows, a secluded strip of white sand and good coral for snorkelling.

Hat Khuat (Bottle Beach)

If the sea is not too rough, longtail boats run several times a day for most of the year from Ban Chaloaklam (east of the fishing pier; B100/person or about B600/boat) to isolated **HAT KHUAT** (**BOTTLE BEACH**), the best of the beaches on the north coast, sitting between steep, jungle-clad hills in a perfect cup of a bay that's good for swimming. You could also walk there along a testing trail from Hat Khom in around ninety minutes.

ACCOMMODATION	THE NORTH COAST

Coral Bay Hat Khom ☎077 374245. Friendly, laidback outfit with plenty of space and great views on the grassy, flower-strewn promontory dividing Hat Khom from Ao Chaloaklam. The sturdy bungalows range from simple affairs with shared bathrooms and no fans to large pads with a/c and hot showers, some with funky bathrooms built into the rock; snorkelling equipment can be rented to make the most of Hat Khom's reef. Phone ahead to ask about their daily transfers from Thong Sala. Fan B200, a/c B1200

Haad Khuad Resort Hat Khuat ☎077 445153–4, ⓦhaadkhuadresort.com. Well-organized spot in the middle of the bay, offering deluxe rooms in a two-storey hotel block with view-filled French windows, a/c, hot water, TV, DVD-players, mini-bars and breakfast included. Also has a choice of wooden or concrete fan bungalows with cold showers on the beachfront and in the garden. Kayaks available. Four daily transfers from Thong Sala (B400/person). Closed mid-Oct to mid-Dec. Fan B250, a/c B1500

EATING

L'Oasi 1km south of Ban Chaloaklam on the main road ☎086 470 4253. A handy, congenial spot for lunch on a round-island tour. As well as burgers and barbecues, it serves up tasty Italian specialities such as pizza, panini and spaghetti with pesto (B250) and decent wine by the glass, in a pretty garden setting with a small kids' playground. Daily 11am–9.30pm.

The west coast

Pha Ngan's **west coast** has attracted about the same amount of development as the forgettable south coast, but the landscape here is more attractive and varied, broken up into a series of long sandy inlets with good sunset views over the islands of the Ang Thong National Marine Park to the west. Most of the bays, however, are sheltered by reefs which can keep the sea too shallow for a decent swim, especially between May and October.

Laem Son Lake and Ao Chaophao

About halfway up the west coast from Thong Sala, there's a surprise in store in the shape of **Laem Son Lake**, a tranquil stretch of clear water cordoned by pines; however, you should avoid swimming here, as the lake, site of a former tin mine, is apparently considered toxic. Beyond, on the small, pretty bay of **AO CHAOPHAO**, there's good accommodation and food at *Seaflower*.

Hat Yao

North of Chaophao, the long, gently curved, fine-sand beach of **HAT YAO** is gradually and justifiably becoming busier and more popular, with several stand-alone bars, diving outfits, a 7-Eleven supermarket, a currency-exchange booth, ATMs and jeep and bike rental, as well as a nonstop line of bungalows. **Boat trips** from here to Hat Salad, Ao Mae Hat, Hat Khom, Bottle Beach and either Thong Nai Pan or Than Sadet waterfall (B750/person, including snorkels) can be arranged, for example, through *Ibiza Bungalows* or directly with Khun Tonan (☎086 279 0166 or ☎077 349139).

Hat Salad

To the north of Hat Yao, **HAT SALAD** is another pretty bay, sheltered and sandy, with good snorkelling off the northern tip. On the access road behind the beach is a rather untidy service village of shops, travel agents, bike and jeep rental outlets and internet offices. Take your pick from a dozen or so bungalow outfits.

Ao Mae Hat

On the island's northwest corner, **AO MAE HAT** is good for swimming and snorkelling among the coral that lines the sandy causeway to the tiny islet of Ko Maa. The broad, coarse-sand bay supports several bungalow resorts.

ARRIVAL AND GETTING AROUND · THE WEST COAST

There's a paved coastal road up as far as Hat Salad, where it loops inland to meet the main inland road from Thong Sala via the hospital to Ao Mae Hat.

By songthaew Songthaews from Thong Sala, the island capital, serve all of the beaches on the west coast, charging B150/person to go as far as Hat Yao, for example.

ACCOMMODATION

AO SEETHANU

Loy Fa ☎077 377319, ⓦloyfanaturalresort.com. Well-run, flower-strewn place that commands good views from its perch on the steep southern cape of otherwise nondescript Ao Seethanu. There's good snorkelling and swimming from its private beach below, as well as a decent-sized pool. Bungalows are scattered around the hilltop and the slope down on the beach, and come with fan and hot showers (one with an outdoor bathroom) or a/c, hot water and mini-bar (some with TV); villas with private pools are planned. Internet access, free wi-fi, kayaks and bicycles are available. Fan B1000, a/c B1800

AO CHAOPHAO

Seaflower ☎077 349090, ⓦseaflowerbungalows.com. Quiet spot, set in a lush garden, with good veggie and non-veggie food. En-suite bungalows with their own hot-water bathrooms vary in price according to their size and age: the newer ones – more like cottages – have marble open-air bathrooms and big balcony seating areas. Wi-fi and snorkels available, as well as fishing and snorkelling day-trips and occasional overnighters to Ang Thong National Marine Park (see p.254). Fan B650, a/c B1700

HAT YAO

Ibiza Bungalows ☎077 349121, ⓦibizabungalow .com. Lively, central spot on a spacious lawn with mature trees for shade. The 34 airy bungalows run the full gamut, from fan and cold-water offerings near the beach (pay B100 extra to be right on the beach) to a/c, hot-shower affairs. There's also internet access, snorkelling equipment, a branch of Lotus Diving (see p.256) and an ATM. Fan B500, a/c B800

Long Bay Resort ☎077 349057, ⓦphangan.info /longbay. Hat Yao's nicest upmarket spot boasts a long stretch of beach and spacious gardens towards the north end of the bay. Choose between small but smart bungalows and a range of large cottages, all with a/c and hot water. There's an attractive swimming pool and kayaks and snorkels to rent. Breakfast included. B2000

Shiralea ☎080 719 9256 or ☎077 349217, ⓦshiralea .net. On a broad, grassy bank beneath coconut trees behind the north end of the beach, the spacious, very attractive thatched bungalows here all come with hot water, and there's a seductive pool, a dive school and free wi-fi. Fan B600, a/c B1200

HAT SALAD

★ **Salad Hut** ☎077 349246, ⓦsaladhut.com. Among the dozen or so bungalow outfits here, this congenial, family-friendly and well-run old-timer stands out. Parallel to the beachfront behind a swimming pool, in a shady, colourful garden, are twelve stylish bungalows done out in dark woods, red and white, with day beds with axe cushions and large verandas. All come with hot water, mini-bar and TV, and a cooked breakfast at the chic bar-restaurant is included. Computers, wi-fi and snorkel and kayak rental. Fan B1900, a/c B2200

AO MAE HAT

Wang Sai Resort ☎077 374238, ⓔwangsaikohma @live.com. Popular, friendly spot by a shady creek at the south end of the bay. On a huge plot of land, most of the en-suite bungalows are set back from the beach, with fans and cold showers – pay B200 extra for those that are up the slope, with great sunset views. The best and most expensive are across the creek on the beach, all with a/c, some with hot water. Free wi-fi in the restaurant, on-site dive school and kayaks and snorkels for rent. Fan B600, a/c B1000

EATING AND DRINKING

Most people staying on the west coast eat and drink at their resort, but one bar here is worth a detour.

AO CHAOPHAO

Pirates Bar ☎ 084 728 6064. On its own tiny beach cove (reached by a short wooden walkway at the south end of Ao Chaophao), with a stonking sound system right on the sand, this is a great place for regular parties, especially its popular Moon Set party, three nights before the full moon. Evenings till late.

Ko Tao

KO TAO (Turtle Island) is so named because its outline resembles a turtle nose-diving towards Ko Pha Ngan, 40km to the south. The rugged shell of the turtle, to the east, is crenellated with secluded coves where one or two bungalows hide among the rocks. On the western side, the turtle's underbelly is a long curve of classic beach, **Hat Sai Ree**, facing **Ko Nang Yuan**, a beautiful Y-shaped group of islands offshore, also known as Ko Hang Tao (Turtle's Tail Island). The 21 square kilometres of granite in between is topped by dense forest on the higher slopes and dotted with huge boulders that look as if they await some Easter Island sculptor. It's fun to spend a couple of days exploring the network of rough trails, after which you'll probably know all 1700 of the island's inhabitants. Ko Tao is now best known as a venue for **scuba-diving courses**, with a wide variety of dive sites in close proximity (see p.270).

The island is the last and most remote of the archipelago that continues the line of Surat Thani's mountains into the sea. It served as a jail for political prisoners from 1933 to 1947, then was settled by a family from Ko Pha Ngan. Now, there are around 150 sets of **bungalows** for visitors, just about enough to cope during the peak seasons of December to March and August, concentrated along the west and south sides; they include a rapidly growing number of upscale resorts with such luxuries as air conditioning, hot water and swimming pools. There's a limited government supply of electricity, so some of it still comes from private generators on the remotest beaches, usually evenings only.

If you're just arriving and want to stay on one of the less accessible beaches, it might be a good idea to go with one of the touts who meet the ferries at **Mae Hat**, the island's main village, with pick-up or boat on hand, since at least you'll know their bungalows aren't full; otherwise call ahead, as even the remotest bungalows now have landlines or mobile phones and most owners come to market once a day (pick-ups are either free or B50–150/person). Some resorts with attached scuba-diving operations have been known to refuse guests who don't sign up for diving trips or courses; on the other hand, most of the dive companies now have their own lodgings, available free or at a discounted price to divers. With a year-round customer base of divers – and resident dive instructors – a growing number of sophisticated Western **restaurants** and **bars** are springing up all the time, notably in Mae Hat and on Hat Sai Ree. For nightlife, your best bet is to watch out for posters advertising weekly and monthly parties around the island, which keep the crowds rotating.

BOAT TOURS AND SNORKELLING ON KO TAO

Round-island **boat tours** are available at Mae Hat or through your bungalow, with stops for snorkelling and swimming (B650/person, including lunch and pick-ups, or around B2000 to hire your own longtail boat for the day); these take in snorkelling in the Japanese Gardens off Ko Nang Yuan, but you'll have to pay the B100 entrance fee if you set foot on the island to climb up to the viewpoint. Some dive companies will take along **snorkellers**, usually on their afternoon trips, when they visit the shallower sites; Davy Jones' Locker (☎ 077 456604, ⓦ davyjoneslockerasia.com) at *Silver Sands Resort* in Ban Hat Sai Ree, for example, charges B650.

KO TAO

ACCOMMODATION
Ananda Villa	15
Ao Leuk II	20
Blue Wind	7
Family	18
Hin Wong Bungalows	6
Jamahkiri	23
Koh Tao Backpackers Hostel	11
Koh Tao Cabana	4
Koh Tao Coral Grand Resort	5
Mango Bay Grand Resort	1
Mr J's Bungalows	14
Nangyuan Island Dive Resort	2
New Heaven Huts	24
New Heaven Resort	25
Sai Ree Cottages	13
Sattva Gardens	19
Save Bungalows	16
Seashell Resort	12
Sensi Paradise	17
Silver Sands	10
Sunsetburi Resort	8
Tao Thong Villa	21
Thipwimarn Resort	3
Viewpoint Bungalows	22
Wind Beach Resort	9

The **weather** is much the same as on Pha Ngan and Samui (see p.55), but being that bit further off the mainland, Ko Tao feels the effect of the southwest monsoon more: June to October can have strong winds and rain, with a lot of debris blown onto the windward coasts.

ARRIVAL AND DEPARTURE

KO TAO

All boats to Ko Tao dock at Mae Hat. Boat services and prices fluctuate according to demand, and in high season extra boats may appear. Voyages to and from Ko Tao may also be affected by the weather at any time between June and January.

FROM CHUMPHON AND BANGKOK
The main jumping-off point for boats to Ko Tao is Chumphon (see p.230), which is connected to Bangkok by train and bus. The two main Chumphon–Ko Tao boat companies both offer through-tickets from Bangkok; with Lomprayah (on Ko Tao ☎ 077 456176, ⓦ lomprayah .com), for example, this costs B950–1050, including a VIP bus from their office on Thanon Ram Bhuttri (☎ 02 629 2569–70), via Hua Hin (see p.217). It's better to buy a Bangkok–Tao through-ticket direct from the boat company's office in the capital rather than from a travel agency, otherwise you're unlikely to get your money back if the boat turns out to be full, which is possible in high season, or is cancelled because of very bad weather.

FROM KO PHA NGAN AND KO SAMUI
Three companies currently operate daily scheduled boats between Thong Sala on Ko Pha Ngan and Ko Tao. Songserm (on Ko Tao ☎ 086 273 0389 or ☎ 077 456274, ⓦ songserm-expressboat.com) does the voyage in around 2hr (1 daily; B300). Lomprayah (see above) and Seatran (on Ko Tao ☎ 077 456497–8, ⓦ seatrandiscovery.com) cover the ground in about 1hr 15min (both 2 daily; B400). The Lomprayah catamaran originates at Maenam, Seatran at Bangrak, on Ko Samui (total journey time to Ko Tao on either about 2hr; B600).

FROM SURAT THANI
With Lomprayah If you're coming from Surat Thani, you could take Lomprayah's Don Sak–Na Thon (Samui)–Thong Sala catamaran all the way to Ko Pha Ngan, then change onto its Maenam (Samui)–Thong Sala–Ko Tao service (total journey time from Surat about 6hr; B700).
With the night boat There's a night boat from Ban Don pier in Surat Thani town, departing at 11pm (☎ 077 284928 or ☎ 081 326 8973; 8hr; B550); in the opposite direction, this leaves Ko Tao at 9pm.

3

GETTING AROUND
You can **get around** easily enough on foot, but there are roads of sorts now to most of the resorts, though many are still very rough tracks, suitable for four-wheel drive only.

By motorbike taxi or pick-up Motorbike taxis (B100 to Chaloke Ban Kao, for example) and pick-ups (B100/person to Chaloke Ban Kao, for example, minimum 2 people; rates are higher at night, or for a 4WD to somewhere more remote) are available in Mae Hat.
By moped Rental mopeds are available from B150/day. If you can, resist the temptation to rent a quad bike, or ATV – not only do they have a disproportionate number of accidents, but they're also very polluting. As on Ko Phangan, there have been lots of reports of travellers being charged exorbitant amounts if they bring the vehicle back with even the most minor damage – avoid the outfits in front of the main pier in Mae Hat, and rent from your bungalow or someone reliable like Mr J (see p.272) or Save

---

ECO TAO

With so many divers and other visitors coming to this tiny island, the pressures on the environment, both above and below the waterline, are immense. To minimize your impact, look out for the work of a community group, **Save Koh Tao** (ⓦ savekohtao.com), which has been formed among concerned locals and resident Westerners, with a sub-group devoted to marine conservation (ⓦ marineconservationkohtao.com, which features a list of the dive schools that are involved in the various conservation projects). Activities include a turtle-release programme, erosion control, a campaign for septic tanks to stop waste water being run straight into the sea, coral nurseries and more than half a dozen artificial reefs around Ko Tao, which allow divers to practise their skills without damaging coral. Their monthly land and underwater clean-ups are given a big splash once a year, during the two-day **Underwater Festival** in March, which involves mass beach-cleaning, fundraising, live bands and turtle releasing. Look out also for **Sabai Jai**, a free quarterly eco-travel magazine produced by the owner of Yakuzen Japanese Bath Village.

Much of what visitors can do to help is common sense: avoiding littering, recycling where possible and turning down plastic bags when you're shopping. The island suffers from a scarcity of water, with occasional droughts during the hot season after a poor rainy season, so conserve water whenever possible. In the sea, the main rule is not to touch the coral, which may mean avoiding snorkelling when the water is low from April to September – if in doubt, ask locally for advice, be careful and go out at high tide. Don't take away dead shells, and don't buy coral or shell jewellery. If you're feeling really keen, check whether your bungalow resort has a septic tank. And some dive schools have a Save Koh Tao donation box.

DIVING OFF KO TAO

Some of the best **dive sites** in Thailand are found off Ko Tao, which is blessed with outstandingly clear (visibility up to 35m), safe and relatively deep water close in to shore. On top of that, there's a kaleidoscopic array of coral species and other marine life, and you may be lucky enough to encounter whale sharks, barracudas, leatherback turtles and pilot whales. Diving is possible at any time of year, with sheltered sites on one or other side of the island in any **season** – the changeover from southwest to northeast monsoon in November is the worst time, while **visibility** is best from April to July, in September (usually best of all) and October. Ko Tao supports several evacuation centres, clinics that specialize in diving medicine, while the nearest recompression chamber is on Ko Samui, ninety minutes away by speedboat (see p.237).

DIVE COMPANIES, COURSES AND TRIPS

Ko Tao has about fifty **dive companies**, making this the largest dive-training centre in Southeast Asia; most of them are staffed by Westerners and based at Mae Hat, Hat Sai Ree or Ao Chaloke Ban Kao. You'll generally be offered discounted or free accommodation while you're diving, but ask exactly how long it's for (three or four nights for an Openwater course), where it is and what it's like. **Operators** on Ko Tao include Crystal (☎077 456106–7, ✆crystaldive.com), a large, lively, sociable PADI 5-Star Career Development Centre, with two swimming pools, three big boats and a speedboat, offering courses in fifteen languages and the chance to buy videos of your dives plus a wide choice of good accommodation in two resorts on the north side of Mae Hat. At the other end of the scale are schools that are small, personal and laidback (though with no compromising on safety) such as New Heaven in Chaloke Ban Kao (☎077 457045, ✆newheavendiveschool.com), which boasts of later starts and a maximum of four people on each course, and will take snorkellers along on their dive trips. Both of these companies have a strong commitment to marine conservation (also check out the website of Crystal's marine conservation department, ✆ecokohtao.com, which features internships in various specialities) and run reef conservation and research programmes for qualified divers among many other activities. You'll find further advice on choosing a dive company in Basics (see p.51).

By far the most popular **course**, PADI's four-day "Openwater" for beginners, costs around B9800 in high season with a reputable dive centre. One-day introductions to diving are also available for B2000, as is the full menu of PADI courses, up to "Instructor".

For **qualified divers**, one dive typically costs B1000, a ten-dive package B7000, with fifteen-percent discounts if you bring your own gear. Among specialities, Crystal (see above) offers nitrox and underwater photography and videography courses, while Tech Thailand (✆techthailand.com), affiliated to Master Divers in Mae Hat, covers technical and wreck diving.

Shop, on the front street, just south of the piers (☎077 456347).

By mountain bike Mountain bikes can be rented from in front of the mini-golf course, on the southern edge of Mae Hat on the Chaloke Ban Kao road (☎089 675 5798; B100/day, or B80/day for rentals of two days or more).

INFORMATION

Koh Tao Info There isn't a TAT office on Ko Tao, but the regularly updated and widely available free booklet, *Koh Tao Info*, is a useful source of information, along with its associated website, ✆kohtaoonline.com, which allows online accommodation booking.

Mae Hat and around

MAE HAT, a small, lively village and port in a pleasant, beachfront setting, boasts the lion's share of the island's amenities. A paved high street heads straight up the hill from the main pier (eventually ending up in Ao Chaloke Ban Kao), with a narrower front street running at right angles, parallel to the seafront. Three of the ferry companies each have their own pier, Lomprayah and Songserm to the south of the main one, Seatran to the north.

MAIN DIVE SITES

Ko Nang Yuan Surrounded by a variety of sites, with assorted hard and soft corals and an abundance of fish: the Nang Yuan Pinnacle, a granite pinnacle with boulder swim-throughs, morays and reef sharks; Green Rock, a maze of boulder swim-throughs, caves and canyons, featuring stingrays and occasional reef sharks; Twins, two rock formations covered in corals and sponges, with a colourful coral garden as a backdrop; and the Japanese Gardens, on the east side of the sand causeway, which get their name from the hundreds of hard and soft coral formations here and are good for beginners and popular among snorkellers.

White Rock (**Hin Khao**) Between Hat Sai Ree and Ko Nang Yuan, where sarcophyton leather coral turns the granite boulders white when seen from the surface; also wire, antipatharian and colourful soft corals, and gorgonian sea fans. Plenty of fish, including titan triggerfish, butterfly fish, angelfish, clown fish and morays.

Shark Island Large granite boulders with acropora, wire and bushy antipatharian corals, sea whips, gorgonian sea fans and barrel sponges. Reef fish include angelfish, triggerfish and barracuda; there's a resident turtle, and leopard and reef sharks may be found as well as occasional whale sharks.

Hinwong Pinnacle At Ao Hinwong; generally for experienced divers, often with strong currents. Similar scenery to White Rock, over a larger area, with beautiful soft coral at 30m depth. A wide range of fish, including blue-spotted fantail stingrays,

sweetlips pufferfish and boxfish, as well as hawksbill turtles.

Chumphon or **Northwest Pinnacle** A granite pinnacle for experienced divers, starting 14m underwater and dropping off to over 36m, its top covered in anemones; surrounded by several smaller formations and offering the possibility of exceptional visibility. Barrel sponges, tree and antipatharian corals at deeper levels; a wide variety of fish, in large numbers, attract local fishermen; barracudas, batfish, whale sharks (seasonal) and huge groupers.

Southwest Pinnacle One of the top sites in terms of visibility, scenery and marine life for experienced divers. A huge pyramid-like pinnacle rising to 6m below the surface, its upper part covered in anemones, with smaller pinnacles around; at lower levels, granite boulders, barrel sponges, sea whips, bushy antipatharian and tree corals. Big groupers, snappers and barracudas; occasionally, large rays, leopard and sand sharks, swordfish, finback whales and whale sharks.

Sail Rock (**Hin Bai**) Midway between Ko Tao and Ko Pha Ngan, emerging from the sand at a depth of 40m and rising 15m above the sea's surface. Visibility of up to 30m, and an amazing 10m underwater chimney (vertical swim-through). Antipatharian corals, both bushes and whips, and carpets of anemones. Large groupers, snappers and fusiliers, blue-ringed angelfish, batfish, kingfish, juvenile clown sweetlips and barracuda; a possible spot for sighting whale sharks and mantas.

Yakuzen Japanese Bath Village

Up a small hill on the southeast side of the village, inland from the Songserm pier • B500 per person, minimum 5 people • Visits by appointment on ☎ 084 837 3385

The delightful, eco-friendly **Yakuzen Japanese Bath Village** is highly recommended. Under the stars and the coconut palms here, you can relax in five landscaped bathing pools among the boulders, each set at a different temperature and made with different textures of rock and wood, and massage yourself with herbal compresses. There's also a daytime café (closed Wed) serving drinks, snacks and desserts, and a very good restaurant, *Kakureya* (see p.272).

ACCOMMODATION

Ananda Villa North end of the village, on the beach ☎ 077 456478, ⓦ anandavilla.com. Cute, well-designed and maintained a/c rooms in a two-storey block, sporting French windows that give onto balconies with wooden balustrades. Inside, silks and other decorative touches set off the dark-wood furniture; facilities include large,

MAE HAT AND AROUND

hot-water bathrooms, TVs, DVD-players and fridges. Also has some fan rooms that are tiny but boast hot showers. Fan B500, a/c B1800

Mr J's Bungalows Behind Mr J's supermarket (see p.272), a 5min walk north of Mae Hat ☎ 077 456066–7. If you just want functional, reliable, good-value accommodation, come to this place, which offers large, clean rooms, with hot showers in some of the a/c offerings. Fan with shared bathroom B250, a/c B800

Save Bungalows At the Save Shop supermarket on the front street, just south of the piers ☎077 456347. Owned by the same family as Mr J's, with a similar ethos: clean, good-value, functional bungalows, most with en-suite cold or hot showers. Fan with shared bathroom B250, fan en-suite B500, a/c B1000

Sensi Paradise On the lower slopes of the headland just south of the village ☎077 456244, ✆kohtao paradise.com. Charming resort in flower-covered grounds, offering a pretty beachside restaurant, an attractive free-

form pool, free snorkelling equipment and some of the best upmarket accommodation on the island: well-designed wooden Thai-style cottages and villas with mini-bars, some with a/c and hot showers and some with large terraces and open-air bathrooms. Breakfast included. B2900

Tao Thong Villa 50min walk south of Mae Hat (about B150/person in a taxi-boat) ☎077 456078. Sturdy, en-suite bungalows dotted around a rocky outcrop and the slope behind, with a breezy restaurant on the tiny, grassy isthmus with two small beaches in between. Plenty of shady seclusion, great views and good snorkelling and swimming. B500

EATING AND DRINKING

Cappuccino 100m from the pier, up the high street on the left ☎077 456870. French-run café and bakery that does a mean pain au chocolat, plus gourmet sandwiches and burgers and salads. Daily 6.30am–6pm.

★ **Kakureya** Yakuzen Japanese Bath Village (see p.271) ☎087 936 2160 or ☎086 059 0408. Small, relaxing and thoroughly authentic Japanese restaurant, serving the best food on the island. Don't miss the excellent tasting set (B140) as a starter, which you might follow with grilled salmon (B180), sashimi (from B340 for a set) or hot or cold noodles. Asahi beer on draught and a good choice of sake. Closed June & Nov. Daily except Wed 5–9.30pm.

Moov On the southeast side of the village, inland from the Songserm pier. Chilled-out bar-restaurant with a Belgian chef and plenty of sofas to recline on in the house and on the big lawn at the back. Tasty global tapas

(under B100) include wonton and sweet potato falafels. Fleamarket first Sun of every month. Daily 3pm–late.

Tukta About 2km out on the Chaloke Ban Kao road. Relaxing, cheap restaurant – open-sided with a few garden tables – serving a wide choice of tasty Thai food, including a good kaeng matsaman with chicken. Daily 8am–10pm.

★ **Whitening** 200m south of the main pier down the front street ☎077 456199. Congenial, mellow and chic bar-restaurant with a great deck and relaxing beach tables overlooking the bay. It dishes up some very tasty Thai food, such as green curries (B130), and more creative, pricier Western food, as well as good cocktails. Daily 1pm–midnight (kitchen closes 11pm).

Zest 100m from the pier up the high street ☎077 456178. Very good coffees, pastries, salads and a huge range of sandwiches (roast beef and horseradish sauce B75). Delivery service available. Daily 6am–6pm.

SHOPPING

Little Book and Old Dog Just off the high street on the south side, in front of the main pier. Sells second-hand books and newspapers and magazines. Daily 9.30am–4.30pm & 6.30–9.30pm.

Mr J 5min walk north of Mae Hat. At the top of a small

rise opposite the primary school you'll find the head office of Ko Tao's all-purpose fixer and all-round character, Mr J. Here you can rent motorbikes, recycle batteries and buy and sell secondhand books.

DIRECTORY

Banks Thanachat (Siam City Bank), up the high street on the left, with an ATM.

Health Mae Hat has a small government health centre (halfway up the high street, turn right) plus several private clinics and pharmacies.

Police station A 5min walk north of Mat Hat, on the

narrow road towards Hat Sai Ree (☎077 456631).

Post office At the top of the village (turn left and left again at the top of the high street), near the start of the main paved road to Ban Hat Sai Ree (Mon–Fri 9am–5pm, Sat 9am–noon).

Hat Sai Ree

To the north of Mae Hat, beyond a small promontory, you'll find **Hat Sai Ree**, Ko Tao's only long beach. The strip of white sand stretches for 2km in a gentle curve, backed by a smattering of coconut palms and scores of bungalow resorts. Around the northerly end of the beach spreads **BAN HAT SAI REE**, a burgeoning village of supermarkets,

HAT SAI REE ACTIVITIES

The main organizers of activities on Hat Sai Ree are the folk at Goodtime Adventures, towards the southern end of the beach (☎087 275 3604, ⓦgtadventures.com), who specialize in **rock-climbing** and **bouldering**, including courses for beginners. They also organize **abseiling**, **hiking** and a **zipline** adventure on Ko Nang Yuan, as well as pub crawls. **Yoga** classes are held at Blue Wind Bungalows (see below; 1–2 daily, not Sun; B300; ☎084 440 6755, ⓔshambhalayoga@yahoo.co.nz).

clinics, pharmacies, travel agents, internet outlets, a Thanachat (Siam City Bank) currency-exchange booth with an ATM, restaurants and bars. A narrow, mostly paved track runs along the back of the beach between Mae Hat and Ban Hat Sai Ree, paralleled by the main road further inland.

ACCOMMODATION HAT SAI REE

★ **Blue Wind** Two doors north of Sunsetburi Resort ☎077 456116, ⓔbluewindkohtao@hotmail.com. This popular old-timer offers a variety of well-kept, en-suite rooms and bungalows scattered about a shady compound, including some very smart new constructions with clapboard walls, four-poster beds with mosquito nets and nice balcony furniture. It also has a good restaurant with free wi-fi (see p.274). Fan and cold shower B350, fan and hot water B800, a/c and hot water B1400

Koh Tao Backpackers Hostel Ban Hat Sai Ree, inland from Silver Sands Resort ☎077 601828, ⓦkohtao backpackers.com. Functional, eight-bed dorms with a/c and hot showers in a small, concrete building set back from the beach. Free use of Davy Jones' Locker's pool, discounts on their dive courses and at their bar-restaurant. Dorm B300

Koh Tao Cabana Far north end of beach ☎077 456504–5, ⓦkohtaocabana.com. Welcoming, rustic-chic luxury resort and spa on a long beach frontage, backed by pleasant lawns that are dotted with elegant day beds. All the thatched, a/c rooms feature open-air bathrooms with hot water: choose between round, adobe-style villas up the slope behind the beach and stilted cottages on the headland, some with fantastic views and some with private pools. Breakfast included. B3700

Koh Tao Coral Grand Resort North of Ban Hat Sai Ree ☎077 456432, ⓦkohtaocoral.com. Welcoming luxury beachfront development with a dive school, where the sandstone-pink octagonal cottages with polished coconut-wood floors and attractive bathrooms gather – some a little tightly – around a pretty, Y-shaped pool; all have hot water, TV, free wi-fi and a/c. Breakfast included. B4050

Sai Ree Cottages Towards the midpoint of the beach, a 20min walk from Mae Hat ☎077 456374, ⓦsairee cottagediving.com. In a large, beautiful, flower-strewn garden, the full spectrum of digs, all en suite and well maintained, from basic rooms and bungalows with cold showers, all the way up to Thai-style villas on the beach with TV, fridge and breakfast included (fan B2000, a/c B2500). Also offers dorm beds with access to hot shower,

TV and fridge (fan B250, a/c B350). Kayaks and snorkels for rent, dive school and excellent grub. Fan and cold shower B350, fan and hot shower B800, a/c and hot shower B1300

Seashell Resort Near the midpoint of the beach, next door to Sai Ree Cottages ☎077 456299–300, ⓦseashell-resort.com. In a spacious, tidy compound, a friendly, well-run place with a dive school that's been very successfully upgraded. Facilities now include two pools, one with a jacuzzi, a spa, a popular seafood restaurant and computers and free wi-fi in the lobby (paid wi-fi available in the rooms). Among the a/c, hot-water rooms, it's well worth paying a little extra for the new "Superior Garden View" offerings (B2420), which have a very attractive, contemporary look with dark wood furniture; those on the first floor have nice big balconies. Breakfast included. B2130

Silver Sands Ban Hat Sai Ree ☎077 456603–6, ⓦsilver-sands-resort.com. Clean, well-kept bungalows and rooms, nearly all of them with hot water, on a narrow but lush and shady plot. Among its bungalows, the cheapest are simple wooden affairs well off the beach, while the priciest are beachside, a/c and cottage-like. New, distressed-concrete rooms, however, in a two-storey hotel block at the back of the compound are more industrial than chic and probably not worth the money. Guests can use the adjacent pool at the affiliated dive company, Davy Jones' Locker. Fan and free wi-fi at reception and snorkels to rent. Fan B800, a/c bungalow B1800, a/c room B2500

Sunsetburi Resort Ban Hat Sai Ree ☎077 457101, ☎077 456101. On a narrow but flower-strewn strip of land with a beachside swimming pool, modern, concrete cottages with TVs and mini-bars, many with a/c and some with the luxury of hot water, as well as a hotel block of a/c, hot-water rooms right at the back on the main road. Fan B700, a/c B1200

Thipwimarn Resort North of Hat Sai Ree, opposite Ko Nang Yuan ☎077 456409, ⓦthipwimarnresort .com. Stylish, eco-friendly, upscale spot with a spa, which

3

tumbles down a steep slope, past an elevated, infinity-edge swimming pool, to its own small beach. Dotted around the hillside, smart, thatched, whitewashed, a/c villas, most with hot water, enjoy a fair measure of seclusion, satellite TV, DVD-players, mini-bars and fine sunset views. Breakfast included. **B3800**

Wind Beach Resort Ban Hat Sai Ree ☏ 077 456082, ⊛ windbeach-resort.com. Welcoming, recently renovated resort lined with mature trees and offering lots of facilities: free wi-fi in the restaurant and nearby rooms, a travel agency, a dive school, massage, and kayaks and snorkels for rent. The choice of rooms and bungalows is also wide-ranging, including some large, very stylish, a/c hotel rooms in two-storey buildings with hot showers, TVs, fridges and breakfast included (B2000). Fan and cold water **B500**, fan and hot water **B700**, a/c and hot water **B1300**

EATING AND DRINKING

★ **Blue Wind** Two doors north of Sunsetburi Resort ☏ 077 456116. Very good beachside restaurant serving home-made breads, cakes, croissants and fruit shakes, as well as Indian and Thai food (B70 for a green curry), home-made pasta, pizzas and other Western meals. Daily 8am–10pm.

Choppers On the main transverse road down to the beach. Popular, well-run, full-service bar, with good food, plenty of imported bottled and draught beers and no fewer than sixteen screens for TV sports. Plenty of offers on drink, including happy hours 4–8pm. Live music from 9pm. Daily 9am–late.

Fizz On the beach at Silver Sands Resort. Chic bar-restaurant, where you can sink into the green beanbags and soak up some mellow sounds over a drink, or sit up for some very good food: there's a long menu of Thai dishes (most under B100) and Western food, including veggie options, pasta, salads and very tasty grilled tuna with mango salsa (B260). Evenings till late.

Lotus Bar On the beach near New Heaven Deli & Bakery. Raucous, very popular late-night haunt for drinking and dancing, with fire shows and regular parties. Happy hour 4–7pm. Evenings till very late.

New Heaven Deli & Bakery On the beach road on the south side of the village. Stylish spot offering great home-baked breads and cakes, as well as sandwiches, salads, pizzas, ice cream, espressos and booster juices, plus free wi-fi. Daily 7am–8pm.

Ko Nang Yuan

One kilometre off the northwest of Ko Tao, **KO NANG YUAN**, a close-knit group of three tiny islands, provides the most spectacular beach scenery in these parts, thanks to the causeway of fine white sand that joins up the islands. You can easily swim off the east side of the causeway to snorkel over the Japanese Gardens, which feature hundreds of hard and soft coral formations.

ARRIVAL AND DEPARTURE   KO NANG YUAN

By boat Boats from the Lomprayah pier in Mae Hat, just south of the main pier, run back and forth twice a day (B200 return), and there are other, irregular services from Hat Sai Ree. Note that rules to protect the environment here include banning all visitors from bringing cans, plastic bottles and fins with them, and day-trippers are charged B100 to land on the island. Lomprayah charge B550 for an all-in day-trip, including boat transfers, snorkelling, buffet lunch and island fee.

ACCOMMODATION AND EATING

Nangyuan Island Dive Resort ☏ 077 456088–93, ⊛ nangyuan.com. The decor at this resort is not much to write home about but it makes the most of its beautiful location, its bungalows, all with en-suite bathrooms, TVs and fridges, most with hot water and some with a/c, spreading over all three islands. There's also a restaurant, a coffee shop and an on-site dive shop. Transfers from and to Mae Hat free for guests. Breakfast included. Fan **B1500**, a/c **B2000**

The north and east coasts

Ao Mamuang (Mango Bay), the lone bay on the **north coast**, is a beautiful, tree-clad bowl, whose shallow reef is a popular stop on snorkelling day-trips, though there's little in the way of a beach. The attractive bar-restaurant of *Mango Bay Grand Resort* spreads its large deck over the rocks here.

The sheltered inlets of the **east coast**, most of them containing one or two sets of bungalows, can be reached by boat, pick-up or four-wheel-drive. The most northerly habitation here is at **Ao Hinwong**, a deeply recessed, limpid bay strewn with large boulders and great coral reefs, which has a particularly remote, almost desolate air.

In the middle of the coast, the dramatic tiered promontory of Laem Thian shelters on its south side a tiny beach and a colourful reef, which stretches down towards the east coast's most developed bay, **Ao Ta Note**, with half a dozen resorts; the paved road from Mae Hat was about to be completed at the time of writing. Ta Note's horseshoe inlet is sprinkled with boulders and plenty of coarse sand, with excellent snorkelling just north of the bay's mouth.

The last bay carved out of the turtle's shell, **Ao Leuk**, has a well-recessed beach and water that's deep enough for good swimming and snorkelling, featuring hard and soft coral gardens. Snorkels and kayaks are available to rent at the beachfront bar.

ACCOMMODATION   **THE NORTH AND EAST COASTS**

AO MAMUANG

Mango Bay Grand Resort ☏ 077 456948–9, ⓦ kohtao mangobay.com. At this remote resort, the well-appointed, colourful, heavily varnished wooden bungalows on stilts all come with hot water, and some have a/c and TV. Transfers from Mae Hat included. Fan B1500, a/c B2800

AO HINWONG

Hin Wong Bungalows ☏ 077 456006 or ☏ 081 229 4810. The most spacious of this bay's small handful of resorts is welcoming and provides good en-suite accommodation on a steep, grassy slope above the rocks, in wooden bungalows with mosquito nets and large bathrooms. It has a nice waterside deck in front of its restaurant and rents out kayaks and snorkels. B400

AO TA NOTE

Family (Ta Note Bay Resort) ☏ 077 456757–8, ✉ tanotebay@hotmail.com. The pick of the half-dozen resorts here, with a dive centre and plenty of well-designed en-suite wooden bungalows, set among thick bougainvillea, some enjoying large verandas and views out towards Ko Pha

Ngan and Ko Samui. Snorkelling equipment is available, as are computers and wi-fi. Breakfast included with the more expensive rooms. Fan B600, fan and hot shower B1000, a/c and hot shower B1800

AO LEUK

Ao Leuk II ☏ 077 456779, ⓦ aowleuk2.com. Large bungalows and family rooms, with big balconies, fans and hot showers, on the bay's southern cape. Discounts for longer stays. If there happens to be no room here, don't worry – the same friendly family own the bay's other two resorts (including some cheaper, cold-shower bungalows), its taxis and the beachfront bar. B1000

Sattva Gardens (Baan Talay) ☏ 077 457045, ⓦ newheavendiveschool.com. Sustainable, secluded retreat with great views from the hillside above the north side of the bay, owned by New Heaven Dive School (see p.270). Stylish bungalows on stilts sport big verandas, mosquito nets on the beds and indoor-outdoor bathrooms. Big discounts for divers. Fan B1200, fan and hot shower B1800, a/c and hot shower B2500

The south coast

The southeast corner of the island sticks out in a long, thin mole of land, which points towards Shark Island, a colourful diving and snorkelling site just offshore; the headland shelters the sandy beach of **Hat Sai Daeng** on one side if the wind's coming from the northeast, or the rocky cove on the other side if it's blowing from the southwest. Beyond quiet, sandy **Ao Thian Ok**, the next bay along on the south coast, the deep indent of **Ao Chaloke Ban Kao** is protected from the worst of both monsoons, and consequently has seen a fair amount of development, with several dive resorts taking advantage of the large, sheltered, shallow bay, which sometimes gets muddy at low tide. Behind the beach are clinics, ATMs, bike rental shops, bars and restaurants. At New Heaven dive school (see p.270), **yoga** classes are held daily between 5 and 7pm on a veranda overlooking the bay (B300).

On the east side of Ao Chaloke Ban Kao, carved out of the Laem Tato headland, the idyllic white sand of **Freedom Beach** is a secluded palm-lined spot with a beach bar; it's reached by walking through *Taatoh Freedom Beach Bungalows*. A fifteen-minute walk above the bungalows, the last stretch up a steep hillside, will bring you to **Jon-Suwan Mountain Viewpoint**, which affords fantastic views, especially at sunset, over the neighbouring bays of Chaloke Ban Kao and Thian Ok and across to Ko Pha Ngan and Ko Samui.

ACCOMMODATION AND EATING   THE SOUTH COAST

HAT SAI DAENG AND AO THIAN OK

Jamahkiri ☎ 077 456400, ⊕ jamahkiri.com. The remote, rocky coastline between Sai Daeng and Thian Ok provides the spectacular location for this luxurious spa resort. There's a panoramic bar-restaurant, a dive centre and a tiered swimming pool, as well as opulent, secluded rooms and bungalows, in a chic mix of Thai and Western design, with great sea views. Their spa offers saunas, body wraps and massages to guests and non-guests (call for reservation and information about the free, thrice-daily transfers from their Mae Hat office, just north of the main pier). Breakfast included. B6900

New Heaven Huts ☎ 087 933 1329, ⊕ newheaven kohtao.com. Straddling the headland on the east side of Hat Sai Daeng, a laidback, well-equipped place with a good kitchen and snorkelling equipment, whose fourteen pleasantly idiosyncratic, en-suite bungalows – some with hot showers and some big enough for a family – enjoy plenty of elbow room and good views. B600

New Heaven Resort ☎ 077 456462, ⊕ newheaven kohtao.com. A scenic restaurant and attractive bungalows that are easily reached by paved road from Ao Chaloke Ban Kao. On a beautiful deck perched on the eastern flank of Laem Tato, the kitchen (daily 7.30am–9.30pm) specializes in seafood in the evenings (B180 for prawns stir-fried with cashew nuts), as well as offering plenty of vegetarian

options. During the day, you can tuck into sandwiches (such as chicken pesto for B110), pasta and simple Thai fare. The bungalows, set on a tree-covered slope running down to a private sandy beach, feature large bathrooms and verandas with great views, and include a/c rooms with hot showers. Wi-fi. Snorkels for rent. Fan B1700, a/c B2700

AO CHALOKE BAN KAO

Koppee On the main road near the centre of the beach. Lovely little bakery-café with books and magazines to browse and free wi-fi. It offers tasty gourmet sandwiches on a choice of breads, salads such as tuna niçoise (B100), all-day breakfasts and a good choice of drinks and sweet treats. Daily 7.30am–6.30pm (low season) or 8/9pm (high season).

Viewpoint Bungalows ☎ 077 456444, ⊕ kohtao viewpoint.com. Run by a friendly bunch, these distinctive bungalows sprawl along the western side of the bay and around the headland beyond, with great sunset views; architect-designed in chic Balinese style, they boast rock bathrooms, lovely polished hardwood floors, mosquito nets and attractive verandas. There are also half a dozen tasty a/c villas with their own infinity-edge pools (from B8000), as well as kayaks and snorkels to explore the reef just offshore. B1000

Nakhon Si Thammarat

NAKHON SI THAMMARAT, the south's second-largest town, occupies a blind spot in the eyes of most tourists, whose focus is fixed on Ko Samui, 100km to the north. Nakhon's neglect is unfortunate, for it's an absorbing place: the south's major pilgrimage site and home to a huge military base, it's relaxed, self-confident and sophisticated, well known for its excellent cuisine and traditional **handicrafts**. The stores on Thanon Thachang are especially good for local nielloware (*kruang tom*), household items and jewellery, elegantly patterned in gold or silver, often on black, and *yan lipao*, sturdy basketware made from intricately woven fern stems of different colours. Nakhon is also the best place in the country to see how Thai **shadow plays** work, at Suchart Subsin's workshop, and the main jumping-off point for towering **Khao Luang National Park** and its beautiful waterfall, **Krung Ching** (see p.282).

The town is recorded under the name of Ligor (or Lakhon), the capital of the kingdom of Lankasuka, as early as the second century, and classical dance-drama, *lakhon*, is supposed to have been developed here. Well placed for trade with China and southern India (via an overland route from the port of Trang, on the Andaman Sea), Nakhon was the point through which the Theravada form of Buddhism was imported from Sri Lanka and spread to Sukhothai, the capital of the new Thai state, in the thirteenth century.

Orientation in Nakhon is simple, though the layout of the town is puzzling at first sight: it runs in a straight line for 7km from north to south and is rarely more than a few hundred metres wide, a layout originally dictated by the availability of fresh water. The

FESTIVALS IN NAKHON

Known as *muang phra*, the "city of monks", Nakhon is still the religious capital of the south, and the main centre for **festivals**. The most important of these are the **Tamboon Deuan Sip**, held during the waning of the moon in the tenth lunar month (either Sept or Oct), and the **Hae Pha Khun That**, which is held several times a year, but most importantly on Makha Puja, the February full moon, and on Visakha Puja, the May full moon (see p.47). The purpose of Tamboon Deuan Sip is to pay homage to dead relatives and friends; it is believed that during this fifteen-day period all *pret* – ancestors who have been damned to hell – are allowed out to visit the world, and so their relatives perform a merit-making ceremony in the temples, presenting offerings from the first harvest to ease their suffering. A huge ten-day fair takes place at Thung Talaat park on the north side of town at this time, as well as processions, shadow plays and other theatrical performances. The Hae Pha Khun That also attracts people from all over the south, to pay homage to the relics of the Buddha at Wat Mahathat. The centrepiece of this ceremony is the Pha Phra Bot, a strip of yellow cloth many hundreds of metres long, which is carried in a spectacular procession around the chedi.

3

modern centre for businesses and shops sits at the north end around the landmark **Tha Wang intersection**, where Thanon Neramit meets Thanon Ratchadamnoen. To the south, centred on the elegant, traditional mosque on Thanon Karom, lies the old Muslim quarter; south again is the start of the old city walls, of which few remains can be seen, and the historic centre, with the town's main places of interest now set in a leafy residential area.

Wat Mahathat

Main entrance faces Thanon Ratchadamnoen, about 2km south of the modern centre

Missing out **Wat Mahathat** would be like going to Rome and not visiting St Peter's, for the Buddha relics in the vast chedi make this the south's most important shrine. In the courtyard inside the temple cloisters, row upon row of smaller chedis, spiked like bayonets, surround the main chedi, the 60m-tall **Phra Boromathat**. This huge, stubby Sri Lankan bell supports a slender, ringed spire, which is in turn topped by a shiny pinnacle said to be covered in 600kg of gold leaf. According to the chronicles, relics of the Buddha were brought here from Sri Lanka two thousand years ago by an Indian prince and princess and enshrined in a chedi. It's undergone plenty of face-lifts since then: an earlier Srivijayan version, a model of which stands at one corner, is encased in the present twelfth-century chedi. The most recent restoration work, funded by donations from all over Thailand, rescued it from collapse, although it still seems to be leaning dangerously to the southeast. Worshippers head for the north side's vast enclosed stairway, framed by lions and giants, which they liberally decorate with gold leaf to add to the shrine's radiance and gain some merit.

Viharn Phra Kien Museum

Extends north from the chedi • Hours irregular, but usually daily 9am–4pm • Free

An Aladdin's cave of bric-a-brac, the **Viharn Phra Kien Museum** is said to house fifty thousand artefacts donated by worshippers, ranging from ships made out of seashells to gold and silver models of the Bodhi Tree. At the entrance to the museum, you'll pass the Phra Puay, an image of the Buddha giving a gesture of reassurance. Women pray to the image when they want to have children, and the lucky ones return to give thanks and leave photos of their chubby progeny.

Viharn Luang

Outside the cloister to the south

The eighteenth-century **Viharn Luang**, raised on elegant slanting columns, is a beautiful example of Ayutthayan architecture. The interior is austere at ground level, but the red coffered ceiling shines with carved and gilded stars and lotus blooms. In the spacious grounds on the viharn's south side, cheerful, inexpensive stalls peddle local handicrafts such as shadow puppets, bronzeware and basketware.

The National Museum

Thanon Ratchadamnoen, a 10min walk south from Wat Mahathat • Wed–Sun 9am–noon & 1–4pm • B150 • ⓦ thailandmuseum.com

The **National Museum** houses a small but diverse collection, mostly of artefacts from southern Thailand. In the prehistory room **downstairs**, look out for the two impressive ceremonial bronze kettledrums dating from the fifth century BC; they were beaten in rainmaking rituals and one of them is topped with chunky frogs (the local frogs are said to be the biggest in Thailand and a prized delicacy). Also on the ground floor are some interesting Hindu finds, including several stone lingams from the seventh to ninth centuries AD and later bronze statues of Ganesh, the elephant-headed god of wisdom and the arts. Look out especially for a vivacious, well-preserved bronze of Shiva here, dancing within a ring of fire on the body of a dwarf demon, who holds a cobra symbolizing stupidity. Among the collections of ceramics **upstairs**, you can't miss the seat panel from Rama V's barge, a dazzling example of the nielloware for which Nakhon is famous – the delicate animals and landscapes have been etched onto a layer of gold which covers the silver base, and then picked out by inlaying a black alloy into the background. The nearby exhibition on local wisdom includes interesting displays on Buddhist ordinations and weddings, and on *manohra*, the southern Thai dramatic dance form.

The shadow puppet workshop

Ban Nang Thalung Suchart Subsin, 110/18 Soi 3, Thanon Si Thammasok, a 10min walk east of Wat Mahathat • Free • ☎ 075 346394

The best possible introduction to *nang thalung*, southern Thailand's **shadow puppet theatre** (see box, p.280), is to head for the atmospheric compound of Suchart Subsin, a designated National Artist and one of the south's leading exponents of *nang thalung*. He and his sons have opened up their workshop to the public, including a small museum of puppets dating back as far as the eighteenth century, and, especially if you

■ ACCOMMODATION	
Bue Loung	1
Grand Park	3
Nakorn Garden Inn	4
Twin Lotus	2

● RESTAURANTS & CAFÉS	
Hao Coffee	3
Krua Thale	4
Khanom Jiin Muangkorn	2
Wang Derm	1

phone in advance, they'll usually be able to show you a few scenes from a shadow play in the small open-air theatre, for which you might want to leave a tip or donation. You can also see the intricate process of making the leather puppets and can buy the finished products as souvenirs: puppets sold here are of much better quality and design than those usually found on southern Thailand's souvenir stalls.

The Phra Buddha Sihing shrine

In the provincial administration complex on Thanon Ratchadamnoen • Mon–Fri 8.30am–noon & 1–4.30pm • Free

Magically created in Sri Lanka in the second century, the **Phra Buddha Sihing** statue was, according to legend, sent by ship to the king of Sukhothai in the thirteenth century, but the vessel sank and the image miraculously floated on a plank to Nakhon. Two other images, one in the National Museum in Bangkok, one in Wat Phra Singh in Chiang Mai, claim to be the authentic Phra Buddha Sihing, but none of the three is in the Sri Lankan style, so they are all probably derived from a lost original. Although similar to the other two in size and shape, the image in Nakhon has a style unique to this area, distinguished by the heavily pleated flap of its robe over the left shoulder, a beaky nose and harsh features, which sit uneasily on the short, corpulent body. The image's plumpness has given the style the name *khanom tom* – "banana and rice pudding".

ARRIVAL AND DEPARTURE
NAKHON SI THAMMARAT

BY PLANE

The airport (❶ 075 369540–2), served daily by Nok Air and Air Asia, is about 20km northwest of the city off the Surat Thani road. From here, taxis charge around B300 to take you into Nakhon while big hotels such as the *Twin Lotus* and *Grand Park* offer airport shuttle buses. Nok Air offer flight-and-boat through-tickets to Ko Samui and Ko Pha Ngan.

Destinations Bangkok (7 daily; 1hr 10min).

BY TRAIN

The train station is very central.

Destinations Bangkok (2 daily; 15–16hr); Hat Yai (2 daily; 4–5hr).

BY BUS

All buses (including a/c vehicles to Surat Thani) use the terminal on the west side of the centre, except for a local, non-a/c service to Surat Thani, which starts about 1km north of the centre on the left-hand side of Thanon

3

SHADOW PUPPETS

Found throughout southern Asia, **shadow puppets** are one of the oldest forms of theatre, featuring in Buddhist literature as early as 400 BC. The art form seems to have come from India, via Java, to Thailand, where it's called *nang*, meaning "hide": the puppets are made from the skins of water buffalo or cows, which are softened in water, then pounded until almost transparent, before being carved and painted to represent the characters of the play. The puppets are then manipulated on bamboo rods in front of a bright light, to project their image onto a large white screen, while the story is narrated to the audience.

The grander version of the art, **nang yai** – "big hide", so called because the figures are life-size – deals only with the *Ramayana* story (see p.451). It's known to have been part of the entertainment at official ceremonies in the Ayutthayan period, but has now almost died out. The more populist version, **nang thalung** – *thalung* is probably a shortening of the town name, Phatthalung (which is just down the road from Nakhon), where this version of the art form is said to have originated – is also in decline now: performances are generally limited to temple festivals, marriages, funerals and ordinations, lasting usually from 9pm to dawn. As well as working the 60cm-high *nang thalung* puppets, the puppet master narrates the story, impersonates the characters, chants and cracks jokes to the accompaniment of flutes, fiddles and percussion instruments. Not surprisingly, in view of this virtuoso semi-improvised display, puppet masters are esteemed as possessed geniuses by their public.

At big festivals, companies often perform the *Ramayana*, sometimes in competition with each other; at smaller events they put on more down-to-earth stories, with stock characters such as the jokers Yor Thong, an angry man with a pot belly and a sword, and Kaew Kop, a man with a frog's head. Yogi, a wizard and teacher, is thought to protect the puppet master and his company from evil spirits with his magic, so he is always the first puppet on at the beginning of every performance.

In an attempt to halt their decline as a form of popular entertainment, the puppet companies are now incorporating modern instruments and characters in modern dress into their shows, and are boosting the love element in their stories. They're fighting a battle they can't win against television and cinemas, although at least the debt owed to shadow puppets has been acknowledged – *nang* has become the Thai word for "movie".

Ratchadamnoen near Wat Pradu.
Destinations Bangkok (Southern Terminal; 19 daily; 12hr); Hat Yai (14 daily; 3hr 30min); Krabi (7 daily; 4hr); Phuket (7 daily; 6hr); Ranong (1 daily; 6hr); Surat Thani (21 daily; 2hr 30min).

BY MINIBUS

A/c minibus offices around town include one for Ko Samui (via the Don Sak ferry), 1km north of the centre on the right-hand side of Thanon Ratchadamnoen opposite the stop for Surat Thani buses; others are marked on our map.

GETTING AROUND

By share-songthaew Small blue share-songthaews ply up and down Thanon Ratchadamnoen (B10).

By car Avis have a branch at Nakhon Si Thammarat airport (ⓦavisthailand.com).

INFORMATION

Tourist information TAT has an office in a restored 1920s government officers' club on Sanam Na Muang (daily 8.30am–4.30pm; ☎075 346515–6, ⓔtatnksri@tat.or.th).

Internet access Klickzone, Bovorn Bazaar, Thanon Ratchadamnoen (daily 9am–6pm).

ACCOMMODATION

Nakhon has no guesthouses or traveller-oriented accommodation, but the best of its hotels offer very good value in all price ranges.

Bue Loung (Bua Luang) Hotel 1487/19 Soi Luang Muang, Thanon Chamroenwithi ☎075 341518, ☎075 343418. Friendly and central but reasonably quiet; gets the thumbs-up from visiting sales reps, with a choice of fan and cold water or a/c, cable TV and hot water in basic double or twin rooms. Fan **B180**, a/c **B340**

OPPOSITE WAT MAHATHAT, NAKHON SI THAMMARAT (P.277) >

Grand Park Hotel 1204/79 Thanon Pak Nakhon ☎075 317666–75, ⊚grandparknakhon.com. If you're looking for an upmarket option in the centre of town, this place, set back a little from the busy road, is worth considering – it's large, smart and bright, with a/c, hot water, TV and mini-bar in every room, free wi-fi in the lobby and cheery and attentive staff. **B600**

★ **Nakorn Garden Inn** 1/4 Thanon Pak Nakhon ☎075 313333, ⊕075 342926. A rustic but sophisticated haven in two three-storey, red-brick buildings overlooking a tree-shaded courtyard. Large, attractive rooms come with a/c, hot water, cable TV and mini-bars. Free wi-fi in the lobby and some rooms. **B445**

Twin Lotus About 3km southeast of the centre at 97/8 Thanon Patanakarn Kukwang ☎075 323777, ⊚twinlotushotel.net. Gets pride of place in Nakhon – though not for its location; sports five bars and restaurants, a large, attractive outdoor swimming pool, a sauna and a fitness centre. **B1600**

EATING AND DRINKING

Nakhon is a great place for inexpensive food, not least at the busy, colourful **night market** on Thanon Chamroenwithi near the *Bue Loung Hotel*.

Hao Coffee In the Bovorn Bazaar, Thanon Ratchadamnoen. Popular place in a quiet courtyard, modelled on an old Chinese-style coffee shop and packed full of ageing lamps, clocks and other antiques. Offers a wide selection of inexpensive Thai dishes, Western breakfasts, cakes, teas, juices and coffees, including Thai filter coffee and delicious iced cappuccinos. Daily 7am–5pm.

Khanom Jiin Muangkorn Thanon Panyom, near Wat Mahathat. Justly famous, inexpensive outdoor restaurant dishing up one of the local specialities, *khanom jiin*, noodles topped with hot, sweet or fishy sauce served with *pak ruam*, a platter of crispy raw vegetables. Daily 8am–3pm.

★ **Krua Thale** Thanon Pak Nakhon, opposite the Nakorn Garden Inn (no English sign – look for the Coke sign). The town's best restaurant, renowned among locals for its excellent, varied and inexpensive seafood. Plain and very clean, with an open kitchen and the day's catch displayed out front, and relaxing patio tables and an a/c room at the back. Recommended dishes include a very good *yam plaa duk foo*, shredded and deep-fried catfish with a mango salad dip (B80), whole baked fish and king prawns, and *hoy maleang poo op mordin*, large green mussels in a delicious herb soup containing lemon grass, basil and mint (B60). Daily 4–10pm.

Wang Derm Thanon Nang Ngam (no English sign). A great place to sample southern food, buffet-style in a big, open-air pavilion in an interesting complex of coffee shops and bakeries, with good *khanom jiin* and other very cheap local dishes (from B15): *kaeng som*, a mild yellow curry; *kaeng tai plaa*, fish stomach curry; *khao yam*, a delicious southern salad of rice and vegetables; and various *khanom wan*, coconut milk puddings. Daily 7am–5pm.

Khao Luang National Park

Headquarters to the south of the summit near Karom Waterfall • National park admission fee B200 • ☎075 391240 or ☎075 391218, ⊚dnp.go.th

Rising to the west of Nakhon Si Thammarat and temptingly visible from all over town is 1835m-high **Khao Luang**, southern Thailand's highest mountain. A huge **national park** encompasses Khao Luang's jagged green peaks, beautiful streams with numerous waterfalls, tropical rainforest and fruit orchards. The mountain is also the source of the Tapi River, one of the peninsula's main waterways, which flows into the Gulf of Thailand at Surat Thani. **Fauna** here include macaques, musk deer, civets and binturongs, as well as more difficult-to-see Malayan tapirs, serows, tigers, panthers and clouded leopards, plus over two hundred bird species. There's an astonishing diversity of **flora** too, notably rhododendrons and begonias, dense mosses, ferns and lichens, plus more than three hundred species of both ground-growing and epiphytic orchids, some of which are unique to the park.

The best **time to visit** is after the rainy season, from January onwards, when there should still be a decent flow in the waterfalls, but the trails will be dry and the leeches not so bad. However, the park's most distinguishing feature for visitors is probably its difficulty of **access**: main roads run around the 570-square-kilometre park with spurs into some of the waterfalls, but there are no roads across the park and very sparse public transport along the spur roads. The Ban Khiriwong Ecotourism Club

(☎075 533113) can arrange **treks** to the peak between January and June, beginning at Ban Khiriwong on the southeast side of the park and including two nights camping on the mountain, meals and guides, as well as homestays in the village. Otherwise only **Krung Ching Waterfall**, one of Thailand's most spectacular, really justifies the hassle of getting to the park.

Krung Ching Waterfall

A trip to **Krung Ching**, a nine-tier waterfall on the north side of the park, makes for a highly satisfying day out with a **nature trail** taking you through dense, steamy jungle to the most beautiful, third tier. Starting at the Krung Ching park office, which lies 13km south of Ban Huai Phan, this shady, mostly paved, 4km trail is very steep in parts, so you should allow four hours at least there and back. On the way you'll pass giant ferns, including a variety known as *maha sadam*, the largest fern in the world, gnarled banyan trees, forests of mangosteen and beautiful, thick stands of bamboo. You're bound to see colourful birds and insects, but you may well only hear macaques and other mammals. At the end, a long, stepped descent brings you to a perfectly positioned wooden platform with fantastic views of the 40m fall, which used to appear on the back of thousand-baht notes; here you can see how, shrouded in thick spray, it earns its Thai name, Fon Saen Ha, meaning "thousands of rainfalls".

ARRIVAL AND DEPARTURE

KHAO LUANG

By songthaew Irregular songthaews on the main roads around the park and to Ban Khiriwong congregate on Thanon Klong Tha south of the *Bue Loung Hotel* in Nakhon. None of them is scheduled to go to Krung Ching – you'd have to catch one to Ban Huai Phan (about 1hr) and then do a deal with the driver to take you the extra 13km to the Krung Ching park office.

By car Rental cars, with or without driver, are available from Muang Tai Tour on Thanon Yomarat in Nakhon (☎075

343996 or ☎075 342768; around B1500/day plus petrol) or from Avis at the airport (see p.280). The easiest way to get to Krung Ching from Nakhon with your own transport is to head north on Highway 401 towards Surat Thani, turning west at Tha Sala on to Highway 4140, then north again at Ban Nopphitam on to Highway 4186, before heading south from Ban Huai Phan on Highway 4188, the spur road to the Krung Ching park office, a total journey of about 70km.

ACCOMMODATION AND EATING

National park accommodation ☎075 391240 or ☎075 391218, �W dnp.go.th. Two- to twenty-person bungalows, most with hot water, are available at the Krung

Ching park office. There's also a campsite. Bungalows B600
National park canteen There's a basic canteen near the park office, where food needs to be ordered in advance.

Southern Thailand: the Andaman coast

KO PANYI, AO PHA NGA

Southern Thailand: the Andaman coast

As Highway 4 switches from the east flank of the Thailand peninsula to the Andaman coast it enters a markedly different country: nourished by rain nearly all the year round, the vegetation down here is lushly tropical, with forests reaching up to 80m in height, and massive rubber, palm-oil and coconut plantations replacing the rice and sugar-cane fields of central Thailand. Sheer limestone crags spike every horizon and the translucent Andaman Sea laps the most dazzlingly beautiful islands in the country, not to mention its finest coral reefs. This is of course the same sea whose terrifyingly powerful tsunami waves battered the coastline in December 2004, killing thousands and changing countless lives and communities forever. The legacies of that horrific day are widespread (see p.312), but all the affected holiday resorts have been rebuilt, with the tourist dollar now arguably more crucial to the region's well-being than ever before.

4

The **cultural mix** along the Andaman coast is also different from central Thailand. Many southern Thais are Muslim, with a heritage that connects them to Malaysia and beyond. This is also the traditional province of nomadic *chao ley*, or sea gypsies, many of whom have now settled but still work as boat captains and fishermen. The commercial fishing industry, on the other hand, is mostly staffed by immigrants – legal and not – from neighbouring Burma, just a few kilometres away along the northern Andaman coast.

The attractions of the northern Andaman coast are often ignored in the race down to the high-profile honeypots around Phuket and Krabi, but there are many quiet gems up here, beginning with the low-key little sister islands of **Ko Chang** (quite different from

SNORKELLING OFF KO SIMILAN

Highlights

❶ Island idylls Tranquillity rules on the uncommercial islands of Ko Phayam, Ko Ra, Ko Yao Noi and Ko Jum. **See p.297, p.301, p.345 & p.380**

❷ Khao Sok National Park Sleep in a jungle treehouse or on a lake amid spectacular karst scenery, and wake to the sound of hooting gibbons. **See p.306**

❸ Ko Similan Remote island chain offering the finest snorkelling and diving, and easily accessible on day-trips and live-aboards. **See p.316**

❹ Phuket Town Handsome Sino-Portuguese architecture and some of the most interesting

sleeping, eating and drinking options on the island. **See p.323**

❺ Sea-canoeing in Ao Phang Nga The perfect way to explore the limestone karsts and hidden lagoons of this spectacular bay. **See p.352**

❻ Rock-climbing Even novices can get a bird's-eye view of the Railay peninsula's fabulous coastal scenery. **See p.368**

❼ Ko Lanta Yai The "island of long beaches", with an atmospheric old town, offers an appealing choice of relaxing mid-range facilities. **See p.384**

HIGHLIGHTS ARE MARKED ON THE MAP ON P.288

SOUTHERN THAILAND: THE ANDAMAN COAST

HIGHLIGHTS
1. Island idylls
2. Khao Sok National Park
3. Ko Similan
4. Phuket Town
5. Sea-canoeing in Ao Phang Nga
6. Rock-climbing
7. Ko Lanta Yai

BURMA

Chumphon

Kra Isthmus

Kraburi

Kaw Thaung

Ranong
Saphan Pla

GULF OF THAILAND

St Matthew's Island

Nam Tok Ngao

Lang Suan

Ko Chang

Pha To

Ko Phayam

Kapoe

Chaiya

Ko Surin Nua

Ban Talae Nok

Ko Surin Tai

Tung Nang Dam

Surat Thani

ANDAMAN SEA

Khuraburi

Ko Ra

Phunphin

KHAO SOK NATIONAL PARK

Cheow Lan Lake

Ko Phra Thong

Ratchabrap Dam

Takua Pa

Khao Sok National Park Headquarters

Ban Ta Khun

Ko Kho Khao

Phanom

Sai Rung Falls

Khao Lak

Thap Lamu

Ko Similan

SA NANG MANORA FOREST PARK

Thep Phut

Phang Nga

Thai Muang

Ao Luk

Khokkloi

Ao Phang Nga

Laem Sak

Ao Thalen

Talat Kao

Khao Phanom

Krabi

Nua Klong

Ko Yao Noi

Phuket

Ko Yao Yai

Ao Nang

Railay Peninsula

Laem Kruat

Khlong Thom

Ban Huay Nam Khao

Phuket Town

Ko Jum

Ban Hua Hin

Bo Muang

Trang

Ko Phi Phi

Ko Lanta Noi

Ko Lanta Yai

Pak Meng

Ko Racha Yai

Ko Hai

Ko Racha Noi

N

0   50
kilometres

THE KRA ISTHMUS

Thailand's Andaman coast begins at **Kraburi**, where, at kilometre-stone 545 (the distance from Bangkok), a signpost welcomes you to the **Kra Isthmus**, the narrowest part of peninsular Thailand. Just 44km separates the Gulf of Thailand from the Andaman Sea's Chan River estuary, and Burmese border, here. Though a seemingly obvious short cut for shipping traffic between the Indian Ocean and the South China Sea, avoiding the 1500km detour via the Strait of Malacca, the much-discussed **Kra Canal** project has yet to be realized, despite being on the table for over three hundred years.

---

its larger, more famous East Coast namesake) and **Ko Phayam**, where the hammocks and paraffin lamps offer an old-style travellers' vibe that's harder to find further south. Snorkellers and divers are drawn in their hundreds to the reefs of the remote National Park island chains of **Ko Surin** and **Ko Similan**, with many choosing to base themselves at the mainland beach resort of **Khao Lak**, though homestay programmes around **Khuraburi** offer an interesting alternative. Inland, it's all about the jungle – with twenty-first-century amenities – at the enjoyable **Khao Sok National Park**, where accommodation is on rafts on the lake and treehouses beneath the limestone crags.

Phuket, Thailand's largest island, is the region's major resort destination for families, package tourists and novice divers; its dining, shopping and entertainment facilities are second to none, but the high-rises and hectic consumerism dilute the Thai-ness of the experience. There's Thai life in spades across on the quiet rural island of **Ko Yao Noi**, scenically located within the spectacular bay of **Ao Phang Nga**, whose scattered karst islets are one of the country's top natural wonders, best appreciated from a sea-canoe. The Andaman coast's second hub is **Krabi** province, rightly famous for its turquoise seas and dramatic islands. Flashiest of these is the flawed but still handsome **Ko Phi Phi**, with its great diving, gorgeous beaches and high-octane nightlife. Mainland and mainstream **Ao Nang** can't really compete, but is at least close to the majestic cliffs and superb rock-climbing of the **Railay** peninsula at **Laem Phra Nang**. Offshore again, there's horizon-gazing aplenty at mellow, barely developed **Ko Jum** and the choice of half a dozen luxuriously long beaches, and plentiful resort facilities, at **Ko Lanta Yai**.

Unlike the Gulf coast, the Andaman coast is hit by the **southwest monsoon**, which usually generally lasts from the end of May until at least the middle of October. During this period, heavy rain and high seas render some of the outer islands inaccessible, but conditions aren't usually severe enough to ruin a holiday on the other islands, or on the mainland, and you'll get tempting discounts on accommodation. Some bungalows at the smaller resorts shut down entirely during low season (highlighted in the text), but most beaches keep at least one place open, and some dive shops lead expeditions year-round.

ARRIVAL AND DEPARTURE   **THE ANDAMAN COAST**

There is no rail line down the Andaman coast, but many travellers take the **train** from Bangkok to the Gulf coast and then nip across by bus; most direct **buses** from the capital travel south overnight. The fastest option is to arrive by plane: both Phuket and Krabi have international **airports**, and there's a domestic airport at Trang, not far from Ko Lanta in the deep south.

Ranong

Despite being the soggiest town in the country, with over 5000mm of rain a year, **RANONG** has a pleasing buzz about it, fuelled by the mix of Burmese, Thai, Chinese and Malay inhabitants. It's a prosperous town, the lucrative nineteenth-century tin-mining concessions now replaced by a thriving fishing industry centred around the port of Saphan Pla, 5km southwest of town, and its scores of fishing boats and fish-processing factories staffed mainly by notoriously poorly treated Burmese workers. As with most border areas, there's also said to be a flourishing illegal trade in amphetamines, guns and labour, not to mention the inevitable tensions over international fishing rights, which sometimes end in shoot-outs, though the closest encounter you're likely to have will be in the pages of the *Bangkok Post*. Thai tourists have been coming here for years, to savour the health-giving properties of the local spring water, but foreign travellers have only quite recently discovered it as a useful departure point for the alluring nearby little islands of **Ko Chang** and **Ko Phayam**. The other reason to stop off in Ranong is to make a visa run to the Burmese town of **Kaw Thaung**.

A stroll along the town centre's main road, **Thanon Ruangrat**, brings its history and geography to mind. The handsome, if faded, shopfront architecture bears many of the hallmarks of nineteenth-century Sino-Portuguese design (see p.324), with its arched "five-foot" walkways shading pedestrians, pastel paintwork and shuttered windows. Chinese goods fill many of the shops – this is a good place to stock up on cheap clothes too – and many signs are written in the town's three main languages: Thai, Chinese and curly Burmese script.

The geothermal springs

Raksawarin Park, about 3km east of the Thanon Ruangrat market • **Raksawarin Hot Springs** daily 7am–9pm • B40 or B60 including transfer from *Tinidee Hotel* (see p.293) • **Siam Hot Spa Ranong** daily noon–9pm • treatments from B200 ☎ 077 813551–4, ⓦ siamhotsparanong.com • Accessible on red songthaew #2 from the market or by motorbike taxi

Though there's little in Ranong to warrant a sightseeing tour, it can be fun to follow the crowds of domestic tourists in their quest for the medicinal and stress-relieving

ACCOMMODATION
Asia Hotel	3
Luang Poj	2
Suta House Bungalows	1
Tinidee Hotel & Inn	4

RESTAURANTS & CAFÉS
Pon's Place	2
Sophon's Hideaway	1

RANONG

properties of Ranong's famously pure **geothermal springs**. They're the focus of forested Raksawarin Park, which is set in a narrow, lush river valley, surrounded by restaurants and souvenir shops. At the park, you can bathe or paddle in either the open-access, public mineral spa pools or the better-appointed and deeper, jacuzzi-type spa pools of Raksawarin Hot Springs, which are run by the *Tinidee Hotel*. Alternatively, you can opt for a more leisurely soak at the indoor Siam Hot Spa Ranong across the road, which offers public and private jacuzzi pools, private bathrooms and inexpensive massage and steam treatments.

First Governor's House

West off Thanon Ruangrat on the northern edge of town • Daily 9am–4.30pm • Free

Ranong's history is closely associated with its most famous son, Khaw Soo Cheang, a poor Hokkien Chinese emigrant turned tin baron who became the first governor of Ranong province in 1854; he is still so esteemed that politicians continue to pay public homage at his grave, and his descendants bear the respected aristocratic surname "na Ranong" ("of Ranong"). Little now remains of Khaw Soo Cheang's house, but in its grounds stands a Khaw clan house and small museum, the **First Governor's House** (Nai Khai Ranong).

ARRIVAL AND DEPARTURE   RANONG

There are currently no services to Ranong airport, 20km south of town on Highway 4.

By bus or minibus Most Andaman-coast buses travelling between Bangkok or Chumphon and Khuraburi, Takua Pa or Phuket stop briefly at Ranong's bus station on Highway 4 (Thanon Phetkasem), 1500m southeast of the central market. If coming from Khao Sok or Surat Thani, you'll usually need to change buses at Takua Pa, though there is also an a/c minibus service from and to Surat Thani (hourly 7am–3pm; 3hr; B190). There are direct buses operated by Rungkit from Chumphon (4 daily; 2–3hr), as well as faster a/c minibuses (hourly 7am–5pm; 2hr; B120), so from Bangkok it's often more comfortable to take a night train to Chumphon and then change on to a bus or minibus. Alternatively, Chokeanan and New Mittour run VIP buses from opposite Wat Bowoniwes and the Siam Commercial Bank in Banglamphu, via the Southern Bus Terminal, to Chumphon's Thanon Tha Muang. Rungkit buses to Chumphon and Phuket and the a/c minibuses operate out of Ranong Bus Station; a/c minibuses to Phuket may be in

the pipeline – check at *Pon's Place* (see below) or Phuket Town bus station.

Destinations: Bangkok (15 daily; 9hr); Chumphon (4 daily; 2–3hr); Khao Lak (7 daily; 3hr 45min); Khuraburi (7 daily; 2hr); Krabi (1–2 daily; 5hr); Phang Nga (1–2 daily; 4hr); Phuket (7 daily; 5hr 30min); Surat Thani (10 daily; 4–5hr); Takua Pa (7 daily; 3hr).

By boat to the islands via Saphan Pla Boats to Ko Chang (see p.296) and Ko Phayam (see p.299) leave from Ranong's port at Saphan Pla, 5km southwest of the town centre and served by songthaews (see below) or by share-taxi from *Pon's Place* (B50). Songthaews drop passengers on the main road through Saphan Pla, from where it's a 500m walk south to the Islands Pier, while share-taxis take you to the pier itself; phone *Pon's Place* if you want to arrange a pick-up from the pier on your return from the islands.

Destinations: Ko Chang (1–5 daily; 1hr–1hr 30min); Ko Phayam (1–5 daily; 45min–2hr).

GETTING AROUND

By songthaew Songthaews shuttle across and around Ranong, starting from the Thanon Ruangrat market, close to the town-centre hotels. Many have their destinations written in English on the side, and most charge around B15 per ride. Several songthaews pass Ranong bus station, including the #2 (red), which runs to the Thanon Ruangrat hotels and day market, and the #6 (blue), which starts at the

day market and heads on to the port area at Saphan Pla, 5km to the southwest (for boats to Ko Chang, Ko Phayam and Kaw Thaung); red #3 songthaew runs direct from the market on Thanon Ruangrat to the Saphan Pla port area.

Car and bike rental *Pon's Place*, 129 Thanon Ruangrat (daily 7.30am–9pm; ☎081 597 4549, ⊛ponplace-ranong .com), rents bicycles, motorbikes and cars.

INFORMATION AND TOURS

Tourist information The best source of tourist information in town is the ever helpful Pon at *Pon's Place*

restaurant and tour agency, 129 Thanon Ruangrat (daily 7.30am–9pm; ☎081 597 4549, ⊛ponplace-ranong.com), where you can also organize a visa run to Burma and back, arrange tours of the local area, book accommodation on Ko Chang and Ko Phayam, and buy air, bus and minibus tickets, as well as train tickets from Chumphon or Surat Thani. There's a branch of A-One Diving (see p.299) at 256 Thanon Ruangrat (☎077 832984).

ACCOMMODATION

Asia Hotel 39/9 Thanon Ruangrat ☎077 811113. Typical, basic Chinese–Thai hotel just south of the market, a bit battered but reasonably clean, with most rooms set back from the road. Airy en-suite fan rooms or large a/c versions with hot water, TV and two big beds (B500). B160

Luang Poj 225 Thanon Ruangrat ☎077 833377, ✉luangpoj@gmail.com. Appealing conversion of a Sino-Portuguese shophouse, maintaining its polished wooden floors, which styles itself as a "boutique hostel" though there are no dorms. The smart, modern bedrooms come with attractive murals: heavy sleepers who like to be in the thick of the action will like the two fan rooms with wooden shutters facing the street; others will want to plump for the windowless a/c options. Hot showers are shared, though en-suite a/c rooms with TV and fridge are planned in the building at the back (as well as a coffee shop and bar with garden seating). Wi-fi throughout. B400

Suta House Bungalows Thanon Ruangrat ☎077 832707–8. Set back 50m from the road, this is an unusual find in a city, with its row of small but well-maintained a/c bungalows, all of them with clean tiled floors, built-in beds, hot showers, fridges, cable TV and free wi-fi. They're set round a small yard, with car parking, a little bar-coffee shop and a restaurant. Open 24hr. B350

TCDF Eco-Logic Pak Song, near Pha To, 45km southeast of Ranong ⊛tcdf-ecologic.jimdo.com. Thai–Dutch eco-tourism guesthouse on a farm in the mountains (and on the Ranong–Surat Thani bus route), with artistically decorated en-suite rooms and bungalows set in lovely grounds, some with garden bathrooms. Lots of activities for adults and kids, including bamboo rafting, hiking and Thai cooking classes.

INTO BURMA: VISA RUNS AND KAW THAUNG (KO SONG)

The southernmost tip of Burma – known as **Kaw Thaung** in Burmese, Ko Song in Thai, and Victoria Point when it was a British colony – lies just a few kilometres west of Ranong across the gaping Chan River estuary, and is easily reached by longtail boat from Saphan Pla fishing port just outside Ranong town centre. It's quite straightforward for foreign tourists to hop across to **Burma** at this point, and hop back for a new fifteen-day stay in Thailand (the "tourist visa exemption"). You can either do it independently, as described below, or you can make use of one of the all-inclusive **"visa run" services** advertised all over town, including at *Pon's Place* (B850 including visa). Most visa-run operators use the Saphan Pla route, but they can also book you on the faster, more luxurious **Andaman Club boat** (6 daily 7am–4pm, later boats available for those staying overnight; 20min each way; B1000 including visa), which departs from the Andaman Club pier 5km north of Ranong's town centre and travels to and from the swanky *Andaman Club* hotel (⊛andamanclub.com), casino and duty-free complex, located on a tiny island in Burmese waters just south of Kaw Thaung.

Boats to Kaw Thaung leave from the so-called Burmese Pier (go through the PTT petrol station on the main road) in the port of Saphan Pla, 5km southwest of town and served by songthaews from Ranong market (B15) – the blue #6 goes via the bus station but the red #3 is more direct. Thai exit formalities are done at the pier (daily 8am–6pm), after which longtail boats take you to Kaw Thaung (B300–400 return per boat – pay at the end; 30min each way) and **Burmese immigration**. Here you pay US$10 (or B500) for a pass that should entitle you to stay in Kaw Thaung for a week but forbids travel further than 8km inland. Note that Burma time is thirty minutes behind Thailand time, and that to get back into Thailand you'll have to be at the immigration office in Saphan Pla before it closes at 6pm. The photocopy shop at the pier in Saphan Pla often keeps US dollars, and you should be able to haggle them down to B400 for a $10 bill. Thai money is perfectly acceptable in Kaw Thaung.

There's nothing much to do in **Kaw Thaung** itself, but it has quite a different vibe to Thai towns. As you arrive at the quay, the market, immigration office and tiny town centre lie before you, while over to your right, about twenty minutes' walk away, you can't miss the hilltop **Pyi Taw Aye Pagoda**, surmounted by a huge reclining Buddha and a ring of smaller ones. Once you've explored the covered market behind the quay and picked your way through the piles of tin trunks and sacks of rice that crowd the surrounding streets, all that remains is to take a coffee break in one of the quayside pastry shops.

In support of the Thai Child Development Foundation (see p.55). Dorm B200, double B750

★ **Tinidee Hotel** 41/144 Thanon Tha Muang ☎ 077 835240, ⓦ tinidee-ranong.com. The top digs in town are at this welcoming, good-value high-rise hotel, a 10min walk from the market, which fully lives up to its name ("It's good here"). The large, bright a/c rooms are tastefully furnished and all come with mini-bars, TVs and bathtubs fed by the local mineral water; there's also a spa and an attractive swimming pool and jacuzzi. B1100

Tinidee Inn 41/144 Thanon Tha Muang ☎ 077 834112, ⓦ tinidee-ranong.com. A wing of the *Tinidee Hotel* has been converted into this low-cost inn, offering less style and smaller rooms, but all with a/c, hot showers, TV and fridge. Guests get access to the hotel's pool and jacuzzi; wi-fi is payable, or you can go across to the hotel's lobby to use it for free. B550

EATING AND DRINKING

Ranong's ethnic diversity ensures a tasty range of eating options, and a stroll up Thanon Ruangrat takes you past Muslim foodstalls and Chinese pastry shops as well as a small but typically Thai night market. A bigger night market convenes at dusk just east of the CAT phone office off Thanon Phoem Phon. The stretch of Thanon Ruangrat between the Thanon Luwang junction and *Sophon's Hideaway* is also abuzz after dark, especially at weekends, with urbane little local bars that keep reinventing themselves.

Pon's Place 129 Thanon Ruangrat ☎ 081 597 4549. This nice little restaurant hung with orchids is the obvious place for farang-style breakfast (French toast B55) with traditional Thai coffee, free wi-fi and as much local information as you care to gather. It also offers sandwiches and standard Thai dishes, including plenty of seafood and some veggie options. Daily 7.30am–9pm.

Sophon's Hideaway Thanon Ruangrat. Lively, enjoyable bar and rustic-style restaurant, where Thai families and expats congregate for the wide-ranging menu, which includes chicken with cashew nuts (B85), T-bone steaks (B350), pizzas, pastas, ice cream and breakfast. The cheapish beer and friendly staff are a plus and there's international sports on the TV, a free pool table and free wi-fi. Daily 10am–12.30am.

4

Ko Chang

Not to be confused with the much larger Ko Chang off Thailand's east coast (see p.180), Ranong's **KO CHANG** is a forested little island about 5km offshore, whose car-free, ultra laidback, roll-your-own vibe more than compensates for the less than perfect beaches. The pace of life here is very slow, encouraging long stays, and for the relatively small number of tourists who make it to the island the emphasis is strongly on kicking back and chilling out – bring your own hammock and you'll fit right in. Those in search of (slightly) livelier scenes head across the water to sister-island Ko Phayam (see p.297). Most islanders make their living from fishing and from the rubber, palm and cashew nut plantations that dominate the flatter patches of the interior. The beaches are connected by tracks through the trees and there are only sporadic, self-generated supplies of electricity for a few hours each evening.

The best of Ko Chang's beaches are on the west coast, and of these the longest, nicest and most popular is **Ao Yai**. The tiny bays to the north and south mostly hold just one set of bungalows each and are good for getting away from it all, though access to Ao Yai is easy enough if you don't mind the hike. About halfway between the west and east coasts, a crossroads bisects Ko Chang's only **village**, a tiny settlement that is home to most of the islanders and holds just a few shops, restaurants and a clinic.

Nearly all the bungalows on Ko Chang **close** down from about late April or early May until mid- or late October, when the island is subjected to very heavy rain, the beaches fill with flotsam, paths become dangerously slippery and food supplies dwindle with no ice available to keep things fresh. Many bungalow staff relocate to the mainland for this period, so you should phone ahead to check first.

KO CHANG

N

Ao Ko

Ko Plai

Nice View

Ko Bonsai

Army Base

Main pier

Om Tao

Aladdin Dive Safari

Ao Yai

Wat Pah Ko Chang

Minimarket

Minimarket

Black Bird Minimarket

Ao Chao Ley

373m

Ao Daddaeng

Saphan Hin

Ao Kai Tao

National Park Ranger Station

Ao Lek

Ao Siad (Ao Lek)

0   approx.   1
kilometre

■ ACCOMMODATION

Cashew Resort	3
Chang Tong	5
Crocodile Rock	8
Full Moon	7
Hornbill	2
Ko Chang Resort	6
Little Italy	4
Mama's Bungalows	10
Sawasdee Resort	9
Sea Eagle	1

ACTIVITIES ON KO CHANG

Going for walks (and not minding getting lost) is the most popular activity on this large, traffic-free island, but several resorts, including *Ko Chang Resort*, run **fishing, snorkelling and camping trips** to Ko Kham, which is famed for its beautiful beaches and reefs, and to Ko Phayam. For **divers**, Ko Chang is particularly well placed for the sites in the Mergui Archipelago across the border in Burma, while the top local dive sites in Thailand are Ko Surin, Ko Bon, Ko Tachai, Ko Similan and Richelieu Rock.

Aladdin Dive Safari Cashew Resort, Ao Yai, and at the Islands Pier in Saphan Pla ☎087 278 6908, ⓦaladdindivesafari.com. This German–Dutch-run dive shop teaches PADI dive courses and runs a huge selection of live-aboards that take in all the local dive sites (from

B14,900 for three days excluding equipment and national park fees).
Om Tao North of Cashew Resort, Ao Yai. Morning yoga classes and t'ai chi in season.

Ao Yai (Long Beach) and Ao Daddaeng

Effectively divided in two by a khlong (canal) and the stumps of a long wooden pier, **Ao Yai**, or **Long Beach**, enjoys a fine view of the brooding silhouette of Burma's St Matthew's Island, which dominates the western horizon. The 800m-long stretch of Ao Yai that runs north from the khlong is the most attractive on the island, nice and wide even at high tide, and especially good for kids. South of the khlong, the beach is very narrow at high tide, but when the water goes out you have to walk a longish distance to find any depth. Further south still, around a rocky headland, tiny secluded gold-sand **Ao Daddaeng** (Tadang) is sandwiched between massive boulders and holds just a few bungalows: reach it via a five-minute footpath from behind *Tadang Bay Bungalows*.

A narrow concrete road connects central Ao Yai with the mangrove-filled little harbour on the east coast, a distance of around 1700m that can be walked in under half an hour. The western end of the road begins beside the island's only temple, **Wat Pah Ko Chang**, whose bot and monks' quarters are partially hidden among the trees beside the beach, with a sign that asks tourists to dress modestly when in the area and not to swim or sunbathe in front of it.

Northern Ko Chang

North of Ao Yai, the crenellated coast reveals a series of tiny bays occupied by just one set of bungalows apiece. The gritty gold-sand beaches are secluded and feel quite remote, accessible only via a track through forest and rubber plantations. Even if you don't want to base yourself up here, you can do an enjoyable **loop** around the northern bays in well under three hours from Ao Yai. Alternatively, you could make use of the Ranong boats, which charge about B50 for any hop up or down the west coast.

Following **the track** inland from just north of Om Tao, a ten-minute walk north brings you to the top of the first of several hills and the barbed-wire perimeters of a military camp, established here to monitor activity along the (maritime) Thai–Burma border. Ten minutes further on, *Nice View* restaurant and bungalows are aptly named: perched atop an outcrop with glorious panoramas over the unfolding little bays and islets beyond, it's a perfect spot to break for lunch or a drink. It's another twenty minutes to *Sea Eagle* (you need to go via the beach at *Hornbill* before returning inland), the last of the northern bay bungalows, beyond which a ten-minute walk up and over the next hill takes you to the edge of the northeast-facing fishing village, an unprepossessing place complete with incongruous Christian church. This is **Ao Ko**, which is linked by road to the east coast's rainy season pier, and also to Ao Yai.

Southern Ko Chang

Ao Siad, at the southern end of the island, is even more isolated than the north coast and makes a good focus for a day-walk. It's sometimes known as Ao Lek, though the real **Ao Lek** is the mangrove-lined bay fifteen minutes' walk to the northeast, on the other coast. From Ao Daddaeng, a clear path takes you south, in about an hour, to **Ao Kai Tao**, a pretty beach and site of the national park ranger station. From Ao Kai Tao, the route then follows an indistinct path across the saddle between two hills and along a creek bed to reach east-coast Ao Lek (this takes another hour), after which it's fifteen minutes south to Ao Siad. Retracing your steps to Ao Lek to start with, it's then about 5km (2hr) to the crossroads in the village.

ARRIVAL AND DEPARTURE   KO CHANG

Cashew Resort (see below) can arrange bus tickets.

BY BOAT

To/from Ranong The island's main link with the outside world is the daily boat service from the Islands Pier in Saphan Pla (see p.291) to the pier on the east coast (currently 2pm; 1hr; B100; sometimes cancelled in the rainy season). You should be able to arrange some kind of a pick-up from the pier through your resort; otherwise it's a 3km walk to Ao Yai. From about early November to late April, there are also three or four daily boat departures to Ko Chang's west coast, stopping at most resorts, from Saphan Pla's Islands Pier (1hr 30min; B150); ask your resort or at *Pon's Place* in Ranong for the latest schedules.

To/from Ko Phayam The easiest and cheapest option for getting to or from Ko Phayam is to use the day-trippers' boat run by *Ko Chang Resort* several times a week in high season (B150); a charter between the two islands costs about B1500 per boat.

INFORMATION

Tourist information For general information on the island see ⓦ kohchang-ranong.com.

ACCOMMODATION

Most of the bungalows on Ko Chang are simple, old-school wooden-plank or woven bamboo constructions with mosquito nets on the beds; you shouldn't necessarily expect flush toilets (buckets and dippers are provided), curtains or a door on your bathroom. Though the bungalow resorts nearly all have their own generators (which usually only operate in the evenings), some stick to candles and paraffin lamps in the bungalows so it's best to bring a torch; very few bungalows have fans. There are no stand-alone restaurants, and as the distances between resorts are long and there's no transport, most visitors dine at their own resort's restaurant.

AO YAI (LONG BEACH)

Cashew Resort ⓣ077 820226 or ⓣ084 538 5385, ⓔ cashew_resort@hotmail.com. The longest-running accommodation on the island, and also the largest, *Cashew* feels like a tiny village, with its forty en-suite bungalows spread among the cashew trees along 700m of prime beachfront, and returnees personalizing their bungalows like mini homes. All the wood or brick bungalows enjoy both a sea view and some privacy, and some have big glass windows. The resort offers the most facilities on the island, including internet access, foreign exchange, Visa and MasterCard capability, an overseas phone service, transport bookings, massage and books to borrow. Its restaurant bakes bread and serves Thai and a few German dishes. May open year-round in the future. B300

Chang Tong ⓣ080 526 8422 or ⓣ089 875 3353, ⓔ aoy_changthong@hotmail.com. The cheapest wood and bamboo bungalows at this friendly spot are very basic, though they're all en suite and are well spaced beneath the shoreside trees; pay a bit more for newer, better appointed ones on the beachfront. B150

★ **Crocodile Rock** ⓣ081 370 1434 or ⓣ087 040 8087, ⓔ tonn1970@yahoo.com. In a shady, secluded, elevated position at the start of Ao Yai's southern headland, with great views of the whole bay, on which the friendly owners have capitalized, with attractive decks at the restaurant and picture windows in some of the bathrooms. Bungalows, some of which have nice pebbledash bathrooms, have a touch more style than the Ko Chang average. The restaurant bakes its own bread, cookies and banana muffins, and serves fresh juices and espresso coffee. Internet access. B300

Full Moon ⓣ084 850 3809, ⓔ familymoon99 @hotmail.com. Though simple, the attractive wooden en-suite bungalows here are well designed and a cut above many others on Ao Yai. The cheaper ones are prettily painted, with cute stencil work in the bathrooms, and there are larger, pastel-painted, clapboard versions with big decks. Beach bar and massage *sala*. B300

Ko Chang Resort ☎ 081 896 1839, ⓦ kohchang andaman.com. Occupying a fabulous spot high on the rocks right over the water, the best of the en-suite wooden bungalows here have fine sea views from their balconies; the cheaper bamboo ones are set further back beside the path. Interiors are very rudimentary but the decks are huge, and there's also a large, more luxurious family bungalow, and two concrete bungalows with fans (all B1000). You can swim below the rocks at low tide, or the more reliable beach is just a couple of minutes' scramble to south or north. There's internet on site, plus the very chilled, fairy-lit *Air Bar*. May open year-round in the future. B300

Little Italy ☎ 084 851 2760, ⓔ daniel060863 @yahoo.it. This tiny Italian–Thai-run outfit has just two attractive bungalows set in a shady, secluded garden of paperbark trees 100m inland from *Cashew Resort*. Bungalows are two-storey, with exceptionally clean, smartly tiled papaya-coloured bathrooms downstairs and Thai-style bamboo-walled sleeping quarters upstairs, with varnished wood floors and big decks. The garden restaurant serves deliciously authentic pastas. Wi-fi available. B250

Sawasdee Resort ☎ 084 846 5828, ⓦ sawasdee kohchang.com. This welcoming place by a khlong at the far southern end of Ao Yai is a little pricier than many but more style-conscious too and tends to attract slightly older, less hammock-bound guests. The eleven thoughtfully designed wooden bungalows have big decks and good bathrooms, and a couple of them, by the beach, are especially large and well equipped, including fans (B800). There's a good, attractive restaurant, serving a wide variety of Thai dishes and plenty of vegetarian options, with decks and terraces under the shady trees. B350

AO DADDAENG

★ **Mama's Bungalows** 5min walk south over the headland from Ao Yai, on Ao Daddaeng ☎ 077 820180 or ☎ 088 476 7144, ⓔ mamas-bungalows@hotmail .com. At this congenial spot, the fourteen attractive, well-maintained wooden and bamboo bungalows with colourfully decorated bathrooms come in several sizes, some of them with big decks. They're built in a pretty flower garden staggered up the hillside; several are on the beach and the uppermost ones overlook the bay from the edge of a rubber plantation. The restaurant serves espresso coffee and generous portions of carefully prepared food, including tasty tzatziki and many German specialities. Very popular, so book ahead. B250

NORTHERN BAYS

Hornbill North around two headlands from Ao Yai, about a 35min walk ☎ 077 870240, ⓔ 66_hornbill @hotmail.com. Set among the trees fronting their own little gold-sand bay, the unobtrusive en-suite bungalows here are constructed to different designs, some of them extremely comfortable, and all enjoy sea views. The food here has a good reputation and the owner is very welcoming. It lives up to its name, as majestic black-and-white hornbills are a common sight. Internet access, kayaks and boat trips on offer. B200

Sea Eagle About 40min walk from Ao Yai ☎ 082 289 0683, ⓦ seaeaglebangkalow.com. The sole occupants of the longest and widest of the northern bays, which is graced by an attractive band of gold sand, the en-suite bamboo and wooden bungalows here are set among trees just back from the shore. They have comfy deck furniture for soaking up the sea views and there are kayaks and windsurfers for rent and a beach volleyball net. The restaurant serves Thai and European food and has internet access. B300

Ko Phayam

The diminutive kangaroo-shaped island of **KO PHAYAM** offers fine white-sand beaches and coral reefs and is home to around five hundred people, most of whom either make their living from prawn, squid and crab fishing, or from growing cashew nuts, *sator* beans, coconut palms and rubber trees. Many islanders live in Ko Phayam's only **village**, behind the pier on the northeast coast, which connects to other corners of the island by a network of concrete roads and rutted tracks. The bays either side of the village have a couple of nice places to stay, but the main beaches and accommodation centres are on the west coast, at **Ao Yai** and **Ao Kao Kwai**. A motorbike taxi service covers all routes, but no journey is very great as the island measures just five by eight kilometres at its widest points.

Ko Phayam has a livelier, younger and slightly more developed feel than neighbouring Ko Chang (see p.293), underlined by a low-key beach-bar scene – all hand-painted signs and driftwood sculptures – and the presence of a significant number of foreigners who choose to spend six or more months here every year. Some expats even take up the

rainy-season challenge, staying on through the downpours and rough seas that lash the island from June to October, but a number of bungalows close down during this time and staff take refuge in Ranong. As the island gets more popular, residents and expats are beginning to try and forestall the inevitable negative impact on the island's **environment**. In particular, they are urging visitors not to accept plastic bags from the few shops on the island, to take non-degradable rubbish such as batteries and plastic items back to the mainland, and to minimize plastic water-bottle usage by buying the biggest possible bottles and by asking to refill them from the water coolers that all bungalow resorts have.

The village and around

The tiny cluster of homes and shops that constitute Ko Phayam's only **village** is within a few minutes' walk of the pier. There are a few little general stores here, plus several restaurants and a **clinic**. North a little way up the shoreline stands the island **temple**, with its circular viharn resting on a huge concrete lotus flower at the end of its own pier.

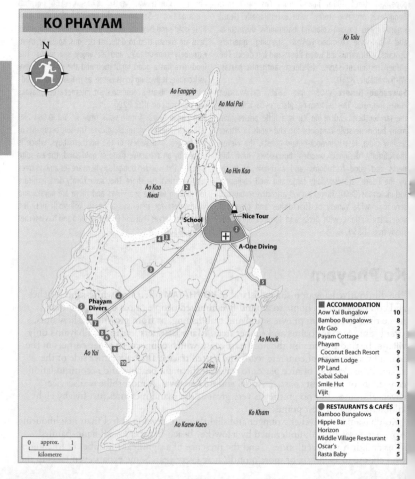

KO PHAYAM

N

Ko Talu

Ao Fangpip

Ao Mai Pai

1

Ao Hin Kao

Ao Kao Kwai

2 **1**

School

Nice Tour

2

A-One Diving

4 3

3

5

Phayam Divers

6

7

8 6

9

Ao Yai

10

224m

Ao Mouk

Ko Kham

Ao Kaew Kaeo

0   approx.   1
kilometre

■ ACCOMMODATION
Aow Yai Bungalow	10
Bamboo Bungalows	8
Mr Gao	2
Payam Cottage	3
Phayam Coconut Beach Resort	9
Phayam Lodge	6
PP Land	1
Sabai Sabai	5
Smile Hut	7
Vijit	4

● RESTAURANTS & CAFÉS
Bamboo Bungalows	6
Hippie Bar	1
Horizon	4
Middle Village Restaurant	3
Oscar's	2
Rasta Baby	5

ACTIVITIES ON KO PHAYAM

Most bungalows can arrange fishing and snorkelling day-trips, while *Oscar's* in the village takes people wakeboarding in the bay. The dive companies teach PADI courses and run liveaboards to Ko Surin, Richelieu Rock, Ko Tachai, Ko Bon and Ko Similan (from about B16,000 for three days, not including equipment).

A-One Diving In the village ☎081 891 5510, ⓦa-one-diving.com. Also does live-aboards to Burma Banks and the Mergui archipelago across the Burmese border.

Mr Gao Ao Kao Kwai ☎077 870222, ⓦmr-trip -phayam.com. Runs occasional two-day snorkelling trips to Ko Surin at B4000 per person, including accommodation in national park tents.

Phayam Divers Phayam Lodge, Ao Yai ☎086 995 2598, ⓦphayamlodge.com. Also does one-day trips to Ko Surin or Richelieu Rock for B4900 (plus equipment rental and national park fee).

Ao Yai

Ko Phayam's main beach is the 3km-long **AO YAI** on the southwest coast, a wide and handsome sweep of powdery white sand backed by an unbroken line of casuarina trees, which curves quite deeply at its northern and southern ends into rocky outcrops that offer some snorkelling possibilities. The shore is pounded by decent waves that are fun for boogie-boarding and pretty safe; the sunsets are quite spectacular too. For the moment Ao Yai's bungalow operations are mostly widely spaced along the shoreline, and much of the forest behind the beach is still intact. You're more than likely to see – and hear – some of the resident black-and-white hornbills at dawn and dusk, along with many white-bellied sea eagles, and sightings of crab-eating macaques are also common.

Ao Kao Kwai and around

The northwest coast is scalloped into **AO KAO KWAI**, a name that's pronounced locally as **Ao Kao Fai** and translates as **Buffalo Horn Bay**; from the cliffside midway along the bay you can see how the two halves of the beach curve out into buffalo-like horns. The southern half of Ao Kao Kwai is subject to both very low and very high tides, which makes it unreliable for swimming, but the northern stretch, from *Mr Gao* bungalows onwards, is exceptionally pretty, secluded between outcrops with decent swimming at any tide, and none of the big waves that characterize Ao Yai.

From the northern end of Ao Kao Kwai, a thirty-minute walk brings you to the pretty little sandy beach at **Ao Fangpip** (also spelt Ao Kwang Pib), which is the best spot on the island for snorkelling. There's also some snorkellable reef at **Ao Hin Kao** on the northeast coast.

ARRIVAL AND DEPARTURE   KO PHAYAM

Nice Tour and Travel, north of the pier-head in the village (☎089 651 5177, ✉nicetour40@hotmail.com), sells bus, train, airline and boat tickets. Nearby *Oscar's* (☎084 842 5070) also sells transport tickets and charters speedboats to other islands. Most bungalows also sell boat tickets, and some sell bus tickets, too.

BY BOAT

To/from Ranong From November to May there are two daily slow boats to Ko Phayam from the Islands Pier in Saphan Pla (see p.291), 5km south of Ranong town centre (currently 9.30am & 2pm, returning from the island at 8am & 2pm; 2hr; B150), as well as up to three speedboat services (45min; B350). During the rainy season only the 2pm slow boat runs, returning from the island at 8am; *Pon's Place* in Ranong keeps the latest timetables.

To/from Ko Chang The easiest and cheapest way of travelling between Ko Phayam and Ko Chang is on the day-trippers' boat organized by *Ko Chang Resort* several times a week in high season (see p.296).

GETTING AROUND

Many travellers heading into the village from one of the beaches opt to walk at least one way: from Ao Yai's *Smile Hut* it's an enjoyable 7km stroll along the narrow concrete road that cuts through the cashew plantations, with the possibility of stopping for a breather at the aptly named *Middle Village Restaurant*. From southern Ao Kao Kwai to the village takes less than an hour.

Motorbike taxis Motorbikes meet incoming boats at the pier and can be booked through any bungalow; a ride between the village and the beaches costs about B80 (there are no cars on the island).

Motorbike rental You can rent your own motorbike through resorts on the beaches and outlets in the village, including *Oscar's* and *Nice Tour and Travel*.
Bike rental *Nice Tour and Travel* in the village.

INFORMATION

Nice Tour and Travel In the village ☎089 651 5177. Changes money and does Visa cash advances, can arrange boat hire and fishing tours, has a book exchange, and offers internet access and an international phone service.

Oscar's Bar In the village ☎084 842 5070. A good source of island information and tickets; also changes money at good rates.

ACCOMMODATION

Most bungalows only provide electricity from around 6 to 11pm and the cheapest rooms often don't have a fan. There's internet access at many, and wi-fi at an increasing number. Unless otherwise stated, all bungalows open year-round.

THE VILLAGE AREA

Most people choose to stay at the west-coast beach centres, but there are a couple of nice little hideaways within easy reach of the village and its facilities.
PP Land ☎081 678 4310, ⓦpayampplandbeach.com. Fronting a small beach about a 10min walk north from the village, this Belgian–Thai place with an organic garden is a cut above many places to stay on the island. Its tasteful, green-painted shaggy thatched bungalows and family rooms line the beach and boast pretty furnishings, polished wood floors inside and out, nice bathrooms, and big comfy decks. There's an attractive swimming pool, plus internet, wi-fi and 24-hour electricity. B800
Sabai Sabai ☎087 895 4653, ⓦsabai-bungalows .com. On their own little beach, a 5min walk south of the pier, are these seven wooden bungalows, some with 24-hour electricity and all but one en suite; cute, stylish touches give them a modern look. Tents are also available, and there's a cool shisha lounge, regular movie nights, TV sports and other events, including live music. Internet access, motorbikes, bicycles, kayaks and snorkels available. B200

AO YAI

Aow Yai Bungalow ☎083 389 8688 or ☎084 061 3283, ⓦaowyai.com. Established by a French–Thai couple, this was the first set of bungalows on the island and remains one of the most popular, especially with return guests. The 26 good-quality en-suite bungalows are dotted around an extensive garden of flowers, fruit trees and palms and come in various styles: the cheapest wooden or thatched bamboo affairs come with mosquito nets but no fans, while the most expensive are built with

concrete and have hot showers. There's wi-fi and internet access, plus snorkels and kayaks. B300
Bamboo Bungalows ☎077 820012, ⓦbamboo -bungalows.com. Ao Yai's liveliest accommodation is Israeli–Thai managed and very traveller-savvy, with free wi-fi, plus snorkels, kayaks, surf- and boogie-boards, currency exchange and overseas phone services. Its en-suite bungalows are set under the trees in a well-tended flower garden and range from luxuriously large chalets with pretty furnishings to shell-studded concrete bungalows and a choice of bamboo and wood huts with mosquito nets. Electricity is 24hr in high season, but with more limited hours in low season. B500
Phayam Coconut Beach Resort ☎089 920 8145 or ☎083 389 6408, ⓦkoh-phayam.com. Occupying a great spot in the centre of the bay and run by a Ko Phayam family, the 27 good-value bungalows here are of a high standard, each set in its own tiny garden. Accommodation ranges from small bamboo en-suite huts through larger wood or bamboo versions to big concrete or clapboard bungalows at the top end (up to B1200). Wi-fi planned. Closed during the worst of the rainy season. B300
Phayam Lodge ☎086 995 2598, ⓦphayamlodge .com. Not quite finished at the time of writing – and with not much shade – but this welcoming place is probably a sign of things to come on Ko Phayam: rows of large, smart concrete villas with attractive teak fittings, proper bathrooms, a/c and hot showers (though electricity is not 24hr). Wi-fi available. B2200
Smile Hut ☎077 820335 or ☎081 515 0856, ⓦsmilehutthai.com. Like *Bamboo*, this is very popular with travellers. The 35 split-bamboo and wooden huts with mosquito nets are simple but en suite and are spread

among the shorefront trees, with the slightly cheaper versions set one row behind. Has internet access and kayaks. **B400**

AO KAO KWAI

Ao Kao Kwai is particularly popular both with long-stay guests and returnees, so you might want to book your accommodation in advance. *PP Land* (see opposite) have recently opened a branch over here, *Heaven Beach* (ⓦ payamheavenbeach.com).

★ **Mr Gao** ☎ 077 870222, ⓦ mr-gao-phayam.com. Located on the best stretch of the beach, this is one of the most famous and popular spots, a well-established operation comprising a good restaurant and just nine well-designed bungalows, in assorted sizes and luxury,

set in a spacious, lovingly tended garden of shrubs and bamboos. All have good bathrooms and generous decks and most have polished wood floors, screened windows and thoughtfully furnished interiors. Internet access. **B500**

Payam Cottage ☎ 085 222 1847, ⓦ payamcottage .com. More resort-like in style and facilities than others on Ko Phayam, with 24hr electricity, the option of a/c, a kids' play area and a good-sized swimming pool. Bungalows are tastefully furnished and built in angled rows across a central garden to give each one some sort of sea view. Internet access and free wi-fi. **B1600**

Vijit ☎ 077 834082, ⓦ ohpayam-vijit.com. This long-running outfit in a lush garden is very popular. Some of the en-suite, clapboard bungalows are designed for families and they're all reasonably spacious and have fans. Free wi-fi. **B400**

EATING AND DRINKING

Several laidback little beach-bars, including the long-running *Rasta Baby* on Ao Yai and *Hippie Bar* on Ao Kao Khwai, put on fireshows and occasional parties.

THE VILLAGE

★ **Oscar's** Just north of the pier-head ☎ 084 842 5070. Offers breakfasts, including home-baked bread, Thai standards such as *tom yam kung* (B90), pizzas, Indian curries, shepherd's pie (B180) and other English favourites, but is most famous for its partially open-air bar, which is the focal point of the expat social scene. Wi-fi planned. Daily 7am–late.

AO YAI

Bamboo Bungalows Tasty spaghetti with pesto (B150), schnitzels, sandwiches and Western breakfasts at this

beachfront restaurant, as well as lots of Thai standards, including seafood priced by weight. Also does wine by the glass and Middle Eastern coffee. Daily 7.45am–10pm.

Horizon Just inland on the Ao Yai road. Congenial outdoor restaurant for very tasty Thai food, all of it offered vegetarian, with the option of adding meat: a toothsome *matsaman* curry with carrot, pumpkin and potatoes costs B60, and you can add chicken for B20. Also does a few Western main courses, sandwiches, a wide choice of breakfasts, Thai desserts, and all kinds of teas, juices and lassis. High season daily 7/8am–8/9pm, closed evenings in shoulder season, closed in low season.

Khuraburi

The small town of **KHURABURI**, 110km south of Ranong on Highway 4, is the main departure point for the magnificent national park island chain of Ko Surin. Much closer to Khuraburi are the islands of **Ko Ra** and **Ko Phra Thong**, which offer empty beaches and decent snorkelling and bird-watching, or there's the chance to participate in typical village life at **homestays** in mainland coastal communities.

Khuraburi's commercial heart is a 500m strip of shops and businesses either side of Highway 4. Most travellers use the town just as a staging post en route to or from the Surin islands: the main pier for boats to the islands is just 7.5km away, and Khuraburi's tour agents sell boat tickets and offer transport to the pier. Though lacking in famous attractions, the local area is nonetheless scenic, both offshore and inland: with an afternoon or more to spare, you could either rent a motorbike, mountain bike or kayak to explore it independently, or charter a motorbike taxi or longtail boat.

Ko Ra

Hilly, forested **Ko Ra** (measuring about 10km north to south and 3km across) sits just off Khuraburi pier's mangrove-lined estuary and is graced with intact rainforest full of towering trees, hornbills and wild, empty beaches. The island is home to some two

---

ANDAMAN DISCOVERIES HOMESTAY PROGRAMME

Khuraburi is the headquarters of the community-based tourism initiative Andaman Discoveries (☎087 917 7165, ⒲andamandiscoveries.com), which runs a recommended **day-trip and homestay programme** in several local villages, as well as interesting trips to Ko Surin (see p.305). It was established after the tsunami to help the area's many devastated fishing communities get back on their feet and has since developed a range of stimulating one- to five-day packages (from B1600 per person per day) featuring all sort of village jobs and activities, from soap-making and batik design to cashew nut-farming and roof-thatching. The office is just east off the highway (south of the bus station), up the soi beside the police box, across from the post office.

---

dozen *chao ley* people (see p.304), plus just one place to stay, the rather special American–Thai *Ko Ra Ecolodge*. On offer are half-day guided tours to the nearby Moken village on Ko Ra; kayak rental and guided day and multi-day sea-kayaking trips; guided and self-guided hiking and bird-watching; yoga classes and retreats; snorkelling trips to nearby Ko Surin (B2900 per person, all-inclusive), as well as to the little-visited islands of Laem Son National Park; and diving to the Surin islands (B6900 for two dives, not including national park entrance fee and equipment rental) and Reef Check courses to monitor the local coral.

Ko Phra Thong

Immediately to the south of Ko Ra, just 1km or so off the Khuraburi coast, **Ko Phra Thong** (Golden Buddha Island) also has some lovely beaches, the nicest of which, on the west coast, is 10km long and blessed with fine gold sand. This is the site of the *Golden Buddha Beach Resort* and of the British-run Blue Guru Dive Centre (☎080 144 0551, ⒲blue-guru.org). The resort offers kayaking, trekking and yoga, while Blue Guru runs all manner of snorkelling tours, PADI courses and dive trips and live-aboards to Ko Tachai, Ko Surin, Richelieu Rock and into Burma, including unique one-day dive trips to Richelieu and overnighters on Ko Surin (diving Richelieu). Blue Guru's owners also organize longtail tours of the island's mangroves and maintain a website to promote the island, ⒲kohphrathong.com, which includes information about homestays and budget bungalows.

ARRIVAL AND DEPARTURE   KHURABURI, KO RA AND KO PHRA THONG

KHURABURI

By bus The bus station is just off the east side of Highway 4 in the centre of town, but some long-distance through buses stop only on the highway.

Destinations: Bangkok (6 daily to Southern Bus Terminal, of which 2 continue to Mo Chit; 10hr); Khao Lak (6 daily; 1hr 45min); Phuket (6 daily; 3hr 30min–4hr); Ranong (6 daily; 2hr); Takua Pa (6 daily; 1hr).

KO RA

By boat A longtail transfer to the *Ecolodge* from the pier at Khuraburi costs B600 (20min).

KO PHRA THONG

By boat A longtail transfer to *Golden Buddha Beach Resort* from the pier at Khuraburi costs B1800 (90min).

GETTING AROUND

KHURABURI

Bike and motorbike rental Tom & Am Tour, who have their office on the west side of the main road in the town centre and maintain a desk in the bus station in high

season (☎086 272 0588, ✉tom_am01@hotmail.com), rent bicycles, motorbikes and cars. *Boon Piya Resort* also rent motorbikes.

ACCOMMODATION

KHURABURI

Boon Piya Resort 100m north of the bus station, on

the same side of the main road ☎081 752 5457. Well-appointed, if rather tightly packed, motel-style concrete bungalows in a tree-strewn courtyard set just back off the road. All have a/c and powerful hot showers; they're the usual choice of sales reps and NGOs. Wi-fi available. B650

Mr Tom's Bungalows On the north bank of the river, east of the bridge ☎086 272 0588, @tom_am01 @hotmail.com. Decent bungalows in a pleasant setting on the north bank of the river, with wi-fi and breakfast included, and kayaks for rent; call in at Tom & Am Tour (see opposite) first. B290

Tararin On the south bank of the river towards the northern end of town, about 200m north of the bus station ☎076 491789. This cute, rustic-style place has just a handful of simple but appealing en-suite wooden and concrete bungalows, some of them on stilts with balconies right over the water, plus an attractive riverside restaurant and eating deck. All rooms have TVs; a/c (B500) have hot showers. B300

KO RA

★ **Ko Ra Ecolodge** ☎089 867 5288, @thaiecolodge .com. This ecotourism venture fronts a curve of bronze sand on the north coast, with magnificent views to the Khuraburi hills, but its star feature is its wild, forty-acre, forest garden. Filled with screw palms, red-barked *samet daeng* trees, dipterocarps and over seventeen epiphytic orchids, the private forest is crossed by trails and home both to a rich bird life, especially sunbirds and oriental pied hornbills, and to monitor lizards, crab-eating macaques and dusky langurs. Accommodation is in eighteen plain but spacious rooms in split-bamboo longhouses just back from the shore, communal meals are taken in the beach-side *sala* (full board B75/day) and there's a genuine focus on community and environmental projects (volunteer placements and internships are offered). Closed May–Oct. B1100

KO PHRA THONG

Golden Buddha Beach Resort ☎081 892 2208, @goldenbuddharesort.com. Tasteful complex of 25 individually styled wooden Thai-style homes, sleeping two to six, with a spa and clubhouse. B4000

EATING AND DRINKING

KHURABURI

At night, many people eat at the night market south of the bus station, where the roti stall is a particular favourite, flipping out a constant pile of sizzling *roti mataba* (chicken) and *roti kluay* (banana). The morning market (daily from 5am) across from *Boon Piya* is the place to stock up on food for the Surin islands.

Tararin Bungalows On the south bank of the river towards the northern end of town, about 200m north of the bus station. Popular with visiting Thais, this riverside deck restaurant hits the spot with specialities such as *nam phrik kapii*, a southern relish made with shrimp paste, and *kaeng liang*, peppery vegetable soup, as well as loads of salads, fish and seafood. Mon–Sat 10am–9pm.

Ko Surin

Mu Ko Surin National Park, about 60km offshore • Nov 1–April 30 • B400 entry fee, valid for 5 days • @dnp.go.th

Unusually shallow reefs, a palette of awesomely clear turquoise waters and dazzling white sands, and dense forests of lofty dipterocarps combine to make the islands of **Ko Surin** one of the most popular destinations in south Thailand. However, Ko Surin's most famous feature, its spectacular and diverse coral lying in fields just below the surface at the perfect depth for snorkelling, was severely bleached by a sudden rise in sea temperature in early 2010. Four of the most popular reefs are now closed to visitors, though half a dozen other sites that were less severely affected by the bleaching remain open; the national park is still a good spot for snorkellers, with plenty of fish to see, but it will take many years for the reefs to recover.

Ko Surin is very much an outdoors experience, with the bulk of accommodation in national park tents, no commerce on the islands at all, and twice-daily snorkelling the main activity. Several tour operators run snorkelling day-trips from Khuraburi, and there are diving trips too, most of which also take in nearby Richelieu Rock, considered to be Thailand's top dive site (see p.338), but independent travel is also recommended. Because the islands are so far out at sea, Ko Surin is closed to visitors from roughly May to October, when monsoon weather renders the 60km trip a potentially suicidal undertaking.

THE CHAO LEY: MOKEN AND URAK LAWOY

Sometimes called sea gypsies, the **chao ley** or *chao nam* ("people of the sea" or "water people") have been living off the seas around the west coast of the Malay peninsula for hundreds of years. Some still pursue a traditional nomadic existence, living in self-contained houseboats known as **kabang**, but many have now made permanent homes in Andaman coast settlements in Thailand, Burma and Malaysia. Dark-skinned and sometimes with an auburn tinge to their hair, the *chao ley* of the Andaman Sea are thought to number around five thousand, divided into five groups, with distinct lifestyles and dialects.

Of the different groups, the **Urak Lawoy**, who have settled on the islands of Ko Lanta, Ko Jum, Ko Phi Phi, Phuket and Ko Lipe, are the most integrated into Thai society. They came north to Thailand from Malaysia around two hundred years ago (having possibly migrated from the Nicobar Islands in the Indian Ocean some two centuries prior) and are known as *Thai Mai*, or "New Thai". Thailand's Urak Lawoy have been recognized as Thai citizens since the 1960s, when the late Queen Mother granted them five family names, thereby enabling them to possess ID cards and go to school. Many work on coconut plantations or as fishermen, while others continue in the more traditional *chao ley* **occupations** of hunting for pearls and seashells on the ocean floor, attaching stones to their waists to dive to depths of 60m with only an air-hose connecting them to the surface; sometimes they fish in this way too, taking down enormous nets into which they herd the fish as they walk along the sea bed. Their agility and courage make them good bird's-nesters as well (see box, p.376).

The **Moken** of Thailand's Ko Surin islands and Burma's Mergui archipelago probably came originally from Burma and are the most traditional of the *chao ley* communities. Some still lead remote, itinerant lives, and most are unregistered as Thai citizens, owning no land or property, but dependent on fresh water and beaches to collect shells and sea slugs to sell to Thai traders. They have extensive knowledge of the plants that grow in the remaining jungles on Thailand's west-coast islands, using eighty different species for food alone, and thirty for medicinal purposes.

The *chao ley* are **animists**, with a strong connection both to the natural spirits of island and sea and to their own ancestral spirits. On some beaches they set up totem poles as a contact point between the spirits, their ancestors and their shaman. The sea gypsies have a rich **musical heritage** too. The Moken do not use any instruments as such, making do with found objects for percussion; the Urak Lawoy, on the other hand, due to their closer proximity to the Thai and Malay cultures, are excellent violin- and drum-players. During community entertainments, such as the Urak Lawoy's twice-yearly full-moon **festivals** on Ko Lanta (see p.384), the male musicians form a semicircle around the old women, who dance and sing about the sea, the jungle and their families.

Building a new boat is the ultimate expression of what it is to be a *chao ley*, and tradition holds that every newly married couple has a *kabang* built for them. But the complex art of constructing a seaworthy home from a single tree trunk, and the way of life it represents, is disappearing. In Thailand, where **assimilation** is actively promoted by the government, the truly nomadic flotillas have become increasingly marginalized, and the number of undeveloped islands they can visit unhindered gets smaller year by year. The 2004 tsunami further threatened their cultural integrity: when the waves destroyed the Moken's boats and homes on Ko Surin, they were obliged to take refuge on the mainland, where some were encouraged by missionaries to convert from their animist religion. Though the Moken have since returned to the Surin islands, inappropriate donations and the merging of two villages have exacerbated family rivalries and caused divisions that may prove lethal to their traditional way of life.

Surin Nua and Surin Tai

The most easily explored of the reefs are those off the two main islands in the group, Ko Surin Nua (north) and Ko Surin Tai (south), which are separated only by a narrow channel. **Surin Nua**, slightly the larger at about 5km across, holds the national park headquarters, visitor centre and park accommodation.

Across the channel, **Surin Tai** is the long-established home of a community of **Moken** *chao ley*, who are no longer allowed to fish in national park waters but make their living mostly as longtail boatmen for snorkellers staying on Surin Nua. Their recent history has been an unhappy one: not only were their settlements destroyed in the 2004 tsunami, but the aid and outside intervention that followed has changed the community forever, amalgamating two villages, building new homes too close together and introducing various modern-day vices; on top of that, tourist numbers are down since the coral bleaching in 2010. In **Ao Bon** village, Bangkok's Chulalongkorn University has recently built a visitor centre with English display boards, where you can hire a Moken guide to lead you on a nature trail around the village; don't go just in your swimwear, but take a sarong for modesty's sake. You can also make a positive contribution by buying one of the woven pandanus-leaf souvenirs or wooden model boats the villagers make; donations of toothpaste and clothes would also be appreciated. One of the Moken traditions that does persist is the new year celebration that's held every April, during Songkhran, when *chao ley* from nearby islands (including those in Burmese waters) congregate here and, among other rites, release several hundred turtles into the sea, a symbol of longevity.

ARRIVAL AND DEPARTURE
KO SURIN

By boat There are no public boats to Ko Surin, but if you want to stay on the islands, it's perfectly possible to come over on one of the tour boats from Khuraburi and return on another day.

GETTING AROUND

By longtail Once on the islands, there's an efficient system of boat hire: Moken longtails depart twice a day from the national park campsites to the different reefs and Ao Bon village and charge B100/person for about two hours (snorkel sets cost B80/day). You can also charter your own longtail for B2500/day.

TOURS

Most visitors either do **snorkelling day-trips** to the islands from Khuraburi or opt for **dive trips** or live-aboards out of Ko Ra, Ko Phra Thong, Khao Lak, Phuket, Ranong, Ko Chang or Ko Phayam. For snorkellers, there are also day-trips from Ko Ra and Ko Phra Thong, and two-day trips run by *Mr Gao* on Ko Phayam. During the season, speedboat snorkelling trips to Ko Surin depart from Khuraburi pier, 7.5km northwest of Khuraburi town, most days; big, slow, wooden boats (2–3hr; B1300 return) only run at weekends and on national holidays for large groups of Thai tourists.

Andaman Discoveries Khuraburi (see p.302). Four-day trips, with two nights on Ko Surin, focusing on learning about Moken life, including guided forest, village and snorkelling tours and cooking classes (B14,500).
Blue Guru Dive Centre Ko Phra Thong (see p.302). Upmarket day-trips on a dive cruiser or speedboat, including "gourmet lunch", for snorkelling (from B3500) or diving (two dives; from B4900); transfers from Khuraburi hotels included. Also offers multi-day trips to Surin; and transfers from Khao Lak.
Boon Piya Resort Khuraburi (see p.302). Sells boat

tickets and packages, including discounts on national park bungalows on weekdays.
Tom & Am Tour Office on the west side of the main road in Khuraburi town centre, but they also maintain a desk in the bus station in high season ☎086 272 0588, ✉tom_am01@yahoo.co.th. Speedboats to Ko Surin (1hr 15min–2hr), departing the pier at 8.30am, leaving the islands at about 2pm; B1600 including transfers. They also rent tents (B50–100/day), bedding sets (B20/day), snorkel sets (B50/day) and fins (B50/day) for Ko Surin (all cheaper than national park prices).

ACCOMMODATION

All island accommodation is on Surin Nua and is provided by the national park. Both campsites have bathrooms, lockers (B100/day) and dining rooms where meals are served at fixed times three times a day (B80–220); many people take their own supplies from Khuraburi instead. Bungalows need to be booked in advance either through the national parks websites (ⓦdnp.go.th or ⓦthaiforestbooking.com) or at the Khuraburi pier office (☎076 472145–6), but tents should be available on spec except during public holidays and long weekends.

Ao Chong Khad On the beach here, near the park headquarters and pier, you have the choice between en-suite national park bungalows (for 2 people) and either renting a national park tent (B300–450/day) or pitching your own (available for rent in Khuraburi) for B80/day;

bedding sets cost B60/day. Bungalow <u>B2000</u>
Ao Mai Ngam Home to the nicer campsite, with tents (B300–450/day) and pitches (B80/day) but no bungalows, and reached via a 2km trail from headquarters or by longtail.

Khao Sok National Park

🕿 077 395154, 🌐 dnp.go.th • B200, payable at the checkpoint at headquarters and valid for 24hr; you'll have to pay again at Cheow Lan Lake if you arrive more than 24hr later

Most of the Andaman coast's highlights are, unsurprisingly, along the shoreline, but the stunning jungle-clad karsts of **KHAO SOK NATIONAL PARK** are well worth heading inland for. Located about halfway between the southern peninsula's two coasts and easily accessible from Khao Lak, Phuket and Surat Thani, the park has become a popular stop on the travellers' route, offering a number of easy trails, a bit of amateur spelunking and some scenic rafthouse accommodation on Cheow Lan Lake. Much of the park, which protects the watershed of the Sok River and rises to a peak of nearly

KHAO SOK NATIONAL PARK

Sip-et Chan Falls

Ton Klai Falls

National Park
Headquarters

0   250
metres

Bang Laen River

Khao Sok
Track & Trail

1

2

4   1

3

2

$ Morning Mist
Minimarket
& ATM

5

7

6

Sok River

Minimarket

N

Minimarket

Wat Tham Phanturat

Bus stop
Takua Pa   401   🚌 Ban Ta Khun, Cheow Lan Lake & Surat Thani
Bus stop

■ ACCOMMODATION	
Art's Riverview Jungle Lodge	6
Bamboo House	1
Khao Sok Green Mountain View	8
Khao Sok Rainforest Resort	4
Morning Mist Resort	3
Nung House	2
Our Jungle House	5
Thanyamundra Organic Resort	7

● RESTAURANTS & CAFÉS	
Da Pipino	1
Thai Herb Restaurant	2

GUIDED TREKS AND TOURS OF KHAO SOK

PARK TREKS AND NIGHT SAFARIS

The vast majority of visitors choose to join a **guided trek** at some point during their stay in the park. Though the trails are waymarked and easy to navigate alone, the guided experience alerts you to details you'd certainly miss on your own – the claw marks left by a sun-bear scaling a tree in search of honey, for example, or the medicinal plants used for malarial fevers and stomach upsets – and is both fun and inexpensive; prices are fixed but exclude the national park entrance fee.

The usual **day trek** (B700–900) goes to Ton Kloi waterfall, and from about December to March there's also a special route that takes in the blooming of the world's second-biggest flower, the **rafflesia kerrii meier**, a rather unprepossessing brown, cabbage-like plant whose enormous russet-coloured petals unfurl to a diameter of up to 80cm; it's also known as "stinking corpse lily" because it gives off a stink like rotting flesh.

After-dinner **night safaris** along the main park trails (B600–800 for 2–4hr) are also popular, not least because they're good for spotting civets, mouse deer and slow loris and, if you're exceptionally lucky, elephants and clouded leopards as well – more likely on darker nights away from the full moon.

You get to stay out in the jungle on the **overnight camping trips** (about B2300), usually around Tan Sawan falls.

Reputable and long-serving **guides** include those booked through *Bamboo House*, *Nung House* and *Khao Sok Rainforest Resort* and at Khao Sok Track & Trail (☎081 958 0629, ⓦkhaosoktrackandtrail.info).

Any guesthouse can also arrange **elephant-rides** (B800–900) and fix you up with equipment and transfers for **tubing** and **canoeing** trips along the Sok River (from B300/B600).

CHEOW LAN LAKE TOURS

The Australian–Thai-run Limestone Lake Rainforest Tours (☎087 268 8017, ⓦlimestonelaketours .com) offers a big range of **lake-based tours**, including a two-hour trip (B1800/boat) and a full-day trip with optional overnight in a rafthouse (from B2500/3700 per person for up to three people, including park entry fee, or cheaper with larger groups).

Khao Sok guesthouses charge B1500 for a day-trip to the lake and around B2500 for two-day, one-night trips. It's also possible to simply turn up at the dam and hire a boat for around B2000.

1000m, is carpeted in impenetrable rainforest, home to gaurs, leopard cats and tigers among others – and up to 155 species of bird. The limestone crags that dominate almost every vista both on and away from the lake are breathtaking, never more so than in the early morning: waking up to the sound of hooting gibbons and the sight of thick white mist curling around the karst formations is an experience not quickly forgotten.

The park has two centres: the **tourist village** that has grown up around the park headquarters and trailheads, which offers all essential services, including an **ATM** at Morning Mist Minimarket and currency exchange and overseas phone services at Khao Sok Track & Trail; and the dam, 65km further east, at the head of **Cheow Lan Lake**. Most visitors stay in the tourist village and organize their lake trips from there, but it's also feasible to do one or more nights at the lake first. Take plenty of water when hiking as Khao Sok is notoriously humid.

The trails

Seven of the park's nine attractions (waterfalls, pools, gorges and viewpoints) branch off the clearly signed main **trail** that runs west of the park headquarters and visitor centre, along the Sok River. The first 3.5km constitute the **interpretative trail** described in *Waterfalls and Gibbon Calls* (see p.309), an unexceptional ninety-minute one-way trail along a broad, road-like track. Most people continue along the river to **Ton Kloi waterfall**, 7km from headquarters (allow 3hr each way), which flows year-round and tumbles into a pool that's good for swimming. En route, signs point to **Bang Liap Nam waterfall** (4.5km from headquarters), which is a straightforward hike; and **Tan Sawan waterfall** (6km from headquarters), which involves wading along a river bed for the final kilometre and should not be attempted during the rainy season. The trail to the rather spectacular eleven-tiered **Sip-et Chan waterfall**, which shoots off north from the park headquarters and follows the course of the Bang Laen River, is no longer much used and can be quite indistinct. Though the falls are only 4km from headquarters, there's a fair bit of climbing on the way, plus half a dozen river crossings, so you should allow three hours each way.

Cheow Lan Lake

65km from national park headquarters

Dubbed Thailand's Guilin because of its photogenic karst islands, forested inlets and mist-clad mountains encircling jade-coloured waters, the vast 28km-long **Cheow Lan Lake** (also known as **Ratchabrapa Dam** reservoir) is Khao Sok's most famous feature and the most popular destination for guided tours. It was created in the 1980s when the Khlong Saeng River was dammed to power a new hydroelectricity plant, and its forested shores and hundred-plus islands now harbour abundant bird life, as well as some primates, most easily spotted in the very early morning. Tours generally combine a trip on the lake with a wade through the nearby flooded cave system and a night on a floating rafthouse. The lake can only be explored by longtail boat tour, arranged either from Khao Sok or from Ratchabrapa Dam.

For many people, the highlight of their lake excursion is the adventurous three-hour trek to and through the 800m-long horseshoe-shaped **Nam Talu cave**, a five-minute boat ride from the national park rafthouses, or about an hour's boat ride from the dam. The **trek** is not for everyone, however, as the cave section entails an hour-long wade through the river that hollowed out this tunnel: it's slippery underfoot and pitch black and there will be at least one 20m section where you have to swim. When the river level is high there will be longer swims. Never attempt the cave without an authorized park guide and heed any closure signs posted because of high water levels and strong currents; in October 2007 a flash flood caused nine fatalities here and the park authorities are now stricter. Wear sandals with decent grip and request (or take) your own torch.

Part of the appeal of a night in a rafthouse on Cheow Lan Lake is the **dawn safari** the next morning, when you've a good chance of seeing langurs, macaques and gibbons on the lakeshore; some tours include this option, or you can usually borrow a kayak from your accommodation and paddle around the shore yourself.

ARRIVAL AND DEPARTURE   KHAO SOK NATIONAL PARK

Khao Sok National Park headquarters, its tourist village and Cheow Lan Lake are all north off Highway 401, which is served by frequent **buses**: all services between the junction town of **Takua Pa**, 40km south of Khuraburi, and Surat Thani come this way, including some Surat Thani services to and from Khao Lak and Phuket. Coming from Bangkok, Hua Hin or Chumphon, take a Surat Thani-bound bus as far as the Highway 401 junction, about 20km before Surat Thani, and change onto one for Takua Pa.

PARK HEADQUARTERS

The access road to the tourist village and trailheads is at kilometre-stone 109 on Highway 401, where guesthouse staff meet bus passengers and offer free lifts to their accommodation, the furthest of which is about 3km from the main road.

Khao Sok Track & Trail in the tourist village (☎ 081 958 0629, ⊕ khaosoktrackandtrail.info) sells bus (including a VIP bus to Bangkok), boat, plane and train tickets, as well as tickets for a/c minibuses to destinations that include Krabi (2hr), Surat Thani's Talat Kaset II via the train station at Phunphin (1hr 45min), Ko Samui (3hr) and Trang (4hr 30min).

Bus destinations: Bangkok (1 daily; 11hr); Khao Lak (9 daily; 1hr 30min); Surat Thani (every 90min; 2hr); Takua Pa (every 90min; 50min).

CHEOW LAN LAKE

Access to the lake is via the town of **Ban Ta Khun**, 50km east of Khao Sok on Route 401, from where it's 12km north to the dam. Many travellers book their tour of the lake from their Khao Sok accommodation, in which case all transport is included, but if coming from Surat Thani or Phang Nga, you could do the lake first. There's a regular **minibus service** from Talat Kaset II in Surat Thani, via Phunphin train station, to Cheow Lan Lake (about every 2hr; 1hr), or you could take a Surat Thani–Takua Pa bus, alight at Ban Ta Khun and get a motorbike taxi to the dam.

INFORMATION

Map The checkpoint office at headquarters supplies a small sketch map of the park and trails.

Guidebooks The best introduction to Khao Sok is the guidebook *Waterfalls and Gibbon Calls* by Thom Henley, which is available at some Khao Sok minimarkets and bungalows.

ACCOMMODATION

PARK HEADQUARTERS

The bulk of the budget accommodation is scenically sited beneath the karsts near the park headquarters, but despite the edge-of-the rainforest location, it can get noisy of an evening, with the sound systems at some backpacker bars pitched against the chattering of the cicadas. Some guesthouses (not listed here) can make life difficult for guests who choose not to book park trips through them.

★ **Art's Riverview Jungle Lodge** ☎ 086 479 3234 or ☎ 087 885 6185. Popular place nicely located away from the main fray next to a good swimming hole, surrounded by jungle and enjoying pretty river views from its terrace restaurant (though the food's no great shakes). The cheaper bungalows are spacious, tastefully designed wooden affairs, with shutters and a deck, while the deluxe versions are bigger still and attractively furnished, some with red-brick outdoor bathrooms and waterfall-style showers; there are also treehouse-style bungalows and family cottages. All rooms have fans and mosquito nets. **B650**

Bamboo House ☎ 081 787 7484, ⓦ krabidir.com /bamboohouse/index.htm. Set in a grassy orchard, this was one of the first guesthouses in the park and is run by welcoming members of the park warden's family. The simple, stilted, en-suite, wooden huts with mosquito nets here are the cheapest in this part of the park and there are also pebble-dashed concrete versions, a couple of treehouse-style bungalows and large, wooden affairs with hot showers and balconies on stilts right over the river (B800). **B200**

Khao Sok Green Mountain View 1500m north up a mostly paved road from Highway 401, just east of the km 106 marker ☎ 087 263 2481, ⓦ khaosok -greenmountainview.com. In a very quiet spot far from almost everyone else, this is a great budget option if you want a remote location. The seven good-quality bamboo and wood bungalows of varying sizes are all en suite and have some nice touches, with pretty open-roofed bath-rooms, fans, mosquito nets, decks and hammocks. They sit on the edge of a rubber plantation on the other side of the karsts from the main accommodation area. There's free transport to the park village or you can walk to *Our Jungle House* across the river in 15min and on to the park headquarters in another 25. **B300**

Khao Sok Rainforest Resort ☎ 077 395135, ⓦ khaosokrainforest.com. This welcoming place has some spectacularly sited "mountain view" bungalows – set high on a jungle slope and affording unsurpassed karst views – plus a/c treehouses and fan or a/c riverside bungalows. The a/c options have hot showers, TVs and mini-bars, and include breakfast in the price. Interiors are decent enough though lacking style. Fan **B500**, a/c **B1650**

★ **Morning Mist Resort** ☎ 089 971 8794, ⓦ khaosok morningmistresort.com. Built within a profuse riverside garden that's filled with carefully tended tropical blooms and a big herb garden that supplies the excellent restaurant, this well-run place offers large, immaculate rooms in variously styled wooden and concrete bungalows, all with hot water and either river, mountain or garden view. It's nicely set up for families, with some rooms sleeping up to four, plus lots of space for kids to play in and a small swimming pool. Good rates for singles. **B550**

Nung House ☎ 077 395147, ⓦ nunghouse.com. Friendly place run by the park warden's son and his family, with eighteen very good huts set around an attractive grassy garden full of rambutan trees. Choose between simple but sturdy bamboo and wood constructions with en-suite facilities, brick and concrete bungalows, and treehouses; some have hot showers and large verandas. **B300**

Our Jungle House ☎ 081 417 0546, ⓦ khaosok accommodation.com. Peaceful, riverside option, a 20min walk from park headquarters, secluded in lush rainforest where you might spot hornbills and several species of monkey. Choose between airy, well-designed, wood and bamboo bungalows and treehouses; all have fans and mosquito nets and most are on the river bank, which has a small beach. Free internet access and wi-fi. Bungalows **B800**, treehouses **B1300**

Thanyamundra Organic Resort ☎ 077 336000, ⓦ thanyamundra.com. Quiet and charming luxury

4

retreat set amid extensive sloping lawns, with a lovely 50m pool and spectacular views over its own organic farm and rice paddies to the karst mountains. Across two buildings, arranged in southern Thai-style compounds, there are just nine rooms and suites, constructed mostly of golden teak wood, with Chinese antique furniture, brass rain showers, free wi-fi, iPod docks and espresso machines. Full-service spa planned. B6290

CHEOW LAN LAKE
On overnight tours to the lake (see p.308), accommodation is either in tents in the jungle or at rafthouses on the lake.

There are both private and national park rafthouses moored at various scenic spots around the lake shore, mostly around an hour's boat ride from the dam. All rafthouse huts are rudimentary bamboo structures with nets and mattresses, offering fabulous lake views from your pillow. If you've arranged your own boat transport, you can fix accommodation at any of the lake's rafthouses for B600 per person including three meals. Jungle Yoga runs yoga, meditation and massage retreats at the remote *Praiwan* rafthouses from December to April (⊕ jungleyoga.com).

EATING AND DRINKING

In the tourist village near park headquarters, there are just a couple of places that might tempt you away from your guesthouse restaurant.

PARK HEADQUARTERS
Da Pipino Homely, rustic, not to say scruffy, Italian restaurant, strewn with lovely plants in a scenic spot by the river. The menu runs to seafood antipasti, decent fettuccine bolognese (B195), a few Italian main courses and a wide range of tasty handmade pizzas. Daily noon–10pm.

Thai Herb Restaurant Morning Mist Resort. Exceptionally tasty and inventive spicy *yam* salads (B70) and other Thai classics, plus a wide choice for vegetarians and breakfasting Westerners; staff grow much of their own produce. Also does Thai desserts and lassis, shakes and herb juices such as roselle. Daily 8am–9pm.

Khao Lak

Handily located just an hour north of Phuket International Airport, and some 30km south of Takua Pa, **KHAO LAK** has established itself as a thriving, mid-market beach resort with plentiful opportunities for diving and snorkelling, easy access to the supreme national park reefs of Ko Similan, and a style that is determinedly unseedy. It lacks sophistication, and is mostly a bit pricey for backpackers, but is ideal for families and extremely popular with northern European tourists. High season here runs from November to April, when the weather and the swimming are at their best and the Similan Islands are open to the public; during the rest of the year, Khao Lak quietens down a lot – and becomes much cheaper too.

The area usually referred to as Khao Lak is in fact a string of beaches west off Highway 4. **Khao Lak** proper is the southernmost and least developed, 5km from the most commercial part of the resort, **Nang Thong** (aka Bang La On), which throngs with shops, restaurants, dive centres and countless places to stay, both on the beachfront and inland from Highway 4. North again about 3km (5min by taxi or a 45min walk up the beach) is lower-key, slightly more youthful **Bang Niang**, a lovely long stretch of golden sand that's backed by a developing tourist village whose network of sois is away from the highway and feels more enticing than its neighbour. Removed from all this commerce, **Laem Pakarang**, 12km further up the coast, a headland and popular sunset-watching spot that gives onto 11km Hat Pakweeb (Hat Bang Sak), is where you find the area's most exclusive accommodation.

There is, thankfully, little obvious evidence these days of the area's devastating experience during the December 2004 **tsunami**, when the undersea earthquake off Sumatra sent a series of murderous waves on to Khao Lak's shores (and the rest of the Andaman coast), vaporizing almost every shorefront home and hotel here and killing thousands. Nang Thong quickly became the centre of a huge reconstruction effort, with thousands of volunteers arriving to help, and rebuilding was mostly

▲ **1** , Laem Pakarang, Bang Sak, Ban Nam Khem, Takua Pa & Surat Thani

KHAO LAK, NANG THONG & BANG NIANG

★ Bus Station

Bang Niang River

Bang Niang

THAI HAT BANG NIANG

SEE INSET BELOW LEFT

N

SEE INSET BELOW RIGHT

Chong Fah Falls

✉ **1**

Nang Thong

THANON NANG THONG

Khao Lak-Lam Ru National Park Headquarters

Police

Tong Pling Falls

Khao Lak

0   1
kilometre

4

▼ **1** , Thap Lamu, Phang Nga, Phuket & Krabi

■ ACCOMMODATION	
Amsterdam Resort	7
Ayara Villas	4, 5, 8
Fair House	6
Jai	10
Khao Lak Banana	13
Khao Lak Green Beach	11
Khao Lak Seafood Family House	9
Nang Thong Bay Resort	12
Phu Khao Lak Resort	14
Poseidon Bungalows	2
Sanuk Bungalows	3
The Sarojin	1

● RESTAURANTS & CAFÉS	
Bussaba	9
The Candle	2
Dive In	10
Jai	7
Khao Niau	5
Navy Club Restaurant	1
O Rendezvous	6
Phu Khao Lak	11
Pinocchio	3
Stempfer Café	8
Takieang	4

■ BARS	
Degree Bar	1
Happy Snapper	2

● SHOPS	
Book Tree	1
Community Crafts	2

4

Bang Niang Beach

Bang Niang River

THAI HAT BANG NIANG

5
8
4 3
7
6
2
@
4
2

Green Biking Club

Police Boat Memorial

Bang Niang Market

Tsunami Museum

Khao Lak Community Appeal Foundation

0   500
metres

BANG NIANG

Sea Dragon Dive Centre

Khao Lak Inter Clinic

6
2
3
9 10

Khao Lak Land Discovery

Nang Thong Supermarket

Police Box

THANON NANG THONG

@

8 9

IQ Dive

11

12

SOI BANG LA ON

13 10

11 14

Everyday 2

0   500
metres

NANG THONG

completed within a couple of years, though for many survivors recovery will probably take a lifetime.

Tsunami Museum

Bang Niang • Daily 9am–7pm • B100 • ⓦ tsunamimuseum.net

This small museum presents a rather dry summary of the facts about the 2004 tsunami, through display boards and videos; the admission fee helps to support local charitable work, as do the crafts on sale.

AFTER THE TSUNAMI

The **Boxing Day tsunami** hit Thailand's Andaman coast just after 9.30am on December 26 2004. The first place to suffer significant damage was Phuket, and the next two hours saw village after resort get battered or decimated by the towering waves thundering in from the Sumatra fault line, 1000km away. The entire coastline from Ranong to Satun was affected, but not all of it with the same intensity: the worst-hit province was Phang Nga, where 4200 people were recorded dead or missing, many of them in the resort of Khao Lak; over 2000 suffered a similar fate on Ko Phi Phi; and more than 900 died on the beaches of Phuket, especially on Patong and Kamala. There were 8212 fatalities in all, a third of them holidaymakers. Another 6000 people were made homeless and some 150,000 lost their jobs, mostly in the tourism and fishing industries. By the end of that day, nearly a quarter of a million people in a dozen countries around the Indian Ocean had lost their lives in the worst natural disaster in recorded history.

Many homes, shops and hotels were quite swiftly rebuilt, but the emotional and social **legacy** of the tsunami endures and most residents along the Andaman coast have a story of terror and bereavement to tell. It's no surprise that many survivors are now afraid of the sea: fearing ghosts, some longtail boatmen won't motor solo past where villages once stood, and hundreds of hotel staff have since sought new jobs in the northern city of Chiang Mai, as far from the sea as they could go.

Immediately after the tsunami, many were surprised when then prime minister Thaksin Shinawatra declined offers of **aid** from foreign governments. But help poured in instead from the Thai government and from royal foundations and local and foreign NGOs and individuals. Of the many **projects** established to help support and rebuild affected communities, the majority have now completed their task; others have evolved into longer-term NGO ventures, including an English-teaching programme in Khao Lak (see p.65), and the community-based tourism company Andaman Discoveries in Khuraburi (see p.302).

Generosity and altruism were not the only responses to the disaster, however. Almost every tsunami-affected community talks of **dishonourable practice** and **corruption**, experiences which have caused bitterness and rifts. Many allegations concern donated money and goods being held back by the local leaders charged with distributing them, and in some cases big business interests muscled in on land deemed "ownerless" because the paperwork had been lost to the waves. Most small businesses had no insurance, and government **compensation** was inconsistently awarded and invariably lacking. In a country where most family enterprises scrape by season to season, it's sobering to contemplate the number of tsunami victims who simply picked up and started over.

Determined not to be caught unawares again, in the unlikely event of Thailand being struck by a second tsunami, the government has created a **tsunami early-warning system** that relays public announcements from towers all the way down the Andaman coast. They have also mapped out evacuation routes, flagged by innumerable "Tsunami Hazard Zone" signs in all the big resorts. For their part, Phuket authorities have remodelled stretches of Ao Patong's beachfront as a building-free zone, creating a park that doubles as a tsunami **memorial**. Krabi officials now require all new buildings to be constructed at least 30m inland from a high-tide boundary, and they even forbid the use of sunloungers below that point. In Khao Lak, a beached police boat (see opposite) has become an eloquent memorial: it rests where it was hurtled by the wave, 2km inland, on the other side of the highway.

Police Boat Memorial

Bang Niang

Inland from the highway – and accessible from it across a field and a bridge – a **beached police boat** has become a memorial to the extraordinary power of the tsunami waves. It was propelled up here, 2km inland, while patrolling the waters in front of *La Flora* resort, where Princess Ubolrat and her children, one of whom perished in the disaster, were staying.

Ban Nam Khem Memorial

13km north of Laem Pakarang up Highway 4, then left for a signposted 3km

The main local tsunami memorial is on the beach at **Ban Nam Khem**, the worst-hit village in Thailand, where half of the four thousand inhabitants died in the waves, as described in Erich Krauss' *Wave of Destruction* (see p.441). Built by the Thai army, it's an evocative installation: you walk down a path between a curling, 4m-high, concrete "wave" and a grassy bank, representing the land, on which plaques commemorate individual victims. Through a window in the concrete wave, a fishing boat looms over you – this "miracle boat" was swept inland but stopped just short of devastating a house and its occupants.

While you're out here, it's worth popping in on the **Saori weaving factory and shop** (not Sun), on the left about 1km further up Highway 4 from the Ban Nam Khem turn-off, towards the northern end of Ban Bang Muang village. It's a regeneration and occupational therapy project, where you can watch the women weaving and buy some lovely scarves.

4

ARRIVAL AND DEPARTURE KHAO LAK

Boats to the Similans depart from the pier at Thap Lamu, which is 6km south of Nang Thong, then 5km west off Highway 4 (see p.318).

By plane Khao Lak is just 70km north of Phuket airport (1hr; B1700–2200 by taxi; see p.321).

By bus and minibus All buses running from Phuket to Takua Pa and Ranong (and vice versa) pass through Khao Lak and can drop you anywhere along Highway 4; coming from Krabi or Phang Nga you'll generally need to change buses in Khokkloi, from Khao Sok, in Takua Pa. On departure, you can flag down most buses on the main road, but the Bangkok services use a bus station at the far north end of Bang Niang. There are also a/c tourist minibuses that

run at least daily to Surat Thani (via Khokkloi, not Khao Sok; 4hr), Krabi/Ao Nang (3hr/3hr 30min) and Trang (change in Krabi; 5hr 30min). Bus and a/c minibus tickets can be booked through, for example, Khao Lak Land Discovery in Nang Thong (☏ 076 485411, ⦿ khaolaklanddiscovery .com), who also offer transfers to and from Phuket Airport (B600/person or B1500/minibus).

Destinations: Bangkok (3 daily; 12hr); Phuket (20 daily; 2hr 30min); Ranong (8 daily; 2hr 30min–3hr); Takua Pa (18 daily; 30min).

GETTING AROUND

By songthaew In the Khao Lak area, a few public songthaews shuttle between Nang Thong and Bang Niang (where they have a base in front of the market), charging B10–20, but mostly they act as private taxis instead and charge B100 or more.

Motorbike and car rental Many hotels can rent motorbikes, and rental cars are available through tour operators; Budget also has an agent on the soi down to *Nang Thong Resort* (☏ 076 443454, ⦿ budget.co.th).

ACCOMMODATION

LAEM PAKARANG

⭐ **The Sarojin** 12km north of Khao Lak ☏ 076 427905, ⦿ thesarojin.com. With a staff-to-guest ratio of two to one and a style and attitude that exudes understated, unpretentious class, this is the top place to stay around Khao Lak. The 56 sleek, tastefully simple rooms are discreetly sited around the wide beachfront garden and

stunning square turquoise swimming pool. It's an obvious honeymoon choice, with a policy of no under-10s, a range of excursions designed for two, and private candlelit tables for dinner on the beach or at a nearby waterfall. There are complimentary non-motorized watersports and mountain bikes, free wi-fi and a spa. All-day breakfast with sparkling wine included. Special promotions often available. **B13,500**

BANG NIANG

Amsterdam Resort Soi 3 ☎081 857 5881, ⓦamsterdamresortkhaolak.com. Just 200m inland from the beach, this helpful Dutch-run little complex offers some of the cheapest accommodation in Bang Niang and serves good food. The rooms and red-brick bungalows of varying size have either fans or a/c; most have hot water. Also has internet and free wi-fi, cycle and motorbike rental and a tour desk. Fan B̲6̲0̲0̲, a/c B̲9̲0̲0̲

Ayara Villas ☎076 486478–9, ⓦayara-villas.com. An attractive upper-mid-range option, spread over three different compounds with two swimming pools. At the top end are beachfront villas right on the sand; many others are terraced bungalows just a few metres from the sea, and the rest are in a three-storey building, with ground-floor rooms enjoying direct pool access. Interiors are a/c and nicely furnished with dark wood in contemporary style and all have kitchenettes. Breakfast included. B̲4̲5̲0̲0̲

Fair House ☎089 473 7985. Currently one of the cheapest places to stay in Bang Niang, with its handful of large, neat, fan-cooled concrete bungalows and rooms with fridges and hot showers, widely spaced around a pretty little garden set back about 50m from the highway, about 1km walk from the beach. B̲6̲0̲0̲

Sanuk Bungalows ☎081 979 0308, ⓦsanukresort .com. Dinky little Swiss-managed group of five comfortable and spacious brick bungalows in a small garden with a heart-shaped whirlpool, just 100m from the beach. Bungalows come with a/c, hot showers, fridges, kitchenettes and wi-fi. B̲1̲0̲0̲0̲

NANG THONG

Jai ☎076 485390, ✉jai_bungalow@hotmail.com. A busy, family-run place that offers some of the cheapest accommodation in Khao Lak. The good-quality, decent-sized, en-suite concrete bungalows are set around a lawn dotted with trees behind the popular restaurant, quite close to the highway and about 600m from the beach; a/c options have hot showers and fridges. Fan B̲4̲0̲0̲, a/c B̲6̲0̲0̲

Khao Lak Banana Soi Bang La On ☎076 485889, ⓦkhaolakbanana.com. Dozens of thoughtfully designed fan and a/c bungalows packed into a garden of banana trees and tropical flowers. All have a safety box, hot shower, wi-fi and fridge and there's a tiny swimming pool. Fan B̲7̲0̲0̲, a/c B̲9̲0̲0̲

★**Khao Lak Green Beach** ☎076 485845, ⓦgreenbeach.de. The attractive design and shorefront location of the bungalows here make this a good-value option, and the staff are great too. Arrayed around a pond, the cream-painted chalet-style bungalows have a/c, hot showers, polished wood floors, pretty furnishings and nice bathrooms and most have a fridge. Price mainly depends on location: some are right on the shore and none is more than a few metres away. Discounts for singles. B̲1̲4̲0̲0̲

DIVING AND SNORKELLING AROUND KHAO LAK

Khao Lak is the closest and most convenient departure point for **diving and snorkelling trips** to the awesome national park islands of **Ko Similan** (see p.316), which can be reached in three to four hours on a live-aboard or other large boat or in two hours in a much less comfortable speedboat. The islands are currently only open from approximately November to April and all divers have to pay a one-off national park fee of B400 plus a B200-a-day diving fee, usually on top of dive-trip prices. **Local Khao Lak dives** are generally possible year-round, especially the highly rated **wreck** of a tin-mining boat near Bang Sak, which is especially rich in marine life such as ghost pipefish, moray eels, scorpion fish, nudibranchs and yellow-tail barracuda. All Khao Lak dive shops also teach PADI **dive courses**, with the last two days of the Openwater course often done on location in the Similans; for advice on choosing a dive shop see "Basics" (see p.51).

IQ Dive Nang Thong, opposite McDonald's ☎076 485614, ⓦiq-dive.com. Swiss–Thai-run PADI Five-Star Centre that specializes in one-day dive trips to the Similans, on a big dive boat (B4700 plus equipment; B2800 for snorkellers). Their Openwater courses cost B17,000 with two days spent diving the Similans.

Sea Dragon Dive Center Nang Thong ☎076 485420, ⓦseadragondivecenter.com. Highly recommended PADI Five-Star Instructor Development Centre which has three live-aboard boats – including budget and deluxe options – running frequent three-day trips to the Similans and Ko Bon (from B11,900 including equipment), and four-day trips to the Similans, Surin islands, Ko Bon, Ko Tachai and Richelieu Rock (from B17,900). Snorkellers get about one-third off. Also offers local wreck and other dives (starting from B1000, not including equipment, for a two-tank dive) and PADI dive courses: the four-day Openwater is B9800, or B15,900 (plus B1200 national park fees) with two day-trips diving the Similans.

Similan Tour At Poseidon Bungalows, 7km south of central Nang Thong, in Khao Lak ☎076 443258, ⓦsimilantour.com. Highly recommended three-day live-aboard snorkelling trips to the Similans (B8200). Current departures are twice weekly on Tuesdays and Fridays, from roughly the end of October to May.

KHAO LAK DAY-TRIPS AND OTHER ACTIVITIES

Aside from diving and snorkelling trips (see opposite), there are several other attractions within day-tripping distance of Khao Lak, including a number of local **waterfalls**. Of these, Sai Rung (Rainbow Falls), about 16km north of Nang Thong in Bang Sak, is the most satisfying. Others include Tong Pling, across from the *Merlin* resort in Khao Lak; Nam Tok Lumphi, about 20km south of Khao Lak; and Chong Fah Falls, located less than 5km east of Bang Niang, but subject to a B100 entry fee because it's part of Khao Lak–Lam Ru National Park (⬤dnp.go.th). The national park's headquarters is on the headland between Nang Thong and Khao Lak beaches, and about 1km south of it, you can easily walk down to a quiet, pretty sandy cove – look for a sign saying "small sandy beach" on the west side of the main road, opposite a layby.

Everyday 2 Restaurant South end of Nang Thong ⬤085 299 0410. Morning Thai cooking courses for B1200, including pick-ups.

The Green Biking Club Bang Niang ⬤076 443211, ⬤greenbikingclub.com. Runs interesting guided mountain-bike trips around rural and coastal Khao Lak (from B1850 for half a day).

Khao Lak Land Discovery Nang Thong ⬤076 485411, ⬤khaolaklanddiscovery.com. One of the best and most reputable, though not the cheapest, local tour operators, whose day-trips include elephant-riding (from B1600), kayaking around Ao Phang Nga (B3200) and trekking, canoeing and elephant-riding in Khao Sok National Park (B2800).

The Yoga Studio Khao Lak Community Appeal Foundation, Bang Niang ⬤089 710 5770, ⬤yoga khaolak.com. High-season yoga classes (B500 for one class) – see the website for the schedule.

Khao Lak Seafood Family House Soi Noen Thong ⬤076 485318, ⬤khaolakseafood.com. The large, good-quality bungalows here are set well back from the road in a garden behind the eponymous restaurant. The fan ones are especially good value for Khao Lak: roomy and nicely designed with good, hot-water bathrooms; a/c rooms in a couple of two-storey blocks are also available. It's a family business and very popular with returning guests and long stayers. Wi-fi available. Fan B600, a/c B1200

Nang Thong Bay Resort ⬤076 485088–9, ⬤nangthong.com. Well priced considering its on-the-beach location, this popular, long-established place offers smartly maintained a/c bungalows that are well spaced around the shorefront garden and mostly enjoy sea views, plus some hotel-style rooms. There's a sea-view swimming pool and restaurant as well. B2000

★ **Phu Khao Lak Resort** ⬤076 485141, ⬤phukhaolak.com. There is a luxurious amount of space at this well-run place, where the thirty large, spotlessly clean bungalows sit prettily amid a grassy park-style coconut plantation. Fan rooms have tiled floors and most have hot-water bathrooms; a/c ones have picture windows and quite stylish interiors. There's a swimming pool, good restaurant and wi-fi in the lounge-library. About 500m walk from the beach. Fan B500, a/c B1500

KHAO LAK

Poseidon Bungalows ⬤076 443258, ⬤similantour .com. Seven kilometres south of central Nang Thong, surrounded by rubber plantations and set above a sandy shore of wave-smoothed rocks just north of the Thai navy's private beach, this Swedish–Thai-run guesthouse is both a quiet place to hang out for a few days and a long-established organizer of snorkelling expeditions to the Similan islands (see opposite). All fifteen bungalows are en suite and fan cooled, with generous amounts of space, hot showers and balconies, some enjoying sea views; there's also internet access, free wi-fi and motorbike rental. Get off the bus at the *Poseidon* sign between kilometre-stones 53 and 54, then phone for a pick-up or walk 1km. B900

EATING AND DRINKING

BANG NIANG

The Candle ⬤076 486123, ⬤thecandlerestaurant .com. White-tablecloth bistro, with an a/c room and outdoor tables, serving tasty Thai traditional and fusion dishes, such as green curry with deep-fried crispy chicken and sweet peppers (B215), and Thai desserts. Daily 11.30am–10.30pm.

Degree Bar With its wooden tables, water-buffalo skulls and folksy, Thai-country vibe, this cheap, welcoming and enjoyably local bar-restaurant is a fun place to listen to live bands, from 10pm every night, playing Thai and Western pop, *luk thung* and "Songs for Life". Daily 9pm–2am.

Khao Niau Rustic, open-sided restaurant dishing up very good northeastern Thai food, including loads of salads such as *som tam* (from B60), *laap* and *nam tok*. Daily 1–10pm; closed 9th and 23rd of each month.

Pinocchio ⬤076 443079. Home-made pastas, decent pizzas made in a wood-fired oven (around B300), a few Italian meat main courses and lots of seafood, topped off with tiramisu and other home-made desserts. Look for the white picket fence and fairy lights. Daily noon–11pm.

Takieang Wooden roadside restaurant that's gone slightly upmarket, offering authentic Thai food, including good *tom yum kung* (B150), banana-flower salad (B120) and exceptional seafood hotplates (B250). Daily noon–10pm.

NANG THONG

Bussaba Welcoming bistro with a long menu of Thai food, including seafood and fish priced by weight and some slightly more unusual dishes such as shrimp green curry with roti bread (B189). Also does sandwiches and a few other Western choices, and good espressos. Daily 1.30–11pm.

★ **Dive In** Khao Lak Banana Resort, Soi Bang La On. Owner and chef Sunny cooks up a storm here and is a favourite with expats, locals and returning tourists. Highlights include a deliciously aromatic *matsaman* curry (B90), *khanom jiin* Phuket-style noodles with fish and red curry, and deep-fried fish topped with mango. The Western menu runs to home-made cakes and bread, breakfasts and espressos. Free wi-fi. Daily 6.30am–11pm.

Happy Snapper ☉ happysnapperbar.com. Khao Lak's most famous dive-staff hangout is chilled and pleasant, with a folksy lounge ambience and a drinks menu that runs to over a hundred cocktails. There's live music, including punk, Mon–Sat from around 10.30pm, and a chill-out DJ on Sun – plus the occasional open-mike session. Daily 8.30pm–1am.

Jai This lofty, open-sided, roadside restaurant is deservedly popular for its hearty, often fiery curries in good-sized portions (B80), including *kaeng phanaeng* and *matsaman*, seafood and *tom yam kung*. Also does a few Thai desserts

and Western breakfasts. Daily 8.30am–10pm.

O Rendezvous ☎ 076 485108, ☉ orendezvouskhaolak .com. Thatched, indoor-outdoor, French–Thai bar-restaurant, very popular with local expats, where you can feast on duck in orange and wine sauce (B420) or Thai specialities like shrimp and banana-flower salad, as well as cheaper standard dishes such as chicken *matsaman* curry (B110). Daily 4–11pm.

Phu Khao Lak Well-known and good-value restaurant attached to the bungalows of the same name serving exceptionally good Thai food from a picture menu that stretches to over a hundred dishes. Everything from red, yellow and green curries (B120–150) to seafood platters. Daily 7am–10pm.

Stempfer Café Genteel, German-style café serving good breakfasts, espresso coffees, hot chocolate and all kinds of teas, lots of bread and cakes including apple tart (B100), plus salads and sandwiches. Free wi-fi. Daily 8.30am–9.30pm.

THAP LAMU

Navy Club Restaurant On the right by the pier, 11km southwest of Nang Thong ☎ 081 648 8656. It's worth the trip out here for some authentic Thai food and the freshest seafood, at prices lower than in Khao Lak itself. Specialities include soft-shell crab, white snapper, pomfret (B35/100g), king prawns and squid, and there are dozens of Thai salads (B80). The restaurant is unprepossessing, but you could phone ahead to book a table on the terrace overlooking the harbour. Daily 10am–10pm.

SHOPPING

Nang Thong offers plenty of shopping, mainly for clothes, souvenirs and handicrafts, with countless tailors and opticians too.

Book Tree Far north end of Nang Thong. New and secondhand books plus magazines, newspapers and art cards, and also serves coffee. Daily 9am–9pm.

Community Crafts Khao Lak Community Appeal Foundation, on the east side of the main road in Bang

Niang ☉ khaolakappeal.com. Non-profit shop selling bead jewellery, batiks, bags and lanterns, made by Thai, Moken and immigrant Burmese groups. Mon–Sat 1–6pm, sometimes open Mon–Fri mornings.

Ko Similan

Mu Ko Similan National Park • B400, valid for 5 days if staying within the national park • Closed May to Oct

Rated as one of the world's best spots for both above-water and underwater beauty, the eleven islands at the heart of the Mu **Ko Similan** National Park are among the most exciting **diving** destinations in Thailand. Massive granite boulders set magnificently against turquoise waters give the islands their distinctive character, but it's the 30m visibility that draws the divers. The 5000-year-old reefs are said to be the oldest in Thailand, so there's an enormous diversity of species, and the underwater scenery is nothing short of overwhelming: the reefs teem with coral fish, and you'll also see turtles, manta rays, moray eels, jacks, reef sharks, sea snakes, red grouper and quite possibly white-tip sharks, barracuda, giant lobster and enormous tuna.

The **islands** lie 64km off the mainland and include the eponymous Ko Similan chain of nine islands as well as two more northerly islands, Ko Bon and Ko Tachai, which are both favoured haunts of manta rays and whale sharks and are halfway between the Similan chain and the islands of Ko Surin. The Similans are numbered north–south from nine to one and are often referred to by number: Ko Ba Ngu (9), Ko Similan (8), Ko Payoo (7), Ko Hin Posar (aka Ko Hok; 6), Ko Ha (5), Ko Miang (4), Ko Pahyan (3), Ko Pahyang (2) and Ko Hu Yong (1). The national park headquarters and accommodation is on Ko Miang and there's also a campsite and restaurant on Ko Similan. Ko Similan is the largest island in the chain, blessed with a beautiful, fine white-sand bay and impressive boulders and traversed by two nature trails; Ko Miang has two pretty beaches, twenty minutes' walk apart, and three nature trails; Ko Hu Yong has an exceptionally long white-sand bay but access is restricted by the Thai navy as **turtles** lay their eggs there from November to February.

Such beauty has not gone unnoticed and the islands are extremely popular with day-trippers from Phuket and Khao Lak, as well as with divers and snorkellers on longer live-aboard trips. This has caused the inevitable congestion and environmental problems and the Similan reefs have been damaged in places by anchors and by the local practice of using dynamite in fishing. National parks authorities have responded by banning fishermen and enforcing strict regulations for tourist boats, including **closing the islands** during the monsoon season, from May to October.

ARRIVAL AND DEPARTURE — KO SIMILAN

Independent travellers wanting to stay on the island for a few days can usually use the snorkelling tour boats for transfers. There are also plenty of live-aboard diving or snorkelling trips to the islands, the best and cheapest of which run out of Khao Lak (see p.314).

Snorkelling tours Most travel agents in Khao Lak, Phuket and Phang Nga sell snorkelling packages to Ko Similan, usually as day-trips featuring at least four island stops (from B3100 including national park fees); two-day, one-night (B5800 staying in tents), and three-day, two-night (B7200) packages, staying on Ko Miang, are also available. The majority of these trips carry quite large groups and use fast boats that depart from Thap Lamu pier, about 11km southwest of Khao Lak's Nang Thong, 90km north of Phuket town, at about 8.30am and get to the islands in under two hours. They depart the islands at around 3pm. Companies offering this service, all of which offer pick-ups in Khao Lak and Phuket, include Medsye Travel and Tours, who also do pick-ups in Krabi (☎076 443276, ⓦmedsye.com), and Jack Similan (☎081 648 8656, ⓦjacksimilan.com), both of which have offices at the Thap Lamu pier; and Khao Lak Land Discovery in Nang Thong (☎076 485411, ⓦkhaolaklanddiscovery.com).

GETTING AROUND

If travelling independently, you'll need to use Ko Similan longtail boats to travel **between the islands** and to explore different reefs: prices are fixed and cost around B200 per person for a half-day trip.

ACCOMMODATION AND EATING

Limited accommodation is available on **Ko Miang**, in the shape of national park rooms and bungalows (fan B1000, a/c B2000) and tents (B300–450), and there's a campsite on **Ko Similan** too; both islands also have a restaurant. Accommodation should be booked ahead, either at the national parks office 500m east of Thap Lamu pier (☎076 453272) or online (ⓦdnp.go.th or ⓦthaiforestbooking.com), as facilities can get crowded with tour groups, especially on weekends and holidays.

Phuket

Thailand's largest island and a province in its own right, **PHUKET** (pronounced "Poo-ket") has been a prosperous region since the nineteenth century, when Chinese merchants got in on its tin-mining and sea-borne trade, before turning to the rubber industry. It remains the wealthiest province in Thailand, with the highest per-capita income, but what mints the

PHUKET DAY-TRIPS AND OTHER ACTIVITIES

Bookings for most of the following **Phuket day-trips and activities** can be made through any tour agent and should include return transport from your hotel (though not for the cooking classes). In addition to the trips listed below, diving is also available (see p.338). Other **sights** worth checking out, especially for kids, include the Phuket Butterfly Garden and Insect World in Phuket town (see p.325), the Aquarium on Laem Panwa (p.342), the Shell Museum in Rawai (p.342), the Big Buddha near Chalong (p.342) and the Gibbon Rehabilitation Project near Thalang (p.345). Avoid any tour that features Ko Siray (Ko Sireh), the island across the narrow channel from Phuket town, which merely encourages tour-bus passengers to gawp at Phuket's largest and longest-established indigenous *chao ley* community (see p.304).

Bicycle touring Full- and half-day guided mountain-bike rides into Phuket's rural hinterlands and to Ko Yao Noi, as well as multi-day rides around Phang Nga Bay, with Action Holidays Phuket (☎076 263575, ⓦbike toursthailand.com; full day from B2400).

Elephant trekking Award-winning, conservation-conscious Siam Safari (☎076 280116, ⓦsiamsafari .com) runs Four-in-One tours featuring their hillside elephant camp plus rubber tapping, buffalo-cart riding and a sail on a Burmese junk (B2350); tours to Khao Sok National Park are also on offer.

Kiteboarding One- (B4000) and three-day courses (B11,000) at Hat Nai Yang and Ao Chalong (depending on the season) are offered by Kiteboarding Asia (☎081 591 4594, ⓦkiteboardingasia.com).

Mini-golf If you just need a little time off from the beach, head for the eighteen-hole Dino Park mini-golf (daily 10am–midnight; B240; ⓦdinopark.com), next to *Marina Phuket Resort* on the headland between Ao Karon and Ao Kata, which is part of a pseudo-prehistoric theme park comprising a dinosaur restaurant and an erupting "volcano" (evenings only).

Sea-canoeing There are dozens of companies offering canoeing and kayaking in Phuket, but the two with the best reputations are John Gray's Sea Canoe (☎076 254505–7, ⓦjohngray-seacanoe.com), who offer "Starlight" afternoon and evening trips around the spectacular limestone karsts of Ao Phang Nga (B3900), as well as multi-day and self-paddle trips; and Paddle Asia (☎076 241519, ⓦpaddleasia.com), who run day-trips to Ao Phang Nga (B4200) and multi-day trips, which can include Khao Sok National Park and other adventure activities.

Surfing The rainy season (roughly May–Oct) is the best time for surfing off Phuket's west coast; courses (B1500 for a 90min private lesson) and board rental are available from Phuket Surf on Ao Kata Yai (☎087 889 7308, ⓦphuketsurf.com).

Thai cookery courses Most famously, every Sat and Sun morning at *The Boathouse* hotel on Ao Kata Yai (B2200; ☎076 330015, ⓦboathousephuket.com); but also at the *Holiday Inn Phuket*, 86/11 Thanon Thavee Wong, Patong (Mon–Sat afternoons; B1800; ☎076 340608, ⓦphuket.holiday-inn.com); and the *Blue Elephant Restaurant*, 96 Thanon Krabi, Phuket town (B3300 for a half-day class; ☎076 354355, ⓦblueelephant.com).

Thai culture and wildlife tours Plan to Phuket (☎081 691 1955, ⓦplantophuket.com; B1500) run a number of tours, including full-day "Culture Tours" that include market and temple visits, batik-making and rubber production; and "Jungle Tours" to Ton Sai waterfall and the Gibbon Rehabilitation project (see p.345); or a combination of both.

money nowadays is **tourism**: with an annual influx of visitors that tops five million, Phuket ranks second in popularity only to Pattaya, and the package-tour traffic has wrought its usual transformations. Thoughtless tourist developments have scarred much of the island, and the trend is upmarket, with very few budget possibilities (expect to shell out up to twice what you'd pay on the mainland for accommodation and food, and sometimes more than double for transport, which is a particular headache on Phuket). However, many of the beaches are still strikingly handsome, resort facilities are second to none, and the offshore snorkelling and diving is exceptional. Away from the tourist hubs, many inland neighbourhoods are clustered round the local mosque – 35 percent of Phuketians are **Muslim**, and there are said to be more mosques on the island than Buddhist temples; though the atmosphere is generally as easy-going as elsewhere in Thailand, it's especially important to dress with some modesty outside the main resorts, and not to sunbathe topless on any of the beaches.

Phuket's capital, Muang Phuket or **Phuket town**, is on the southeast coast, 42km south of the Sarasin Bridge causeway to the mainland. Though it's the most

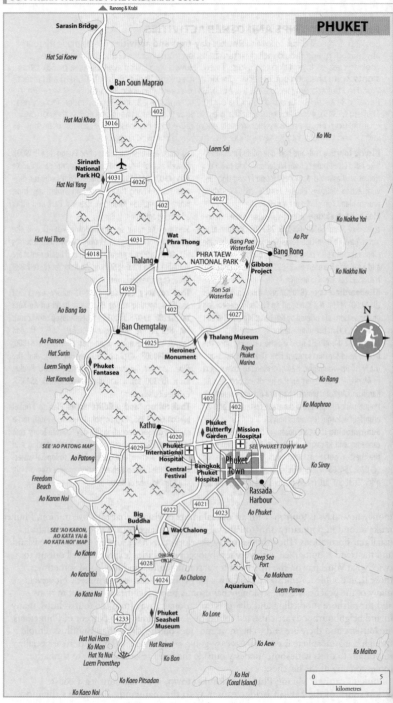

PHUKET

Ranong & Krabi

Sarasin Bridge

Hat Sai Kaew

Ban Soun Maprao

Hat Mai Khao

3016

402

Ko Wa

Laem Sai

Sirinath National Park HQ

4031

4026

Hat Nai Yang

4027

Ko Nakha Yai

Hat Nai Thon

4031

Wat Phra Thong

Bang Pae Waterfall

Ao Por

Bang Rong

4018

Thalang

PHRA TAEW NATIONAL PARK

Gibbon Project

Ko Nakha Noi

4030

Ton Sai Waterfall

402

4027

Ao Bang Tao

Ban Cherngtalay

4025

Thalang Museum

Ao Pansea

Heroines' Monument

Royal Phuket Marina

Hat Surin

Laem Singh

Phuket Fantasea

Hat Kamala

Ko Rang

Ko Maphrao

402

402

Kathu

4020

Phuket Butterfly Garden

Mission Hospital

SEE 'AO PATONG MAP'

4029

Phuket International Hospital

Central Festival

Bangkok Phuket Hospital

SEE PHUKET TOWN MAP

Ao Patong

Phuket Town

Ko Siray

Freedom Beach

Ao Karon Noi

Rassada Harbour

Ao Phuket

Big Buddha

4022

4021

4023

SEE 'AO KARON, AO KATA YAI & AO KATA NOI' MAP

Wat Chalong

Ao Karon

4028

CHALONG CIRCLE

Deep Sea Port

Ao Kata Yai

4024

Ao Chalong

Ao Makham

Laem Panwa

Aquarium

Ao Kata Noi

4233

Phuket Seashell Museum

Ko Lone

Hat Nai Harn

Ko Man

Hat Ya Nui

Laem Promthep

Hat Rawai

Ko Aew

Ko Maiton

Ko Bon

Ko Kaeo Pitsadan

Ko Hai (Coral Island)

Ko Kaeo Noi

N

0   5
kilometres

culturally stimulating place on Phuket, most visitors pass straight through the town on their way to the **west coast**, where three resorts corner the bulk of the trade: high-rise **Ao Patong**, the most developed and expensive, with an increasingly seedy nightlife; the slightly nicer, if unexceptional, **Ao Karon**; and adjacent **Ao Kata**, the smallest of the trio. If you're after a more peaceful spot, aim for the 17km-long national park beach of **Hat Mai Khao**, its more developed neighbour **Hat Nai Yang**, or one of the smaller alternatives at **Hat Nai Thon** or **Hat Kamala**. Most of the other west-coast beaches are dominated by just a few upmarket hotels, specifically **Hat Nai Harn**, **Ao Pansea** and **Ao Bang Tao**; the southern and eastern beaches are better for seafood than swimming.

As with the rest of the Andaman coast, the sea around Phuket is at its least inviting during the **monsoon**, from June to October, when the west-coast beaches in particular become quite rough and windswept. At any time of year, beware the strong **undertow** and heed any red warning flags; there are dozens of fatalities in the water each year, but there is currently no official lifeguard service on the island. Some stretches of Phuket's coast were very badly damaged by the December 2004 **tsunami** (see box, p.312), which caused significant loss of life and destroyed a lot of property. Reconstruction was swift, however, and a first-time visitor to the island is now unlikely to notice any major post-tsunami effect.

ARRIVAL AND DEPARTURE
PHUKET

BY PLANE
Phuket International Airport (☎076 327230–79) is near the northern tip of the island, between Hat Mai Khao and Hat Nai Yang, 32km northwest of Phuket town. It has ATMs, currency exchange, a post office, a Bangkok Hospital clinic, a hotel booking and travel agency counters plus a left-luggage service (daily 6am–10pm; B80 per item per day). There are scores of international flights into Phuket, including several direct services from Australia and dozens of mostly seasonal flights from northern Europe. Between them, Thai Airways, Air Asia, Bangkok Airways, Orient Thai and Nok Air run around thirty domestic flights a day between Bangkok and Phuket, while Thai Airways and Air Asia fly direct from Chiang Mai and Bangkok Airways connects Phuket with Pattaya and Ko Samui.

Onward transport The airport bus (☎076 232371, ✇airportbusphuket.com; B85; 1hr 20min) runs approximately hourly to the bus station in Phuket town, via Thalang; as it doesn't serve the beaches, you'll need to change on to the songthaews in town to reach those. Travel agents in the arrivals hall organize a/c minibuses, which leave when they have ten passengers, to Phuket town (B100), Rassada pier (B150), Patong (B150) and Kata (B180). Outside the arrivals hall at the south end of the building, you'll find a booth for metered taxis (though even here the drivers often need a lot of persuading to turn their meters on): to get to Patong, for instance, will set you back around B450, including a B100 airport charge. On departure from the beaches, most people use taxis organized by their hotel – about B500 for the hour's ride from Patong or Karon. If you're landing at the airport and want to catch a bus north, you can save going into Phuket town by getting a taxi or the airport bus to Ban Muang Mai,

about 6km southeast of the airport on Highway 402, where you can pick up your northbound bus.
Destinations: Bangkok (30 daily; 1hr 20min); Chiang Mai (3 daily; 2hr); Ko Samui (2–5 daily; 50min); Pattaya/U-Tapao (daily; 1hr 35min).

BY BUS AND MINIBUS
Nearly all buses to and from Phuket use the Baw Khaw Saw bus station off the eastern end of Thanon Phang Nga in Phuket town (though there is talk of a possible move to a more spacious location to the north of town). From there it's a 10min walk or a short tuk-tuk ride to the town's central hotel area, and slightly further to the Thanon Ranong departure point for songthaews to the beaches. On the west side of the bus station, licensed private companies offer a/c minibuses to Krabi, Ko Lanta, Surat Thani, Nakhon Si Thammarat, Trang and Hat Yai (a service to Ranong may be granted a licence soon).
From Bangkok Most a/c buses from Bangkok's Southern Bus Terminal make the journey overnight, departing from mid-afternoon onwards. There's no train service to Phuket, but you could book an overnight sleeper train to Surat Thani, about 290km east of Phuket, and take one of the regular buses from there to Phuket (about 5hr).
Bus destinations: Bangkok (30 daily; 10–14hr); Chumphon (17 daily; 6hr 30min); Hat Yai (roughly hourly; 7hr); Khao Lak (20 daily; 2hr 30min); Khao Sok (4 daily; 3–4hr); Khuraburi (20 daily; 3hr 30min–4hr); Ko Samui (daily; 8hr); Krabi (at least hourly; 3hr 30min); Nakhon Si Thammarat (8 daily; 7hr); Phang Nga (at least hourly; 2hr 30min); Ranong (20 daily; 5hr); Satun (4 daily; 7hr); Surat Thani (13 daily; 4hr 30min–5hr 30min); Takua Pa (20 daily; 2hr 30min–3hr); Trang (roughly hourly; 5–6hr).

4

BY BOAT

If you're coming to Phuket from Ko Lanta or Ao Nang in Krabi province, the quickest and most scenic option is to take the boat.

To/from Ko Phi Phi During peak season, up to three ferries a day, plus a speedboat or two, make the trip to and from Ko Phi Phi, docking at Rassada Harbour on Phuket's east coast; during low season, there's at least one ferry a day in both directions.

To/from Ko Yao Noi Boats from Ko Yao Noi and the high-season speedboat service from Ao Nang via Ko Yao Noi terminate at Bang Rong on Phuket's northeast coast.

To/from Ko Lanta Travellers from Sala Dan on Ko Lanta (Nov–May only) may have to change boats at Ao Nang or Ko Phi Phi to get to Phuket's Rassada Harbour.

To/from Ao Nang Ferries go to Rassada Harbour; the speedboat service from Ao Nang via Ko Yao Noi terminates at Bang Rong.

Onward transport from Rassada Harbour Shared a/c minibuses meet the ferries at Rassada Harbour and charge B50 per person for transfers to Phuket town hotels, B150 to Patong and B200 to the airport; taxis charge B500–600 per car to the major west-coast beaches or the airport (leave plenty of extra time if you have a flight to catch as boats are notoriously tardy).

Onward transport from Bang Rong Infrequent songthaews shuttle between Bang Rong and Phuket town (about 1hr; B40), while taxis charge B500–800 to the airport or the west-coast beaches.

Destinations: Ao Nang (Nov–May 2 daily; 2hr); Ko Lanta Yai (Nov–May 2 daily; 4hr 30min); Ko Phi Phi Don (1–3 daily; 2hr); Ko Yao Noi (roughly hourly; 40min–1hr 10min).

GETTING AROUND

Getting around the island is a nightmare: on one hand, tuk-tuks and taxis know that they have a captive audience and charge through the nose; on the other, Phuket has probably the worst, most dangerous drivers in Thailand, driving on roads that are often steep and winding, with quite a few hairpin bends – which all discourages renting a vehicle. If you do decide to drive yourself, stay alert and be defensive. There is a system of public songthaews (supplemented by buses) radiating out from Phuket town, but to get from one beach to another by this method you nearly always have to go back into town. For transport within resorts, the cheapest option is to make use of the public songthaews where possible, or to hail a motorbike taxi where available (B30–100).

By songthaew Songthaews run regularly throughout the day (when they have a full complement of passengers) from Thanon Ranong in the centre of Phuket town to the coast and cost B25–45.

By tuk-tuk or taxi Tuk-tuks and taxis do travel directly between major beaches, but are notoriously overpriced (there are almost no metered taxis on the island), charging at least B100 from Kata to Karon or B250 between Patong and Karon and often doubling their prices after dark – they have been known to ask for B1000 to go from Patong to Karon at night. Phuket TAT (see p.326) issues a list of price guidelines but you'll have to bargain hard to get near the quoted prices.

Motorbike rental Many tourists rent their own motorbike or moped, which are widely available (from B250/day), but be warned that there is a very sobering average of 10,000 motorbike injuries a year on Phuket, and about a hundred fatalities; it makes sense to obey the compulsory helmet law, which is anyway strictly enforced in most areas of Phuket, with flouters subject to a B500 fine.

Car rental At the airport, there are offices of Avis (☎ 076 351244, ⓦ avisthailand.com) and Budget (☎ 076 327744, ⓦ budget.co.th), who also have a branch on Patong (see p.333); both charge from around B1200/day.

INFORMATION

On the web There's a wide-ranging website about Phuket, ⓦ phuket.com, which is particularly good for discounted accommodation.

Guidebooks For a detailed historical and cultural guide to the island, it's hard to better Oliver Hargreave's impressive *Exploring Phuket & Phi Phi* (Within Books).

Tourist office Phuket's TAT office is in Phuket Town (see p.326), though it's not worth going out of your way to visit.

DIRECTORY

Dentists At Phuket International Hospital and Bangkok Hospital Phuket (see below).

Hospitals Phuket International Hospital (☎ 076 249400, emergencies ☎ 076 210935, ⓦ phuketinternationalhospital .com), north of Central Festival shopping centre on Highway 402, just west of Phuket town, is considered to have Phuket's best facilities, including an emergency department and an ambulance service. Reputable alternatives include Bangkok

Hospital Phuket, on the northwestern edge of Phuket town just off Thanon Yaowarat at 2/1 Thanon Hongyok Uthis (☎ 076 254425, ⓦ phukethospital.com), and the Mission Hospital (aka Phuket Adventist Hospital), on the northern outskirts at 4/1 Thanon Thepkasatri (☎ 076 237220–6, emergencies ☎ 076 237227, ⓦ missionhospitalphuket.com).

Immigration office At the southern end of Thanon Phuket, in the suburb of Saphan Hin, Phuket town (☎ 076

221905, ⓦphuketimmigration.go.th; Mon–Fri 8.30am–noon & 1–4.30pm), plus an information centre in Patong (see p.335).
Tourist police For all emergencies, contact the tourist police, either on the free, 24hr phone line (☏1155), at their main office at 327 Thanon Yaowarat in Phuket town (☏076 223891, ⓦphukettouristpolice.go.th), or at their branch in Patong (see p.335).

Phuket town

Though it has plenty of hotels and restaurants, **PHUKET TOWN** (Muang Phuket) stands distinct from the tailor-made tourist settlements along the beaches as a place of tangible history and culture. Most visitors hang about just long enough to jump on a beach-bound songthaew, but you may find yourself returning for a welcome dose of real life; there's plenty to engage you in a stroll through the small but atmospherically restored heart of the Old Town, along with many idiosyncratic cafés and art shops, several notable restaurants and some good handicraft shops. The town works well as an overnight transit point between the islands and the bus station or airport, but is also

4

■ ACCOMMODATION	
Baan Suwantawe	3
Casa 104	1
Crystal Inn Hotel	8
On On Hotel	5
Phuket Backpacker Hostel	6
Royal Phuket City	7
Sino House	2
Thalang 37 Guest House	4

■ BARS	
Sanaeha	1
Soi Romanee	2, 3

● RESTAURANTS & CAFÉS	
Bo(ok)hemian Arthouse	1
China Inn Café	2
Ka Jok See	6
Natural Restaurant (Thammachat)	5
On On Café	3
Siam Indigo	4

worth considering as a base for exploring the island, with more interesting and affordable accommodation, eating and drinking options than the beaches, but linked to them by regular songthaews.

The Old Town
Between Thanon Dibuk and Thanon Rat Sada; ⓦ lestariheritage.net/Phuket

Phuket town's most interesting features are clustered together in the **Old Town** conservation zone, a grid of streets between Thanon Dibuk and Thanon Rat Sada whose colonial-style **Sino-Portuguese shophouses** (see below) date back to the nineteenth century, the former homes of emigrant Chinese merchants from Penang, Singapore and Melaka. Modern-day residents have put a lot of effort into restoring these handsome old neighbourhoods and there's an engagingly bohemian style to a number of the businesses here. The Phuket Old Town Foundation helps to publish the excellent free **Phuket Town Treasure Map**, available all over the Old Town, and also stages the **Old Town Festival** just before Chinese New Year (sometime between Jan & March).

Some of the Old Town's most elegant buildings line the western arm of **Thanon Thalang**, where a dozen signboards – including at *Thalang Guest House* at no. 37 (see p.326) and outside the *China Inn Café* at no. 20 (see p.326) – highlight the special features worth an upward or sideways glance: pastel-coloured doors and shutters, elaborate stucco mouldings, ornate wooden doors, and the distinctively arched "five-foot walkways" that link them. Further east along Thanon Thalang there's more of an Islamic emphasis, with many old-style shops selling fabric and dressmaking accessories, including lots of good-value sarongs from Malaysia and Indonesia. The road's former red-light alley, **Soi Romanee**, has also been given a major multicoloured face-lift and these days buzzes come sundown with arty little bars, while on nearby **Thanon Dibuk** the doors and window shutters of *Dibuk Restaurant* at no. 69 display intricate wooden and gold-leaf fretwork. You'll find other renovated Sino-Portuguese

---

PHUKET TOWN SINO-PORTUGUESE ARCHITECTURE

As Chinese immigrant merchants got rich on tin-mining profits so they started building homes. Though the very richest commissioned enormous mansions, a number of which survive in Phuket town today, the vast majority bought themselves eminently practical terraced **shophouses** at the heart of the merchant district. Phuket's Old Town retains south Thailand's finest examples, some of which are open to the public, but there are also intact, if less well-conserved, shophouse neighbourhoods in many other southern cities, including Ranong and Takua Pa.

Shophouse design followed a standard prototype favoured by the mixed-race Chinese–Malay ("Baba", or "Straits Chinese") immigrants from Melaka and other parts of the Malay Peninsula. It's a style now widely dubbed **Sino-Portuguese** because Melakan architecture of the time was itself strongly influenced by the territory's Portuguese former colonists, though it also incorporates traits from Dutch and Anglo-Indian colonial architecture. Although some features have evolved with changing fashions the basic look is still recognizably mid-nineteenth century.

Because streetside space was at a premium, shophouses were always long and thin, with narrow frontages, recessed entrances and connecting porches that linked up all the way down the block to make shady, arched colonnades known as **five-foot walkways**, ideal for pedestrians and shoppers. The front room was (and often still is) the business premises, leaving the rest of the two- or three-storey building for living. A light well behind the front room encouraged natural ventilation and sometimes fed a small courtyard garden at its base, and the household shrine would always occupy a prominent and auspicious position. Outside, the hallmark features that make the neighbourhoods so striking today include pastel-painted **louvred windows** that might be arched or rectangular and perhaps topped by a pretty glass fantail, lacquered and inlaid wooden doors, fancy gold-leaf fretwork, detailed **stucco mouldings** and perhaps Neoclassical pilasters.

NGAN KIN JEH: THE VEGETARIAN FESTIVAL

For nine days, usually in October or November, at the start of the ninth lunar month (see
ⓦphuketvegetarian.com for exact dates), the celebrations for **Ngan Kin Jeh** – the Vegetarian
Festival – set the streets of Phuket buzzing with processions, theatre shows and food stalls,
culminating in the unnerving spectacle of men and women parading about with steel rods
through their cheeks and tongues. The festival marks the beginning of **Taoist Lent**, a
month-long period of purification observed by devout Chinese all over the world, but
celebrated most ostentatiously in Phuket, by devotees of the island's five Chinese temples.
After six days' abstention from meat (hence the festival's name), alcohol and sex, the white-clad
worshippers flock to their local temple, where drum rhythms help induce a trance state in
which they become possessed by spirits. As proof of their new-found transcendence of the
physical world they skewer themselves with any available sharp instrument – fishing rods and
car wing-mirrors have done service in the past – before walking over red-hot coals or up
ladders of swords as further testament to their otherworldliness. In the meantime there's
singing and dancing and almost continuous firework displays, with the grandest festivities
held at Wat Jui Tui on Thanon Ranong in Phuket town.

The ceremony dates back to the mid-nineteenth century, when a travelling Chinese opera
company turned up on the island to entertain emigrant Chinese working in the tin mines.
They had been there almost a year when suddenly the whole troupe – together with a
number of the miners – came down with a life-endangering fever. Realizing that they'd
neglected their gods, the actors performed elaborate rites and kept to a vegetarian diet, and
most were soon cured. The festival has been held ever since, though the self-mortification rites
are a later modification, possibly of Hindu origin.

4

buildings on **Thanon Yaowarat**, and on **Thanon Ranong** (where the Thai Airways office
occupies a fine old mansion), **Thanon Phang Nga** (especially the *On On Hotel*) and
Thanon Damrong, whose town hall, just east of the Provincial Court, stood in for
Phnom Penh's US embassy in the film *The Killing Fields*.

Phuket Thaihua Museum

28 Thanon Krabi • Daily 9am–5pm • B200 • ⓦ thaihuamuseum.com

This 1930s Neoclassical former school – complete with grand columns, stucco
decoration, shuttered windows and central light well – has been turned into the
Phuket Thaihua Museum. Some of the old school desks are still *in situ*, but the focus
of the museum's excellent displays, videos and historic photos is on the role and
traditions of Phuket's main immigrant groups, namely the Chinese and mixed-race
Baba (Malay–Chinese) communities who arrived to work in the island's burgeoning
tin-mining industry.

San Jao Saeng Tham (Shrine of Serene Light)

Accessed via a soi through the narrow archway next to South Wind Books on Thanon Phang Nga • Daily 8.30am–noon & 1.30–5.30pm

The spiritual heritage of Phuket's Chinese immigrants is kept very much alive by their
descendants, notably in the extraordinary spectacle of the annual Vegetarian Festival
(see above). They also maintain many shrines around town, including **San Jao Saeng
Tham**, the tiny **Shrine of Serene Light**, whose roof is decorated with intensely coloured
ceramic figurines of dragons, carp and sages in bright blues, greens and reds.

Phuket Butterfly Garden

2km beyond the northern end of Thanon Yaowarat at 71/6 Soi Paneang in Ban Sam Kong • Daily 9am–5pm • B300 • ☏ 076 210861,
ⓦ phuketbutterfly.com • A tuk-tuk from the town centre should cost around B150 return

Kids usually enjoy the **Phuket Butterfly Garden and Insect World**, whose thousands
of butterflies of some twenty indigenous species flit around the prettily landscaped
grounds; there's also a silk museum documenting the amazingly industrious short life
of the silkworm, plus scorpions, tarantulas and other notorious creepy-crawlies.

ARRIVAL AND DEPARTURE PHUKET TOWN

By songthaew Songthaews run regularly throughout the day (when they have a full complement of passengers) from Thanon Ranong in the centre of Phuket town to the coast and cost B25–45.

INFORMATION

Tourist information The TAT office is at 191 Thanon Thalang (daily 8.30am–4.30pm; ☏076 212213, ✉tatphket@tat.or.th), though it's not worth going out of your way to visit.

ACCOMMODATION

★**Baan Suwantawe** 1/10 Thanon Dibuk ☏076 212879, ⓦbaansuwantawe.com. Offering four-star rooms at two-star prices, this apartment-style hotel is designed with long-stay residents in mind but is also exceptionally comfortable for tourists. The huge, pleasantly decorated a/c rooms all have a balcony overlooking the small swimming pool and come with TV, broadband, fridge and kettle. There's no restaurant or hotel services but the front desk is helpful and the location very handy for the Old Town. **B1500**

Casa 104 104 Thanon Yaowarat ☏076 221268, ✉casa 104phuket@gmail.com. Friendly, popular establishment offering four chic but windowless rooms away from the street noise, behind a French bistro, with access to a lovely, shady garden at the back; all have a/c, flat-screen TVs and attractive, hot-water bathrooms. Substantial Continental breakfast with home-baked bread included. **B1200**

Crystal Inn Hotel 2/1–10 Soi Surin, Thanon Montri ☏076 256789, ⓦphuketcrystalinn.com. Surprisingly stylish and contemporary cream- and dark-wood decor makes this small, 54-room downtown hotel an inviting and good-value option. All rooms have a/c and there's internet downstairs. Breakfast included. **B950**

On On Hotel 19 Thanon Phang Nga ☏076 211154. This attractive, colonial-style 1920s building is a long-running travellers' favourite, mainly because the rooms are so cheap. They're pretty basic, with very thin walls, holes in the floorboards and ancient plumbing, but they're adequate and there are lots of them; the cheapest share bathrooms, the most expensive have a/c. There's wi-fi, an internet café and a tour agent in the lobby. Shared bathroom **B180**, en suite **B250**, a/c **B400**

Phuket Backpacker Hostel 167 Thanon Ranong ☏076 256680, ⓦphuketbackpacker.com. Popular, sociable and well-organized hostel, with lots of tours and information available and a lively bar downstairs. Dorms squeeze in up to ten guests, but there are some nice, clean and small fan rooms with TVs and hot showers overlooking the quiet garden at the back. Internet access, free wi-fi, bicycle rental and a common room for showing movies. Fan dorm **B250**, a/c dorm **B300**, fan double **B550**, a/c double **B650**

Royal Phuket City 154 Thanon Phang Nga ☏076 233333, ⓦroyalphuketcity.com. Large, high-rise business hotel, with large swimming pool, gym, business centre and light, bright, comfortable a/c rooms, most of them with fine views over the city and all with broadband. **B2200**

Sino House 1 Thanon Montri ☏076 232494–5, ⓦsino housephuket.com. Beautifully styled with Chinoiserie artefacts and elegant flourishes, the apartment-style rooms in this striking Art Deco building are huge and light and all come with a/c, fridge, DVD player, complimentary wi-fi, coffee-making facilities and Continental breakfast. There's a restaurant and the Raintree Spa on site, plus some tour services, but no pool. **B2000**

Thalang 37 Guest House 37 Thanon Thalang ☏076 214225, ⓦthalangguesthouse.com. Housed in a 1940s, Sino-Portuguese, wood-floored shophouse in one of the Old Town's most attractive streets, this place is fairly simple but full of character, traveller-friendly and good value. The twelve fan and a/c rooms are large and en suite – the best of them are up on the rooftop, affording unusual panoramic views. It's very popular, so it's best to book ahead; rates include a simple breakfast. Fan **B400**, a/c **B500**

EATING AND DRINKING

Phuket town has much the largest concentration of good Thai food on the island, well worth making the trip for. Unlike Thais in most other parts of the country, Phuketians like to breakfast on noodles rather than rice; spindly white *khanom jiin* noodles, made with rice-flour and ladled over with one of several different fiery, soupy curry sauces, are a local speciality and served at some of the restaurants listed below.

Bo(ok)hemian Arthouse 61 Thanon Thalang. Artsy little hangout for cappuccinos (B60), free wi-fi, DVD rental and occasional film screenings. Daily 10am–9pm.

China Inn Café 20 Thanon Thalang ☏076 356239. This beautifully renovated heritage house and courtyard garden would be reason enough to stop by for a meal, but the menu is also enticing, proffering Thai dishes such as *phat thai* (B190) and spicy salads, as well as a few Western, mostly Italian, dishes including delicious mozzarella salad (B290). Streetside, the gallery shop displays Asian antiques, textiles and lacquerware. High season Mon–Wed 11am–6pm, Thurs–Sat

11am–10pm, low season Mon–Sat 11am–6pm.

Ka Jok See 26 Thanon Takuapa ☎076 217903. A Phuket institution, housed in a charmingly restored traditional shophouse (unsigned), this place serves fabulous Thai food on a pricey set menu (B1500) and fosters a fun, sociable atmosphere. Mains are sophisticated and beautifully presented – their *goong sarong*, individual shrimps bound in a crisp-noodle wrap, is famous island-wide. Reservations are essential. Tues–Sun 7.30–10.30pm.

★ **Natural Restaurant (Thammachat)** 62/5 Soi Putorn ☎076 214037. There are plenty of reasons to linger over dinner at this rambling, informal, hugely popular, plant-wreathed restaurant, not least the two hundred different choices on the menu, and the affordable prices (main dishes around B100). Highlights include fried sea bass with chilli paste, fried chicken with Muslim herbs, soft-shelled crab with garlic and pepper, and spicy Phuket bean salad. Daily 10.30am–11.30pm.

On On Café Thanon Phang Nga. Sociable spot for cheap, mostly Thai–Chinese meals, as well as breakfasts, including fry-ups (B120 for an "American" set breakfast) and espresso coffee. Mon–Sat 7am–7pm, Sun 7am–noon.

Sanaeha Thanon Yaowarat. Lively, hip bar in an old mansion, all done out in blue and white with chandeliers and mirror balls, with live bands playing jazz and other stuff on the central stage from 9pm. Daily 6/7pm–12.30am.

Siam Indigo 8 Thanon Phang Nga ☎076 256697, ⊚siamindigo.com. In a hundred-year-old house with an attractive rear patio, this stylish bar-restaurant and clothes boutique is festooned with chandeliers, red velvet curtains and striking mosaic portraits of film stars. The menu features tapas and lots of local dishes such as *nam prik kung siab* (a spicy relish with dried shrimps; B120); happy hour 5–7pm. Daily 2pm till late.

Soi Romanee This artfully restored, plant-strewn soi connecting Dibuk and Thalang roads shows off its handsome new pastel paintwork and stuccoed Old Town facades with half a dozen little café-bars whose seating spills out on to the pavement for ultimate architectural appreciation.

ENTERTAINMENT

Siam Niramit Phuket North of town off Thanon Chalerm Prakiat ☎076 335000, ⊚siamniramit.com. Recently opened offshoot of the Siam Niramit Bangkok extravaganza, this 70min show presents a tourist-oriented rendering of traditional Thai theatre, in a high-tech spectacular of fantastic costumes and huge chorus numbers, enlivened by acrobatics and flashy special effects. Tickets from B1300. Daily except Tues 8.30pm.

SHOPPING

The two most fruitful shopping roads for handicrafts and antiques are Thanon Yaowarat and Thanon Rat Sada, while the shops on eastern Thanon Thalang keep a phenomenal range of well-priced sarongs, mostly of Burmese, Malaysian and Indonesian designs. *Art and Culture South*, a useful, free, quarterly booklet that's available at TAT and other outlets, details shops and galleries in the town and around.

The Books Thanon Phuket. Decent selection of new English-language books and magazines, with a coffee corner and internet access. Daily 8.30am–9.30pm.

South Wind Books Thanon Phang Nga. Big, sprawling range of secondhand books. Mon–Sat 9am–6pm, Sun 10am–3pm.

DIRECTORY

Travel agent Mark Travel, in the lobby of the *On On Hotel* on Thanon Phang Nga (☎076 225741 or 081 693 6207), is a helpful agent, good for all kinds of transport tickets, including cheap boat tickets, as well as activities and day-trips.

Hat Mai Khao

Phuket's longest and quietest beach, the 17km **HAT MAI KHAO**, unfurls along the island's upper northwest coast, beginning some 3km south of the Sarasin Bridge causeway and ending just north of the airport (34km from Phuket town). It's a beautiful piece of casuarina- and palm-shaded coastline, minimally developed and protected in part as **Sirinath National Park** because of the few giant marine turtles that lay their eggs here between October and February.

ACCOMMODATION   HAT MAI KHAO

Accommodation on Hat Mai Khao is predominantly five-star: an enclave of half a dozen luxury hotels is elegantly spaced behind the sloping shoreline towards the north end of the beach, accessed by an all-but-private road that is not served by any public transport. Most of the resorts have a swimming pool as the undertow here can be fierce and unpredictable.

★**Anantara Phuket Villas** ☏076 336100–9, ⓦanantara.com. Set amid stylishly landscaped grounds and lagoons, all the secluded villas here have their own plunge pool, outdoor bath and garden *sala*, while the luxurious interiors feature antique furniture, lots of dark wood, dressing rooms, espresso machines and free wi-fi. There's an impressive selection of free activities, including sailing and yoga, a kids' club, a beautiful spa and excellent seafood at the stylish restaurant, *Sea Fire Salt*. Rates are sometimes reduced by more than half in low season. **B18,000**

JW Marriott Phuket Resort and Spa ☏076 338000, ⓦmarriott.com. Complemented by high standards of service, this luxury resort offers well-appointed rooms, a spa, two tennis courts and no less than seven restaurants. Two swimming pools, a well-equipped children's pavilion, good sports facilities and extensive landscaped lawns all help make it a favourite with families. **B6960**

Mai Khao Beach Bungalows ☏081 895 1233, ⓦmaikhaobeach.wordpress.com. Six simple en-suite bungalows sit in spacious, grassy grounds just behind the shore beneath coconut palms hung with hammocks, next door to the *Holiday Inn*. There's a restaurant and motorbike rental here too, but not much else. Easiest access to *Mai Khao Beach Bungalows* is by bus to or from Phuket town: ask to be dropped at Thachatchai police box, 4km away on Highway 402, from where you can phone the bungalows for a pick-up. Closed Aug, sometimes longer, during the rainy season. Fan **B900**, a/c **B1300**, with hot water **B1800**

Sala Phuket ☏076 338888, ⓦsalaphuket.com. The sharp, Sino-modern architecture of the villa compounds here – all done out in cool creams and silver, with colour-coordinated planting and the occasional lacquered screen – attract mainly couples, especially honeymooners, who enjoy the style and privacy, especially of the pool villas. There's an enticing open-air seafront lounging area here too, with deliciously squishy sofas, plus a rooftop terrace, a spa and three swimming pools. Breakfast and wi-fi included. **B10,100**

Hat Nai Yang

The long curved sweep of **HAT NAI YANG**, 5km south of Hat Mai Khao and 30km north of Phuket town, is partly under the protection of Sirinath National Park and has only fairly low-key development. In the plentiful shade cast by the feathery casuarinas and cajeput trees that run most of the length of the bay stand more than a dozen small seafood restaurants, and a small, low-rise tourist village of travel agents, a few accommodation options, ATMs, a massage pavilion, internet and dive shops. The beach is clean and good for swimming at the southern end, and there's a reasonable, shallow **reef** about 1km offshore (10min by longtail boat) from the Sirinath National Park headquarters, which is a fifteen-minute walk north of the tourist village (if you're driving yourself to Hat Nai Yang, when the main access road hits the beach, turn left for the tourist village, right for the national park).

ARRIVAL AND DEPARTURE

HAT NAI YANG

By taxi Hat Nai Yang is just 2km south of the airport, about B150 by taxi.

By songthaew An infrequent songthaew service (B35; 1hr 45min) runs between Phuket town and Hat Nai Yang.

ACCOMMODATION

Indigo Pearl ☏076 327006, ⓦindigo-pearl.com. Luxurious rooms and villas look on to attractively landscaped plantation-style gardens that run down to the southern end of the beachfront road; facilities include a meandering lagoon-like salt-water swimming pool, a dive shop, an inventively programmed activities centre, a spa and kids' club. Interiors are designed to evoke Phuket's tin-mining history, with metallic colour schemes, polished cement floors and a penchant for industrial art, but the look is softened by very comfortable furniture, generous balconies and plenty of greenery. **B11,700**

Nai Yang Beach Resort ☏076 328300, ⓦnaiyang beachresort.com. Good upper-mid-range option at the south end of the beach, its cosy, modern, whitewashed a/c rooms fitted with attractive dark-wood furniture and ranged in two- and three-storey wings around pretty tropical gardens; there are three swimming pools, a dive centre and wi-fi throughout. Breakfast included. **B2700**

EATING AND DRINKING

The tourist village in Nai Yang is locally famous for its small shorefront restaurants that serve mostly barbecued seafood (and the odd wood-fired pizza), on mats under the trees and at tables on the sand, which are candlelit and exceptionally tranquil at night.

The Beach Club One of several little beach bars in the tourist village, a cool, relaxed place for a drink in its low-slung track-side chairs or on one of its day beds with triangular cushions on the beach. Happy hour 3–5pm & 10–11pm. Daily noon–1am.

Black Ginger Indigo Pearl ☎076 327006. For a really top-notch romantic dinner, you can't top the intimate, black-painted *sala* here. Highlights from the very classy menu here (from B300) include the Phuket lobster with red coconut curry, fresh Vietnamese-style rice-flour pancakes stuffed with shrimps, coriander and herbs and local *kaeng leuang*, yellow curry with fish fillet. Reservations advisable. Daily 6.30–11pm.

Hat Nai Thon

The next bay south down the coast from Hat Nai Yang is the small but perfectly formed 500m-long gold-sand **HAT NAI THON**, with good snorkelling at reefs a brief longtail ride offshore. Shops, hotels and restaurants line the inland side of its narrow little shorefront road, but there's still a low-key, village-like atmosphere here.

ARRIVAL AND DEPARTURE   HAT NAI THON

Most visitors rent their own transport as songthaews don't make the detour from the highway and taxis are thin on the ground.

ACCOMMODATION

Andaman White Beach Resort ☎076 316300, ⓦandamanwhitebeach.com. About 2km south over the southern headland, occupying secluded cliffside land that runs down to a gorgeous little private bay of white sand and turquoise water (sometimes known as Hat Nai Thon Noia), this resort offers luxurious rooms and villas with unsurpassed views, including some designed for families, plus a 40m swimming pool, a spa and wi-fi. B7750

Naithonburi Beach Resort ☎076 318700, ⓦnaithonburi.com. Huge resort, with over two hundred posh a/c rooms in a U-shaped complex enclosing an enormous pool, some of them with direct pool access, though it doesn't dominate the bay. B2800

Ao Bang Tao

Re-landscaped from a former tin-mining concession to encompass lagoons, parkland and Phuket's best eighteen-hole golf course, **AO BANG TAO** is dominated by the vast, upscale *Laguna Phuket*, a gated "integrated resort" of seven luxury hotels on an impressive 8km shorefront. It's a world away from the thrust and hustle of Patong and a popular choice for families, with no need to leave the *Laguna* village, though beware of the undertow off the coast here, which confines many guests to the hotel pools. There's free transport between the seven hotels, which between them offer a huge range of leisure and sports facilities, as well as a shopping centre.

ARRIVAL AND DEPARTURE   AO BANG TAO

Half-hourly **songthaews** (B25; 1hr 15min) cover the 24km from Phuket town to Ao Bang Tao during the day, or there are resort shuttle **buses** and on-site car rental.

ACCOMMODATION

Laguna Phuket ☎076 362300, ⓦlagunaphuket.com. The main website sometimes has discounted rates at *Laguna's* seven hotels, while the family-oriented *Best Western Allamanda Laguna* (☎076 362700, ⓦallamanda.com), comprising 150 apartment-style suites with kitchenette and separate living area, has the cheapest rates in the complex (B5000). Haunt of high society and sports stars, the exclusive *Banyan Tree Phuket* (☎076 324374, ⓦbanyantree.com) offers lavish villas in private gardens, many with private pools, and the gloriously indulgent, award-winning, Banyan Tree spa (B20,000).

Hat Surin and Ao Pansea

South around Laem Son headland from Ao Bang Tao, handsome little **HAT SURIN** is a favourite weekend getaway for sophisticated Phuketians and a big draw for expats, who inhabit the ever-expanding forest of condo developments inland from the small, pretty beach. The shorefront gets very crowded, however, packed with sunloungers and beach restaurants, so it can be hard to appreciate the setting. Eating and shopping facilities cater to the upmarket clientele, and beachfront dining and drinking is the main pastime. Things are much quieter on Hat Surin's northern bay, **AO PANSEA**, which is divided from the main beach by a rocky promontory.

ARRIVAL AND DEPARTURE — HAT SURIN AND AO PANSEA

By songthaew Songthaews travel the 24km between the fresh-food market on Thanon Ranong in Phuket town and Hat Surin approximately every half-hour during the day and cost B30.

ACCOMMODATION

Amanpuri ☎076 324333, ⓦamanresorts.com. Secluded from the riffraff on Ao Pansea, this is a favourite haunt of royalty and Hollywood stars, who stay in the butler-staffed pavilions, some with their own pools, relax in the spa and charter the hotel's yachts. B31,500

Benyada Lodge 103 Thanon Hat Surin ☎076 271261, ⓦbenyadalodge-phuket.com. Just across the small park from the beach, this thirty-room lodge with high standards of service has had a recent makeover in a crisp, bright contemporary style, with the addition of a rooftop pool and bar-restaurant. The spacious a/c rooms all have wi-fi, hot showers, TV and fridge. Breakfast included. B2800

Surin Bay Inn 106 Thanon Hat Surin ☎076 271601, ⓦsurinbayinn.com. Large, attractive rooms above a restaurant and bar near *Benyada Lodge*, with in-room a/c, hot showers, free wi-fi, TV and fridge. Breakfast included. B1800

EATING AND DRINKING

Opus One ☎076 386562, ⓦopusonephuket.com. Chic, atmospherically lit lounge-bar and bistro done out in black and red, serving very tasty dishes, such as risotto with mushrooms and truffles, in large portions (B450); live soul band Fri from 9.30pm. Daily 6pm–midnight/1am, kitchen closes 10pm.

Taste ☎076 270090, ⓦtastesurinbeach.com. This sophisticated seafront restaurant and art gallery is especially known for its great seafood, such as steamed red snapper fillet with a lemon and butter sauce (B390) and wild ginger and green pepper shrimp (B390). Tues–Sun 2pm–midnight.

Hat Kamala and Laem Singh

With its cheerfully painted houses and absence of high-rises, the small, village-like tourist development at **HAT KAMALA** is low-key and mid-market, sandwiched between the beach and the predominantly Muslim town of Ban Kamala, about 300m west of the main Patong–Surin road, 6km north of Patong and 26km northwest of Phuket town. Accommodation, shops, restaurants and other tourist services are mostly clustered either side of shoreside Thanon Rim Had (also spelt Rim Hat) which, despite its limited choice, is a much pleasanter place to browse than the big resorts. The beach gets prettier and quieter the further north you go, away from Thanon Rim Had, with restaurant shacks renting sunloungers along most of its course. A stretch of this area is backed by the Muslim cemetery, so it's particularly important to respect local sensibilities and avoid going topless.

Kamala was very badly hit by the 2004 **tsunami**, which killed many residents and wiped out the beachfront school, the temple and countless homes and businesses. Though extensive rebuilding has extinguished most of the physical scars, a copper sculpture in the park opposite *Print Kamala* bears witness to the devastation, and a volunteer English-teaching programme at the school, Phuket Has Been Good to Us (see p.65), aims to help rebuild some of the young lives affected.

About 1km northeast of Hat Kamala, a couple of steep paths lead west off the main Patong–Surin road down to **Laem Singh** cape, a pretty little sandy cove whose picturesque combination of turquoise water and smooth granite boulders makes it one of Phuket's finest. It's good for swimming and very secluded, plus there's a decent patch of shade throughout the day.

ARRIVAL AND DEPARTURE

By songthaew The cheapest way to get to Hat Kamala is by songthaew from the fresh-food market on Thanon

HAT KAMALA AND LAEM SINGH

Ranong in Phuket town (about every 30min during the day, 1hr 15min; B35).

ACCOMMODATION

Hat Kamala is popular with long-stay tourists, and several hotels offer rooms with kitchenettes; there's also a preponderance of small-scale places.

Benjamin Resort 83 Thanon Rim Had, opposite the school at the southerly end of the beachfront road ⊕076 385146–7, ⊛phuketdir.com/benjaminresort. Set right on the beach and about the best and friendliest deal in Kamala, this block of 37 a/c rooms lacks character but couldn't be closer to the sea. Although views are obstructed from all but the most expensive rooms, the spacious interiors are almost identical and all have balcony, fridge, TV, hot water and breakfast included, plus use of sunloungers out front. **B500**

Coconut Garden Soi Police Station ⊕081 477 3331, ⊛coconutgarden.se. The best thing about the dozen good-sized but unexceptional concrete a/c bungalows, two- and three-bedroom houses here is their location on the nicer northerly stretch of the central beach; all have a/c, hot shower, fridge, TV and DVD. **B2000**

Kamala Dreams 74/1 Thanon Rim Had ⊕076 279131, ⊛kamaladreams.net. Epitomizing all the best things about Kamala, this is a really nice, small hotel set right on the shore, in the middle of the tourist village. Its eighteen

rooms are large and furnished in contemporary style, and all have a/c, TVs, a kitchenette and a large balcony overlooking the pool and the sea. **B2300**

Malinee House 75/4 Thanon Rim Had ⊕081 691 7879, ⊛malineehouse.com. Very friendly, traveller-oriented guesthouse in the middle of the tourist village, with internet access and the Jackie Lee travel agency downstairs, and large, comfortably furnished and cheerfully painted a/c rooms upstairs, all of them with balconies, hot showers and fridges. **B1000**

Print Kamala Resort 74/8 Thanon Rim Had ⊕076 385396–8, ⊛printkamalaresort.net. The best accommodation here is in a village-like complex of very generously sized bungalows, connected via stilted walkways around a tropical Bali-style garden. The bungalows all have prettily furnished a/c bedrooms plus separate living rooms, and capacious, shaded decks. The hotel also has some less interesting, but more expensive, rooms in a hotel wing, and a large pool. Breakfast included. **B3500**

EATING AND DRINKING

Most people eat and drink on the beach, especially at the restaurant shacks and bars that pretty much line the shore all the way north from opposite *Print Kamala*; seafood is the big seller here, and you can bury your feet in the sand.

Rockfish Kamala Beach Estate Hotel ⊕076 279732, ⊛rockfishrestaurant.com. This Australian-run restaurant enjoys lovely views from its southern headland location and an island-wide reputation for great food, mostly

Asian fusion and seafood dishes such as tiger prawns in tamarind sauce (B600) or a blue crab and mango salad starter (B350); simpler, cheaper dishes available for breakfast and lunch. Daily 8am–10pm.

ENTERTAINMENT

Phuket FantaSea About 1km northeast of Hat Kamala off the main Patong–Surin road ⊕076 385111, ⊛phuket-fantasea.com. The enjoyable, hi-tech mega-spectacular, "Fantasy of a Kingdom, Cultural Illusion Show", is staged at the enormous FantaSea entertainments

complex, featuring high-wire trapeze acts, acrobatics, pyrotechnics, illusionists, comedy and traditional dance – plus a depressing baby elephant circus. B1500 or B1900 including the unexciting pre-show dinner. Daily except Thurs 9pm.

Ao Patong

The busiest and most popular of all Phuket's beaches, **AO PATONG** – 5km south of Ao Kamala and 15km west of Phuket town – is vastly overdeveloped and hard to recommend. A congestion of high-rise hotels, tour agents and souvenir shops disfigures the beachfront road, tireless and tiresome touts are everywhere, and hostess bars and strip joints dominate the nightlife, attracting an increasing number of single Western men to the most active scene between Bangkok and Hat Yai. On the plus side, the broad, 3km-long beach offers good sand and plenty of shade beneath the parasols and there are hundreds of shops and bars plus a surprising number of good restaurants to keep you busy after dark.

ARRIVAL AND DEPARTURE

AO PATONG

Songthaews from Phuket town (approx every 15min, 6am–6pm; 30min; B25) approach Patong from the northeast, driving south along one-way Thanon Raja Uthit Song Roi Phi (Thanon Raja Uthit 200 Phi) then

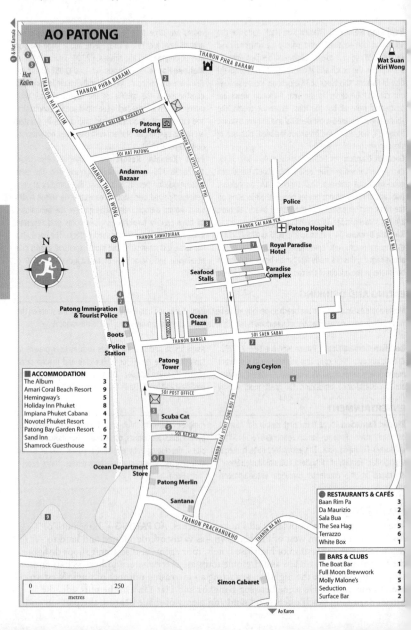

AO PATONG

ACCOMMODATION
The Album	3
Amari Coral Beach Resort	9
Hemingway's	5
Holiday Inn Phuket	8
Impiana Phuket Cabana	4
Novotel Phuket Resort	1
Patong Bay Garden Resort	6
Sand Inn	7
Shamrock Guesthouse	2

RESTAURANTS & CAFÉS
Baan Rim Pa	3
Da Maurizio	2
Sala Bua	4
The Sea Hag	5
Terrazzo	6
White Box	1

BARS & CLUBS
The Boat Bar	1
Full Moon Brewwork	4
Molly Malone's	5
Seduction	3
Surface Bar	2

circling back north along beachfront Thanon Thavee Wong (also one-way) via the *Patong Merlin*, where they wait to pick up passengers for the return trip.

GETTING AROUND

National **car rental** (☎076 340608, ⓦnationalcarthailand.com) has a desk inside the *Holiday Inn*, the local Budget agent is at the nearby *Patong Merlin* (☎076 292389, ⓦbudget.co.th), or you can rent jeeps and motorbikes from any transport tout on Thanon Thavee Wong. Otherwise, aim to stroll – tuk-tuks ask for as much as B200 for short trips within the resort.

INFORMATION AND TOURS

Most of the **tour agents** have offices on the southern stretch of Thanon Thavee Wong, offering a number of day-trips and activities (see box, p.319); this is also where you'll find many of the **dive operators** (see box, p.338).

ACCOMMODATION

It's hard to find much accommodation under B900 in Patong, and there are no backpacker places, but upper-end hotels are reasonable value and all have excellent facilities.

The Album 29 Thanon Sawatdirak ☎076 297023, ⓦthealbumhotel.com. Tiny urban-chic boutique inn, where the 22 carefully designed a/c rooms all have a flatscreen TV, DVD player, free wi-fi, and a petite balcony. There's a small jacuzzi pool on the fourth-floor roof terrace and rates include Continental breakfast and high tea. B2900

Amari Coral Beach Resort 104 Thanon Traitrang ☎076 340106, ⓦamari.com. Occupying its own secluded little beach on a headland at the southernmost end of the bay, this upmarket Thai chain hotel offers contemporary-chic rooms with generous sea-view balconies, plus two swimming pools, romantic spa facilities, tennis courts and several restaurants. The views are exceptional and the location peaceful but convenient; as it's ranged up a slope it's not ideal for guests with mobility problems. B5700

Hemingway's 179/95–8 Soi Saen Sabai ☎076 343264–5, ⓦpatonghemingways.com. Smart, modern, a/c rooms done out in dark wood, black and red, with small, hot-water bathrooms, TVs, fridges and free wi-fi. Wicker chairs and old-fashioned ceiling fans downstairs are all that conjure up the ghost of Papa Hemingway, but the big plus-point of this place is the small rooftop pool, jacuzzi and bar with views of the surrounding hills. B2500

★ **Holiday Inn Phuket** 86/11 Thanon Thavee Wong ☎076 340608, ⓦphuket.holiday-inn.com. Well-run, innovative, upmarket chain hotel that offers smart, contemporary rooms just across the road from the beach, in two differently styled wings, and fosters an informal, unpretentious atmosphere. The poshest Busakorn villa rooms have their own interconnected pools and there are also large, attractive pools for each wing, plus several restaurants and an interesting programme of daily activities. The hotel makes a big effort to be family-friendly, with special "kidsuites" for children, an all-day kids' club and a teens' club and two children's pools. Also offers wheelchair-accessible rooms. Breakfast and wi-fi included. B6300

Impiana Phuket Cabana 94 Thanon Thavee Wong ☎076 340138, ⓦimpiana.com. Located right on the beach and in the heart of the resort, the very tastefully designed a/c cabanas here are set around a garden and smallish swimming pool; also has a kids' pool and a spa. B7600

Novotel Phuket Resort Thanon Phra Barami/Thanon Hat Kalim ☎076 342777, ⓦnovotelphuket.com. Luxurious and relaxing chain hotel built on the hillside above Kalim Bay, the quieter, northern end of the resort, a 10min walk or a free shuttle ride to Patong's main beach and shops, but very close to some of the best restaurants. Occupying sloping landscaped tropical gardens and offering exceptional high-level sea views, it's especially popular with families as it offers heaps of activities plus a multi-level swimming pool. B4500

Patong Bay Garden Resort 33/1 Thanon Thavee Wong ☎076 340297–8, ⓦpatongbaygarden.com. Lively, mid-sized 71-room hotel set right on the beach, with the top "studio" rooms having uninterrupted sea views, quite unusual in central Patong. Other rooms look out on the small shorefront pool or have no view at all. Rooms are quite elegantly furnished and all have a/c, free wi-fi and TV. Breakfast included. B3200

Sand Inn 171 Soi Saen Sabai ☎076 340275, ⓦsandinn phuket.com. Thirty well-appointed a/c rooms, a little on the compact side, but maintained to a good standard and in the ideal location for nightlife, just east off bar-packed Thanon Bangla. There's TV, hot showers and fridges in all rooms, a *Euro Deli* restaurant downstairs, and use of a small swimming pool just a few metres up the soi. B1600

Shamrock Guesthouse Above The Deli supermarket, 31 Thanon Raja Uthit Song Roi Phi ☎076 340991, ⓦdeliguesthouse.com. Friendly, good-value three-storey hotel at the northern end of the resort with large, pleasant, well-maintained and cheerily painted a/c rooms, all with TVs, fridges, and safety boxes. Ask for a room on the north side of the building: they're cooler, have balconies and are away from the noise of the adjacent Irish bar. B800

4

EATING

Much of the food on Patong is dire, but in among the disastrous little cafés advertising everything from Hungarian to Swedish "home cooking" you'll find a few genuinely reputable, long-running, upmarket favourites; reservations are recommended at all the places listed here. For well-priced Thai fast food, there are the regional speciality stalls at the *Food Haven* food centre in Jung Ceylon, the *Patong Food Park* night market that sets up around 5pm towards the northern end of Thanon Raja Uthit Song Roi Phi, and the row of seafood stall-restaurants further south, opposite the *Royal Paradise Hotel* complex.

★ **Baan Rim Pa** Across from the Novotel on Thanon Hat Kalim ☎076 340789, ⓦbaanrimpa.com. One of Phuket's most famous fine-dining restaurants, this is an elegant spot that's beautifully set in a teak building on a clifftop overlooking the bay, with tables also on its sea-view terrace. Known for its classic "Royal Thai" cuisine (mains from about B400), including banana blossom salad, creamy duck curry and fried tiger prawns with tamarind sauce, as well as for its wine cellar. Live jazz every night in the *Piano Bar*. Daily 1pm–midnight.

Da Maurizio Across from the Novotel on Thanon Hat Kalim ☎076 344079, ⓦdamaurizio.com. Superior Italian restaurant in a stunning location set over the rocks beside the sea. Serves authentic antipasti and home-made pasta such as pappardelle with scallops and crab in a spicy tomato sauce, Phuket lobsters and other great seafood, and a good wine list. Main dishes from B450. Daily noon–11pm.

Sala Bua 41 Thanon Thavee Wong ☎076 340138, ⓦsala-bua.com. Fabulously stylish, breezy, beach-view restaurant attached to the *Impiana Phuket Cabana* hotel. The innovative, pricey, Pacific Rim and Thai menus include Cajun-style red snapper with fermented black bean sauce (B485) and desserts such as sticky-rice sushi rolls with green mango shake (B250). Daily 6am–midnight.

★ **The Sea Hag** Soi Dr Wattana (Soi Permpong 3) ☎076 341111, ⓦkenyaphuket.com. The same chef has been cooking great seafood here for two decades and this is where expat hoteliers come for a good Patong feed. Fish and seafood cooked any number of Thai-style ways for B200–400. Daily noon–4pm & 6pm–midnight.

Terrazzo Holiday Inn Phuket, 86/11 Thanon Thavee Wong ☎076 340608, ⓦphuket.holiday-inn.com. Good, crispy, thin pizzas (around B300) and tasty pastas including home-made ravioli and gnocchi, in a very pleasant, open-plan garden setting, with a popular oval bar, on the main beachfront drag. Daily 6–11.15pm.

White Box Thanon Hat Kalim, 1.5km north of the Novotel ☎076 346271, ⓦwhiteboxphuket.com. This chic, sophisticated waterside restaurant and bar, strikingly designed as a modernist cube with panoramic picture windows, is a magnet for visiting celebs and style-conscious expats. The very expensive menu (mains from B480) mixes Thai and Mediterranean flavours – grilled Phuket lobster with mint and ginger, beef carpaccio, red curry with roasted duck – and the rooftop sofas are ideal for a pre- or post-dinner drink. Daily 11am–11.30pm.

NIGHTLIFE AND ENTERTAINMENT

After dark, everyone heads to pedestrianized Thanon Bangla for their own taste of Patong's notorious **nightlife** and the road teems with a cross section of Phuket tourists, from elderly couples and young parents with strollers, to glammed-up girlfriends and groups of lads. The big draw for the more innocent onlookers is Thanon Bangla's Soi Crocodile, better known as Soi Katoey, or "Trannie Alley", where pouting, barely clad transvestites jiggle their implants on podiums at the mouth of the soi and charge for photos with giggling tourists. But the real action happens further down the many bar-filled sois shooting off Thanon Bangla, where open-air bar-beers and neon-lit go-go clubs packed with strippers and goggle-eyed punters pulsate through the night. The pick-up trade pervades most bars in Patong, and though many of these joints are welcoming enough to couples and female tourists, there are a few alternatives, listed below, for anyone not in that kind of mood. The **gay** entertainment district is concentrated around the Paradise Complex, a network of small sois and dozens of bar-beers in front of *Royal Paradise Hotel* on Thanon Raja Uthit Song Roi Phi: see ⓦgaypatong.com for events listings, including dates for the annual Gay Pride festival, which has recently been held in late April. If you're looking for something else to do with yourself (or your kids) in the evening, check out the transvestite Simon Cabaret, or the spectacular show at nearby Phuket FantaSea (see p.331). The Jung Ceylon shopping centre has a seven-screen **cinema**, SF Cinema City.

The Boat Bar Soi 5, Paradise Complex, off Thanon Raja Uthit Song Roi Phi ⓦboatbar.com. Long-running, very popular gay bar and disco, with two cabaret shows nightly, at around midnight and 1.30am. Daily 9pm–late.

Full Moon Brewwork Port Zone (next to the replica junk), Jung Ceylon shopping centre, Thanon Raja Uthit Song Roi Phi ⓦfacebook.com/fullmoonbrewwork. The best of this microbrewery's offerings is their dark ale, a decent bitter that might appease homesick Brits, and there's good food, too, including tom yam kung (B145). Live music upstairs (daily except Tues & Thurs 7.30–10pm). Daily 11am–midnight.

Molly Malone's 94/1 Thanon Thavee Wong ⓦmolly malonesphuket.com. Genial Thai–Irish pub chain that serves draught Guinness and Kilkenny, shows international sports TV, stages live bands playing pub rock from 9.30pm and has pool tables, a small beer garden and no overt hostess presence. Daily 10am–2am.

Seduction Soi Happy, off Thanon Bangla ⓦseduction disco.com. Currently the favourite dance venue for partying couples and others not looking for freelance company, this three-storey bar and club has fairly classy lounge areas, hi-tech lighting and a catholic music policy, and occasionally brings in big-name international DJs. Free

until midnight, B200 thereafter. Daily 10pm–4am.

Simon Cabaret Thanon Prachanukho, south end of Patong ☎076 342011–5, ⓦphuket-simoncabaret .com. Famously flamboyant extravaganza starring a troupe of transvestites. It's all very Hollywood – a little bit risqué but not at all sleazy – and popular with tour groups and families. B700. Nightly 6pm, 7.45pm & 9.30pm.

Surface Bar Top floor, La Flora Resort Patong, 39 Thanon Thavee Wong ☎076 344241. The perfect place for a sophisticated sundowner, enjoyed from the comfort of enormous sofas on the hotel's wide rooftop terrace. Expansive ocean views and a sea breeze as well. Daily 5pm–midnight.

SHOPPING

Jung Ceylon Thanon Raja Uthit Song Roi Phi ⓦjungceylon.com. Though you can't move for shops in downtown Patong, by far the best, and least hectic, place to browse is this enormous shopping centre, whose refreshingly tasteful and spacious design includes fountains and plaza seating plus countless shops and restaurants.

There are branches of Robinsons Department Store and, on the ground floor at the front end, Boots the Chemist and Asia Books (for English-language books, magazines and newspapers), plus the That's Siam Thai handicrafts emporium in the basement. Daily 11am–10pm.

DIRECTORY

Immigration The tiny Patong branch (information only) of Phuket's Immigration office is next to *Sala Bua* restaurant on Thanon Thavee Wong (☎076 340477; Mon–Fri 10am–noon & 1–3pm).

Post office Thanon Thavee Wong (daily 9am–7pm).
Tourist police In front of the Immigration office on Thanon Thavee Wong (☎076 340244 or 1155).

Ao Karon

AO KARON, Phuket's second resort, after Patong, is very much a middle-of-the-road destination. Far less lively, or congested, than Patong, but more commercial and less individual than the smaller beaches, it's the domain of affordable guesthouses and package-tour hotels and appeals chiefly to mid-budget tourists, many of them from Scandinavia. The 2.5km-long **beach** is graced with squeaky soft golden sand and is completely free of developments, though there's very little natural shade; an embankment screens most of the southern half of the beach from the road running alongside, but north of the *Hilton* the road is more often in view and parts of the shore back on to lagoons and wasteland. Karon's main **shopping and eating areas**, with all the usual resort facilities, are grouped around the *Centara Karon Resort* on the northern curve of Thanon Patak; along and around Thanon Luang Pho Chuain, location of the Kata Plaza enclave of accommodation, restaurants and bars; and along Thanon Taina (sometimes referred to as Kata Centre).

The **undertow** off Ao Karon is treacherously strong during the monsoon season from June to October, so you should heed the warning signs and flags and ask for local advice – fatalities are not uncommon. The tiny bay just north of Ao Karon – known as **Karon Noi** or Relax Bay – is almost exclusively patronized by guests of the *Le Meridien* hotel, but non-guests are quite welcome to swim and sunbathe here.

ARRIVAL AND DEPARTURE   AO KARON

Ao Karon is 5km south of Patong and 20km southwest of Phuket town. Most **songthaews** from Phuket town (approx every 20min; 30min; B30) arrive in Karon via Thanon Patak, hitting the beach at the northern end of Ao Karon and then driving south along beachfront Thanon Karon, continuing over the headland as far as *Kata Beach Resort* on Ao Kata Yai. To catch a songthaew back into town, just stand on the other side of the road and flag one down. Transport touts throughout the resort rent motorbikes and jeeps.

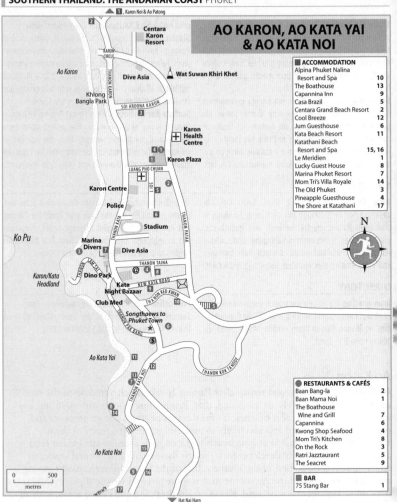

AO KARON, AO KATA YAI & AO KATA NOI

ACCOMMODATION

Alpina Phuket Nalina Resort and Spa	10
The Boathouse	13
Capannina Inn	9
Casa Brazil	5
Centara Grand Beach Resort	2
Cool Breeze	12
Jum Guesthouse	6
Kata Beach Resort	11
Katathani Beach Resort and Spa	15, 16
Le Meridien	1
Lucky Guest House	8
Marina Phuket Resort	7
Mom Tri's Villa Royale	14
The Old Phuket	3
Pineapple Guesthouse	4
The Shore at Katathani	17

RESTAURANTS & CAFÉS

Baan Bang-la	2
Baan Mama Noi	1
The Boathouse Wine and Grill	7
Capannina	6
Kwong Shop Seafood	4
Mom Tri's Kitchen	8
On the Rock	3
Ratri Jazztaurant	5
The Seacret	9

BAR

75 Stang Bar	1

ACCOMMODATION

★ **Casa Brazil** 9 Soi 1, Thanon Luang Pho Chuain ☎076 396317, ⓦphukethomestay.com. Appealingly arty little hotel, designed in Santa Fe style, with adobe-look walls, earth-toned paintwork, and funky decor and furnishings. The 21 rooms are comfortable, with hot showers, fridges and TVs, and nearly all have a/c. Choose rooms at the back for a rare green and peaceful view of Karon's hilly backdrop, best enjoyed from the French windows and private balconies. Rates include breakfast and there's wi-fi. Fan B1200, a/c B1400

Centara Grand Beach Resort 683 Thanon Patak ☎076 201234, ⓦcentarahotelsresorts.com. Huge, low-rise, beachfront luxury hotel, which very loosely echoes Phuket's Sino-Portuguese architecture, all in different

shades of pink. It's particularly good for children, with two kids' clubs, a kids' pool, a free-form main pool and a "Lazy River", an artificial river that runs under bridges and under tunnels for exploration on inner tubes. There's an adults-only pool too, and grown-ups can also enjoy kayaking, windsurfing, tennis, the spa and a long menu of other activities. B10,500

Jum Guesthouse Off Thanon Kata, about 100m from the beach, directly behind and accessible through Andaman Seaview Hotel ☎076 396570. Friendly place in a lush, shady garden with just five large, concrete bungalows, all with fridges, TVs, wardrobes, free wi-fi and a few decorative touches; the big, well-equipped bathrooms have hot showers. Fan B1000, a/c B1200

Le Meridien Ao Karon Noi (also known as Relax Bay), north of Ao Karon ☎076 370100, ⓦlemeridien.com. This huge hotel complex has the tiny bay all to itself and boasts an amazing breadth of facilities, including ten restaurants and bars, two lagoon-style swimming pools (with islands), a spa, squash and tennis courts, free non-motorized watersports and private woods. It's a good choice for kids, with reliable babysitting services and a kids' club. Breakfast included. **B9200**

Lucky Guest House 110/44–45 Thanon Taina, Kata Centre ☎076 330572, ⓔluckyguesthousekata @hotmail.com. Good-value place offering unusually large, bright en-suite rooms in a low-rise block (the best have balconies) and some rather plain but very clean semi-detached bungalows on land further back; set back a bit down a small soi, this guesthouse has a refreshing sense of space that's at a premium on this road packed with shops, bars and restaurants. Fan **B450**, a/c **B650**

Marina Phuket Resort 47 Thanon Karon, far southern end of Ao Karon, on the Karon/Kata headland ☎076 330625, ⓦmarinaphuket.com. Enjoying both a very central location, backing on to the beach and just steps from restaurants and shops, and a luxuriously spacious and secluded tropical garden in a former coconut plantation, this is a good upper-end choice. Accommodation is in a/c cottages – Garden View options are old-fashioned and plain, but Jungle View versions are very appealing – and there's a pool, wi-fi and the prettily located *On the Rock* restaurant. Breakfast included. **B6000**

The Old Phuket Soi Aroona Karon, 192/36 Thanon Karon ☎076 396353–6, ⓦtheoldphuket.com. The Sino Wing at this attractive, peacefully secluded, heritage-conscious hotel is designed to evoke Sino-Portuguese shophouse architecture. Its rooms are both pretty and modern, with coloured glass window panels and East Indies-style wooden doors. Furnishings in the more expensive Serene Wing are much more contemporary and minimalist and many of its rooms have direct access to the lagoon-like pool. **B8200**

Pineapple Guesthouse Karon Plaza, off Patak and Luang Pho Chuain rds ☎076 396223, ⓦpineapple phuket.com. Good-value British–Thai guesthouse offering 21 sprucely kept, tiled-floor rooms, all with fridges, TV and hot water, most with a/c, plus a ten-bed mixed dorm, with lockers and several fans. The downstairs restaurant serves full English breakfasts and the guesthouse is surrounded by other expat bars and restaurants in the enclave known as Karon Plaza (not to be confused with the Karon Plaza market stalls at the north end of Karon beachfront). Free internet access and free wi-fi throughout. Dorm **B200**, fan **B500**, a/c **B900**

EATING AND DRINKING

Karon's choice of restaurants is underwhelming, lacking either the big-name restaurants of Patong or Kata, or the authenticity of Phuket town. Though go-go bars haven't arrived yet, clusters of outdoor bar-beers with hostess service are popping up at a depressing rate.

75 Stang Bar Karon Plaza, up a lane off Thanon Luang Pho Chuain, near Thanon Patak. In among the sports bars and rooms for rent in Karon Plaza are a couple of "art bars" run by cool local creative types, including this invitingly bohemian little outdoor place. It's a mess of driftwood and found objects, where the only things that seem to have been designed are the red, gold and green stools, which match the wall-to-wall reggae on the sound system. Drinks aren't quite 75 *satang*, but they're certainly cheap. Daily 6pm–2am.

Baan Bang-la 6 Soi Patak, off Thanon Patak. The seafood here has a good reputation and there are also pasta dishes and pizzas – made in a brick oven by an Italian *pizzaiolo* – on the menu too. Dining is mostly alfresco in Thai *salas* set around a pretty little garden. Mains B180–300. Daily 6pm–late.

Baan Mama Noi Karon Plaza, next door but one to Pineapple Guesthouse on a lane off Thanon Patak.

Expats, dive staff and Italian tourists fill this place at lunch and dinnertime, savouring the home-from-home taste of the excellent, mid-priced, Italian food, such as spaghetti bolognese (B130). Daily 7am–10pm.

Kwong Shop Seafood 114 Thanon Taina. Unassuming but very popular, friendly family-run institution sporting gingham tablecloths that's famous for its well-priced fresh fish (all B40 per 100 grammes) and seafood cooked to order. Daily 8am–midnight.

On the Rock In the grounds of Marina Phuket Resort, Kata/Karon headland ☎076 330625, ⓦmarinaphuket .com. Occupying a fine spot above the rocks at the southern end of Ao Karon, this open-air restaurant serves especially good baskets of grilled and deep-fried seafood, baked mussels and mixed seafood satay. Especially romantic at night. Main dishes from B350. Daily 11am–10.30pm.

Ao Kata Yai and Ao Kata Noi

Broad, curving **AO KATA YAI** (Big Kata Bay) is only a few minutes' drive around the headland from Karon (17km from Phuket town), but both prettier and safer

DIVING AND SNORKELLING OFF PHUKET

The reefs and islands within sailing distance of Phuket rate among the most spectacular in the world, and **diving and snorkelling** trips are both good value and hugely popular. Many trips operate year-round, though some of the more remote islands and reefs become too dangerous to reach during part or all of the monsoon season, roughly June to October.

DIVE SHOPS AND TRIPS

All the dive **shops** listed below are established and accredited PADI Five-Star Instructor or Career Development Centres; they teach courses, organize dive trips and rent equipment. Advice on choosing a dive shop and other general diving information can be found in "Basics" (see p.51). Expect to pay around B4500 for a one-day introductory **diving course**, and B14,500 for the four-day Openwater course, including equipment. **Day-trips** to the closest of the dive sites listed below, including at least two dives, cost around B3800, while multi-day **live-aboard** cruises to the more distant top-rated reefs of Ko Similan and Ko Surin, Hin Daeng and Hin Muang, and the Mergui archipelago can cost as much as B33,000 for four days, including sixteen dives and full board but excluding equipment and national park fees.

There are **recompression chambers** at Phuket International Hospital in Phuket town (see p.322), and at Vachira Hospital, Soi Wachira, Thanon Yaowarat, Phuket town (☏076 211114, ⊛vachiraphuket.go.th).

Dive Asia 24 Thanon Karon, Kata/Karon headland, Ao Karon, and 623 Thanon Patak, Karon Circle, Ao Karon ☏076 330598, ⊛diveasia.com.

Marina Divers Next to *Marina Phuket Resort* at 45 Thanon Karon, Ao Karon ☏076 330272,
⊛marinadivers.com.

Santana 240 Thanon Raja Uthit Song Roi Phi, Ao Patong ☏076 294220, ⊛santanaphuket.com.

Scuba Cat 94 Thanon Thavee Wong, Ao Patong ☏076 293120, ⊛scubacat.com.

SNORKELLING TRIPS

The most popular snorkelling destination from Phuket is **Ko Phi Phi** (see p.370). All travel agents sell mass-market day-trips there, on huge ferries with capacities of a hundred plus; prices average B1600 and include snorkelling stops at Phi Phi Leh and Phi Phi Don, snorkel rental and a seafood lunch. Smaller speedboat trips to Ko Phi Phi are usually worth the extra money to avoid the big groups; those run by Offspray Leisure (B3200; ☏076 281375, ⊛offsprayleisure.com) get good reviews, and they also run speedboat snorkel trips to **Ko Racha Yai** (B3200). Day-trips to the remote but beautiful **Ko Similan** islands start from B2600 (see p.316). Many of the dive companies listed welcome snorkellers

for swimming, thanks to the protective rocky promontories at either end. It's also a good distance from the main road. The northern stretch of Kata Yai is overlooked by the unobtrusive buildings of the *Club Med* resort, and the southern by *Kata Beach Resort*: in between the soft sand is busy with sunloungers and the occasional drink and fruit stall. The rest of the accommodation, and the bulk of the tourist village, with its restaurants, bars, tour operators and many shops, fans out eastwards from the walled *Club Med* compound, up to the main road, Thanon Patak.

Beyond the southern headland, **AO KATA NOI**'s (Little Kata Bay) smaller white-sand bay feels secluded, being at the end of a no-through road, but is very popular and filled with loungers and parasols. Kata Noi has its own low-key but rather charmless cluster of businesses, including an ATM and minimarket, though it's dominated by the various sections of the enormous *Katathani* hotel; public access to the beach is down to the right just beyond the hotel's Thani wing.

ARRIVAL AND DEPARTURE   AO KATA YAI AND AO KATA NOI

Most **songthaews** from Phuket go first to Karon, then drive south past *Club Med* and terminate beside *Kata Beach Resort* on the headland between Kata Yai and Kata Noi (B30; returning songthaews depart approx every 20min 5am–4.30pm). To get to Kata Noi, continue walking over the hill for about ten minutes, or take a tuk-tuk for about B100.

on board their day-trips, and sometimes on the live-aboards too, for a discount of about thirty percent.

ANDAMAN COAST DIVE AND SNORKEL SITES

Anemone Reef About 22km east of Phuket. Submerged reef of soft coral and sea anemones starting about 5m deep. Lots of fish, including leopard sharks, tuna and barracuda. Usually combined with a dive at nearby Shark Point. Unsuitable for snorkellers.

Burma Banks About 250km northwest of Phuket; only accessible on live-aboards. A series of submerged "banks", well away from any landmass and very close to the Burmese border. Only worth the trip for its sharks. Visibility up to 25m.

Hin Daeng and **Hin Muang** 56km southwest of Ko Lanta. Hin Daeng is an exceptional reef wall, named after the red soft corals that cover the rocks, with visibility up to 30m. One hundred metres away, Hin Muang also drops to 50m and is good for stingrays, manta rays, whale sharks and silvertip sharks. Visibility up to 50m. Because of the depth and the current, both places are considered too risky for novice divers who have logged fewer than twenty dives. Unsuitable for snorkellers.

King Cruiser Near Shark Point, between Phuket and Ko Phi Phi. Dubbed the *Thai Tanic*, this became a wreck dive in May 1997, when a tourist ferry sank on its way to Ko Phi Phi. Visibility up to 20m, but hopeless for snorkellers because of the depth, and collapsed sections make it dangerous for any but the most experienced divers.

Ko Phi Phi 48km east of Phuket's Ao Chalong (see p.370). Visibility up to 30m. The most popular destination

for Phuket divers and snorkellers. Spectacular drop-offs; good chance of seeing whale sharks.

Ko Racha Noi and **Ko Racha Yai** About 33km and 28km south of Phuket's Ao Chalong respectively. Visibility up to 40m. Racha Yai (aka Raya Yai) is good for beginners and for snorkellers; at the more challenging Racha Noi there's a good chance of seeing manta rays, eagle rays and whale sharks.

Ko Rok Nok and **Ko Rok Nai** 100km southeast of Phuket, south of Ko Lanta (see box, p.387). Visibility up to 18m. Shallow reefs that are excellent for snorkelling.

Ko Similan 96km northwest of Phuket; easiest access from Khao Lak (see p.316). One of the world's top diving spots. Visibility up to 30m. Leopard sharks, whale sharks and manta rays, plus caves and gorges.

Ko Surin 174km northwest of Phuket; easiest access from Khuraburi (see p.303). Shallow reefs of soft and hard corals that are good for snorkelling.

Richelieu Rock Just east of Ko Surin, close to Burmese waters. A sunken pinnacle that's famous for its whale sharks. Considered by many to be Thailand's top dive spot.

Shark Point (Hin Mu Sang) 24km east of Phuket's Laem Panwa. Protected as a marine sanctuary. Visibility up to 10m. Notable for soft corals, sea fans and leopard sharks. Often combined with the *King Cruiser* dive and/or Anemone Reef; unrewarding for snorkellers.

ACCOMMODATION

Alpina Phuket Nalina Resort and Spa 7/1 Thanon Ked Kwan, Kata Yai **☎** 076 370999, **ⓦ** phuketnalina .com. Very pleasant hotel with comfortable, tastefully Thai-style rooms and a surprisingly quiet location that's close to shops and restaurants and about 10min walk from the beach. A free shuttle also runs guests to the hotel's private beach club in front of *Club Med*. Rooms have generous balconies overlooking the free-form pool and the hills beyond, with some enjoying direct pool access; suites and private pool villas are enormous. Also has a spa, several restaurants and wi-fi throughout. Breakfast included. **B6150**

The Boathouse Thanon Kok Tanode, Kata Yai **☎** 076 330015–7, **ⓦ** boathousephuket.com. Exclusive beach-front boutique hotel in a graceful, contemporary style, with just 38 elegantly furnished sea-front rooms, a reputation for classy service, and a famously top-notch restaurant. All rooms have free wi-fi, there's a pool, a spa and weekend cooking classes. Advance booking essential. **B9600**

Capannina Inn The Beach Centre, "New Kata Road", Kata Yai **☎** 076 284450, **ⓦ** phuket-capannina-inn .com. Smart, modern, large bedrooms and well-equipped bathrooms, with a/c, cable TV, hot water, fridges and espresso machines. Guests have the use of an attractive, shared, garden pool in front. It's set in a new development of shops and hotels, a 5min walk from the beach – or there's a free tuk-tuk to the beach and the restaurant (see p.340). Continental breakfast included. **B2000**

Cool Breeze 225 Thanon Kok Tanode, Kata Yai **☎** 076 330484 or **☎** 085 900 3681, **ⓦ** phuketindex.com /coolbreezebungalows. Though one of the cheapest places in Kata, for your money you get a spacious private bungalow, plus a view of sorts from the terrace (either of the distant sea or of the hilltop Big Buddha in profile), the bungalows being ranged steeply up the hillside, in a grassy palm- and shrub-filled garden. Interiors are nothing fancy but good value, with hot shower (in most), TV and fridge, and are sufficiently far above the narrow, noisy road. Fan B800, a/c B1000

Kata Beach Resort Thanon Kata, Kata Yai ☏ 076 330530–4, ⓦ katagroup.com. This huge 275-room, four-storey hotel occupies a great spot right on the edge of the southern end of Kata Yai's white-sand beach. It has a shorefront restaurant and two swimming pools, a palm-shaded seaside garden, a spa and a dive shop. Some of the attractive, balconied, wooden-floored rooms have direct pool access, and some have sea views. B9300

Katathani Beach Resort and Spa 14 Thanon Kata Noi, Kata Noi ☏ 076 330124–6, ⓦ katathani.com. The various wings and offshoots of the enormous and luxurious *Katathani* now occupy almost the entire shoreline of small, secluded Kata Noi. The beachfront all-suite Thani wing has the prime position, with the narrow lawn dropping seamlessly onto the white sand; all rooms here have sea-view balconies. Across the effectively private, no-through road, the cheaper, garden-view Bhuri wing has a distinctively contemporary, pastel-coloured look and its rooms

too are very deluxe. There's broadband throughout (free in the lobby) and a daily shuttle service to town and to Patong. The hotel has six restaurants, six swimming pools and a spa, plus an arm-long menu of activities and a kids' club. Breakfast included. B8750

Mom Tri's Villa Royale 12 Thanon Kata Noi, Kata Noi ☏ 076 333569, ⓦ villaroyalephuket.com. Luxurious suites, richly decorated with fine textiles and teak, a renowned restaurant (see below), an excellent spa and two saltwater and one freshwater pools, set in landscaped tropical gardens with fine views above Kata Noi. Free wi-fi throughout. B12,900

The Shore at Katathani 18 Thanon Kata Noi, Kata Noi ☏ 076 330124, ⓦ theshore.katathani.com. The sister hotel of the *Katathani* has its own spa, restaurant and infinity pool, and targets couples (no under-12s allowed). Stacked up the hillside at the south end of the beach, the relaxing, 130-square metre pool villas sport a fresh, breezy modern design and ample space to lounge inside and out, as well as thoughtful extras such as espresso machines and iPod docks. B25,000

EATING AND DRINKING

The Boathouse Wine and Grill Thanon Kok Tanode, Kata Yai ☏ 076 330015–7, ⓦ boathousephuket.com. One of the best-known restaurants on Phuket – not least for its famously extensive, award-winning wine list – where the skills of the French chef are best sampled on four-course Thai or French tasting menus (B1500, or just over B3000 with paired wines). The beachside terrace and dining room, decorated with nautical touches and attached to the boutique hotel of the same name, enjoy fine sunset views, and there are cooking classes here every weekend. Reservations recommended. Daily 6.30am–11pm.

Capannina Down a short alley of shops off Kata Road, Kata Yai ☏ 076 284318, ⓦ capannina-phuket.com. Done out in cool red and black, this Italian-run, open-sided restaurant (with an a/c room) prepares good, home-made pastas (tagliatelle bolognese B230), pizzas from a wood-fired oven and a wide range of seafood and meat main courses; finish off with your choice of grappas and an Illy espresso. Daily 11am–late.

Mom Tri's Kitchen Mom Tri's Villa Royale, 12 Thanon Kata Noi, Kata Noi ☏ 076 333569, ⓦ villaroyalephuket .com. Highly regarded luxury restaurant, offering Thai

and European fine dining, in dishes such as veal parmigiana and jumbo prawns in red curry. Mains from B460. Reservations recommended. Daily 6.30am–11.30pm.

Ratri Jazztaurant Reached by a vertiginous but short climb (or by road) east off Thanon Patak ☏ 076 333538, ⓦ ratrijazztaurant.com. This rather sophisticated eyrie makes a panoramic spot for cocktails at sundown, with high-level views across Kata, plenty of squishy sofas to sink into and a good if pricey menu of Thai food (B220–850), including *matsaman* and Indian–Thai curries. The enthusiastic in-house jazz band plays from about 8.30pm late into the night and is worth lingering for. Daily 3pm–late.

★ **The Seacret** Katathani Beach Resort and Spa, 14 Thanon Kata Noi, Kata Noi ☏ 076 330124–6, ⓦ katathani.com. Excellent Phuket and southern Thai cuisine, such as the classic dried-shrimp relish, *nam prik kung siap* (B220), *pla thawt khamin* (deep-fried fish with turmeric and pineapple relish) and *muu hong* (stewed pork belly with cinnamon). All this and an attractive, open-air setting by the swimming pool, with the best tables on a deck under fairy-lit trees by the beach. Daily 11am–5pm & 6–10.30pm.

Hat Nai Harn

The favourite beach of the many expats who live in nearby Rawai, **HAT NAI HARN**, 18km southwest of Phuket town, is an exceptionally beautiful curved bay of white sand backed by a stand of casuarinas and plenty of foodstalls but only minimal development. It does get crowded with parasols and loungers, however, and during the monsoon the waves here are huge.

ARRIVAL AND DEPARTURE   **HAT NAI HARN**

By songthaew Songthaews from the market on Thanon Ranong in Phuket town (approx every 30min; 45min; B40) go to Hat Nai Harn, via Hat Rawai, with the last one returning at about 5pm.

ACCOMMODATION

All Seasons Naiharn Phuket ☎076 289327, ⊚allseasons-naiharn-phuket.com. Run by the French Accor group, this well-sited, though architecturally unexciting, hotel offers contemporary-styled concrete row rooms with ocean or garden view, five restaurants and bars, a spa, a kids' club and a decent-sized pool, just over the narrow road from the shore, next door to *The Royal Phuket Yacht Club*. **B3470**

The Royal Phuket Yacht Club ☎076 380200, ⊚pura -varna.com. The beach's northern headland is dominated by this long-standing luxurious hotel, whose rooms are raked up the hill amid terraced gardens of bougainvillaea; all have huge bathrooms and living-room sized balconies to make the most of the fine sea views. A spa, a swimming pool, tennis courts and lots of watersports complete the picture. **B6000**

EATING AND DRINKING

★ **Trattoria del Buongustaio** ☎087 467 2554, ⊚trattoriabuongustaio.ilmiosito.net. From a lovely balcony above the rocks on the northern headland, this Italian-run restaurant offers gorgeous views of the bay; reach it via the paved road through *The Royal Phuket Yacht Club* (the road may appear to be private, but persevere).

The full menu covers a wide choice of starters and meat and especially seafood main courses, plus risottos and pastas such as delicious seafood ravioli with sage and butter (B350). Daily noon–12.30am; the kitchen closes at 11pm, while the downstairs lounge bar closes at 2am.

Hat Ya Nui and Laem Promthep

Follow the coastal road 2km south around the lumpy headland from Hat Nai Harn and you reach the tiny roadside beach of **Hat Ya Nui**, which gets a surprising number of visitors despite being so small and right next to the admittedly quiet road. There are coral reefs very close to shore, though the currents are strong, and kayaks and sunloungers for rent.

The rugged, wind-blasted, grassy flanked headland of **Laem Promthep**, 1km beyond Hat Ya Nui, marks Phuket's southernmost tip, jutting dramatically – and photogenically – into the deep blue of the Andaman Sea. The cape is one of the island's top beauty spots, and at sunset busloads of tour groups get shipped in to admire the spectacle; Thais pay their respects at the Hindu shrine here, offering elephant figurines in honour of the enshrined four-headed god Brahma and his elephant mount, Erawan. You can escape the crowds by following the trail along the ridge and down to the rocks just above the water.

ARRIVAL AND DEPARTURE   **HAT YA NUI AND LAEM PROMTHEP**

You could catch a **songthaew** from Phuket town to Nai Harn, then walk up and around the promontory in a couple of hours, to pick up another songthaew back to town from Rawai.

ACCOMMODATION

Nai Ya Beach Bungalow ☎076 238179 or ☎076 288817. Two hundred metres uphill from Ya Nui beach towards the cape, this friendly and very pleasant place has attractive, sturdy, thatch-roofed bamboo bungalows with fans, en-suite cold showers and verandas. They're set in a flowery garden that's nicely shaded by cashew nut trees and bougainvillaea and enjoys high-level sea views. Closed May–Oct. **B950**

Hat Rawai

Phuket's southernmost beach, **HAT RAWAI**, was the first to be exploited for tourist purposes, but, half a century on, the hoteliers have moved to the far more appealing sands of Kata and Karon, leaving Rawai to its former inhabitants, the Urak Lawoy *chao ley* (see p.304), and to an expanding expat population. Most visitors are here for the many alfresco **seafood restaurants** along Thanon Viset's beachside promenade.

Phuket Seashell Museum
1500m north of the beach on Highway 4024 • Daily 8am–5.30pm • B200

Aside from its seafront restaurants, Rawai's chief attraction is the **Phuket Seashell Museum**, which displays some two thousand species of shell, including 380-million-year-old fossils, giant clams, and a 140-carat gold pearl.

ARRIVAL AND DEPARTURE   HAT RAWAI
Songthaews from Phuket town pass through Rawai (35min; B30) on their way to and from Nai Harn.

EATING AND DRINKING

Nikita's Towards the northern end of the promenade ☎076 288703, ⓦnikitas-phuket.com. A standout among the many expat-favoured bar-restaurants in the area, not least for the horizon-gazing potential from its peaceful tables on the sand (candle-lit at night). Pizzas from a wood-fired oven (from B200) feature on its Thai and Western menu, alongside well-priced cocktails, wines by the glass and espresso coffees. Daily 10am–2am

at the latest, kitchen closes 11pm.
Salaloy Opposite Nikita's, towards the northern end of the promenade ☎076 613740. The best and most famous of Rawai's restaurants, whose highlights include *pla thawt khamin* (fried fish with turmeric) and omelette topped with baby oysters (B90); it has some lovely outdoor tables right on the shorefront under the casuarinas. Daily 10am–9.30pm.

Ao Chalong, Laem Panwa and around

North of Rawai, the sizeable offshore island of Ko Lone protects the broad sweep of **AO CHALONG**, where many a Chinese fortune was made from the huge quantities of tin mined in the bay. These days, Ao Chalong is the main departure point for dive excursions and snorkelling and fishing trips, which mostly leave from Chalong Pier, east of the bottle-neck roundabout known as Chalong Circle, or Chalong Ha Yaek.

Wat Chalong
8km southwest of Phuket town, on Thanon Chao Fa Nok, aka Route 4022 • Phuket–Karon songthaews pass the entrance

For islanders, Chalong is important as the site of **Wat Chalong**, Phuket's loveliest and most famous temple, which enshrines the statue of revered monk Luang Pho Saem, who helped resolve a violent rebellion by migrant Chinese tin-miners in 1876. Elsewhere in the temple compound, the Phra Mahathat chedi is believed to contain a relic of the Buddha.

Big Buddha of Phuket
Access is via the very steep and winding 6km Soi Jao Fa 51, signed west off Thanon Chao Fa Nok (Route 422), 2km south of Wat Chalong, or 1km north of Chalong Circle • ⓦmingmongkolphuket.com

With your own transport, a visit to Wat Chalong combines well with a pilgrimage to the newly erected **Big Buddha of Phuket** (officially Phra Phuttha Mingmongkol Eaknakakeeree), a towering 45m statue atop the aptly named Khao Nakkerd hill, which dominates many island vistas, including from Kata Yai to the southwest, and is easily spotted from aeroplane windows. Made of concrete but faced with glistening white-marble tiles, the eastward-looking Buddha boasts enormous proportions: he sits on a lotus flower that's nearly 25m across and even his individual hair curls measure almost 1m each. Views from the base of the statue extend east over Ao Chalong to hilly Ko Lone beyond, while western panoramas take in Kata Noi; it's a popular sunset-viewing spot.

Phuket Aquarium
Laem Panwa, 10km south of Phuket town • Daily 8.30am–4.30pm, feeding show Sat & Sun 11am • B100 • ⓦphuketaquarium.org • Songthaews from the market in Phuket town (B25), the last one returning at about 3.30pm

Ao Chalong tapers off eastwards into **Laem Panwa**, at the tip of which you'll find the **Phuket Aquarium**. Run by the island's Marine Biological Centre, it's not a bad primer

for what you might see on a reef and has walk-through tunnels, a sea-turtle pool and a shark-feeding show.

ARRIVAL AND DEPARTURE   **AO CHALONG**

Songthaews to Ao Chalong from Phuket town charge B25.

ACCOMMODATION

Shanti Lodge Soi Bangrae, 1500m south down Thanon Chao Fa Nok from Wat Chalong (the Phuket–Karon songthaew can drop you close by) ☎ 076 280233, ⓦ shantilodge.com. Though there's no special reason to stay in this part of the island, you might make an exception for this alternative, traveller-oriented place. It's set in a relaxing garden, with salt-water swimming pool, book exchange and predominantly vegetarian restaurant, and has fan and a/c doubles with or without private hot-water bathrooms, some of them wheelchair accessible, and family rooms. Fan B750, a/c B850

EATING AND DRINKING

Kan Eang @ Pier Ao Chalong ☎ 076 381212, ⓦ kaneang-pier.com. Classy, long-running restaurant, which is handily, and scenically, sited on a 200m frontage at the mouth of Chalong Pier. The big draw here is the seafood, the best of it barbecued old-style on burning coconut husks (from B1200/kg); deep-fried seaweed with shrimps and chilli sauce is also good and the *haw mok* (fish curry steamed in a banana leaf) is exceptional. Sister restaurant *Kan Eang Seafood*, north up the beach (☎ 076 381323, ⓦ phuket-seafood.com), enjoys a similarly good reputation and offers free pick-ups. Daily 10.30am–11pm.

Thalang and around

There's not a great deal for tourists in the northeast of Phuket island around the district town of **THALANG**, but you're quite likely to pass the landmark **Heroines' Monument**, which stands in the centre of the Tha Rua junction, 12km north of Phuket town on Highway 402. The monument commemorates the repulse of the Burmese army by the widow of the governor of Phuket and her sister in 1785; together they rallied the island's womenfolk who, legend has it, frightened the Burmese away by cutting their hair short and rolling up banana leaves to look like musket barrels – a victory that's celebrated every March 13 to 15 with a monks' ordination ceremony and processions.

Thalang National Museum

On Route 4027, 200m east of the Heroines' Monument • Daily 8.30am–4pm • B30 • ⓦ thailandmuseum.com • All mainland-bound traffic and all songthaews between Phuket and Hat Surin and Hat Nai Yang pass the monument

As the only official introduction to Phuket's rich and intriguing history, **Thalang National Museum** doesn't really match up to the task, but taken in conjunction with the privately funded Thaihua Museum in Phuket town (see p.325), the picture starts to flesh out. Displays include some interesting exhibits on the local tin and rubber industries, accounts of some of the more colourful folkloric traditions and photos of the masochistic feats of the Vegetarian Festival (see box, p.325).

Wat Phra Thong

Just beyond the crossroads in Thalang town, 8km north of the Heroines' Monument

Wat Phra Thong is one of Phuket's most revered temples on account of the power of the Buddha statue it enshrines. The solid gold image is half-buried and no one dares dig it up for fear of a curse that has struck down excavators in the past. After the wat was built around the statue, the image was encased in plaster to deter would-be robbers.

Khao Phra Taew Forest Reserve

Visitor centre 3km east of the crossroads in Thalang town

Several paths cross the small hilly enclave of **Khao Phra Taew Wildlife Park and Forest Reserve**, leading you through the forest habitat of macaques and wild boar, but the most popular features of the park are the Gibbon Rehabilitation Project and the Ton Sai and Bang Pae waterfalls, which combine well as a day-trip or on a tour (see p.319). You can get drinks and snacks at the foodstall next to the Rehabilitation Centre, and the route to the waterfalls is signed from here.

The Gibbon Rehabilitation Project

10km northeast of the Heroines' Monument, off Route 4027 • Daily 9am–4.30pm • National park admission fee B200 • Ⓦ gibbonproject.org • Songthaews from Phuket town, will be more frequent in the morning, will take you most of the way: ask to be dropped off at Bang Pae (a 40min drive from town) and then follow the signed track for about 1km to get to the project centre

Phuket's forests used to resound with the whooping calls of indigenous white-handed lar gibbons (see p.438), but they make such charismatic pets that they were poached to extinction on the island by the mid-1980s. The lar is now an endangered species, and in 1992 it became illegal in Thailand to keep them as pets, to sell them or to kill them. Despite this, you'll come across a depressing number of pet gibbons on Phuket, kept in chains by bar and hotel owners as entertainment for their customers. The **Gibbon Rehabilitation Centre** aims to reverse this state of affairs, first by rescuing as many pet gibbons as they can, and then by resocializing and re-educating them for the wild before finally releasing them back into the forests. It is apparently not unusual for gibbons to be severely traumatized by their experience as pets: not only will they have been taken forcibly from their mothers, but they may also have been abused by their owners.

Visitors are welcome at the project, which is centred in the forests of Khao Phra Taew Reserve, protected as a "non-hunting area", close to Bang Pae waterfall, but because the whole point of the rehab project is to minimize the gibbons' contact with humans, you can only admire the creatures from afar. There's a small exhibition here on the aims of the project, and the well-informed volunteer guides will fill you in on the details of each case and on the idiosyncratic habits of the lar gibbon. Should you want to become a **project volunteer** yourself, adopt a gibbon, or make a donation, email the project centre.

Bang Pae and Ton Sai waterfalls

If you follow the track along the river from the Gibbon Project, you'll soon arrive at **Bang Pae Falls**, a popular picnic and bathing spot, ten to fifteen minutes' walk away. Continue on the track for another 2.8km (about 1hr 30min on foot) and you should reach **Ton Sai Falls**: though not a difficult climb, the route is unsigned and indistinct, is steep in places and rough underfoot. There are plenty of opportunities for cool dips in the river en route. Once at Ton Sai you can either walk back down to the access road to the Khao Phra Taew Reserve visitor centre and try to hitch a ride back home, or return the way you came.

Ko Yao Noi

Located in an idyllic spot in Phang Nga bay, almost equidistant from Phuket, Phang Nga and Krabi, the island of **KO YAO NOI** enjoys magnificent maritime views from almost every angle and makes a refreshingly tranquil getaway. Measuring about 12km at its longest point, it's home to some four thousand islanders, the vast majority of them Muslim, who earn their living from rubber and coconut plantations, fishing and shrimp-farming. Tourism here is low-key, not least because the beaches lack the wow factor of more sparkling nearby sands, and visitors are drawn instead by the rural ambience and lack of commercial pressures. Nonetheless, there's decent swimming off the east coast at high tide, and at low tide too in a few places, and plenty of potential for kayaking, rock-climbing and other activities.

Most tourists stay on the east side, which has the bulk of the accommodation, at **Hat Tha Khao**, **Hat Khlong Jaak** (**Long Beach**), **Hat Pasai** and **Laem Sai**. Exploring the interior is a particular pleasure, either via the barely trafficked round-island road as it runs through tiny villages and the island's diminutive town, **Ban Tha Khai**, or via the trails that crisscross the forested interior, where you've a good chance of encountering monkeys as well as cobras and even pythons, not to mention plenty of birds, including majestic oriental pied hornbills.

Hat Tha Kao and Hat Sai Taew

The most northerly of the main eastern beaches is **HAT THA KAO**, site of a small village, **BAN THA KAO**, with a couple of shops and restaurants, the pier for boats to

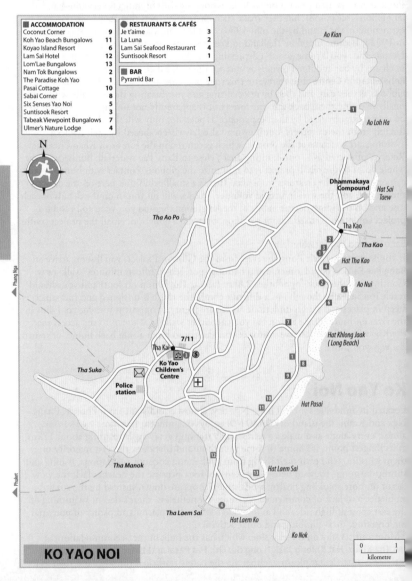

◼ ACCOMMODATION	
Coconut Corner	9
Koh Yao Beach Bungalows	11
Koyao Island Resort	6
Lam Sai Hotel	12
Lom'Lae Bungalows	13
Nam Tok Bungalows	2
The Paradise Koh Yao	1
Pasai Cottage	10
Sabai Corner	8
Six Senses Yao Noi	5
Suntisook Resort	3
Tabeak Viewpoint Bungalows	7
Ulmer's Nature Lodge	4

● RESTAURANTS & CAFÉS	
Je t'aime	3
La Luna	2
Lam Sai Seafood Restaurant	4
Suntisook Resort	1

◼ BAR	
Pyramid Bar	1

KO YAO NOI

and from Krabi, and the cheapest and most backpacker-oriented bungalows on the island. It's not an attractive beach itself, barely swimmable, but is the closest point to Ko Yao's nicest beach, so-called **Temple Beach** or **Hat Sai Taew**, 2km away, whose pretty, gold-sand shore is great for swimming at any tide. However, it's backed by private land that belongs to the Dhammakaya Foundation, a populist Buddhist sect, and is unsigned and a bit tricky to find. From Tha Kao pier, head inland and take the first right behind the shops, walk alongside the khlong and its sheltered marina, over the bridge, then via the faint trail over the hill to the beach. Or just kayak there from the pier.

Hat Khlong Jaak (Long Beach)

A couple of kilometres south of Hat Tha Kao, **HAT KHLONG JAAK**, more commonly referred to as **Long Beach**, is the site of the longest-running and best-known tourist accommodation and the liveliest places to eat and drink. The beach is indeed long, around 1500m from the northern end to *Sabai Corner* on the southern headland. Much of it is rocky and all but unswimmable at low tide, except in front of *Koyao Island Resort*, the smoothest stretch. The seaward views are glorious from every angle, however, taking in the many lovely islets of eastern Ao Phang Nga.

Hat Pasai

A minute's walk south from *Sabai Corner* on Hat Khlong Jaak and you're on **HAT PASAI**, a rather pretty little beach, with some shade, several resorts and a few simple beach restaurants with tables under the casuarinas at the south end.

Laem Sai

Beyond Hat Pasai, tiny **HAT LAEM SAI** is often known simply as **Hat Lom'Lae**, after the appealing Thai–Canadian *Lom'Lae Bungalows*, which sits on the shore (see p.350).

A few hundred metres west from the *Lom'Lae* turn-off, about 3km from Tha Kai, another side-road takes you down towards **Laem Sai pier**, along a coast that has no real beach but is scenically dotted with houses on stilts, fishing platforms, dozens of longtails and some inviting views of Ko Yao Noi's larger twin, Ko Yao Yai, just across the channel. At the tip of the peninsula stands a good seafood restaurant (see p.350), and there's a nice little beach 300m east further around the rocks.

Ban Tha Kai and north

The island's commercial and administrative centre is **BAN THA KAI**, inland from the main piers on the southwest coast. This is where you'll find the post office, banks, hospital, police station, obligatory 7-Eleven shop with ATM, as well as several internet centres, the main market and several roti stalls.

Visitors are very much encouraged to drop by the **Ko Yao Children's Community Centre** (☎087 929 4320, ⊛koyao-ccc.com), at the western end of town, an NGO that aims to help improve the English-language, arts, handicraft and computer skills of island children and adults, as well as organizing regular beach clean-ups.

The road running **north from Tha Kai**'s 7-Eleven is particularly scenic, taking you through several hamlets with their mosques and latex-pressing mangles, and past rice fields and their resident buffaloes, framed by mangroves in the middle distance, sea eagles hovering overhead, and the rounded hills of nearby islands in the background. At a junction about 3km from Tha Khai, the northbound road soon turns into a rough track leading to the beautiful beach at **AO LOH HA**, while veering right will take you over the hill and down to Tha Kao on the east coast, about 4km away.

KO YAO NOI ACTIVITIES

KAYAKING AND SNORKELLING

Kayaking around the coast is a very enjoyable pastime, and the dozens of tiny islands visible from eastern shorelines make enticing destinations for experienced paddlers; kayaks can be rented through Ko Yao Noi hotels for about B300 per day. Just about every hotel and travel agent sells kayaking and snorkelling trips to Ko Hong and other islands in Ao Phang Nga.

Koh Kayak Expeditions Just south of Coconut Corner on Hat Pasai ☎087 929 4320. Good-quality kayaks, fully equipped for self-guided overnight expeditions that can last anything from 24 hours to a month, for rent (B1500 per single or B2000 per tandem per 24hr, including camping equipment plus an itinerary and maps).

Ko Yao Islander Tour Next to Pasai Cottage on Hat Pasai ☎084 744 3686. Friendly place offering local snorkelling trips from B600 per person (minimum 4 people) or B1700 per boat, and kayaking and snorkelling day-trips in Phang Nga bay from B1400 per person (minimum 4 people).

DIVING

Koh Yao Diver Lom'Lae Resort, Laem Sai ☎076 597406, 🌐kohyaodiver.com. Diving trips and courses on the island are the speciality of Koh Yao Diver, where two local dives cost B3600, two dives at the reefs around Phi Phi in a longtail B5520, and the Openwater course is B16,680.

ROCK-CLIMBING

Ko Yao Noi is fast becoming a respected destination for **rock-climbers**, who appreciate the fresh sites and uncrowded routes compared to the hectic scene at nearby Ton Sai and Railay. There are over 150 bolted routes on the island, from beginner level to advanced (5 to 8A), established by the American and Thai climbers who run The Mountain Shop in Ban Tha Kao. Many routes are over water and accessible only by boat, or at the least via a hike off the dirt track to *Paradise* hotel.

The Mountain Shop At Sea Gypsy Restaurant in Ban Tha Kao ☎083 969 2023, 🌐themountainshop .org. For beginners, prices start from B2500 for a half-day's course, with multi-day courses also available; there are guides and rental gear for experienced climbers.

OTHER CLASSES AND ACTIVITIES

Lam Sai Hotel Laem Sai 🌐phuket-krabi-muaythai .com. B300 for a two-hour Thai boxing class or B2500 for a week of classes.

Tappi Thai Cookery School Ban Tha Kai ☎087 887 3161. Three-hour classes, morning or afternoon, for B1600, including transfers.

Ulmer's Nature Lodge Hat Tha Kao ☎084 690 3731, 🌐thailandyogaretreats.com. Daily drop-in yoga classes (B300), plus diverse workshops and retreats.

ARRIVAL AND DEPARTURE   **KO YAO NOI**

There are three mainland departure points for **boats** to Ko Yao Noi – from Phuket, Krabi's Ao Thalen, and Phang Nga – plus services from Ao Nang. On Ko Yao Noi, shared songthaew **taxis** meet all arriving boats and charge up to B100 per person (depending on distance) for transfers to accommodation, or up to B150 if chartered for a single traveller.

To/from Phuket The most common route is from Bang Rong on Phuket's northeast coast to Tha Manok on Ko Yao Noi's southwest coast, which is covered by five longtail boats a day (1hr 10min; B120) and seven speedboats a day (40min; B200), with the last service at around 5pm. Returning to Bang Rong, boats depart Tha Manok every hour or so until 4.40pm. Infrequent songthaews run between Phuket town's Thanon Ranong market and the pier at Bang Rong, via the Heroines' Monument (about 1hr; B40). A taxi to Bang Rong from town or the main beaches costs about B500, from Phuket airport B350, or about B260 if you can cajole the driver into turning his meter on; the taxi service at Bang Rong pier charges B500 to the airport, B800 to Patong.

To/from Ao Thalen Most of the Krabi province boats leave from Ao Thalen, 33km northwest of Krabi town, and arrive at the Tha Kao pier on Ko Yao Noi's northeast coast: three longtail boats a day (1hr; B120) and four speedboats (30min; B200), with the last service at 5pm. Songthaews from Krabi town connect with most boats, leaving about an hour before from the morning market on Maharat Soi 7, passing the 7-Eleven on Thanon Maharat and Talat Kao bus terminal.

To/from Ao Nang In high season, the Green Planet speedboat service connects Ao Nang's Hat Nopparat Thara with Ko Yao Noi once a day (30min; B550, including pick-ups in the Krabi area), and continues to Bang Rong in

Phuket; there's also a daily big boat from Ao Nang (about 1hr; B350).

To/from Phang Nga The most scenic journey to Ko Yao Noi is the daily (Mon–Sat) service from Phang Nga, which takes you through the heart of Ao Phang Nga, passing close by the stilt-house island of Ko Panyi (see p.351). It departs the Phang Nga bay pier at Tha Dan, 9km south of Phang Nga town, at 1pm and returns from Tha Suka on Ko Yao Noi at 7.30am (90min; B200); songthaews connect Phang Nga town with the pier.

GETTING AROUND

Songthaew taxis are easily arranged and many hotels can organize **motorbike** (B200–350/day) and **bicycle** (B200) rental.

INFORMATION

A good, free, regularly updated **map** of the island and its tourist businesses, produced by Pakorn Photo Classic, is available on the island. There's an **ATM** at the 7-Eleven in Ban Tha Kai and in front of *Six Senses* on Hat Khlong Jaak.

ACCOMMODATION

HAT THA KAO

Nam Tok Bungalows ☏ 087 292 1102. Set back from the beach around a khlong, a 5min walk south from the Tha Kao ferry pier, this ultra laidback set of bungalows is one of the cheapest places to stay on the island. The budget options are comfortable bamboo and wood huts, with cute bathrooms and hammocks on the deck, encircling a small garden full of flowers and a fishpond; the more luxurious ones have hot water. *Nam Tok*'s manager, Danny, occasionally takes guests on camping trips to Ko Pak Bia (from B4000 per boat). **B400**

★ **Suntisook Resort** ☏ 089 781 6456, ⓦ suntisook kohyao.com. Genial, well-organized place where the bungalows are nicely spaced around a garden and come with TVs, fridges and good, hot-water bathrooms. They're all a bit different but each has a deck and a hammock and some have a/c and three beds. Internet access and free wi-fi, as well as motorbikes, mountain bikes and kayaks for rent. Fan **B900**, a/c **B1500**

Ulmer's Nature Lodge ☏ 084 848 5112, ⓔ almar_k @hotmail.com. Occupying a peaceful spot by a mangrove swamp, down a track at the far southern end of the bay, *Ulmer's Nature Lodge* is establishing itself as a centre for yoga, though of course anyone is welcome to stay at its en-suite shoreside bungalows, which are either small and thatched or large and smart, with lots of polished wood. Fan **B600**, a/c **B1500**

HAT KHLONG JAAK (LONG BEACH)

Koyao Island Resort ☏ 076 597474, ⓦ koyao.com. This lovely, stylish resort occupies the best part of the beach and comprises just eighteen chic, thatched, mostly fan-cooled cottage compounds, all of them with separate living areas, huge bathrooms with open-air showers, and sliding doors that give access to the spacious garden and its fine bay views. There's a swimming pool and spa, internet access, wi-fi, mountain bikes and kayaks. Breakfast included. **B7000**

Sabai Corner ☏ 081 892 1827, ⓦ sabaicorner bungalows.com. Occupying Long Beach's rocky southern headland, this long-established, Italian–Thai, laidback little outfit has eleven thoughtfully designed wooden bungalows, all with fans, nets and rustic bathrooms, plus decks and hammocks. They're dotted along a rise between the road and the beach, under cashew and jackfruit trees. There's a good restaurant, serving home-made bread and yoghurt, plus Italian and Thai food, and kayak hire on site. **B1000**

Six Senses Yao Noi ☏ 076 418500, ⓦ sixsenses.com. Extraordinarily luxurious and expensive retreat, hidden in its own little bay and accessed by a private road. The huge villas are designed in natural-chic style, mostly wood and thatch, but all come with private pool, expansive sun deck and personal staff. **B28,000**

Tabeak Viewpoint Bungalows ☏ 089 590 4182, ⓦ kohyaotravel.com. Two hundred metres inland, on a cross-island track, this Japanese–Thai place has large, well-outfitted, fan-cooled, wood and bamboo bungalows, all with hot showers, polished wood floors and French windows and balconies that give commanding views of the islands. The Thai owner is a community policeman and enthusiastic fisherman, and an excellent source of island information. **B900**

HAT PASAI

Coconut Corner ☏ 076 454221, ⓦ kohyaotravel.com. Offering some of the cheapest and most traveller-friendly accommodation on the island, in simple en-suite bungalows set around a small garden just across the road from the northern end of Hat Pasai beach. It's just a few minutes' walk from *Pyramid Bar* on Long Beach and has internet access, bicycle and motorbike rental. **B500**

Koh Yao Beach Bungalows ☏ 076 454213, ⓦ kohyao beach.com. Clean, well-kept bungalows around a pretty, well-tended lawn, across the main road from the south end of the beach. The smaller fan bungalows – thatched, with mosquito nets and small, cold-water bathrooms – are better value than the larger ones with TVs (B800); there are

4

also some big, smart, a/c options with hot showers, TVs and fridges. Free wi-fi. Fan **B500**, a/c **B1500**

Pasai Cottage ☎ 076 454235, ✉ pasaicottage @hotmail.com. The ten bamboo cottages here, just across from Pasai's beach but set back from the road, have unexpectedly tasteful interiors, folding glass doors and prettily tiled bathrooms. **B800**

LAEM SAI

Lam Sai Hotel ☎ 084 746 3861, ⊛ lamsaihotel.com. British-run hotel and *muay thai* training camp (see p.348) on the less appealing western side of the peninsula, with a two-storey block of good-quality tiled rooms and a few bungalows, all with TVs, hot showers, wi-fi and balconies and use of the small swimming pool. Kayaks and motorbikes for rent, free bicycles. Fan **B1000**, a/c **B1700**

Lom'Lae Bungalows ☎ 076 597486, ⊛ lomlae.com. Beautiful, secluded haven, backed by rice fields and rubber

plantations and enjoying stunning bay views from its palm-fringed beach and grassy garden. The attractive, airy, wooden, fan-cooled bungalows are thatched and widely spaced, and have sliding doors, decks and hammocks to capitalize on the vistas. Some have additional upstairs loft beds, and there are two-bedroom family houses as well; all have free wi-fi. Kayaks, bikes and motorbikes are available for rent and there's a dive shop. Twenty percent discount for stays of five nights or more. **B2500**

AO LOH HA

The Paradise Koh Yao ☎ 076 584450, ⊛ theparadise .biz. Set on a lovely but isolated beach, these large, deluxe, thatched, a/c rooms and villas all have plenty of outdoor space and semi-outdoor bathrooms, some with private jacuzzis. There's a huge pool, a spa, wi-fi throughout, kayaks and yoga classes. Breakfast included. **B8500**

EATING AND DRINKING

HAT THA KAO

Suntisook Resort Charming restaurant serving a long menu of Thai food, including fish (according to market price) and a good, generous chicken *matsaman* curry, as well as spaghetti, mashed potato and Western breakfasts. Daily 7.30am–9pm.

HAT KHLONG JAAK (LONG BEACH)

★ **La Luna** ☎ 084 629 1550, ⊛ lalunakohyao.com. Congenial, Italian-owned bar-restaurant in a garden setting with hammocks. On offer are home-made pastas, including very tasty tagliatelle with cream and prosciutto (B230), proper pizzas (around B200), Italian desserts and lots of cocktails. Daily from roughly 2pm till late (kitchen closes 9.30/10pm).

Pyramid Bar Famous island meeting place, with a pool table, sports TV and extensive menu of cocktails, wine and Thai and Western food, including sandwiches (from B120), breakfasts and seafood; it's at its liveliest on Friday nights

when half the island turns up for the very enjoyable weekly sets by island musicians. Daily 9/10am till late (kitchen closes 10pm).

LAEM SAI

Lam Sai Seafood Restaurant ☎ 081 446 0689. About 1.5km further down the road from the *Lam Sai Hotel*, just beyond where the paving stops, this is a great place for seafood, which is pulled up fresh from nets off a pontoon according to your order (priced according to weight). Tables are set on a deck over the water with good views across to Ko Yao Yai. Daily 10am–10pm.

BAN THA KAI

Je t'aime ☎ 076 597495. At the T-junction at the heart of the village, this welcoming French- and Danish-owned restaurant is especially good for locally caught fish and seafood – try the green curry for B180 – but also does a bit of Western food, including breakfasts. Daily 9am–10pm.

Ao Phang Nga

National Park admission B200 • ⊛ dnp.go.th

Protected from the ravages of the Andaman Sea by Phuket, **AO PHANG NGA** has a seascape both bizarre and beautiful. Covering some four hundred square kilometres of coast between Phuket and Krabi, the mangrove-edged bay is spiked with limestone karst formations up to 300m in height, jungle-clad and craggily profiled. This is Thailand's own version of Vietnam's world-famous Ha Long Bay, reminiscent too of Guilin's scenery in China, and much of it is now preserved as **national park**. The bay is thought to have been formed about twelve thousand years ago when a dramatic rise in sea level flooded the summits of mountain ranges, which over millions of years had been eroded by an acidic mixture of atmospheric carbon dioxide and rainwater. Some of these karst islands have been further eroded in such a way that they are now hollow, hiding secret lagoons or *hongs* that can only be accessed at certain tides and only by kayak. The main *hong* islands are in the **western** and **eastern** bay areas – to the west or east of Ko Yao Noi, which sits roughly midway between Phuket and Krabi. But the most famous scenery is in the **central bay** area, which boasts the biggest concentration of karst islands, and the weirdest rock formations.

The central bay

On tours of the **central bay**, the standard itinerary follows a circular or figure-of-eight route, passing extraordinary karst silhouettes that change character with the shifting light – in the eerie glow of an early morning mist it can be a breathtaking experience. Some of the formations have nicknames suggested by their weird outlines – like **Khao Machu (Marju)**, which translates as "Pekinese Rock". Others have titles derived from other attributes – **Tham Nak** (or Nark, meaning Naga Cave) gets its name from the serpentine stalagmites inside; **Ko Thalu** (Pierced Cave) has a tunnel through it; and a close inspection of **Khao Kien** (Painting Rock) reveals a cliff wall decorated with paintings of elephants, monkeys, fish, crabs and hunting weapons, believed to be between three thousand and five thousand years old.

Ao Phang Nga's most celebrated features, however, earned their tag from a movie: the cleft **Khao Ping Gan** (Leaning Rock) and its tapered outcrop **Khao Tapu** (Nail Rock) are better known as **James Bond Island**, having starred as Scaramanga's hideaway in *The Man with the Golden Gun*. Every boat stops off here so tourists can pose in front of the iconic rock – whose narrowing base is a good example of how wave action is shaping the bay – and the island crawls with seashell and trinket vendors.

The central bay's other major attraction is **Ko Panyi**, a Muslim village built almost entirely on stilts around the rock that supports the mosque. Nearly all boat tours stop here for lunch, so you're best off avoiding the pricey seafood restaurants around the jetty, and heading instead towards the islanders' foodstalls near the mosque. You can enjoy a more tranquil Ko Panyi experience by joining one of the overnight tours from Phang Nga town (see p.353), which include an evening meal and guesthouse accommodation on the island – and the chance to watch the sun set and rise over the bay; you can also rent a kayak from the jetty and go exploring yourself.

At some point on your central-bay tour you should pass several small brick **kilns** on the edge of a mangrove swamp, which were once used for producing charcoal from mangrove wood. You'll also be ferried beneath **Tham Lod**, a photogenic archway roofed with stalactites that opens onto spectacular limestone and mangrove vistas.

THE HONGS

Hongs are the *pièce de résistance* of Ao Phang Nga: invisible to any passing vessel, these secret tidal lagoons are enclosed within the core of seemingly impenetrable limestone outcrops, accessible via murky tunnels that can only be navigated at certain tides in kayaks small enough to slip beneath and between low-lying rocky overhangs. Like the karsts themselves, the *hongs* have taken millions of years to form, with the softer limestone hollowed out from above by the wind and the rain, and from the side by the pounding waves. Eventually, when the two hollows met, the heart of the karst was able to fill with water via the wave-eroded passageway at sea level, creating a lagoon. The world inside these roofless hollows is an extraordinary one, protected from the open bay by a ring of cliff faces hung with vertiginous prehistoric-looking gardens of upside-down cycads, twisted bonsai palms and tangled ferns. And as the tide withdraws, the *hong's* resident creatures emerge to forage on the muddy floor, among them fiddler crabs, mudskippers, dusky langurs and crab-eating macaques, with white-bellied sea eagles often hovering overhead.

The western bay: Ko Panak and Ko Hong

The main attraction of **the western bay** is **Ko Panak**, whose limestone cliffs hide secret tunnels to no less than five different **hongs** within its hollowed heart. These are probably Ao Phang Nga's most spectacular hidden worlds, the pitch-black tunnel approaches infested by bats and the bright, roofless *hongs* an entire other world, draped in hanging gardens of lianas and miniature screw pines and busy with cicadas and the occasional family of crab-eating macaques. Western-bay tours also usually take in nearby **Ko Hong** (different from the Ko Hong in the eastern bay), whose exterior walls are coated with red, yellow and orange encrusting sponges, oyster shells and chitons (560-million-year-old slipper-shaped shells), which all make good camouflage for the scuttling red, blue and black crabs. Ko Hong's interior passageways light up with bioluminescent plankton in the dark and lead to a series of cave-lagoons.

The eastern bay: Ko Hong, Ao Thalen and Ao Luk

The principal *hong* island in the **eastern bay**, known both as **Ko Hong** and **Ko Lao Bileh**, lies about midway between Krabi's Hat Klong Muang beach and the southeast coast of Ko Yao Noi. The island is fringed by white-sand beaches and exceptionally clear aquamarine waters that make it a popular snorkelling destination. The island's actual *hong* lacks the drama of Ao Phang Nga's best *hongs* because it's not fully enclosed or accessed via dark tunnels as at Ko Panak, but it is pretty, full of starfish, and tidal, so can only be explored at certain times.

The eastern bay's other big attractions are the mangrove-fringed inlets along the mainland coast between Krabi and Phang Nga, particularly around **Ao Luk** and **Ao Thalen** (sometimes Ao Talin or Talane), though the latter can get very crowded with tour groups. Trips around here take you through complex networks of channels that weave through the mangrove swamps, between fissures in the limestone cliffs, beneath karst outcrops and into the occasional cave. Many of these passageways are *hongs*, isolated havens that might be up to 2km long, all but cut off from the main bay and accessible only at certain tides. The **Ban Bor Tor** (or Ban Bho Tho) area of Ao Luk bay is especially known for **Tham Lod**, a long tunnel hung with stalactites whose entrance is obscured by vines, and for nearby **Tham Phi Hua Toe**, whose walls display around a hundred prehistoric cave-paintings, as well as some interestingly twisted stalactite formations.

TOURS OF THE BAY · AO PHANG NGA

By sea canoe The most rewarding, and generally the most expensive option is to join a sea-canoeing trip (either guided or self-paddle), which enables you both to explore inside the *hongs* and to see at close quarters the extraordinary ecosystems around and inside the karst islands. Most sea-canoeing tours use large support boats carrying groups of up to thirty people. They can be arranged from any resort in Phuket, or through the specialist operators John Gray's Sea Canoe and Paddle Asia (see p.319); at Khao Lak, for example through Khao Lak Land Discovery (see p.313); at all Krabi beaches and

islands and in Krabi town (see p.364), and on Ko Yao No (see p.348). The itinerary is usually determined by you departure point, with Phuket trips focusing on the wester bay and Krabi tours concentrating on the eastern half.
By tour boat Most tours of the central bay are eithe in large tour boats booked out of Phuket or Krabi, whic generally feature snorkelling and beach stops rather tha kayaking, or in inexpensive, small-group longtail boat that depart from Phang Nga town (see opposite), as well a from Phuket and Ko Yao Noi. All the main areas of the ba are extremely popular so don't expect a solitary experience

Phang Nga town

Friendly if unexciting little **PHANG NGA TOWN**, beautifully located under looming limestone cliffs edged with palm groves midway between Phuket and Krabi, serves mainly as a point from which to organize budget longtail trips around the spectacular

TOURS FROM PHANG NGA TOWN

AO PHANG NGA

The most popular budget tours of Ao Phang Nga (see p.350) are the **longtail-boat trips** run by tour operators based inside Phang Nga bus station. Competition between these outfits is fierce and the itineraries they offer are almost identical, so it's best to get recommendations from other tourists fresh from a bay trip, especially as reputations fluctuate with every change of staff. To date the one that's remained most constant is Mr Kean Tour (076 430619 or 089 871 6092); next door but one is Sayan Tour (076 430348, sayantour .com). Both offer half-day tours of the bay (daily at about 8.30am & 2pm; 3–4hr) costing B500 per person (including national park fee; minimum four people), as well as full-day trips, which cost B800, including lunch and national park fee; take the 8.30am tour to avoid seeing the bay at its most crowded. All tours include a chance to swim in the bay, and most offer the option of an hour's canoeing around Ko Thalu as well, for an extra B350.

All tour operators also offer the chance to **stay** overnight at their own guesthouse on **Ko Panyi**. This can be tacked onto the half- or full-day tour for an extra B250–300; dinner, accommodation, and breakfast are included in the price. Mr Kean can also sometimes offer (dependent on the tides) an interesting alternative overnight programme on his home island of **Ban Mai Phai**, a much less commercial version of Ko Panyi, with the chance to trek, cycle and kayak.

LOCAL SIGHTS AROUND PHANG NGA TOWN

Mr Kean can arrange trips (B500) to **Tham Phung Chang**, or **Elephant Belly Cave**, a natural 1200m-long tunnel through the massive 800m-high wooded cliff that towers over the Provincial Hall, about 4km west of the town centre. With a bit of imagination, the cliff's outline resembles a kneeling elephant, and the hollow interior is, of course, its belly. You can travel through the elephant's belly to the other side of the cliff and back on a two-hour excursion that involves wading, rafting and canoeing along the freshwater stream, Khlong Tham, that has eroded the channel.

Mr Kean also offers tours (B450) that take in several other local caves, plus **Sa Nang Manora Forest Park**, which has hiking trails through thick, impressive rainforest and several waterfalls with swimmable pools, 9km north of the town centre.

4

---

karst islands of Ao Phang Nga (see above). But there are also several caves and waterfalls nearby, accessible on cheap tours run by Phang Nga tour operators.

ARRIVAL AND DEPARTURE   PHANG NGA TOWN

Tour operators inside the bus station compound sell bus and boat tickets and will store your baggage for a few hours.

By bus Phang Nga has good bus connections: during the day, all services between Krabi and Phuket detour off Highway 415 to make a stop at the bus station (076 412014) on Thanon Phetkasem, located towards the northern end of this long, thin town; evening services don't make the detour, but Mr Kean (see above) will give you a free lift to the junction of Highway 415 and Highway 4, 4km west of town, if you buy your bus ticket from him. If you're heading to Khao Sok National Park headquarters (see p.306), it's usually fastest to take a Surat Thani bus and change in Phanom. Some of the services to Bangkok's

Southern Bus Terminal continue to Mo Chit station on the north side of the city.

Destinations: Bangkok (8 daily; 11hr); Ko Samui (daily; 6hr); Krabi (every 30min; 1hr 30min–2hr); Phuket (at least hourly; 1hr 30min–2hr 30min); Ranong (1–2 daily; 4hr); Satun (4 daily; 5hr 30min); Surat Thani (5 daily; 4hr); Takua Pa (hourly; 1hr); Trang (every 30min; 3hr).

By boat The pier for boats around Ao Phang Nga, and to Ko Yao Noi, is at Tha Dan, 9km south of town and served by songthaews that pass the bus station (B25).

Destinations: Ko Yao Noi (daily; 90min).

INFORMATION

Tourist information The TAT information office for Phang Nga is inconveniently located 2km south of the town on Highway 4 (daily 8.30am–4.30pm; 076

411586). You may find the tour operators inside the bus station compound (see above) more helpful.

ACCOMMODATION

Phang Nga's best hotels are all within 250m of the bus station, heading northeast (right) up Thanon Phetkasem (Highway 4).

Baan Phang Nga 100/2 Thanon Phetkasem (on the left-hand side) ☎ 076 413276, ⌨ baanphangnga.com. Friendly, new, upmarket guesthouse above a café, offering a/c rooms with TVs, small, hot-water bathrooms and a few touches of kitsch contemporary decor. There's also internet access and free wi-fi. **B650**

Phang Nga Guest House 99/1 Thanon Phetkasem (on the right-hand side, next to Krung Thai Bank) ☎ 076 411358. The public areas here have been recently redecorated with some colourful touches, but the clean

and comfortable rooms with small, mostly cold-water, en-suite bathrooms and TVs remain much the same; few have anything but a brick-wall view. Fan **B380**, a/c **B480**

Thawisuk Hotel 77 Thanon Phetkasem (just beyond Phang Nga Guest House on the right-hand side) ☎ 076 412100. The choice of local civil servants, this is an old-style, well-maintained hotel with very clean and bright fan rooms, a couple of huge a/c options, and a rooftop terrace. Fan **B180**, a/c **B500**

EATING

Duang Thanon Phetkasem, a couple of doors away from Baan Phang Nga Guesthouse (a tiny sticker shows the name in English). Locals rate this simple but friendly restaurant with a few outdoor tables as the best in town; it's been going 30 years and serves a good squid salad (*yam pla meuk*; B150), as well as rice and noodle dishes for about B70. Daily 10.30am–10pm.

Kafeh Thanon Phetkasem (no English sign). For a great

Thai breakfast, go left down Phetkasem about 100m from the bus station to find this hugely popular dessert shop on the left. Fill your tray with assorted Thai *khanom* – banana-leaf parcels of sticky rice laced with sweet coconut milk and stuffed with banana, mango or other delights – at about B5 apiece, then order from the selection of hot and cold coffees and watch Thai breakfast TV with everyone else. Daily 6am–6pm.

Krabi town

The estuarine town of **KRABI** is both provincial capital and major hub for onward travel to some of the region's most popular islands and beaches, including Ko Phi Phi, Ko Lanta, Ao Nang, Klong Muang and Laem Phra Nang (Railay). So efficient are the transport links that you don't really need to stop here, but it also makes an appealing base, strung out along the west bank of the Krabi estuary, with mangrove-lined shorelines to the east, craggy limestone outcrops on every horizon, and plenty of guesthouses. The beaches of **Ao Nang** (see p.360) and **Railay** (see p.366) are both within 45 minutes of town, and other nearby attractions include the **mangrove swamps** and **Ko Klang** peninsula across the estuary, the dramatically sited Tiger Cave Temple at **Wat Tham Seua** and **Khao Phanom Bencha National Park**. A number of

KRABI MANGROVE TOURS

A boat trip through the eerily scenic **mangrove**-lined channels of the Krabi estuary is a fun way to gain a different perspective on the area. As well as a close-up view of the weird creatures that inhabit the swamps (see box, p.356), you'll get to visit a riverside cave or two. **Tours** are best organized directly with the longtail boatmen who hang around Krabi's two piers and the surrounding streets (B300–500/boat/hr), but can also be arranged through most tour agents.

The estuary's most famous features are the twin limestone outcrops known as **Khao Kanab Nam**, which rise a hundred metres above the water from opposite sides of the Krabi River near the *Maritime Park and Spa Resort* and are so distinctive that they've become the symbol of Krabi. One of the twin karsts hides caves, which can be explored – many skeletons have been found here over the centuries, thought to be those of immigrants who got stranded by a flood before reaching the mainland. You can also choose to visit the Muslim island of Ko Klang (see p.356).

KRABI TOWN

Tha Thara Park & Boats to Ko Klang

organized **day-trips in the Krabi area**, including snorkelling and kayaking excursions, are available (see box, p.364).

Krabi town has no unmissable sights, but is small enough for a pleasant stroll around its main landmarks. Its chief attraction is its setting, and a good way to appreciate this is to follow the paved **riverside walkway** down to the fishing port, about 800m south of Tha Chao Fa; several hotels capitalize on the views here, across to mangrove-ringed Ko Klang, and towards the southern end the walkway borders the municipal Thara Park.

Inland, in the centre of town, you can't fail to notice the bizarre sculptures of hulking **anthropoid apes** clutching two sets of traffic lights apiece at the Thanon Maharat/Soi 10 crossroads. They are meant to represent Krabi's most famous ancestors, the tailless *Siamopithecus oceanus*, whose forty-million-year-old remains were found in a lignite mine in the south of the province and are believed by scientists to be among the earliest examples worldwide of the ape-to-human evolutionary process.

Wat Kaew Korawaram and Krabi Museum of Contemporary Art

West off Thanon Maharat • **Krabi Museum of Contemporary Art** Tues–Sun 10am–1pm & 2–5pm • Free

It's hard to miss the striking white walls of the minimalist modern bot at the town-centre temple, **Wat Kaew Korawaram** (Grovaram), approached via a grand naga staircase. The interior murals depict traditional scenes, including Jataka episodes from the lives of the Buddha, but are spiced up with some modern twists – including warring hairy foreigners on either side of the door. Just across Thanon Isara from the wat's extensive compound, **Krabi Museum of Contemporary Art** stages temporary exhibitions of modern paintings by artists from the Krabi area and beyond.

Ko Klang

Across the river from Krabi town • Frequent longtails from Tha Chao Fa (B20; 10min) and Tha Thara Park (B20; 3min; bicycles carried)

Most of Krabi's longtail boatmen come from **Ko Klang**, the mangrove-encircled peninsula just across the channel from Tha Chao Fa and Tha Thara Park. On a two-hour mangrove tour you can choose to stop off on the peninsula for a visit, or you can go there yourself, on one of the public longtail **boats** that shuttle across from Krabi town throughout the day. You can also stay in Ban Ko Klang as part of a **homestay** programme, which can be booked locally through Krabi Friendly Tour (see p.359) or in advance as part of a package with Tell Tale Travel (⊚ telltaletravel.co.uk).

The predominantly Muslim peninsula is home to three small **villages** housing a total of around four thousand people, most of whom earn their living from tourism and fishing. The island is no great beauty but therein lies its charm, offering the chance to experience a little of typical southern Thai life. You can swim off Ko Klang's long, wild southwestern **beach**, from where you also get an excellent view of the distinctive profiles of all the famous local **islands** – Laem Phra Nang (30min boat ride away), Ko Poda (45min), Bamboo Island, Ko Phi Phi (2hr) and Ko Jum; any Ko Klang boatman will take you out there for the same price as from Krabi town.

LIFE IN A MANGROVE SWAMP

Mangrove swamps are at their creepiest at low tide, when their aerial roots are fully exposed to form gnarled and knotted archways above the muddy banks. Not only are these roots essential parts of the tree's breathing apparatus, they also reclaim land for future mangroves, trapping and accumulating water-borne debris into which the metre-long mangrove seedlings can fall. In this way, mangrove swamps also fulfil a vital ecological function: stabilizing shifting mud and protecting coastlines from erosion and the impact of tropical storms.

Mangrove swamp mud harbours some interesting creatures too, like the instantly recognizable **fiddler crab**, named after the male's single outsized reddish claw, which it brandishes for communication and defence purposes; the claw is so powerful it could open a can of baked beans. If you keep your eyes peeled you should be able to make out a few **mudskippers**. These specially adapted fish can absorb atmospheric oxygen through their skins as long as they keep their outsides damp, which is why they spend so much time slithering around in the sludge; they move in tiny hops by flicking their tails, aided by their extra-strong pectoral fins. You might well also come across **kingfishers** and white-bellied **sea eagles**, or even a **crab-eating macaque**.

Though the Krabi mangroves have not escaped the **environmentally damaging** attentions of invasive industry, or the cutting down of the bigger trees to make commercial charcoal, around fifteen percent of the Andaman coastline is still fringed with mangrove forest, the healthiest concentration of this rich, complex ecosystem in Thailand.

4

Wat Tham Seua

10km northeast of Krabi town, about 2km north of Highway 4 • Red songthaews from Krabi town, heading for the Tesco Lotus supermarket (about B20), pass the T-junction on Highway 4, from where you could take a motorbike taxi (about B30); you might be able to persuade the songthaew driver to detour to the temple for an extra fee (about B50) or you could walk the last 2km

Spectacularly situated amid limestone cliffs within a tropical forest, **Wat Tham Seua** (Tiger Cave Temple) is a famous meditation temple of caves, wooded trails and panoramic viewpoints. As it's a working monastery, visitors are required to wear respectable dress (no shorts or sleeveless tops for men or women).

Wat Tham Seua's abbot is a renowned teacher of Vipassana meditation, and some of his educational tools are displayed in the main **bot**, on the left under the cliff overhang, in the main temple compound. Though these close-up photos of human entrails and internal organs may seem shockingly unorthodox, they are there as reminders of the impermanence of the body, a fundamental tenet of Buddhist philosophy; the human skulls and skeletons dotted around the rest of the compound serve the same purpose. Beyond the bot, follow the path past the nuns' quarters to reach the pair of steep **staircases** that scale the 600m-high cliffside. The first staircase is long (1272 steps) and very steep, and takes about an hour to climb, but the vista from the summit is quite spectacular, affording fabulous views over the limestone outcrops and out to the islands beyond. There's a large seated Buddha image and chedi at the top, and a few monks' cells hidden among the trees. The second staircase, next to the large statue of the Chinese Goddess of Mercy, Kuan Im, takes you on a less arduous route down into a deep dell encircled by high limestone walls. Here the monks have built themselves self-sufficient meditation cells (*kuti*) in and around the rocky crannies, linked by paths through the lush ravine: if you continue along the main path you'll eventually find yourself back where you began, at the foot of the staircase. The valley is home to squirrels and monkeys as well as a pair of remarkable trees with overground **buttress roots** over 10m high.

Khao Phanom Bencha National Park

25km north of Krabi • B200 • ⓦ dnp.go.th

With your own transport, you could combine a visit to Wat Tham Seua with a meander around the scenic backroads and a plunge into **Huay Toh Falls**, a five-tiered cascade that lies within **Khao Phanom Bencha National Park**.

You can buy bus, a/c minibus, boat, train and air tickets, including combination bus and train tickets, to Bangkok via Surat Thani and through-tickets to Ko Samui and Ko Pha Ngan, from clued-up, helpful Krabi Friendly Tour & Travel, 9/3 Thanon Chao Fa (☎ 075 612558).

BY PLANE

Krabi **airport** (☎ 075 636541–2, ⓦ krabiairport.org) is just off Highway 4, 18km east of Krabi town, 35km from Ao Nang. It's served by international Air Asia flights from Kuala Lumpur and by domestic flights from Bangkok with Thai Airways, Bangkok Airways, Nok Air, Orient Thai and Air Asia, and from Ko Samui with Bangkok Airways. An airport shuttle bus runs to Krabi town at B100 per person, or there are fixed-price taxis at B350 per car to Krabi town and port. Car rental is also available (see below).
Destinations: Bangkok (up to 15 daily; 1hr 20min); Ko Samui (1 daily; 50min).

BY BUS

Numerous long-distance buses run to Krabi's bus terminal, which is 5km north of the town centre in the suburb of Talat Kao, beside Highway 4. Frequent red songthaews (B20) shuttle between the town centre (where they do a little circuit to pick up passengers, starting from the 7-Eleven on Thanon Maharat or *Pak-up Hostel* on Thanon Utrakit) and the bus station.
To/from Bangkok A/c and VIP buses between Bangkok's Southern Bus Terminal and Krabi depart mainly in the late afternoon or evening, arriving at the other end in the early morning. Think twice before taking a private bus direct from Thanon Khao San (see p.116).
By a/c minibus Private a/c minibus services (all roughly hourly) run from Krabi to Surat Thani, Nakhon Si Thammarat, Trang and Ko Lanta (see map, p.355). Aimed specifically at tourists, in competition with the boats, the Lanta service will pick up from hotels in Krabi and charges B250–350, depending on which beach you want to be dropped off at on Ko Lanta Yai. From the Talat Kao bus terminal, you can also catch an a/c minibus that originates on Lanta to Phuket airport and town (roughly every 2hr; bookable through Krabi hotels and travel agents).
Bus destinations: Bangkok (12 daily; 12hr); Hat Yai (13 daily; 4–5hr); Nakhon Si Thammarat (at least hourly; 3hr);

Phang Nga (every 30min; 2hr); Phuket (at least hourly; 3hr 30min); Ranong (2 daily; 5hr); Satun (4 daily; 5hr); Surat Thani (at least hourly; 2hr); Takua Pa (4 daily; 3hr 30min–4hr 30min); Trang (at least hourly; 2–3hr).

BY TRAIN AND BUS

A more comfortable alternative to taking a bus from Bangkok is to catch an overnight train from the capital to Surat Thani and then change on to one of the frequent a/c buses or minibuses to Krabi (hourly; 2hr).

BY BOAT

Ferries to Ko Phi Phi, Ko Lanta and Ko Jum leave from **Krabi Passenger Port** (sometimes referred to as Tha Khlong Jilad; ☎ 075 620052), a couple of kilometres southwest of Krabi town centre. Ferry tickets bought from tour operators in town should include a free transfer to Krabi Passenger Port, but there are also red songthaews that do a circuit of the town centre before heading out to the port.
Ko Phi Phi Ferries to Ko Phi Phi from Krabi Passenger Port depart four times daily in high season and at least twice daily in low season (2hr; B350–400).
Ko Lanta Yai Going by a/c minibus to Ko Lanta is more popular these days, but there's still one ferry a day from Krabi Passenger Port, via Ko Jum, in peak season (roughly mid-Nov to mid-April 11.30am; 2hr 30min; B400).
Laem Phra Nang (East Railay) Longtail boats for East Railay on Laem Phra Nang (45min; B1500 per boat or B150 per person if there are 8–10 passengers) leave on demand from the town-centre pier at Tha Chao Fa on Thanon Kong Ka.
Ko Yao Noi As well as boats from Ao Nang, there are services from the pier at Ao Thalen, 33km northwest of Krabi town, to Ko Yao Noi (see p.348).
Destinations: Ko Jum (roughly mid-Nov to mid-April daily; 1hr 30min–2hr); Ko Lanta Yai (roughly mid-Nov to mid-April daily; 2hr 30min); Ko Phi Phi Don (2–4 daily; 2hr); Ko Yao Noi (from Ao Thalen; 6–7 daily; 1hr).

GETTING AROUND

By songthaew Most of the public songthaew services to local beaches, towns and attractions circulate around town before heading out, making stops outside the 7-Eleven just south of the Soi 8 intersection on Thanon Maharat and along Thanon Utrakit; most run at least twice an hour from dawn till noon, and then less frequently until dusk. For getting around town, the most useful are probably the red songthaews that run between Tesco Lotus, out on Highway 4 beyond the Wat Tham Seua turn-off, and Krabi Passenger

Port. White songthaews start at Talat Kao bus terminal and do a spin around town before heading out to Ao Nang (B50 daytime, B60 after 6pm).
By car or motorbike Budget (☎ 075 636171, ⓦ budget .co.th) and Avis (☎ 089 969 8676, ⓦ avisthailand.com) have desks at the airport, or try Krabi Friendly Tour in town at 9/3 Thanon Chao Fa (☎ 075 612558).
By bicycle *Pak-up Hostel* (see opposite) rents mountain bikes for B150/day.

INFORMATION AND TOURS

Tourist information Krabi's unhelpful TAT office (daily 8.30am–4.30pm; ☎075 612812, ✉tatkrabi@tat.or.th) is inconveniently located 2km north of the centre on Thanon Maharat.

Books If you're spending some time in this region, it's worth buying a copy of *Krabi: Caught in the Spell – A Guide to Thailand's Enchanted Province*, expat environmentalist Thom Henley's lively and opinionated book about Krabi

people, islands and traditions (see p.442).

Tour agents Any of the town's numerous tour agents will fill you in on the many organized day-trip options (see p.364), and fix you up with a room on one of the beaches – a service that's worth considering for your first night or two, particularly during the notoriously oversubscribed Christmas–New Year period. Recommended agents include Krabi Friendly Tour & Travel, 9/3 Thanon Chao Fa (☎075 612558).

ACCOMMODATION

★ **Chan-Cha-Lay** 55 Thanon Utrakit ☎075 620952, chanchalay.com. With its stylish blue-and-white theme throughout, funky bathrooms, white-painted wooden furniture and blue shutters, this is the most charming and arty place to stay in Krabi. The en suites in the garden come with fan or a/c and are by far the nicest option; rooms in the main building share bathrooms and some don't have windows. Internet access. Shared bathroom B250, en suite fan B450, a/c B700

City Hotel 15/2–4 Soi 10, Thanon Maharat ☎075 611961, ⓦcitykrabi.com. Comfortable, friendly, modern hotel where most of the rooms are set well back from the road; choose between fan with cold shower and a/c with hot shower (all come with TVs). Wi-fi in the lobby and the most expensive rooms. Fan B450, a/c B650

K Guest House 15–25 Thanon Chao Fa ☎075 623166, ✉kguesthouse@yahoo.com. Deservedly popular and well run, in a peaceful but central spot, this long, timber-clad row house has bedrooms with wooden floors, panelled walls, streetside balconies and hot showers – ask for a more attractive upstairs room. Also offers some cheaper rooms with shared bathroom downstairs and at the back. Internet access and free wi-fi. Shared bathroom B200, en suite B350, a/c B500

Krabi River Hotel 73/1 Thanon Kong Ka ☎075 612321, ⓦkrabiriverhotel.com. Occupying a scenic spot beside the estuary on the southern edge of Krabi town, a few minutes' walk south of Tha Chao Fa pier, this place offers high-standard a/c rooms, the best of which have big river-view balconies; the smaller, cheaper ones look onto the wall of the adjacent hotel. There's a riverside eating area too. Standard B800, river view B1200

Kyo Ngean (Ngoen) Mansion 2 25/1 Thanon Chao Fa, ☎075 621111, ✉kyo-ngean@hotmail.com. Good-value

little hotel in a modern block, popular with long-stay guests, with very clean and well-appointed rooms, all of them with a/c, TV, free wi-fi, fridge, hot water and balconies; some on the upper floors have long-range river views. Staff are friendly but don't speak much English. B600

Kyo Thong Mansion 31 Thanon Chao Fa ☎075 613001, ✉baankyothong@hotmail.com. Very similar setup to *Kyo Ngean*, three doors away, with large, well-appointed, modern rooms with small, hot-water bathrooms, a/c, TV, free wi-fi, fridge and balconies. B600

Maritime Park and Spa Resort 2km north of town off Thanon Utrakit ☎075 620028–35, ⓦmaritimepark andspa.com. Beautifully located upper-end hotel, set beside the limestone karsts and mangroves of the Krabi River. Rooms are a little old-fashioned but large and comfortable, and have fine views over the extensive landscaped grounds and lake. There's a big pool and a spa, and shuttles into Krabi town and Ao Nang. Good-value packages sometimes available on their website. Breakfast included. B3200

Pak-up Hostel 87 Thanon Utrakit ☎075 611955, ⓦfacebook.com/pakuphostel. Colourful, modern hostel in a short tower block on probably Krabi's busiest corner, with smart ten-bed dorms. Lots of tours available, as well as free wi-fi throughout and pay computers. There are plenty of guesthouses in town with cheaper private rooms for groups of two or more, but this is the place to come to be sociable, with lots of common areas, a rooftop bar and an adjacent garden bar. Fan dorm B180, a/c dorm B200

Swallow 31 Soi 4, Thanon Maharat ☎075 612464. Tiny six-roomed guesthouse that's kept spotlessly clean and is a good budget option. All rooms have windows and fans; the cheapest share bathrooms. No advance booking. Shared bathroom B250, en suite B350

EATING AND DRINKING

Krabi offers plenty of traveller-oriented restaurants – and Krabi Friendly Tour has a good juice bar if you need a healthy shot-in-the-arm – but there's also inexpensive local-style dining at the night markets on riverside Thanon Kong Ka and on Maharat Soi 10. The Walking Street **night bazaar** on Soi 8 (Fri, Sat & Sun 5–10pm) also brims with excellent food stalls, as well as an entertainments stage and trinket and craft stalls.

Bai Toei Just south of Thara Guesthouse on Thanon Kong Ka ☎075 611509 (English sign on the riverside only; look

for a Pepsi sign on the roadside). A good place for a sundowner, with pleasing views over the promenade to the river and Ko Klang, and great seafood: try the local *nam prik kung siap* (on the menu as "smoke-shrimp paste"; B120) or the fried squid with salted eggs; fried rice and noodles start as low as B60. Mon–Sat 10am–10pm, Sun 4–10pm.

Chalita Thanon Chao Fa. Congenial, Italian–Thai restaurant that serves mostly Thai food, but also steaks, burgers, pastas and one or two fusion dishes such as spaghetti with chicken green curry (B110), which works surprisingly well. Daily 4–10.30pm.

Good Dream 83 Thanon Utrakit ☎ 075 622993. A great, farang-run place for breakfast – very good French toast (B70), mega fry-ups (B170), Continental sets, muesli and fruit, all served with fresh coffee – plus plenty more Western and Thai dishes and cocktails later in the day. There's free wi-fi and internet access for customers too. Daily 8am–11pm.

★ **Ko Tung** 36 Thanon Kong Ka ☎ 075 611522. Though it looks nothing much, this little Thai restaurant is always packed with locals savouring the excellent, good-value, southern-style seafood. Special highlights include the sweet mussels (*hawy wan*), baked crab, and mushroom, long bean and shrimp *yam* salads. Most dishes around B80. Mon–Sat 11am–10pm.

May and Mark Soi 2, Thanon Maharat. Early hours, home-baked bread, fresh coffee and full-English fry-ups make this a popular spot for breakfast. Also does tacos, sandwiches, cheese and tuna melts (B160), pizzas and Thai, German and vegetarian food. Daily 6.30am–9pm.

Old West Thanon Utrakit. All bare wood and Wild West photos, with racks of imported spirits behind the long bar that get mixed into some serious cocktails. The top-notch sound system churns out wall-to-wall rock and there are a couple of pool tables. Daily 4pm–4am.

Pizzeria Firenze Thanon Kong Ka. Authentic Italian dishes, including twenty different thin-crust pizzas (from B175), home-made pasta, ice cream, tiramisu, espresso coffee and Italian wines. Daily 9am–9.30pm.

Ruen Mai About 2km north of the town centre at 315/5 Thanon Maharat. Popular with locals and well regarded, this inviting, artfully planted garden restaurant is well worth making the effort to get to. Among the many highlights of its mostly Thai menu (B60–180), standouts include the perfectly spiced *tom yam kung* with satisfyingly large prawns, juicy deep-fried ribs, and fried butterfish with tamarind and ginger. Daily 11am–9pm.

SHOPPING

Bookshops The Books, next to Vogue Department Store on Thanon Maharat (daily 8am–9.30pm), has a decent selection of new English-language books, and the well-stocked Pakarang on Thanon Utrakit (daily 8am–9pm) buys and sells secondhand books, as well as selling handicrafts and espresso coffees.

DIRECTORY

Hospitals Krabi Hospital is about 1km north of the town centre at 325 Thanon Utrakit (☎ 075 611202) and also has dental facilities, but the better hospital is considered to be the private Muslim hospital, Jariyatham Ruam Phet Hospital (☎ 075 611223), which is about 3km north of town at 514 Thanon Utrakit and has English-speaking staff.

Immigration office In the compound of government offices on the way to Krabi Passenger Port (Mon–Fri 8.30am–4.30pm; ☎ 075 611097).

Police For all emergencies, call the tourist police on the free, 24hr phone line ☎ 1155, or contact the local branch of the tourist police in Ao Nang on ☎ 075 637208.

Ao Nang

AO NANG (sometimes confusingly signed as Ao Phra Nang), 22km west of Krabi town, is a busy, continually expanding, rather faceless mainland resort that mainly caters for mid-budget and package-holiday tourists. Although it lacks the fine beaches of the nearby Railay peninsula (an easy 10min boat-ride away), it is less claustrophobic, and has a much greater choice of restaurants and bars, masses of shopping (mostly beachwear, DVDs and souvenirs), plus a wealth of dive shops, day-tripping and snorkelling possibilities and other typical resort facilities. Adjacent **Hat Nopparat Thara**, part of which comes under the protection of a national marine park, is prettier, and divided into two separate beaches by a khlong. The uncrowded, 2km-long **eastern beach** is effectively linked to Ao Nang by a conurbation of accommodation and shops, but the **western beach**, sometimes known as **Hat Ton Son**, across the khlong, is an altogether quieter and more beautiful little enclave, accessible only via longtail or a circuitous back road. Fifteen kilometres' drive west of Ao Nang, **Hat Klong Muang** is no great shakes as a beach but does have some attractive four- and five-star accommodation.

Central Ao Nang and Ao Phai Plong

Ao Nang's central beach is unexceptional and busy with longtail traffic, though it's backed by a pleasantly landscaped promenade. The nicer stretch is east beyond *Ao Nang Villa Resort*, accessed by the pavement that takes you all the way along the shore to the appropriately named *Last Café*, a very pleasant spot for a shady drink. Follow the wooden walkway from beyond *The Last Café* and scale the steps up and over the headland to reach, in about ten minutes, the beach at diminutive **Ao Phai Plong**, which is the sole province of the luxurious *Centara Grand* hotel.

Hat Nopparat Thara east

Immediately west of Ao Nang, beyond the headland occupied by *Krabi Resort* but reached by simply following the road (on foot or in one of the frequent Krabi-bound songthaews), **Hat Nopparat Thara east** is long and pretty, with the road running along a landscaped promenade behind it. Its eastern hinterland is developing fast with hotels and restaurants, but the other end, close to the T-junction with Route 4202, is the site of the Hat Nopparat Thara–Mu Ko Phi Phi **national park headquarters** and accommodation. Here too is the **tsunami memorial**, *Hold Me Close* by Louise Bourgeois (2005), a broken, roofless, wood-slatted corncob structure enclosing two pairs of hands, joined, prayer like and pleading, extending from a lumpy sea.

At low tide it's almost impossible to swim on this beach, but the sands come alive with thousands of starfish and hermit crabs, and the view out towards the islands is glorious; you can walk to the nearest outcrop at low water.

The **national park visitor centre** is at the end of the beach, beside the khlong and its sheltered marina and jetty, Tha Nopparat Thara, which is the departure point for Ao Nang ferry services to Phuket, Phi Phi and Ko Lanta, as well as for longtails to the western beach. The visitor centre's car park is famous for its **seafood restaurants**, and Krabi residents also like to picnic under the shorefront casuarina trees here.

Hat Nopparat Thara west

Hat Nopparat Thara west has a quite different atmosphere from its eastern counterpart: just a handful of small bungalow hotels and a few private residences share its long swathe of peaceful casuarina- and palm-shaded shoreline, making it a great place to

---

DIVING FROM AO NANG

Ao Nang is Krabi's main centre for **dive shops**, with a dozen or more outlets, the most reputable of which include Kon-Tiki (☎075 637826, ⓦkontiki-thailand.com) and Poseidon (☎075 637263, ⓦposeidon-diving.com); they have a price agreement for PADI courses, but Poseidon is cheaper for dive trips. Diving with Ao Nang operators is possible year-round, with some dive staff claiming that off-season diving is more rewarding, not least because the sites are much less crowded.

Most one-day **dive trips** head for the area round Ko Phi Phi (from B3500 including two tanks; B1700 for snorkellers with Poseidon) and often include dives at Shark Point and the "King Cruiser" wreck dive (see p.338); the Ko Ha island group, near Ko Lanta, is also popular but more expensive (see p.387).

Two dives in the Ao Nang area – at Ko Poda and Ko Yawasam – cost B2700–3200 (B1900 for snorkellers), much less if you go in a longtail with Poseidon. PADI dive courses cost B5500 for the introductory Discover Scuba day, or B14,900 for the Openwater.

The nearest recompression chambers are on Phuket (see p.338); check to see that your dive operator is insured to use one of them. General information on diving in Thailand can be found in Basics (see p.51).

escape the crowds and commerce of other Krabi beaches. The views of the karst islands are magnificent, though swimming here is also tide-dependent. Without your own transport you can only get here by longtail across the narrow but deep khlong beside the national park visitor's centre, but with a car or bike you can arrive via the very quiet back road that snakes through the mangroves from the Klong Muang road to the edge of the bungalow properties.

ARRIVAL AND DEPARTURE
AO NANG

Ao Nang has no proper transport terminals of its own so most long-distance journeys entail going **via Krabi town** (see p.358). Taxis charge about B500 from Krabi to Ao Nang. From the **airport** (see p.358), a shuttle bus runs to Ao Nang for B150, while taxis charge B600–900 to Ao Nang and Klong Muang.

By songthaew The cheapest onward connection from Krabi to Ao Nang is by white songthaews, which run regularly throughout the day from Krabi town centre and bus station (every 10min or so; 45min; B50 daytime, B60 after dark) and pass eastern Nopparat Thara en route. Alight at the Nopparat Thara national park T-Junction and car park for longtails across the narrow khlong to the western beach (B100) or, with your own transport, follow the Klong Muang road until signs direct you off it. There's also a songthaew service from Krabi town to Klong Muang.
By boat In addition to the ferries listed below, also

available are longtails to Laem Phra Nang (see p.368) and boats to Ko Yao Noi (see p.348); the latter is a daily, high-season Green Planet speedboat that continues to Bang Rong in Phuket (B900 from Ao Nang). There are once-daily ferry services from Tha Nopparat Thara, near the national park visitors' centre, to Ko Phi Phi Don (2hr 30min; B450) and to Phuket (3hr; B650–700), both year-round in theory though they sometimes don't run in the monsoon season; and to Ko Lanta (2hr 30min; B470) from roughly November to May. Transfers from Ao Nang hotels are included in the ticket price.

GETTING AROUND

The Krabi **songthaews** are useful for nipping between Ao Nang, Hat Nopparat Thara and town, and motorcycle taxis with sidecars buzz around Ao Nang and Hat Nopparat Thara; **motorbikes** and **jeeps** are **available** for rent throughout the resort; and there are kayaks on the beach in front of *The Last Café* at the far east end of Ao Nang (B100–150/hr), from where, in calm seas, it's an easy 15min paddle to Ao Phai Plong or about 45min to Ao Ton Sai and West Railay.

ACCOMMODATION

During high season, it's almost impossible to get a double room under B600 in Ao Nang, though there is one exceptional travellers' place, *Laughing Gecko*, on contiguous Hat Nopparat Thara east. For a simple bungalow on the beach you need to go to Hat Nopparat Thara west. Mid- and upper-end accommodation is plentiful throughout and of a high standard; you can usually get decent discounts through online booking agents. Prices across the board drop by up to fifty percent during the rainy season, from May to October.

AO PHAI PLONG

Centara Grand Beach Resort Ao Phai Plong, east end of Ao Nang ☎075 637789, ⓦcentarahotelsresorts .com. Ao Nang's top hotel has the secluded sandy bay of Ao Phai Plong all to itself, but is connected by longtail boat to the shops and restaurants of Ao Nang or free speedboat shuttle to Hat Nopparat Thara east. Designed to sit almost seamlessly against the forested crags behind, there's a lovely green feel here and seaward vistas are also beautiful. Nearly all rooms in the four-storey hotel buildings and detached villas have sea views. Interiors are modern and generous with sun-balconies and shaded outdoor daybeds; all have wi-fi. There's a big pool, a diving and watersports centre, kids' club, gym and spa. B̲1̲0̲,̲7̲0̲0̲

CENTRAL AO NANG

Ao Nang Orchid Resort 141 Thanon Ao Nang ☎075 638426–8, ⓦaonangorchid-resort.com. This medium-sized but well-appointed hotel is good value for Ao Nang. Choose from rooms in the hotel wing, where the nicest overlook the pool and karst mountains beyond (rather than those with "city" views), or go for stand-alone villas with direct access to the lagoon pool. Interiors are chic and attractive, rooms and bungalows all have decks, and many have hardwood floors. Wi-fi in some areas. B̲3̲8̲5̲0̲

Ao Nang Villa Resort 113 Thanon Ao Nang ☎075 637270, ⓦaonangvilla.com. A very popular hotel and spa whose grounds run down to the beachfront walkway. The upscale, a/c rooms are contained within several

low-rise wings, a few of them enjoying a sea view, but most overlooking the garden or the bigger of the resort's two pools. Breakfast included. B̲4̲5̲0̲0̲

Centara Anda Dhevi Resort Ao Nang Soi 8 ☎075 626222, ⓦcentarahotelsresorts.com. New luxury hotel that cleverly squeezes in 130 spacious, contemporary-style rooms with rain showers and wi-fi around an attractive 43m pool, which features a water-slide and a swim-up bar; ground-floor rooms have direct pool access, others have balconies. There's also a very good spa and kids' club. B̲4̲5̲9̲0̲

J Mansion Off Thanon Ao Nang ☎075 695128, ⓦjmansionaonang.com. The best-known and most popular of the mini-hotels in Ao Nang's travellers' enclave, this place has very good, large, fan and a/c rooms, all with hot showers, satellite TVs, fridges and wi-fi. Most have high-level views, some of which extend to the green-clad cliffs behind. The rooftop terrace also has a panoramic outlook. Fan B̲1̲0̲0̲0̲, a/c B̲1̲2̲0̲0̲

PK Mansion and **Top View** Off Thanon Ao Nang ☎075 637431, ⓦkrabidir.com/pkmansion. Offering rates similar to its budget-oriented neighbours, *PK Mansion* and its adjacent, slightly pricier, sister hotel, *Top View*, have a range of mostly very good-quality rooms, with hot-water bathrooms, fan or a/c, balconies (many with partial sea views), TVs and fridges. Reservations advisable. Fan B̲7̲0̲0̲, a/c B̲8̲0̲0̲

Red Ginger Ao Nang Soi 8 ☎075 637999, ⓦred gingerkrabi.com. Located between the two beaches and a

ACTIVITIES AROUND KRABI, AO NANG AND LAEM PHRA NANG

Any tour agent in Krabi town, Ao Nang, Klong Muang or Railay can set you up on these **snorkelling day-trips** and other **activities**; prices usually include transport from your accommodation. Diving (see p.361) and rock-climbing (see p.368) are also available.

SNORKELLING DAY-TRIPS

By far the most popular organized outings from Krabi, Ao Nang and Laem Phra Nang are the **snorkelling trips** to nearby islands. The main **islands** in question are Ko Poda, Ko Tub and Chicken Island, all of them less than half an hour's longtail ride from Ao Nang or Railay. There are various permutations, offered by numerous companies, including the number of islands you visit (usually three, four or five) and whether you go in a longtail boat, a larger wooden boat or speedboat; prices start as low as B450 for a longtail trip to three islands, including packed lunch and snorkel set. In all cases you should be prepared to share the experience with dozens, even hundreds, of others, because pretty much everyone congregates at the same spots. It's a lot more fun than it sounds though – so long as you're not expecting a solitary experience.

It's also possible to organize your own boat trip with the **longtail boatmen** on Ao Nang waterfront. Their prices are fixed, but don't include snorkelling equipment or lunch: for the return trip to either Ko Poda, Ko Tub or Chicken Island (8am–4pm), they charge B300 per person, minimum six people; for Ko Hong (see p.352) it's B2500 per boat per full day, for Bamboo Island, near Ko Phi Phi (see p.372), B3800 per boat per full day. Krabi town is quite a bit further away so its boatmen charge B1800–2300 for the three main islands.

From some angles, one of the pinnacles on **Chicken Island** does indeed look like the scrawny neck and beaky head of a chicken. There's decent snorkelling off its coast, with a fair range of reef fish and quite a lot of giant clams, though most of the reef is either bleached or dead. Its dazzlingly white-sand northeastern shore, which has a food stall, toilets and kayak rental, is connected to the islets of **Ko Tup** by a sandbank, which is walkable at low tide – quite a striking sight as you arrive to see other visitors seemingly walking on water. Nearby **Ko Poda**, which sits directly in front of the Ao Nang beachfront, is encircled by lovely white-sand beaches and clear turquoise water. There's a restaurant here and plenty of shade under the casuarina trees, so this is the typical lunch stop; sandwich-selling boats dock here too. Though you might get three hundred people lunching on the shore here at any one time, it's big enough to cope. Some itineraries also feature **Ao Phra Nang** and its cave, on the Laem Phra Nang (Railay) peninsula (see p.367), and this is the one to avoid unless you enjoy scrambling for your metre of sand on this overrun little bay.

OTHER ACTIVITIES

Cycle rides Half- and full-day rides into the Krabi countryside, or to Ko Klang, Khao Phanom Bencha falls or Khlong Tom's Emerald Pool, with Krabi Eco Cycle, based about 2km inland from the Hat Nopparat Thara National Park visitors' centre on Route 4202 (from B800; ☎081 607 4162, ⊛krabiecocycle.com).

Elephant trekking Nosey Parker's Elephant Trekking (☎075 612258, ⊛krabidir.com/noseyparkers), 7km north of Ao Nang, has a good reputation. From B800 for an hour's trek along the river and elephant bathing.

Sea canoeing Guided and self-paddle trips around the spectacular karst islands and secret lagoons of

Ao Phang Nga, usually focusing on Ao Luk, Ao Thalen and Ko Hong in the eastern bay (see p.352). Dozens of companies offer this, including Sea Kayak Krabi, Soi 2, Thanon Maharat, Krabi town (☎075 630270, ⊛seakayak-krabi.com), who offer a multitude of day and multi-day trips, charging B1500 for a full-day trip to Ao Thalen, for example.

Thai cookery lessons Ya's Thai Cookery School, about 4km inland of Ao Nang off Route 4203, runs morning and afternoon courses (Mon–Sat 9am–1pm & 2–6pm; from B1000 including transport; ☎081 979 0677, ⊛thaicookeryschool.net).

short walk from central Ao Nang shops, this contemporary Sino-Thai hotel has jut 63 rooms, some of them duplexes, set round a saltwater pool. Lines are clean and simple with modern Chinese styling and it all feels bright and upbeat. Breakfast included. **B3300**
Somkietburi Resort Thanon Ao Nang ☎075 637990–1,

⊛somkietburi.com. Guests here enjoy one of the most delightful settings in Ao Nang, with the 26 rooms and swimming pools surrounded by a feral, jungle-style garden that's full of hanging vines and lotus ponds. Rooms are perfectly pleasant but nothing special; all have a/c and TV, and there's a spa. Breakfast included. **B3000**

HAT NOPPARAT THARA EAST

Cashew Nut Soi Hat Nopparat Thara 13 ☎ 075 637560, ⓦ cashewnutbungalows.com. Good, sturdy en-suite brick and concrete bungalows with fan or a/c and hot showers ranged around a peaceful garden full of cashew trees, just 5min walk from Hat Nopparat Thara east. Family-run, welcoming and peaceful, with free wi-fi in the restaurant. Fan **B500**, a/c **B1000**

★ **Laughing Gecko** Soi Hat Nopparat Thara 13 ☎ 081 270 5028, ⓦ laughinggeckothailand.com. Perhaps the last of the old-style bungalows left in the Ao Nang area, this is an easy-going and exceptionally traveller-friendly haven run by a Thai–Canadian couple. Choose from a range of simple, thatched, fan-cooled, en-suite bamboo huts set around a garden dotted with cashew trees, including four-person dorms. Also has free wi-fi and nightly all-you-can-eat Thai buffets (B150–200). Dorm **B150**, double **B500**

National park bungalows Beside the national park headquarters on Thanon Nopparat Thara east ☎ 075 637200, ⓦ dnp.go.th. Standard-issue, fan-cooled, en-suite bungalows, 2km from Ao Nang's main facilities but just across the (quite busy) road from a nice stretch of beach and a 5min walk from the seafood restaurants near the visitors' centre. **B1000**

HAT NOPPARAT THARA WEST

Long Beach Bungalow 600m west from the khlong ☎ 089 777 5853, ⓦ longbeachkrabivillas.com; map p.357. Set round a grassy, tree-strewn lawn, the main offerings at this place are attractive wood-and-bamboo huts with fans, mosquito nets and en-suite bathrooms; it also has some simple, shared-bathroom versions for single travellers (B350) and large, two-bedroom concrete bungalows that are available with fan (B1840) or a/c (B3000). Electricity at night only. Informal cooking classes, snorkelling trips and reasonably priced pick-ups. **B750**

PAN Beach At the westernmost end of the beach, about 700m walk from the khlong ☎ 089 866 4373, ⓦ panbeachkrabi.com; map p.357. Sturdy, simply furnished wooden bungalows in two sizes and styles, each with screened windows, fans and bathrooms, set just back from the shore around a lawn. Also has internet access, motorbikes and cars for rent, and organizes local boat trips. Electricity at night only. Free pick-ups in the morning from Ao Nang. **B800**

HAT KLONG MUANG

Sheraton Krabi Beach Resort ☎ 075 628000, ⓦ sheraton.com/krabi; map p.357. Unusually for a top-notch beachfront hotel, the *Sheraton Krabi* does not boast of its sea views because the entire low-rise resort has been built among the mangroves and alongside a khlong; the result is refreshingly green and cool – and full of birdsong. The sandy shore – the nicest in Klong Muang – is anyway just a few steps away, accessed via a series of wooden walkways, and there's a seafront lawn for lounging. Rooms are large, sleek and very comfortable; there's a big pool, a spa, a tennis court, a watersports centre and bicycle rental. Wi-fi is free in public areas, payable in the rooms. Breakfast included. **B6800**

EATING AND DRINKING

Eating and drinking options in Ao Nang are not sophisticated and there are few places that stand out from the crowd. At weekends, locals flock to the seafood restaurants in the national park visitors' centre car park on Hat Nopparat Thara, or buy fried chicken from nearby stalls and picnic on mats under the shorefront trees. In central Ao Nang, there are cheap hot-food stalls on the road outside *Krabi Resort*, opposite Kontiki Diving, and handcarts selling Muslim roti pancakes (filled with milk, banana or chocolate) pitch up all over the resort. The bar scene is mainly focused around Ao Nang Center Point Walking Street, a U-shaped passageway behind the beachfront shops that's packed with rock, reggae and all-sorts bars, including Krabi's first pole-dancing club. There's also a small knot of makeshift little bars on the beach next to *Wang Sai Restaurant* on Thanon Nopparat Thara.

CENTRAL AO NANG

Chanaya Thai-Dutch Thanon Ao Nang. With its fairy lights, trailing plants and wooden tables, this place always gets a good crowd. The menu is mostly European – T-bone steaks done various ways, ostrich steaks, asparagus, ham and cheese bake – and there are tempting set dinners rounded off with Dutch apple pie and cream. Mains from B160; sets from B515. Daily 8am–2am.

The Last Fisherman Bar Soi Ao Nang 17. On the sand at the far easternmost end of the beach, serving simple Thai food and a huge range of sandwiches for lunch, but most famous for its evening barbecues (from B350 per set),

which come with baked potatoes, corn-on-the-cob, salads and desserts. Daily 11.30am–4.30pm & 6–9pm.

Longtail Boat Soi Seafood ☎ 075 638093. All the Thai standards, including plenty of fish and seafood, which is displayed on ice and in tanks at the entrance, but especially good for thick, toothsome *matsaman* curries served with roti pancakes (B280). Daily 2–10.30pm.

Sala Bua and Lo Spuntino Soi Seafood, a pedestrianized alley of restaurants running off the promenade ☎ 075 637110, ⓦ salabua-lospuntino.com. Enjoying great sea views, especially at sunset, this is a welcoming two-in-one restaurant with two chefs. One does the Thai dishes under *Sala Bua*, including excellent

4

phanaeng curries (B175) and seafood, while the other cooks authentic Italian off a wide-ranging menu – lots of appetizers and home-made pastas, pizzas, and imported Australian meats for the main courses – for *Lo Spuntino*. Daily 11am–10pm.

Sally O'Malley's Up a small soi off the promenade. Friendly, Scottish-run, Irish theme pub with a long bar, Kilkenny bitter, Guinness and cider on draught, regular live guitar music and a pool table. Daily 11am–1/2am.

Ton Sai 150m north of McDonald's on Thanon Ao Nang. Home-style Thai cooking is the calling card at this bamboo-shack family-run restaurant. The curries are delicious, there's plenty of seafood and you can get almost any dish cooked to order. Most mains B80–100. Daily 8.30am–10pm.

HAT NOPPARAT THARA EAST

Krua Thara (After the Tsunami) National park visitors' centre car park. Hugely popular with locals, expats and visiting Thais for its reasonably priced fresh seafood (mostly sold by weight), but also serves north-eastern salads, rice and noodle dishes (around B70) and excellent espresso coffees. Daily 11am–10pm.

★ **Wang Sai** Beside the bridge at the eastern end of Thanon Nopparat Thara ☎075 638128. Good sunset views from its beachfront tables, an enormous range of seafood and lots of southern Thai specialities. The hearty *haw mok thalay* (on the menu as "steam seafood curry sauce"; B180) is excellent, stuffed with all kinds of fish and seafood, or you can get seafood fried rice for just B70. Daily 10.30am–10pm.

DIRECTORY

Tourist police On the main road between Ao Nang and Hat Nopparat Thara (☎075 637208).

Laem Phra Nang: Railay and Ton Sai

Seen from the close quarters of a longtail boat, the combination of sheer limestone cliffs, pure white sand and emerald waters around the **LAEM PHRA NANG** peninsula is spectacular – and would be even more so without the hundreds of other admirers gathered on its four beaches. The peninsula (often known simply as **Railay**) is effectively a tiny island, embraced by impenetrable limestone massifs that make road access impossible – but do offer excellent, world-famous **rock-climbing**; transport is by boat only, from Krabi town or, most commonly, from nearby Ao Nang. It has four beaches within ten minutes' walk of each other: **Ao Phra Nang** graces the southwestern edge, and is flanked by **East and West Railay**, just 500m apart; **Ao Ton Sai** is beyond West Railay, on the other side of a rocky promontory. Almost every patch of buildable land fronting East and West Railay has been taken over by bungalow resorts, and development is creeping up the cliffsides and into the forest behind. But at least high-rises don't feature, and much of the construction is hidden among trees or set amid prettily landscaped gardens. Accommodation is at a premium and not cheap, so the scene on West and East Railay, and Ao Phra Nang, is predominantly holidaymakers on short breaks rather than backpackers. The opposite is true on adjacent Ao Ton Sai, Krabi's main travellers' hub and the heart of the rock-climbing scene.

West Railay

The loveliest and most popular beach on the cape is **WEST RAILAY**, with its gorgeous white sand, crystal-clear water and impressive karst scenery at every turn. The best of the peninsula's bungalow hotels front this shoreline, and longtail boats from Ao Nang pull in here too, so it gets crowded.

East Railay

Follow any of the tracks inland, through the resort developments, and within a few minutes you reach **EAST RAILAY** on the other coast, lined with mangrove swamps and a muddy shore that make it unsuitable for swimming; boats from Krabi town dock here. Accommodation on this side is a bit cheaper, and there's more variety in price too, though – aside from a couple of gems – it's mostly an uncomfortable mix of uninspired, low-grade developments and unsubtle bars with names like *Skunk* and *Stone*. Depressingly, much of East Railay's hinterland is despoiled by trash and building rubble, but inland it's another story, with a majestic amphitheatre of forested karst turrets just ten minutes' walk away, on the back route to Ao Ton Sai.

Ao Phra Nang

Head to the far south end of East Railay's shoreline to pick up the path to the diminutive, cliff-bound beach at **AO PHRA NANG** (also called **Hat Tham Phra Nang**). Though exceptionally pretty, the bay can be hard to appreciate beneath the trinket sellers and crowds of day-trippers who are deposited here in their hundreds, by boats that pollute the coastal waters. Better to visit before 10am or after 4pm if you can.

The walkway from East Railay winds between the super-lux *Rayavadee* hotel and the lip of a massive karst before emerging at the beach beside **Tham Phra Nang**, or **Princess Cave**. The beach and cave, and indeed the peninsula, are named for this princess (*phra nang* means "revered lady"): according to legend, a boat carrying an Indian princess sank in a storm here and the royal spirit took up residence in the cave. Local fisherfolk believe she controls the fertility of the sea and, to encourage large catches, leave red-tipped wooden phalluses as offerings to her at the cave entrance. Buried deep

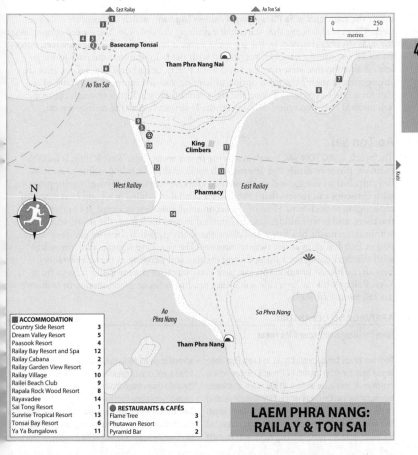

ACCOMMODATION	
Country Side Resort	3
Dream Valley Resort	5
Paasook Resort	4
Railay Bay Resort and Spa	12
Railay Cabana	2
Railay Garden View Resort	7
Railay Village	10
Railei Beach Club	9
Rapala Rock Wood Resort	8
Rayavadee	
Sai Tong Resort	1
Sunrise Tropical Resort	13
Tonsai Bay Resort	6
Ya Ya Bungalows	11

RESTAURANTS & CAFÉS	
Flame Tree	3
Phutawan Resort	1
Pyramid Bar	2

LAEM PHRA NANG: RAILAY & TON SAI

ROCK-CLIMBING AND KAYAKING ON LAEM PHRA NANG

Ton Sai and Railay are Thailand's biggest **rock-climbing** centres, attracting thousands of experienced and novice climbers every year to the peninsula's seven hundred bolted routes, which range in difficulty from 5a to 8c (see ⊕railay.com for a full rundown). Of the many climbing **schools** that rent out equipment and lead guided climbs, the most established include King Climbers at *Ya Ya Resort* on East Railay (☎075 662096, ⊕www.railay.com/railay /climbing/climbing_king_climbers.shtml) and Basecamp Tonsai on Ton Sai (☎081 149 9745, ⊕weesclimbingschool.com). A typical half-day introduction costs B1000, a full day B1800, while B6000 will get you a three-day course, learning all rope skills; equipment can be rented for about B1300 per day for two people. If you don't need instruction, the locally published and regularly updated guidebooks, Basecamp Tonsai's *Rock Climbing in Thailand and Laos* and King Climbers' Thailand *Route Guide Book*, will give you all the route information you need. Unaided over-water climbing on cliffs and outcrops out at sea, known as **deep-water soloing**, with no ropes, bolts or partner, is also becoming a big thing around here and can be arranged through most climbing schools for about B1000.

Kayaking around this area is also very rewarding – you can get to Ao Nang in less than an hour; kayaks cost B200 per hour to rent, for example on the beach in front of *Flame Tree* restaurant on West Railay. There are plenty of other activities in the Krabi area that you could hook up with from Laem Phra Nang (see p.364).

---

inside the same cliff is **Sa Phra Nang (Princess Lagoon)**, which is accessible only via a steep 45-minute descent that starts halfway along the walkway. You'll need proper shoes for it, as slippery descents and sharp rocks make it hard in flip-flops or bare feet. After an initial ten-minute clamber, negotiated with the help of ropes, the path forks: go left for a panoramic view over East and West Railay, or right for the lagoon. (For the strong-armed, there's the third option of hauling yourself up ropes to the top of the cliff for a bird's-eye view.) Taking the right-hand fork, you'll pass through the tropical dell dubbed "big tree valley" before eventually descending to the murky lagoon.

Ao Ton Sai

The beach at **AO TON SAI**, north across the oyster rocks from West Railay, is not the prettiest, prone to murk and littered with rocks that make it impossible to swim at low tide. But its orange-and-ochre-striped cliffs are magnificently scenic, dripping with curlicues and turrets that tower over a central tree-filled bowl and host scores of challenging rock climbs. Most of the accommodation here is aimed at climbers and travellers, and is well hidden several hundred metres back from the shore, scattered within the remains of a forest and along the shady path that, beyond *Sai Tong*, takes you to East Railay in about twenty minutes. The vibe here is green and comradely, with climbers doing their thing during the day and partying at the several chilled bars after dark. At low tide you can pick your way over the razor-sharp rocks from West Railay, while at high tide you either need to swim or get a longtail, or walk over the hill from East Railay.

ARRIVAL AND DEPARTURE   LAEM PHRA NANG

Laem Phra Nang is only accessible by **boat**.

To/from Krabi town Longtail boats to Laem Phra Nang depart from the Krabi riverfront (45min; B150 per person, minimum 8 people, or around B1500 when chartered), leaving throughout the day as soon as they fill up. Depending on the tide, all Krabi boats land on or off East Railay, so you may have to wade; they do run during the rainy season, but the waves make it a nerve-wracking experience, so you're

advised to go via Ao Nang instead. Coming back, contact a travel agent or your guesthouse on Laem Phra Nang about the half a dozen timed departures a day, if you need to make onward connections from Krabi town.

To/from Ao Nang and beyond Ao Nang is much closer than Krabi town to Laem Phra Nang, and shared longtails run from the beachfront here to West Railay, Ao Phra Nang and Ao Ton Sai when full (minimum 8 people; 10min; B100, B150 after dark). There are several longtail boat stations, including one at the Hat Nopparat Thara national park visitor centre, all charging the same price; the one at the eastern end of the beachfront road is the most popular,

so you'll probably have the shortest wait for the boat to fill up here. During high season there should also be daily ferries from Ao Nang via West Railay to Ko Phi Phi (2hr 30min), Ko Lanta (2hr 30min) and Phuket (3hr); if not, you'll need to travel via Ao Nang.

GETTING AROUND

Shared **longtail boats** between Ao Ton Sai and West Railay cost B50 per person (minimum 4 people).

ACCOMMODATION

Because demand is so high, from November to March it's often hard to get a room on spec on West or East Railay, though you should have more luck on Ao Ton Sai. Mains electricity hasn't yet reached Ton Sai: very few of the bungalows have electricity during daylight hours, and in the cheapest places you'll just get a few hours' worth out of the generator in the evening.

WEST RAILAY

Railay Bay Resort and Spa ☎ 075 819407, ⓦ railaybay resort.com. There's a huge range of rooms and bungalows here (all with free wi-fi), in a shady coconut grove that runs down to both East and West Railay, plus two swimming pools and a spa. The pick of the bunch are the very large beachfront suites, which have marble bathrooms with jacuzzi tubs and great sea views from their verandas. B4100
Railay Village ☎ 075 819412–3, ⓦ railayvillagekrabi .com. Occupying very pretty gardens in between the two beaches, with nowhere more than 300m from the West Railay shore, the style here is elegant tropical, in whitewashed jacuzzi villas and pool-access hotel rooms, all roofed in low-impact wooden tiles, with wooden floors and Thai furnishings completing the look. There are two pools and a spa. Breakfast included. B6750
Railei Beach Club ☎ 086 685 9359, ⓦ raileibeachclub .com. Unusual compound of charming, mostly fan-cooled private houses, built of wood in idiosyncratic Thai style and rented out by their owners. One- to four-bed houses are available, all well spaced, and there are a couple of cheaper private rooms; most have kitchen facilities and there's wi-fi throughout. The compound is only minimally screened from the beach, so seafront houses get good views but may lack privacy and bear the brunt of the noisy longtail traffic. Minimum stays of three nights, rising to seven from mid-Dec to mid-Jan. B2500

AO PHRA NANG

Rayavadee ☎ 075 620740, ⓦ rayavadee.com. The supremely elegant two-storey spiral-shaped pavilions here, some set in enclosed gardens, some with whirlpools, are set in a beautifully landscaped, eco-friendly compound with lotus ponds that borders all three beaches. Facilities include a pool with a kids' pool, a spa, a squash court and tennis courts, a gym and two restaurants. B22,300

EAST RAILAY

Railay Cabana ☎ 084 057 7167. In a spacious, grassy, tree-filled amphitheatre of majestic karst cliffs, a 5min

walk from the beach on the track to Ton Sai, this friendly family-run place offers simple bamboo bungalows with thick mattresses, mosquito nets, fans and bathrooms. It's a lovely quiet spot, away from the East Railay crassness. Staff can help transport luggage from the pier. B450
★ **Railay Garden View Resort** ☎ 085 888 5143, ⓦ railaygardenview.com. This place really stands out for it simple rustic-chic style, great high-level views over the mangroves and sea beyond, and green surrounds in a garden of jackfruit, banana and papaya trees. The fan-cooled bungalows, built from good-quality split bamboo, are widely spaced and on stilts, with colour-washed cold-water bathrooms, wooden-floored bedrooms and decks, and plenty of triangular cushions for lounging. The drawback is that it's up a steep stairway beyond the far north end of East Railay, accessed via a short walkway beyond *The Last Bar*, about 15min walk from West Railay. Free wi-fi. Breakfast included. B1000
Rapala Rock Wood Resort Climb a steep flight of stairs to reach the thirty rough-hewn, fan-cooled timber and brick huts here, which are among the cheapest on Railay, set around a scruffy, breezy garden high above the beach, with some enjoying dramatic karst views from their verandas. There's also a nice communal deck among the treetops, and a friendly restaurant that serves Indian food and bakes its own tasty biscuits and bread. No advance bookings, walk-ins only. Shared bathroom B200, en suite B400
★ **Sunrise Tropical Resort** ☎ 075 819418–20, ⓦ sunrisetropical.com. The most stylish of the affordable hotels on the cape offers just forty rooms, most in elegantly designed a/c bungalows, and some in a couple of two-storey buildings, all with Thai furnishings and generously spacious living areas, set around a landscaped tropical garden with a pool and spa. Wi-fi throughout. Rooms B2550, villas B3700
Ya Ya Bungalows (Railay Princess Budget) ☎ 075 819401–3, ⓦ yaya-resort.com. This idiosyncratic place has some of the cheapest accommodation on Railay and is built almost entirely of wood, with most rooms contained in a series of sturdy, quite well-designed,

4

three-storey buildings. They all have verandas and en-suite bathrooms and many have hot showers, but soundproofing is not great and most rooms are quite dark. It's recently been taken over by the *Railay Princess*, so there may be changes and a rise in prices. Fan B850, a/c (breakfast included) B1880

AO TON SAI
Country Side Resort ☎ 084 848 0146, ☞ countryside -resort.com. Solar-powered eco-resort offering airy and attractive wooden bungalows on stilts, some with stunning views of the karsts, some with hot showers – including the a/c rooms, which have iPod docks and can fit three people. Wi-fi throughout. Fan B850, a/c B1380

Dream Valley Resort ☎ 075 819810–2, ☞ dream valleyresortkrabi.com. The ninety bungalows here are ranged discreetly among the trees, running far back towards the cliff-face, offering a range of good-quality accommodation in various categories, from wooden bungalows with fans, mosquito screens and bathrooms through to a/c villas with hot showers, the best of which

are the premier accommodation on Ao Ton Sai. Breakfast included. Fan B900, a/c B1400

Pasook Resort ☎ 089 645 3013. Friendly, welcoming spot, set on sloping lawns amid flowers and small trees, offering en-suite, fan-cooled concrete rooms and clapboard bungalows – best value are the larger concrete rooms with nice bathrooms (B450). Prices change frequently, according to demand. Room B300, bungalow B600

Sai Tong Resort 400m along the track to East Railay ☎ 081 079 6583. This friendly, good-value little place offers cheap, woven-bamboo huts with nets, fans and bathrooms, and bigger, more comfy, cute-looking split-bamboo ones, also en suite and with nets, fans and proper beds. B200

Tonsai Bay Resort ☎ 075 695599, ☞ tonsaibay.co.th. With its large, widely spaced and plain but comfortable bungalows, this is one of the top places to stay on Ao Ton Sai. The detached and semi-detached bungalows boast huge glass windows and big decks from which to soak up the pretty location in a grove of trees set back from the shore, and all have a/c, hot shower, satellite TV, fridge and safety box. Breakfast included. B2250

EATING AND DRINKING

There's no shortage of traveller-style bars on Laem Phra Nang, especially at the north end of East Railay and on the beach at Ton Sai, with their fire-juggling, driftwood furniture, chillums and occasional parties.

WEST RAILAY
Flame Tree On the seafront. This sprawling, laidback, semi-outdoor place has a more varied menu than most of the restaurants on Laem Phra Nang, including cashew nut salad (B175), some southern Thai dishes, mushroom sauce steak (B395), pastas, sandwiches, a variety of breakfasts and espresso coffees. Daily 7am–9.30pm.

EAST RAILAY
Phutawan Resort Quietly located in the middle of the

spectacular cliff-lined basin on the track to Ton Sai, a 10min walk from both East and West Railay, the restaurant here offers fine views and good food, mostly seafood and Thai curries, and largely in the reasonable B100–120 range. Daily 7.30am–10pm.

AO TON SAI
Pyramid Bar Busy day and night with climbers scoffing the fresh coffees, tuna and cheese melts (B100), ciabatta sandwiches and Thai food. High season only, hours variable.

DIRECTORY

ATM Several in the resort, including one next to *Flame Tree* restaurant.

Ko Phi Phi Don

About 40km south of Krabi, the island of **KO PHI PHI DON** looks breathtakingly handsome as you approach from the sea, its classic arcs of pure white sand framed by dramatic cliffs and lapped by water that's a mouthwatering shade of turquoise. A flat sandy isthmus connects the hilly east and west halves of the island, scalloped into the much photographed symmetrical double bays of Ao Ton Sai and Ao Loh Dalum. The vast majority of the tourist accommodation is squashed in here, as is the island's wild nightlife, with just a few alternatives scattered along eastern coasts. Phi Phi's few indigenous islanders mostly live in the northeast.

Such beauty, however, belies the island's turbulent recent history. By the early 1990s, Phi Phi's reputation as a tropical idyll was bringing unfeasibly huge crowds of backpackers to its shores, and the problem worsened after uninhabited little sister

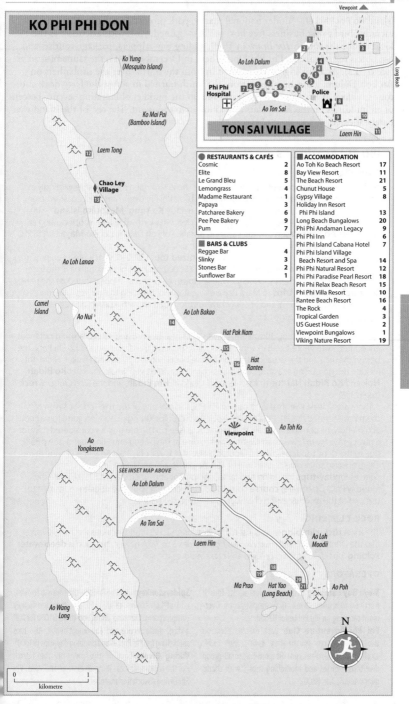

KO PHI PHI DON

Ko Yung
(Mosquito Island)

Ko Mai Pai
(Bamboo Island)

Laem Tong

Chao Ley Village

Ao Loh Lanaa

Camel Island

Ao Nui

Ao Loh Bakao

Hat Pak Nam

Hat Rantee

Ao Loh Moodii

Viewpoint

Ao Toh Ko

Ao Yongkasem

SEE INSET MAP ABOVE

Ao Loh Dalum

Ao Ton Sai

Laem Hin

Ma Prao

Hat Yao
(Long Beach)

Ao Poh

Ao Wang Long

TON SAI VILLAGE

Viewpoint ▲

Ao Loh Dalum

Phi Phi Hospital ✚

Ao Ton Sai

Police

Long Beach

Laem Hin

● RESTAURANTS & CAFÉS

Cosmic	2
Elite	8
Le Grand Bleu	5
Lemongrass	4
Madame Restaurant	1
Papaya	3
Patcharee Bakery	6
Pee Pee Bakery	9
Pum	7

■ BARS & CLUBS

Reggae Bar	4
Slinky	3
Stones Bar	2
Sunflower Bar	1

■ ACCOMMODATION

Ao Toh Ko Beach Resort	17
Bay View Resort	11
The Beach Resort	21
Chunut House	5
Gypsy Village	8
Holiday Inn Resort	
Phi Phi Island	13
Long Beach Bungalows	20
Phi Phi Andaman Legacy	9
Phi Phi Inn	6
Phi Phi Island Cabana Hotel	7
Phi Phi Island Village	
Beach Resort and Spa	14
Phi Phi Natural Resort	12
Phi Phi Paradise Pearl Resort	18
Phi Phi Relax Beach Resort	15
Phi Phi Villa Resort	10
Rantee Beach Resort	16
The Rock	4
Tropical Garden	3
US Guest House	2
Viewpoint Bungalows	1
Viking Nature Resort	19

4

0 _____ 1
kilometre

N

island **Ko Phi Phi Leh** – under national marine park protection on account of its lucrative bird's-nest business (see box, p.376) – gained worldwide attention as the location for the movie *The Beach* in 1999, adding day-trippers, package-tourists and big hotels to the mix on Phi Phi Don. Then, in December 2004, the **tsunami** struck (see p.312). As a 5m-high wave crashed in from the north, over the sunbathers on Ao Loh Dalum, a 3m-high wave from the south hurtled in across the ferry dock and tourist village at Ao Ton Sai. The waves met in the middle, obliterating seventy percent of all buildings on the sandy flats and killing two thousand. The rest of the island was barely affected.

PHI PHI ACTIVITIES

SNORKELLING

There's some great **snorkelling** around Phi Phi's shallow fringing reefs, most rewardingly at strikingly beautiful **Ko Mai Pai** (**Bamboo Island**), off Phi Phi Don's northeast coast, where much of the reef lies close to the surface, and at nearby **Ko Yung** (**Mosquito Island**), with its spectacular, steep-sided drop. Phi Phi Don has its own worthwhile reefs too, including at west-coast **Ao Yongkasem**, within kayaking distance of Loh Dalum, but **Ao Maya** on Phi Phi Leh is more famous, and a lot more crowded (see p.374).

Outings are easily arranged as part of an **organized tour** (B500–800 including equipment) or by **hiring your own longtail** boatman (B1500/3000 per boat per half/full day), the latter far preferable to the largest tour boats, whose groups of forty-plus trippers inundate the reefs. **Overnight camping trips** to Maya Bay are a neat way of avoiding the crowds, offering late-afternoon snorkelling, and possibly kayaking, rounded off with a beach barbecue.

DIVING

Offering visibility touching 30m, a great diversity of healthy hard and soft corals, and potential encounters with white-tip sharks, moray eels and stingrays, the diving around Ko Phi Phi is the best in the area and the usual destination of dive boats from Ao Nang and Phuket. Highlights include the gorgonian sea fans, barracudas, manta rays and even whale sharks at **Ko Bidah Nok** and **Ko Bidah Nai**, the mass of leopard sharks at **Hin Bidah**, and the *King Cruiser* **wreck** (see p.338).

There are at least twenty dive shops on Phi Phi, the majority of them in Ton Sai; seven of them have formed the Phi Phi Diving Association (phiphidivingassociation.com) to promote eco-friendly, responsible and safe diving practices (see p.51). Note that it's considered risky for a novice diver with fewer than twenty dives to dive at Hin Daeng and Hin Muang (see p.338), due to the depth and the current; reputable dive shops will only take Advanced Divers there. There are also small dive centres on Hat Yao, Ao Loh Bakao and Laem Tong.

Prices for **day-trips** including two tanks, equipment and lunch start at B2500, while the four-day PADI Openwater **course** costs B13,800. Check that your dive operator is insured to use one of the recompression chambers on Phuket (see p.338).

ROCK-CLIMBING

The main **rock-climbing** area is just to the west of Ao Ton Sai, and includes the Ton Sai Tower and the Drinking Wall, with thirty routes from grades 5 to 7a. A newer attraction is **deep-water soloing**, unaided climbing on cliffs and outcrops over the sea.

OPERATORS

Maya Bay Camping East of the pier, on the fourth north–south alley mayabaycamping.com. Overnight camping on Phi Phi Le for B2500.
Phi Phi Adventure Club East of the pier, on the fourth north–south alley 081 895 1334, phi-phi-adventures.com. Responsible, small-group dive trips, courses and snorkelling trips ("with sharks guaranteed"; 3hr; B800).

Spidermonkey Near The Rock on the route to the east end of Loh Dalum 075 819384, spidermonkey climbing.com. Climbing instruction (from B1000 for half a day), guide service and equipment rental. Also runs snorkelling (on Phi Phi Le) and climbing day-trips (B1600).
Viking Divers East of the pier, on the fourth north–south alley vikingdiversthailand.com. Phi Phi Diving Association member.

Volunteers and donations poured in to help the island back on its feet, and though the rebuild was dogged by much political wrangling, the Phi Phi of today thrives much as it ever did, firmly re-established as the destination to be ticked off on almost any itinerary in southern Thailand. Unfortunately, few of the pre-tsunami **problems** have been properly resolved – in part because tsunami survivors were desperate to make a new start as fast as they could. The island is now once again floundering under unregulated, unsightly and unsustainable development, with inadequate rubbish disposal and a plague of overpriced accommodation, at its most acute around the Ton Sai–Loh Dalum hub. There's always more building work going on, while thousands of visitors from all corners of the world fight for space in the narrow maze of pedestrianized alleys in Ton Sai village, sometimes generating an unusually aggressive atmosphere for Thailand. The noise pollution from the untrammelled outdoor bars and clubs is an additional turn-off for some – though it is a fun place to party, and there are enough more remote escapes for a peaceful stay too.

All boats dock in **Ao Ton Sai**, from where it's a short walk to the main accommodation centres – in **Ton Sai village**, at **Laem Hin**, the next little stretch of sand to the east, and on **Ao Loh Dalum**, the still attractive, deeply curved bay across the isthmus. **Hat Yao**, another fine beach just a short boat ride away, is also very popular. To escape the crowds you need to aim for one of the smaller bays further north: **Hat Toh Ko**, **Ao Rantee** and **Hat Pak Nam** are all good for moderately priced breakaways, while **Ao Loh Bakao** and **Laem Tong** are pricier and more luxurious.

Ton Sai village, Ao Loh Dalum and Laem Hin

Ton Sai village is a hectic warren of a place, both strangely old-fashioned with its alley traffic of bicycles and pushcarts, its fresh market tucked away in the middle and its squalid shanty town and stinky sewers hidden along the edges, and bang up to date, the narrow lanes bursting with state-of-the-art dive companies, shops advertising DVD players for rent and trendy boutiques.

West of the pier, **Ao Ton Sai** beach is an attractive little retreat under the limestone karsts, though it gets busy for a couple of hours around lunchtime and you're not far from the longtail moorings. Most people simply head for **Ao Loh Dalum** instead, less than 300m north across the narrow isthmus, which looks astonishingly pretty at high tide, with its glorious curve of powder-white sand beautifully set off by pale blue water; it's a different story at low water, however, as the tide goes out for miles. There's a tiny Tsunami Memorial Park of carefully tended shrubs, epitaphs and photos at the eastern end, near *Sunflower Bar*.

East along the coast from the Ton Sai pier, about ten minutes' walk along the main alley, is the promontory known as **Laem Hin**, beyond which lies a small beach and bungalows that enjoy a little more space. Inland, there are island homes and a mosque.

The viewpoint

The **viewpoint** that overlooks eastern Ao Loh Dalum affords a magnificent panorama over the twin bays and every evening a stream of people makes the steep fifteen-minute climb up the steps for sunset shots; early morning is also photogenic, and the shop at the "Topview" summit, set within a pretty tropical garden, serves coffee as well as cold drinks. From the viewpoint, you can descend the rocky and at times almost sheer paths to the trio of little east-coast bays at Ao Toh Ko, Ao Rantee (Lanti) and Hat Pak Nam, each of which takes about thirty minutes.

Hat Yao (Long Beach)

With its deluxe sand and large reefs packed with polychromatic marine life just 20m offshore, **HAT YAO** (Long Beach) is considered the best of Phi Phi's main beaches, but it's lined with hotels so gets very busy. UK-run Long Beach Divers (@longbeachdivers.com) here runs all the same **dive** trips and courses as shops in the village and offers discounted stays at *Long Beach Bungalows* for dive students.

Longtail **boats** do the ten-minute shuttle between Hat Yao and Ao Ton Sai (B100 per person, or B150 after dark), but at low tide it's also possible to **walk** between the two in half an hour, via the coast in front of *Bay View Resort* on Laem Hin and then via *Viking*. The island's single **road** follows an inland route to *The Beach Resort* from *The Rock* junction in the village, passing the post-tsunami housing project and Water Hill reservoir en route; it's a hot, hilly and unshaded forty-minute walk.

Ao Toh Ko, Hat Rantee and Hat Pak Nam

Travellers wanting to escape the crowds around Ton Sai and Hat Yao without spending a fortune head for the trio of little bays midway along the east coast: **AO TOH KO** and adjacent **HAT RANTEE** (Lanti) and **HAT PAK NAM**. You can reach the bays inland, via steep forest trails that run from the Viewpoint above Ao Loh Dalum (see p.373) in half an hour, while you can walk from Ao Toh Ko to Hat Rantee in five minutes at low tide. Rantee is probably the pick of the three, a palm- and casuarina-fringed white-sand bay, with great snorkelling at the reef right off the beach.

Ao Loh Bakao and Laem Tong

Far removed from the hustle of Ao Ton Sai and its environs, the beautiful, secluded northern beaches at Ao Loh Bakao and Laem Tong are the domain of just a few upscale resorts. *Phi Phi Island Village Beach Resort and Spa* (see p.378) has the gorgeous 800m-long white-sand beach and turquoise waters of **AO LOH BAKAO** all to itself. If you tire of these sands, and the hotel's four restaurants, there's a cluster of reasonably priced local restaurants behind the resort, and you can walk to the long, semicircular beach at **Ao Loh Lanaa**, across on the west coast, in ten minutes, or to Laem Tong in half an hour.

Almost right at Phi Phi's northernmost tip, **LAEM TONG** is busier and more commercial than Loh Bakao, with several upmarket resorts and stand-alone restaurants along its white-sand shores, and views across to nearby Bamboo and Mosquito islands. The beach is home to a group of Urak Lawoy *chao ley* "sea gypsies" (see p.304), whose village is next to the *Holiday Inn*; all longtail boat tours and transfers are run by Laem Tong's *chao ley* cooperative.

Ko Phi Phi Leh

More rugged than its twin, Ko Phi Phi Don, and a quarter the size, **KO PHI PHI LEH** is the number one day-tripping destination from Phi Phi Don, twenty minutes north, and a feature of snorkelling tours out of Phuket and Ao Nang (the national park admission fee of B200 is only levied if you set foot on the island, but not if you only snorkel offshore). It is very scenic indeed, and world famous, following its starring role in the film *The Beach*, so expect huge crowds, a plethora of discarded polystyrene lunch boxes, and a fair bit of damage to the reefs from the carelessly dropped anchors of tourist and fishing boats. The best way to appreciate the island is probably on one of the overnight camping and snorkelling trips from Phi Phi Don (see p.372).

Most idyllic of all the island's bays is **Ao Maya** on the southwest coast, where the water is still and very clear and the coral extremely varied; **Ao Phi Leh**, an almost completely enclosed east-coast lagoon of breathtakingly turquoise water, is also beautiful. Nearby, the **Viking Cave** gets its misleading name from the scratchy wall-paintings of Chinese junks inside, but more interesting than this 400-year-old graffiti is the **bird's-nesting** that goes on here (see p.376): rickety bamboo scaffolding extends hundreds of metres

BIRD'S-NESTING

Prized for its aphrodisiac and energizing qualities, **bird's-nest soup** is such a delicacy in Taiwan, Singapore and Hong Kong that ludicrous sums of money change hands for a dish whose basic ingredients are tiny twigs glued together with bird's spit. Collecting these nests is a lucrative but life-endangering business: sea swifts (known as edible-nest swiftlets) build their nests in rock crevices hundreds of metres above sea level, often on sheer cliff-faces or in cavernous hollowed-out karst. **Nest-building** begins in January and the harvesting season usually lasts from February to May, during which time the female swiftlet builds three nests on the same spot, none of them more than 12cm across, by secreting an unbroken thread of saliva, which she winds round as if making a coil pot. **Gatherers** will only steal the first two nests made by each bird, prising them off the cave walls with special metal forks. This in theory allows the bird to build a final nest and raise her chicks in peace. Gathering the nests demands faultless agility and balance, skills that seem to come naturally to the *chao ley* (see p.304), whose six-man teams bring about four hundred nests down the perilous bamboo scaffolds each day, weighing about 4kg in total. At a market rate of up to $2000 per kilo, so much money is at stake that a government franchise must be granted before any collecting commences, and armed guards often protect the sites at night. The *chao ley* seek spiritual protection from the dangers of the job by making offerings to the spirits of the cliff or cave at the beginning of the season; in the Viking Cave, they place buffalo flesh, horns and tails at the foot of one of the stalagmites.

In recent years, entrepreneurs in Ban Laem, near Phetchaburi, across on south Thailand's Gulf coast, have started competing with the *chao lay* – by constructing **sea swift condominiums** and trying to attract the swiftlets that frequent the attic of the nearby temple. The theory is that by constructing windowless concrete towers that mimic the Andaman Sea caves – complete with cool dark interiors and droppings-smeared walls, plus swiftlet soundtracks on continuous replay – they can entice the birds in to build their nests and harvest them with ease. To date, the main beneficiary seems to have been the construction company that builds these ugly towers, as the local swiftlet population suddenly has an awful lot of new accommodation to choose from.

up to the roof of the cave, where intrepid *chao ley* harvesters spend the day scraping the unfeasibly valuable nests made by tiny sea swifts off the rockface, for export to specialist Chinese restaurants all over the world.

ARRIVAL AND DEPARTURE

KO PHI PHI DON

Tour agents in Phuket, Ao Nang, Krabi town and Ko Lanta all organize snorkelling day-trips to Phi Phi Don and Phi Phi Leh. Touts and bungalow staff always meet the ferries at the pier in Ton Sai; if you've pre-booked accommodation your luggage will usually be transported in a handcart. There are also boat transfers to Ko Jum (see p.382), which can be arranged, for example, through Parntawan Tour, a helpful travel agent on the main alley running east of the pier in Ton Sai village (☎ 075 601412), who can also book bus tickets on the mainland.

To/from Phuket Several companies run large, crowded ferries from Rassada Harbour (see p.322) in Phuket to Ko Phi Phi Don twice daily in high season (currently 8.30am & 1.30pm; 2hr), and there's at least one boat a day out of season. From an agent such as Mark Travel in Phuket town (see p.327), prices can start as low as B300 single, B550 return, including transfer from Phuket town. Andaman Wave Master's boats call in at Ao Ton Sai, but continue up the west coast to Laem Tong (B500 single), where the resorts send out longtail boats to pick up guests from the ship. Mark Travel also offers deals such as Phuket–Ko Lanta, breaking the journey on Phi Phi, for B650; Phuket–Phi Phi–Krabi for B650; and Phuket–Phi Phi–Ao Nang/Railay for B800. There's also a daily speedboat from Rassada to Phi Phi (which continues to Ko Lanta), but it costs B1500 for the 50min journey.

To/from Krabi From Krabi Passenger Port, there are boats to Phi Phi daily year-round, with at least four a day in high season (2hr; B350–400). You can also reach Phi Phi by once-daily ferries from Ao Nang, via West Railay (2hr 30min; B450), which are year-round in theory though they sometimes don't run in the monsoon season.

To/from Ko Lanta Yai From Ban Sala Dan on Ko Lanta Yai, there are two daily departures to Ko Phi Phi in high season (1hr 30min; B400).

GETTING AROUND

It's possible to **walk** along the paths across the steep and at times rugged interior (see p.373). There are only a few short motorbike tracks and one road, from the back of Ton Sai village to *The Beach Resort* on Long Beach, which takes around forty minutes on foot.

By boat From Ao Ton Sai, east of the main pier, you can catch a longtail to any of the other beaches, which range in price from B100 per person (minimum two people) to Hat Yao, to B1000 per boat to Laem Tong; prices often double after dark. The Andaman Wave Master ferry (see opposite) and a smaller shuttle boat each run twice a day between Ton Sai and the east-coast bays as far as Laem Tong (both B200). You could also get about by kayak (B700 per day from in front of *Slinky Bar* on Ao Loh Dalum), which is the perfect way to explore the limestone cliffs and secluded bays, without the roar of an accompanying longtail or cruise ship.

ACCOMMODATION

As demand for accommodation frequently outstrips supply on Phi Phi, if you haven't made a reservation, it's worth using the agents' booking service at the pier head, where pictures and – genuine – room prices for hotels in all categories are posted for easy browsing; staff then call ahead to secure your room, and might even carry your bag there. Be warned though that rooms are very expensive on Phi Phi, and often poorly maintained. We've quoted rates for high season, which runs from November to April, but most places slap on a thirty- to fifty-percent surcharge during Christmas and New Year and, conversely, will discount up to fifty percent in quiet periods between May and October.

TON SAI VILLAGE AND AO LOH DALUM

Ton Sai hotels are the least good value on the island and almost none, however expensive, is out of earshot of the thumping all-night beats cranked up by the various bars and clubs; bring some heavy-duty earplugs if you're not planning to party every night.

★ **Chunut House** Turn right at The Rock and walk for about 5min back towards Laem Hin ☏ 075 601227, ⓦ phiphichunuthouse.com. Very welcoming, relaxing place in a leafy, sloping garden, in a relatively quiet location. Big, stylish, thatched cottages come with a/c, free wi-fi, flat-screen TVs, mini-bars and spacious, attractive, hot-water bathrooms. The owners have recently opened a similar branch, *Hin Puu Village*, on the slopes above Loh Dalum, about 10min walk beyond *Phi Phi Viewpoint*. Breakfast included. B2300

Phi Phi Inn Straight ahead from the pier next to the landmark Phi Phi Hotel ☏ 081 797 2088, ⓔ phiphi_inn @hotmail.com. Small, sparklingly clean hotel in a white clapboard house, where all fifteen rooms have a/c, TVs, hot showers, mini-bars, safety boxes and balconies, though only the upstairs ones have the chance of a view and also enjoy more privacy. Free wi-fi. B1650

Phi Phi Island Cabana Hotel West of the pier on Ton Sai ☏ 075 601170–7, ⓦ phiphi-cabana.com. The views from the contemporary rooms at this large, imposing hotel are breathtakingly lovely. Most look out across the scoop of Ao Loh Dalum and its framing cliffs, and ground-floor ones have direct access to the sand. There's a huge pool too. On the minus side, the hotel lacks atmosphere, has a cavernous restaurant and some rooms are affected by late-night club noise. B8000

The Rock ☏ 081 607 3897 or ☏ 075 601021. Traveller-oriented hangout behind a landmark bar-restaurant, offering the cheapest beds on the island, in large mixed-sex dorms; up to seventeen bunk beds are crammed in each, but there are fans and lockers. Also has a few singles (B400) and doubles with shared, cold-water bathrooms. Dorm B300, double B800

Tropical Garden Beyond the turn-off for the path to the viewpoint ☏ 081 968 1436, ⓦ thailandphiphitravel.com. Here you'll find a wide variety of rooms and good-sized rough-timber bungalows, which are mostly built on stilts up the side of an outcrop. The better ones have a breezy veranda (though not much of a view) and there's a refreshing amount of greenery around, plus a small pool, despite being surrounded by other accommodation. Free wi-fi, book exchange and crafts shop. Fan B1000, a/c B1600

US Guest House Close to the base of the viewpoint access steps ☏ 075 601400, ⓔ jo_uspp @hotmail.com. This functional two-storey block with wi-fi throughout has the look and feel of a city guesthouse, and offers some of the cheaper en-suite rooms in the area, as well as a/c versions with hot water and TV. Interiors aren't bad at all and there's a long shared deck with seating beside the narrow lane. Fan B800, a/c B1500

Viewpoint Bungalows ☏ 075 601200, ⓦ phiphi viewpoint.com. Strung out across and up the cliffside at the far eastern end of Ao Loh Dalum, the rooms and bungalows here enjoy great views over the bay, though interiors are nothing to write home about and the all-night bars are too near to ignore. Facilities include a scenically sited restaurant, a tour desk and a small, idyllically situated, infinity-edged bayview pool. Breakfast included. Fan B1600, a/c B2500

LAEM HIN

Bay View Resort ☏ 075 601127, ⓦ phiphibayview .com. The draw at the seventy large, a/c bungalows here is

4

their prime location: they're set high on the cliffside at the far eastern end of Laem Hin beach, strung out along the ridge almost as far as Hat Yao. All have massive windows and decks to enjoy the great views and there's a pool here too. Be prepared for lots of steps though. Breakfast included. **B3600**

Gypsy Village About 150m down the track between the mosque and Phi Phi Andaman Legacy ☎075 601045, ⍟krabidir.com/ppgypsyvillage. The thirty plain and pretty shabby pink-painted concrete bungalows here are relatively cheap, but they're all en suite and fan-cooled, and are set round a big dry lawn. **B900**

Phi Phi Andaman Legacy ☎075 601106, ⍟ppandamanlegacy.com. Set in a secluded enclosure just a few metres back from the beach, the rather old-fashioned bungalows here are arranged in a square around a large lawn and small central swimming pool, while the 36 more modern rooms occupy a three-storey hotel building at the back. All rooms are a/c and come with TVs, hot water, fridges, wi-fi and safety boxes. Breakfast included. **B2090**

Phi Phi Villa Resort ☎075 601100, ⍟phiphivilla resort.com. The best of the many options at this outfit are the huge a/c family cottages occupying the front section of the prettily landscaped garden, near the pool. Also available are smaller bungalows and stylish new rooms in an annexe set back from the beach, all with a/c, hot water, fridge, TV and payable wi-fi. Breakfast included. **B3100**

LONG BEACH (HAT YAO)

The Beach Resort ☎075 819206, ⍟phiphithebeach .com. Currently the poshest option on Hat Yao, this place has a throng of large, timber-clad chalets built on stilts up the hillside, with the tallest, most deluxe ones enjoying commanding views of Phi Phi Leh. Interiors are fairly upscale, with a/c and liberal use of wood for flooring and wall panels. There's wi-fi and a small beachfront pool. **B4300**

Long Beach Bungalows ☎086 470 8984, ✉longbeach@gmail.com. The first choice of most budget travellers, this relatively cheap, well-located and long-running option has dozens of tightly packed huts for rent, ranging from simple, clean bamboo huts with fans, mosquito nets and cold-water bathrooms, to smart beachfront cottages with hot water. The room price includes a B100 food and drinks voucher for the restaurant, and there are discounts for divers (see p.373). **B1000**

Phi Phi Paradise Pearl Resort ☎075 601246, ⍟phiphiparadisepearl.com. The 35 bungalows and rooms at this efficiently run place are fairly well spaced along the western half of the beach, with none more than a few steps from the shore. Interiors are unremarkable but perfectly comfortable and all have a/c, hot water and verandas. There's internet access here, plus a tour counter;

free longtail pick-ups from the pier are offered. Breakfast included. **B3000**

Viking Nature Resort ☎075 819399, ⍟vikingnature resort.com. Tucked away on and above two private little coves just west of Hat Yao, with easy access via a rocky path, this is a very stylish take on classic Thai beach-bungalow architecture. It's nearly all wood and bamboo here, with no a/c, but interiors are styled with Asian boho-chic artefacts. The most glamorous accommodation is in the enormous, high-level, one- to four-bedroom "Makmai" tree houses, with their massive living-room decks overlooking the bay. There's a stylish lounge and dining area on the beach, with wi-fi; kayaks and snorkels are available. **B1500**

AO TOH KO

★ **Ao Toh Ko Beach Resort** ☎081 537 0528, ⍟www .tohkobeachresort.com. The exceptionally welcoming family who run this place keep people staying and returning – and they're great cooks too. The comfortable accommodation varies from attractive, breezy, en-suite, bamboo huts with mossie nets, some sitting right over the sea on the rocks, to smart, bright, concrete bungalows with a/c, hot water, fridge and TV. Kayaks and snorkels for rent. Fan **B1800**, a/c **B2500**

HAT RANTEE

Rantee Beach Resort ☎089 725 4411, ⍟krabidir .com/ranteeresort. At this shady resort, you can choose between en-suite, thatched, bamboo huts and spacious, arched, Bali-style villas with a/c, hot showers and TV. Kayaks and internet access are available, while transfers from the pier cost B200 per person. Breakfast included. Fan **B1800**, a/c **B2900**

HAT PAK NAM

Phi Phi Relax Beach Resort ☎089 725 4411, ⍟phiphirelaxbeach.com. Rustic but comfortable and very welcoming accommodation, in 51 attractive, en-suite wood and bamboo bungalows, set in rows in among the beachfront trees. Internet access, kayaks and pick-ups from the pier twice a day (B150 per person). **B1800**

AO LOH BAKAO

Phi Phi Island Village Beach Resort and Spa ☎075 628999, ⍟ppisland.com. This plush, a/c resort on a lovely beach is a popular honeymoon spot, and a great location for anyone looking for a quiet, comfortable break. The thatched, split-bamboo bungalows and pool villas are mostly designed in traditional Thai style and furnished with character and elegance. There's a large pool and a spa in the prettily landscaped tropical gardens, as well as a dive centre. The resort was about to be taken over by the luxury Outrigger group at the time of writing, so prices may go up. **B8300**

LAEM TONG

Holiday Inn Resort Phi Phi Island ☎075 627300, ⊕phiphi.holidayinn.com. The *Holiday Inn* enjoys nearly a kilometre of beachfront at the southern end of the bay, but its 120 deluxe a/c bungalows and spacious, balconied, sea-view rooms (all with wi-fi and DVD players) are nicely hidden by the shoreline trees and sit in graceful gardens of tidy lawns and flowering shrubs. There's a popular sunset bar at the top of the ridge, two swimming pools, a dive centre, a massage pavilion and tennis courts, and cooking classes, free kayaks and snorkelling equipment are available. **B7000**

Phi Phi Natural Resort ☎075 819030–1, ⊕phiphi natural.com. Up at the northern end of the bay, the a/c rooms, wooden chalets and pool villas here are scattered around an extensive tropical shorefront garden, with pool, that stretches along the coast to the next tiny uninhabited bay. All come with a/c, TV, mini-bar, hot water, free breakfast and a fairly traditional Thai-style decor. **B3600**

EATING

Ton Sai is the best place to eat on the island; elsewhere, visitors tend to eat at their resort's restaurant.

TON SAI VILLAGE

Cosmic East of the pier, on the fourth north–south alley, heading north from the yellow Phi Phi Divers shop. Popular, well-priced pasta, including home-made ravioli and gnocchi (B150), and pizzas (B150). Daily 8am–10.30pm.

Elite On the main alley running east from the pier. A/c café serving delicious Italian ice cream made in Phuket (from B80 for one scoop) and excellent Illy espressos. Daily 10am–10pm.

Le Grand Bleu Just east of the pier on the main east–west alley. Classy place serving a French-inspired menu that includes lots of fresh seafood, including risotto with scallops (B190), sirloin steak and changing dishes of the day. Daily 6.30–10.30pm.

Lemongrass East of the pier, on the first north–south alley. Friendly, basic restaurant with an open kitchen, serving very tasty Thai standards, starting with chicken fried rice for B80. Daily 10/10.30am–10.30/11pm.

Madame Restaurant East of the pier, off the fourth north–south alley, on the main route heading towards The Rock. Deservedly popular for its curries – *phanaeng, matsaman,* green and red – mostly B80. Also offers thin-crust pizzas and a decent vegetarian selection, as well as Western breakfasts and espresso coffees. Daily 8am–11pm.

Papaya East of the pier, just off the fourth north–south alley. One of the best of several village-style kitchens whose authentic and reasonably cheap Thai standards, including noodle soups, *phat thai*, fried rice dishes and fiery curries (B150), make it very popular with locals and dive staff. Daily 3pm–1am.

Patcharee Bakery On the main alley running east from the pier. This place and *Pee Pee Bakery* square up to each other across the narrow alley, vying for the breakfast trade. Croissants – plain, chocolate (B25), almond or savoury – are the thing here, washed down with espresso coffees. Daily 7am–8pm.

Pee Pee Bakery On the main alley running east from the pier, opposite Patcharee Bakery. Good choice for breakfast or lunch, with espresso coffees, set breakfasts (from B100), sandwiches and piles of home-made breads, cakes and cookies. Daily 7am–5pm.

Pum East of the pier, on the fourth north–south alley ☎081 521 8904, ⊕pumthaifoodchain.com. Small, comfy, contemporary chain restaurant, serving basic Thai dishes, such as noodles (B89), fried rice and curries, in some strange combinations that sometimes work. They also offer cooking classes at their school on the next alley west for B1200 for 3hr. Daily 11am–9pm.

NIGHTLIFE AND ENTERTAINMENT

TON SAI VILLAGE AND AO LOH DALUM

Concentrated on the beach at Loh Dalum, Ton Sai nightlife is young and drunken, involving endless buckets of Sansom and red bull, dance music played until dawn, and fire-juggling shows on the beach. Most of the bars offer a pretty similar formula, so it's often the one-off events and happy hours that make the difference.

Reggae Bar East of the pier, off the fourth north–south alley, on the main route heading towards The Rock. A Phi Phi institution in the heart of the village that's been running for years in various incarnations. These days it arranges regular amateur *muay thai* bouts in its boxing ring at around 9pm – "beat up your friend and win free buckets" – and has pool tables and a bar around the sides. There's even reggae karaoke. Daily roughly 10am–1am.

Slinky Towards the east end of Loh Dalum, where the left fork just before The Rock hits the beach. The messy, throbbing heart of Phi Phi nightlife, with a booming sound system, fire shows, and buckets and buckets of booze. Daily 6pm–late.

Stones Bar On the beach at the east end of Loh Dalum. One of the bars of the moment, with dozens of nifty red, gold and green axe cushions scattered on the beach and on platforms under the trees, and a DJ station in a treehouse. Claims to be open 24hr.

Sunflower Bar On the beach at the east end of Loh Dalum. Timber-built chillout spot with tables, axe cushions and plants strewn around the garden, plus great views, good music, free wi-fi and a pool table. Happy hour daily 5.30–8.30pm. Daily roughly 10am–2pm.

4

DIRECTORY

ATMs and exchange Plenty of machines in Ton Sai village, including next to the Siam Commercial Bank exchange counter (daily 9am–8.30pm), on the main alley running east of the pier.

Hospital Phi Phi Hospital (☎075 622151 or ☎081 270 4481), at the western end of Ao Ton Sai.

Police As well as a police station (☎075 611177), next to *Carlito's Bar* on the main alley running east of the pier, out towards Laem Hin, there's a tourist policeman on Phi Phi (☎1155), who's looking for new premises, probably just west of the pier near the *Phi Phi Island Cabana Hotel*.

Ko Jum

Situated halfway between Krabi and Ko Lanta Yai, **KO JUM** (whose northern half is known as **Ko Pu**) is the sort of laidback spot that people come to for a couple of days, then can't bring themselves to leave. Though there's plenty of accommodation on the island, there's nothing more than a handful of beach bars for evening entertainment, and little to do during the day except try out the half-dozen west-coast beaches. The beaches may not be pristine, and are in some places unswimmably rocky at low tide, but they're mostly long and wild, and all but empty of people. Nights are also low-key: it's paraffin lamps and starlight after about 11pm (or earlier) at those places that are off the main grid, and many don't even provide fans as island breezes are sufficiently cooling.

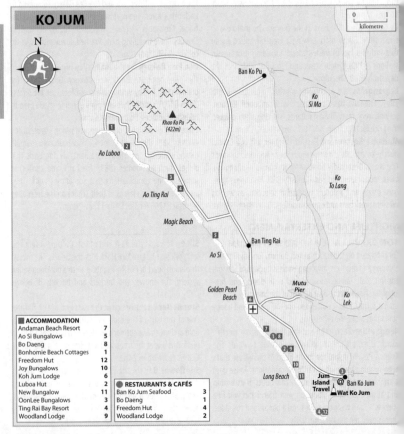

■ ACCOMMODATION	
Andaman Beach Resort	7
Ao Si Bungalows	5
Bo Daeng	8
Bonhomie Beach Cottages	1
Freedom Hut	12
Joy Bungalows	10
Koh Jum Lodge	6
Luboa Hut	2
New Bungalow	11
OonLee Bungalows	3
Ting Rai Bay Resort	4
Woodland Lodge	9

● RESTAURANTS & CAFÉS	
Ban Ko Jum Seafood	3
Bo Daeng	1
Freedom Hut	4
Woodland Lodge	2

ACTIVITIES ON KO JUM

Most bungalows can organize **day-trips**, as will tour agencies in Ban Ko Jum, for example to Ko Phi Phi, Bamboo Island and Mosquito Island (about B3500–4000 per boat), or around Ko Jum (B2500 per boat). Many offer guided hikes up **Khao Ko Pu** (about B1000, including lunch). Ko Jum Divers, at *Ko Jum Beach Villas* at the north end of Long Beach (☎082 273 7603, ⓦkohjum-divers.com), run daily **dive** trips to Ko Phi Phi (B4200), with snorkellers welcome (B2100), and diving courses on offer (Discover Scuba B4900; Openwater B14,900).

The island is home to around three thousand people, the majority of them Muslim, though there are also communities of *chao ley* sea gypsies on Ko Jum (see p.304), as well as Buddhists. The main village is **Ban Ko Jum**, on the island's southeastern tip, comprising a few local shops and small restaurants, one of the island's three piers for boats to and from Laem Kruat on the mainland, and a beachfront school. It's about 1km from the village to the southern end of the island's most popular beach, the appropriately named **Long Beach**. Long Beach is connected to **Golden Pearl Beach**, which sits just south of **Ban Ting Rai**, the middle-island village that's about halfway down the west coast. North of Ban Ting Rai, a trio of smaller, increasingly remote beaches at **Ao Si**, **Ao Ting Rai**, and **Ao Luboa** complete the picture. The island's third village, **Ban Ko Pu**, occupies the northeastern tip, about 5km beyond Ban Ting Rai, and has another Laem Kruat ferry pier. Many islanders refer to the north of the island, from Ban Ting Rai upwards, as Ko Pu, and define only the south as Ko Jum. Much of the north is made inaccessible by the breastbone of forested hills, whose highest peak (422m) is Khao Ko Pu.

Very high winds and heavy seas mean that Ko Jum becomes an acquired taste from May through October, so nearly all accommodation and restaurants **close** for that period: the few exceptions are highlighted in the text.

Long Beach and Golden Pearl Beach

LONG BEACH (sometimes known as **Andaman Beach**) is the main backpackers' beach and is indeed long – at around 2.5km – with large chunks of the shoreline still uncultivated, backed with trees and wilderness, and well beyond sight of the island road. From *New Bungalow* towards the southern end it's a twenty-minute walk into Ban Ko Jum village.

At its northern end, Long Beach segues into **GOLDEN PEARL BEACH**, which is about 750m/fifteen minutes' walk north up the beach from *Bo Daeng*, 5km by road from Ban Ko Jum and 1km south of Ban Ting Rai. Like Long Beach, it also has only a few bungalow outfits along its curving shoreline, though these are close by the island road.

Ao Si

Around the rocky headland from Golden Pearl Beach, accessible in ten minutes at low tide or quite a bit further by road, long and beautifully uncluttered **AO SI** is good for swimming. There are a few places to stay, and a big troupe of monkeys makes its home here too. A ten-minute walk through the rubber trees from the uppermost of *Ao Si*'s bungalows brings you to Magic Beach, just south of Ao Ting Rai.

Ban Ting Rai, Khao Ko Pu and Ao Ting Rai

The road begins to climb as soon as you leave Golden Pearl Beach, taking you up through the ribbon-like village of **Ban Ting Rai**, pretty with bougainvillea and wooden houses, and location of a few small restaurants and noodle shops. **Khao Ko Pu** which rises in the distance is, at 422m, the island's highest mountain and home to macaques that sometimes come down to forage on the rocks around the northern beaches; guided treks up the eastern flank to the summit take about an hour and reward you with fine 360-degree panoramas encompassing the entire island, the mainland and the outer islands.

The little bay of **AO TING RAI**, sometimes known as **Hat Kidon**, has some nice places to stay and good snorkelling off its shore, with reef to explore and plenty of fish. At low tide it's too rocky for swimming though, when you'll need either to pick your way over the rocks, rent a kayak, or walk south 500m along the coastal road, to get to the little sandy crescent known as **Magic Beach**, which is swimmable at any tide. You can walk to Ao Ting Rai from Ao Si in about twenty minutes along the coast road.

Ao Luboa

Ko Jum's peaceful northernmost beach, **AO LUBOA**, feels remote. It's accessed chiefly by a loop in the main island road that circles the northeastern slopes of Khao Ko Pu and terminates at the north end of the bay, though the steeply undulating coast road from Ao Ting Rai can also be walked (about 45min from *OonLee Bungalows*). Like Ao Ting Rai, Ao Luboa's shorefront reef gets exposed at low tide, making it impossible to swim, though at high water things are fine and it's anyway a supremely quiet, laidback beach with just a few bungalows.

ARRIVAL AND DEPARTURE   KO JUM

To/from Krabi/Ko Lanta During high season, usual access to Ko Jum is via the Krabi–Ko Lanta ferry (daily; 1hr 30min–2hr from Krabi, currently leaving at 11am, or about 45min from Ko Lanta, currently leaving at 8am; B400). Ko Jum bungalows send longtails out to meet the ferries as they make two stops off the west coast: coming from Krabi, stop one is for the northern "*Ko Pu*" bungalows (on Ao Ting Rai and Ao Luboa) and the second, "Ko Jum", stop is for bungalows on *Ao Si, Golden Pearl* and *Long Beach*.

To/from Ko Phi Phi This service isn't set in stone, but there should be a boat from Ton Sai to Ko Jum every afternoon in high season (1hr 30min; B500) – ask at Parntawan Tour (see p.376).

To/from Laem Kruat In the rainy season you have to travel to Ko Jum overland, and an increasing number of

visitors now use this route year-round; some bungalow operators, for example, offer transfers from Krabi airport using this route (about B800 per car to Laem Kruat). Coming from Krabi town, you need to take a blue songthaew, passing the airport, either all the way through to Laem Kruat (B100) or changing in Nua Klong. Boats run from Laem Kruat to all three east-coast "village" piers on Ko Jum (45min–1hr; B50–70), from where a motorbike taxi with sidecar (best arranged in advance through your resort) will transfer you to your bungalow, charging from B50 per person. Boats to Ban Ko Pu depart Laem Kruat about every two hours during the day, while the thrice-daily services to Mutu and Ban Ko Jum are mostly in the afternoon, timed for shoppers and traders to return to the island.

GETTING AROUND

Most bungalows can arrange **kayak** (about B600 per day) and **motorbike** (about B350 per day) rental, while *Bo Daeng* has mountain bikes (B120 per day). The main island road is slowly being paved north from Ban Ko Jum, but the track on the west side of Khao Ko Pu remains a bumpy nightmare.

INFORMATION

For a comprehensive **guide** to life on the island and pictures of all the bungalow operations, see ⓦ kohjumonline.com.

ACCOMMODATION

LONG BEACH

Accommodation on Long Beach is in three clusters, each about 15min' walk apart.

Andaman Beach Resort ☏089 724 1544, ✉andaman_kohjum@yahoo.com. You can't miss the steeply roofed concrete bungalows at this friendly, well-run place, painted in shocking pink, yellow and other

"lucky" colours like gingerbread houses, complete with false first-floor windows. Set in a pleasant garden, they're all bright, clean and en suite with mosquito screens and terraces, and are priced according to size and proximity to the beach (rising to B3000 for a big, a/c, beachfront pad with hot water and breakfast). The food's good and reasonably priced, too. B350

Bo Daeng ☎ 081 494 8760. This funky, ultra-cheap and ultra-basic travellers' classic is run by a famously welcoming charismatic island *chao ley* family and has legendary food. The rudimentary bamboo huts come with or without private bathrooms – the latter are among the very cheapest on the island, but all have nets and electricity during the evening. Open all year. Shared bathroom B150, en suite B200

Freedom Hut ☎ 084 991 0881 or ☎ 084 746 2964, ✉ yakohjum@hotmail.co.th. Large, beautifully simple, thatched bungalows (including a treehouse) in rustic-contemporary style, way off on their own at the southernmost point, with loads of space for hammocks and chairs on the deck. Some have nice outdoor rock bathrooms, and one occupies an unparalleled spot on a tiny rocky promontory, with awesome 360-degree sea views (B3000). B500

Joy Bungalows ☎ 075 618199, ⓦ kohjum-joybungalow .com. This is the longest-running and most famous place to stay on the island, though not necessarily the friendliest. It has a big spread of accommodation set in a very shady grove of trees behind the shorefront, the majority of them smart wooden bungalows in varying sizes and proximity to the sea, plus some cheaper thatched ones and two-bedroom houses. The resort has electricity but not the bungalows, so it's paraffin lamps all round at night. B650

New Bungalow ☎ 075 618116, ✉ nbkohjum @hotmail.com. The two-dozen differently styled bungalows at this friendly, long-established place include a few cheapie bamboo ones with and without private bathrooms, some plain, en-suite wooden huts, and a couple of treehouses set 5m or so up in the branches by the beach, with idyllic sea views and shared bathrooms. Electricity evenings only. Shared bathroom B200, en-suite B300, treehouse B400

★ **Woodland Lodge** ☎ 081 893 5330, ⓦ woodland -koh-jum.com. Welcoming, helpful and peaceful spot owned by a UK–Thai couple and one of the few places on the island to stay open year-round (with big discounts in the rainy season). Its large, attractive, well-designed bungalows with 24hr electricity are widely set beneath the trees of its shorefront garden and all have good, spacious bathrooms; the doubles have platform beds, mosquito nets, varnished wooden floors and deep shady decks, while the bigger ones are designed for families. B1000

GOLDEN PEARL BEACH

Koh Jum Lodge ☎ 089 921 1621, ⓦ kohjumlodge .com. This French–Thai place is one of the most upscale resorts on the island, with nineteen thatched wooden

chalets designed in charming rustic-chic style. Thoughtfully constructed to make the most of the island breezes, they have doors onto the veranda to avoid the need for a/c, plus low beds and elegantly simple furniture. The resort has a small pool, internet access, a TV and DVD area, a massage service and a restaurant. Minimum stay four nights, seven in peak season. Breakfast included. B5000

AO SI

Ao Si Bungalows ☎ 081 747 2664, ⓦ aosibungalow .com. On Ao Si's northern headland, the woven-bamboo, en-suite bungalows here are built on piles up the side of the cliff and have wrap-around verandas for soaking up the commanding views of the bay and the southern half of the island. B500

AO TING RAI

OonLee Bungalows ☎ 087 200 8053, ⓦ kohjumoonlee bungalows.com. Small, enthusiastically run and well-liked French–Thai place with sturdy accommodation in various styles stacked up the cliffside. The wooden bungalows have plenty of storage, appealing bathrooms and sea-view verandas; there's a stylish upper-level lounge area and good restaurant, and a bar and massage area at beach level, plus kayaks for rent and free snorkels for guests. *OonLee* offers lots of organized activities and tours, including guided half-day treks up Khao Ko Pu and fishing trips. B600

Ting Rai Bay Resort ☎ 087 277 7379, ⓦ tingrai.com. Popular spot whose nicely designed wooden bungalows are ranged up the sloping shorefront on stilts, most offering fine views from capacious decks (especially the "honeymoon" ones). Interiors have fans, four-poster style beds, and plenty of attention to detail. The food here is also good and there's internet access. B600

AO LUBOA

Bonhomie Beach Cottages ☎ 086 560 7977, ⓦ bonhomiebeach.com. At the far northern end of the beach, very large, attractively designed en-suite wooden chalets with mosquito nets, many with sea view; price depends on proximity to the sea. B700

Luboa Hut ☎ 081 388 9241, ⓦ luboahut.com. Friendly establishment with ten en-suite bamboo and wooden bungalows with sea views from their verandas in a well-shaded spot under shoreside trees; many of them are roomy and good quality, some have extra beds or sofas and all have mosquito nets. The owners offer free kayaks, cooking classes and internet. B500

EATING AND DRINKING

LONG BEACH

★ **Bo Daeng** For an outstanding Thai meal, at some of the cheapest prices on the island, you should join the (sometimes

lengthy) queue here, whose highlights include baked fish, vegetable tempura (B80), curries including southern yellow curry (B80), plus Thai desserts, home-baked bread and

4

coconut shakes. Daily 7.30am–9pm.

Freedom Hut Many people round off the night with a drink around the camp fire at this easy-going place, right down at the bottom end of Long Beach. Choose between cocktails, wine and cheapish beer; an espresso machine and pizza oven are planned. Daily 7.30am–12.30am.

Woodland Lodge Delicious curries – try the Indian curry with prawns (B200) – plenty of choice for vegetarians, including tasty vegetable tempura (B80), plus Western food, including breakfast and fish and chips. Daily roughly 7am–8.30/9pm.

BAN KO JUM

Ban Ko Jum Seafood ☎ 081 893 6380. The big name here is this very popular and very good restaurant, whose tables occupy a scenically sited jetty near the pier, and enjoy fine views across the mangrove channel. Among its big menu of fresh seafood cooked any number of ways (B100–400), the juicy fat prawns barbecued with honey are a standout, and their crab and lobster dishes are famous too. Daily 9am–10pm.

DIRECTORY

Clinic The island medical centre is on the road near *Ko Jum Lodge*, beyond the southern edge of Ban Ting Rai.

Exchange There's no ATM on the island, so it's best to bring all the cash you'll need with you. At a pinch, you can change money at Jum Island Travel, next to the pier in Ban Ko Jum, at expensive rates.

Internet access In Ban Ko Jum and at one or more of the hotels on almost every beach.

Ko Lanta Yai

Although **KO LANTA YAI** can't quite compete with Phi Phi's stupendous scenery, the thickly forested 25km-long island has the longest beaches in the Krabi area – and plenty of them. There's decent snorkelling and diving nearby, plus caves to explore, kayaking and other watersports, so many tourists base themselves here for their entire holiday fortnight. The island is especially popular with families, in part because of the local laws that have so far prevented jet-skis, beachfront parasols and girlie bars from turning it into another Phuket, though resort facilities are expanding fast. Lanta is also rapidly being colonized by Scandinavian expats, with villa homes and associated businesses popping up all over the place, at a pace that not all islanders are happy about. The majority of Ko Lanta Yai's ten thousand indigenous residents are mixed-blood descendants of Muslim Chinese–Malay or animist *chao ley* ("sea gypsy") peoples (see box, p.304), most of whom supported themselves by fishing and cultivating the land before the tourist boom brought new jobs, and challenges.

One of those challenges is that the **tourist season** is quite short, with the weather and seas at their calmest and safest from November to April; the main ferries don't run outside that period, and some hotels close, though most do stay open and offer huge discounts. The short money-making window, however, means that accommodation prices on Ko Lanta fluctuate more wildly than many other south Thailand destinations.

The local *chao ley* name for Ko Lanta Yai is *Pulao Satak*, "Island of Long Beaches", an apt description of the string of beaches along the **west coast**, each separated by

---

LANTA FESTIVALS

Every March, Ko Lanta Yai celebrates its rich ethnic heritage at the **Laanta Lanta Festival** (*laanta* meaning roughly "eye-dazzling"), which is held over five days in Lanta Old Town and features both traditional and modern music and entertainments, countless specialist foodstalls and crafts for sale (check ⓦ lantaoldtown.com for dates and specifics). Traditional *chao ley* rituals are celebrated on Ko Lanta twice a year, on the full moons of the sixth and eleventh lunar months – usually June and Oct/Nov (see p.389). Meanwhile, the Chinese shrine in Lanta Old Town is the focus of the island's version of the **Vegetarian Festival** (see p.325), which involves processions, cultural performances and walking on hot coals.

KO LANTA

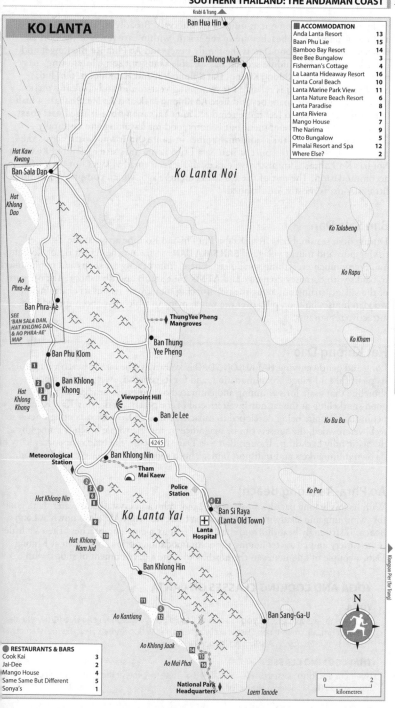

Krabi & Trang ▲

Ban Hua Hin ●

Ban Khlong Mark ●

Ko Lanta Noi

Hat Kaw Kwang

Ban Sala Dan ●

Hat Khlong Dao

Ko Talabeng

Ko Rapu

Ao Phra-Ae

Ban Phra-Ae ●

SEE 'BAN SALA DAN, HAT KHLONG DAO & AO PHRA-AE' MAP

ThungYee Pheng Mangroves

Ban Thung Yee Pheng ●

Ko Kham

4

Ban Phu Klom ●

1

Ban Khlong Khong ●

2
3
1
4

Viewpoint Hill

Ban Je Lee ●

Ko Bu Bu

Hat Khlong Khong

4245

Meteorological Station

Ban Khlong Nin ●

Tham Mai Kaew

Police Station

6 7

Ban Si Raya (Lanta Old Town)

Ko Por

2
5
3
6

Hat Khlong Nin

Lanta Hospital

Ko Lanta Yai

9

Hat Khlong Nam Jud

10

Ban Khlong Hin ●

Ban Sang-Ga-U ●

11

Ao Kantiang

5
12

13

Ao Khlong Jaak

14
15
16

Ao Mai Phai

N

● Ban Sang-Ga-U

Klongson Pier (for Trang) ▶

National Park Headquarters

Laem Tanode

0   2
kilometres

rocky points and strung out at quite wide intervals. Broadly speaking, the busiest and most mainstream beaches are in the north, within easy reach of the port at **Ban Sala Dan**: Hat Khlong Dao is the family beach and **Ao Phra-Ae** the longer and more beautiful. The middle section has variable sands but some interesting, artsy places to stay, at **Hat Khlong Khong**, **Hat Khlong Nin** and **Hat Khlong Nam Jud**. Southerly **Ao Kantiang** is reliable for swimming year-round and currently marks the end of the made road; beyond here **Ao Khlong Jaak** and **Ao Mai Phai** are a little harder to get to and so feel more remote. Lanta Yai's mangrove-fringed **east coast** has no real tourist development but is both good for kayaking and culturally interesting because of the traditional homes in **Lanta Old Town**. North across the narrow channel from the port at Ban Sala Dan, Lanta Yai's sister island of **Ko Lanta Noi** has Ko Lanta's administrative offices and several small villages but no tourist accommodation. The rest of the Ko Lanta archipelago, which comprises over fifty little islands, is mostly uninhabited.

Ban Sala Dan

During high season, boats from Krabi, Phi Phi and Ko Lipe arrive at the T-shaped fishing port and tourist village of **BAN SALA DAN**, on the northernmost tip of Ko Lanta Yai. Pretty much everything you'll need is here, from beachwear shops and minimarkets to banks with currency exchange and ATMs, tour agents and dive shops. The old part of the village, strung out along the north-facing shorefront, retains its charming old wooden houses built on piles over the water, many of which have been turned into attractive restaurants.

Hat Khlong Dao

Long and gently curving **HAT KHLONG DAO** is known as "the family beach", both for its plentiful mid-range accommodation, and for its generous sweep of flat sandy shoreline that's safe for swimming and embraced by protective headlands; there's good snorkelling at the far northwestern end of the beach, off the tiny Kaw Kwang peninsula. Despite being developed to capacity, Khlong Dao is broad enough never to feel overcrowded, the sunsets can be magnificent, and the whole beach is framed by a dramatic hilly backdrop. Though Ban Sala Dan is close by, the beach supports plenty of its own minimarkets and transport outlets, both shoreside and along the main road.

Ao Phra-Ae (Long Beach)

With its lovely long parade of soft, white sand, calm and crystal-clear water that's good for swimming and shady fringe of casuarina trees, **AO PHRA-AE** (also known as **Long Beach**) is strikingly beautiful and the best of Lanta's many long beaches. There's a little more variety and character among the accommodation options here than at Khlong Dao, a couple of kilometres to the north, and quite a development of shops, with

---

YOGA AND COOKING CLASSES ON LANTA

YOGA

During high season there are **yoga** classes at *Cha Ba* bungalows on Khlong Dao (ⓦ theretreat thailand.com; also meditation classes and yoga and meditation retreats), but the most famous teacher is at *Relax Bay* on Ao Phra-Ae (ⓦ monayoga.com).

THAI COOKING CLASSES

Five-hour **cooking** classes (B1800) are offered by Time for Lime, at the south end of Hat Khlong Dao (☏ 075 684590, ⓦ timeforlime.net).

SNORKELLING TRIPS AND WATERSPORTS ON LANTA

SNORKELLING TRIPS

The best and most popular **snorkelling** is at the islands of **Ko Rok Nai** and **Ko Rok Nok**, 47km south of Ko Lanta; these forested twins are graced with stunning white-sand beaches and accessible waterfalls and separated by a narrow channel full of fabulous shallow reefs. Also hugely popular is the "**four island**" snorkelling trip that takes in the much nearer islands off Trang – the enclosed emerald lagoon on **Ko Mook** (see p.409), plus nearby **Ko Hai** (Ko Ngai), **Ko Ma** and **Ko Kradan** – but these sites can get very crowded. Another option is the day-trip to **Phi Phi Don**, Phi Phi Leh and Bamboo Island (see p.370). The trips cost around B1500 in a speedboat or B900 in a big boat, including lunch, snorkelling equipment and national park entry fee. For a smaller, more personal experience, contact Sun Island Tours or Freedom Adventures.

DIVING

The **reefs** around Ko Lanta are quieter and in some cases more pristine than those round Phi Phi and Phuket, and excellent for seeing whale sharks. The **diving season** runs from November to April, though a few dive shops continue to run successful trips from May to August. All dive boats depart from Ban Sala Dan, and nearly all dive courses are taught either in Sala Dan or on Hat Khlong Dao, though there are dive shops on every beach.

Some of Lanta's best **dive sites** are located between Ko Lanta and Ko Phi Phi, including the soft coral at **Ko Bidah**, where you get lots of leopard sharks, barracuda and tuna. West and south of Lanta, the **Ko Ha** island group offers four different dives on each of its five islands, including steep drop-offs and an "underwater cathedral" and other caves; visibility is often very good. Much further south, about 56km from Ko Lanta, are **Hin Daeng** and **Hin Muang** (see p.338).

The nearest recompression chambers are located on Phuket (see p.338); check to see that your dive operator is insured to use one of them (see p.51).

KAYAKING

There are several rewarding **kayaking** destinations, rich in mangroves and caves, around Ko Lanta Yai's east coast and around Ko Lanta Noi and its eastern islands, including **Ko Talabeng** and **Ko Bubu**; a few companies also offer kayak-snorkel trips to the four islands described above.

OPERATORS

Freedom Adventures ☎ 084 910 9132, ⌨ freedom-adventures.net. A variety of snorkelling day-trips, as well as overnight camping trips on Ko Rok and Ko Kradan (from B2600).

Ko Lanta Diving Centre On the main road into Ban Sala Dan ☎ 075 668065, ⌨ kolantadivingcenter.com. German-run outfit charging B3000 for two dives, excluding equipment, B1600 for accompanying snorkellers and B15,650 for the Openwater course.

Lanta Diver On the main road into Ban Sala Dan ☎ 075 684208, ⌨ lantadiver.com. Swedish-owned, PADI Five-star Instructor Development Centre charging from B2900 for two dives, excluding equipment, and B14,300 for the Openwater course.

Lanta Garden Hill Speed Boat ☎ 075 684042,

⌨ lantaislandtours.com. One of the main operators of snorkelling trips, which can be booked through any agent on Ko Lanta.

Lanta Kayaking ☎ 081 787 1040. Kayaking trips to Ko Talabeng for B1300, bookable through most travel agents.

Lanta Paddlesports On the main road in Hat Khlong Dao and on several beaches ☎ 075 668096, ⌨ lantapaddlesports.com. Paddleboard lessons, rental and tours, as well as windsurfing, kayaking, surfing and snorkelling trips.

Sun Island Tours ☎ 087 891 6619, ⌨ lantalongtail.com. Various longtail trips to the four islands, around Ko Lanta, and to Lanta's eastern islands (where there's also an overnight camping option), which come very highly rated and cost B1500.

TMs, restaurants and tour agents along the main road. The main stretch of the beach is divided from the southern rocky extremity by a shallow, easily wadeable khlong; *Lanta Marina Resort* marks the southern reaches of the beach and is about half an hour's walk along the beach from *Sayang* at the northern end. Phra-Ae's budget enclave clusters along a network of sandy tracks behind the *Ozone Bar*.

Hat Khlong Khong

The luxuriously long beach at **HAT KHLONG KHONG**, 2km south of Ao Phra-Ae's *Relax Bay Resort*, is peppered with rocks and in most parts only really swimmable at high tide, though the snorkelling is good. Another big draw is the traveller-oriented bungalows, among them the most creatively designed places to stay on the island. There are several funky little beach bars too, notably at *Bee Bee Bungalows*.

Hat Khlong Nin

About 4km south of Hat Khlong Khong the road forks at kilometre-stone 13, at the edge of the village of **Ban Khlong Nin**. The left-hand, east-bound arm runs across to Ko Lanta Yai's east coast, via the caves and viewpoint (see opposite). The right-hand fork is the route to the southern beaches and continues southwards along the west coast for 14km to the southern tip.

Just beyond the junction, the little enclave of bungalows, restaurants, bars and tour agents at **HAT KHLONG NIN** lends this beach more of a village atmosphere than the northern beaches. The beach itself is lovely, long and sandy and good for swimming, though the road runs close alongside it. There are several reasonably priced places to stay here, with the cheapest beds in some hotels located in separate little garden compounds on the inland side of the road, and a low-key collection of shoreside bar-restaurants with plenty of character and mellow vibes.

There are minimarkets, ATMs and a clinic at the Ban Khlong Nin junction, and from here you could walk the 3km to the Tham Mai Kaew caves from Khlong Nin in about an hour.

Hat Khlong Nam Jud

Just over 1km south of Hat Khlong Nin, the road passes the two tiny little bays known as **HAT KHLONG NAM JUD**. The northerly one is the domain of *The Narima* (see p.393). A brief scramble around the rocky point to the south, the next tiny cove is rocky in parts but enjoys a swimmable beach and is home to *Lanta Coral Beach* (see p.393).

Ao Kantiang

The secluded cove of **AO KANTIANG**, some 7km beyond Hat Khlong Nam Jud, is an impressively long curve, backed by jungle-clad hillsides and dominated by one luxury hotel, which keeps the southern half of the beach in pristine condition. Unusually for Lanta, the bay is protected enough to be good for swimming year-round, and there's some coral at the northern end; snorkelling and fishing trips are easily arranged. The small but lively roadside village covers most necessities, including tours, onward transport, motorbike rental and internet access.

Ao Khlong Jaak and Ao Mai Phai

The road beyond Ao Kantiang to Lanta's southern tip, about 4km away, is steeply undulating and rutted, but is slowly being paved. The next bay south of Kantiang is **AO KHLONG JAAK**, site of some accommodation including the lively *Anda Lanta Resort* (see p.394). Though it's not much more than a trickle, the **waterfall** inland from Ao Khlong Jaak can be reached from the bay by walking along the course of the stream for about two hours. South around the next headland, western Lanta plays its final card in the shape of handsome white-sand **AO MAI PHAI**, a peaceful getaway because of its remote position on the largely unmade road. There's good coral close to shore here, but this makes it too rocky for low-tide swimming, when you'll need to kayak up to Ao Khlong Jaak instead.

Tham Mai Kaew caves

3km from the Khlong Nin junction • Two-hour tours available Mon–Thurs, Sat & Sun 9am–4pm, Fri 8–10am & 1.30–4pm (☎ 089 288 8954) • B300, including national park entry fee and head torch • A motorcycle taxi costs about B200 each way from Khlong Dao or Ao Phra-Ae

The myriad chambers at **Tham Mai Kaew caves**, some of which you can only just crawl into, are Ko Lanta's biggest inland attraction. They are filled with stalactites and interesting rock formations, and there's a creepy cave pool too, as well as the inevitable bats. Tours of the cave are given by the local family who first properly explored the cave system in the 1980s; as well as the standard tour they sometimes offer longer cave tours and overnight jungle treks. Most of Thailand's countless caves are underwhelming and certainly not worth B300, but this is one of the better ones, not least because the caretakers have resisted stringing it with electric lights so you're left to wonder both at what you catch with your torch and at what you don't see. Among its star features are crystallized waterfalls, fossils and ammonites embedded in the cave walls and overhangs, stalagmites and stalactites young and old and a tangible sense of there being endless passageways to explore. In the rainy season it's a more slippery, challenging experience, with some wading likely and the option of a dip in the wet-season-only lagoon. Even in the dry season it's moderately arduous and best done in sensible shoes and clothes you're happy to get grubby in.

The viewpoint

3km beyond the turn-off to the Tham Mai Kaew caves • Café daily 8am–8pm

Three kilometres beyond the turn-off to the caves, the eastbound road drops down over the central spine of hills and you pass *Viewpoint* café, where nearly everyone stops for a drink and a gawp at the stunning panorama. The **view over the east coast** is glorious, encompassing the southeast coast of mangrove-fringed Ko Lanta Noi, dozens of islets – including Ko Bubu and Ko Por – adrift in the milky blue sea, and the hilly profile of the mainland along the horizon.

Lanta Old Town (Ban Si Raya)

🌐 lantaoldtown.com

The seductively atmospheric little waterfront settlement of **LANTA OLD TOWN**, officially known as **Ban Si Raya**, is Ko Lanta's oldest town. It began life as a sheltered staging post for ships and served as the island's administrative capital from 1901 to 1998. The government offices have since moved to Ko Lanta Noi, and Ban Sala Dan has assumed the role of harbour, island gateway and commercial hub, so Ban Si Raya has been left much as it was a century ago, with its historic charm intact. There's little more to the Old Town than its peaceful main street, which runs right along the coast parallel to Route 4245 and is lined with traditional, hundred-year-old sea- and wind-blasted wooden homes and shops, many of them constructed on stilted jetties over the sea, their first-floor overhangs shading the pavements and plant-filled doorways. The Chinese shrine midway down the street is evidence of the town's cultural mix: Ban Si Raya is home to a long-established Buddhist Chinese–Thai community as well as to Muslims and, in its southern neighbourhood, communities of animist Urak Lawoy *chao ley* ("sea gypsies").

The **Urak Lawoy** *chao ley* (see box, p.304) are thought to have been Ko Lanta's first inhabitants, perhaps as long as five hundred years ago, living along the shoreline during the monsoon season and setting off along the coast again when the winds abated. They have now settled permanently in their own villages on the island, including at **Ban Sang-Ga-U**, 4km to the south of Lanta Old Town; other Urak Lawoy living elsewhere in the Andaman Sea, around Trang and beyond, consider Ko Lanta their capital and will always stop at Sang-Ga-U when making a journey. One of the accessible elements of Urak Lawoy culture is their **music**, an interesting fusion of far-flung influences, featuring violins (from the Dutch East Indies), drums (from Persia) and gongs (from China), as well as singing, dancing and ritual elements. A good time to hear their music is at one of their twice-yearly three-day full-moon **festivals**, or at the Laanta Lanta Festival (see p.384).

As an additional incentive to linger among the wooden architecture of the main street, there are several browsable **shops** selling batik sarongs and souvenirs, plus the charming Hammock House (ⓦjumbohammock.com), whose amazing range of hammocks includes ones woven by people of the endangered Mrabri tribe of northern Thailand. The hourly Krabi air-conditioned minibus service starts from and terminates in Lanta Old Town.

Koh Lanta Community Museum

Across the small grassy park from the pier and parking lot • Daily 9am–3pm • B40

There's an attempt to introduce the cultures of Ban Si Raya's three distinct but peaceable communities at the **Koh Lanta Community Museum**, which is housed in the attractive 1901 wooden building that used to serve as the local district office. Archive photos and one or two English-language captions describe the main occupations for the communities, including fishing and making charcoal from mangrove wood; you can sometimes watch an interesting video in which villagers air their concerns about the recent explosion in tourism on the island and the effect that the influx of incomers and investors is having on traditional lifestyles and livelihoods.

Thung Yee Pheng mangroves

About 1km north of the junction of Route 4245 and the road across from Ao Phra-Ae, take the right turn for a couple of hundred metres • Daily 8am–4pm • B20

This community tourism project allows you to take a short, not very compelling stroll along a 200m boardwalk out into the mangrove swamps that line Ko Lanta Yai's east coast. More interesting are the one-hour longtail tours available here (B1000 per boat, including guide), and you can also hire a two-person kayak to have a look around (B500/2hr, B300 extra for a guide).

ARRIVAL AND DEPARTURE   KO LANTA YAI

The principal mainland gateways to Ko Lanta are Krabi, Phuket and Trang, all of which have good long-distance bus services, and **airports**. Trang also has a train station, and a new combined boat and road transfer to Lanta run by KK Travel (see p.403): a/c minibus to Klongson pier, north of Pak Meng, followed by speedboat to Lanta Old Town, then free transfers on Lanta (2 daily in high season; roughly 1hr 30min in total; B450, though currently on promotion at B300).

By boat In high season, there are boats to Ko Lanta Yai, as detailed below, from Krabi (B400), via Ko Jum (B400); from Ko Phi Phi (ferry B400, speedboat B600), with connections from Phuket (ferry B800, speedboat B1500); and from Ao Nang (B400) via West Railay (B470). There are also high-season services to Ko Lanta from the Trang islands and Ko Lipe, with connections to Langkawi (see p.406). All of these ferries dock at Ban Sala Dan and are met by bungalow touts who usually transport you to the beach of your choice for free. If you need to use the motorbike sidecar taxi service instead, be warned that drivers will try and charge arrivals way over the normal fares; walk 250m from the pier head to the main road to get a ride at more reasonable rates.

Destinations: Ao Nang, via West Railay (daily; 2hr 30min); Ko Phi Phi Don (2 daily; 1hr 30min); Krabi, via Ko Jum (daily; 2hr 30min); Phuket (1–2 daily; 4hr 30min).

By road The alternative to the ferries is the overland route to Ko Lanta Yai – essential during the rainy season but increasingly popular at any time of year. Access is via Ban Hua Hin on the mainland, 75km south of Krabi, from where a small ferry crosses to Ban Khlong Mark on Ko Lanta Noi, after which there's a 7km drive across to Lanta Noi's southwest tip, then another ferry over the narrow channel to the car-ferry port on Ko Lanta Yai's northeastern coast (though a bridge between Lanta Noi and Lanta Yai is being planned); both ferries run approximately every 20min from about 7am to 10pm (B120 in total per car). This is the route used by a/c minibuses from Krabi town (hourly; 2hr; B250–350 depending on which beach you get dropped at; terminates in Lanta Old Town); from Phuket (9 daily; 5hr; B500); from Trang (roughly hourly; 3hr; B300); and by anyone bringing their own vehicle. On departure from

Lanta, the Krabi minibuses will drop you off at Krabi Airport; on arrival, you'll need to call ☎081 606 3591 to ask them to pick you up at the airport. There's also a daily bus between Ban Hua Hin and Bangkok's Mo Chit bus terminal (12hr), fed by a/c minibuses to and from Ko Lanta Yai.

GETTING AROUND

There's no public transport on the island, but motorbikes are widely available for rent and there are jeeps too.

Share-taxis and songthaews A fleet of motorbike sidecar share-taxis, with drivers in numbered vests, and a few white songthaews operate out of Ban Sala Dan and will go pretty much anywhere on the island, though they usually need to be phoned (by staff at hotels or restaurants) for pick-ups from anywhere outside Sala Dan. Lanta has its share of scamming taxi-drivers, so bear in mind the following approximate per-person rates for rides out of Sala Dan: B40 to Hat Khlong Dao, B60 to Ao Phra-Ae, B90 to Hat Khlong Kong, or about B50 between the above.

ACCOMMODATION

Ko Lanta Yai is extremely popular during high season (Nov–Feb), when it's worth either booking your first night's accommodation in advance or taking up the suggestions of the bungalow touts who ride the boats from the mainland. A confirmed booking also means you should get free transport from the port to your hotel. Accommodation pricing on Ko Lanta is disconcertingly flexible and alters according to the number of tourists on the island: bungalow rates can double between mid-December and mid-January (and some resorts extend their "peak season" to include the whole of January and February), while during the rainy season between May and October rates are vastly discounted.

HAT KHLONG DAO

There are a couple of budget-oriented places to stay on Hat Khlong Dao, but the emphasis is on accommodation for families and others looking for a/c comfort.

Cha-Ba Bungalows ☎075 684118, ⊛krabidir.com /chababungalows. There's plenty of kitsch creativity at this welcoming, idiosyncratic complex of bungalows, set among model dinosaurs and Flintstone boulders. The tightly packed bungalows are simple and flimsy, but cute, decorated with loud retro-look fabrics and wallpapers. Fan ones come with hot showers, while the a/c ones also have TVs, fridges and free breakfasts. There's free wi-fi in the restaurant and some rooms, and a small swimming pool is planned. Fan **B1300**, a/c **B2000**

Costa Lanta ☎075 684630, ⊛costalanta.com. You're either going to love or hate this ultra-brutal minimalist grouping of 22 polished-grey concrete boxes, each bungalow consisting of an unadorned bedroom all in grey and white with a mosquito net, a similarly styled bathroom with rain shower and a large terrace. They're set in a broad garden bisected by khlongs, with a big, sleek pool and a striking bar-restaurant. Breakfast included. **B6200**

Crown Lanta ☎075 626999, ⊛crownlanta.com. Upmarket, German-managed resort on the island's very northwestern tip, where crown motifs feature heavily on the rooftops. The hotel divides into two zones: standard with very large balconies and pool-access rooms near the lobby; up on the hill, villas and another free-form pool, plus a panoramic restaurant, a spa and steps down to a part-sandy, part-rocky private beach. **B6500**

Hans Restaurant ☎075 684152, ⊛krabidir.com /hansrestaurant. By far the cheapest place on this beach, with fifteen huts ranged along a narrow, scruffy strip of garden behind the shorefront restaurant, next to the *Royal Lanta* resort in the heart of the beach. Choose between very simple, rickety bamboo bungalows with mosquito nets and bathrooms, and slightly better-furnished wooden versions. All bungalows are wi-fi accessible. High season only. **B300**

Kaw Kwang Beach Resort At the northernmost end of Khlong Dao ☎075 668260–1, ⊛lanta -kawkwangresort.com. Welcoming, family-run outfit with good-value (for Lanta) rooms, occupying a large area of beachfront land on Hat Kaw Kwang adjacent to *Crown Lanta*. There are many options here, all with hot showers and TVs, from cheap, decent, old-style en-suite wood and concrete huts among the trees above the shore, to bigger, beachside a/c bungalows, family bungalows and hotel-style rooms. Has an infinity-edged pool and wi-fi in some rooms, plus computers for guest use. Snorkel rental and free transfers to and from Sala Dan pier. Fan **B650**, a/c **B1700**

The Noble House ☎075 668096, ⊛lantanoblehouse .com. Appealingly small-scale, Swiss-run place where the inviting a/c bungalows have big glass windows and hot showers. They're set in facing rows, in a pretty shrub-filled garden, mostly around the little swimming pool. Also has a few a/c hotel rooms at the back of the compound. Free wi-fi in the restaurant. Buffet breakfast included. **B2000**

Slow Down ☎083 632 1551, ⊛slowdownlanta.se. This Swedish-run resort at the far southern end of the beach, with a very attractive dark blue pool and kids' pool and a good restaurant, rents out villas and apartments by the week, but also has two hotel rooms (misleadingly called "bungalows"). They're a little dark, but successfully mix Swedish and southern Thai aesthetics, with lots of wood, white walls and wooden-tiled roofs, as well as a/c, hot

4

RESTAURANTS & CAFÉS

Catfish	2
Costa Lanta	3
Faim de Loup	6
Laanta Seafood	1
Red Snapper	7
Sayang Beach Resort	5
Slow Down	4

BARS

Indian Bar	1
Irish Embassy	4
Klapa Klum	3
Ozone Bar	2

ACCOMMODATION

Cha-Ba Bungalows	7
Costa Lanta	3
Crown Lanta	1
Hans Restaurant	5
Kaw Kwang Beach Resort	2
Lanta LD Beach	10
Lanta Marina Resort	14
Lanta Palm Beach	12
Layana	13
The Noble House	4
Relax Bay Resort	15
Sayang Beach Resort	9
Slow Down	8
Somewhere Else	11
Southern Lanta Resort	6

BAN SALA DAN, HAT KHLONG DAO & AO PHRA-AE

water, mini-bars and DVD players. **B2600**
Southern Lanta Resort ☎075 684175–7, ⓦsouthern
lanta.com. One of the biggest hotels on the beach,
offering dozens of very spacious a/c bungalows set at
decent intervals around a garden of shrubs, clipped hedges
and shady trees. There's a good-sized swimming pool too
and wi-fi throughout. Popular with families and package
tourists. Breakfast included. **B1800**

AO PHRA-AE (LONG BEACH)

Lanta LD Beach ☎075 684548, ⓦsandybeachlanta
.com. In a grassy lot by the beach, south of *Somewhere Else*,
this place offers a fair amount of shade and cheapish
en-suite bamboo bungalows with fans and mosquito nets,
plus more robust concrete alternatives with either fans
or a/c, TVs, fridges and hot water; most have hammocks,
all have small bathrooms. Fan **B500**, a/c **B1000**
★ **Lanta Marina Resort** ☎075 684168,
ⓦlantamarina.com. At the far southern end of Ao
Phra-Ae by a rocky point, this friendly place has 23 shaggily
thatched wood-and-split-bamboo bungalows, connected
by wooden walkways, that circle a very pretty lawn and
flower garden. All the huts have nice beds, well-designed
bathrooms, high palm-leaf roofs, fans and wi-fi access
(payable, though there's also a free computer for guests),
and the larger, more expensive ones on the beach have
hot showers. **B700**
Lanta Palm Beach ☎075 684406, ⓦlantapalm
beachresort.com. A busy, central and popular spot
within stumbling distance of several beach bars. The
concrete bungalows and large, bright cottages sit back
from the shore a little, within a garden of neat clipped
hedges and come with a/c and hot water. Has internet
access and a dive centre. Breakfast included. **B2500**
★ **Layana** ☎075 607100, ⓦlayanaresort.com.
Located plumb in the middle of the beautiful beach, this
is currently the top spot on Ao Phra-Ae and one of the
best and most liked on the whole island, not least for its
calm ambience (the hotel has a no-under-18s policy) and
attentive service. Its 44 a/c rooms occupy chunky, two-
storey villas designed in modern-Thai style and set around
a tidy beachfront garden of lawns and mature shrubs.
There's a gorgeous shorefront salt-water infinity pool,
a spa and plenty of activities and day-trips, plus wi-fi
throughout. Breakfast included. **B11,300**
Relax Bay Resort ☎075 684194, ⓦrelaxbay.com. On
a tiny bay south around the next rocky point (and quite a
hike) from *Lanta Marina*, the style of this French-managed
place is affordable rustic chic. Accommodation is in forty
tastefully simple thatched bungalows, all with large sea
view decks. Also has a luxury safari-style tent on a large
deck with a chic outdoor bathroom. There's a pool, a dive
centre and yoga classes during high season (see p.386).
Breakfast included. Fan **B1400**, a/c **B2300**
Sayang Beach Resort ☎075 684156, ⓦsayangbeach
resort.com. Welcoming, family-run place whose thirty
a/c bungalows are nicely spaced beneath the palm trees
in the expansive shorefront grounds. Some bungalows are
designed for families and there's also a beachfront suite.
Prices include buffet breakfasts and there's a very good
restaurant here too. Daily free transfers to Sala Dan. **B2550**
Somewhere Else ☎081 536 0858. Located in the heart
of the liveliest part of Ao Phra-Ae, with bars to the left

right and seaward, this cheap, congenial place on a beachside lawn is one of the main travellers' centres on the beach. Its spacious, unusually designed hexagonal bungalows made of tightly woven bamboo come with pretty bathrooms, some with hot showers. The drawback is that most are close together and lack a sense of privacy, though many have sea views. There's free wi-fi in the restaurant. **B300**

HAT KHLONG KHONG

★ **Bee Bee Bungalow** ☎081 537 9932, ✉beebee piya02@hotmail.com. A special, friendly place that stands out for its fourteen highly individual huts, each one a charmingly idiosyncratic experiment in bamboo architecture. All are simple but comfortably furnished, given style with batik fabric flourishes, and have fans, mosquito nets and partially open-air bathrooms; some have an upstairs room as well. There's a good bar-restaurant, too, with similarly experimental but lovely wood and thatch *salas*. **B550**

★ **Fisherman's Cottage** ☎081 476 1529, ⓦfishermanscottage.biz. This quiet, low-key chummy place at the southern end of the beach has just nine thatched-roof and concrete bungalows, each with big windows, quite spartan one-off beach-modern interiors — whitewashed concrete, nutty mural artworks, splashes of strong colour — mosquito nets, fans and good bathrooms. Free wi-fi throughout. Closed July–Oct. **B1500**

Lanta Riviera ☎075 667043, ⓦlantariviera.net. There are rows and rows of good, standard-issue, comfortably furnished fan and a/c concrete bungalows here, plus a few rooms in a two-storey building, set among shady beds of shrubs and flowers at the far northern end of the beach. Many of the rooms sleep three so it's popular with families. Also has a pool and jacuzzi near the shore. Fan **B800**, a/c **B1300**

Where Else? ☎081 536 4870, ⓦlanta-where-else .com. This charming collection of 22 bungalows has a laidback vibe and lots of personality, though it's more of a party place than *Bee Bee*. The artfully and individually designed bamboo and coconut-wood bungalows all have fans, mosquito nets, hammocks and open-air bathrooms filled with plants, and there are shell mobiles, driftwood sculptures and pot plants all over the place. The pricier bungalows are larger and nearer the sea, and some even have bamboo sunroofs and turrets. **B500**

HAT KHLONG NIN

Lanta Nature Beach Resort ☎075 662560, ⓦlanta naturebeachresort.com. In the cluster of concrete bungalow operations right on the beach at the southern end of Khlong Nin, this one has rows of cream-and-lilac painted fan and a/c concrete huts, with spacious tiled interiors. There are even bigger, cheaper bungalows in a garden inland, across the road. Fan **B800**, a/c **B1000**

Lanta Paradise ☎075 662569, ⓦlantaparadise beachresort.com. Though the shorefront concrete bungalows at this friendly spot are packed uncomfortably close together, they feel spacious inside and are well maintained; they lack style and are plain, but are all a/c with hot showers, and there's a pool here too. Breakfast included. **B1600**

Otto Bungalow ☎084 051 7180, ✉otto_lanta @hotmail.com. Tightly packed compound right by the road, containing four shorefront A-frame cabins, with thatched roofs, concrete walls, mosquito nets and fans, as well as a variety of a/c rooms, including one in a small converted bus. Fan **B800**, a/c **B1500**

HAT KHLONG NAM JUD

Lanta Coral Beach ☎075 662535, ⓦlantacoralresort .com. Friendly resort with a lovely, lofty restaurant — especially nice at sunset — up on the rocky point, with wi-fi. The twenty, good-sized, plain but very clean and en-suite bamboo and concrete huts here are scattered over a lawn among the palms (some of which are hung with hammocks); the concrete options, whether fan or a/c, boast hot showers. Fan **B300**, a/c **B800**

The Narima ☎075 662668, ⓦnarima-lanta.com. Very quiet but welcoming, elegantly designed, environmentally conscious resort of 32 posh but unadorned thatch-roofed bamboo bungalows set in three rows in a palm-filled garden. The bungalows all have polished wood floors, verandas with sea view, hot showers and fans as well as a/c (but no TV); there's also a three-tiered pool (with kids' level) and a dive centre, and staff rent out jeeps, motorbikes and mountain bikes. Breakfast included. **B2300**

AO KANTIANG

Lanta Marine Park View ☎075 665063, ⓦlanta marine.com. The thirty bungalows here are ranged up a slope at the northern end of the beach, with steps leading down to the shore. The best of them, though pricey, are great value as they're on stilts and enjoy glorious bay views from their balconies and glass-fronted interiors, and the furnishings are chic and modern. The plain, cheap fan-cooled wood and bamboo bungalows sit further back. There's also a small cliffside bar affording great views, plus wi-fi in the public areas and a tour agency. Fan **B600**, a/c **B1100**

Pimalai Resort and Spa ☎075 607999, ⓦwww .pimalai.com. At the southern end of Ao Kantiang is one of Ko Lanta's poshest hotels, which spreads over such an extensive area that guests are shuttled around in golf buggies. All rooms are luxuriously and elegantly designed in contemporary style, and there's a delightful spa, two infinity-edge swimming pools, a dive centre and lots of other watersports, tennis courts and free bicycles. However, only the more expensive accommodation gets a sea view

4

(the pool villas and walled beach villas are particularly stunning). In high season, guests are usually transferred direct to the resort by boat, landing at the *Pimalai*'s private floating jetty. B11,900

AO KHLONG JAAK
Anda Lanta Resort ☎075 665018, ⓦandalanta.com. Lively, buzzing resort that offers well-furnished, well-maintained a/c bungalows and rooms (all with hot showers, balconies, DVD players and free wi-fi), set around the shorefront garden and swimming pool. It's popular with families and has free kayaks and plenty of day-tripping options. B3200

AO MAI PHAI
Baan Phu Lae ☎081 201 1704, ⓦbaanphulae.com. Occupying the centre of the bay, this tastefully camp place manages to combine a whiff of Bangkok sophistication with laidback island charm. Its fan-cooled bamboo bungalows are stylishly simple and nearly all enjoy direct sea views; the a/c rooms high above the shore are less interesting. Massage, cooking classes and motorbike rental available. Fan B1180, a/c B1480
Bamboo Bay Resort ☎075 665023, ⓦbamboobay .net. At the northern end of the bay, this welcoming and very popular Thai–Danish resort offers 21 concrete

bungalows with hot showers, stepped up the cliffside above the headland. Nearly all have great sea views and interiors are spacious and of a high standard. Its *pièce de résistance* is its idyllically sited deck restaurant and bar, which jut out over the rocks just above the water. Fan B1000, a/c B2100
La Laanta Hideaway Resort ☎075 665066, ⓦlalaanta.com. Luxurious bolthole at the far southern end, which is very well liked for its attentive staff and chic, thatched, wooden-floored villas – all with a/c, hot showers, DVD players, low beds and free wi-fi – built to a cosy, village-style layout, around two pools and a beachfront garden. Breakfast included. B2800

LANTA OLD TOWN (BAN SI RAYA)
★ **Mango House** ☎086 948 6836, ⓦmangohouses .com. The rooms and villas built on stilts over the water here make an attractive and unusual Ko Lanta base. Several century-old wooden buildings, one of them a former charcoal store, have been charmingly converted into accommodation that can sleep between two and six people; interiors are furnished in fishing-village chic, with elegant contemporary bathrooms, DVD players, free wi-fi and kitchenette. The big draw though is the large waterside decks, which afford fine views of seven islands. B2000

EATING AND DRINKING

BAN SALA DAN
Many charming old wooden houses built on piles over the water have been turned into attractive jetty restaurants, perfect for whiling away a breezy hour with views of marine activity.
Catfish Named for its cats rather than its fish, and a good place to come for a change from seafood, with a chance to shop for secondhand books. As well as standard Thai food (fried rice B70), there's a wide choice of Western dishes, including falafels (B180), spaghetti, sandwiches, breakfasts, ice cream and espressos. Daily 8.30am–9pm.
Laanta Seafood The oldest restaurant in town and the most highly rated – its seafood, displayed on ice at the front, is great, including *haw mok thalay* (curried seafood soufflé; B120) and local dishes such as *nam prik kung siab*, smoked prawn dip with vegetables. Daily 10am–9.30pm.

HAT KHLONG DAO
Restaurant tables fill the shoreline in the evening, illuminated with fairy lights and lanterns, which lends a nice mellow atmosphere. The formula is very similar at most of them, with fresh seafood barbecues the main attraction during the season. Clusters of little beach bars serve cocktails on deckchairs and cushions, often with chill-out music and a campfire to gather round.

Costa Lanta ☎075 684630 (see p.391). The most sophisticated venue on the beach is a great place for a sundowner, with sea-view daybeds, plump bolsters, cool sounds and lemon-grass martinis. The food, however, doesn't match up to its hefty price tag. Daily 11am–midnight.
Indian Bar Three doors south of Cha-Ba Bungalows. One of the most genial bars on the beach, where the host, dressed as a Hollywood-style American Indian, makes a mean cocktail and does good fire-juggling shows. Claims to open 24hr.
Slow Down ☎075 684982 (see p.391). Serves up excellent spaghetti bolognese (B160), Swedish specialities such as cold shrimp plate, and Thai food, with set menus available. It's a good place to keep the family happy, with its special kids' menu, cushion seating in a converted longtail boat and, most importantly, its volleyball net within sight of adult dining areas. Daily 8am–10pm.

AO PHRA-AE (LONG BEACH)
Most of Ao Phra-Ae's most interesting restaurants are along the main road, while down on the beach you get small, mellow bars.
★ **Faim de Loup** On the main road towards the south end of the bay. Very good French bakery, where the croissants, pains au chocolat, fruit tarts and excellent

espressos just hit the spot. Also does sandwiches, quiches, potato and sausage salad (B75) and a few *plats du jour* such as aubergine gratin and salad (B250); free wi-fi, too. Daily 7.30am–5pm, sometimes closed on Sun.

Irish Embassy On the main road near the centre of the bay. Very friendly little Irish bar, serving back-home food such as fish and chips and offering quiz nights, TV sports and occasional live music. Daily 4pm–1am.

Klapa Klum Near Lanta Palm bungalows. There are bamboo love-booths and private seating areas at this beachfront bar, plus happy hours (5–8pm), cheap cocktails all night long and weekly on-the-beach parties with international DJs (currently Wed). Daily 5pm–late.

Ozone Bar On the beach, near Somewhere Else bungalows. One of the most famous bars on the beach, especially for its weekly DJ parties (currently Thurs), which usually draw a lively crowd. Daily roughly 11am–late.

Red Snapper On the main road, inland from Lanta Marina bungalows at the southern end of Phra-Ae. Tapas and creative European cuisine using imported meats, such as pork loin with apple chutney and gorgonzola (B290), are the hallmarks of this highly rated, Dutch-run, garden restaurant. Sometimes serves daytime sandwiches, too. Daily 5–11pm.

Sayang Beach Resort On the beach, at Sayang Beach Resort. This is a lovely spot for dinner, with tables set out under shoreside casuarinas strung with fairy lights. The kitchen here has a tandoori oven and serves a long menu of authentic Indian dishes, including dhal (B90) and chicken tikka masala (B200), as well as Thai and Western food, plus fresh seafood nightly and a big veggie menu. Daily roughly 10am–10pm.

HAT KHLONG KHONG

Sonya's On the main road, just north of 7-Eleven. Very popular, cheap, garden restaurant with free wi-fi (and pay computers), where you can "build your own" pasta from a wide choice of pastas, sauces, meats and extras. Also has a

big selection of Thai food (from B60), Western breakfasts and teas, as well as sandwiches and espresso coffees. Daily 8.30am–9.30pm.

HAT KHLONG NIN

A dozen or so mellow little beachfront bar-restaurants make inviting places to while away a few hours, day or night, with mats and cushions on the sand, tables under the shade of the spiky shoreside pandanus trees, and appropriately chilled sounds.

Cook Kai Diagonally north across the road from Nice Beach ⓦ cook-kai.com. Friendly restaurant hung with shell mobiles and lamps, dishing up hearty portions of all the Thai classics, plus famous hotplate dishes such as sizzling squid with garlic and pepper (B190) and a few Western dishes including breakfast. Daily 7.30am–10.30pm.

Jai-Dee North end of the beach, squeezed between the road and the beach. Bar-restaurant with a lovely shady deck and hammocks, internet access and free wi-fi, and a good menu of Thai curries and sandwiches (bacon B80), fresh coffee and breakfasts. Daily 9am–late, kitchen closes 9pm.

AO KANTIANG

Same Same But Different On the beach to the south of Pimalai. Tranquil haven of a bar-restaurant, where the tables and thatched *salas* are set beneath a tangled growth of shrubs and vines, surrounded by shell-mobiles and driftwood sculptures; it's run by the man behind the renowned *Ruen Mai* restaurant in Krabi (see p.360), and the mid-priced menu of mainly Thai and seafood dishes is of a similarly high standard. Daily 8am–11pm.

LANTA OLD TOWN (BAN SI RAYA)

Mango House Sophisticated little bar-café all done out in stylish dark wood, which does burgers, salads and sandwiches, as well as wine and freshly roasted coffee. High season daily 8am–8pm.

DIRECTORY

Banks and ATMs Several banks and ATMs in Ban Sala Dan, and there are ATMs beside the road at most of the beaches and in Lanta Old Town.

Hospitals Nearly every beach has a clinic, there's a larger health centre in Ban Sala Dan, and the rather basic island hospital is in Lanta Old Town (☏ 075 697017), though for anything serious you'll need to go to Phuket.

Post offices At the south end of Ban Sala Dan and in Lanta

Old Town.

Tourist police On the main road in Ao Phra-Ae (Long Beach; ☏ 1155).

Travel agent A helpful, clued-up travel agent is Otto Lanta Tour at *Otto Bungalows* on Hat Khlong Nin (☏ 083 634 8882, ✉ ottolantatour@gmail.com), who sell plane, train and bus tickets, as well as booking tours (see p.387) and accommodation.

The deep south

KARST SCENERY ON THE TRANG COAST

5

The deep south

The frontier between Thailand and Malaysia carves across the peninsula six degrees north of the equator, but the cultures of the two countries shade into each other much further north. According to official divisions, the southern Thais – the Thai Pak Tai – begin around Chumphon, and as you move further down the peninsula into Thailand's deep south you'll see ever more sarongs, yashmaks and towering mosques, and hear with increasing frequency a staccato dialect that baffles many Thais. Here too, you'll come across caged singing doves outside many houses, as well as strange-looking areas spiked with tall metal poles, on which the cages are hung during regular cooing competitions; and you'll spot huge, hump-backed Brahma bulls on the back of pick-up trucks, on their way to bullfights (in the Thai version, beast is pitted against beast, and the first to back off is the loser).

In Trang and Phatthalung provinces, the Muslim population is generally accepted as being Thai, but the inhabitants of the southernmost provinces – Satun, Pattani, Yala, Narathiwat and most of Songkhla – are ethnically more akin to the Malays: most of the 1.5 million followers of Islam here speak a dialect of Malay and write Yawi, an old modification of Arabic script to reflect Malay pronunciation. To add to the ethnic confusion, the region has a large urban population of Chinese, whose comparative wealth makes them stand out sharply from the Muslim farmers and fishermen.

The touristic interest in the deep south is currently all over on the beautiful **west coast**, where sheer limestone outcrops, pristine sands and fish-laden coral stretch down to the Malaysian border. Along Trang's **mainland coast**, there's a 30km stretch of attractive beaches, dotted with mangroves and impressive caves that can be explored by sea canoe, but the real draw down here is the offshore **islands**, which offer gorgeous panoramas and beaches, great snorkelling and at least a modicum of comfort in their small clusters of resorts. An added attraction is the recently introduced, scheduled boat services which have set up the intriguing possibility of **island-hopping**: it would now be possible to work your way down from Phuket as far as Penang without setting foot on the peninsula. The spread of tourism outwards from Phuket has been inching its way south down this coast for some time, but for now, apart from the tiny, remote but overcrowded honeypot of Ko Lipe, the islands remain largely undeveloped.

ARRIVAL AND GETTING AROUND   THE DEEP SOUTH

As well as the usual bus services, the area covered in this chapter is served by **flights** and **trains** to Trang (see p.402), as well as by **boats** between the islands (see p.406) and from the mainland to the islands.

HEADING FOR THE EMERALD CAVE, KO MOOK

Highlights

❶ Nature Resorts Not-for-profit resorts at Ban Chao Mai, on Ko Mook and Ko Libong, with great tours through the mangroves to Tham Chao Mai cave and to see the dugongs and birds on Libong. **See p.405, 409 & 411**

❷ Ko Hai A variety of good resorts for all budgets and gorgeous views. **See p.406**

❸ Tham Morakhot Ko Mook's Emerald Cave, with its inland beach of powdery sand at the base of an awesome natural chimney, is best visited by kayak. **See p.409**

❹ Ko Kradan Remote island with a long, white, east-facing strand, crystal-clear waters and a reef for snorkellers to explore. **See p.410**

❺ Ko Sukorn For a glimpse of how islanders live and an outstanding beach resort. **See p.411**

❻ Ko Tarutao Huge national park island with mangroves and jungle tracks to explore, and the most unspoilt beaches in the area. **See p.414**

HIGHLIGHTS ARE MARKED ON THE MAP ON P.400

5

By share-taxi The deep south has traditionally been the territory of share-taxis, which connect certain towns for about twice the fare of ordinary buses. The cars leave when they're full, which usually means six passengers, and sometimes a long wait, though there's always the option of buying up extra seats or chartering the whole car if you're in a hurry. They are a quick way of getting around and you should get dropped off at the door of your journey's end.

By minibus Inexorably, share taxis are being replaced by a/c minibuses, which run on almost exactly the same principles at similar prices; on these you'll be more comfortable, with a seat to yourself, and most of the various ranks publish a rough timetable – though the minibuses also tend to leave as soon as they're full.

Brief history

The central area of the Malay peninsula first entered Thai history when it came under the sway of Sukhothai, probably around the beginning of the fourteenth century.

Islam was introduced to the area by the end of that century, by which time Ayutthaya was taking a firmer grip on the peninsula. **Songkhla** and **Pattani** then rose to be the major cities, prospering on the goods passed through the two ports across the peninsula to avoid the pirates in the Straits of Malacca between Malaysia and Sumatra. More closely tied to the Muslim Malay states to the south, the Sultanate of Pattani began to **rebel** against the power of Ayutthaya in the sixteenth century, but the fight for self-determination only weakened Pattani's strength. The town's last rebellious fling was in 1902, after which it was

THE DEEP SOUTH

TRAVEL WARNING

Because of the ongoing **violence** in the deep south (see below), all major Western governments are currently advising people **not to travel** to or through Pattani, Yala and Narathiwat provinces unless essential, and nearly all are advising against travel to Songkhla province too; following on from this, insurance companies are refusing to cover travel in the affected areas. The four provinces encompass the city and transport hub of **Hat Yai** and several of the main border crossings to Malaysia: by rail from Hat Yai (and Bangkok) to Butterworth via Padang Besar and to Sungai Kolok; and by road from Hat Yai via Sadao, from Yala via Betong, and down the east coast to Kota Bharu.

The routes to Sungai Kolok, Betong and Kota Bharu pass through particularly volatile territory, with **martial law** declared in Pattani, Yala and Narathiwat provinces; however, martial law is only in effect in certain districts of Songkhla province, and not in Hat Yai itself.

The provinces of **Trang** and **Satun** are not affected, and it's still perfectly possible to continue overland to Malaysia via Satun: by a/c minibus from nearby Ban Khuan to Kangar, or by ferry from Thammalang to Kuala Perlis or the Malaysian island of Langkawi (see p.420); or by boat from Ko Lipe to Langkawi (see p.417). For up-to-the-minute advice, consult your government travel advisory (see p.57).

definitively and brutally absorbed into the Thai kingdom, while its allies, Kedah, Kelantan and Trengganu, were transferred into the suzerainty of the British in Malaysia.

During World War II the **Communist Party of Malaya** made its home in the jungle around the Thai border to fight the occupying Japanese. After the war they turned their guns against the British colonialists, but having been excluded from power after independence, descended into general banditry and racketeering around Betong. The Thai authorities eventually succeeded in breaking up the bandit gangs in 1989 through a combination of pardons and bribes, but the stability of the region soon faced disruption from another source, a rise in Islamic militancy.

The troubles: 2004 to the present

Armed resistance to the Thai state by **Muslim separatists** had fluctuated at a relatively low level since the 1960s, but in early 2004 the violence escalated dramatically. Since then, there have been thousands of deaths on both sides in the troubles, and barely a day goes by without a fatal incident of one kind or another. The insurgents have viciously targeted Buddhist monks, police, soldiers, teachers and other civil servants, as well as attacking a train on the Hat Yai–Sungai Kolok line and setting off bombs in marketplaces, near tourist hotels and bars and at Hat Yai airport. Increasingly, they have attacked other Muslims who are seen to be too sympathetic to the Thai state.

Often writing the militants off as bandits, the authorities have stirred up hatred – and undermined moderate Muslim voices – by reacting violently, notably in crushing protests at Tak Bai and the much-revered Krue Se Mosque in Pattani in 2004, in which a total of over two hundred alleged insurgents died. Meanwhile, the army has "subcontracted" much of its work to rangers, untrained village militias, thus inflaming the situation further and deepening the ethnic divide. In 2005, the government announced a **serious state of emergency** in Pattani, Yala and Narathiwat provinces, and imposed **martial law** here and in southern parts of Songkhla province. This, however, has exacerbated economic and unemployment problems in what is Thailand's poorest region.

A large part of the problem is that a wide variety of shadowy groups – with names like the Pattani Islamic Mujahideen, the Barisan Revolusi Nasional-Coordinate and Runda Kumpulan Kecil – are operating against the government, generally working in small cells at village level without central control. Rather than religious issues, the most likely causes of their militancy are ethnic grievances: prejudice, lack of opportunity and disempowerment, accompanied by resentment towards not only Thais but also the remote and corrupt Muslim elite. However, it's unclear exactly who they are or what they want and, faced with such shifting sands, all attempts to broker a ceasefire have failed.

5

Trang town

TRANG (also known as Taptieng) is gradually developing as a popular jumping-off point for travellers drawn south from the crowded sands of Krabi to the pristine beaches and islands of the nearby coast. The town, which prospers on rubber, oil palms, fisheries and – increasingly – tourism, is a sociable place whose wide, clean streets are dotted with crumbling, wooden-shuttered houses. In the evening, the streets are festooned with colourful lights, and during the day, many of the town's Chinese inhabitants hang out in the cafés, drinking the local filtered coffee. Trang's Chinese population makes the **Vegetarian Festival** in October or November almost as frenetic as Phuket's (see box, p.325) – and for veggie travellers it's an opportunity to feast at the stalls set up around the temples.

ARRIVAL AND DEPARTURE   TRANG TOWN

By plane Air Asia and Nok Air run daily flights between Bangkok and Trang airport (1hr 30min), which is connected to Trang town, 3km to the north, by a/c minibuses (B100), operated by, for example, BB Tour, 23 Thanon Sathanee (☎ 075 219054).

By train Two overnight trains from Bangkok (15–16hr) run down a branch of the southern line to Trang.

By bus Buses arrive at and depart from the new terminal on Thanon Phattalung (Highway 4), opposite Robinson department store, about 3km northeast of the centre, including an a/c service between Satun and Phuket four times daily; Satun buses also make a stop on Thanon Rama VI, just east of the central clocktower.

Destinations Bangkok (11 daily; 12–14hr); Krabi (roughly every 30min; 2hr); Phuket (hourly; 5hr); Satun (every 30min; 2hr 30min–3hr).

By minibus A/c minibuses to Surat Thani, Nakhon Si Thammarat and Hat Yai use the new bus terminal on Thanon Phattalung, while the services to Pak Meng and Ban Chao Mai have an office on Thanon Tha Klang northwest of the train station. Among a/c minibuses aimed specifically at tourists, Andaman Tour travel agency, opposite the station (☎ 075 216110), runs a service to Pak Bara at least once daily (2hr; B150), and Kanokwan Tour, just east of the *Sri Trang Hotel* (☎ 075 215235), goes to Ko Lanta (6 daily; 3hr; B250, including drop-off anywhere as far south as Hat Khlong

TRANG TOWN

Krabi & Phuket

Bus Terminal, Phatthalung & Hat Yai

ACCOMMODATION
Ban Aothong	6
Koh Teng Hotel	3
Sri Trang Hotel	5
Thumrin Hotel	4
Thumrin Thana Hotel	1
Trang Hotel	2

RESTAURANTS & CAFÉS
Fatimah	1
Nam Mui	3
Richy Station	5
See Far Lifestyle	2
Sin-o-cha	6
Wunderbar	4

Kantang & Hat Yao

Airport, Langu, Pak Bara & Satun

Khong). There are also faster minibus and speedboat transfers to Ko Lanta (see p.390) through KK Travel, opposite the train station (☎ 075 211198, ⌨ kktravelandtour.com).
By share taxi Share taxis for Pak Bara and Satun

congregate on Thanon Ratsada, out on the southeast side of town, for Krabi on Thanon Huay Yod, opposite the old bus station on the north side of town (about 500m north of the junction with Thanon Wisetkul).

GETTING AROUND

By car or motorbike Trang Island Hopping Tour (see below) and Avis at the airport (⌨ avisthailand.com)

rent cars, while motorbikes can be rented at *Koh Teng Hotel* (see below), (B250/day).

INFORMATION AND TOURS

Tourist information TAT have a helpful office on Thanon Wisetkul (daily 8.30am–4.30pm, sometimes closed for lunch on Sat & Sun; ☎ 075 215867, ✉ tattrang@tat.or.th).
Travel agents The best travel agent in town is Trang Island Hopping Tour, directly opposite the station at 28/2 Thanon Sathanee (☎ 075 211457 or ☎ 082 804 0583, ⌨ trang-island-hopping.com). This well-organized outfit offers a huge range of services, including mainland and island transfers and tickets, and accommodation booking

on any island. The friendly staff are a great source of impartial information on the area, and their office makes a good first stop in town. They also offer one-day boat trips around the islands and day-trips and camping trips to Ko Rok, and inland excursions to waterfalls and caves, as well as trekking and kayaking. *Wunderbar*, just around the corner (☎ 075 214563, ⌨ wunderbar-trang.com), also acts as a very helpful and clued-up travel agent, especially for island bookings.

ACCOMMODATION

Ban Aothong 25/28–31 Thanon Sathanee ☎ 075 225611, ✉ banaothong@yahoo.com. An overblown pink facade announces this upmarket guesthouse that's popular with Thai businesspeople, with its chunky wooden furniture, half-tester beds and rather kitsch decor. Double rooms are compact, while the slightly pricier twins have more space, though the bathrooms are still small; all have a/c, hot showers, fridges, free wi-fi and DVD players. __B790__
Koh Teng Hotel 77–79 Thanon Rama VI ☎ 075 218622 or ☎ 075 218148. This characterful 1940s Chinese hotel is a little battered and dusty but offers large, mostly clean en-suite rooms, some with cable TV and a/c, above a popular restaurant and coffee shop that serves southern Thai and Chinese food and Western breakfasts. Fan __B180__, a/c __B280__
Sri Trang Hotel 22 Thanon Sathanee ☎ 075 218122, ⌨ sritranghotel.com. Welcoming, recently updated hotel offering spacious rooms with some colourful decorative

touches, free wi-fi, hot water, cable TV and fridges. Has a few fan-cooled single rooms (B450–500) but otherwise a/c throughout. Internet access. __B650__
Thumrin Hotel Thanon Rama VI ☎ 075 211011–4, ⌨ thumrin.com. Good-value hotel offering international-standard facilities – a/c, hot water, TV, wi-fi and internet access – at cheap prices, in a high-rise block above its popular bakery-cum-coffee shop. __B850__
Thumrin Thana Hotel 69/8 Thanon Huay Yod ☎ 075 211211, ⌨ thumrin.com. The best hotel in town, though not in the same league as the *Anantara* on the coast (see p.405). Spacious, well-equipped rooms, a pool and fitness centre, wi-fi and internet access. __B1400__
Trang Hotel 134/2–5 Thanon Wisetkul ☎ 075 218944, ☎ 075 218451. Good, welcoming, moderately priced choice, with large, comfortable twin rooms with a/c, hot water, fridge and TV. __B590__

EATING AND DRINKING

Trang's streets are dotted with dozens of traditional cafés, which serve up gallons of **kopii** (local filtered coffee) accompanied by various tidbits and light meals. Most famous of these is the local speciality, **muu yaang**, delicious charcoal-grilled pork, which is generally eaten for breakfast. At the excellent **night market**, around the back of the city hall on Thanon Ruenrom, you can try another tasty southern dish, *khanom jiin*, soft noodles topped with hot, sweet or fishy sauces and eaten with crispy greens.

Fatimah Thanon Sathanee. Simple halal restaurant that's especially popular in the evenings. Buffet of southern curries, tasty *phat thai* (B35), *kopii* and tea. Tues–Sun roughly 8.30am–10pm.
Nam Mui Thanon Rama VI (no English sign but it's directly opposite the Koh Teng Hotel). With a pleasant patio at the back, this Thai–Chinese restaurant is popular with locals for its seafood and for very tasty, generously

portioned dishes such as deep-fried chicken with cashew nuts (B150). The English-language menu is a lot shorter than the Thai version, so it may be time to practise your Thai. Daily 11.30am–9pm.
Richy Station Thanon Sathanee ☎ 075 218431. Genteel bakery-café serving croissants, cakes, ice cream, lots of juices and espresso coffees, as well as tasty grilled ham and cheese sandwiches (B80), spaghetti and

breakfasts, and an extensive menu of Thai and Chinese dishes. Daily 7am–8pm (Wed drinks and baked goods only).

See Far Lifestyle 37 Thanon Phattalung (no English sign, but it's right by the entrance to Soi 3) ☎075 210139. Good, inexpensive restaurant with a varied menu of carefully prepared dishes, specializing in healthy cuisine and local food, such as *tom som plakapong*, a light, refreshing soup of sea bass, mushrooms and cumin, and *kao yok* (B120), a Chinese-style dish of steamed pork with taro found only in Trang. Daily 10.30am–8pm.

Sin-o-cha Next to the station at 25/25–26 Thanon Sathanee. Very popular, updated traditional café: *kopii* with Thai and Western cakes and main courses (fried rice B45), or espresso, various teas and Western breakfasts. Daily 7am–5pm.

Wunderbar Thanon Sathanee ☎075 214563, ⊛wunderbar-trang.com. Multipurpose farang bar-restaurant with free wi-fi that serves a wide selection of drinks (including wine and espressos), Thai food, and burgers (B60), salads, pizzas, breakfasts and other Western standards, as well as cheese platters (B290). Daily 7.30am–10pm.

DIRECTORY

Internet access Available at *Wunderbar* and at Click Corner, opposite, both on Thanon Sathanee.

The Trang coast

From Pak Meng, 40km due west of Trang town, down to the mouth of the Trang River runs a 30km-long stretch of lovely beaches, broken only by dramatic limestone outcrops. A paved road roughly parallels this stretch of coast, but otherwise there's surprisingly little development, as the shoreline is technically part of Hat Chao Mai National Park.

Pak Meng and Hat Chang Lang

Although it has a fine outlook to the headlands and islands to the west (with regular boats to the biggest, Ko Hai), the beach at **PAK MENG** is not the most attractive on the coast, becoming a rather muddy strip of sand at low tide. At other times, however, it offers quiet, calm swimming, and there's always the possibility of a meal at one of the many tree-shaded foodstalls and restaurants that line the back of the beach.

Immediately south of Pak Meng's beach is the white sand of **Hat Chang Lang**, famous for its oysters, which shelters at its north end the finest luxury hotel in the province, *Anantara Si Kao*.

Hat Chao Mai National Park HQ

The turning for the headquarters is 3km on from Hat Chang Lang · B200 · ☎075 213260, ⊛dnp.go.th

Hat Chao Mai National Park covers 230 square kilometres, including parts of Ko Mook and Ko Kradan, but the park admission fee is only rigidly enforced if you visit its headquarters. From the HQ a short trail leads to the south end of the beach and a viewpoint partway up a karst pinnacle, from which you can see Ko Mook and occasionally dugongs in the bay below. At headquarters there's a simple café as well as accommodation.

Hat Yong Ling and Hat Yao

About 5km south of the national park HQ, beyond Kuantunku, the pier for Ko Mook, is **Hat Yong Ling**. This quiet and attractive convex beach, which shelters a national park ranger station, is probably the nicest along this stretch of coast, with a large cave which you can swim into at high tide or walk into at low tide. Immediately beyond comes **Hat Yao**, which runs in a broad 5km white-sand strip, backed by casuarina trees and some simple restaurants.

Ban Chao Mai

At the south end of Hat Yao is **BAN CHAO MAI** (also called **Ban Hat Yao**), a straggle of houses on stilts, which exists on fishing, especially for crabs. From the harbour, boats run regularly across to Ko Libong, and this is the mainland ferry stop on Tigerline's Lanta–Lipe route. The owners of *Had Yao Nature Resort* by the harbour organize guided and fully insured trips by longtail and canoe through the mangroves to the nearby cave of **Tham Chao Mai** (B800/person in a group of four or more, including lunch; ten percent discount for guests at the resort); inside are impressively huge rock pillars and a natural theatre, its stage framed by rock curtains. The resort also rents out two-person kayaks (B200 for the first hour, B100/hr thereafter) if you want to do the trip by yourself, with a map and head-torch (B100 rental), as well as offering tours to the local islands, including highly recommended dugong-watching trips to Ko Libong (see p.411).

ARRIVAL AND GETTING AROUND   THE TRANG COAST

Air-conditioned **minibuses**, departing only when full, run from Thanon Tha Klang in Trang to Pak Meng (45min; B60), as well as via Hat Yao to Ban Chao Mai (1hr; B70), but if you want to explore the whole coastline, you'll need to rent a **motorbike** or **car** in Trang (see p.403).

ACCOMMODATION AND EATING

PAK MENG

Lay Trang Resort ☎ 075 274027–8, 🖥 laytrang.com. The nicest place to stay and eat at Pak Meng, a stone's throw from the pier at the far north end of the beach. Ranged around a large, peaceful garden with lawns and orchids set back from the beach, its bright concrete chalets with huge bathrooms and smart brick rooms come with verandas, hot showers, a/c and TV. Its welcoming, reasonably priced restaurant is renowned for its seafood, including *nam prik kung siap* (dried shrimp relish) and *kaeng som* soup with sea bass. B1200

HAT CHANG LANG

★ **Anantara Si Kao** ☎ 075 205888, 🖥 anantara.com. The finest luxury hotel in the province, where the low-rise blocks of stylish bedrooms and pool suites, all with large balconies, are set behind a line of casuarina trees. Facilities encompass a beautiful, large pool, Italian and international restaurants, a fitness centre and a spa. Watersports on offer include diving and sailing, and there's plenty of other activities, notably cooking and Thai-language lessons and some interesting local tours. The hotel also has its own beach club and restaurant on the main strand on Ko Kradan

(see p.410), reached by daily boat transfer. Breakfast included. B6000

HAT CHAO MAI NATIONAL PARK HQ

National park bungalows 🖥 dnp.go.th. Fan-cooled, en-suite bungalows and rooms for two to six people, set under the casuarinas at the back of the sandy beach, and a simple café. B800

BAN CHAO MAI

★ **Had Yao Nature Resort** ☎ 087 885 7815 or ☎ 081 894 6936, 🖥 natureresortsgroup.com. Eco-friendly, non-profit resort, where your custom will go towards helping local people and the environment (see p.55); the same people own *Libong Nature Beach Resort* (see p.411) and *Ko Mook Nature Beach Resort* (see p.409). Many of the smart a/c rooms and bungalows with wi-fi face directly onto the water, and some have hot showers and satellite TV. The breezy, waterside restaurant serves up Western breakfasts, vegetarian food and excellent squid and other seafood dishes. There's also kayak, bike and snorkel rental, and internet access. Breakfast included. B1200

The Trang and Satun islands

Generally blessed with blinding white beaches, great coral and amazing marine life, the islands off the coast of Trang and Satun provinces have managed, mostly with just a handful of resorts on each, to cling onto some of that illusory desert-island atmosphere which better-known places like Phuket and Samui lost long ago. Indeed, islands such as **Ko Hai** and **Ko Kradan** support no permanent settlements other than the bungalow concerns, while on **Ko Tarutao** and **Ko Adang** in the far south, the peace and quiet is maintained by the national parks department; at the other end of the scale, however,

5

ISLAND-HOPPING AND TOURS

Access to the Trang and Satun islands from their nearest mainland ports is described in the individual island accounts, but what sets this area apart are the enticing opportunities for **island-hopping**, thanks to regular boat services in the tourist season out of Ko Lanta, further up the coast (see p.384), which can be booked through any travel agent in the area. If you just fancy a day exploring some of the islands, any travel agent in Trang can book you on a **boat trip** (mid-Oct to mid-May only) to Ko Kradan, the Emerald Cave on Ko Mook, and other small nearby islands for snorkelling, for around B700/person including packed lunch and soft drinks.

LANTA–LIPE AND BEYOND

Bundhaya Speedboat ☏074 783643–4, ⦿ bundhayaresort.com. Speedboats between Lanta and Lipe (1 daily; about 4hr; B1900) via Ko Hai, Hat Farang on Ko Mook and Ko Bulon Lae. Onward, same-day connections to Langkawi.

Satun Pakbara Speedboat Club ☏074 783643–4, ⦿ tarutaolipeisland.com. Speedboats between Lanta and Lipe (1 daily; about 4hr; B1900) via Ko Hai, Hat Farang on Ko Mook, Ko Kradan and Ko Bulon Lae. Onward, same-day connections between Lipe and

Langkawi, and between Lanta and Ko Phi Phi, Phuket and Krabi.

Tigerline ☏081 092 8800, ⦿ tigerlinetravel.com. Ferries between Lanta and Lipe (1 daily; about 5hr 30min; B1700), via Ko Hai, Hat Farang on Ko Mook (with longtail transfers to Ko Kradan), and Ban Chao Mai on the mainland (usually with a change of boat). Onward, same-day connections between Lipe and Langkawi, and between Lanta and Ko Phi Phi, Phuket, Krabi, Ao Nang and Railay.

LANTA–KRADAN

Petpailin and Lanta Princess day-trip boats The cheapest way to travel between Ko Lanta, Ko Hai, Ko Mook and Ko Kradan is generally on the big day-trip boats run by Petpailin and Lanta Princess out of Lanta, which will drop you at, or transfer you between, any of the islands; Lanta to Ko Hai, for instance, costs B500.

Garden Hill speedboat Garden Hill (see p.387) sends out a speedboat from Lanta every day on the same three-island route, charging B700 between Lanta and Hai, for example, about the same as on the three Lanta–Lipe boats described above.

---

nearby **Ko Lipe** is developing at its own merry pace and now boasts over forty resorts, as well as a substantial *chao ley* village (see p.304).

Accommodation on the islands, much of which is mid-priced, is now often fully booked at the very busiest times. Most of the resorts open year-round, though in practice many can't be reached out of season (roughly June–Oct) due to treacherous seas. It's sensible to get in touch ahead of time to check whether the resort you're interested in is open or has vacancies, and in many cases to arrange transfers from Trang; a few of the resorts maintain offices or have agents in Trang town to make this easier.

Ko Hai (Ko Ngai)

KO HAI (also known as **KO NGAI**), 16km southwest of Pak Meng, is the most developed of the Trang islands, though it's still decidedly low-key. The island's action, such as it is, centres on the east coast, where half a dozen resorts enjoy a dreamy panorama of jagged limestone outcrops, whose crags glow pink and blue against the setting sun, stretching across the sea to the mainland behind. The gently sloping beach of fine, white sand here runs unbroken for over 2km (though at low tide, swimming is not so good at the northern end, which is scattered with dead coral), and there's some good snorkelling in the shallow, clear water off the island's southeastern tip.

ARRIVAL AND DEPARTURE   KO HAI

If you're planning to **fly** into Trang or Krabi airports, contact your resort in advance about transfers. There are also plenty of island-hopping options (see above).

KO HAI ACTIVITIES

You can rent **snorkelling equipment** (B100/day at *Coco Cottage*, for example) and **kayaks** (B50/hr at *Koh Ngai Villa*, for example) at most of the resorts. All the resorts offer **boat trips** (B1500/boat, or B300/person in a group of six, at *Ko Hai Seafood*, for example) that take in the Emerald Cave on Ko Mook and some snorkelling off Ko Hai. (Ko Cheuak, just to the southeast of Ko Hai, is currently off-limits to visitors to protect the coral, which was badly bleached during a sudden rise in sea temperatures in 2010 – avoid any place that offers trips there.) *Ko Hai Seafood* can also put together overnight snorkelling and camping trips to Ko Rok (see p.387) for B2300 per person.

Towards the southern end of the beach, *Fantasy Resort* has a well-organized **dive shop**, the German-run Rainbow Divers (☎075 206962, ⊕rainbow-diver.com; Nov–April).

By ferry The resorts on Ko Hai's east coast currently rely on ferries owned by *Koh Ngai Villa* and *Fantasea* resorts to transfer their guests from Pak Meng (45min–1hr); longtail boats come out to meet the ferries and shuttle passengers to the various resorts up and down the beach. Both ferries depart at around 11.30am; *Villa's* is the cheaper of the two,

charging B350 from Pak Meng, or B450 including a/c minibus from their office in Trang town (see map, p.402).
By chartered longtail If you miss the ferries, you can charter a longtail boat for around B1000, for example through *Koh Ngai Villa* (see below).

INFORMATION

Hat Chao Mai National Park maintains a booth at Pak Meng pier, where visitors to Ko Hai will usually be charged B200 entrance fee; hang on to your ticket as this should also cover you if you take a trip to Ko Mook's Emerald Cave.

ACCOMMODATION

★ **Coco Cottage** Towards the northern end of the beach ☎087 898 6522, ⊕coco-cottage.com. Charming, helpful and family-friendly resort in a grassy palm grove, where the chic, thatched wooden bungalows (both detached and semi-detached) sport verandas, a/c and well-designed bathrooms with outdoor bamboo hot showers, wooden basins and indoor toilets. Also has wi-fi, internet access, a stylish beach bar and a very good restaurant that serves creative Thai food, Thai desserts and espresso coffees. Breakfast included. B2800

Ko Hai Paradise Resort Ao Kauntong on the south coast ☎089 646 5731, ⊕kohhaiparadise.com; Trang office at The Meeting Point restaurant opposite the station ☎075 216420. With a tranquil bay all to themselves, the simple but sturdy en-suite bungalows with mosquito nets at this friendly resort are sheltered by tall palms in spacious, grassy grounds. The food's good and the long, white-sand beach slopes down towards some great coral for snorkelling right in front of the resort. The resort arranges its own transfers from Trang town via Kuantunku pier (B450). Open only at the height of the high season (roughly Dec–April). B500

Ko Hai Seafood Near the centre of the beach, north of Koh Ngai Villa ☎081 367 8497. Large, well-built, thatched, woven-bamboo bungalows with wall fans, mosquito screens and well-equipped bathrooms, in a single row facing the beach across a nice lawn. Internet access available. B1200

Koh Ngai Villa Near the centre of the main beach ☎075 203263, ⊕kohngaivillathai.com; Trang office

opposite the station ☎075 210496. Friendly, old-style beach resort with plenty of space. Simple, well-organized bamboo bungalows boast verandas, mosquito nets and small toilets, or you could opt for a large room with two double beds in a concrete longhouse or a smart concrete bungalow with a/c, or even a two-person tent (B200, including bedding). Breakfast included with most rooms. Fan B850, a/c B1800

Mayalay Beach Near the centre of the main beach, south of Koh Ngai Villa ☎083 590 7523, ⊕mayalay beachresort.com. Welcoming place with nineteen deluxe, a/c, woven-bamboo bungalows with thatched roofs, day beds, fridges and capacious hot-water bathrooms. The restaurant is no great shakes but has free wi-fi and access to a computer (payable). Often open all year round. Breakfast included. B3000

Thanya South end of the beach ☎075 206965, ⊕kohngaithanyaresort.com. A large, very attractive beachside swimming pool with jacuzzis, set on a spacious lawn, is the main draw here. As well as a/c, hot water and fridges, the villas feature verandas, big French windows and lots of polished teak, while the restaurant has a varied menu of Thai food, including some interesting seafood dishes. Breakfast included. B3500

Thapwarin Resort Towards the northern end of the main beach, north of Coco Cottage ☎081 894 3585, ⊕thapwarin.com. Welcoming, shady resort, where you can choose between well-appointed bamboo and rattan cottages with semi-outdoor bathrooms, and large, very smart, beachfront wooden bungalows; all are thatched and have a/c and hot showers. There's internet access and free wi-fi, a massage spa, beach bar and good restaurant, serving Thai and Western food, including seafood barbecues in the evening. Breakfast included. B3000

Ko Mook

KO MOOK, about 8km southeast of Ko Hai, supports a comparatively busy fishing village on its eastern side, around which – apart from the sandbar that runs out to the very pricey *Sivalai Resort* – most of the beaches are disappointing, reduced to dirty mud flats when the tide goes out. However, across on the island's west coast lies beautiful **Hat Farang**, with gently shelving white sand, crystal-clear water that's good for swimming and snorkelling, and gorgeous sunsets.

Tham Morakhot

Part of Hat Chao Mai National Park • Open Oct–June • B200 admission fee if the park rangers are around

The island's main source of renown is **Tham Morakhot**, the stunning "Emerald Cave" north of Hat Farang on the west coast, which can only be visited by boat, but shouldn't be missed. An 80m swim through the cave – 10m or so of which is in pitch darkness – brings you to a *hong* (see p.351) with an **inland beach** of powdery sand open to the sky, at the base of a spectacular natural chimney whose walls are coated with dripping vegetation. Chartering your own longtail or taking a trip with *Ko Mook Nature Beach Resort* (B200/person, in a group of four or more) is preferable to taking one of the big day-trip boats that originate on Lanta or Pak Meng: if you time it right, you'll get the inland beach all to yourself, an experience not to be forgotten. It's also easy enough to **kayak** there from Hat Farang (from B100/hr from *Sawaddee*), and at low tide you can paddle right through to the inland beach: buoys mark the cave entrance, from where a tunnel heads straight back into the rock; about halfway along, there's a small, right-hand kink in the tunnel which will plunge you briefly into darkness, but you should soon be able to see light ahead from the *hong*. Mid-afternoon is often a good time to paddle off on this trip, after the tour boats have left and providing the tide is right.

ARRIVAL AND DEPARTURE — KO MOOK

In addition to the services mentioned below, there are plenty of island-hopping options (see p.406).

Minibus-and-boat packages The easiest way to get to Ko Mook is to book a minibus-and-boat package to Hat Farang through a travel agent in Trang, which costs B350, including the 30min longtail ride.

By public boat There's a pretty reliable public boat (B60) at around midday to Ko Mook's village from Kuantunku

pier, 8km south of Pak Meng, between Hat Chang Lang and Hat Yong Ling; Ban Chao Mai a/c minibuses from Trang (see p.405) will usually detour to Kuantunku if asked (around B100/person from Trang). Once landed at the village, you're left with a 30min walk or B50 motorbike-taxi ride over to Hat Farang.

ACCOMMODATION

Most of Hat Farang is unfortunately occupied by the disappointing *Charlie's Resort*, leaving room only for one other resort, *Sawaddee*. However, *Rubber Tree* and *Had Farang* make the best of the attractive, shady slopes behind the beach, while *Ko Mook Nature Beach Resort* is away on the east side of the island near the village.

Had Farang Bungalows 087 884 4785, kohmookhadfarang.com. The nineteen bungalows and rooms at this friendly place are basic bamboo and wood affairs, but most are en-suite with their own verandas and the restaurant is very good. Sometimes open in the rainy season. B400

★ **Ko Mook Nature Beach Resort** 087 885 7815 or 081 894 6936, natureresortsgroup.com. Recently

opened branch of the non-profit *Had Yao Nature Resort*, which promotes conservation and sustainable tourism (see p.405). On the south-facing shore of the sandbar that ends at *Sivalai Resort*, the bright, concrete bungalows all have mosquito-screened French windows directly facing the sea, as well as a/c, satellite TV, DVD player and free wi-fi. Bicycles, kayaks, snorkels, trips to the Emerald Cave and Ko Kradan, and internet access available. Breakfast included. B2800

5

Rubber Tree ☎081 606 9358, ⓦmookrubbertree .com; or contact Sea Breeze restaurant in front of the station in Trang (☎075 215972). On a well-tended, landscaped slope that's also a working rubber plantation, fan bungalows with cold-water bathrooms and crisp, white linen, or spacious, smartly designed a/c versions with rubber-wood furniture and hot showers. Occasionally puts together overnight camping trips to Ko Rok. Breakfast included. Fan B800, a/c B1990

Sawaddee ☎081 508 0432, ⓔsawaddeeresort64 @yahoo.com; or contact Wunderbar in Trang (see p.403). Laidback, old-style, concrete or stilted wooden bungalows with mosquito nets parallel to the beach, with en-suite bathrooms, plenty of shade and largely uninterrupted sea views. High season only. B800

Ko Kradan

About 6km to the southwest of Ko Mook, **KO KRADAN** is the remotest of the inhabited islands off Trang, and one of the most beautiful, with crystal-clear waters. On this slender triangle of thick jungle, the **main beach** is a long strand of steeply sloping, powdery sand on the east coast, with fine views of Ko Mook, Ko Libong and the karst-strewn mainland, and an offshore reef to the north with a great variety of hard coral; such beauty, however, has not escaped the attention of the day-trip boats from Ko Lanta, who turn the beach into a lunchtime picnic ground most days in summer. From a short way north of the *Anantara* beach club (see p.405), which is located towards the south end of this beach, a path across the island will bring you after about fifteen minutes to **Sunset Beach**, another lovely stretch of fine, white sand in a cove; a branch off this path at *Paradise Lost* leads to a beach on the short south coast, which enjoys good reef snorkelling (also about 15min from the *Anantara* beach club).

ARRIVAL AND DEPARTURE

KO KRADAN

By minibus-and-longtail transfer Agencies such as Trang Island Hopping Tour (see p.403) can arrange minibus-and-longtail transfers from Trang town, via Kuantunku pier (twice daily in season; B450). There are also plenty of island-hopping options (see p.406).

ACCOMMODATION

Kalume ☎089 650 3283, ⓦkalumekradan.com. Italian-run resort on the beach next to *Seven Seas*, with small, basic, thatched bamboo huts with mosquito nets and en-suite bathrooms and smart, large, wooden bungalows with French windows and nice verandas (B1500). Good Italian food at the bar-restaurant and free wi-fi. B900

Paradise Lost ☎089 587 2409; for further information, go to ⓦkokradan.wordpress.com or contact Sea Breeze restaurant in front of the station in Trang (☎075 215972). In the middle of the island, roughly halfway along the path to *Sunset Beach* is Kradan's best-value accommodation, run by an American and his dogs. Set in a grassy, palm-shaded grove, it offers simple, clean, thatched rattan bungalows with shared bathrooms or larger, en-suite, wooden affairs, as well as an open-sided dorm with mosquito nets and fans (B250/person), kayaks, snorkels and good Thai and Western food. B700

Seven Seas ☎075 203389–90, ⓦsevenseasresorts .com. By far the best of several resorts on the east coast, *Seven Seas* adds a surprising splash of contemporary luxury to this remote spot. Behind a small, black, infinity pool, the large bungalows and rooms with outdoor warm-water bathrooms are stylishly done out in greys and whites, and sport a/c, wi-fi, fridges, TVs and DVDs. There's a small massage spa and breakfast is included. B6500

Ko Libong

The largest of the Trang islands with a population of six thousand, **KO LIBONG** lies 10km southeast of Ko Mook, opposite Ban Chao Mai on the mainland. Less visited than its northern neighbours, it's known mostly for its wildlife, although it has its fair share of golden beaches too. Libong is one of the most significant remaining refuges in Thailand of the **dugong**, a large marine mammal similar to the manatee, which feeds on sea grasses growing on the sea floor – the sea-grass meadow around Libong is reckoned to be the largest in Southeast Asia. Sadly, dugongs are now an endangered species, traditionally hunted for their blubber (used as fuel) and meat, and increasingly

5

KO LIBONG BOAT TRIPS AND DIVING

Libong Nature Beach Resort runs award-winning, day-long **boat trips around Libong** (B1200/person, including lunch, in a group of four or more; ten percent discount for guests), which are safe, insured and licensed with TAT, and staffed by local *chao ley* (sea gypsies) who know the dugong well. As well as visiting a *chao ley* village, these give you the chance to kayak into the sanctuary to observe the rare birds and to snorkel at the sea-grass beds – with, they reckon, an eighty percent chance of seeing a dugong. They also run day-trips to the Emerald Cave on Ko Mook and Ko Kradan (B1200/person, including lunch, in a group of four or more; ten percent discount for guests). If you'd rather explore below water than above, there's a PADI **dive shop**, Jolly Roger, at *Libong Beach Resort* on the north side of Ban Lan Khao (ⓦ trangdiving.com).

affected by fishing practices such as scooping, and by coastal pollution, which destroys their source of food. The dugong has now been adopted as one of fifteen "reserved animals" of Thailand and is the official mascot of Trang province.

Libong is also well known for its migratory **birds**, which stop off here on their way south from Siberia, drawn by the island's food-rich mud flats (now protected by the Libong Archipelago Sanctuary, which covers the eastern third of the island). For those seriously interested in ornithology, the best time to come is during March and April, when you can expect to see brown-winged kingfishers, masked finfoots and even the rare black-necked stork, not seen elsewhere on the Thai–Malay peninsula.

The island's handful of resorts occupy a long, thin strip of golden sand at the fishing village of **Ban Lan Khao** on the southwestern coast. At low tide here, the sea retreats for hundreds of metres, exposing rock pools that are great for splashing about in but not so good for a dip.

ARRIVAL AND DEPARTURE   KO LIBONG

By public longtail Public longtails depart daily year-round from Ban Chao Mai (see p.405) when full (most frequent in the morning and around lunchtime; B50/person), arriving 20min later at Ban Phrao on Ko Libong's north side. From here motorbike taxis (B100) transport you to Ban Lan Khao.

By private transfer You can arrange a direct boat transfer from Ban Chao Mai to *Libong Nature Beach Resort* for about B1000/boat.

ACCOMMODATION

Libong Beach Resort ⓣ 075 225205, ⓦ libongbeach resort.com. Friendly resort on the north side of Ban Lan Khao with a wide variety of accommodation set amid lawns and flowers, ranging from small, en-suite concrete and wood bungalows at the back to spacious, bright, stilted, wooden cabins with a/c and nice decks on the beachfront (B2500). Internet access, kayak and motorbike rental are available. Fan B700, a/c B1000

★ **Libong Nature Beach Resort** ⓣ 087 885 7815 or ⓣ 081 894 6936, ⓦ natureresortsgroup.com. Run by the same charitable foundation that operates the Had Yao Nature Resort (see p.405), with neat, en-suite bungalows, all with wi-fi and some with hot water and a/c, stretching back from a secluded part of the beach; it's a 10min walk south of Ban Lan Khao, and there's another sheltered cove a further 5min walk (or kayak) to the south. There's a good restaurant attached too, with internet access, and mountain bikes and snorkelling gear are available to rent. Breakfast included. Fan B1200, a/c B1500

Ko Sukorn

A good way south of the other Trang islands, low-lying **KO SUKORN** lacks the white-sand beaches and beautiful coral of its neighbours, but makes up for it with its friendly inhabitants, a laidback ambience and one excellent resort; for a glimpse of how islanders live and work, this is the place to come.

The lush interior is mainly given over to rubber plantations, interspersed with rice paddies, banana and coconut palms; the island also produces famously delicious watermelons, which are plentiful in March and April. Hat Talo Yai, the main **beach**

5

KO SUKORN BOAT TRIPS AND OTHER ACTIVITIES

Boat excursions from *Sukorn Beach Bungalows* include trips out to the islands of Ko Lao Liang and Ko Takieng, which are part of the Mu Ko Phetra National Marine Park, for some excellent snorkelling. These run nearly every day from November to May; at other times of year, the sea is sometimes calm enough but you're usually restricted to fishing trips – and to looking round the island itself, which, at thirty square kilometres, is a good size for exploring. The resort offers **guided tours**, and has motorbikes (B250/half-day) and mountain bikes (B150/ half-day) for rent, as well as a handy map that marks all the sights, including the three villages and seafood market.

– 500m of gently shelving brown sand, backed by coconut palms – runs along the southwestern shore.

ARRIVAL AND DEPARTURE   **KO SUKORN**

A songthaew-and-boat transfer to Ko Sukorn (B250/person), via the public ferry from Laem Ta Sae, leaves Trang Island Hopping Tours (see p.403) daily at 11am and takes a couple of hours, or you can arrange a private transfer. *Sukorn Beach Bungalows* can also organize pricey longtail-boat transfers to or from any of the nearby islands.

ACCOMMODATION

Ko Sukorn Cabana ☎ 089 724 2326, ⓦ sukorncabana .com. After *Sukorn Beach Bungalows*, the best of the rest of the island's handful of resorts is *Ko Sukorn Cabana*, a friendly and peaceful place offering stilted, a/c bungalows with attractive bathrooms and large, well-appointed log cabins on a secluded beach to the north of Hat Talo Yai. Day-trips to Lao Liang and Takieng, kayaks, motorbikes, internet and wi-fi are also available; private transfers from Trang can be arranged for B2100 all-in. B1500

★ **Sukorn Beach Bungalows** ☎ 075 207707, ⓦ sukorn-island-trang.com; for further information in Trang, go to Trang Island Hopping Tours (see p.403). This outstanding place is one of the few Trang resorts that's reliably accessible all year round (discounts of up to forty percent are available in low season). The clued-up and

congenial Thai–Dutch duo who run the place are keen to keep it low-key and quiet (no children under 7), and work with the locals as much as possible, something that's reflected in the friendly welcome you get all over the island. Attractively decorated and well-designed bungalows and rooms – all spotlessly clean and with en-suite hot showers – are set around a lush garden dotted with deckchairs and umbrellas, and there's an excellent, well-priced restaurant. At the resort, you can access the internet (including wi-fi), make overseas calls, exchange money and get a good massage, and you're free to paddle around in kayaks; the owners can even put together pricey but very appealing, five-night island-hopping packages. Good breakfast included. Fan B1000, a/c B1250

Ko Bulon Lae

The scenery at tiny **KO BULON LAE**, 20km west of Pak Bara in Satun province, isn't as beautiful as that generally found in Ko Tarutao National Park just to the south, but it's not at all bad: a 2km strip of fine white sand runs the length of the casuarina-lined east coast, while *chao ley* fishermen make their ramshackle homes in the tight coves of the rest of the island. A reef of curiously shaped hard coral closely parallels the eastern beach, while **White Rock** to the south of the island has beautifully coloured soft coral and equally dazzling fish.

KO LAO LIANG

The beautiful, twin islets of **Ko Lao Liang**, with their white-sand beaches, abundant corals and dramatic rock faces, lie to the west of Ko Sukorn. They're deserted apart from a single adventure-sport camp, *Lao Liang Resort* (ⓦ laoliangresort.com; open mid-Nov to April; B1500). All-in costs at the resort comprise camping in deluxe tents on the beach, three meals, including seafood barbecues in the evening, and snorkelling gear; kayak rental, rock-climbing (instruction, equipment rental, deep-water soloing) and snorkelling tours are extra. Trang Island Hopping Tours (see p.403) can arrange transfers via Laem Ta Sae for B850 per person.

ARRIVAL AND DEPARTURE

From/to Pak Bara Boats for Ko Bulon Lae currently leave Pak Bara (see box, p.414) daily at about 12.30pm (1hr 30min; B450). As there's no pier on Bulon Lae, boat arrivals are met by longtails to transfer visitors to shore (B50). Boats return from Bulon Lae to Pak Bara at around 9.30am. There are also island-hopping options (see p.406).

ACCOMMODATION

The island's resorts are open roughly from late October to mid-May.

Bulone ☎ 081 897 9084 or ☎ 086 960 0468, ⓦ bulone -resort.net. Friendly spot in a huge grassy compound under the casuarinas at the north end of the main beach. Airy, en-suite bungalows on stilts come with fans, mosquito nets and verandas, while the restaurant features plenty of vegetarian options and a small selection of tasty Italian favourites, as well as internet access and wi-fi; kayaks and snorkelling gear are also available. B1250

Pansand ☎ 081 693 3667, ⓦ pansand-resort.com; Trang office at First Andaman Travel on Thanon Wisetkul. The oldest and largest resort on the island, on the east-coast beach, where large, smart, peaceful cottages come with verandas, fans, mosquito screens, cold-water bathrooms and plenty of room to breathe. On the beach side of the shady, well-tended grounds, there's a sociable restaurant serving up good seafood and other Thai dishes; internet access and snorkelling gear are also available. Breakfast included. B1500

Ko Tarutao National Marine Park

B200 admission fee • ⓦ dnp.go.th

The unspoilt **KO TARUTAO NATIONAL MARINE PARK** is probably the most beautiful of all Thailand's accessible beach destinations. Occupying 1400 square kilometres of the Andaman Sea in Satun province, the park covers 51 mostly uninhabited islands. Site of the park headquarters, the main island, **Ko Tarutao**, offers a variety of government-issue accommodation and things to do, while **Ko Adang** to the west is much more low-key and a springboard to some excellent snorkelling. The port of **Pak Bara** (see box, p.414) is the main jumping-off point for the park, and houses a **national park visitor centre** (☎ 074 783485), set back on the left just before the pier, where you can gather information and book a room on Tarutao or Adang before boarding your boat.

The park's forests and seas support an incredible variety of **fauna**: langurs, crab-eating macaques and wild pigs are common on the islands, which also shelter several unique subspecies of squirrel, tree shrew and lesser mouse deer; among the hundred-plus bird species found here, reef egrets and hornbills are regularly seen, while white-bellied sea eagles, frigate birds and pied imperial pigeons are more

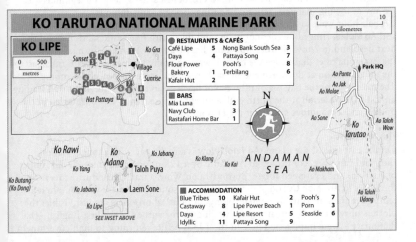

KO TARUTAO NATIONAL MARINE PARK

RESTAURANTS & CAFÉS			
Café Lipe	5	Nong Bank South Sea	3
Daya	4	Pattaya Song	7
Flour Power		Pooh's	8
Bakery		Terbilang	6
Kafair Hut	2		

BARS	
Mia Luna	2
Navy Club	3
Rastafari Home Bar	1

ACCOMMODATION					
Blue Tribes	10	Kafair Hut	2	Pooh's	7
Castaway	8	Lipe Power Beach	1	Porn	3
Daya	4	Lipe Resort	5	Seaside	6
Idyllic	11	Pattaya Song	9		

ANDAMAN SEA

5

TRANSPORT TO AND FROM PAK BARA

The main port for Bulon Lae, Tarutao and Lipe is **PAK BARA**, towards the north end of Satun province. **From Trang**, there are direct a/c minibuses and share taxis to Pak Bara (see p.402); otherwise you'll need to take a Satun-bound bus (2hr–2hr 30min) to the inland town of **Langu** and change there to a red songthaew for the 10km hop to the port. There are also direct a/c minibuses **from Hat Yai** (see p.420), while **from Satun**, frequent buses and a/c minibuses make the 50km trip to Langu, where you'll have to change onto a songthaew. Andrew Tour in Pak Bara (☏081 897 6482) lays on a/c minibuses to and from Krabi and Hat Yai when they have enough customers.

---

rarely encountered; and the park is the habitat of about 25 percent of the world's tropical fish species, as well as dugongs, sperm whales, dolphins and a dwindling population of turtles.

The park amenities on Adang, though not on Tarutao, are officially closed to tourists in the monsoon season from mid-May to mid-November (the exact dates vary from year to year). Accommodation is especially likely to get full around the three New Years (Thai, Chinese and Western), when it's best to book national park rooms in advance (see p.38).

Ko Tarutao

The largest of the national park's islands, **KO TARUTAO** offers the greatest natural variety: mountains covered in semi-evergreen rainforest rise steeply to a high point of 700m; limestone caves and mangrove swamps dot the shoreline; and the west coast is lined with perfect beaches for most of its 26km length. For a different perspective on Ko Tarutao, John Gray's Sea Canoe in Phuket runs multi-day **sea-kayaking** trips, either guided or self-paddle, around the island (☏076 254505–7, ⊛johngray-seacanoe.com).

The west coast

At **Ao Pante**, site of the **park headquarters**, you'll find the only shop on the island, selling basic supplies, as well as a visitor centre. Behind the settlement, the steep, half-hour climb to **To-Boo cliff** is a must, especially at sunset, for the view of the surrounding islands and the crocodile's-head cape at the north end of the bay. A fun ninety-minute trip by boat (B400/boat; contact the visitor centre to book) or kayak can also be made near Ao Pante, up the canal which leads 2km inland from the pier, through a bird-filled mangrove swamp, to **Crocodile Cave** – where you're unlikely to see any of the big snappers, reported sightings being highly dubious.

A half-hour walk south from Ao Pante brings you to the two quiet bays of **Ao Jak** and **Ao Molae**, fringed by coconut palms and filled with fine white sand. Beyond the next headland (a 2hr walk from Ao Pante) lies **Ao Sone** (which gets its name from the casuarina trees that fringe the beach), where a pretty freshwater stream runs past the ranger station at the north end of the bay, a good place for peaceful camping. The main part of the bay is a 3km sweep of flawless sand, with a one-hour trail leading up to **Lu Du Waterfall** at the north end, a ninety-minute trail to **Lo Po Waterfall** in the middle and a **mangrove swamp** at the far south end.

The east coast

On the east side of the island, **Ao Taloh Wow** is a rocky bay with a ranger station, shop and campsite, connected to Ao Pante by a 12km-long road through old rubber plantations and evergreen forest. Beyond Taloh Wow, a trail (5hr return) cuts through the forest to **Ao Taloh Udang**, a sandy bay on the south side where you can pitch a tent. Here the remnants of a penal colony for political prisoners are just visible: the plotters of two failed coup attempts – including the author of the first English–Thai dictionary – were imprisoned here in the 1930s before returning to high government posts. The ordinary convicts, who used to be imprisoned here and at Ao Taloh Wow, had a much harsher time, and during World War II, when supplies from the mainland dried up, prisoners and guards ganged together to turn to piracy. This turned into a lucrative business, which was not suppressed until 1946 when the Thai government asked the British in Malaysia to send in three hundred troops. Pirates and smugglers still occasionally hide out in the Tarutao archipelago, but the main problem now is illegal trawlers fishing in national park waters.

ARRIVAL AND DEPARTURE   KO TARUTAO

From Pak Bara and Ko Lipe At least once a day, the speedboat services between Pak Bara and Ko Lipe (see p.417) call in at Ko Tarutao; currently it's the 11.30am boat from Pak Bara (30min; B300–350) and the 9.30am boat from Lipe (1hr; B350). If you're planning to visit both

islands, you can buy a ticket for B500 that will allow you to stop off at Tarutao on your way to Lipe. Boats drop passengers off at Ao Pante on Tarutao; the pier at Ao Pante is sometimes inaccessible at low tide, when longtails (B30) shuttle people to shore.

GETTING AROUND

By truck The visitor centre can arrange transport by road, usually in an open truck, to several of the island's beaches, charging B50 per person to Ao Molae, around B400 per vehicle to Ao Sone and B600 per vehicle to Ao Taloh Wow.
By boat Transfers to the same places by boat cost at least

twice as much, though you may be tempted by a round-island boat trip for B3000.
By kayak or mountain bike Kayaks and mountain bikes are available at headquarters.

ACCOMMODATION

National park accommodation At park headquarters, the bungalows (sleeping four people, or available as twin rooms), which are spread over a large, quiet park behind the beach, are for the main part national park standard issue with cold-water bathrooms, but there are also some basic mattress-on-floor four-person rooms in longhouses, sharing bathrooms, as well as a restaurant. There are also

bungalows containing en-suite twin rooms and a small restaurant at Ao Molae. HQ bungalow B1000, HQ twin room from B600, HQ longhouse room B500, Ao Molae twin room B600
Camping There are campsites at Ao Pante, Ao Molae and Ao Taloh Wow. Two-person tents can be rented from Ao Pante for B150/night (plus B50/person for bedding).

Ko Adang

At **KO ADANG**, a wild, rugged island covered in tropical rainforest 40km west of Ko Tarutao, the park station is at **Laem Sone** on the southern shore, where the beach is steep and narrow and backed by a thick canopy of pines. The half-hour climb to **Sha-do** cliff on the steep slope above Laem Sone gives good views over Ko Lipe to the south, while about 2km west along the coast from the park station, a twenty-minute trail leads inland to the small **Pirate Waterfall**.

ARRIVAL AND DEPARTURE   KO ADANG

To get to Ko Adang, take any boat to Ko Lipe (see p.416): if the boat moors off Lipe's Hat Pattaya, a longtail transfer to Adang will cost B100/person; if it stops in the channel between the two islands, the transfer to Adang will cost B50.

ACCOMMODATION

There are **rooms** in bamboo longhouses at the park station at **Laem Sone** (B300/room sleeping three), **bungalows** sleeping two–eight people (B600–1800), and two/three-person **tents** can be rented (B150–225/night). There's a **restaurant** here, too.

SNORKELLING TRIPS AROUND KO ADANG

You can charter **longtail boats** (and rent snorkels and masks, for around B50/day) through the rangers for excellent snorkelling trips to nearby islands such as Ko Rawi and Ko Jabang (around B1500–2500 for up to ten people, depending on how far you want to go).

5

Ko Lipe

Home to a population of around a thousand *chao ley*, tiny **KO LIPE**, 2km south of Ko Adang (see the map on p.413), is something of a frontier maverick, attracting ever more travellers with one dazzling beach, fifty or so private bungalow resorts and a rough-and-ready atmosphere. It's technically a part of Ko Tarutao National Marine Park, but the authorities seem to have given up on the island and don't collect an admission fee from visitors. A small, flat triangle, Lipe is covered in coconut plantations and supports a school and a health centre in the village on the eastern side. By rights, such a settlement should never have been allowed to develop within the national park boundaries, but the *chao ley* on Lipe are well entrenched: Satun's governor forced the community to move here from Phuket and Ko Lanta between the world wars, to reinforce the island's Thai character and prevent the British rulers of Malaya from laying claim to it.

More recently, a huge, diverse influx of tourists – Westerners, Thais and Malaysians, families and backpackers – has been enticed here by the gorgeous beach of **Hat Pattaya**, a shining crescent of squeaky-soft white sand with an offshore reef to explore on its eastern side, as well as by the relaxed, anything-goes atmosphere and mellow nightlife. Many of Lipe's *chao ley* have now sold their beachfront land to Thai–Chinese speculators from the mainland, who have increased the island's capacity to over two thousand guest rooms; with the money earned, the *chao ley* have bought the scores of longtail boats that clog up the bay at Hat Pattaya. Lipe's main drag is **Walking Street**, a paved path lined with tourist businesses between the eastern end of Hat Pattaya and the south end of the village, which lies on east-facing **Sunrise**, an exposed, largely featureless beach that gives access to some good snorkelling around Ko Gra; a few other narrow roads also radiate out from the village. The other island track that's most likely to be useful runs from *Daya Resort* at the west end of Pattaya across to **Sunset** beach, a shady, attractive spot with good views of Ko Adang, in around ten minutes.

ARRIVAL AND DEPARTURE
KO LIPE

As well as being one of the hubs for island-hopping boats (see p.406), Ko Lipe is served by **ferries** from Thammalang pier near Satun town, **speedboats** from Pak Bara in the north of Satun province, and ferries and speedboats from the Malaysian island of Langkawi. However, services to Lipe seem to change by the year, due to competition between the boat companies and local politicking; for up-to-date **transport information**, contact Koh Lipe Thailand.com (see opposite). There is no pier on Lipe, so boats anchor off Hat Pattaya or sometimes in the channel between the island and Ko Adang, where they're met by **longtails** (B50/person to any beach on Lipe).

Via Thammalang From roughly November to the beginning of May, Andaman Express (☎ 086 964 8929, ⓦ andaman-express.com) operates a daily ferry between Thammalang and Ko Lipe, currently departing from the

---

SNORKELLING AND DIVING AROUND KO LIPE

The prime **diving and snorkelling sites** around Ko Lipe are around Ko Adang, Ko Rawi and Ko Dong, just to the north and west in Ko Tarutao National Marine Park, where encounters with reef and even whale sharks, dolphins and stingrays are not uncommon. Further afield to the south, advanced divers head for Eight Mile Rock, a pinnacle that rises to about 14m from the surface, with soft corals, mantas, leopard and whale sharks. A handful of dive shops operate on Lipe, and there are dozens of places offering snorkelling day-trips on *chao ley* longtail boats; snorkellers are liable to pay the park admission fee of B200, though some longtail captains will try to dodge the park rangers.

Koh Lipe Thailand.com See opposite. Snorkelling trips to the best sites around the islands on the west side of Ko Adang for B550–650/person, including lunch.
Sabye Sports On the east side of Porn Resort, behind Flour Power Bakery, on Sunset beach

☎089 464 5884, ⓦsabye-sports.com. Canadian-run dive shop, Lipe's oldest, which offers daily trips (from B2000, plus equipment rental, for two dives) and PADI courses (B12,900 for the Openwater). Also does snorkelling equipment rental (B150/day including fins).

mainland at 12.30pm, from the island at 9.30am (2hr 15min; B600). Orange songthaews (roughly every 30min; B40), as well as chartered tuk-tuks (B150) and motorcycle taxis (B60–70), cover the 10km between Thammalang and Satun town.

Via Pak Bara Several companies run speedboats between Pak Bara (see box, p.414) and Ko Lipe in high season (at least 5 daily; 1hr 30min; B400–650). In the rainy season,

there's at least one crossing a day, usually heading out at either 11.30am or 1pm.

Via Langkawi Speedboats operate between Ko Lipe and Langkawi, the large Malaysian island to the southeast, four times a day in high season (1hr; B1200); there's also a daily ferry (1hr 30min; B1100). During the season, a Thai immigration post is set up at the far east end of Lipe's Hat Pattaya to cover this route.

GETTING AROUND

By mountain bike You can rent mountain bikes from several places, including the shop next to *Pooh's* on the Walking Street between Hat Pattaya and Sunrise (see p.418) for B200/day.

INFORMATION

Koh Lipe Thailand.com The best travel agent and source of information on the island, including a good website, is Koh Lipe Thailand.com (Boi's Travel; ☏ 089 464 5854 or ☏ 081 541 4489, ⌨ kohlipethailand.com), which currently has two outlets on Walking Street between Hat Pattaya and the village, with the main one hard by the beach (the second shop, further inland towards *Pooh's*, has a book exchange). On offer are all manner of transport tickets (including discounted boat tickets) plus accommodation bookings (including on the website).

ACCOMMODATION

The majority of Lipe's bungalows are on **Hat Pattaya**, the prettiest but most crowded and expensive beach on the island. *Porn Resort* has **Sunset** beach on the northwest side to itself, while a dozen or so resorts have set up shop on **Sunrise**, on the east side near the village. Plenty of accommodation options are bookable in advance through ⌨ kohlipethailand.com; if you turn up on the island and are struggling to find a vacant room, head for one of their offices on Walking Street for booking assistance (see above).

★ **Blue Tribes** East end of Hat Pattaya ☏ 083 654 0316, ⌨ bluetribeslipe.com. Congenial, Italian-run resort and restaurant with very spacious, well-spread and well-designed bungalows and rooms, either in lovely dark wood or in thatched white concrete, sporting large, attractive tiled bathrooms with hot showers; some are two-storey with a balcony and chill-out room/extra bedroom upstairs. B1700

Castaway Sunrise ☏ 083 138 7472, ⌨ castaway-resorts .com. Airy, thatched, mostly two-storey bungalows featuring well-equipped bathrooms with cold rain showers, ceiling fans, big decks, hammocks and a certain amount of style, mostly bestowed by the distinctive red Indonesian hardwood that they're made from. On a sandy patch with a dive shop, a mellow, multi-tiered bar-restaurant and a massage spa; kayaks and snorkels for rent. B2000

Daya West end of Hat Pattaya ☏ 081 479 0682, ✉ dayaresort@hotmail.com. *Chao ley*-owned resort with over thirty colourful, en-suite rooms and bungalows in a large, shady, flower-strewn garden, ranging from simple concrete rooms to clapboard bungalows in a great position on the beach. Wi-fi, kayaks and snorkels available. B500

Idyllic South end of Sunrise ☏ 081 802 5453, ⌨ idyllic resort.com. This welcoming "concept resort" comes as a big surprise out here in Thailand's far maritime corner, with its angular contemporary architecture in white, grey and wood. Set in an attractive garden, the minimalist rooms boast huge windows, a/c, hot outdoor rain showers, DVD players and nice

touches such as sun hats for guests' use. There are two pools – one infinity-edged and beachside, with a swim-up bar, the other with a jacuzzi – as well as kayaks and other watersports, and free wi-fi in the restaurant. Breakfast included. B5900

Kafair Hut 150m inland from Sunset Beach, on the track to the village ☏ 081 541 9870, bookable online through ⌨ kohlipethailand.com. Gentle, welcoming café and resort, offering three attractive, breezy, red-wood bungalows on high stilts, with mosquito nets, fans and modern, semi-outdoor bathrooms. Good breakfast included. B1500

Lipe Power Beach Sunrise, in the village near the school ☏ 081 970 0741, ⌨ lipepowerbeach.com. Seven rows of five clapboard bungalows each, very tightly packed together though scattered with colourful flowers. All have polished-concrete bathrooms with hot showers, a/c, TVs, mini-bars and safety boxes, and there's a small saltwater swimming pool, internet access and wi-fi (payable). Buffet breakfast included. B3000

Lipe Resort Towards the west end of Hat Pattaya ☏ 074 750291, ⌨ liperesort.com. Welcoming place owned by the village chief in a good position on the beach. Though the grounds are scruffy and few of the rooms are on the sand, the accommodation is neat and clean and represents decent value for a/c and hot showers in large, modern bathrooms. Free kayak, snorkels and basic buffet breakfasts. B3000

Pattaya Song Far west end of Hat Pattaya ☏ 086 960

5

0418, ⓦpattayasongresort.com. Italian-run resort, the oldest on the beach (the name means "Pattaya no. 2"), where plain, good-sized, en-suite clapboard or concrete bungalows are strung out away from the beach (the cheapest, with small bathrooms) or in a lovely location up on a steep promontory with great views of the bay; kayaks for rent. **B500**

Pooh's On Walking Street between Sunrise and Hat Pattaya ☎074 750345, ⓦpoohlipe.com. Well inland behind the popular restaurant, but a good, functional choice if you get stuck for somewhere to stay. The eight concrete single-storey rooms have small terraces, a/c, hot showers and TVs, and there's free wi-fi and a dive centre.

Breakfast included. **B1800**

★ **Porn Resort** Sunset ☎084 691 8743. Popular, attractive and well-run spot in a pleasant, spacious, sloping setting under the trees on the beach. Well-designed bungalows come with verandas, mosquito nets and en-suite bathrooms, or you can pitch your own tent in a prime spot by the beach (B100). Snorkelling equipment for rent. **B400**

Seaside Near the midpoint of Hat Pattaya ☎087 398 7932. Good-value, *chao ley*-owned resort, offering basic but sturdy woven-bamboo, en-suite bungalows with mosquito nets, in plenty of space on a grassy patch and under a little shade, behind the popular *Family* restaurant. **B600**

EATING AND DRINKING

Besides the **bars** reviewed below, there are a couple of beach bars on Sunset, but the east end of Pattaya has the biggest concentration, with low candlelit tables and cushions sprawled on the sand, fire shows and names like *Peace and Love*. Also check out ⓦpirates4ever.de for details of their electronic underground **parties** at *Mia Luna* bar on a small cove beach to the west of Sunset (weekly, according to the moon's phases; camping available).

Café Lipe Near the midpoint of Hat Pattaya. Eco-conscious, solar-powered place behind a thick screen of foliage that serves up decent veggie choices among its inexpensive Thai dishes, sandwiches, salads and espressos, as well as home-made bread, cakes and muesli. Daily 6am–5pm.

Daya West end of Hat Pattaya ☎081 479 0682. One of the most popular of half a dozen restaurants that lay out candlelit tables and seafood barbecues on the beach at night. It also offers a long menu of mostly Thai dishes, such as prawn tempura (B120), lots of tofu options for vegetarians, Thai desserts and Western breakfasts. Daily 8am–10pm.

★ **Flour Power Bakery** Sunset. At shady, beachfront tables, you can feast on delicious home-made brownies, croissants (B60), baguettes and blueberry pie as well as sandwiches (from B100), spaghetti and Thai dishes including vegetarian options. There are also wines by the glass, cocktails, water refills from their cooler and rental kayaks if you want to burn off the calories. Daily 7.30am–8.30pm.

Kafair Hut 150m inland from Sunset Beach, on the track to the village ☎081 541 9870. Tiny, mellow café for deli sandwiches (from B80), simple Thai food, breakfasts, shakes and espresso coffees. Daily 7.30am–6/7pm.

Navy Club Far east end of Hat Pattaya. On the edge of the navy base, this friendly, jerry-built bar and shop with a few wooden benches is the best spot for a quiet, cheap, ice-cold beer watching the sun set. Daily 6/7am till midnight or later, depending on who's in.

Nong Bank South Sea Towards the west end of Hat Pattaya, just east of Lipe Resort. Friendly restaurant with

tables on the beach, which are shaded in the mornings, serving tasty Thai and Western food, including breakfasts, lots of curries (B80 for a small plate), Thai desserts, juices and shakes. Daily 7am–11.30pm.

Pattaya Song Far west end of Hat Pattaya ☎086 960 0418. At tables on the sand here, tuck into very tasty gnocchi bolognese (B240) and other home-made pasta, Italian sausages, Thai-style seafood and, in the evenings, authentic pizzas (from B180), all washed down with Italian wines. Daily 8am–10pm.

Pooh's On Walking Street between Sunrise and Hat Pattaya ☎074 750345. Well-run and welcoming bar-restaurant that's a popular hive of activity, with free wi-fi. Offers tasty Thai food, including chicken with cashew nuts (B150) and vegetarian dishes, as well as sandwiches, cakes, evening barbecues and live music, plus a wide choice of breakfasts and espresso coffees. Daily roughly 9am–10pm.

Rastafari Home Bar Just north of the main track from Sunset to the village, next to the entrance to Mountain Resort. Genial and eccentric outdoor rasta bar serving plenty of cocktails and furnished with driftwood painted red, gold and green, a campfire and a circle of filled-in yellow toilet bowls to get sociable on. Their motto is "open when closed".

Terbilang Walking Street, about 50m inland from Hat Pattaya on the right-hand side. Famous outlet for all manner of outlandish roti pancakes – basil chicken cheese roti, anyone? – as well as the more familiar roti with chicken curry (*matabah*; B60) and banana roti (B50). Also does strong, traditional Thai coffee, teas and shakes. Daily noon–midnight.

DIRECTORY

Currency exchange There are currently no ATMs on Ko Lipe (the nearest are in Satun and Pak Bara), but Koh Lipe Thailand.com, for instance (see p.417), offers currency

exchange and cash advances.

Internet access Available at Koh Lipe Thailand.com (B3, minute, discounted for travel agency customers).

5

Tourist police At *Pooh's* restaurant on Walking Street between Sunrise and Hat Pattaya ☎ 1155.

Satun town

Nestling in the last wedge of Thailand's west coast, the remote town of **SATUN** is served by just one road, Highway 406, which approaches through forbidding karst outcrops. Set in a green valley bordered by limestone hills, the town is leafy and relaxing but not especially interesting, except during its small version of the Vegetarian Festival (see p.325) and its International Kite Festival at the end of February; the boat services to and from Kuala Perlis and Langkawi in Malaysia and Ko Lipe are the main reason for foreigners to come here.

National Museum

Soi 5, Thanon Satun Thani, on the north side of the centre • Wed–Sun 9am–4pm • B30

If you find yourself with time on your hands in Satun, it's worth seeking out the **National Museum**. It's memorable, as much as anything else, for its setting, in the graceful **Kuden Mansion**, which was built in British colonial style, with some Thai and Malay features, by craftsmen from Penang, and inaugurated in 1902 as the Satun governor's official residence. The exhibits and audiovisuals in English have a distinctive anthropological tone, but are diverting enough, notably concerning Thai Muslims, the *chao ley* on Ko Lipe, and the **Sakai**, a dwindling band of nomadic hunter-gatherers who still live in the jungle of southern Thailand.

Map

▲ Pak Bara, Trang & Hat Yai

SATUN

■ ACCOMMODATION
On's Guest House	2
Rian Thong	4
Satunthanee Hotel	1
Sinkiat Thani Hotel	3

Wangmai Hotel

406

Minibuses to Hat Yai
THANON YATRA SAWATAL

▲ Khao To Yong Kong

National Museum

Police Station

Khlong Mambang

THANON SATUN THANI

Night Market

Satun Hospital ✚

HATTHAKAM SUEKSA

Baw Khaw Saw Office

BUREEWANIT

Mambang Mosque

Share-taxis to Hat Yai

THANON SARIT PHUMINAT

THANON PHUNGA TRIMUK

THANON SAMAN PRADIT

N

THANON SULAKANUKUL

Minibuses to Langu

THANON SAKHI UTITHAM

0   200
metres

WISET MAYURA

Songthaews to Thammalang

● RESTAURANTS & CAFÉS
| Go Ho | 2 |
| On's | 1 |

▼ Thammalang Pier

By bus Satun's new bus station is far to the southeast of the centre on the new bypass, but Hat Yai and non-a/c Trang buses usually do a tour of the town centre, stopping, for example, in front of the *Sinkiat Thani Hotel* on Thanon Bureewanit; incoming a/c buses from Phuket via Trang (4 daily) will set you down on Thanon Satun Thani by the *Wangmai* hotel; and you can book tickets in advance at the central Baw Khaw Saw office on Thanon Hatthakam Sueksa.

Destinations: Bangkok (4 daily; 16hr); Hat Yai (hourly; 2hr); Phuket (4 daily; 7hr); Trang (hourly; 2hr 30min–3hr).
By minibus or **share-taxi** The bases for a/c minibuses to Langu and Hat Yai and share taxis to Hat Yai are marked on our map.
By ferry There are high-season ferries from nearby Thammalang pier to Ko Lipe (see p.416), as well as boats to Kuala Perlis and Langkawi in Malaysia (see box, p.420).

GETTING AROUND

By motorbike or car On Kongnual (see below) offers motorbike (B250/day) and car rental (B1500/day).

INFORMATION AND TOURS

On Kongnual 36 Thanon Bureewanit ☎ 074 724133 or ☎ 081 097 9783, ✉ onmarch13@hotmail.com. From her restaurant, *On's: The Kitchen*, near the *Sinkiat Thani Hotel*, On

Kongnual dispenses helpful tourist information, sells all kinds of transport tickets and can organize local river-kayaking trips and cave visits.

5

CROSSING INTO MALAYSIA FROM SATUN

From **Thammalang** pier, 10km south of Satun at the mouth of the river, boats leave when full on 45-minute trips (B150/person) to **Kuala Perlis** on the northwest tip of Malaysia, from where there are plentiful transport connections down the west coast; 9am is usually a good time to turn up at Thammalang for these boats, but they need a minimum of ten passengers (or B1500), which means that on some days they don't run. Three ferry boats a day cross from Thammalang to the Malaysian island of **Langkawi** (1hr 15min; B300). The journey from Satun town to Thammalang is covered by orange songthaews (roughly every 30min; B40) from near the 7-Eleven supermarket on Thanon Sulakanukul, as well as chartered tuk-tuks (B150) and motorcycle taxis (B60–70).

It's also possible to cross by road to Malaysia's **Kangar** (which has bus connections to Penang and Kuala Lumpur) and Alor Setar through Thale Ban National Park, though a little tricky as the a/c minibuses (B300; about 2hr) depart from Ban Khuan, 20km or so up Highway 406 from Satun – contact local fixer On (see p.419) to arrange this.

ACCOMMODATION

On's Guest House 36 Thanon Bureewanit ✆ 074 724133 or ✆ 081 097 9783, ✉ onmarch13@hotmail.com. Three big, bright rooms in a modern, Sino-Portuguese-style building above *On's: The Kitchen* restaurant, with wooden shutters, coloured-glass windows, a/c, hot showers, fridges, satellite TV and free wi-fi. B650

Rian Thong 4 Thanon Saman Pradit ✆ 074 711036. Just on the west side of the centre, this is a decent budget hotel with friendly owners, where some of the large, en-suite rooms with TVs overlook the canal. B200

Satunthanee Hotel Thanon Satun Thani ✆ 074 711010. This centrally placed, good-value, traditional Chinese hotel offers battered but clean rooms with small bathrooms and TVs, though it suffers from noise from the road and the mosque. Fan B280, a/c B350

Sinkiat Thani Hotel 50 Thanon Bureewanit ✆ 074 721055–8, ✉ sinkiathotel@hotmail.com. Satun's top hotel, offering large, carpeted bedrooms with a/c, hot water, fridges, TVs and good views over the surrounding countryside from the upper floors; a more deluxe wing at the back of the building was being built at the time of writing. B680

EATING AND DRINKING

For a meal in the evening, you can't do much better than the lively and popular night market, north of the centre on the west side of Thanon Satun Thani.

Go Ho Thanon Saman Pradit opposite the Chinese temple. A cheap, busy, friendly restaurant with leafy pavement tables that serves tasty Thai and Chinese food, including plenty of seafood (according to market price), salads and southern specialities such as *kaeng som* (B70). Daily 5pm–midnight.

On's: The Kitchen 36 Thanon Bureewanit ✆ 074 724133. Very tasty Thai food, including southern specialities, some interesting fish dishes and handy set menus, such as green curry with prawn patties (*thawt man kung*) and rice for B120. Also offers a wide array of Western food, including good breakfasts, jacket potatoes and pies, espresso coffees and free wi-fi. (On's bar, a couple of doors away, *The Living Room*, has a computer for customers' use, as well as free wi-fi, and stays open late.) Daily 8am–10pm.

Hat Yai

Travelling to or through **HAT YAI**, the biggest city in the region, is currently **not recommended** because of the troubles in the south (see p.401). To be honest, you're not missing much, but as it's a major transport axis, we've provided a few, rudimentary practicalities and a map of the city, in case you get stuck there. The three main Niphat Uthit roads are known locally as *sai neung*, *sai sawng* and *sai saam*.

ARRIVAL AND DEPARTURE

The helpful Cathay Tour (✆ 074 235044, 🌐 cathaytourthailand.com), a **travel agency** on the ground floor of the guesthouse of the same name (see opposite), handles onward flight, bus, share-taxi and a/c minibus bookings, both within Thailand and into Malaysia.

By plane About 5km south of town, Hat Yai airport is connected to the downtown area by a/c minibuses (B80) and has Avis (☎074 227259, ⓦavisthailand.com) and Budget (☎074 227268, ⓦbudget.co.th) car rental desks.

By train The train station is on the west side of the centre at the end of Thanon Thamnoon Vithi.

By bus or minibus The bus terminal is southeast of the centre on Thanon Kanchanawanit, while the a/c minibus terminal at Talat Kaset is about 5km west of town, both leaving you with a songthaew ride to the centre.

INFORMATION

Tourist information The TAT office is at 1/1 Soi 2, Thanon Niphat Uthit 3 (daily 8.30am–4.30pm; ☎074 243747 or ☎074 238518, ⓔtatsgkhl@tat.or.th).

ACCOMMODATION

Cathay Guest House 93 Thanon Niphat Uthit 2 ☎074 243815. This friendly place in the heart of town has long been Hat Yai's main travellers' hub, and the café, which has internet access, acts as a sociable meeting place; the rooms have fans and en-suite cold-water bathrooms but are rather run-down. B200

Lee Gardens Plaza Hotel 29 Thanon Prachatipat ☎074 261111, ⓦleeplaza.com. Characterless but good-value and central upmarket option with great views of the city from its four hundred comfortable a/c rooms. Facilities include a fitness centre, a rooftop pool and a 33rd-floor panoramic restaurant. Breakfast included. B1300

Centara Hotel 3 Thanon Sanehanusorn ☎074 352222, ⓦcentarahotelsresorts.com. Luxury hotel in a good location next to the Central Department Store, featuring contemporary-styled rooms with wi-fi, a spa, fitness centre, sauna, swimming pool and Thai, Chinese and Japanese food at its several restaurants. B1800

DIRECTORY

Tourist police Thanon Niphat Uthit 3, near the TAT office ☎074 246733 or ☎1155.

MEDITATING BUDDHA, WAT KHLONG PHRAO, KO CHANG (TRA

Contexts

History

Thailand's history is complex and fascinating, but what follows can be only a brief account of the major events in the country's past. For more detailed coverage, get hold of a copy of David Wyatt's excellent *Thailand: A Short History* (see p.441).

Early history

The region's first distinctive civilization, **Dvaravati**, which encompassed city-states in central and northern Thailand, was established around two thousand years ago by an Austroasiatic-speaking people known as the Mon. One of its mainstays was Theravada Buddhism, which had probably been introduced to Thailand during the third century BC by Indian missionaries. In the eighth century, peninsular Thailand to the south of Dvaravati came under the control of **Srivijaya**, a Mahayana Buddhist state centred on Sumatra, which had strong ties with India.

From the ninth century onwards, both Dvaravati and Srivijaya Thailand succumbed to invading **Khmers** from Cambodia, who took control of northeastern, central and peninsular Thailand. They ruled from Angkor and left dozens of spectacular temple complexes throughout the region. By the thirteenth century, however, the Khmers had overreached themselves and were in no position to resist the onslaught of a vibrant new force in Southeast Asia: the **Thais**. The earliest traceable history of the Thai people picks them up in southern China around the fifth century AD, when they were squeezed by Chinese and Vietnamese expansionism into sparsely inhabited northeastern Laos. Their first significant entry into what is now Thailand seems to have happened in the north, where, some time after the seventh century, the Thais formed a state known as Yonok. Theravada Buddhism spread to Yonok via Dvaravati around the end of the tenth century, which served not only to unify the Thais themselves, but also to link them to the wider community of Buddhists.

By the end of the twelfth century, they formed the majority of the population in Thailand, then under the control of the Khmer empire. The Khmers' main outpost, at Lopburi, was by this time regarded as the administrative capital of a land called "Syam".

Sukhothai

Some time around 1238, Thais in the upper Chao Phraya valley captured the main Khmer outpost in the region at **Sukhothai** and established a kingdom there. When the young Ramkhamhaeng came to the throne around 1278, he seized control of much of the Chao Phraya valley, and over the next twenty years gained the submission of most of Thailand under a complex system of tribute-giving and protection – the political system that persisted in Thailand until the end of the nineteenth century.

Although the kingdom of Sukhothai extended Thai control over a vast area, its

6800 BC	3rd century BC	6th–9th centuries AD
Date of earliest pottery found in Thailand	Theravada Buddhism probably first enters Thailand	Dvaravati civilization flourishes

greatest contribution to the Thais' development was at home, in cultural and political matters. A famous inscription by Ramkhamhaeng, now housed in the Bangkok National Museum, describes a prosperous era of benevolent rule, and it is generally agreed that Ramkhamhaeng ruled justly according to Theravada Buddhist doctrine. A further sign of the Thais' growing self-confidence was the invention of a new script to make their tonal language understood by the non-Thai inhabitants of the land.

Ayutthaya

After the death of Ramkhamhaeng around 1299, however, Sukhothai's power waned, and **Ayutthaya** became the most powerful Thai city-state. Soon after founding the city in 1351, the ambitious King Ramathibodi united the principalities of the lower Chao Phraya valley, which had formed the western provinces of the Khmer empire. When he recruited his bureaucracy from the urban elite of Lopburi, Ramathibodi set the style of government at Ayutthaya, elements of which persist to the present day. The elaborate etiquette, language and rituals of Angkor were adopted, and, most importantly, so was the concept of the ruler as *devaraja* (divine king).

The site chosen by Ramathibodi for an international port was the best in the region, and so began Ayutthaya's rise to prosperity, based on exploiting the upswing in trade in the middle of the fourteenth century along the routes between India and China. By 1540, Ayutthaya held sway over most of the area of modern-day Thailand. Despite a 1568 invasion by the Burmese, which led to twenty years of foreign rule, Ayutthaya made a spectacular comeback, and in the seventeenth century its foreign trade boomed. In 1511, the Portuguese had become the first Western power to trade with Ayutthaya, while a treaty with Spain in 1598 was followed by similar agreements with Holland and England in 1608 and 1612 respectively. European merchants flocked to Thailand, not only to buy Thai products, but also for the Chinese and Japanese goods on sale there.

In the mid-eighteenth century, however, the rumbling in the Burmese jungle to the north began to make itself heard again. After an unsuccessful siege in 1760, February 1766 saw the **Burmese** descend upon the city for the last time. The Thais held out for over a year but, finally, in April 1767, the city was taken. The Burmese savagely razed everything to the ground, led off tens of thousands of prisoners to Burma and abandoned the city to the jungle.

From Taksin to Rama III

Out of this lawless mess emerged **Phraya Taksin**, a charismatic general, who was crowned king in December 1768 at his new capital of **Thonburi**, on the opposite bank of the river from modern-day Bangkok. Within two years, he had restored all of Ayutthaya's territories and, by the end of the next decade, had brought Cambodia and much of Laos under Thai control.

However, by 1779 all was not well with the king. Taksin was becoming increasingly irrational and sadistic, and in March 1782 he was ousted in a coup. Chao Phraya Chakri, Taksin's military commander, was invited to take power and had Taksin executed.

1278	1351	1511
Ramkhamhaeng "the Great" comes to the throne of Sukhothai	Ramathibodi founds Ayutthaya	The first Western power, Portugal, begins trading with Ayutthaya

With the support of the Ayutthayan aristocracy, Chakri – reigning as **Rama I** (1782–1809) – set about consolidating the Thai kingdom. His first act was to move the capital across the river to what we know as Bangkok, on the more defensible east bank. Borrowing from the layout of Ayutthaya, he built a new royal palace and impressive monasteries in the area of Ratanakosin within a defensive ring of two (later expanded to three) canals. In the palace temple, Wat Phra Kaeo, he enshrined the talismanic Emerald Buddha, which he had snatched during his campaigns in Laos. Trade with China revived, and the style of government was put on a more modern footing: while retaining many of the features of a *devaraja*, he shared more responsibility with his courtiers, as a first among equals.

The peaceful accession of Rama I's son as **Rama II** (1809–24) signalled the establishment of the Chakri dynasty, which is still in place today. This Second Reign is best remembered as a fertile period for Thai literature; indeed, Rama II himself is renowned as one of the great Thai poets.

By the reign of **Rama III** (1824–51), the Thais were starting to get alarmed by British colonialism in the region. In 1826, Rama III was obliged to sign the Burney Treaty, a limited trade agreement with the British, by which the Thais won some political security in return for reducing their taxes on goods passing through Bangkok.

Mongkut and Chulalongkorn

Rama IV, commonly known to foreigners as **Mongkut** (in Thai, *Phra Chom Klao*; 1851–68), had been a Buddhist monk for 27 years when he succeeded his brother. But far from leading a cloistered life, Mongkut had travelled widely throughout Thailand, and had taken an interest in Western learning, studying English, Latin and the sciences. Realizing that Thailand would be unable to resist the military might of the British, the king reduced import and export taxes, allowed British subjects to live and own land in Thailand and granted them freedom of trade under the Bowring Treaty. Within a decade, similar agreements had been signed with France, the United States and a score of other nations. Thus, by skilful diplomacy the king avoided a close relationship with just one power, which could easily have led to Thailand's annexation.

Mongkut's son, **Chulalongkorn**, took the throne as Rama V (1868–1910) at the age of only fifteen, but was well prepared by an education which mixed traditional Thai and modern Western elements – provided by Mrs Anna Leonowens, subject of *The King and I*. One of his first acts was to scrap the custom by which subjects were required to prostrate themselves in the presence of the king. In the 1880s, he began to restructure the government to meet the country's needs, setting up a host of departments – for education, public health, the army and the like – and bringing in scores of foreign advisors to help with everything from foreign affairs to railway lines.

Throughout this period, however, the Western powers maintained their pressure on the region. The most serious threat to Thai sovereignty was the Franco-Siamese Crisis of 1893, which culminated in the French sending gunboats up the Chao Phraya River to Bangkok. Flouting numerous international laws, France claimed control over Laos and made other outrageous demands, which Chulalongkorn had no option but to agree to. During the course of his reign, the country ceded control over huge areas of tributary states, and forewent large sums of tax revenue in order to preserve its

1767	1782	1893
Ayutthaya is razed to the ground by the Burmese	A grandiose new capital, Bangkok, is established, modelled on Ayutthaya	The Franco-Siamese Crisis obliges Thailand to give up its claims to Laos and Cambodia

independence. However, by Chulalongkorn's death in 1910, the frontiers were fixed as they are today.

The end of absolute monarchy and World War II

Chulalongkorn was succeeded by a flamboyant, British-educated prince, **Vajiravudh** (Rama VI, 1910–25), and by the time the young and inexperienced **Prajadhipok** – 76th child of Chulalongkorn – was catapulted to the throne as Rama VII (1925–35), Vajiravudh's extravagance had created severe financial problems, which were exacerbated by the onset of the Great Depression.

On June 24, 1932, a small group of middle-ranking officials, dissatisfied with the injustices of monarchical government and led by a lawyer, **Pridi Phanomyong**, and an army major, Luang Phibunsongkhram (**Phibun**), staged a coup with only a handful of troops. Prajadhipok weakly submitted to the conspirators, and a hundred and fifty years of **absolute monarchy** in Bangkok came to a sudden end. The king was sidelined to a position of symbolic significance, and in 1935 he abdicated in favour of his ten-year-old nephew, Ananda, then a schoolboy living in Switzerland.

Phibun emerged as prime minister after the decisive elections of 1938, and a year later officially renamed the country Thailand ("Land of the Free") – Siam, it was argued, was a name bestowed by external forces, and the new title made it clear that the country belonged to the Thais rather than the economically dominant Chinese.

The Thais were dragged into **World War II** on December 8, 1941, when, almost at the same time as the assault on Pearl Harbor, the Japanese invaded the east coast of peninsular Thailand, with their sights set on Singapore to the south. The Thais at first resisted fiercely, but realizing that the position was hopeless, Phibun quickly ordered a ceasefire.

The Thai government concluded a military alliance with Japan and declared war against the United States and Great Britain in January 1942, probably in the belief that the Japanese would win. However, the Thai minister in Washington, Seni Pramoj, refused to deliver the declaration of war against the US, and, in cooperation with the Americans, began organizing a resistance movement called Seri Thai. Pridi Phanomyong, now acting as regent to the young king, secretly coordinated the movement, smuggling in American agents and housing them in Bangkok. By 1944, Japan's defeat looked likely, and in July, Phibun, who had been most closely associated with them, was forced to resign by the National Assembly.

Postwar upheavals

With the fading of the military, the election of January 1946 was the first one contested by organized political parties. Pridi became prime minister, a new constitution was drafted, and the outlook for democratic, civilian government seemed bright. Hopes were shattered, however, on June 9, 1946, when King Ananda was found dead in his bed, with a bullet wound in his forehead. Three palace servants were tried and executed, but the murder has never been satisfactorily explained. Pridi resigned as prime minister, and in April 1948, Phibun, playing on the threat of communism, took

1932	1939	1941
A coup brings the end of the absolute monarchy and introduces Thailand's first constitution	The country's name is changed from Siam to the more nationalistic Thailand	The Japanese invade, and Thailand forms an alliance with them

over the premiership again.

As **communism** developed its hold in the region with the takeover of China in 1949 and the French defeat in Indochina in 1954, the US increasingly viewed Thailand as a bulwark against the red menace. Between 1951 and 1957, when its annual state budget was only about $200 million a year, Thailand received a total of $149 million in American economic aid and $222 million in military aid.

Phibun narrowly won a general election in 1957, but only by blatant vote-rigging and coercion. After vehement public outcry, General Sarit, the commander-in-chief of the army, overthrew the new government in September the same year. Believing that Thailand would prosper best under a unifying authority – an ideology that still has plenty of supporters today – Sarit set about re-establishing the monarchy as the head of the social hierarchy and the source of legitimacy for the government. Ananda's successor, **Bhumibol** (Rama IX), was pushed into an active role, while Sarit ruthlessly silenced critics and pressed ahead with a plan for economic development.

The Vietnam War and the democracy movement

Sarit died in 1963, whereupon the military succession passed to General Thanom. His most pressing problem was the **Vietnam War**. The Thais, with the backing of the US, quietly began to conduct military operations in Laos, to which North Vietnam and China responded by supporting anti-government insurgency in Thailand. By 1968, around 45,000 US military personnel were on Thai soil, which became the base for US bombing raids against North Vietnam and Laos. The effects of the American presence were profound. The economy swelled with dollars, and hundreds of thousands of Thais became reliant on the Americans for a living, with a consequent proliferation of prostitution – centred on Bangkok's infamous Patpong district – and corruption. Moreover, the sudden exposure to Western culture led many to question traditional Thai values and the political status quo.

Poor farmers in particular were becoming increasingly disillusioned with their lot, and many turned against the Bangkok government. At the end of 1964, the Communist Party of Thailand and other groups formed a broad left coalition which soon had the support of several thousand insurgents in remote areas of the northeast and the north. By 1967, a separate threat had arisen in southern Thailand, involving Muslim dissidents and the Chinese-dominated Communist Party of Malaysia.

Thanom was now facing a major security crisis, and in November 1971 he imposed repressive military rule. In response, **student demonstrations** began in June 1973, and in October as many as 500,000 people turned out at Thammasat University in Bangkok to demand a new constitution. Clashes with the police ensued on October 14, during which over 350 people were reported killed, but elements in the army, backed by King Bhumibol, refused to provide enough troops to crush the demonstrators. Later that day, Thanom was forced to resign and leave the country.

In a new climate of openness, **Kukrit Pramoj** formed a coalition of seventeen elected parties and secured a promise of US withdrawal from Thailand, but his government was riven with feuding. In October 1976, the students demonstrated again, protesting against the return of Thanom to Bangkok. This time there was no restraint: supported by elements of the military and the government, the police and reactionary students

1946	1973	1976
Rama VIII is mysteriously shot dead; the present king, Rama IX (Bhumibol), accedes	Bloody student demonstrations bring the downfall of General Thanom	The brutal suppression of further student demos ushers the military back in

launched a massive assault on Thammasat University. On October 6, hundreds of students were brutally beaten, scores were lynched and some even burnt alive; the military took control and suspended the constitution.

"Premocracy"

Soon after, the military-appointed prime minister, Thanin Kraivichien, forced dissidents to undergo anti-communist indoctrination, but his measures seem to have been too repressive even for the military, who forced him to resign in October 1977. General Kriangsak Chomanand took over, and began to break up the insurgency with shrewd offers of amnesty. He in turn was displaced in February 1980 by **General Prem Tinsulanonda**, backed by a broad parliamentary coalition. Untainted by corruption, Prem achieved widespread support, including that of the monarchy. Overseeing a period of rapid economic growth, Prem maintained the premiership until 1988, with a unique mixture of dictatorship and democracy sometimes called **Premocracy**: although never standing for parliament himself, Prem was asked by the legislature after every election to become prime minister. He eventually stepped down (though he remains a powerful privy councillor and very close to the king) because, he said, it was time for the country's leader to be chosen from among its elected representatives.

The 1992 demonstrations and the 1997 constitution

The new prime minister was indeed an elected MP, Chatichai Choonhavan. He pursued a vigorous policy of economic development, but this fostered widespread corruption. Following an economic downturn and Chatichai's attempts to downgrade the political role of the military, the armed forces staged a bloodless coup on February 23, 1991, led by Supreme Commander Sunthorn and General Suchinda, the army commander-in-chief, who became premier.

When Suchinda reneged on promises to make democratic amendments to the constitution, hundreds of thousands of ordinary Thais poured onto the streets around Bangkok's Democracy Monument in **mass demonstrations** between May 17 and 20, 1992. Suchinda brutally crushed the protests, leaving hundreds dead or injured, but was then forced to resign when King Bhumibol expressed his disapproval in a ticking-off that was broadcast on world television.

Elections were held in September, with the **Democrat Party**, led by Chuan Leekpai, a noted upholder of democracy and the rule of law, emerging victorious. Chuan was succeeded in turn by Banharn Silpa-archa – nicknamed by the local press "the walking ATM", a reference to his reputation for buying votes – and General Chavalit Yongchaiyudh. The most significant positive event of the latter's tenure was the approval of a **new constitution** in 1997. Drawn up by an independent drafting assembly, its main points included: direct elections to the senate, rather than appointment of senators by the prime minister; acceptance of the right of assembly as the basis of a democratic society and guarantees of individual rights and freedoms; greater public accountability; and increased popular participation in local administration. The eventual aim of the new charter was to end the traditional system of patronage, vested interests and vote-buying.

1980–88	1991	1992
Period of Premocracy, General Prem's hybrid of military rule and democracy	The military launch a coup, protesting the corruption of the recently democratically elected government	Mass demonstrations lead to bloodshed – and the return of democracy

Tom yam kung: the 1997 economic crisis

In February 1997 foreign-exchange dealers began to mount speculative attacks on the **baht**, alarmed at the size of Thailand's private foreign debt – 250 billion baht in the unproductive property sector alone, much of it accrued through the proliferation of prestigious skyscrapers in Bangkok. Chavalit's government defended the pegged exchange rate, spending $23 billion of the country's formerly healthy foreign-exchange reserves, but at the beginning of July was forced to give up the ghost – the baht was floated and soon went into free-fall. Thailand was forced to seek help from the **IMF**, which in August put together a $17-billion **rescue package**, coupled with severe austerity measures.

In November, the inept Chavalit was replaced by Chuan Leekpai, who immediately took a hard line in following the IMF's advice, which involved maintaining cripplingly high interest rates to protect the baht and slashing government budgets. Although this played well abroad, at home the government encountered increasing hostility from its newly impoverished citizens – the downturn struck with such speed and severity that it was dubbed the **tom yam kung crisis**, after the searingly hot Thai soup. Chuan's tough stance paid off, however, with the baht stabilizing and inflation falling back, and in October 1999 he announced that he was forgoing almost $4 billion of the IMF's package.

Thaksin

The general election of January 2001 was the first to be held under the 1997 constitution, which was intended to take vote-buying out of politics. However, this election coincided with the emergence of a new party, **Thai Rak Thai** ("Thai Loves Thai"), formed by one of Thailand's wealthiest men, **Thaksin Shinawatra**, an ex-policeman who had made a personal fortune from government telecommunications concessions.

Thaksin duly won the election but, instead of moving towards greater democracy, as envisaged by the new constitution, he began to apply commercial and legal pressure, including several lawsuits, to try to silence critics in the media and parliament, and to manipulate the Senate and supposedly independent institutions such as the Election Commission to consolidate his own power. As his standing became more firmly entrenched, he rejected constitutional reforms designed to rein in his power – famously declaring that "democracy is only a tool" for achieving other goals.

Thaksin did, however, maintain his reputation for being a populist reformer by carrying through nearly all of his election promises. He issued a three-year loan moratorium for perennially indebted farmers and set up a one-million-baht development fund for each of the country's seventy thousand villages – though many villages just used the money as a lending tool to cover past debts, rather than creating productive projects for the future as intended. To improve public health access, a standard charge of B30 per hospital visit was introduced nationwide. However, too little was invested in the health service to cope with the increased demand that was generated.

Despite a sharp escalation of violence in the Islamic southern provinces in early 2004 (see p.401), Thaksin breezed through the February 2005 election, becoming the first prime minister in Thai history to win an outright majority at the polls but causing alarm among a wide spectrum of Thailand's elites. When Thaksin's relatives sold their

1997	2001	2004
Tom yam kung: Thailand is ravaged by economic crisis	Thaksin Shinawatra, loved and hated in roughly equal measure, wins the general election	The violence in the Islamic southern provinces sharply escalates

shares in the family's Shin Corporation in January 2006 for £1.1 billion, without paying tax, tens of thousands of mostly middle-class Thais flocked to Bangkok to take part in protracted demonstrations, under the umbrella of the **People's Alliance for Democracy (PAD)**. After further allegations of corruption and cronyism, in September 2006 Thaksin was ousted by a military government in a **coup**, while on official business in the United States.

... and the spectre of Thaksin

Thaksin set up home in London, but his supporters, now the People's Power Party (PPP), won the December 2007 general election; its leader, Samak Sundaravej, an irascible TV chef, openly confessed to being a proxy for Thaksin. In response, the PAD – its nationalist and royalist credentials and its trademark **yellow shirts** (the colour of the king) now firmly established – restarted its mass protests, eventually occupying the government's offices for several months. Meanwhile, there was a merry-go-round of tribunals and court cases, including the conviction of Thaksin *in absentia* for corruption.

Matters came to a head in November and December 2008: the PAD seized and closed down Bangkok's Suvarnabhumi airport; the ruling People's Power Party was declared illegal by the courts, which persuaded the yellow shirts to lift their sit-in; and **Pheu Thai** (sometimes "Peua Thai"; meaning "For Thais"), the PPP's swift reincarnation, found itself unable to form a new coalition government. Instead, led by the Eton- and Oxford-educated **Abhisit Vejjajiva**, the Democrat Party jumped into bed with the Bhumjaithai Party, formerly staunch supporters of Thaksin, to take the helm.

This in turn prompted Thaksin's supporters – now **red-shirted** and organized into the **UDD** (United Front for Democracy against Dictatorship) – to hold mass protest meetings. In March 2009, Thaksin claimed by video broadcast that Privy Council President, Prem Tinsulanonda, had masterminded the 2006 coup and Abhisit's appointment as prime minister, and called for the overthrow of the *amat* (elite). In the following month, the red shirts forced the ASEAN (Association of Southeast Asian Nations) summit meeting in Pattaya to be embarrassingly abandoned and closed down central Bangkok for several days, before being dispersed by the army.

Amid a clampdown by the Democrat government on free speech, including heavy-handed use of the Computer Crimes Act and Article 112, the *lèse majesté* law, much more violent protests took place early the following year. Calling on Abhisit to hold new elections, thousands of red shirts set up a heavily defended camp around the **Ratchaprasong** intersection in central Bangkok in early April. On May 19, Abhisit sent in the army to break up the camp by force; altogether 91 people died on both sides in the two months of protests.

Mass popular support for Thaksin, however, did not wane, and in the general election of May 2011, Pheu Thai – now led by his younger sister, **Yingluck Shinawatra** – romped home with an absolute majority. At the time of writing, the main issues facing the government are what to do about the 2007 Constitution, which was imposed by the coup-makers – whether to amend it, or scrap it in favour of the 1997 Constitution; and how to engineer a pardon for Thaksin and bring him home. Intertwined with these are the failing health of the 84-year-old king – now the world's longest-running head of state – and the likely turmoil of the succession.

2006	2010	2011
While in the US, Thaksin is ousted in a military coup and goes into exile	Red-shirted supporters of Thaksin set up a month-long protest camp in Bangkok	Thaksin's sister, Yingluck, wins the general election with an outright majority

Religion: Thai Buddhism

Over 85 percent of Thais consider themselves Theravada Buddhists, followers
of the teachings of a holy man usually referred to as the Buddha (Enlightened
One), though more precisely known as Gautama Buddha to distinguish him
from lesser-known Buddhas who preceded him. Theravada Buddhism is one
of the two main schools of Buddhism practised in Asia, and in Thailand it has
absorbed an eclectic assortment of animist and Hindu elements.

Islam is the biggest of the minority religions in Thailand, practised by between five and
ten percent of the population. Most Muslims live in the south, especially in the
deep-south provinces of Yala, Pattani and Narithiwat, along the Malaysian border,
whose populations are over eighty percent Muslim. The separatist violence in this
region has caused great tension between local Buddhist and Muslim communities,
which have traditionally co-existed peacefully; it has not, however, obviously affected
inter-faith relationships elsewhere in Thailand. The rest of the Thai population
comprises Mahayana Buddhists, Hindus, Sikhs, Christians and animists.

The Buddha: his life and beliefs

Gautama Buddha was born as **Prince Gautama Siddhartha** in Nepal, in the seventh
century BC according to the calculations for the Thai calendar, though scholars now
think it may have been a century or two later. At his birth, astrologers predicted that he
would become either a famous king or a celebrated holy man, depending on which
path he chose. Much preferring the former, the prince's father forbade the boy from
leaving the palace grounds, and set about educating Gautama in all aspects of the high
life. Most statues of the Buddha depict him with elongated earlobes, which is a
reference to this early pampered existence, when he would have worn heavy precious
stones in his ears.

The prince married and became a father, but at the age of 29 he flouted his father's
authority and sneaked out into the world beyond the palace. On this fateful trip he
encountered successively an old man, a sick man, a corpse and a hermit, and thus for
the first time was made aware that pain and suffering were intrinsic to human life.
Contemplation seemed the only means of discovering why this was so – and therefore
Gautama decided to leave the palace and become a **Hindu ascetic**.

For several years he wandered the countryside leading a life of self-denial and
self-mortification, but failed to come any closer to the answer. Eventually concluding
that the best course of action must be to follow a "Middle Way" – neither indulgent
nor overly ascetic – Gautama sat down beneath the famous riverside bodhi tree at **Bodh
Gaya** in India, facing the rising sun, to **meditate** until he achieved enlightenment. For
49 days he sat cross-legged in the "lotus position", contemplating the causes of
suffering and wrestling with temptations that materialized to distract him. Most of
these were sent by **Mara**, the Evil One, who was finally subdued when Gautama
summoned the earth goddess **Mae Toranee** by pointing the fingers of his right hand at
the ground – the gesture known as **Calling the Earth to Witness**, or *Bhumisparsa Mudra*,
which has been immortalized by thousands of Thai sculptors. Mae Toranee wrung
torrents of water from her hair and engulfed Mara's demonic emissaries in a flood, an
episode that's also commonly reproduced, especially in temple murals.

Temptations dealt with, Gautama soon came to attain **enlightenment** and so become
a Buddha. As the place of his enlightenment, the **bodhi tree** (*bodhi* means
"enlightenment" in Sanskrit and Pali; it's sometimes also known as the bo tree, in Thai

ton po) has assumed special significance for Buddhists: not only does it appear in many Buddhist paintings, but there's often a real bodhi tree (*Ficus religiosa*, or sacred fig) planted in temple compounds as well. In addition, the bot is nearly always built facing either a body of water or facing east (preferably both).

The Buddha preached his **first sermon** in the deer park at Sarnath in India, where he characterized his doctrine, or **Dharma**, as a wheel. From this episode comes the early Buddhist symbol the **Dharmachakra**, known as the Wheel of Law, which is often accompanied by a statue of a deer. Thais celebrate this first sermon with a public holiday in July known as **Asanha Puja**. On another occasion 1250 people spontaneously gathered to hear the Buddha speak, an event remembered in Thailand as **Makha Puja** and marked by a public holiday in February.

For the next forty-odd years the Buddha travelled the region converting non-believers and performing miracles. One rainy season he even ascended into the **Tavatimsa heaven** (Heaven of the 33 Gods) to visit his mother and to preach the doctrine to her. His descent from this heaven is quite a common theme of paintings and sculptures, and the **Standing Buddha** pose of numerous Buddha statues comes from this story.

The Buddha "died" at the age of eighty on the banks of a river at Kusinari in India – an event often dated to 543 BC, which is why the **Thai calendar** is 543 years out of synch with the Western one, so that the year 2013 AD becomes 2556 BE (Buddhist Era). Lying on his side, propping up his head on his hand, the Buddha passed into **Nirvana** (giving rise to another classic pose, the **Reclining Buddha**), the unimaginable state of nothingness which knows no suffering and from which there is no reincarnation. Buddhists believe that the day the Buddha entered Nirvana was the same date on which he was born and on which he achieved enlightenment, a triply significant day that Thais honour with the **Visakha Puja** festival in May.

Buddhists believe that Gautama Buddha was the five-hundredth incarnation of a single being: the stories of these five hundred lives, collectively known as the **Jataka**, provide the inspiration for much Thai art. Hindus also accept Gautama Buddha into their pantheon, perceiving him as the ninth manifestation of their god Vishnu.

The spread of Buddhism

After the Buddha entered Nirvana, his **doctrine** spread relatively quickly across India, and probably was first promulgated in Thailand in about the third century BC, when the Indian emperor, Ashoka (in Thai, Asoke), sent out missionaries. His teachings, the *Tripitaka*, were written down in the Pali language – a then-vernacular derivative of Sanskrit – in a form that became known as **Theravada**, or "The Doctrine of the Elders".

By the beginning of the first millennium, a new movement called **Mahayana** (Great Vehicle) had emerged within the Theravada school, attempting to make Buddhism more accessible by introducing a pantheon of **bodhisattva**, or Buddhist saints, who, although they had achieved enlightenment, postponed entering Nirvana in order to inspire the populace. Mahayana Buddhism spread north into China, Korea, Vietnam and Japan, also entering southern Thailand via the Srivijayan empire around the eighth century and parts of Khmer Cambodia in about the eleventh century. Meanwhile Theravada Buddhism (which the Mahayanists disparagingly renamed "Hinayana" or "Lesser Vehicle") established itself most significantly in Sri Lanka, northern and central Thailand and Burma.

Buddhist doctrine and practice

Central to Theravada Buddhism is a belief in **karma** – every action has a consequence – and **reincarnation**, along with an understanding that craving is at the root of human suffering. The ultimate aim for a Buddhist is to get off the cycle of perpetual reincarnation and suffering and instead to enter the blissful state of non-being that is **Nirvana**. This enlightened state can take many lifetimes to achieve so the more realistic goal for most is to be reborn slightly higher up the karmic ladder each time. As Thai Buddhists see it, animals are at the bottom of the karmic scale and monks at the top, with women on a lower rung than men.

Living a good life, specifically a life of "pure intention", creates good karma and Buddhist doctrine focuses a great deal on how to achieve this. Psychology and an understanding of human weaknesses play a big part. Key is the concept of *dukka* or **suffering**, which holds that craving is the root cause of all suffering or, to put it simplistically, human unhappiness is caused by the unquenchable dissatisfaction experienced when one's sensual, spiritual or material desires are not met. The concepts concerning suffering and craving are known as the **Four Noble Truths** of Buddhism. The route to enlightenment depends on a person being sufficiently detached from earthly desires so that *dukka* can't take hold. One acknowledges that the physical world is impermanent and ever changing, and that all things – including the self – are therefore not worth craving. A Buddhist works towards this realization by following the **Eightfold Path**, or **Middle Way**, that is by developing a set of highly moral personal qualities such as "right speech", "right action" and "right mindfulness". Meditation is particularly helpful in this.

A devout Thai Buddhist commits to the **five basic precepts**, namely not to kill or steal, to refrain from sexual misconduct and incorrect speech (lies, gossip and abuse) and to eschew intoxicating liquor and drugs. There are **three extra precepts** for special *wan phra* holy days and for those laypeople including foreign students who study meditation at Thai temples: no eating after noon, no entertainment (including TV and music) and no sleeping on a soft bed; in addition, the no-sexual-misconduct precept turns into no sex at all.

Making merit

Merit-making in popular Thai Buddhism has become slightly skewed, so that some people act on the assumption that they'll climb the karmic ladder faster if they make bigger and better offerings to the temple and its monks. However, it is of course the purity of the intention behind one's **merit-making** (*tham buun*) that's fundamental.

Merit can be made in many ways, from giving a monk his breakfast to attending a Buddhist service or donating money and gifts to the neighbourhood temple, and most **festivals** are essentially communal merit-making opportunities. Between the big festivals, the most common days for making merit and visiting the temple are **wan phra** (holy days), which are determined by the phase of the moon and occur four times a month. The simplest **offering** inside a temple consists of lotus buds, candles and three incense sticks (representing the three gems of Buddhism – the Buddha himself, the Dharma or doctrine, and the monkhood). One of the more bizarre but common merit-making activities involves **releasing caged birds**: worshippers buy tiny finches from vendors at wat compounds and, by liberating them from their cage, prove their Buddhist compassion towards all living things. The fact that the birds were free until netted earlier that morning doesn't seem to detract from the ritual. In riverside and seaside wats, fish or even baby turtles are released instead.

For an insightful introduction to the philosophy and practice of Thai Buddhism, see ⓦthaibuddhism.net. A number of Thai temples welcome foreign students of Buddhism and meditation (see p.50).

The monkhood

It's the duty of Thailand's 200,000-strong **Sangha** (monkhood) to set an example to the Theravada Buddhist community by living a life as close to the Middle Way as possible and by preaching the Dharma to the people. The life of a monk (*bhikkhu*) is governed by 227 precepts that include celibacy and the rejection of all personal possessions except gifts.

Each day begins with an alms round in the neighbourhood so that the laity can donate food and thereby gain themselves merit, and then is chiefly spent in meditation, chanting, teaching and study. As the most respected members of any community, monks act as teachers, counsellors and arbiters in local disputes, and sometimes become spokesmen for villagers' rights. They also perform rituals at cremations, weddings and other events, such as the launching of a new business or even the purchase of a new car. Many young boys from poor families find themselves almost obliged to become either a *dek wat* (temple boy) or a **novice monk** because that's the only way they can get accommodation, food and, crucially, an education. This is provided free in exchange for duties around the wat, and novices are required to adhere to ten rather than 227 Buddhist precepts.

Monkhood doesn't have to be for life: a man may leave the Sangha three times without stigma and in fact every Thai male (including royalty) is expected to **enter the monkhood** for a short period, ideally between leaving school and marrying, as a rite of passage into adulthood. Thai government departments and some private companies grant their employees paid leave for their time as a monk, but the custom is in decline as young men increasingly have to consider the effect their absence may have on their career prospects. Instead, many men now enter the monkhood for a brief period after the death of a parent, to make merit both for the deceased and for the rest of the family. The most popular time for temporary ordination is the three-month Buddhist retreat period – **Pansa**, sometimes referred to as "Buddhist Lent" – which begins in July and lasts for the duration of the rainy season. (The monks' confinement is said to originate from the earliest years of Buddhist history, when farmers complained that perambulating monks were squashing their sprouting rice crops.)

Monks in contemporary society

Some monks extend their role as village spokesmen to become influential activists: Wat Tham Krabok near Lopburi and Wat Nong Sam Pran in Kanchanaburi are among a growing number of temples that have established themselves as successful drug rehabilitation centres; monks at Wat Phra Bat Nam Pu in Lopburi run a hospice for people with HIV/AIDS as well as a famously hard-hitting AIDS-awareness museum; monks at Wat Phai Lom near Bangkok have developed the country's largest breeding colony of Asian open-billed storks; and the monks at Wat Pa Luang Ta Bua Yannasampanno in Kanchanaburi have hit the headlines with their tiger sanctuary. Other monks, such as the famous octogenarian Luang Pho Khoon of Wat Ban Rai in Nakhon Ratchasima province, have acquired such a reputation for giving wise counsel and bringing good fortune to their followers that they have become national gurus and their temples now generate great wealth through the production of specially blessed amulets and photographs.

Though the increasing involvement of many monks in the secular world has not met with unanimous approval, far more disappointing to the laity are those monks who **flout the precepts** of the Sangha by succumbing to the temptations of a consumer society, flaunting Raybans, Rolexes and Mercedes (in some cases actually bought with temple funds), chain-smoking and flirting, even making pocket money from predicting lottery results and practising faith-healing. With so much national pride and integrity riding on the sanctity of the Sangha, any whiff of a deeper scandal is bound to strike deep into the national psyche. Cases of monks involved in drug dealing, gun running, even rape and murder have prompted a stream of editorials on the state of the Sangha and the collapse of spiritual values at the heart of Thai society. The inclusivity of the monkhood – which is open to just about any male who wants to join – has been highlighted as a particularly vulnerable aspect, not least because donning saffron robes has always been an accepted way for criminals, reformed or otherwise, to repent of their past deeds.

Interestingly, back in the late 1980s, the influential monk Phra Bodhirak (Photirak) was defrocked after criticizing what he saw as a tide of decadence infecting Thai

Buddhism. He now preaches his ascetic code of anti-materialism through his breakaway **Santi Asoke** sect, famous across the country for its cheap vegetarian restaurants, its philosophy of self-sufficiency and for the simple blue farmers' shirts worn by many of its followers.

Women and the monkhood

Although the Theravada Buddhist hierarchy in some countries permits the ordination of **female monks**, or *bhikkhuni*, the Thai Sangha does not. Instead, Thai women are officially only allowed to become **nuns**, or *mae chii*, shaving their heads, donning white robes and keeping eight rather than 227 precepts. Their status is lower than that of the monks and they are chiefly occupied with temple upkeep rather than conducting religious ceremonies.

However, the progressives are becoming more vocal, and in 2002 a Thai woman became the first of several to break with the Buddhist authorities and get **ordained** as a novice *bhikkhuni* on Thai soil. Thailand's Sangha Council, however, still recognizes neither her ordination nor the temple, Watra Songdhammakalyani in Nakhon Pathom, where the ordination took place. The Watra (rather than Wat) is run by another Thai *bhikkhuni*, Dhammananda Bhikkhuni, the author of several books in English about **women and Buddhism** and of an informative website, ⓦthaibhikkhunis.org.

Hindu deities and animist spirits

The complicated history of the area now known as Thailand has made Thai Buddhism a confusingly syncretic faith, as you'll realize when you enter a Buddhist temple compound to be confronted by a statue of a Hindu deity. While regular Buddhist merit-making insures a Thai for the next life, there are certain **Hindu gods and animist spirits** that many Thais – sophisticated Bangkokians and illiterate farmers alike – also cultivate for help with more immediate problems; and as often as not it's a Buddhist monk who is called in to exorcize a malevolent spirit. Even the Buddhist King Bhumibol employs Brahmin priests and astrologers to determine auspicious days and officiate at certain royal ceremonies and, like his royal predecessors of the Chakri dynasty, he also associates himself with the Hindu god Vishnu by assuming the title Rama IX – Rama, hero of the Hindu epic the *Ramayana*, having been Vishnu's seventh manifestation on earth.

If a Thai wants help in achieving a short-term goal, like passing an exam, becoming pregnant or winning the lottery, he or she will quite likely turn to the **Hindu pantheon**, visiting an enshrined statue of Brahma, Vishnu, Shiva or Ganesh, and making offerings of flowers, incense and maybe food. If the outcome is favourable, the devotee will probably come back to show thanks, bringing more offerings and maybe even hiring a dance troupe to perform a celebratory *lakhon chatri*. Built in honour of Brahma, Bangkok's Erawan Shrine is the most famous place of Hindu-inspired worship in the country.

Spirits and spirit houses

Whereas Hindu deities tend to be benevolent, **spirits** (or *phi*) are not nearly as reliable and need to be mollified more frequently. They come in hundreds of varieties, some more malign than others, and inhabit everything from trees, rivers and caves to public buildings and private homes – even taking over people if they feel like it. So that these *phi* don't pester human inhabitants, each building has a special **spirit house** (*saan phra phum*) in its vicinity, as a dwelling for spirits ousted by the building's construction. Usually raised on a short column to set it at or above eye-level, the spirit house must occupy an auspicious location – not, for example, in the shadow of the main building. It's generally about the size of a dolls' house and designed to look like a wat or a traditional Thai house, but its ornamentation is supposed to reflect the status of the humans' building, so if that building is enlarged or refurbished, the spirit house should be improved accordingly. And as architects become increasingly bold in their designs, so modernist spirit houses are also beginning to appear, especially in Bangkok where an eye-catching new skyscraper might be graced by a spirit house of glass or polished concrete. **Figurines** representing the relevant guardian spirit and his aides are sometimes put inside, and daily offerings of incense, lighted candles and garlands of jasmine are placed alongside them to keep the *phi* happy – a disgruntled spirit is a dangerous spirit, liable to cause sickness, accidents and even death. As with any religious building or icon in Thailand, an unwanted or crumbling spirit house should never be dismantled or destroyed, which is why you'll often see damaged spirit houses placed around the base of a sacred banyan tree, where they are able to rest in peace.

The coastal environment

Spanning some 1650km north to south, Thailand lies in the heart of Southeast Asia's tropical zone, its southern border running less than seven degrees north of the Equator. Coastal Thailand's climate is characterized by high temperatures and even higher humidity, a very fertile combination that nourishes a huge diversity of flora and fauna in the tropical rainforests, mangrove swamps and coral reefs that constitute the region's main habitats.

The habitats

Some of Thailand's most precious habitats are protected as **national park**, including the steamy jungles of Khao Sok; the coastal mud flats of Khao Sam Roi Yot, a favourite haunt of migrating birds; and the island shorelines and reefs of Ko Surin, Ko Similan, plus Ko Tarutao, Ang Thong, Khao Luang, parts of Phang Nga bay, Ko Lanta and Ko Chang.

Tropical rainforests

Thailand's **tropical rainforests** occur in areas of high and prolonged rainfall in the southern peninsula, most accessibly in the national parks of Khao Sok, Tarutao and Khao Luang. Some areas contain as many as two hundred species of tree within a single hectare, along with a host of other flora. Characteristic of a tropical rainforest is the multi-layered series of **canopies**. The uppermost storey sometimes reaches 60m, and will often have enormous buttressed roots for support; beneath this, the dense canopy of 25–35m is often festooned with climbers and epiphytes such as ferns, lianas, mosses and orchids; then comes an uneven layer 5–10m high consisting of palms, rattans, shrubs and small trees. The forest floor in tropical rainforests tends to be relatively open and free of dense undergrowth because the upper three layers shade much of the light.

The family **Dipterocarpaceae** dominate these forests, a group of tropical hardwoods prized for their timber – and as nesting sites for hornbills and lookout posts for gibbons. Also very common are the many different species of **epiphytes**, plants that usually grow on other plants, but aren't parasitic, obtaining their nutrients from the atmosphere instead, and from decaying plant and animal matter. Among the most famous, and most beautiful, epiphytes are Thailand's countless species of wild **orchids**, many of them gratifyingly common in the forest and prized as houseplants in the West, including the golden spiky petalled *Bulbophyllum picturatum*, the bright yellow members of the genus *Dendrobium*, the flame-red *Ascocentrum curvifolium*, and the blue *Vanda coerulea*.

For the early years of its life, the **strangling fig** (*Ficus* sp) is also an epiphyte, often using a dipterocarp as host while it drops its distinctive lattice of roots to the ground. It can then feed normally, so well in fact that, after many years, the fig's roots and crown completely enshroud the support tree and hasten its death. As the host decomposes, it leaves a hollow but structurally sound strangling fig. Strangling figs are excellent places to observe birds and mammals, particularly when in fruit, as they attract hornbills, green pigeons, barbets, gibbons, langurs and macaques.

Mangrove swamps and coastal forests

Mangrove swamps are an important habitat for a wide variety of marine life (including two hundred species of bird, seventy species of fish and fifty types of crab) but, as with much of Thailand's inland forest, they have been significantly degraded by encroachment, as well as by large-scale prawn farming. Huge swathes of Thailand's littoral used to be fringed with mangrove swamps, but now they are mainly found only along the west peninsular coast, between Ranong and Satun, though Chanthaburi's Ao Khung Kraben is a notable east-coast exception. A great way of **exploring the swamps** is to paddle a kayak through the mangrove-clogged inlets and island-lagoons of Ao Phang Nga. Not only do mangrove swamps harbour a rich and important ecosystem of their own, but they also help prevent coastal erosion; in certain areas of the tsunami-hit Andaman coast intact mangrove forest absorbed some of the waves' impact, protecting land and homes from even worse damage.

Nipa palms share the mangrove's penchant for brackish water, and these stubby-stemmed palm trees grow in abundance in the south, though commercial plantations are now replacing the natural colonies. Like most other species of palm indigenous to Thailand, the nipa is a versatile plant that's exploited to the full: alcohol is distilled from its sugary sap, and its fronds are woven into roofs (especially for beach huts and village homes), sticky-rice baskets and chair-backs.

The hardy **coconut palm** is also very tolerant of salty, sandy soil, and is equally useful. On islands such as Ko Kood, it's the backbone of the local economy, with millions of coconuts harvested every month for their milk, their oil-producing meat (copra), and their fibrous husks or coir (used for making ropes, matting, brushes and mattress stuffing); the palm fronds are woven into roof thatching and baskets, and the wood has an attractive grain.

Casuarinas (also known as she-oaks or ironwoods) also flourish in sandy soils and are common on beaches throughout Thailand; fast-growing and tall (up to 20m), they are quite often planted as wind-breaks. Though its feathery profile makes it look like a pine, it's actually made up of tiny twigs, not needles.

The wildlife

Thailand lies in an exceptionally rich "transition zone" of the Indo-Malayan realm, its forests, mountains and national parks attracting wildlife from both Indochina and Indonesia. In all, Thailand is home to three hundred species of mammal (37 of which are considered to be endangered or vulnerable), while 982 species of bird have been recorded here (49 of them globally threatened). For a guide to Thailand's spectacular array of **marine species**, check out the "Underwater Thailand" section (see p.20).

Mammals

In the main national parks like Khao Sok, the animals you're most likely to encounter – with your ears if not your eyes – are **primates**, particularly macaques and gibbons.

The latter are responsible for the distinctive hooting that echoes through the forests. Chief noise-maker is the **white-handed** or **lar gibbon**, a beige- or black-bodied, white-faced animal whose cute appearance, intelligence and dexterity unfortunately make it a popular pet. The poaching and mistreatment of lar gibbons has become so severe that a special Gibbon Rehabilitation Project has been set up in Phuket (see p.345).

Similarly chatty, macaques hang out in gangs of twenty or more. The **long-tailed** or **crab-eating macaque** lives in the lowlands, near rivers, lakes and coasts, including around Ao Phang Nga, Krabi, Ko Tarutao, Ang Thong and Khao Sam Roi Yot. It eats not only crabs, but mussels, other small animals and fruit, transporting and storing food in its big cheek pouch when swimming and diving. The **pig-tailed macaque**, named for its short curly tail, excels at scaling tall trees, a skill which has resulted in many of the males being captured and trained to pick coconuts.

Commonly sighted on night treks in Khao Sam Roi Yot, the **civet** – species of which include the common palm and small Indian – is a small mongoose-type animal which hunts smaller mammals in trees and on the ground; it's known in the West for the powerful smell released from its anal glands, a scent used commercially as a perfume base. Far more elusive is the **Indochinese tiger**, which lives under constant threat from both poachers and the destruction of its habitat by logging interests, both of which have reduced the current population to probably fewer than one hundred; it's thought

THE GECKO

Whether you're staying on a beach or in a town, chances are you'll be sharing your room with a few **geckos**. These pale-green tropical lizards, which are completely harmless to humans and usually measure a cute 4cm to 10cm in length, mostly appear at night, high up on walls and ceilings, where they feed on insects. Because the undersides of their flat toes are covered with hundreds of microscopic hairs that catch at even the tiniest of irregularities, geckos are able to scale almost any surface, including glass, which is why you usually see them in strange, gravity-defying positions. The largest and most vociferous gecko is known as the **tuukae** in Thai, named after the disconcertingly loud sound it makes. *Tuukae* can grow to an alarming 35cm but are welcomed by most householders, as they devour insects and mice; Thais also consider it auspicious if a baby is born within earshot of a crowing *tuukae*.

that some still live in Khao Sok, however. Khao Sok is also potentially one of the easier places to encounter wild, small-eared Asian **elephants**, of which around two thousand now remain in Thailand.

Birds

Even if you don't see many mammals on a trek through a national park, you're certain to spot a satisfying range of birds. The **hornbill** is the most majestic, easily recognizable from its massive, powerful wings (the flapping of which can be heard for long distances) and huge beak surmounted by a bizarre horny casque. The two most commonly spotted species in Thailand are the plain black-and-white **oriental pied hornbill**, frequently sighted on the little islands of Ko Phayam and Ko Chang in Ranong province, among other places, and the flashier **great hornbill**, whose monochromic body and head are broken up with jaunty splashes of yellow. Thailand is also home to the extremely rare **Gurney's pitta**, found only in Khlong Thom national park, inland from Ko Lanta.

Coastal areas attract storks, egrets and herons, and the mud flats of Khao Sam Roi Yot are breeding grounds for the large, long-necked **purple heron**. The magnificent **white-bellied sea eagle** haunts the Thai coast, nesting in the forbidding crags around Ao Phang Nga, Krabi and Ko Tarutao and preying on fish and sea snakes. The tiny **edible nest swiftlet** makes its eponymous nest – the major ingredient of the luxury food, bird's-nest soup – in the limestone crags, too (see p.376).

For information on specific **bird-watching** locations throughout Thailand see ⓦ thai birding.com; for guided birding tours contact Thailand Bird Watching (ⓦ thailandbird watching.com); bird-watching guidebooks are listed in the "Books" section (see p.442).

Snakes

Thailand is home to around 175 different species and subspecies of **snake**, 56 of them dangerously venomous. Death by snakebite is not common, however, but all provincial hospitals should keep a stock of serum.

Found everywhere and highly venomous, the 2m, nocturnal, yellow-and-black-striped **banded krait** is one to avoid, as is the shorter but equally venomous **Thai** or **monocled cobra**, which lurks in low-lying humid areas and close to human habitation and sports a distinctive "eye" mark on its hood. The other most widespread venomous snake is the 60cm **Malayan pit viper**, which has an unnerving ability to camouflage its pinky-brown and black-marked body. The **mangrove snake** lives in the humid swamps south of Chumphon: arboreal, nocturnal and mildly venomous, it can grow to about 2.5m and is black with thin yellow bands.

Environmental issues

Thailand's rapid economic growth has had a significant effect on its environment. Huge new infrastructure projects, an explosion in real-estate developments and the constantly expanding tourist industry have all played a part, and the effects of the subsequent **deforestation** and pollution have been felt nationwide. Such was the devastation caused by floods and mud slides in Surat Thani in 1988 that the government banned commercial logging the following year, though land continues to be denuded for other purposes. There is also the endemic problem of "influence" so that when a big shot wants to clear a previously pristine area for a new property development, for example, it is virtually impossible for a lowly provincial civil servant to reject their plan, or money.

Flooding has always been a feature of the Thai environment, crucial to the fertility of its soil, and its worst effects are obviated by the stilted design of the traditional Thai house. However, there is now an almost annual inundation in certain riverside town centres, and of roads and railways, particularly along the Gulf coast, with especially severe floods in 2011, when towns in the central plains, including the World Heritage Site of Ayutthaya and many suburbs of Bangkok, were under metres of water for weeks on end. And in recent times, far more dangerous **flash floods** have recurred with depressing frequency, most dramatically around the northern town of Pai in 2005, where many homes and guesthouses were washed away. The link between deforestation and floods is disputed, though encroaching cement and tarmac on Thai flood plains surely play a part, as does the clogging of exit channels by garbage and other pollutants, and of course climate change.

Reefs and shorelines

A number of Thailand's **coral reefs** – some of which are thought to be around 450 million years old – are being destroyed by factors attributable to tourism, most significantly the pollution generated by coastal hotels with inadequate sewage systems. Longtail boats that anchor on reefs, souvenirs made from coral, and the use of harpoon guns by irresponsible dive leaders all have a cumulative effect, dwarfed however by the local practice of using dynamite to gather fish, including reef fish for sale to aquariums.

The 2004 **tsunami** also caused significant damage to coastal and marine environments the length of the Andaman coast. Reefs close to shore were crushed by debris (furniture, machinery, even cars) and buried under displaced soil; the sea was temporarily polluted by extensive damage to sewage systems; and tracts of shorefront farmland were rendered unusable by salt water. In 2010, a mass **coral bleaching** event occurred in all of the world's oceans, damaging especially shallow-water reefs in Thailand, such as Ko Surin's; the event was caused by sudden, steep rises in sea temperatures, and has been interpreted as dramatic evidence of the effects of climate change.

National parks

Although Thailand has since the 1970s been protecting some of its natural resources within **national parks**, these have long been caught between commercial and conservationist aims, an issue which the government addressed in 2002 by establishing a new National Park, Wildlife and Plant Conservation Department (DNP; ⑩dnp.go.th), separate from the Royal Forestry Department and its parent Ministry of Agriculture.

With 140 national parks and marine parks across the country, as well as various other protected zones, over thirteen percent of the country is now, in theory at least, protected from encroachment and hunting (a high proportion compared to other nations, such as Japan at 6.5 percent, and the US at 10.5 percent).

However, the **touristification** of certain national parks endures; Ko Phi Phi and Ko Samet in particular have both suffered irreversible environmental damage as a direct result of the number of overnight visitors they receive. While most people understand that the role of the national parks is to conserve vulnerable and precious resources, the dramatic hike in entrance fees payable by foreigner visitors to national parks – from B20 up to B200 in 2000 and up again to B400 for a few special parks – was greeted with cynicism and anger, not least because there is often little sign of anything tangible being done on site with the money.

Books

We have included publishers' details for books that may be hard to find outside Thailand, though some of them can be ordered online through ⓦdcothai.com, which also carries e-books. Other titles should be available worldwide. Titles marked ★ are particularly recommended. There's a good selection of Thai novels and short stories in translation, available to buy as e-books, on ⓦthaifiction.com.

CULTURE AND SOCIETY

Michael Carrithers *The Buddha: A Very Short Introduction*. Accessible account of the life of the Buddha, and the development and significance of his thought.

★ **Philip Cornwel-Smith and John Goss** *Very Thai*. Why do Thais decant their soft drinks into plastic bags, and how does one sniff-kiss? Answers and insights aplenty in this intriguingly observant, fully illustrated guide to contemporary Thai culture. Look out also for Cornwel-Smith's forthcoming *Very Bangkok*.

James Eckardt *Bangkok People*. The collected articles of a renowned expat journalist, whose encounters with a varied cast of Bangkokians – from construction-site workers and street vendors to boxers and political candidates – add texture and context to the city.

Sandra Gregory with Michael Tierney *Forget You Had A Daughter: Doing Time in the "Bangkok Hilton" – Sandra Gregory's Story*. The frank and shocking account of a young British woman's term in Bangkok's notorious Lard Yao prison after being caught trying to smuggle 89g of heroin out of Thailand.

Sebastian Hope *Outcasts of the Islands: The Sea Gypsies of Southeast Asia*. Unusual insight into the lives of the *chao ley* people from a British traveller who spent several months in various sea gypsy communities.

★ **Erich Krauss** *Wave of Destruction: One Thai Village and its Battle with the Tsunami*. A sad and often shocking, clear-eyed account of what Ban Nam Khem went through before, during and after the tsunami. Fills in many gaps left unanswered by news reports at the time.

Father Joe Maier *Welcome to the Bangkok Slaughterhouse: The Battle for Human Dignity in Bangkok's Bleakest Slums*. Catholic priest Father Joe shares the stories of some of the Bangkok street kids and slum-dwellers that his charitable

foundation has been supporting since 1972 (see p.55).

Cleo Odzer *Patpong Sisters*. An American anthropologist's funny and touching account of her life with the prostitutes and bar-girls of Bangkok's notorious red-light district.

James O'Reilly and Larry Habegger (eds) *Travelers' Tales: Thailand*. Absorbing anthology of contemporary writings about Thailand, by Thailand experts, social commentators, travel writers and first-time visitors.

★ **Phra Peter Pannapadipo** *Little Angels: The Real-Life Stories of Twelve Thai Novice Monks*. A dozen young boys, many of them from desperate backgrounds, tell the often poignant stories of why they became novice monks. For some, funding from the Students Education Trust (p.55) has changed their lives.

Phra Peter Pannapadipo *Phra Farang: An English Monk in Thailand*. Behind the scenes in a Thai monastery: the frank, funny and illuminating account of a UK-born former businessman's life as a Thai monk.

Pasuk Phongpaichit and Sungsidh Piriyarangsan *Corruption and Democracy in Thailand*. Fascinating academic study, revealing the nuts and bolts of corruption in Thailand and its links with all levels of political life, and suggesting a route to a stronger society. Their sequel, a study of Thailand's illegal economy, *Guns, Girls, Gambling, Ganja*, co-written with Nualnoi Treerat, makes equally eye-opening and depressing reading.

Tom Vater and Aroon Thaewchatturat *Sacred Skin*. Fascinating, beautifully photographed exploration of Thailand's spirit tattoos, *sak yant*.

William Warren *Living in Thailand*. Luscious gallery of traditional houses, with an emphasis on the homes of Thailand's rich and famous; seductively photographed by Luca Invernizzi Tettoni.

HISTORY

William Warren *Jim Thompson: the Legendary American of Thailand*. The engrossing biography of the ex-intelligence agent, art collector and Thai silk magnate whose disappearance in Malaysia in 1967 has never been satisfactorily resolved.

★ **David K. Wyatt** *Thailand: A Short History*. An excellent, recently updated treatment, scholarly but highly readable, with a good eye for witty, telling details. Good chapters on the story of the Thais before they reached what's now Thailand, and on recent developments.

ART AND ARCHITECTURE

★ **Steve Van Beek** *The Arts of Thailand*. Lavishly produced and perfectly pitched introduction to the history of Thai architecture, sculpture and painting, with superb photographs by Luca Invernizzi Tettoni.

Sumet Jumsai *Naga: Cultural Origins in Siam and the West Pacific*. Wide-ranging discussion of water symbols in Thailand and other parts of Asia, offering a stimulating mix of art, architecture, mythology and cosmology.

Steven Pettifor *Flavours: Thai Contemporary Art*. Takes up the baton from Poshyananda (see below) to look at the newly invigorated art scene in Thailand from 1992 to 2004,

with profiles of 23 leading lights, including painters, multimedia and performance artists.

★ **Apinan Poshyananda** *Modern Art in Thailand*. Excellent introduction which extends up to the early 1990s, with very readable discussions on dozens of individual artists, and lots of colour plates.

William Warren and Luca Invernizzi Tettoni *Arts and Crafts of Thailand*. Good-value large-format paperback, setting the wealth of Thai arts and crafts in cultural context, with plenty of attractive illustrations and colour photographs.

NATURAL HISTORY AND TRAVEL GUIDES

Ashley J. Boyd and Collin Piprell *Diving in Thailand*. A thorough guide to 84 dive sites, plus general introductory sections on Thailand's marine life, conservation and photography tips.

Oliver Hargreaves *Exploring Phuket & Phi Phi: From Tin to Tourism*. Fascinating, thoroughly researched guide to the Andaman coast's big touristic honeypots; especially good on Phuket's history.

★ **Thom Henley** *Krabi: Caught in the Spell – A Guide to Thailand's Enchanted Province* (Thai Nature Education, Phuket). Highly readable features and observations on the attractions and people of south Thailand's most beautiful

region, written by an expat environmentalist.

Boonsong Lekagul and Philip D. Round *Guide to the Birds of Thailand*. Unparalleled illustrated guide to Thailand's birds. Worth scouring secondhand sellers for.

Craig Robson *A Field Guide to the Birds of Thailand*. Expert and beautifully illustrated guide to Thailand's top 950 bird species, with locator maps.

Eric Valli and Diane Summers *The Shadow Hunters*. Beautifully photographed photo-essay on the birds'-nest collectors of southern Thailand, with whom the authors spent over a year, together scaling the phenomenal heights of the sheer limestone walls.

LITERATURE

Alastair Dingwall (ed) *Traveller's Literary Companion: Southeast Asia*. A useful though rather dry reference, with a large section on Thailand, including a book list, well-chosen extracts, biographical details of authors and other literary notes.

★ **Chart Korbjitti** *The Judgement* (Howling Books). Sobering modern-day tragedy about a good-hearted Thai villager who is ostracized by his hypocritical neighbours. Contains lots of interesting details on village life and traditions and thought-provoking passages on the stifling conservatism of rural communities. Winner of the S.E.A. Write award in 1982.

★ **Rattawut Lapcharoensap** *Sightseeing*. This outstanding debut collection of short stories by a young Thai-born author now living overseas highlights big, pertinent themes – cruelty, corruption, racism, pride – in its neighbourhood tales of randy teenagers, bullyboys, a child's friendship with a Cambodian refugee, a young man who uses family influence to dodge the draft.

Nitaya Masavisut (ed) *The S.E.A. Write Anthology of Thai*

Short Stories and Poems (Silkworm Books, Chiang Mai). Interesting medley of short stories and poems by Thai writers who have won Southeast Asian Writers' Awards, providing a good introduction to the contemporary literary scene.

S.P. Somtow *Jasmine Nights*. An engaging and humorous rites-of-passage tale, of an upper-class boy learning what it is to be Thai. *Dragon's Fin Soup and Other Modern Siamese Fables* is an imaginative and entertaining collection of often supernatural short stories, focusing on the collision of East and West.

★ **Khamsing Srinawk** *The Politician and Other Stories*. A collection of brilliantly satiric short stories, full of pithy moral observation and biting irony, which capture the vulnerability of peasant farmers in the north and northeast, as they try to come to grips with the modern world. Written by an insider from a peasant family, who was educated at Chulalongkorn University, became a hero of the left, and joined the communist insurgents after the 1976 clampdown.

THAILAND IN FOREIGN LITERATURE

Dean Barrett *Kingdom of Make-Believe*. Despite the clichéd ingredients – the Patpong go-go bar scene, opium smuggling in the Golden Triangle, Vietnam veterans – this novel about a return to Thailand following a twenty-year

absence turns out to be a rewardingly multi-dimensional take on the farang experience.

John Burdett *Bangkok 8*. Riveting Bangkok thriller that takes in Buddhism, plastic surgery, police corruption, the *yaa baa* drugs trade, hookers, jade-smuggling and the spirit world.

Alex Garland *The Beach*. Gripping cult thriller (later made into a film, shot partly on Ko Phi Phi Leh) that uses a Thai setting to explore the way in which travellers' ceaseless quest for "undiscovered" utopias inevitably leads to them despoiling the idyll.

Andrew Hicks *Thai Girl*. A British backpacker falls for a reticent young beach masseuse on Ko Samet but struggles with age-old cross-cultural confusion in this sensitive attempt at a different kind of expat novel.

Michel Houellebecq *Platform*. Sex tourism in Thailand provides the nucleus of this brilliantly provocative (some would say offensive) novel, in which Houellebecq presents a ferocious critique of Western decadence and cultural colonialism, and of radical Islam too.

Christopher G. Moore *God Of Darkness*. Thailand's best-selling expat novelist sets his most intriguing thriller during the economic crisis of 1997 and includes plenty of meat on endemic corruption and the desperate struggle for power within family and society.

FOOD AND COOKERY

Vatcharin Bhumichitr *The Taste of Thailand*. Another glossy introduction to this eminently photogenic country, this time through its food. The author runs a Thai restaurant in London and provides background colour as well as about 150 recipes adapted for Western kitchens.

Jacqueline M. Piper *Fruits of South-East Asia*. An exploration of the bounteous fruits of the region, tracing their role in cooking, medicine, handicrafts and rituals. Well illustrated with photos, watercolours and early botanical drawings.

★ **David Thompson** *Thai Food*. Comprehensive, impeccably researched celebration of the cuisine, with over three hundred recipes, by the owner of the first Thai restaurant ever to earn a Michelin star.

Language

Thai belongs to one of the oldest families of languages in the world, Austro-Thai, and is radically different from most of the other tongues of Southeast Asia. Being tonal, Thai is very difficult for Westerners to master, but by building up from a small core of set phrases, you should soon have enough to get by. Most Thais who deal with tourists speak some English, but once you stray off the beaten track you'll probably need at least a little Thai. Anywhere you go, you'll impress and get better treatment if you at least make an effort to speak a few words.

Distinct dialects are spoken in the north, the northeast and the south, which can increase the difficulty of comprehending what's said to you. **Thai script** is even more of a problem to Westerners, with 44 consonants and 32 vowels. However, street signs in touristed areas are nearly always written in Roman script as well as Thai, and in other circumstances you're better off asking than trying to unscramble the swirling mess of letters and accents. There's more information on transliteration into Roman script, in the box in this book's introduction (see p.7).

Among **language books**, *Thai: The Rough Guide Phrasebook* covers the essential phrases and expressions in both Thai script and phonetic equivalents, as well as dipping into grammar and providing a menu reader and fuller vocabulary in dictionary format (English-Thai and Thai-English). Probably the best pocket dictionary is Paiboon Publishing's (ⓦpaiboonpublishing.com) *Thai-English, English-Thai Dictionary* (also available as a CD and as an app), which lists words in phonetic Thai as well as Thai script, and features very useful examples of the Thai alphabet in different fonts.

The best **teach-yourself course** is the expensive *Linguaphone Thai* (including eight CDs and an alphabet book), which also has a shorter, cheaper beginner-level PDQ version (with four CDs or downloadable audio files). *Thai for Beginners* by Benjawan Poomsan Becker (Paiboon Publishing) is a cheaper, more manageable textbook and is especially good for getting to grips with the Thai writing system; you can also buy accompanying CDs to help with listening skills, or get the whole thing in CD-ROM or Apple app format. For a more traditional textbook, try Stuart Campbell and Chuan Shaweevongse's *The Fundamentals of the Thai Language*, which is comprehensive, though hard going. The **website** ⓦthai-language.com is an amazing free resource, featuring a searchable dictionary with over fifty thousand entries, complete with Thai script and audio clips, plus a guide to the language, lessons and forums; you can also browse and buy Thai language books and learning materials.

Pronunciation

Mastering **tones** is probably the most difficult part of learning Thai. Five different tones are used – low, middle, high, falling, and rising – by which the meaning of a single syllable can be altered in five different ways. Thus, using four of the five tones, you can make a sentence from just one syllable: "mái mài mâi ma˘i" meaning "New wood burns, doesn't it?" As well as the natural difficulty in becoming attuned to speaking and listening to these different tones, Western efforts are complicated by our habit of denoting the overall meaning of a sentence by modulating our tones – for example, turning a statement into a question through a shift of stress and tone. Listen to native Thai speakers and you'll soon begin to pick up the different approach to tone.

The pitch of each tone is gauged in relation to your vocal range when speaking, but they should all lie within a narrow band, separated by gaps just big enough to differentiate them. The **low tones** (syllables marked `) , **middle tones** (unmarked syllables), and **high tones** (syllables marked ´) should each be pronounced evenly and with no inflection. The **falling tone** (syllables marked ˆ) is spoken with an obvious drop in pitch, as if you were sharply emphasizing a word in English. The **rising tone** (marked ˇ) is pronounced as if you were asking an exaggerated question in English.

As well as the unfamiliar tones, you'll find that, despite the best efforts of the transliterators, there is no precise English equivalent to many **vowel and consonant sounds** in the Thai language. The lists below give a simplified idea of pronunciation.

VOWELS

a as in dad	**eu** as in sir, but heavily nasalized
aa has no precise equivalent, but is pronounced as it looks, with the vowel elongated	**i** as in tip
	ii as in feet
ae as in there	**o** as in knock
ai as in buy	**oe** as in hurt, but more closed
ao as in now	**oh** as in toe
aw as in awe	**u** as in loot
ay as in pay	**uu** as in pool
e as in pen	

CONSONANTS

r as in rip, but with the tongue flapped quickly against the palate – in everyday speech, it's often pronounced like "l"	**th** as in time
	k is unaspirated and unvoiced, and closer to "g"
	p is also unaspirated and unvoiced, and closer to "b"
kh as in keep	**t** is also unaspirated and unvoiced, and closer to "d"
ph as in put	

General words and phrases

GREETINGS AND BASIC PHRASES

When you speak to a stranger in Thailand, you should generally end your sentence in *khráp* if you're a man, *khâ* if you're a woman – these untranslatable politening syllables will gain goodwill, and are nearly always used after *sawàt dii* (hello/goodbye) and *khàwp khun* (thank you). *Khráp* and *khâ* are also often used to answer "yes" to a question, though the most common way is to repeat the verb of the question (precede it with *mâi* for "no"). *Châi* (yes) and *mâi châi* (no) are less frequently used than their English equivalents.

Hello	sawàt dii	**My name is…**	phŏm (men)/diichăn (women) chêu…
Where are you going?	pai năi? (not always meant literally, but used as a general greeting)	**I come from…**	phŏm/diichăn maa jàak…
I'm out having fun/ I'm travelling	pai thîaw (answer to pai năi, almost indefinable pleasantry)	**I don't understand**	mâi khâo jai
		Do you speak English?	khun phûut phasăa angkrìt dâi măi?
Goodbye	sawàt dii/la kàwn	**Do you have…?**	mii…măi?
Good luck/cheers	chôhk dii	**Is…possible?**	…dâi măi?
Excuse me	khăw thâwt	**Can you help me?**	chûay phŏm/ diichăn dâi măi?
Thank you	khàwp khun		
It's nothing/ it doesn't matter	mâi pen rai	**(I) want…**	ao…
		(I) would like to…	yàak jà…
How are you?	sabai dii reŭ?	**(I) like…**	châwp…
I'm fine	sabai dii	**What is this called in Thai?**	níi phasăa thai rîak wâa arai?
What's your name?	khun chêu arai?		

GETTING AROUND

Where is the…?	…yùu thîi nǎi?	west	tawan tòk
How far?	klai thâo rai?	near/far	klâi/klai
I would like to go to…	yàak jà pai…	street	thanǒn
Where have you been?	pai nǎi maa?	train station	sathàanii rót fai
Where is this bus going?	rót níi pai nǎi?	bus station	sathàanii rót mae
When will the bus leave?	rót jà àwk mêua rai?	airport	sanǎam bin
What time does the bus arrive in…?	rót theǔng…kìi mohng?	ticket	tǔa
		hotel	rohng raem
Stop here	jàwt thîi nîi	post office	praisanii
here	thîi nîi	restaurant	raan ahǎan
there/over there	thîi nâan/thîi nôhn	shop	raan
right	khwǎa	market	talàat
left	sái	hospital	rohng pha-yaabaan
straight	trong	motorbike	rót mohtoesai
north	neǔa	taxi	rót táksîi
south	tâi	boat	reua
east	tawan àwk	bicycle	jàkràyaan

ACCOMMODATION AND SHOPPING

How much is…?	…thâo rai/kìi bàat?	Can you reduce the price?	lót raakhaa dâi mǎi?
I don't want a plastic bag, thanks	mâi ao thǔng khráp/khâ	Can I store my bag here?	fàak krapǎo wái thîi nîi dâi mǎi?
How much is a room here per night?	hâwng thîi nîi kheun lá thâo rai?	cheap/expensive	thùuk/phaeng
		air-con room	hâwng ae
Do you have a cheaper room?	mii hâwng thùuk kwàa mǎi?	ordinary room	hâwng thammadaa
		telephone	thohrásàp
Can I/we look at the room?	duu hâwng dâi mǎi?	laundry	sák phâa
		blanket	phâa hòm
I/We'll stay two nights	jà yùu sǎwng kheun	fan	phát lom

GENERAL ADJECTIVES

alone	khon diaw	fun	sanùk
another	ìik…nèung	hot (temperature)	ráwn
bad	mâi dii	hot (spicy)	phèt
big	yài	hungry	hiǔ khâo
clean	sa-àat	ill	mâi sabai
closed	pìt	open	pòet
cold (object)	yen	pretty	sǔay
cold (person or weather)	nǎo	small	lek
delicious	aròi	thirsty	hiǔ nám
difficult	yâak	tired	nèu-ay
dirty	sokaprok	very	mâak
easy	ngâi		

GENERAL NOUNS

Nouns have no plurals or genders, and don't require an article.

bathroom/toilet	hâwng nám	friend	phêuan
boyfriend or girlfriend	faen	money	ngoen
food	ahǎan	water/liquid	nám
foreigner	fàràng		

GENERAL VERBS

Thai verbs do not conjugate at all, and also often double up as nouns and adjectives, which means that foreigners' most unidiomatic attempts to construct sentences are often readily understood.

come	maa	go	pai
do	tham	sit	nâng
eat	kin/thaan khâo	sleep	nawn làp
give	hâi	walk	doen pai

NUMBERS

zero	sǔun	twelve, thirteen…	sìp sǎwng, sìp sǎam…
one	nèung	twenty	yîi sìp/yiip
two	sǎwng	twenty-one	yîi sìp èt
three	sǎam	twenty-two,	yîi sìp sǎwng,
four	sìi	twenty-three…	yîi sìp sǎam…
five	hâa	thirty, forty, etc	sǎam sìp, sìi sìp…
six	hòk	one hundred,	nèung rói, sǎwng rói…
seven	jèt	two hundred…	
eight	pàet	one thousand	nèung phan
nine	kâo	ten thousand	nèung mèun
ten	sìp	one hundred thousand	nèung sǎen
eleven	sìp èt	one million	nèung lǎan

TIME

The most common system for telling the time, as outlined below, is actually a confusing mix of several different systems. The State Railway and government officials use the 24-hour clock (9am is *kâo naalikaa*, 10am *sìp naalikaa*, and so on), which is always worth trying if you get stuck.

1–5am	tii nèung–tii hâa	hour	chûa mohng
6–11am	hòk mohng cháo– sìp èt mohng cháo	day	wan
noon	thîang	week	aathít
1pm	bài mohng	month	deuan
2–4pm	bài sǎwng mohng– bài sìi mohng	year	pii
		today	wan níi
5–6pm	hâa mohng yen– hòk mohng yen	tomorrow	phrûng níi
		yesterday	mêua wan níi
7–11pm	nèung thûm– hâa thûm	now	diǎw níi
midnight	thîang kheun	next week	aathít nâa
What time is it?	kìi mohng láew?	last week	aathít kàwn
How many hours?	kìi chûa mohng?	morning	cháo
How long?	naan thâo rai?	afternoon	bài
minute	naathii	evening	yen
		night	kheun

DAYS

Sunday	wan aathít	Thursday	wan pháréuhàt
Monday	wan jan	Friday	wan sùk
Tuesday	wan angkhaan	Saturday	wan sǎo
Wednesday	wan phút		

Food and drink

BASIC INGREDIENTS

kài	chicken	plaa mèuk	squid
mŭu	pork	kûng	prawn, shrimp
néua	beef, meat	hŏy	shellfish
pèt	duck	hŏy nang rom	oyster
ahăan thalay	seafood	puu	crab
plaa	fish	khài	egg
plaa dùk	catfish	phàk	vegetables

VEGETABLES

makĕua	aubergine	taeng kwaa	cucumber
makĕua thêt	tomato	phrík yùak	green pepper
nàw mái	bamboo shoots	krathiam	garlic
tùa ngâwk	bean sprouts	hèt	mushroom
phrík	chilli	tùa	peas, beans or lentils
man faràng	potato	tôn hŏrm	spring onions
man faràng thâwt	chips		

NOODLES

ba mìi	egg noodles	kwáy tiăw/ba mìi rât nâ (mŭu)	rice noodles/egg noodles fried in gravy-like sauce with vegetables (and pork slices)
kwáy tiăw (sên yài/sên lék)	white rice noodles (wide/thin)		
khanŏm jiin nám yaa	noodles topped with fish curry	mìi kràwp	crisp fried egg noodles with small pieces of meat and a few vegetables
kwáy tiăw/ ba mìi haêng	rice noodle/egg noodles fried with egg, small pieces of meat and a few vegetables		
		phàt thai	thin noodles fried with egg, bean sprouts and tofu, topped with ground peanuts
kwáy tiăw/ba mìi nám (mŭu)	rice noodle/egg noodle soup, made with chicken broth (and pork balls)		
		phàt siyú	wide or thin noodles fried with soy sauce, egg and meat

RICE

khâo	rice	khâo niăw	sticky rice
khâo man kài	slices of chicken served over marinated rice	khâo phàt	fried rice
		khâo kaeng	curry over rice
khâo mŭu daeng	red pork with rice	khâo tôm	rice soup (usually for breakfast)
khâo nâ kài/pèt	chicken/duck served with sauce over rice		

CURRIES AND SOUPS

kaeng phèt	hot, red curry	kaeng liang	peppery vegetable soup
kaeng phánaeng	thick, savoury curry	kaeng sôm	tamarind soup
kaeng khîaw wan	green curry	tôm khà kài	chicken, coconut and galangal soup
kaeng mátsàman	rich Muslim-style curry, usually with beef and potatoes		
		tôm yam kûng	hot and sour prawn soup
		kaeng jèut	mild soup with vegetables and usually pork
kaeng karìi	mild, Indian-style curry		
hàw mòk thalay	seafood curry soufflé		

SALADS

lâap	spicy ground meat salad	yam plaa mèuk	squid salad
nám tòk	grilled beef or pork salad	yam sôm oh	pomelo salad
sôm tam	spicy papaya salad	yam plaa dùk foo	crispy fried catfish salad
yam hua plee	banana flower salad	yam thùa phuu	wing-bean salad
yam néua	grilled beef salad	yam wun sen	noodle and pork salad

OTHER DISHES

hâwy thâwt	omelette stuffed with mussels	néua phàt nám man hâwy	beef in oyster sauce
kài phàt bai kraprao	chicken fried with holy basil leaves	phàt phàk bûng fai daeng	morning glory fried in garlic and bean sauce
kài phàt nàw mái	chicken with bamboo shoots	phàt phàk ruam	stir-fried vegetables
		pàw pía	spring rolls
kài phàt mét mámûang	chicken with cashew nuts	plaa nêung pàe sá	whole fish steamed with vegetables and ginger
kài phàt khîng	chicken with ginger		
kài yâang	grilled chicken	plaa rât phrík	whole fish cooked with chillies
khài yát sài	omelette with pork and vegetables		
		plaa thâwt	fried whole fish
kûng chúp paêng thâwt	prawns fried in batter	sàté	satay
mûu prîaw wǎan	sweet and sour pork	thâwt man plaa	fish cake
néua phàt krathiam phrík thai	beef fried with garlic and pepper		

THAI DESSERTS (KHANǑM)

khanǒm beuang	small crispy pancake folded over with coconut cream and strands of sweet egg inside	khâo niǎw thúrian/ mámûang	sticky rice mixed with coconut cream and durian/mango
		klûay khàek	fried banana
		lûk taan chêum	sweet palm kernels served in syrup
khâo lǎam	sticky rice, coconut cream and black beans cooked and served in bamboo tubes	sǎngkhayaa	coconut custard
		tàkôh	squares of transparent jelly (jello) topped with coconut cream
khâo niǎw daeng	sticky red rice mixed with coconut cream		

DRINKS (KHREÛANG DEÙM)

bia	beer	nám plào	drinking water (boiled or filtered)
chaa ráwn	hot tea		
chaa yen	iced tea	nám sǒdaa	soda water
kaafae ráwn	hot coffee	nám taan	sugar
kâew	glass	kleua	salt
khúat	bottle	nám yen	cold water
mâekhǒng (or anglicized Mekong)	Thai brand-name rice whisky	nom jeùd	milk
		ohlíang	iced black coffee
klûay pan	banana shake	thûay	cup
nám mánao/sôm	lemon/orange juice		

ORDERING

I am vegetarian/vegan	Phǒm (male)/diichǎn (female) kin ahǎan mangsàwirát/jeh	I would like…	Khǎw…
		with/without…	Sài/mâi sài…
Can I see the menu?	Khǎw duù menu nóy?	Can I have the bill please?	Khǎw check bin?

Glossary

Amphoe District.
Amphoe muang Provincial capital.
Ao Bay.
Apsara Female deity.
Avalokitesvara Bodhisattva representing compassion.
Avatar Earthly manifestation of a deity.
Ban Village or house.
Bang Village by a river or the sea.
Bencharong Polychromatic ceramics made in China for the Thai market.
Bhumisparsa mudra Most common gesture of Buddha images; symbolizes the Buddha's victory over temptation.
Bodhisattva In Mahayana Buddhism, an enlightened being who postpones his or her entry into Nirvana.
Bot Main sanctuary of a Buddhist temple.
Brahma One of the Hindu trinity – "The Creator". Usually depicted with four faces and four arms.
Celadon Porcelain with grey-green glaze.
Changwat Province.
Chao ley/chao nam "Sea gypsies" – nomadic fisherfolk of south Thailand.
Chedi Reliquary tower in Buddhist temple.
Chofa Finial on temple roof.
Deva Mythical deity.
Devaraja God-king.
Dharma The teachings or doctrine of the Buddha.
Dharmachakra Buddhist Wheel of Law (also known as Wheel of Doctrine or Wheel of Life).
Doi Mountain.
Erawan Mythical three-headed elephant; Indra's vehicle.
Farang Foreigner/foreign.
Ganesh Hindu elephant-headed deity, remover of obstacles and god of knowledge.
Garuda Mythical Hindu creature – half-man half-bird; Vishnu's vehicle.
Gopura Entrance pavilion to temple precinct (especially Khmer).
Hamsa Sacred mythical goose; Brahma's vehicle.
Hanuman Monkey god and chief of the monkey army in the Ramayana; ally of Rama.
Hat Beach.
Hin Stone.
Hinayana Pejorative term for Theravada school of Buddhism, literally "Lesser Vehicle".
Ho trai A scripture library.
Indra Hindu king of the gods and, in Buddhism, devotee of the Buddha; usually carries a thunderbolt.
Isaan Northeast Thailand.
Jataka Stories of the Buddha's five hundred lives.

Khaen Reed and wood pipe; the characteristic musical instrument of Isaan.
Khao Hill, mountain.
Khlong Canal.
Khon Classical dance-drama.
Kinnari Mythical creature – half woman, half bird.
Kirtimukha Very powerful deity depicted as a lion-head.
Ko Island.
Ku The Lao word for prang; a tower in a temple complex.
Laem Headland or cape.
Lakhon Classical dance-drama.
Lak muang City pillar; revered home for the city's guardian spirit.
Lakshaman/Phra Lak Rama's younger brother.
Lakshana Auspicious signs or "marks of greatness" displayed by the Buddha.
Lanna Northern Thai kingdom that lasted from the thirteenth to the sixteenth century.
Likay Popular folk theatre.
Longyi Burmese sarong.
Luang Pho Abbot or especially revered monk.
Maenam River.
Mahathat Chedi containing relics of the Buddha.
Mahayana School of Buddhism now practised mainly in China, Japan and Korea; literally "the Great Vehicle".
Mara The Evil One; tempter of the Buddha.
Mawn khwaan Traditional triangular or "axe-head" pillow.
Meru/Sineru Mythical mountain at the centre of Hindu and Buddhist cosmologies.
Mondop Small, square temple building to house minor images or religious texts.
Moo/muu Neighbourhood.
Muang City or town.
Muay thai Thai boxing.
Mudra Symbolic gesture of the Buddha.
Mut mee Tie-dyed cotton or silk.
Naga Mythical dragon-headed serpent in Buddhism and Hinduism.
Nakhon Honorific title for a city.
Nam Water.
Nam tok Waterfall.
Nang thalung Shadow-puppet entertainment, found in southern Thailand.
Nielloware Engraved metalwork.
Nirvana Final liberation from the cycle of rebirths; state of non-being to which Buddhists aspire.
Pak Tai Southern Thailand.
Pali Language of ancient India; the script of the original Buddhist scriptures.

Pha sin Woman's sarong.

Phi Animist spirit.

Phra Honorific term – literally "excellent".

Phu Mountain.

Prang Central tower in a Khmer temple.

Prasat Khmer temple complex or central shrine.

Rama/Phra Ram Human manifestation of Hindu deity Vishnu; hero of the Ramayana.

Ramakien Thai version of the Ramayana.

Ramayana Hindu epic of good versus evil: chief characters include Rama, Sita, Ravana, Hanuman.

Ravana see Totsagan.

Reua hang yao Longtail boat.

Rishi Ascetic hermit.

Rot ae/rot tua Air-conditioned bus.

Rot thammadaa Ordinary bus.

Sala Meeting hall, pavilion, bus stop – or any open-sided structure.

Samlor Three-wheeled passenger tricycle.

Sanskrit Sacred language of Hinduism; also used in Buddhism.

Sanuk Fun.

Sema Boundary stone to mark consecrated ground within temple complex.

Shiva One of the Hindu trinity – "The Destroyer".

Shiva lingam Phallic representation of Shiva.

Soi Lane or side road.

Songkhran Thai New Year.

Songthaew Public transport pick-up vehicle; means "two rows", after its two facing benches.

Takraw Game played with a rattan ball.

Talat Market.

Talat nam Floating market.

Talat yen Night market.

Tambon Subdistrict.

Tavatimsa Buddhist heaven.

Tha Pier.

Thale Sea or lake.

Tham Cave.

Thanon Road.

That Chedi.

Thep A divinity.

Theravada Main school of Buddhist thought in Thailand; also known as Hinayana.

Totsagan Rama's evil rival in the Ramayana; also known as Ravana.

Tripitaka Buddhist scriptures.

Trok Alley.

Tuk-tuk Motorized three-wheeled taxi.

Uma Shiva's consort.

Ushnisha Cranial protuberance on Buddha images, signifying an enlightened being.

Viharn Temple assembly hall for the laity; usually contains the principal Buddha image.

Vipassana Buddhist meditation technique; literally "insight".

Vishnu One of the Hindu trinity – "The Preserver". Usually shown with four arms, holding a disc, a conch, a lotus and a club.

Wai Thai greeting expressed by a prayer-like gesture with the hands.

Wang Palace.

Wat Temple.

Wiang Fortified town.

Yaksha Mythical giant.

Yantra Magical combination of numbers and letters, used to ward off danger.

Small print and index

A ROUGH GUIDE TO ROUGH GUIDES

Published in 1982, the first Rough Guide – to Greece – was a student scheme that became a publishing phenomenon. Mark Ellingham, a recent graduate in English from Bristol University, had been travelling in Greece the previous summer and couldn't find the right guidebook. With a small group of friends he wrote his own guide, combining a highly contemporary, journalistic style with a thoroughly practical approach to travellers' needs.

The immediate success of the book spawned a series that rapidly covered dozens of destinations. And, in addition to impecunious backpackers, Rough Guides soon acquired a much broader readership that relished the guides' wit and inquisitiveness as much as their enthusiastic, critical approach and value-for-money ethos.

These days, Rough Guides include recommendations from budget to luxury and cover more than 200 destinations around the globe, as well as producing an ever-growing range of eBooks and apps.

Visit **roughguides.com** to see our latest publications.

Rough Guide credits

Editor: Emma Gibbs
Layout: Pradeep Thapliyal
Cartography: Ed Wright
Picture editor: Roger d'Olivere Mapp
Photographers: Karen Trist & Martin Richardson
Proofreader: Jan McCann
Managing editor: Kathryn Lane
Assistant editor: Dipika Dasgupta
Production: Gemma Sharpe
Cover design: Nicole Newman, Pradeep Thapliyal

Editorial assistant: Eleanor Aldridge
Senior pre-press designer: Dan May
Design director: Scott Stickland
Travel publisher: Joanna Kirby
Digital travel publisher: Peter Buckley
Reference director: Andrew Lockett
Operations coordinator: Becky Doyle
Publishing director (Travel): Clare Currie
Commercial manager: Gino Magnotta
Managing director: John Duhigg

Publishing information

This fifth edition published November 2012 by
Rough Guides Ltd,
80 Strand, London WC2R 0RL
11, Community Centre, Panchsheel Park,
New Delhi 110017, India
Distributed by the Penguin Group
Penguin Books Ltd,
80 Strand, London WC2R 0RL
Penguin Group (USA)
375 Hudson Street, NY 10014, USA
Penguin Group (Australia)
250 Camberwell Road, Camberwell,
Victoria 3124, Australia
Penguin Group (NZ)
67 Apollo Drive, Mairangi Bay, Auckland 1310,
New Zealand
Penguin Group (South Africa)
Block D, Rosebank Office Park, 181 Jan Smuts Avenue,
Parktown North, Gauteng, South Africa 2193
Rough Guides is represented in Canada by Tourmaline
Editions Inc. 662 King Street West, Suite 304, Toronto,
Ontario M5V 1M7
Printed in Singapore by Toppan Security Printing Pte. Ltd.

© Paul Gray and Lucy Ridout, 2012
Maps © Rough Guides
No part of this book may be reproduced in any form
without permission from the publisher except for the
quotation of brief passages in reviews.
464pp includes index
A catalogue record for this book is available from the
British Library
ISBN: 978-1-40539-008-8
The publishers and authors have done their best to
ensure the accuracy and currency of all the information
in **The Rough Guide to Thailand's Beaches & Islands**,
however, they can accept no responsibility for any loss,
injury, or inconvenience sustained by any traveller as a
result of information or advice contained in the guide.
1 3 5 7 9 8 6 4 2

MIX
Paper from
responsible sources
FSC www.fsc.org FSC™ C018179

Help us update

We've gone to a lot of effort to ensure that the fifth edition of **The Rough Guide to Thailand's Beaches & Islands** is accurate and up-to-date. However, things change – places get "discovered", opening hours are notoriously fickle, restaurants and rooms raise prices or lower standards. If you feel we've got it wrong or left something out, we'd like to know, and if you can remember the address, the price, the hours, the phone number, so much the better.

Please send your comments with the subject line "**Rough Guide Thailand's Beaches & Islands Update**" to mail@uk.roughguides.com. We'll credit all contributions and send a copy of the next edition (or any other Rough Guide if you prefer) for the very best emails.

Find more travel information, connect with fellow travellers and book your trip on roughguides.com

ABOUT THE AUTHORS

Paul Gray After twenty years of toing and froing, Paul has recently settled down in Thailand. He is co-author of the *Rough Guide to Thailand's Beaches & Islands*, as well as the *Rough Guide to Ireland*, and has edited and contributed to many other guidebooks, including an update of his native Northeast for the *Rough Guide to England*.

Lucy Ridout has spent all her working life travelling in and writing about Asia. She is co-author of the *Rough Guide to Bangkok*, the *Rough Guide to Thailand's Beaches & Islands* and the *Rough Guide to Bali & Lombok*, and has also co-written *First-Time Asia*, a handbook for travellers making their first visit to the region.

Acknowledgements

The authors would like to thank: Gade Gray; Emma, James, Ed and Kathryn at Rough Guides; staff at TAT offices in Pattaya, Cha-am, Hua Hin, Chumphon, Ko Samui, Nakhon Si Thammarat and Trang; Felix Hude for the original section on cycling; Colonel Prakob Siriphap; Steve Epstein; Kanokros Sakdanares and Marion Walsh in Bangkok; Serge in Trat; Tom Kirk on Ko Chang; Cristina on Ko Mak;

Tom in Phetchaburi; the Hurlers in Prachuap; Suda in Chumphon; Rashi, Bambi and Jorge on Ko Pha Ngan; Matt Bolton, Nathan Cook and Dev on Ko Tao; Pon in Ranong; Richard on Ko Phayam; Karen and Bodhi in Khuraburi; Paul Counihan in Khao Lak; Mai in Krabi; Ray and Sao on Ko Jum; Ekkachai in Trang; On in Satun; and Tuppadit Thaiarry and all the Phuket staff at Avis.

Readers' letters

Thanks to all the readers who have taken the time to write in with comments and suggestions (and apologies if we've inadvertently omitted or misspelt anyone's name):

Allan Dreyer Andersen, Luis F. Arévalogarcia, Keeley Bolger, John Breadman, Andrew Dean, Ruth French, Uschi Gaida, Tim Hare, Jim Hayes, Ian Hodge, Penny Holmes, Hilary Kennedy, Monica Mackaness and John Garratt, Natalie Marchant, Stefania Minuto and Giulia Gionchetta, Graeme

Nicholson, Charlotte Norton, Rob, Lien Roose, Pete Searl, Alex Shields, Paul Smekens, Jeff Stone, Kerrie Taylor Cross, Barry Walden & Mandy Berger, Clive Walker, Denise Williams.

Photo credits

All photos © Rough Guides except the following:
(Key: t-top; c-centre; b-bottom; l-left; r-right)

p.2 SuperStock, Stefano Baldini
p.7 SuperStock, Michael DeFreitas
p.9 Getty Images, Holger Leue (t)
p.10 Getty Images, Reinhard Dirscherl
p.11 Corbis, Martin Puddy (t); SuperStock, Renault-Rieger (b)
p.12 Getty Images, Paul Miles (t)
p.13 Alamy (tr); Getty Images, Megan Ahrens (tl); peru serra (b)
p.14 SuperStock, Norbert Eisele-Hein (bl); SuperStock (t, br)
p.15 SuperStock, Philippe Body (t)
p.16 Getty Images (b); Igor Prahin (t)
p.17 SuperStock, Luca Tettoni (b)
p.18 Getty Images, Ingolf Pompe (tr)
p.21 Getty Images (tl); SuperStock, Georgie Holland (tr); Georgette Douwma (br); Louise Murray (bl); Corbis (cl);
p.23 Reinhard Dirscherl (tc); Getty Images (cr); Franco Banfi (bc); Georgette Douwma (cl)
p.25 Dave Fleetham (tl); Getty Images (tr, bc); SuperStock (cr)
p.93 SuperStock, Gonzalo Azumendi (b)

p.148 Alamy, Markus Braun
p.151 SuperStock, Michael Zegers
p.181 Alamy, Artur Bogacki (t)
p.207 SuperStock
p.219 SuperStock, Franck Guiziou (b)
p.257 SuperStock, Sean White (t); Getty Images (b)
p.281 SuperStock, Heeb Christian
p.284 SuperStock, Walter Allgoewer
p.287 SuperStock
p.317 SuperStock, Paul Picasso (t)
p.375 AWL Images, Travel Pix Collection
p.396 Getty Images, Igor Prahin
p.399 SuperStock
p.407 Corbis, Thomas Marent (tl); Alamy, Andrew Woodley (tr); Getty Images, Otto Stadler (b)
p.422 SuperStock

Front cover Traditional boats © Getty Images/Peter Adams
Back cover Ko Samet © Rough Guides/ Karen Trist; Bangkok Palace © Rough Guides/Karen Trist; Two Monks © Rough Guides/Martin Richardson

Index

Maps are marked in grey

Map symbols

The symbols below are used on maps throughout the book

▬▬ ▪ ▪	International boundary	⊠	Gate
▬ ▬ ▬	Chapter division boundary	∩	Arch
▬ ▬ ▪ ▪	Provincial boundary	⊙	Statue
▨▨▨	Expressway	✈	Airport
▨▨▨	Pedestrianized road	★	Transport stop
══	Road	♦	Point of interest
→	One-way street	♦	National park (country map)
⊞⊞⊞	Steps	♛	Museum
▪▪▪▪▪	Unpaved road	Ⓢ	Bank/ATM
▪ ▪ ▪	Path	@	Internet access
▬▬	Railway	ⓘ	Tourist information
▬ ▬	Ferry route	Ⓒ	Telephone office
──	River/canal	⊗	Airline office
▬▬▬	Wall	⊞	Hospital/clinic
●▪▪▪●	Cable car & stations	⊠	Post office
≍	Footbridge	E	Embassy/consulate
⌣	Bridge	⛫	Market
⟟	Border crossing	⟟	Temple
▲	Peak	⌂	Mosque
⋀⋀	Mountains	⛩	Chinese temple/pagoda
◠	Cave	⬭	Stadium
⟊	Waterfall	▦	Church
⩊	Spring	▦	Building
⁓	Rocks	~ ~	Swamps/marshes
⟊	Lighthouse		Park/forest
↯	Viewpoint		Beach

Listings key

■ Accommodation

● Restaurants & cafés

■ Bars & clubs

● Shops

AVIS Rent a Car

www.AVISThailand.com

Save the money online

Anywhere you go, you will meet us there too.

Safe Car ... Save Money

AVIS Locations

Chiang Mai Airport
Chiang Mai Downtown

AVIS Chiang Rai Airport

AVIS Udon Thani Airport

Phitsanuloke Airport **AVIS**

AVIS Khon Kaen Airport

AVIS Ubon Ratchathani Airport

Suvarnabhumi Airport
Don Muang Airport
Bangkok Downtown

AVIS Pattaya

Cha Am & Hua Hin **AVIS**

AVIS Samui Airport

AVIS Surat Thani Airport

Krabi Airport **AVIS**

Phuket Airport **AVIS**

AVIS Hat Yai Airport

Save up to 50%*
and get more benefit
visit our website now

Please contact us for more information.
Terms and Conditions apply

Available at all Airport Locations, Call us now!

Center: **02 251 1131-2**
www.AVISThailand.com

Limited Offer, please contact us for more information

AVIS

We try
harder.

Bangkok, Chiang Mai, Chiang Rai, Cha Am & Hua Hin, Hat Yai, Khon Kaen, Krabi, Pattaya, Phitsanuloke, Phuket, Surat Thani & Koh Samui, Udon Thani, Ubon Ratchathani

ROUGH
GUIDES

SO NOW WE'VE TOLD YOU
HOW TO MAKE THE MOST
OF YOUR TIME, WE WANT
YOU TO STAY SAFE AND
COVERED WITH OUR
FAVOURITE TRAVEL INSURER

WorldNomads.com
keep travelling safely

GET AN ONLINE QUOTE
roughguides.com/insurance

RECOMMENDED BY

ROUGH
GUIDES

MAKE THE MOST OF YOUR TIME ON EARTH™

ROUGH
GUIDES

WE GET AROUND

ONLINE start your journey at roughguides.com

EBOOKS & MOBILE APPS

GUIDEBOOKS from Amsterdam to Zanzibar

PHRASEBOOKS learn the lingo

MAPS so you don't get lost

GIFTBOOKS inspiration is our middle name

LIFESTYLE from iPads to climate change

...SO YOU CAN TOO

BOOKS | EBOOKS | APPS

Start your journey at **roughguides.com**
MAKE THE MOST OF YOUR TIME ON EARTH™

ROUGH
GUIDES

MAKE THE MOST OF YOUR CITY BREAK

NEW YORK CITY | **HONG KONG** & MACAU | **BERLIN** | **MARRAKESH** | **ROME**

FREE PULL OUT MAP WITH EVERY SIGHT AND LISTING FROM THE GUIDE

ESSENTIAL ITINERARIES AND RELIABLE RECOMMENDATIONS

BOOKS | EBOOKS | APPS